Baseball America
2009 DIRECTORY

YOUR DEFINITIVE GUIDE TO THE GAME

Detailed Information On Baseball In All Leagues At All Levels

MAJORS

MINORS

INDEPENDENT

INTERNATIONAL

COLLEGE

AMATEUR

BASEBALL AMERICA INC. · DURHAM, N.C.

Baseball America 2009 Directory

Editor

Josh Leventhal

Assistant Editors

Ben Badler, Kary Booher, Jesse Burkhart, Brian Chmielewski, J.J. Cooper, Aaron Fitt, Conor Glassey Will Lingo, Nathan Rode, Jim Shonerd

Photo Editor

Nathan Rode

Design & Production

Sara Hiatt, Linwood Webb

Programming & Technical Development

Greg Levine, Brent Lewis

Jacket Photos

Kory Casto by Ed Wolfstein; Walt Jocketty by Larry Goren

Cover Design

Linwood Webb

Baseball America

President/Publisher: Lee Folger

Editors in Chief: Will Lingo, John Manuel

Executive Editor: Jim Callis

Design & Production Director: Sara Hiatt

Distributed by Simon & Schuster

ISBN-13: 978-1-932391-25-1

BaseballAmerica.com

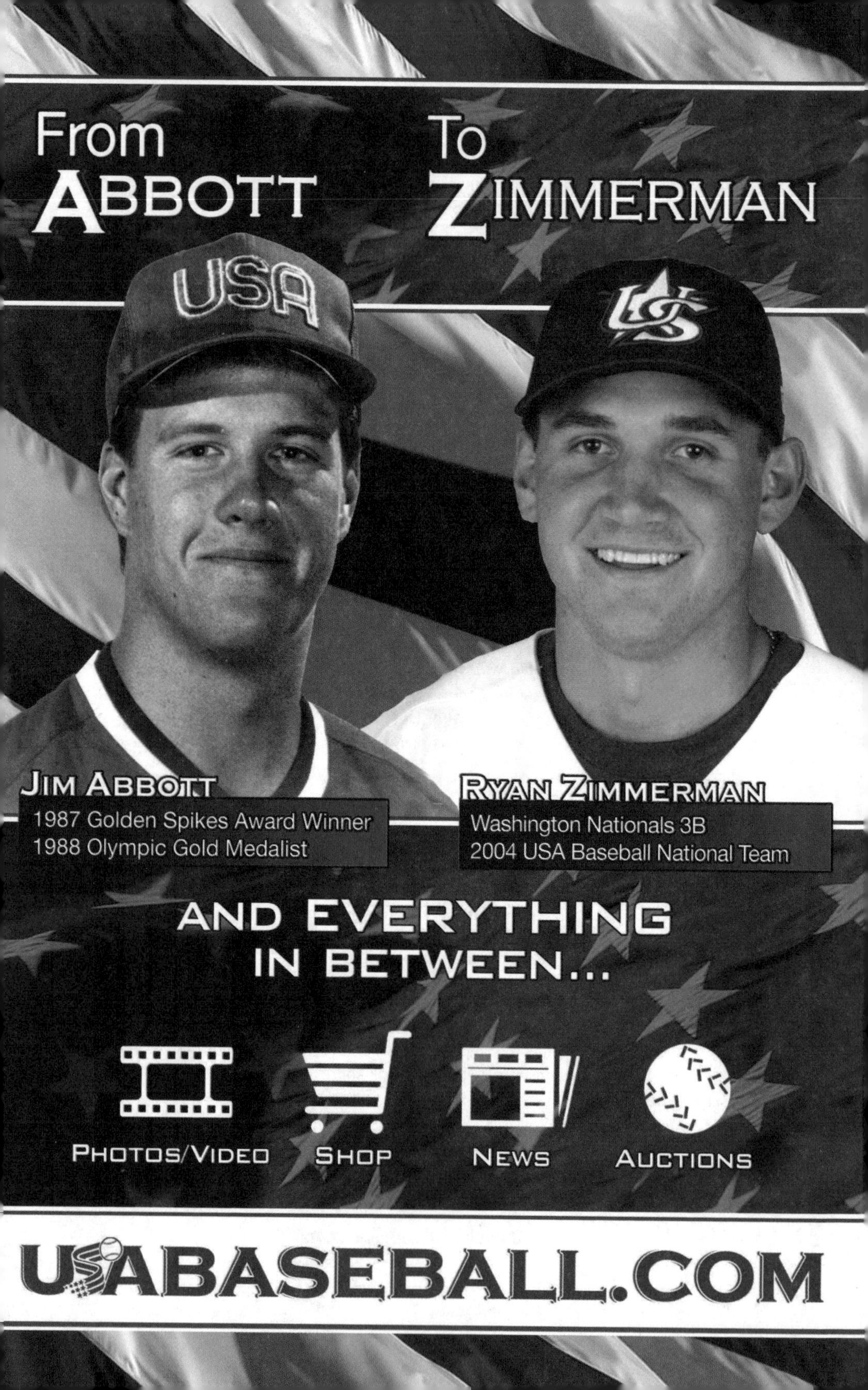
From ABBOTT
To ZIMMERMAN
JIM ABBOTT
1987 Golden Spikes Award Winner
1988 Olympic Gold Medalist
RYAN ZIMMERMAN
Washington Nationals 3B
2004 USA Baseball National Team
AND EVERYTHING IN BETWEEN...
PHOTOS/VIDEO
SHOP
NEWS
AUCTIONS
USABASEBALL.COM

TABLE OF CONTENTS

WHAT'S NEW IN 2009

TRIPLE-A

AFFILIATION CHANGES | Buffalo (International) from Indians to Mets, Columbus (International) from Nationals to Indians, Syracuse (International) from Blue Jays to Nationals

BALLPARK | Buffalo: Huntington Park

FRANCHISE MOVES | Richmond Braves (International) become Gwinnett Braves (Lawrenceville, Ga.); Tucson Sidewinders (PCL) become Reno Aces (Reno, Nev.)

NAME CHANGE | Oklahoma RedHawks (PCL) become Oklahoma City RedHawks.

DOUBLE-A

AFFILIATION CHANGES | Carolina (Southern) from Marlins to Reds, Chattanooga (Southern) from Reds to Dodgers, Jacksonville (Southern) from Dodgers to Marlins

HIGH CLASS A

AFFILIATION CHANGES | Lancaster (California) from Red Sox to Astros, Salem (Carolina) from Astros to Red Sox

BALLPARK | Winston-Salem

FRANCHISE MOVE | Vero Beach Devil Rays (Florida State) become Charlotte Stone Crabs.

NAME CHANGES | Salem Avalanche (Carolina) become Salem Red Sox. Visalia Oaks (California) become Visalia Rawhide, Winston-Salem Warthogs (Carolina) become Winston-Salem Dash.

LOW CLASS A

AFFILIATION CHANGES | Clinton (Midwest) from Rangers to Mariners, Hickory (South Atlantic) from Pirates to Rangers, West Virginia (South Atlantic) from Brewerrs to Pirates, Wisconsin (Midwest) from Mariners to Brewers

BALLPARK | Fort Wayne: Parkview Field.

FRANCHISE MOVE | Columbus Catfish (South Atlantic) to Bowling Green Hot Rods (Bowling Green, Ky.)

NAME CHANGE | Fort Wayne Wizards (Midwest) become Fort Wayne Tincaps

Map illustrations by Paul Trap

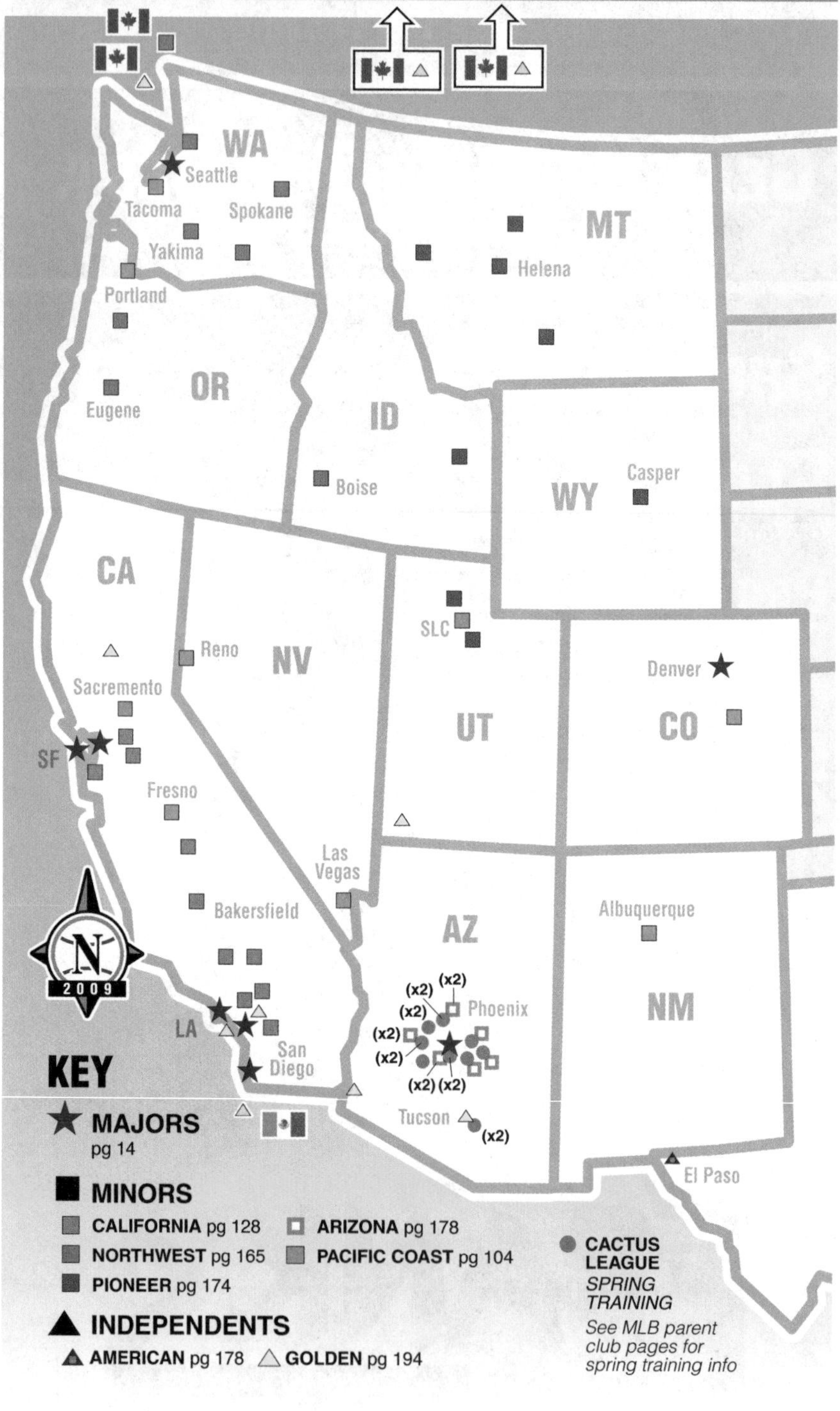
WA
Seattle
Tacoma
Spokane
Yakima
Portland
OR
Eugene
MT
Helena
ID
Boise
WY
Casper
CA
Reno
NV
SLC
UT
Denver
CO
Sacramento
SF
Fresno
Las Vegas
Bakersfield
AZ
Albuquerque
NM
N
2009
(x2)
Phoenix
LA
San Diego
Tucson
El Paso
KEY
MAJORS pg 14
MINORS
CALIFORNIA pg 128
NORTHWEST pg 165
PIONEER pg 174
ARIZONA pg 178
PACIFIC COAST pg 104
CACTUS LEAGUE SPRING TRAINING
See MLB parent club pages for spring training info
INDEPENDENTS
AMERICAN pg 178
GOLDEN pg 194

COMING SOON

THE 2009 SUPER REGISTER

The 2009 Super Register features complete career statistics for every active player in the majors and minors in 2008, from the youngest player in the Gulf Coast League to the oldest players in the major leagues.

You won't find another book that lists every minor and major leaguer—more than 6,000 players, with transactions, awards and major and minor league totals.

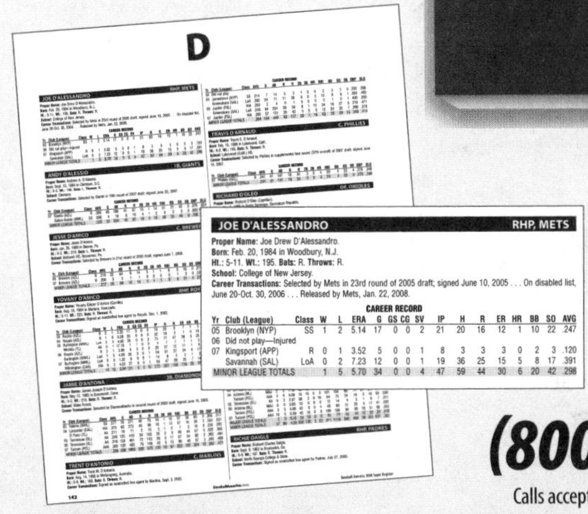

JOE D'ALESSANDRO — **RHP, METS**

Proper Name: Joe Drew D'Alessandro.
Born: Feb. 20, 1984 in Woodbury, N.J.
Ht.: 5-11. **Wt.:** 195. **Bats:** R. **Throws:** R.
School: College of New Jersey.
Career Transactions: Selected by Mets in 23rd round of 2005 draft; signed June 10, 2005 . . . On disabled list, June 20-Oct. 30, 2006 . . . Released by Mets, Jan. 22, 2008.

CAREER RECORD

Yr	Club (League)	Class	W	L	ERA	G	GS	CG	SV	IP	H	R	ER	HR	BB	SO	AVG
05	Brooklyn (NYP)	SS	1	2	5.14	17	0	0	2	21	20	16	12	1	10	22	.247
06	Did not play—Injured																
07	Kingsport (APP)	R	0	1	3.52	5	0	0	1	8	3	3	3	0	2	3	.120
	Savannah (SAL)	LoA	0	2	7.23	12	0	0	1	19	36	25	15	5	8	17	.391
MINOR LEAGUE TOTALS			1	5	5.70	34	0	0	4	47	59	44	30	6	20	42	298

Available late March

$81[95]

(800) 845-2726

Calls accepted Monday–Friday, 9 a.m.-5 p.m. ET.
Please have your credit card ready.

WISH YOU'D GOTTEN YOUR DIRECTORY SOONER?

Now if you order any of Baseball America's books and choose the Premium Shipping and Handling Option, your books will be shipped to you hot off the press via USPS Priority Mail. You'll get your books ***FIRST***, before they hit the stores, giving you the fantasy league advantage or insider scoop you want.

Don't miss out: Pre-order next year's book ***NOW!***

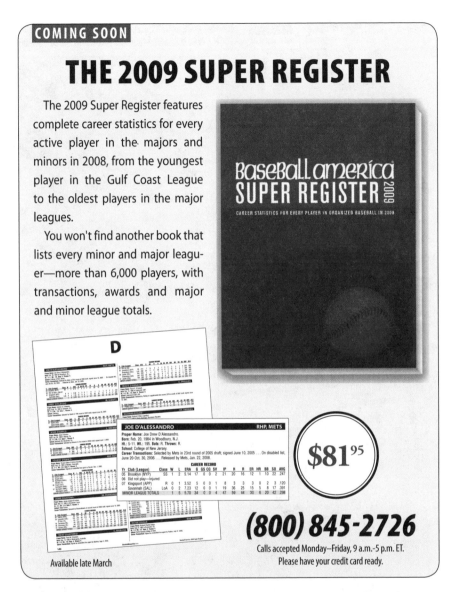

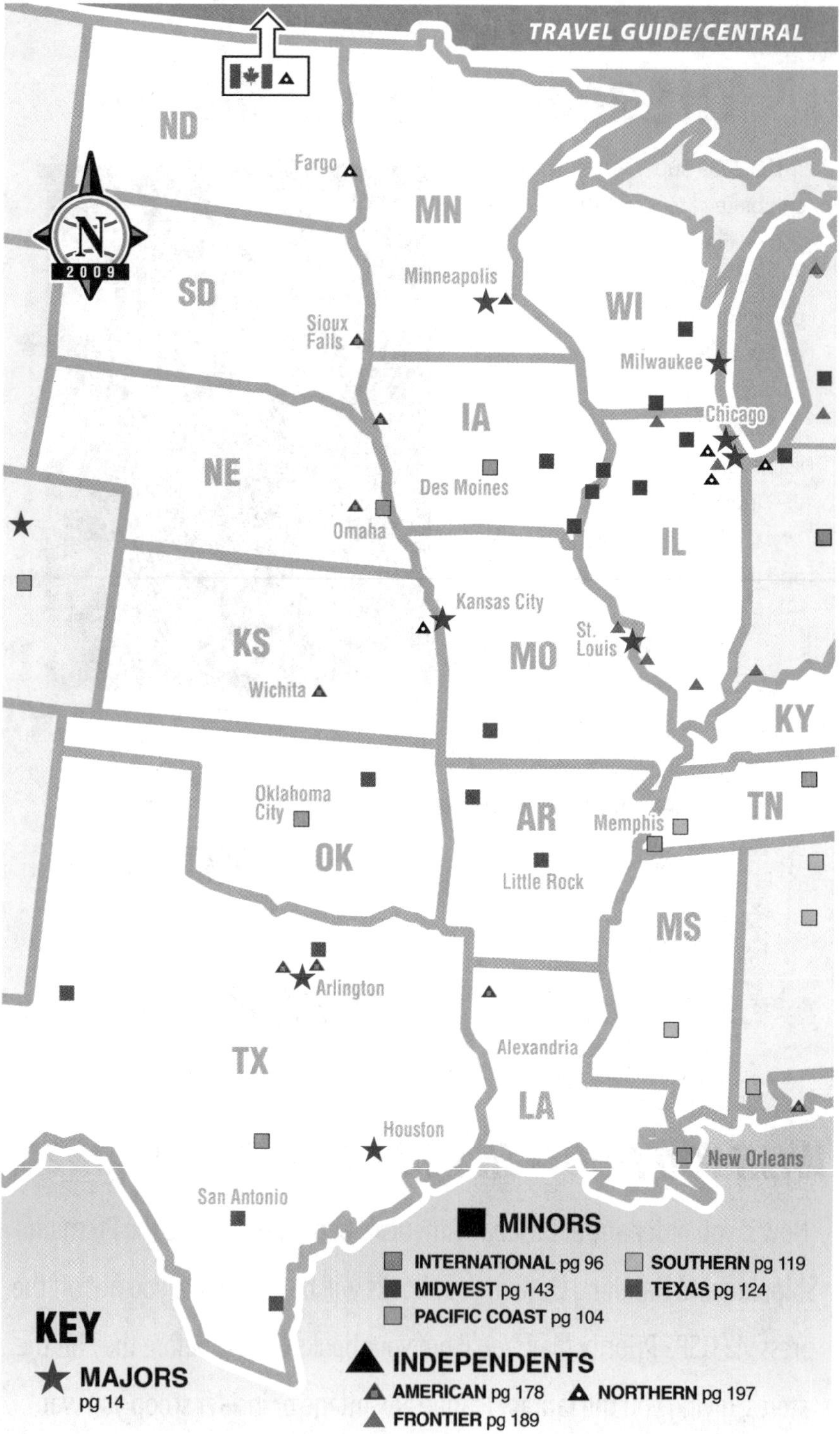
ND
Fargo
MN
2009
SD
Minneapolis
WI
Sioux Falls
Milwaukee
IA
Chicago
NE
Des Moines
Omaha
IL
Kansas City
KS
St. Louis
MO
Wichita
KY
Oklahoma City
AR
Memphis
TN
OK
Little Rock
MS
Arlington
Alexandria
TX
LA
Houston
New Orleans
San Antonio
KEY
MAJORS
pg 14
MINORS
INTERNATIONAL pg 96
SOUTHERN pg 119
MIDWEST pg 143
TEXAS pg 124
PACIFIC COAST pg 104
INDEPENDENTS
AMERICAN pg 178
NORTHERN pg 197
FRONTIER pg 189

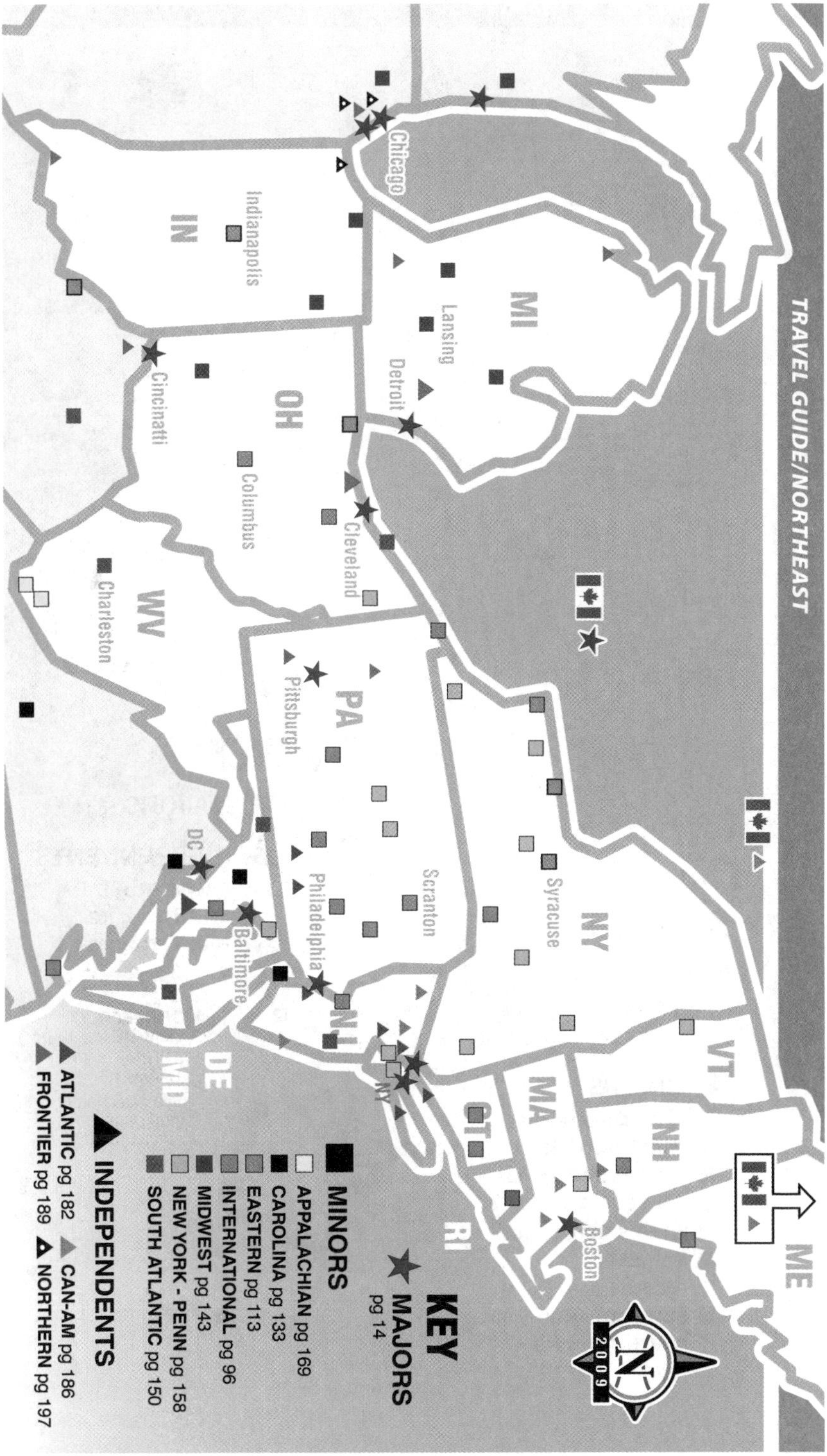

TRAVEL GUIDE/NORTHEAST
IN
Indianapolis
Chicago
MI
Lansing
Detroit
OH
Cincinatti
Columbus
Cleveland
WV
Charleston
PA
Pittsburgh
Philadelphia
Scranton
NY
Syracuse
DC
Baltimore
NJ
NY
DE
MD
CT
MA
RI
VT
NH
ME
Boston
2009
N
KEY
MAJORS pg 14
MINORS
APPALACHIAN pg 169
CAROLINA pg 133
EASTERN pg 113
INTERNATIONAL pg 96
MIDWEST pg 143
NEW YORK - PENN pg 158
SOUTH ATLANTIC pg 150
INDEPENDENTS
ATLANTIC pg 182
CAN-AM pg 186
FRONTIER pg 189
NORTHERN pg 197

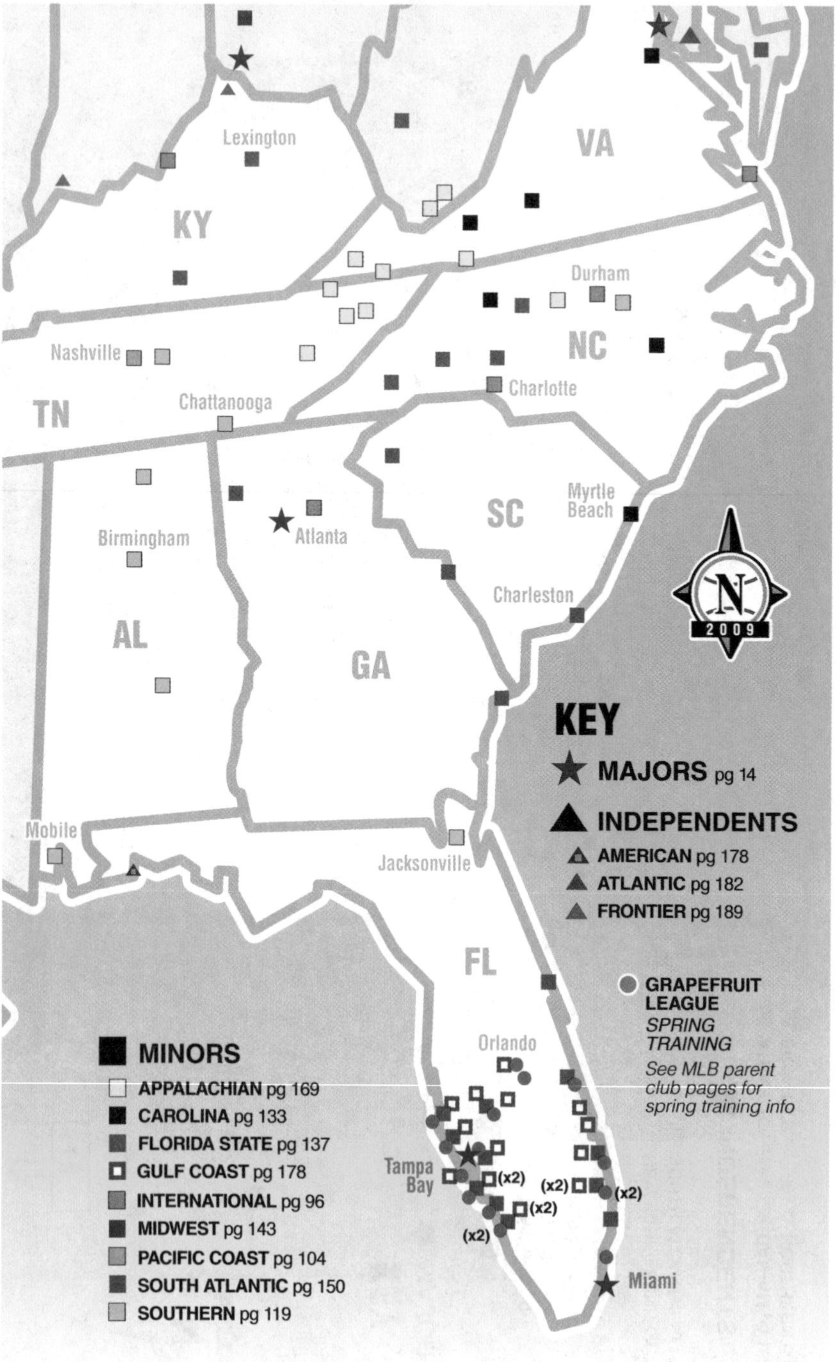
Lexington
VA
KY
Durham
Nashville
NC
TN
Chattanooga
Charlotte
SC
Myrtle Beach
Birmingham
Atlanta
Charleston
2009
AL
GA
KEY
MAJORS pg 14
INDEPENDENTS
AMERICAN pg 178
ATLANTIC pg 182
FRONTIER pg 189
Mobile
Jacksonville
FL
GRAPEFRUIT LEAGUE
SPRING TRAINING
See MLB parent club pages for spring training info
Orlando
MINORS
APPALACHIAN pg 169
CAROLINA pg 133
FLORIDA STATE pg 137
GULF COAST pg 178
INTERNATIONAL pg 96
MIDWEST pg 143
PACIFIC COAST pg 104
SOUTH ATLANTIC pg 150
SOUTHERN pg 119
Tampa Bay
(x2)
(x2)
(x2)
(x2)
(x2)
Miami

MAJOR LEAGUES

MAJOR LEAGUE BASEBALL

Mailing Address: 245 Park Ave. New York, NY 10167.

Telephone: (212) 931-7800.

Website: www.mlb.com.

Commissioner: Allan H. "Bud" Selig.

President/Chief Operating Officer: Bob DuPuy. **Executive Vice President, Business:** Tim Brosnan. **Executive VP, Labor Relations/Human Resources:** Robert Manfred. **Executive VP, Finance:** Jonathan Mariner. **Executive VP/Chief Information Officer:** John McHale. **Executive VP, Baseball Operations:** Jimmie Lee Solomon.

Bud Selig

BASEBALL OPERATIONS

Senior Vice President, Baseball Operations: Joe Garagiola Jr.

VP, Baseball Operations/Administration: Ed Burns. **VP, International Baseball Operations/Administration:** Lou Melendez. **VP, Umpiring:** Mike Port. **VP, On-Field Operations:** Bob Watson.

Special Advisor, Baseball Operations: Frank Robinson. **Senior Director, Major League Operations:** Roy Krasik.

Director, Urban Youth Academy: Darrell Miller. **Director, Minor League Operations:** Sylvia Lind. **Manager, Baseball Operations:** Jeff Pfeifer. **Manager, Dominican Operations:** Ronaldo Peralta. **Senior Specialist, On-Field Operations:** Darryl Hamilton. **Specialist, Major League Operations:** Brian Porter.

Specialist, On-Field Operations: Matt McKendry. **Specialist, Umpiring:** Fred Seymour. **Director, Umpire Administration:** Tom Lepperd.

Director, Umpire Medical Services: Mark Letendre.

Umpiring Supervisors: Rich Garcia, Cris Jones, Jim McKean, Steve Palermo, Rich Rieker, Marty Springstead.

Director, Arizona Fall League: Steve Cobb. **Director, Major League Scouting Bureau:** Frank Marcos. **Assistant Director, Scouting Bureau:** Rick Oliver.

Bob DuPuy

Security

Vice President, Security/Facility Management: Earnell Lucas.

Senior Manager, Facility Operations: Linda Pantell. **Senior Manager, Security:** Leroy Hendricks.

Investigations

Vice President, Investigations: Dan Mullin.

Senior Director, Investigations: George Hanna. **Supervisor, Investigations Operations:** Nancy Zamudio.

Public Relations

Telephone: (212) 931-7878. **FAX:** (212) 949-5654.

Senior Vice President, Public Relations: Richard Levin. **VP, Public Relations Operations:** Patrick Courtney. **VP, Business Public Relations:** Matt Bourne.

Director, Multicultural/Charitable Communications: Silvia Alvarez. **Senior Manager, Baseball Information:** Rob Doelger. **Managers, Media Relations:** John Blundell, Michael Teevan. **Manager, Business Public Relations:** Jeff Heckelman. **Senior Specialist, Business Public Relations:** Daniel Queen. **Specialist, Business Public Relations:** Steven Arrocho, Lauren Verrusio. **Coordinators, Media Relations:** Donald Muller, Sarah Leer. **Senior Administrative Assistant:** Heather Flock. **Administrative Assistant:** Raquel Ramos.

Official Baseball Historian: Jerome Holtzman.

Club Relations

Senior Vice President, Scheduling/Club Relations: Katy Feeney. **Senior Administrative Assistant, Scheduling/Club Relations:** Raxel Concepcion. **Coordinator, Club Relations:** Andrew Davis.

Senior Vice President, Club Relations: Phyllis Merhige. **Senior Administrative Assistant, Club Relations:** Angelica Cintron.

Licensing

Senior Vice President, Licensing: Howard Smith.

VP, Domestic Licensing: Steve Armus. **Vice President, Hard Goods:** Colin Hagen. **Director, Licensing/Minor Leagues:** Eliot Runyon. **Director, National Retail:** Adam Blinderman. **Director, Gifts/Novelties:** Maureen Mason. **Director, Hard Goods:** Mike Napolitano. **Director, Non-Authentics:** Greg Sim. **Director, Authentic Collection:** Ryan Samuelson. **Senior Manager, Presence Marketing:** Robin Jaffe.

Publishing and Photographs

Vice President, Publishing/Photographs: Don Hintze. **Editorial Director:** Mike McCormick. **Art Director, Publications:** Faith Rittenberg. **Director, MLB Photographs:** Rich Pilling.

Special Events

Senior Vice President, Special Events: Marla Miller. **Senior Director, Special Events:** Brian O'Gara. **Director, Special Events:** Eileen Buser. **Senior Manager, Special Events:** Rob Capilli. **Manager, Special Events:** Joe Fitzgerald. **Manager, Special Events:** Jennifer Jacobson.

Broadcasting

Senior Vice President, Broadcasting: Chris Tully. **VP, Broadcast Administration/Operations:** Bernadette McDonald. **Director, Broadcast Administration/Operations:** Chuck Torres.

Corporate Sales & Marketing

Senior Vice President, Corporate Sales/Marketing: John Brody. **VP, Partnership Marketing:** Jeremy Cohen. **Vice President, National Sales:** Ari Roitman. **Director, Local Sales:** Joe Grippo. **Manager, Partnership Marketing:** Jean Marie Glenister.

Advertising

Senior Vice President, Advertising/Marketing: Jacqueline Parkes. **Senior Director, Research:** Dan Derian. **Research Manager, Advertising:** Marc Beck.

Vice President, Design Services: Anne Occi.

Community Affairs/Educational Programming

Vice President, Community Affairs: Tom Brasuell. **Director, Community Relations:** Celia Bobrowsky.

General Administration

Senior Vice President, Accounting/Treasurer: Bob Clark.

Senior Vice President/General Counsel, Labor Relations: Dan Halem. **Senior VP/General Counsel; Business:** Ethan Orlinsky.

Senior Vice President/General Counsel; BOC: Tom Ostertag. **Senior VP, Finance:** Kathleen Torres.

Vice President, Application Development: Mike Morris. **VP, Deputy General Counsel:** Domna Candido. **Senior VP, Diversity/Strategic Alliances:** Wendy Lewis. **VP, Human Resources:** Ray Scott.

Vice President, Deputy General Counsel: Jennifer Simms. **VP, Operations & Tech Support:** Peter Surhoff.

Executive Director, Baseball Assistance Team: Jim Martin. **Senior Director, Office Operations:** Donna Hoder. **Senior Director, Quality Control:** Peggy O'Neill-Janosik.

Director, Recruitment: Francisco Estrada. **Director, Risk Management/Financial Reporting:** Anthony Avitabile. **Senior Manager, Records:** Mildred Delgado.

Manager, Payroll/Pension: Rich Hunt. **Manager, Benefits/HRIS:** Diane Cuddy.

International

Mailing Address: 245 Park Ave., 34th Floor, New York, NY 10167. **Telephone:** (212) 931-7500. **FAX:** (212) 949-5795.

Senior Vice President, International Business Operations: Paul Archey.

Vice President, International Licensing/Sponsorship: Shawn Lawson-Cummings. **VP/Executive Producer:** Russell Gabay. **Tournament Director, World Baseball Classic:** James Pearce. **Director, International Licensing:** Deidra Varona. **Director, International Corporate Marketing and Retail Services:** Jacquelyn Walsh. **Director, Market Development/Communications:** Dominick Balsamo. **VP/Managing Director, MLB Japan:** Jim Small.

Director, China Operations: Leon Xi. **Director, Australian Operations:** Thomas Nicholson. **Director, European Operations:** Clive Russell.

MLB Western Operations

Office Address: 2415 East Camelback Rd., Suite 850, Phoenix, AZ 85016. **Telephone:** (602) 281-7300. **FAX:** (602) 281-7313.

Vice President, Western Operations/Special Projects: Laurel Prieb. **Office Coordinator:** Valerie Dietrich

Major League Baseball Productions

Office Address: 75 Ninth Ave., New York, NY 10011. **Telephone:** (212) 931-7777. **FAX:** (212) 931-7788.

Vice President/Executive In Charge of Production: Dave Gavant. **VP, Programming/Business Affairs:** Elizabeth Scott. **Executive Producer:** David Check. **Director, Operations:** Shannon Valine. **Senior Producer:** Jonathan Nanberg. **Coordinating Producer:** Adam Schlackman. **Coordinating Producer, Field Production:** Robert Haddad.

Umpires

Lance Barksdale, Ted Barrett, Wally Bell, C.B. Bucknor, Mark Carlson, Gary Cederstrom, Eric Cooper, Derryl Cousins, Jerry Crawford, Fieldin Culbreth, Phil Cuzzi, Kerwin Danley, Gary Darling, Bob Davidson, Gerry Davis, Dana DeMuth, Laz Diaz, Mike DiMuro, Bruce Dreckman, Doug Eddings, Paul Emmel, Mike Everitt, Andy Fletcher, Marty Foster, Greg Gibson, Brian Gorman, Tom Hallion, Angel Hernandez, Ed Hickox, John Hirschbeck, Bill Hohn, Sam Holbrook, Marvin Hudson, Dan Iassogna, Jim Joyce, Jeff Kellogg, Ron Kulpa, Jerry Layne, Alfonso Marquez, Randy Marsh, Tim McClelland, Jerry Meals, Chuck Meriwether, Bill Miller, Ed Montague, Paul Nauert, Jeff Nelson, Brian O'Nora, Larry Poncino, Tony Randazzo, Ed Rapuano, Rick Reed, Mike Reilly, Charlie Reliford, Jim Reynolds, Brian Runge, Paul Schrieber, Dale Scott, Tim Timmons, Tim Tschida, Larry Vanover, Mark Wegner, Bill Welke, Tim Welke, Hunter Wendelstedt, Joe West, Mike Winters, Jim Wolf, Larry Young.

Events

2009 All-Star Game: July 14 at Busch Stadium, St. **Louis, MO.**

2009 World Series: TBD.

AMERICAN LEAGUE

Years League Active: 1901-.
2009 Opening Date: April 6. **Closing Date:** Oct 4.
Regular Season: 162 games.
Division Structure: East—Baltimore, Boston, New York, Tampa Bay, Toronto. Central—Chicago, Cleveland, Detroit, Kansas City, Minnesota. West—Los Angeles, Oakland, Seattle, Texas.
Playoff Format: Three division champions and second-place team with best record meet in two best-of-five Division Series. Winners meet in best-of-seven League Championship Series.
All-Star Game: July 14, Busch Stadium, St Louis (American League vs National League).
Roster Limit: 25, through Aug. 31 when rosters expand to 40.
Brand of Baseball: Rawlings.
Statistician: MLB Advanced Media, 75 Ninth Ave., 5th Floor, New York, NY 10011.

STADIUM INFORMATION

		Dimensions				
City	**Stadium**	**LF**	**CF**	**RF**	**Capacity**	**2008 Att.**
Baltimore	Camden Yards	333	410	318	48,190	1,950,075
Boston	Fenway Park	315	390	302	36,525	3,048,250
Chicago	U.S. Cellular Field	330	400	335	40,615	2,500,648
Cleveland	Progressive Field	325	405	325	43,545	2,169,760
Detroit	Comerica Park	345	420	330	41,000	3,202,645
Kansas City	Kauffman Stadium	330	410	330	38,030	1,578,922
Los Angeles	Angel Stadium	333	404	333	45,257	3,336,747
Minnesota	Humphrey Metrodome	343	408	327	46,632	2,302,431
New York	Yankee Stadium	318	408	314	52,325	*4,298,655
Oakland	McAfee Coliseum	330	400	367	34,077	1,665,256
Seattle	Safeco Field	331	405	326	47,447	2,329,702
Tampa Bay	Tropicana Field	315	404	322	41,315	1,811,986
Texas	Rangers Ballpark in Arlington	332	400	325	48,911	1,945,677
Toronto	Rogers Centre	328	400	328	49,539	2,399,786

*Denotes attendance at old Yankee Stadium

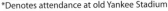

NATIONAL LEAGUE

Years League Active: 1876-.
2009 Opening Date: April 5. **Closing Date:** Oct 4.
Regular Season: 162 games.
Division Structure: East—Atlanta, Florida, New York, Philadelphia, Washington. Central—Chicago, Cincinnati, Houston, Milwaukee, Pittsburgh, St. Louis. West—Arizona, Colorado, Los Angeles, San Diego, San Francisco.
Playoff Format: Three division champions and second-place team with best record meet in two best-of-five Division Series. Winners meet in best-of-seven League Championship Series.
All-Star Game: July 14, Busch Stadium, St Louis (American League vs. National League).
Roster Limit: 25, through Aug. 31 when rosters expand to 40.
Brand of Baseball: Rawlings.
Statistician: MLB Advanced Media, 75 Ninth Ave., 5th Floor, New York, NY 10011.

STADIUM INFORMATION

		Dimensions				
City	**Stadium**	**LF**	**CF**	**RF**	**Capacity**	**2008 Att.**
Phoenix	Chase Field	330	407	334	49,033	2,509,924
Atlanta	Turner Field	335	400	330	49,743	2,532,834
Chicago	Wrigley Field	355	400	353	41,160	3,300,200
Cincinnati	Great American Ball Park	328	404	325	42,319	2,058,632
Colorado	Coors Field	347	415	350	50,499	2,650,218
Florida	Dolphins Stadium	330	434	345	38,560	1,335,076
Houston	Minute Maid Park	315	435	326	40,976	2,779,487
Los Angeles	Dodger Stadium	330	395	330	56,000	3,730,553
Milwaukee	Miller Park	344	400	345	41,900	3,068,458
New York	Citi Field	335	408	330	42,000	*4,042,045
Philadelphia	Citizens Bank Park	329	401	330	43,647	3,422,583
Pittsburgh	PNC Park	325	399	320	38,362	1,609,076
St. Louis	Busch Stadium	336	400	335	43,975	3,432,917
San Diego	PETCO Park	336	396	322	42,685	2,427,535
San Francisco	AT&T Park	339	399	309	41,503	2,863,837
Washington	Nationals Park	336	404	335	42,000	2,320,400

*Denotes attendance at Shea Stadium

Arizona Diamondbacks

Office Address: Chase Field, 401 E. Jefferson St, Phoenix, AZ 85004.
Mailing Address: P.O. Box 2095, Phoenix, AZ 58001.
Telephone: (602) 462-6500. **Fax:** (602) 462-6599.
Website: www.dbacks.com

Ownership

Managing General Partner: Ken Kendrick. **General Partners:** Mike Chipman, Dale Jensen, Jeff Royer.

BUSINESS OPERATIONS

Ken Kendrick

President/CEO: Derrick Hall. **Executive Assistant to President/CEO:** Brooke Mitchell.

Executive Vice President/COO: Tom Garfinkel. **Executive Assistant to Executive VP/COO:** Anita Barton. **Special Assistant to President:** Roland Hemond.

Broadcasting

Vice President, Broadcasting: Scott Geyer.

Corporate Partnerships/Marketing

Senior Vice President, Corporate Partnerships/Marketing: Cullen Maxey.

Senior Director, Marketing: Karina Bohn. **Brand Director:** Doug Alkire. **Directors, Corporate Partnerships:** Tim Emory, Steve Mullins. **Director, Hispanic Media Sales:** Julie Romero.

Finance/Legal

Executive Vice President/CFO: Tom Harris. **Executive Assistant/Office Manager:** Sandy Cox. **VP, Finance:** Craig Bradley. **VP/General Counsel:** Nona Lee. **Associate General Counsel:** Caleb Jay. **Legal Secretary:** Candace Kerege.

Community Affairs

Director, Community Affairs: Amy Buchan. **Manager, Community Affairs:** Pete Flocken.

Communications/Media Relations

Telephone: (602) 462-6519. **Fax:** (602) 462-6527.

Vice President, Communications: Shaun Rachau. **Director, Player/Media Relations:** Mike McNally. **Director, Corporate Communications:** Catherine Herman. **Assistant Director, Player/Media Relations:** Aaron Staenberg. **Coordinator, Player/Media Relations:** Lynita Johnson. **Director, Publications:** Greg Salvatore.

Stadium Operations

Vice President, Facility/Event Services: Russ Amaral. **Director, Security:** Sean Maguire. **Manager, Security:** Greg Green. **Senior Director, Suite/Premium Services:** Diney Ransford. **Director, Building Services:** Jim Hawkins. **Director, Engineering:** Jim White. **Director, Event Services:** Bryan White. **Event Coordinator:** Stephanie Scheidler. **Head Groundskeeper:** Grant Trenbeath. **Official Scorer:** Rodney Johnson.

Manager, Spring Training Operations: Bonnie Faircloth.

Ticketing

Telephone: (602) 514-8400. **Fax:** (602) 462-4141.

Vice President, Ticket Sales/Service: Brent Stehlik. **Senior Director, Suite/Premium Services:** Diney Ransford. **Director, Group/Inside Sales:** Jeremy Walls. **Director, Season Ticket Sales/Service:** John Fisher. **Director, Season Ticket Services:** Luis Calderon. **Director, Premium Seating:** Mike Dunham. **Director, Suite Sales:** Tim Martin. **Director, Ticket Development:** Joel McFadden. **Director, Ticket Operations:** Kenny Farrell.

Travel, Clubhouse

Director, Team Travel: Roger Riley. **Visitor Clubhouse:** Bob Doty.

GENERAL INFORMATION

Stadium (year opened): Chase Field (1998).
Home Dugout: Third Base. **Playing Surface:** Grass.
Team Colors: Sedona red, Sonoran sand and black.
Player Representative: Unavailable.
Driving Directions: I-10 to Seventh Street exit, turn south; I-17 to Seventh Street, turn north.

BASEBALL OPERATIONS

Telephone: (602) 462-6500. **Fax:** (602) 462-6425.

Senior Vice President/General Manager: Josh Byrnes.

Assistant GM: Peter Woodfork. **VP, Special Assistant to GM:** Bob Gebhard. **Manager, Baseball Operations:** Shiraz Rehman. **Baseball Operations Video Coordinator:** Jim Currigan.

Major League Staff

Manager: Bob Melvin.

Coaches: Bench—Kirk Gibson; Pitching—Bryan Price; Batting—Rick Schu; First Base—Lorenzo Bundy; Third Base—Chip Hale; Bullpen—Glenn Sherlock.

Medical, Training

Club Physicians: Dr. Michael Lee, Dr. Roger McCoy. **Head Trainer:** Ken Crenshaw. **Assistant Trainer:** Dave Edwards. **Strength/Conditioning Coach:** Nate Shaw.

Minor Leagues

Telephone: (602) 462-4400. **Fax:** (602) 462-6421.

Director, Player Development: A.J. Hinch.

Manager, Minor League Administration: Susan Webner.

Coordinators: Jack Howell (field), Mel Stottlemyre, Jr. (pitching), Dave Hansen (hitting), Tony Perezchica (infield), Joel Youngblood (outfield/baserunning), Bill Plummer (catching), Hatuey Mendoza (Latin liaison). **Tucson Complex Coordinator:** Bob Bensinger. **Medical Coordinator:** PJ Mainville. **Assistant Medical Coordinator:** Jimmy Southard. **Strength/Conditioning Coordinator:** Brett McCabe.

Farm System

Class	Club	Manager	Coach	Pitching Coach
Triple-A	Reno (PCL)	Brett Butler	Rick Burleson	Mike Parrott
Double-A	Mobile (SL)	Hector De La Cruz	Turner Ward	Jeff Pico
High A	Visalia (CAL)	Mike Bell	Nick Oldroyd	Alan Zinter
Low A	South Bend (MWL)	Mark Haley	Brian Czachowski	Francisco Morales
Short-season	Yakima (NWL)	Bob Didier	Andy Abad	Dan Carlson
Rookie	Missoula (PIO)	Audo Vicente	Jason Hardtke	Steve Merriman

Scouting

Telephone: (602) 462-6518. **Fax:** (602) 462-6527.

Director, Scouting: Tom Allison.

Director, Player Personnel: Jerry Dipoto. **Assistant Director, Scouting/International Supervisor:** Chad MacDonald.

Advance Scout/Consultant to Major League Staff: David Parrish.

Scouting Administrator: Jennifer Blatt. **Scouting Coordinator:** Helen Zelman.

Director, Pacific Rim Operations: Mack Hayashi. **Special Assistant, Pacific Rim Operations:** Jim Marshall.

Pro Scouts: Joe Bohringer (De Kalb, IL), Rico Brogna (Woodbury, CT), Jeff Cirillo (Medina, WA), Bill Earnhart (Point Clear, AL), Mike Piatnik (Winter Haven, FL), Tim Schmidt (San Bernardino, CA), Mike Sgobba (Scottsdale, AZ), Carlos Gomez (Atlanta, GA), Muzzy Jackson (Key Biscayne, FL), Kevin Jarvis (Franklin, TN), John Vander Wal (Grand Rapids, MI).

Amateur Scouting: Northeastern Regional Supervisor—Greg Lonigro (Connellsville, PA), Western Regional Supervisor—Bob Minor (Garden Grove, CA), Midwestern Regional Supervisor—Steve McAllister (Chillicothe, IL), Southeastern Regional Supervisor – Howard McCullough.

Scouts: Shawn Barton (Reading, PA), Ray Blanco (Miami, FL), Darold Brown (Elk Grove, CA), Trip Couch (Sugar Land, TX), Mike Daughtry (St. Charles, IL), Rodney Davis (Glendale, AZ), Jim Dedrick (Granite Falls, WA), Jason Karegeannes (Dallas, TX), Hal Kurtzman (Lake Balboa, CA), T.R. Lewis (Marietta, GA), Matt Merullo (Madison, CT), Jeff Mousser (Huntington Beach, CA), Joe Robinson (St. Louis, MO), George Swain (Wilmington, NC), Frankie Thon, Jr. (Louisville, KY), Luke Wrenn (Lakeland, FL).

Part-Time Scouts: Homer Newlin (Tallahassee, FL), Juan Gonzalez (Puerto Rico).

Special Assistant to GM, Latin American Operations: Junior Noboa (Dominican Republic).

International Scouts: Supervisor—Luis Baez (Santo Domingo, DR), Dominican Republic—Gabriel Berroa, José Ortiz, Rafael Mateo, Panama—José Díaz Perez. Nicaragua—Julio Sanchez. Colombia—Luis Gonzalez. Venezuela—Ubaldo Heredia, Marlon Urdaneta.

Spring Training

Complex Address: Tucson Electric Park, 2500 Ajo Way, Tucson, AZ 85713. **Telephone:** (520) 434-1400. **Seating Capacity:** 11,000. **Location:** I-10 to exit 262 (Park Street) or 263 (Kino Street), south to Ajo Way, left (east) on Ajo Way to park.

Hotel Address: JW Marriott Starr Pass Resort, 3800 W. Starr Pass Blvd., Tucson, AZ 85745. **Telephone:** (520) 792-3500.

Minor League Clubs

Complex Address: Kino Veterans Memorial Sportspark, 3600 S. Country Club, Tucson, AZ 85713. **Telephone:** (520) 434-1400. **Hotel Address:** The Hotel Arizona, 181 W. Broadway, Tucson, AZ 85701. **Telephone:** (520) 624-8711.

2009 SCHEDULE

CHASE FIELD

Standard Game Times: 6:40 p.m.; Sun. 1:40.

APRIL

6-8	Colorado
10-12	Dodgers
13-15	St. Louis
17-19	at San Francisco
20-22	Colorado
17-19	San Francisco
27-29	Cubs
30	at Milwaukee

MAY

1-3	at Milwaukee
4-5	at Dodgers
6-7	San Diego
8-10	Washington
11-13	Cincinnati
15-17	at Atlanta
18-21	at Florida
22-24	at Oakland
25-27	San Diego
28-31	Atlanta

JUNE

1-3	at Dodgers
5-8	at San Diego
9-11	San Francisco
12-14	Houston
16-18	at Kansas City
19-21	at Seattle
23-25	Texas
26-28	Angels
30	at Cincinnati

JULY

1-2	at Cincinnati
3-5	at Colorado
6-8	San Diego
9-12	Florida
17-19	at St. Louis
20-22	at Colorado
23-26	Pittsburgh
27-29	Philadelphia
31	at Mets

AUGUST

1-3	at Mets
4-6	at Pittsburgh
7-9	at Washington
10-12	Mets
14-16	Dodgers
18-20	at Philadelphia
21-23	at Houston
25-27	at San Francisco
28-30	Houston
31	at Dodgers

SEPTEMBER

1-3	at Dodgers
4-6	at Colorado
7-9	Dodgers
11-13	Milwaukee
14-16	at San Diego
18-20	Colorado
21-23	San Francisco
25-27	San Diego
29-30	at San Francisco

OCTOBER

1	at San Francisco
2-4	at Cubs

Atlanta Braves

Office Address: 755 Hank Aaron Dr, Atlanta, GA 30315.
Mailing Address: PO Box 4064, Atlanta, GA 30302.
Telephone: (404) 522-7630. **Fax:** (404) 614-1391.
Website: www.braves.com.

Ownership

Operated/Owned By: Liberty Media.
Chairman Emeritus: Bill Bartholomay. **Chairman/CEO:** Terry McGuirk.
President: John Schuerholz. **Senior Vice President:** Henry Aaron.

Terry McGuirk

BUSINESS OPERATIONS

Executive Vice President, Business Operations: Mike Plant.
VP/General Counsel: Greg Heller.

Finance

Vice President, Controller: Chip Moore.

Marketing, Sales

Executive Vice President, Sales/Marketing: Derek Schiller. **Executive Director, Marketing:** Gus Eurton. **Senior Director, Ticket Sales:** Paul Adams. **Senior Director, Corporate Sales:** Jim Allen.

Media Relations/Public Relations

Telephone: (404) 614-1556. **Fax:** (404) 614-1391.
Director, Media Relations: Brad Hainje. **Director, Public Relations:** Beth Marshall.
Publications Manager: Andy Pressley. **Public Relations Manager:** Meagan Swingle. **Senior Coordinator, Media Relations:** Adam Liberman. **Media Relations Coordinator:** Adrienne Midgley.

Stadium Operations

Director, Stadium Operations/Security: Larry Bowman.
Field Director: Ed Mangan. **Director, Game Entertainment:** Scott Cunningham. **PA Announcer:** Casey Motter. **Official Scorers:** Mike Stamus, Jack Wilkinson.

Ticketing

Telephone: (800) 326-4000. **Fax:** (404) 614-2480.
Director, Ticket Operations: Ed Newman.

Travel, Clubhouse

Director, Team Travel/Equipment Manager: Bill Acree.
Visiting Clubhouse Manager: John Holland.

GENERAL INFORMATION

Stadium (year opened): Turner Field (1997).
Home Dugout: First Base. **Playing Surface:** Grass.
Team Colors: Red, white and blue.
Player Representative: Unavailable.
Driving Directions: I-75/85 northbound/southbound, take exit 246 (Fulton Street); I-20 westbound, take exit 58A (Capitol Avenue); I-20 eastbound, take exit 56B (Windsor Street), right on Windsor Street, left on Fulton Street.

BASEBALL OPERATIONS

Telephone: (404) 522-7630. **Fax:** (404) 614-3308.
Executive Vice President/General Manager: Frank Wren.
Assistant GM: Bruce Manno. **Executive Assistant:** Melissa Stone.

Major League Staff

Manager: Bobby Cox.
Coaches: Bench—Chino Cadahia; Pitching—Roger McDowell; Batting—Terry Pendleton; First Base—Glenn Hubbard; Third Base—Brian Snitker; Bullpen—Eddie Perez.

Medical, Training

Head Team Physician: Dr. Norman Elliot.
Trainer: Jeff Porter. **Assistant Trainer:** Jim Lovell.
Strength/Conditioning Coach: Phil Falco.

Player Development

Telephone: (404) 522-7630. **Fax:** (404) 614-1350.
Special Assistant to the GM, Player Development: Jose Martinez.
Director, Player Development: Kurt Kemp. **Director, Baseball Administration:** John Coppolella. **Director, International Scouting/Operations:** Johnny Almaraz. **Assistant Director, Player Development:** Ronnie Richardson. **Administrative Assistants:** Raquel Davis, Chris Rice.
Minor League Field Coordinator: Tommy Shields. **Pitching Coordinator:** Kent Willis. **Hitting Coordinator:** Leon Roberts. **Roving Instructors:** Mike Alvarez (pitching), Joe Breeden (catching), Lynn Jones (outfield/base running), Jonathan Schuerholz (infield), Luckie Dacosta (strength/conditioning).

Farm System

Class	Club (League)	Manager	Coach	Pitching Coach
Triple-A	Gwinnett County (IL)	Dave Brundage	Jamie Dismuke	Derek Botelho
Double-A	Mississippi (SL)	Phillip Wellman	Roosevelt Brown	Marty Reed
High A	Myrtle Beach (CL)	Rocket Wheeler	Rick Albert	Guy Hansen
Low A	Rome (SAL)	Randy Ingle	Bobby Moore	Jim Czajkowski
Rookie	Danville (APP)	Paul Runge	Carlos Mendez	Derrick Lewis
Rookie	Braves (GCL)	Luis Ortiz	Sixto Lezcano	Gabe Luckert
Rookie	Braves (DSL)	Jose Tartabull	Unavailable	William Martinez

Scouting

Telephone: (404) 614-1359. **Fax:** (404) 614-1350.
Director, Scouting: Roy Clark. **Administrative Assistant, Scouting:** Dixie Keller.
Advance Scout: Bobby Wine (Norristown, PA). **Special Assignment Scouts:** Dick Balderson (Englewood, CO), Dom Chiti (Auburndale, FL), Tim Conroy (Monroeville, PA), Tony DeMacio (Virginia Beach, VA), Jim Fregosi (Tarpon Springs, FL), Chuck McMichael (Keller, TX), Jeff Wren (Senoia, GA).
Professional Scouts: Hep Cronin (Cincinnati, OH), Rod Gilbreath (Lilburn, GA), Lloyd Merritt (Myrtle Beach, SC), John Stewart (Granville, NY), Jonathan Story (Gulfport, MS),
National Supervisors: Jerry Jordan (Kingsport, TN), Terry R. Tripp (Harrisburg, IL). **Regional Supervisors:** West—Tom Battista (Tustin, CA). East—Paul Faulk (Laurinburg, NC). Midwest—Steve Taylor (Shawnee, OK). **Area Supervisors:** John Barron (Cameron, TX), Billy Best (Holly Spings, NC), Brian Bridges (Rome, GA), Stu Cann (Bradley, IL), Blaine Clemmens (San Francisco, CA), Ralph Garr (Richmond, TX), Chris Knabenshue (Fort Collins, CO), Brian Hunter (Murrieta, CA), Tim Moore (Florence, KY), Don Thomas (Geismar, LA), Terry C. Tripp (Raleigh, IL), Gerald Turner (Bedford, TX). Kevin Barry (Cream Ridge, NJ), Dan Cox (Santa Ana, CA), Brett Evert (Salem, OR), Buddy Hernandez (Orlando, FL). **Part-Time Scouts:** Hugh Buchanan (Snellville, GA), Dewayne Kitts (Moncks Corner, SC), Abraham Martinez (Santa Isabel, PR), Mike Spiers (San Bernardino, CA), Stan Teem (Ringgold, GA). Gene Kerns (Hagerstown, MD).
International Coordinators: Latin America—Roberto Aquino (Santo Domingo, Dominican Republic), Eastern Rim—Phil Dale (Victoria, Australia).
International Area Supervisors: Hiroyuki Oya (Japan), Luis Ortiz (Panama), Rolando Petit (Venezuela), Manuel Samaniego (Mexico),.

Spring Training

Stadium Address: Champions Park (1998), The Ballpark at Disney's Wide World of Sports Complex, 700 S. Victory Way, Kissimmee, FL 34747. **Telephone:** (407) 939-2200. **Seating Capacity:** 9,500. **Location:** I-4 to exit 25B (Highway 192 West), follow signs to Magic Kingdom/Wide World of Sports Complex, right on Victory Way.
Hotel Address: World Center Marriott, World Center Drive, Orlando, FL 32821. **Telephone:** (407) 239-4200.
Minor League Clubs
Complex Address: Same as major league club. **Telephone:** (407) 939-2232. **FAX:** (407) 939-2225. **Hotel Address:** Marriot Village at Lake Buena Vista, 8623 Vineland Ave., Orlando, FL 32821. **Telephone:** (407) 938-9001.

2009 SCHEDULE

TURNER FIELD

Standard Game Times:
7:35 p.m.; Mon./Sat. 7:05; Sun. 1:05.

APRIL
5 . . . . at Philadelphia
7-8 . . . . . . at Philadelphia
10-12 . . . . . . Washington
14-16 . . . . Florida
17-19 . . . . . . at Pittsburgh
20-22 . . . . . at Washington
24-26 . . . . . . at Cincinnati
27-29 . . . . St. Louis

MAY
1-3 . . . . Houston
4-5 . . . . Mets
6-7 . . . . at Florida
8-10 . . . . . at Philadelphia
11-13 . . . . at Mets
15-17 . . . . Arizona
18-21 . . . . Colorado
22-24 . . . . Toronto
25-27 . . . . at San Francisco
28-31 . . . . at Arizona

JUNE
2-4 . . . . Cubs
5-7 . . . . Milwaukee
8-11 . . . . Pittsburgh
12-14 . . . . . . at Baltimore
16-18 . . . . . . at Cincinnati
19-21 . . . . at Boston
23-25 . . . . Yankees
26-28 . . . . Boston
30 . . . . Philadelphia

JULY
1-2 . . . . Philadelphia
3-5 . . . . at Washington
6-8 . . . . at Cubs
9-12 . . . . at Colorado
16-19 . . . . Mets
20-23 . . . . . San Francisco
24-26 . . . . . at Milwaukee
28-30 . . . . at Florida
31 . . . . Dodgers

AUGUST
1-2 . . . . Dodgers
3-5 . . . . at San Diego
6-9 . . . . at Dodgers
11-12 . . . . . . Washington
14-16 . . . . . . Philadelphia
18-20 . . . . at Mets
21-23 . . . . Florida
25-27 . . . . San Diego
28-30 . . . . at Philadelphia
31 . . . . at Florida

SEPTEMBER
1-3 . . . . at Florida
4-6 . . . . Cincinnati
8-10 . . . . at Houston
11-13 . . . . at St. Louis
15-17 . . . . Mets
18-20 . . . . . . Philadelphia
21-23 . . . . at Mets
25-27 . . . . . at Washington
28-30 . . . . Florida

OCTOBER
1-4 . . . . Washington

Baltimore Orioles

Office Address: 333 W. Camden St, Baltimore, MD 21201.
Telephone: (888) 848-BIRD. **Fax:** (410) 547-6272.
E-mail Address: birdmail@orioles.com. **Website:** www.orioles.com.

Ownership

Operated By: The Baltimore Orioles Limited Partnership Inc.
Chairman/CEO: Peter Angelos.

BUSINESS OPERATIONS

Peter Angelos

Vice Chairman, Community Projects/Public Affairs: Thomas Clancy. **Executive Vice President:** John Angelos. **VP/Special Liaison to Chairman:** Lou Kousouris. **General Legal Counsel:** Russell Smouse. **Director, Human Resources:** Lisa Tolson. **Director, Information Systems:** James Kline.

Finance

Vice President/CFO: Robert Ames.

Public Relations/Communications

Telephone: (410) 547-6150. **Fax:** (410) 547-6272.

Director, Communications: Greg Bader. **Director, Public Relations:** Monica Barlow. **Manager, Media Relations:** Jeff Lantz. **Coordinator, Baseball Information:** Jay Moskowitz. **Director, Promotion/Community Initiatives:** Kristen Schultz.

Ballpark Operations

Director, Ballpark Operations: Doug Rosenberger. **Head Groundskeeper:** Nicole Sherry.

PA Announcer: David McGowan. **Official Scorers:** Jim Henneman, Marc Jacobsen.

Ticketing

Telephone: (888) 848-BIRD. **Fax:** (410) 547-6270.

Director, Sales/Fan Services: Neil Aloise. **Assistant Director, Sales:** Mark Hromalik. **Ticket Manager:** Audrey Brown.

Travel/Clubhouse

Traveling Secretary: Phil Itzoe.

Equipment Manager (Home): Jim Tyler. **Equipment Manager (Road):** Fred Tyler. **Umpires, Field Attendant:** Ernie Tyler.

GENERAL INFORMATION

Stadium (year opened): Oriole Park at Camden Yards (1992).

Home Dugout: First Base. **Playing Surface:** Grass.

Team Colors: Orange, black and white.

Player Representative: Unavailable.

Driving Directions: From the north and east on I-95, take I-395 (exit 53), downtown to Russell Street; from the south or west on I-95, take exit 52 to Russell Street North.

Andy MacPhail

BASEBALL OPERATIONS

Telephone: (410) 547-6121. **Fax:** (410) 547-6271.

President, Baseball Operations: Andy MacPhail.

Special Assistant: Wayne Krivsky. **Director, Baseball Operations:** Matt Klentak.

Major League Staff

Manager: Dave Trembley.

Coaches: Bench—Dave Jauss; Pitching—Rick Kranitz; Batting—Terry Crowley; First Base—John Shelby; Third Base—Juan Samuel; Bullpen—Alan Dunn.

Medical, Training

Club Physician: Dr. William Goldiner. **Club Physician, Orthopedics:** Dr. Andrew Cosgarea.

Head Athletic Trainer: Richie Bancells. **Assistant Athletic Trainer:** Brian Ebel. **Strength/Conditioning Coach:** Jay Shiner.

Minor Leagues

Telephone: (410) 547-6120. **Fax:** (410) 547-6298.

Director, Player Development: David Stockstill. **Assistant Director, Player Development:** Tripp Norton. **Director, Minor League Instruction:** Brian Graham. **Hitting Coordinator:** Julio Vinas. **Pitching Coordinator:** Dave Schmidt. **Medical Coordinator:** Dave Walker. **Latin American Medical Coordinator:** Manny Lopez. **Strength/Conditioning Coach:** Joe Hogarty. **Facilities Coordinator:** Jaime Rodriguez. **Camp Coordinator:** Len Johnston.

Roving Instructors: Butch Davis (outfield/baserunning), Alex Arias (infield), Larry Jaster (pitching coordinator, Florida operations), Denny Walling (hitting), Don Werner (catching).

Farm System

Class	Club (League)	Manager	Coach	Pitching Coach
Triple-A	Norfolk (IL)	Gary Allenson	Dallas Williams	Mike Griffin
Double-A	Bowie (EL)	Brad Komminsk	Moe Hill	Larry McCall
High A	Frederick (CL)	Richie Hebner	J.J. Cannon	Kennie Steenstra
Low A	Delmarva (SAL)	Orlando Gomez	Ryan Minor	Blaine Beatty
Short-season	Aberdeen (NYP)	Gary Kendall	C. Devarez/J. Alfaro	Scott McGregor
Rookie	Bluefield (App)	Einar Diaz	Jim Saul	Troy Mattes
Rookie	Orioles (GCL)	Ramon Sambo	Unavailable	Calvin Maduro
Rookie	Orioles (DSL)	Miguel Jabalera	B. Adames/R. Lubo/F. Nunez	Evaristo Mercedes

Professional Scouting

Telephone: (410) 547-6121. **Fax:** (410) 547-6298.

Director, International Scouting: John Stockstill.

Director, Professional Scouting: Lee MacPhail IV.

Major League Advance Scout: Jim Thrift. **Major League Scouts:** Dave Engle (San Diego, CA), Bruce Kison (Bradenton, FL). **Professional Scouts:** Todd Frohwirth (Waukesha, WI), Dave Hollins (Orchad Park, NY), Jim Howard (Clifton Park, NY), Deacon Jones (Sugar Land, TX), Ted Lakas (Worcester, MA), Bobby Myrick (Colonial Heights, VA), Gary Roenicke (Nevada City, CA), Fred Uhlman Sr. (Baltimore, MD).

Amateur Scouting

Telephone: (410) 547-6187. **Fax:** (410) 547-6298.

Director, Amateur Scouting: Joe Jordan. **Scouting Administrator:** Marcy Zerhusen.

National Crosschecker: Matt Reubel (Oklahoma City, OK). **Regional Crosscheckers:** East—Nick Presto (Palm Beach Garden, FL), Central—Deron Rombach (Mansfield, TX), West—David Blume (Elk Grove, CA). East-Dean Albany (Baltimore, MD).

Full-Time Scouts: Keith Connolly (Fair Haven, NJ), Dave Dangler (Camas, WA), Adrian Dorsey (Florence, KY), John Gillette (Gilbert, AZ), David Jennings (Daphne, AL), James Keller (Sacremento, CA), Gilbert Kubski (Huntington Beach, CA), John Martin (Tampa, FL), Rich Morales (League City, TX), Mark Ralston (San Diego, CA), Jim Richardson (Marlow, OK), Bob Szymkowski (Chicago, IL), Mike Tullier (River Ridge, NC), Dominic Viola (Cary, NC).

Dominican Summer League, Camp Coordinator: Felipe Alou Jr.

International Scouts: Salvador Ramirez (Dominican), Carlos Bernhardt (Dominican).

Spring Training

Complex Address (first year): Fort Lauderdale Stadium (1996), 1301 NW 55th St., Fort Lauderdale, FL 33309. **Telephone:** (954) 776-1921. **Seating Capacity:** 8,340. **Location:** I-95 to exit 32 (Commercial Blvd.), West on Commercial, right on Orioles Blvd., stadium on left. **Hotel Address:** Sheraton Suites, 555 NW 62nd St., Fort Lauderdale, FL 33309. **Telephone:** (954) 772-5400.

Minor League Clubs

Complex Address: Twin Lakes Park, 6700 Clark Rd., Sarasota, FL 34241. **Telephone:** (941) 923-1996. **Hotel Address:** Ramada Inn Limited, 5774 Clark Rd., Sarasota, FL 34233. **Telephone:** (941) 921-7812; Americinn, 5931 Fruitville Rd., Sarasota, FL 34232. **Telephone:** (941) 342-8778.

2009 SCHEDULE

CAMDEN YARDS

Standard Game Times:
1:35 p.m; Sun. 1:05

APRIL

6-9 . . . Yankees
10-12 . . . Tampa Bay
13-15 . . . at Texas
17-20 . . . at Boston
21-23 . . . White Sox
24-27 . . . Texas
28-29 . . . Angels

MAY

1-3 . . . at Toronto
4-5 . . . at Tampa Bay
6-7 . . . Minnesota
8-10 . . . Yankees
12-13 . . . Tampa Bay
14-17 . . . at Kansas City
19-21 . . . at Yankees
22-24 . . . at Washington
25-27 . . . Toronto
28-31 . . . Detroit

JUNE

1-3 . . . at Seattle
5-7 . . . at Oakland
9-11 . . . Seattle
12-14 . . . Atlanta
16-18 . . . Mets
19-21 . . . at Philadelphia
23-25 . . . at Florida
26-28 . . . Washington
29-30 . . . Boston

JULY

1 . . . Boston
2-5 . . . at Angels
6-8 . . . at Seattle
10-12 . . . Toronto
17-19 . . . at White Sox
20-22 . . . at Yankees
24-26 . . . at Boston
27-30 . . . Kansas City
31 . . . Boston

AUGUST

1-2 . . . Boston
3-6 . . . at Detroit
7-9 . . . at Toronto
10-12 . . . Oakland
14-17 . . . Angels
18-20 . . . at Tampa Bay
21-23 . . . at White Sox
24-26 . . . at Minnesota
27-30 . . . Cleveland
31 . . . Yankees

SEPTEMBER

1-2 . . . Yankees
4-6 . . . Texas
8-9 . . . at Boston
11-13 . . . at Yankees
14-17 . . . Tampa Bay
18-20 . . . Boston
21-23 . . . at Toronto
25-27 . . . at Cleveland
28-30 . . . at Tampa Bay

OCTOBER

1 . . . at Tampa Bay
2-4 . . . Toronto

Boston Red Sox

Office Address: Fenway Park, 4 Yawkey Way, Boston, MA 02215.
Telephone: (617) 226-6000. **Fax:** (617) 226-6416.
Website: www.redsox.com

Ownership

Principal Owner: John Henry. **Chairman:** Thomas Werner. **Vice Chairmen:** David Ginsberg, Phillip Morse.

President/CEO: Larry Lucchino. **Director:** George Mitchell.

BUSINESS OPERATIONS

Larry Lucchino

COO: Mike Dee. **Senior Vice President, Fenway Affairs:** Larry Cancro. **Senior VP, Corporate Relations/Executive Director, Red Sox Foundation:** Meg Vaillancourt. **VP, Emeritus:** Joe McDermott. **Executive Consultant:** Lou Gorman. **Senior Business Analyst:** Tim Zue. **Senior Advisor/Baseball Projects:** Jeremy Kapstein. **Senior Advisor/Strategic Planning:** Michael Porter.

Vice President, Club Counsel: Elaine Steward. **Vice President, Club Counsel:** Jennifer Flynn.

Finance/Human Resources

Vice President, CFO: Bob Furbush. **VP, Finance:** Steve Fitch. **Director, Finance:** Ryan Oremus. **Payroll Administrator:** Mauricio Rosas. **Accounting Manager:** Cathy Fahy. **Senior Tax Accountant:** Erin Walsh. **Senior Accountant:** Tom Williams. **VP, Human Resources/Office Administration:** Mary Sprong. **Human Resources Manager:** Patricia Moseley. **Director, Information Technology:** Steve Conley. **Senior Systems Analyst:** Randy George.

Sales/Corporate Marketing/Broadcasting

Executive Vice President, Chief Sales/Marketing Officer: Sam Kennedy. **VP, Corporate Partnerships:** Joe Januszewski. **VP, Marketing:** Adam Grossman. **Vice President, Client Services:** Troup Parkinson. **Director, Client Services:** Marcell Saporita. **Coordinator, Sponsor Services:** Margaret Gormley. **Senior Manager, State Street Pavillion Club Services:** Carole Alkins. **Manager, Suite Services:** Kim Cameron. **Manager, Community Marketing/Fan Clubs:** Mardi Fuller. **Assistant Director, Fenway Enterprises:** Marcita Thompson. **Manager, Fenway Enterprises/ Broadcasting:** Colin Burch.

Public/Community Relations

VP, Public Affairs: Susan Goodenow. **Director, Media Relations:** Pam Ganley. **Coordinator, Baseball Information:** Henry Mahegan. **VP, Publications/Archives:** Dick Bresciani. **Director, Publications:** Debbie Matson.

Business, Ballpark Operations/Development

Senior Vice President, Planning/Development: Janet Smith. **Senior Manager, Planning/Development:** Paul Hanlon. **Senior Vice President, Business Operations:** Jonathan Gilula. **Director, Security/Emergency Services:** Charles Cellucci. **Director, Facilities Management:** Tom Queenan. **Director, Event Operations:** Jeff Goldenberg. **Director, Grounds:** Dave Mellor. **Director Emeritus, Grounds:** Joe Mooney.

Vice President, Fan Services/ Entertainment: Sarah McKenna. **Manager, Entertainment/Special Event Operations:** Dan Lyons. **Manager, Television Production:** John Carter. **Manager, Video Operations/Scoreboard:** Sarah Logan.

PA Announcer: Carl Beane. **Official Scorers:** Charles Scoggins, Mike Shalin, Bob Ellis, Mike Petraglia.

Ticketing Services/Operations

Telephone: 877-REDSOX9. **Fax:** (617) 226-6640.

Vice President/Ticketing: Ron Bumgarner. **Director, Ticketing:** Richard Beaton. **Assistant Director, Ticketing:** Naomi Calder.

Assistant Director, Ticketing-Season Ticket Services/Information: Joe Matthews. **Senior Manager, Premium Sales:** Corey Bowdre.

Travel/Clubhouse

Traveling Secretary: Jack McCormick. **Equipment Manager/Clubhouse Operations:** Joe Cochran. **Assistant Equipment Manager:** Edward Jackson. **Visiting Clubhouse Manager:** Tom McLaughlin. **Video Coordinator:** Billy Broadbent.

GENERAL INFORMATION

Stadium (year opened): Fenway Park (1912).
Home Dugout: First Base. **Playing Surface:** Grass.
Team Colors: Navy blue, red and white.
Player Representative: Kevin Youkilis.
Driving Directions: Massachusetts Turnpike (I-90) to Prudential exit (stay left), right at first set of lights, right on Dalton Street, left on Boylston Street, right on Ipswich Street.

Theo Epstein

BASEBALL OPERATIONS

Telephone: (617) 226-6000. **Fax:** (617) 226-6695.

Executive Vice President/General Manager: Theo Epstein.

Assistant GM: Jed Hoyer. **Vice President, Player Personnel:** Ben Cherington. **Vice President, International Scouting:** Craig Shipley. **Assistant to GM:** Allard Baird. **Special Assistant:** David Howard. **Senior Advisor:** Bill James. **Director, Baseball Operations:** Brian O'Halloran. **Assistant Director, Baseball Operations:** Zack Scott.

Major League Staff

Manager: Terry Francona.

Coaches: Bench—Brad Mills; Pitching—John Farrell; Batting—Dave Magadan; First Base—Tim Bogar; Third Base—DeMarlo Hale; Bullpen—Gary Tuck.

Medical/Training

Medical Director: Dr. Thomas Gill. **Internist:** Dr. Larry Ronan. **Head Trainer:** Paul Lessard.

Player Development

Telephone: (617) 226-6000. **Fax:** (617) 226-6695.

Director, Player Development: Mike Hazen. **Director, Minor League Operations:** Raquel Ferreira. **Assistant Director, Player Development:** Ethan Faggett. **Assistant, Player Development:** Jared Banner.**Director, Florida Operations:** Todd Stephenson. **Coordinator, Latin American Operations:** Eddie Romero.

Field Coordinator: Rob Leary. **Roving Instructors:** Bruce Crabbe (infield), Tom Goodwin (outfield/baserunning), Victor Rodriguez (hitting), Ralph Treuel (pitching).

Farm System

Class	Club (League)	Manager	Coach(es)	Pitching Coach
Triple-A	Pawtucket (IL)	Ron Johnson	Russ Morman	Rich Sauveur
Double-A	Portland (EL)	Arnie Beyeler	Dave Joppie	Mike Cather
High A	Salem (CL)	Chad Epperson	Carlos Febles	Dick Such
Low A	Greenville (SAL)	Kevin Boles	Billy McMillion	Bob Kipper
Short-season	Lowell (NYP)	Gary DiSarcina	Luis Lopez	Kevin Walker
Rookie	Red Sox (GCL)	Dave Tomlin	U.L. Washington	G. Gregson/W. Miranda
Rookie	Red Sox (DSL)	Jose Zapata	Nelson Paulino	Jose Gonzalez

Scouting

Director, Amateur Scouting: Jason McLeod. **Assistant Director, Amateur Scouting:** Amiel Sawdaye. **Coordinator, Professional Scouting:** Jared Porter. **Advance Scouting Coordinator:** Ben Crockett. **Assistant, International Scouting:** Fernando Tamayo

Advance Scout: Dana Levangie (East Bridgewater, MA).

Major League Scouts: Galen Carr (Burlington, VT), Kyle Evans (Boston, MA), Gus Quattlebaum (Long Beach, CA).

Pro Scouts: Jaymie Bane (Parrish, FL), Dean Decillis (Weston, FL), Dave Klipstein (Roanoke, TX), Bill Latham (Trussville, AL), Curtis Leskanic (Orlando, FL), Joe McDonald (Lakeland, FL), Steve Peck (Scottsdale, AZ), Jerry Stephenson (Fullerton, CA). **National Crosschecker:** David Finley (San Diego, CA). **Regional Crosscheckers:** East—Mike Rikard (Durham, NC); Midwest—Danny Haas (Boston, MA); West—Mark Wasinger (El Paso, TX); Southeast—Fred Petersen (Horshoe Bay, TX).

Area Scouts: John Booher (Austin, TX), Quincy Boyd (Harrisburg, NC), Chris Calciano (Ocean View, DE), Matt Dorey (Vancouver, WA), Raymond Fagnant (East Granby, CT), Duane Gustavson (Westerville, OH), Laz Gutierrez (Miramar, FL), Blair Henry (Roseville, CA), Tim Hyers (Loganville, GA), Ernie Jacobs (Wichita, KS), Wally Komatsubara (Aiea, HI), Dan Madsen (Murrieta, CA), Matt Mahoney (Scottsdale, AZ), Chris Mears (Lake Villa, IL) Edgar Perez (Vega Baja, PR), Jim Robinson (Arlington, TX), Anthony Turco (Tampa, FL), Danny Watkins (Tuscaloosa, AL), Jim Woodward (Claremont, CA).

Director, Dominican Operations: Jesus Alou.

International Scouts: Jose Cabrera (Mexico), Luciano Del Rosario (Dominican), Angel Escobar (Venezuela), Brian Farley (Europe), Julio Guevara (Venezuela), Niko Lin (Taiwan), Santiago Prada (Columbia), Luis Prieto (Venezuela), Juan Carlos Pringle (Panama), Antonio Simon (Curacao), Victor Torres (Dominican), Fernando Veracierto (Venezuela).

Spring Training

Complex Address (First year): City of Palms Park (1993), 2201 Edison Ave., Fort Myers, FL 33901. **Telephone:** (239) 334-4799. **Fax:** (239) 332-8105. **Seating Capacity:** 7575. **Location:** I-75 to exit 138, four miles west to Fowler St., left on Fowler to Edison Ave., right on Edison Ave., park on right. **Hotel Address:** Homewood Suites Hotel, 5255 Big Pine Way, Fort Myers, FL 33907. **Telephone:** (239) 275-6000.

Minor League Clubs

Complex Address: Red Sox Minor League Complex, 4301 Edison Ave., Fort Myers, FL 33916. **Telephone:** (239) 334-4799. **Hotel Address:** Ambassador Hotel, 2500 Edwards Dr., Fort Myers, FL 33901. **Telephone:** (239) 337-0300.

2009 SCHEDULE

FENWAY PARK

Standard Game Times:
7:05; Sun. 2:05

APRIL

4-9 . . . . Tampa Bay
10-12 . . . . at Angels
13-15 . . . . at Oakland
17-20 . . . . Baltimore
21-22 . . . . .Minnesota
24-26 . . . . Yankees
27-29 . . . . . . at Cleveland
30 . . . . at Tampa Bay

MAY

1-3. . . . . at Tampa Bay
4-5. . . . . .at Yankees
6-7. . . . . Cleveland
8-10. . . . . Tampa Bay
12-14 . . . . at Angels
15-17 . . . . at Seattle
19-21 . . . . Toronto
22-24 . . . . Mets
25-28 . . . . . . at Minnesota
39-31 . . . . at Toronto

JUNE

2-4. . . . . at Detroit
5-7. . . . . Texas
9-11 . . . . Yankees
12-14 . . . . .at Philadelphia
16-18 . . . . Florida
19-21 . . . . Atlanta
23-25 . . . . . at Washington
26-28 . . . . at Atlanta
29-30 . . . . . . .at Baltimore

JULY

1 . . . . .at Baltimore
3-5. . . . . Seattle
6-8. . . . . Oakland
9-12. . . . . Kansas City
17-19 . . . . at Toronto
20-22 . . . . at Texas
24-26 . . . . Baltimore
27-30 . . . . Oakland
31 . . . . at Baltimore

AUGUST

1-2. . . . . at Baltimore
4-5. . . . . at Tampa Bay
6-9. . . . . at Yankees
10-13 . . . . Detroit
14-16 . . . . at Texas
18-20 . . . . at Toronto
21-23 . . . . Yankees
24-27 . . . . White Sox
28-30 . . . . Toronto

SEPTEMBER

1-3. . . . . Tampa Bay
4-7. . . . . at White Sox
8-9. . . . . Baltimore
11-13 . . . . Tampa Bay
15-17 . . . . Angels
18-20 . . . . at Baltimore
21-24 . . . . . at Kansas City
25-27 . . . . .at Yankees
28-30 . . . . Toronto

OCTOBER

1-4. . . . . Cleveland

Chicago Cubs

Office Address: Wrigley Field, 1060 W. Addison St, Chicago, IL 60613.
Telephone: (773) 404-2827. **Fax:** (773) 404-4129.
E-mail Address: cubs@cubs.com
Website: www.cubs.com.

Ownership

Owner: Tribune Co. **Chairman:** Crane Kenney.

BUSINESS OPERATIONS

Phone: (773) 404-2827. **Fax:** (773) 404-4111.
Executive Vice President, Business Operations: Mark McGuire.
Executive Coordinator, Business Operations,: Sarah Poontong.

Mark McGuire

Accounting

Co-Directors, Finance: Jodi Reischl, Terri Fleischhacker. **Accounting Manager:** Mike Van Poucke. **Finance Manager:** Jaime Norton. **Payroll Administrator:** Theresa Bacholzky. **Senior Accountants:** Marian Greene, Aimee Sison. **Staff Accountant:** Mario Becerra.

Human Resources

Senior Director, Human Resources: Jenifer Surma. **Employment Manager:** Marisol Widmayer. **Human Resources Coordinator:** Danielle Alexa.

Event Operations/Security

Manager, Event Operations/Security: Mike Hill. **Coordinator, Event Operations/Security:** Julius Farrell. **Coordinator, Facility Management:** Russell Johnson. **Coordinator, Exterior Operations:** Mary Kusmirek. **Switchborad Operator/Receptionist:** Brenda Morgan.

Facility Management/Information Technology

Senior Director, Facility Management/Information Technology: Carl Rice. **Information Systems Analyst:** Sean True. **Information Systems Support Specialist Specialist:** Lucas Luecke. **Coordinator, Office Services:** Randy Skocz. **Head Groundskeeper:** Roger Baird. **Facility Supervisor:** Bill Scott.

Legal/Community Affairs

Senior Vice President, Community Affairs/General Counsel: Michael Lufrano. **Managers, Community Affairs:** Mary Dosek, Jill Lawlor. **Senior Coordinator, Community Affairs/Neighborhood Relations:** Jennifer Dedes Nowak. **Administrative Assistant, Community Affairs:** Vijay Tekchandani.

Marketing/Broadcasting

Director, Sales and Promotions: Matthew Wszolek. **Manager, Mezzanine Suites:** Louis Artiaga. **Manager, Special Events/Player Relations/Entertainment:** Joe Rios. **Manager, Sponsorship Sales:** David Knickerbocker. **Senior Account Executive:** Andrea Burke.

Account Executives: Ryan Balogh, Piper Mead, Jaime Morales, Jim Oboikowitch, Anna Rivera. **Sponsorship Sales Service Representative:** Ryan McDonough. **Mezzanine Suites Account Executive:** Mireya Medina. **Administrative Assistant, Marketing:** Remy Swain.

Media Relations/Publications

Telephone: (773) 404-4191. **Fax:** (773) 404-4129.

Director, Media Relations: Peter Chase. **Assistant Director, Media Relations:** Jason Carr. **Coordinator, Media Relations:** Dani Holmes. **Assistant, Media Relations:** Dusty Harrington. **Director, Publications/Creative Services:** Lena McDonagh. **Photographer:** Stephen Green.

Ticket Operations

Telephone: (773) 404-2827. **Fax:** (773) 404-4014.

Director, Ticket Operations: Frank Maloney. **Assistant Director, Ticket Sales:** Brian Garza. **Assistant Director, Ticket Services:** Joe Kirchen. **Vault Room Supervisor:** Cherie Blake. **Coordinator, Ticket Orders:** Jan Jotzat. **Coordinator, Ticket Sales:** Karry Kerness. **Senior Ticket Sales Representative:** Kevin Enerson.

Game Day Operations

PA Announcers: Paul Friedman, Wayne Messmer, Michael Terson. **Clubhouse Manager:** Tom Hellmann. **Visiting Clubhouse Manager:** Michael Burkhart. **Home Clubhouse Assistant:** Gary Stark.

GENERAL INFORMATION

Stadium (year opened): Wrigley Field (1914).
Home Dugout: Third Base. **Playing Surface:** Grass.
Team Colors: Royal blue, red and white.
Player Representative: Unavailable.
Driving Directions: I-90/94 to Addison Street exit, follow Addison five miles to ballpark. One mile west of Lakeshore Drive, exit at Belmont going northbound, exit at Irving Park going southbound.

Jim Hendry

BASEBALL OPERATIONS

Telephone: (773) 404-2827. **Fax:** (773) 404-4111.

Vice President/General Manager: Jim Hendry. **Assistant GM:** Randy Bush. **Director, Baseball Administration:** Scott Nelson. **Senior Advisor:** Billy Williams. **Special Assistants:** Gary Hughes, Ken Kravec, Dave Littlefield, Ed Lynch, Louie Elijua, Mike Valarezo. **Major League Scouts:** Bill Harford, Brad Kelley. **Manager, Baseball Information:** Chuck Wasserstrom. **Traveling Secretary:** Jimmy Bank. **Major League Advance Scout:** Keith Stohr.

Major League Staff

Manager: Lou Piniella

Coaches: Pitching—Larry Rothschild; Hitting—Gerald Perry; Bench—Alan Trammell; Third Base—Mike Quade; First Base—Mike Sinatro; Bullpen—Lester Strode; Special Assistant—Ivan DeJesus.

Medical/Training

Team Physician: Dr. Stephen Adams. **Team Orthopedist:** Dr. Stephen Gryzlo.
Director Athletic Training: Mark O'Neal. **Strength/Conditioning Coordinator:** Tim Buss.

Player Development

Telephone: (773) 404-4035. **Fax:** (773) 404-4147

Vice President, Player Personnel: Oneri Fleita.

Coordinators: Dave Bialas (field), Mark Riggins (pitching), Bobby Dernier (outfield/baserunning), Franklin Font (infield), Dave Keller (hitting) Jody Davis (catching). **Latin American Field Coordinator:** Carmelo Martinez. **Minor League Training Coordinator:** Justin Sharpe. **Assistant Minor League Training Coordinator:** Chuck Baughman. **Strength and Conditioning Coordinator:** Doug Jarrow. **Strength/Conditioning Coach:** Scott Weberg. **Manager, Player Development Administration:** Patti James. **Equipment Manager:** Dana Noeltner.

Farm System

Class	Club (League)	Manager	Hitting Coach	Pitching Coach
Triple-A	Iowa (PCL)	Bobby Dickerson	Von Joshua	Mike Mason
Double-A	Tennessee (SL)	Ryne Sandberg	Tom Beyers	Dennis Lewallyn
High Class A	Daytona (FSL)	Buddy Bailey	Richie Zisk	Tom Pratt
Low Class A	Peoria (MWL)	Marty Pevey	Barbaro Garbey	Rich Bombard
Short-season	Bosie (NWL)	Casey Kopitzke	Desi Wilson	David Rosario
Rookie	Cubs (AZL)	Juan Cabreja	Ricardo Medina	Rick Tronerud
Rookie	Cubs I (DSL)	Alberto Garcia	Ramon Caraballo	Leo Hernandez
Rookie	Cubs II (DSL)	Franklin Blanco	Leo Perez	Anderson Tavares

Scouting

Telephone: (773) 404-2827. **Fax:** (773) 404-4147.

Director, Amateur/Professional Scouting: Tim Wilken (Dunedin, FL).

Director, International Scouting: Paul Weaver. **Special Assistant:** Steve Hinton (Mather, CA). **Player Development/Scouting Assistant:** Jake Ciarrachi. **Baseball Operations Assistant:** Alex Suarez. **Administrative Assistant:** Patricia Honzik.

Pro Scouts: Tom Bourque (Cambridge, MA), Jim Crawford (Madison, MS), Joe Housey (Hollywood, FL), Demie Mainieri (Ft. Lauderdale, FL), Mark Servais (LaCrosse, WI), Charlie Silvera (Millbrae, CA). **Special Assignment Scouts:** Bob Lofrano (Woodland Hills, CA), Glen Van Proyan (Lisle, IL).

National Crosschecker: Sam Hughes (Atlanta, GA).

Crosscheckers: East—Charles Aliano (Land O'Lakes, FL), Midwest—Steve Riha (Houston, TX), West—Mark Adair (Phoenix, AZ).

Area Scouts: John Bartsch (Rocklin, CA), Billy Blitzer (Brooklyn, NY), Trey Forkerway (Houston, TX), Steve Fuller (Seal Beach, CA), Al Geddes (Canby, OR), Antonio Grissom (College Park, GA), Denny Henderson (Orange, CA), Steve McFarland (Scottsdale, AZ), Lukas McKnight (Westfield, NY), Brandon Mozley (Nixa, MO), Rolando Pino (Pembroke Pines, FL), Keith Ryman (Jefferson City, TN), Billy Swoope (Norfolk, VA), Michael Valarezo (Hoover, AL), Stan Zielinski (Winfield, IL).

International Scouts: Hector Ortega (Venezuela), Jose Serra (Dominican Republic), Steve Wilson (Asia).

Spring Training

Major League Complex Address: HoHoKam Park, 1235 N. Center St., Mesa, AZ 85201. **Telephone:** (480) 668-0500. **Seating Capacity:** 12,632. **Location:** Main Street (U.S. Highway 60) to Center Street, north 1 1/2 miles on Center Street.

Hotel Address: Best Western Dobson Ranch Inn, 1666 S. Dobson Rd., Mesa, AZ 85202. **Telephone:** (480) 831-7000.

Minor League Clubs

Complex Address: Fitch Park, 160 E. Sixth Place, Mesa, AZ 85201. **Telephone:** (480) 668-0500. **FAX:** (480) 668-4501. **Hotel Address:** Best Western Mezona, 250 W. Main St., Mesa, AZ 85201. **Telephone:** (480) 834-9233.

2009 SCHEDULE

WRIGLEY FIELD

Standard Game Times: 1:20 p.m., 7:05.

APRIL

6-8 . . . . . at Houston
10-12 . . . . . at Milwaukee
13 . . . . . Colorado
15 . . . . . Colorado
16-19 . . . . . St. Louis
21-23 . . . . . Cincinnati
24-26 . . . . . at St. Louis
27-29 . . . . . at Arizona
30 . . . . . Florida

MAY

1-3 . . . . . Florida
4-5 . . . . . San Francisco
6-7 . . . . . at Houston
8-10 . . . . . at Milwaukee
12-14 . . . . . San Diego
15-17 . . . . . Houston
19-21 . . . . . at St. Louis
22-24 . . . . . at San Diego
25-27 . . . . . Pittsburgh
28-31 . . . . . Dodgers

JUNE

2-4 . . . . . at Atlanta
5-7 . . . . . at Cincinnati
9-11 . . . . . at Houston
12-14 . . . . . Minnesota
16-18 . . . . . White Sox
19-21 . . . . . Cleveland
23-25 . . . . . at Detroit
26-28 . . . . . at White Sox
29-30 . . . . . at Pittsburgh

JULY

1 . . . . . at Pittsburgh
2-5 . . . . . Milwaukee
6-8 . . . . . Atlanta
10-12 . . . . . St. Louis
16-19 . . . . . at Washington
20-22 . . . . . at Philadelphia
24-26 . . . . . Cincinnati
27-29 . . . . . Houston
31 . . . . . at Florida

AUGUST

1-2 . . . . . at Florida
3-5 . . . . . at Cincinnati
7-10 . . . . . at Colorado
11-13 . . . . . Philadelphia
14-16 . . . . . Pittsburgh
17-19 . . . . . at San Diego
20-23 . . . . . at Dodgers
25-27 . . . . . Washington
28-30 . . . . . Mets
31 . . . . . Houston

SEPTEMBER

1-2 . . . . . Houston
4-6 . . . . . at Mets
7-9 . . . . . at Pittsburgh
11-13 . . . . . Cincinnati
14-17 . . . . . Milwaukee
18-20 . . . . . at St. Louis
21-23 . . . . . at Milwaukee
24-27 . . . . . at San Francisco
29-30 . . . . . Pittsburgh

OCTOBER

1 . . . . . Pittsburgh
2-4 . . . . . Arizona

Chicago White Sox

Office Address: 333 W. 35th St., Chicago, IL 60616.
Telephone: (312) 674-1000. **Fax:** (312) 674-5116.
Website: www.whitesox.com.

Ownership

Chairman: Jerry Reinsdorf. **Vice Chairman:** Eddie Einhorn.

Board of Directors: Robert Judelson, Judd Malkin, Robert Mazer, Allan Muchin, Jay Pinsky, Larry Pogofsky, Lee Stern, Sanford Takiff, Burton Ury, Charles Walsh.

Special Assistant to Chairman: Dennis Gilbert. **Assistant to Chairman:** Anita Fasano.

BUSINESS OPERATIONS

Jerry Reinsdorf

Executive Vice President: Howard Pizer.

Senior Director, Information Services: Don Brown. **Senior Director, Human Resources:** Moira Foy. **Administrators, Human Resources:** Leslie Gaggiano, J.J. Krane.

Finance

Senior Vice President, Administration/Finance: Tim Buzard. **Senior Director, Finance:** Bill Waters. **Accounting Manager:** Chris Taylor.

Marketing/Sales

Vice President, Marketing: Brooks Boyer. **Senior Director, Business Development/ Broadcasting:** Bob Grim. **Manager, Scoreboard Operations/Production:** Jeff Szynal. **Director, Game Operations:** Nichole Manning. **Manager, Game Operations:** Amy Sheridan. **Coordinator, Game Operations:** Dan Mielke.

Senior Director, Corporate Partnerships: Jim Muno. **Manager, Corporate Partnerships:** George McDoniel, Gail Tucker, Brad Dreher. **Manager, Client Services:** Stephanie Johnson. **Coordinator, Corporate Partnership Services:** Jorie Sax.

Director, Ticket Sales: Tom Sheridan. **Manager, Premium Seating Service:** Deb Theobald. **Senior Director, Community Relations:** Christine O'Reilly. **Director, Mass Communications:** Maggie Luellen. **Manager, Design Services:** Gareth Breunlin. **Senior Coordinator, Design Services:** Matt Peterson. **Manager, Community Relations:** Danielle Disch. **Senior Coordinator, Community Relations:** Laina Myers. **Coordinators, Community Relations:** Stacy Tsihlopoulos, Dan Puente.

Public Relations

Telephone: (312) 674-5300. **Fax:** (312) 674-5116.

Vice President, Communications: Scott Reifert.

Director, Media Relations: Bob Beghtol. **Director, Public Relations:** Lou Hernandez. **Manager, Media Relations:** Pat O'Connell. **Coordinator, Public Relations:** Marty Maloney. **Coordinator, Media Services:** Ray Garcia.

Stadium Operations

Senior Vice President, Stadium Operations: Terry Savarise. **Senior Director, Park Operations:** David Schaffer. **Senior Director, Guest Services/Diamond Suite Operations:** Julie Taylor. **Head Groundskeeper:** Roger Bossard. **PA Announcer:** Gene Honda. **Official Scorer:** Bob Rosenberg.

Ticketing

Telephone: (312) 674-1000. **Fax:** (312) 674-5102.

Director, Ticket Operations: Mike Mazza. **Manager, Ticket Accounting Administration:** Ken Wisz.

Travel/Clubhouse

Director, Team Travel: Ed Cassin.

Manager, White Sox Clubhouse: Vince Fresso. **Manager, Visiting Clubhouse:** Gabe Morell. **Manager, Umpires Clubhouse:** Joe McNamara Jr.

GENERAL INFORMATION

Stadium (year opened): U.S. Cellular Field (1991).
Home Dugout: Third Base. **Playing Surface:** Grass.
Team Colors: Black, white and silver.
Player Representative: Unavailable.
Driving Directions: Dan Ryan Expressway (I-90/94) to 35th Street exit.

Ken Williams

BASEBALL OPERATIONS

Senior Vice President, General Manager: Ken Williams.

VP/Assistant GM: Rick Hahn. **Special Assistants:** Bill Scherrer, Dave Yoakum. **Executive Assistant to GM:** Nancy Nesnidal. **Director, Baseball Operations:** Dan Fabian. **Assistant Director, Baseball Operations:** Daniel Zien.

Major League Staff

Manager: Ozzie Guillen.

Coaches: Bench—Joey Cora; Pitching—Don Cooper; Batting—Greg Walker; First Base—Harold Baines; Third Base—Jeff Cox; Bullpen—Juan Nieves.

Medical, Training

Senior Team Physician: Dr. Charles Bush-Joseph.

Head Athletic Trainer: Herm Schneider. **Assistant Athletic Trainer:** Brian Ball. **Director, Conditioning:** Allen Thomas.

Player Development

Telephone: (312) 674-1000. **Fax:** (312) 674-5105.

Director, Player Development: Buddy Bell.

Director, Minor League Operations: Grace Guerrero Zwit. **Assistant Director, Player Development:** J.J. Lally. **Senior Coordinator, Minor League Administration:** Kathy Potoski. **Manager, Clubhouse/Equipment:** Dan Flood.

Roving Instructors: Daryl Boston (outfield), Dale Torborg (conditioning coordinator), Kirk Champion (pitching), Jeff Manto (hitting), John Orton (catching), Ron Oester (infield), Manny Trillo (baserunning/bunting), Art Kusyner (bullpen). **Latin Roving Instructor:** Jose Bautista. **Dominican Player/Development Scouting Supervisor:** Rafael Santana. **Coordinator, Minor League Trainers/Rehabilitation:** Scott Takao. **Dominican Coordinator:** Julio Valdez.

Farm System

Class	Club (League)	Manager	Coach	Pitching Coach
Triple-A	Charlotte (IL)	Chris Chambliss	Gary Ward	Richard Dotson
Double-A	Birmingham (SL)	Everardo Magallanes	Andy Tomberlin	J.R. Perdew
High A	Winston-Salem (CL)	Joe McEwing	Robert Sasser	Bobby Thigpen
Low A	Kannapolis (SAL)	Ernie Young	Greg Briley	Larry Owens
Rookie	Bristol Sox (APP)	Ryan Newman	Jerry Hairston	Brian Drahman
Rookie	Great Falls (PIO)	Chris Cron	Olmedo Saenz	Curt Hasler
Rookie	White Sox (DSL)	Fermin Urbi	Domingo Michel	Melido Perez

Scouting

Telephone: (312) 674-1000. **Fax:** (312) 674-5105.

Pro Scouts: Joe Butler (Long Beach, CA), Gary Pellant (Chandler, AZ), Paul Provas (Arlington, TX), Daraka Shaheed (Vallejo, CA), Bill Young (Long Beach, CA), John Tumminia (Newburgh, NY).

Director, Amateur Scouting: Doug Laumann (Florence, KY).

Manager, Amateur Scouting: Ryan Dorsey. **National Crosscheckers:** Nathan Durst (Sycamore, IL) Ed Pebley (Brigham City, UT). **Regional Crosscheckers:** Nick Hostetler (East Coast) (Union, KY), Derek Valenzuela (West Coast) (Temecula, CA). **Advisor to Baseball Department:** Larry Monroe (Schaumburg, IL).

Area Scouts: Mike Baker (Santa Ana, CA), Kevin Burrell (Sharpsburg, GA), Alex Cosmidis (Raleigh, NC), Dan Durst (Rockford, IL), Chuck Fox (Summit, NJ), Phil Gulley (Morehead, KY), Warren Hughes (Mobile, AL), George Kachigian (Coronado, CA), John Kazanas (Phoenix, AZ), Jose Ortega (Fort Lauderdale, FL), Clay Overcash (Oologan, OK),Andrew Pinter (Raleigh, NC), Mike Shirley (Anderson, IN), Joe Siers (Wesley Chapel, FL), Keith Staab (College Station, TX), Adam Virchis (Modesto, CA), Gary Woods (Solvang, CA).

Part-Time Scouts: Tommy Butler (East Rancho Dominguez, CA), Javier Centeno (Guaynabo, PR), John Doldoorian (Whitinsville, MA), Trent Eckstaine (Lemars, IA), Cade Griffis (Addison, TX), Jack Jolly (Murfreeboro, TN), Jason Morvant (Abbeville, LA), Glenn Murdock (Livonia, MI), Howard Nakagama (Salt Lake City, UT), Al Otto (Schaumburg, IL), Mike Paris (Boone, IA)

International Scouts: Rafael Santana (Dominican), Miguel Ibarra (Panama), Marino DeLeon (Dominican Republic), Miguel Peguero (Dominican), Amador Arias (Venezuela), Jhonny Pantoja (Colombia), Ehire Adrianza (Venezuela).

Spring Training

Complex Address: Tucson Electric Park, 2500 E. Ajo Way, Tucson, AZ 85713. **Telephone:** (520) 434-1300. **Seating Capacity:** 11,000. **Location:** I-10 to exit 262 (Park Street) or 263 (Kino Street), south to Ajo Way, left (east) on Ajo Way to park.

Hotel Address: Doubletree Guest Suites, 6555 E. Speedway Blvd., Tucson, AZ 85710. **Telephone:** (520) 721-7100.

Minor League Clubs

Complex Address: Same as major league club. **Hotel Address:** Ramada Palo Verde, 5251 S. Julian Dr., Tucson, AZ 85706. **Telephone:** (520) 294-5250.

2009 SCHEDULE

U.S. CELLULAR FIELD

Standard Game Times: 7:05 p.m.; Sat. 6:05; Sun. 1:05.

APRIL

6-9 . . . . Kansas City
10-12 . . . . .Minnesota
13-15 . . . . at Detroit
16-19 . . . . . . at Tampa Bay
21-23 . . . . . . .at Baltimore
24-26 . . . . Toronto
27-29 . . . . Seattle

MAY

1-3. . . . . at Texas
4-5. . . . . . . at Kansas City
6-7. . . . . Detroit
8-10 . . . . Texas
11-13 . . . . . . at Cleveland
15-18 . . . . at Toronto
19-21 . . . . .Minnesota
22-24 . . . . Pittsburgh
25-27 . . . . at Angels
29-31 . . . . . at Kansas City

JUNE

1-4. . . . . Athletics
5-7. . . . . Cleveland
8-11 . . . . Detroit
12-14 . . . . . . at Milwaukee
16-18 . . . . .at Cubs
19-21 . . . . . . at Cincinnati
23-25 . . . . Dodgers
26-28 . . . . Cubs
29-30 . . . . at Cleveland

JULY

1 . . . . at Cleveland
2-5. . . . . at Kansas City
7-9. . . . . Cleveland
10-12 . . . . . . at Minnesota
17-19 . . . . Baltimore
20-23 . . . . Tampa Bay
24-26 . . . . at Detroit
27-29 . . . . . . at Minnesota
30-31 . . . . Yankees

AUGUST

1-2. . . . . Yankees
4-6. . . . . Angels
7-9. . . . . Cleveland
10-12 . . . . at Seattle
14-16 . . . . at Oakland
17-19 . . . . Kansas City
21-23 . . . . Baltimore
24-27 . . . . at Boston
28-30 . . . . .at Yankees
31 . . . . at Minnesota

SEPTEMBER

1-2. . . . . at Minnesota
4-6. . . . . Boston
8-9. . . . . Oakland
11-13 . . . . at Angels
15-17 . . . . at Seattle
18-20 . . . . . . Kansas City
21-23 . . . . . . .Minnesota
25-27 . . . . Detroit
28-30 . . . . at Cleveland

OCTOBER

2-4. . . . . at Detroit

Cincinnati Reds

Office Address: 100 Main St., Cincinnati, OH 45202.
Telephone: (513) 765-7000. **Fax:** (513) 765-7342.
Website: www.reds.com.

Ownership

Operated by: The Cincinnati Reds LLC.

President/CEO: Robert Castellini. **Chairman:** Joseph Williams Jr. **Vice Chairman/Treasurer:** Thomas Williams. **COO:** Phillip Castellini. **Executive Assistant to COO:** Sally Greytak. **Secretary:** Christopher Fister.

BUSINESS OPERATIONS

Robert Castellini

Senior Vice President, Business Operations: Karen Forgus. **Vice President, Business Development:** Brad Blettner. **Administrator, Business/Broadcasting:** Ginny Kamp.

Assistant, Business Operations/Speakers Bureau: Emily Chalfant.

Finance/Administration

Vice President, Finance/CFO: Doug Healy. **VP/General Counsel:** James Marx. **Controller:** Bentley Viator. **Assistant, Finance/Administration:** Debbie Hall. **Accounting Manager:** Jill Niemeyer. **Director, Human Resources:** Teddi Mangas-Coon. **Human Resources Manager:** John Hale. **Human Resources Coordinator:** Drew Manley. **Benefits Coordinator:** Allison Spurlock. **Director, Information Technology:** Brian Keys.

Sales

Senior Director, Ticket Sales: John Davis. **Director, Group Sales:** David Ziegler. **Group Sales Manager:** Ryan Niemeyer. **Suite/Premium Services Manager:** Emily Tincher. **Premium Sales Managers:** Christopher Bausano, Ryan Rizzo. **Premium Sales Coordinator:** Ashley Vella. **Season Sales Manager:** Chris Herrell. **Season Ticket Manager:** Bev Bonavita. **Group Ticket Manager:** Brad Callahan. **Group Ticket Coordinator:** John Rieder. **Season Ticket Coordinator:** Shelley Volpenhein. **Director, Special Events:** Jennifer Green. **Event Services Coordinator:** Anne Kirby. **Director, Ticket Client Services:** Craig Warman. **Supervisor, Ticket Client Services:** Nancy Bloss.

Ticket Operations

Director, Ticket Operations: John O'Brien. **Assistant Director, Ticket Operations:** Ken Ayer. **Ticket Operations Administration Manager:** Hallie Kinney.

Media Relations

Director, Media Relations: Rob Butcher. **Assistant Directors, Media Relations:** Larry Herms, Jamie Ramsey.

Communications/Marketing

Director, Creative Services: Ralph Mitchell. **Managing Editor:** Jarrod Rollins. **Senior Director, Entertainment/Events/Production:** Jennifer Berger. **Promotional Events Manager:** Zach Bonkowski. **Media Production Manager:** David Storm. **Coordinator, Events/Community:** Kathryn Braun. **Manager, Public Relations:** Michael Anderson. **Marketing Manager:** Lisa Braun.

Community Relations

Director, Community Relations: Lorrie Platt. **Community Fund Executive Director:** Charley Frank. **Executive Director, Reds Hall of Fame:** Rick Walls. **Operations Manager/Chief Curator Reds Hall of Fame:** Chris Eckes. **Education/Programming Manager, Reds Hall of Fame:** Ken Freeman.

Corporate Sales

Vice President, Corporate Sales: Bill Reinberger. **Assistant, Corporate Sales:** Denise Lockwood. **Corporate Sales Managers:** Dave Collins, Dan Lewis, Mark Scherer. **Broadcast/Affiliates Manager:** Joe Zerhusen. **Corporate Promotions Manager:** Lori Watt. **Corporate Services Managers:** Casandra Ersel, Joanie Roebel. **Trafficking Coordinator:** Brandon Bowman.

Ballpark Operations

Vice President, Ballpark Operations: Declan Mullin.

Director, Ballpark Operations: Sean Brown. **Ballpark Operations Manager:** Colleen Rodenberg. **Ballpark Operations Superintendent:** Bob Harrison. **Facility/Construction Services Manager:** Kim Hoffa. **Manager, Technology Business Center:** Chris Campbell. **Engineer:** Eric Dearing. **Head Groundskeeper:** Doug Gallant.

GENERAL INFORMATION

Stadium (year opened): Great American Ball Park (2003).
Home Dugout: First Base. **Playing Surface:** Grass.
Team Colors: Red, white and black.
Player Representative: Aaron Harang.

Driving Directions: I-75 southbound, take Second Street exit. Ballpark is located off Second Street at Main Street. I-71 southbound, take Third Street exit, right on Broadway. I-75/I-71 northbound, take Second Street exit—far right lane on Brent Spence Bridge. Ballpark is located off Second Street at Main Street.

LARRY GOREN

Walt Jocketty

BASEBALL OPERATIONS

President, Baseball Operations/GM: Walt Jocketty.

Director, Major League Administration: Debbie Bent. **Vice President/Assistant GM:** Bob Miller. **VP, Scouting/Player Development:** Bill Bavasi. **VP/Special Assistant:** Jerry Walker. **VP, Baseball Operations:** Dick Williams. **Assistant Director, Baseball Operations:** Nick Krall. **Manager, Video Scouting Operations:** Jeff Graupe. **Manager, Baseball Research:** Sam Grossman. **Baseball Operations Assistant:** Stephanie Ben.

Major League Staff

Manager: Dusty Baker.

Coaches: Bench—Chris Speier; Pitching—Dick Pole; Batting—Brook Jacoby; First Base—Billy Hatcher; Third Base—Mark Berry; Bullpen—Juan Lopez.

Player Development

Telephone: (513) 765-7700. **Fax:** (513) 765-7799.

Senior Director, Player Development: Terry Reynolds.

Special Assistant: Ken Griffey Sr. **Director, Minor League Administration:** Lori Hudson. **GM, Florida Operations:** Dan Wolfert. **Assistant GM:** Mike Rebok. **Minor League Equipment Manager:** Jonathan Snyder.

Field Coordinator: Freddie Benavides. **Assistant Field Coordinator/Instruction:** Bill Doran. **Coordinators:** Ronnie Ortegon (hitting), Mack Jenkins (pitching), Darren Bragg (outfield/baserunning). **Catching Coordinator/Director, Florida On-Field Operations:** Pat Kelly.

Farm System

Class	Club (League)	Manager	Coach	Pitching Coach
Triple-A	Louisville (IL)	Rick Sweet	Adrian Garrett	Ted Power
Double-A	Carolina (SL)	David Bell	Ryan Jackson	Tom Browning
High A	Sarasota (FSL)	Joe Ayrault	Jorge Orta	Tom Brown
Low A	Dayton (MWL)	Todd Benzinger	Tony Jaramillo	Rigo Beltran
Rookie	Billings (PIO)	Julio Garcia	Delino DeShields	Bob Forsch
Rookie	Reds (GCL)	Pat Kelly	Alex Paleaz	Tony Fossas
Rookie	Reds (DSL)	Joel Noboa	Nilson Antiqua	Francisco Trejo

Scouting

Telephone: (513) 765-7000. **Fax:** (513) 765-7799.

Senior Director, Scouting: Chris Buckley.

Director, Scouting Administration: Wilma Mann. **Assistant Director, Amateur Scouting/Player Development:** Paul Pierson. **Senior Special Assistant, Pro Scouting:** Gene Bennett. **Special Assistants:** Cam Bonifay, J Harrison, Scott Nethery, Mike Squires. **Major League Advance Scout:** Shawn Pender. **Pro Scouts:** Jeff Morris, John Morris, Jamie Quirk, Tom Shafer, Jeff Taylor. **National Crosscheckers:** Butch Baccala (Weimer, CA), Wayne Britton (Waynesboro, VA), Mark McKnight (Tega Cay, SC), Mark Snipp (Humble, TX). **Cross-checker:** Jeff Barton (Gilbert, AZ). **Scouting Supervisors:** Jason Baker (Catonsville, MD), Jeff Brookens (Chambersburg, PA), Keith Chapman (Petaluma, CA), Clark Crist (Tucson, AZ), Rex de la Nuez (Burbank, CA), Jerry Flowers (Cypress, TX), Tyler Jennings (Daphne, AL), Joe Katuska (Cincinnati, OH), Mike Keenan (Manhattan, KS), Steve Kring (Charlotte, NC), Greg McClain (Oakland, CA), Mike Misuraca (Pomona, CA), Rick Sellers (Remus, MI), Lee Seras (Flanders, NJ), Perry Smith (Charlotte, NC), Andy Stack (Milwaukee, WI), Greg Zunino (Cape Coral, FL). **Part-Time Scouts:** George Blackburn (Evans, GA), Edwin Daub (Binghamton, NY), Jim Grief (Paducha, KY), Bill Killian (Stanwood, MI), Ed Mathes (Westbury, NY), Denny Nagel (Cincinnati, OH), Marlon Styles (Cincinnati, OH), Mike Wallace (Escondido, CA), John Walsh (Windsor, CT), Roger Weberg (Bemidji, MN).

Director, Latin American Scouting: Tony Arias. **Director, International Operations:** Jim Stoeckel. **Assistant Director, Latin America Scouting:** Miguel Machado.

International Scouts: Carlos Batista (Dominican), Geronimo Blanco (Colombia), Bill Byckowski (Canada), Cesar Castro (Dominican), Andy Chen (Taiwan), Nathan Davison (Australia), Nick Dempsey (South Africa), Jose Fuentes (Venezuela), Jason Hewitt (Australia), Evert Jan't Hoen (Netherlands), Bob Lindsey (Germany), Robert Morillo (Venezuela), Victor Oramas (Venezuela), Ben Park (Korea), Camilo Pina (Dominican), Luke Prokopec (Australia), Anibal Reluz (Panama), Sal Varriale (Italy), Anibal Vega (Nicagarua), Miguel Victor Pol (Dominican), Randy Yamashiro (Hawaii/Japan).

Spring Training

Major League Complex Address: Ed Smith Stadium, 1090 N. Euclid Ave., Sarasota, FL 34237. **Telephone:** (941) 955-6501. **Seating Capacity:** 7,500. **Location:** I-75 to exit 39, west on Rte 780, right on Tuttle. **Hotel Address:** Marriott Residence Inn, 1040 University Pkwy., Sarasota, FL 34234. **Telephone:** (941) 358-1468.

Minor Leagues

Complex Address: Same as major league club. **Hotel Address:** Holiday Inn, 7150 N. Tamiami Trail, Sarasota, FL 34243. **Telephone:** (941) 355-2781.

2009 SCHEDULE

GREAT AMERICAN BALL PARK

Standard Game Times:
7:10 p.m.; Sun. 1:15

APRIL

6 . . . . . Mets
8-9 . . . . . Mets
10-12 . . . . . Pittsburgh
13-15 . . . . . at Milwaukee
17-20 . . . . . at Houston
21-23 . . . . . at Cubs
24-26 . . . . . Atlanta
27-29 . . . . . Houston

MAY

1-3 . . . . . at Pittsburgh
4-5 . . . . . at Florida
6-7 . . . . . Milwaukee
8-10 . . . . . St. Louis
11-13 . . . . . at Arizona
15-17 . . . . . at San Diego
19-21 . . . . . Philadelphia
22-24 . . . . . Cleveland
25-27 . . . . . Houston
29-31 . . . . . at Milwaukee

JUNE

1-4 . . . . . at St. Louis
5-7 . . . . . Cubs
9-11 . . . . . at Washington
12-14 . . . . . at Kansas City
16-18 . . . . . Atlanta
19-21 . . . . . White Sox
23-25 . . . . . at Toronto
26-28 . . . . . at Cleveland
30 . . . . . Arizona

JULY

1-2 . . . . . Arizona
3-5 . . . . . St. Louis
6-9 . . . . . at Philadelphia
10-12 . . . . . at Mets
16-19 . . . . . Milwaukee
20-22 . . . . . at Dodgers
24-26 . . . . . Cubs
27-30 . . . . . at San Diego
31 . . . . . Colorado

AUGUST

1-2 . . . . . Colorado
3-5 . . . . . Cubs
7-9 . . . . . at San Francisco
10-12 . . . . . at St. Louis
13-16 . . . . . Washington
18-20 . . . . . San Francisco
21-23 . . . . . at Pittsburgh
25-27 . . . . . at Milwaukee
28-30 . . . . . Dodgers
31 . . . . . Pittsburgh

SEPTEMBER

1-2 . . . . . Pittsburgh
4-6 . . . . . at Atlanta
7-10 . . . . . at Colorado
11-13 . . . . . at Cubs
14-16 . . . . . Houston
17-20 . . . . . Florida
22-24 . . . . . at Pittsburgh
25-27 . . . . . at Houston
29-30 . . . . . St. Louis

OCTOBER

1 . . . . . St. Louis
2-4 . . . . . Pittsburgh

Cleveland Indians

Office Address: Progressive Field, 2401 Ontario St, Cleveland, OH 44115.
Telephone: (216) 420-4200. **Fax:** (216) 420-4396.
Website: www.indians.com.

Ownership

Owner, CEO: Lawrence Dolan. **President:** Paul Dolan.

BUSINESS OPERATIONS

Executive Vice President, Business: Dennis Lehman. **Executive Administrative Assistant, Business:** Dru Kosik.

Larry Dolan

Corporate Marketing

Director, Corporate Sales: Ted Baugh. **Manager, New Business Development:** Sheff Webb. **Senior Corporate Marketing Account Executives:** Bryan Hoffart, Jennifer Horn, Dominic Polito.

Finance

Senior Vice President, Finance/CFO: Ken Stefanov. **Vice President/General Counsel:** Joe Znidarsic. **Controller:** Sarah Taylor. **Director, Planning/Analysis/Reporting:** Rich Dorffer. **Senior Director, Human Resources/Benefits:** Sara Lehrke. **Manager, Accounting:** Karen Menzing. **Manager, Payroll Accounting:** Mary Forkapa. **Manager, Merchandise Accounting:** Diane Turner. **Senior Staff Accountant:** Kim Haist. **Staff Accountant:** Samantha Culver. .

Marketing/Merchandising

Senior Vice President, Sales/Marketing: Vic Gregovits. **Director, Marketing:** Sanaa Julien. **Manager, Broadcasting:** Dan Foust. **Manager, Promotions:** Jason Kidik. **Manager, Productions:** Justin White. **Manager, In-Game Entertainment:** Annie Merovich. **Mascot Coordinator:** Dan Kilday. **Broadcast Engineer:** Jim Rosenhaus. **Senior Director, Merchandising:** Kurt Schloss. **Merchandise Manager:** Karen Fox. **rea Supervisor/ Great Northern Manager:** Amy Carter. **Merchandise Buyer:** Iris Delgado. Purchasing Coordinator: Melissa Bilsky. Analyst/Staff Accountant: Bette Prendergast.

Public Relations, Communications

Telephone: (216) 420-4380. **Fax:** (216) 420-4396.

Vice President, Public Relations: Bob DiBiasio. **Director, Media Relations:** Bart Swain. **Manager, Media Relations/ Administration:** Susie Giuliano. **Manager, Media Relations:** Jeff Sibel. **Director, Communications/Creative Services:** Curtis Danburg. **Coordinator, Communications:** Danielle Cherry. **Team Photographer:** Dan Mendlik. **Executive Director, Community Outreach:** Jayne Churchmack. **Manager, Community Relations:** Steve Frohwerk. **Coordinator, Community Relations:** Kate Vale.

Stadium Operations

Vice President, Ballpark Operations: Jim Folk.

Director, Facility Maintenance: Chris Donahoe. **Head Groundskeeper:** Brandon Koehnke. **Director, Ballpark Operations:** Jerry Crabb. **Assistant Director, Ballpark Operations:** Brad Mohr. **Manager, Ballpark Projects:** Jim Goldwire. **Assistant Director, Facility Maintenance:** Seth Cooper.

Ticketing

Telephone: (216) 420-4487. **Fax:** (216) 420-4481.

Director, Ticket Services: Gene Connelly. **Manager, Ticket Services:** David Pike. **Manager, Ticket Office:** Ryan Beech. **Manager, Ticket Operations:** Andrea Zagger.

Senior Director, Tickets/Premium Sales: Mike Mulhall. **Director, Fan Services:** Dave Murray. **Group Sales Manager:** Renee Boerner. **Manager, Premium Services:** Cassy Baskin. **Manager, Premium Seating Development:** Marie Patten. **Manager, Season Ticket Sales:** Nick Arndt.

Travel, Clubhouse

Director, Team Travel: Mike Seghi. **Home Clubhouse/Equipment Manager:** Tony Amato. **Assistant Home Clubhouse Manager:** Marty Bokovitz. **Manager, Video Operations:** Bob Chester. **Video Operations:** Frank Velotta. **Visiting Clubhouse Manager:** Willie Jenks.

GENERAL INFORMATION

Stadium (year opened): Progressive Field (1994).
Home Dugout: Third Base. **Playing Surface:** Grass.
Team Colors: Navy blue, red and silver.
Player Representative: Jake Westbrook.
Driving Directions: From south, I-77 North to East Ninth Street exit, to Ontario Street; From east, I-90/Route 2 west to downtown, remain on Route 2 to East Ninth Street, left to stadium.

Mark Shapiro

BASEBALL OPERATIONS

Telephone: (216) 420-4200. **Fax:** (216) 420-4321.

Executive Vice President/General Manager: Mark Shapiro.

Vice President, Baseball Operations: Chris Antonetti.

Director, Player Personnel: Steve Lubratich. **Director, Baseball Operations:** Mike Chernoff. **Director, Baseball Administration:** Wendy Hoppel. **Special Assistants, Baseball Operations:** Tim Belcher, Jason Bere, Ellis Burks, Robby Thompson.

Director, Latin American Operations: Lino Diaz. **Manager, Baseball Research/Analysis:** Keith Woolner. **Assistant, Baseball Operations:** Andrew Miller. **Executive Administrative Assistant, Baseball Operations:** Marlene Lehky. **Administrative Assistant, Baseball Operations:** Barbara Lessman.

Major League Staff

Manager: Eric Wedge.

Coaches: Bench—Jeff Datz, Pitching—Carl Willis, Hitting—Derek Shelton, First Base/Infield—Luis Rivera, Third Base—Joel Skinner, Bullpen—Chuck Hernandez, Bullpen Catcher—Dan Williams, Dave Wallace.

Medical, Training

Head Team Physician: Dr. Mark Schickendantz.

Director, Medical Services/Head Trainer: Lonnie Soloff. **Strength/Conditioning Coach:** Tim Maxey. **Physical Therapy Consultant:** Jim Mehalik.

Player Development

Telephone: (216) 420-4308. **Fax:** (216) 420-4321.

Director, Player Development: Ross Atkins.

Assistant, Player Development: Meka Asonye. **Administrative Assistant:** Nilda Taffanelli. **Advisor, Player Development:** Johnny Goryl. **Nutrition Consultant:** Jackie Berning.

Field Coordinator: Dave Hudgens. **Coordinators:** Bruce Fields (hitting), Jake Beiting (strength/conditioning), Tim Laker (catching), Steve Lyons (lower level pitching), Dave Miller (pitching), Julio Rangel (mental skills), Gary Thurman (outfield/baserunning).

Field Coordinator, Latin America: Minnie Mendoza.

Farm System

Class	Club	Manager	Coach	Pitching Coach
Triple-A	Columbus (IL)	Torey Lovullo	Jon Nunnally	Scott Radinsky
Double-A	Akron (EL)	Mike Sarbaugh	Lee May Jr.	Ruben Niebla
High A	Kinston (CL)	Chris Tremie	Rouglas Odor	Greg Hibbard
Low A	Lake County (SAL)	Aaron Holbert	Jim Rickon	Tony Arnold
Short-season	Mahoning Valley (NYP)	Travis Fryman	Phil Clark	Ken Rowe
Rookie	Indians (AZL)	Ted Kubiak	D. Malave/A. Medrano	Jeff Harris
Rookie	Indians (DSL)	Wilfredo Tejada	P. Matos/C. Fermin	Kevin Carcamo

Scouting

Telephone: (216) 420-4309. **Fax:** (216) 420-4321.

Assistant General Manager/Scouting Operations: John Mirabelli.

Director, Amateur Scouting: Brad Grant. **Assistant Director, Scouting:** Paul Gillispie. **Assistant Scouting Operations:** Derek Falvey.

Major League Scouts: Dave Malpass (Huntington Beach, CA), Don Poplin (Norwood, NC).

Pro Scouts: Tyrone Brooks (San Francisco, CA), Doug Carpenter (North Palm Beach, FL), Doug Harris (Carlisle, PA), Pat Murtaugh (Lafayette, IN), Bill Schudlich (Dearborn, MI), Greg Smith (Davenport, WA). **National Crosschecker:** Chuck Ricci (Greencastle, PA).

Regional Crosscheckers: Lower Midwest—Scott Barnsby (Brownsboro, AL); West—Paul Cogan (Rocklin, CA); East—Scott Meaney (Apex, NC); Upper Midwest—Derrick Ross (Olmsted Township, OH).

Area Scouts: Steve Abney (Lawrence, KS), Corteze Armstrong (Willowbrook, IL), Chuck Bartlett (Starkville, MS), Kevin Cullen (Dallas, TX), Byron Ewing (Chicago, IL), Don Lyle (Sacramento, CA), Bob Mayer (Somerset, PA), Junie Melendez (Toledo, OH), Les Pajari (Conroe, TX), Vince Sagisi (Encino, CA), Jason Smith (Long Beach, CA), Mike Soper (Tampa, FL), Brad Tyner (Bishop, GA), Jack Uhey (Ridgefiled, WA), Brent Urcheck (Philadelphia, PA).

Latin America Crosschecker: Cesar Geronimo (Aventura, FL).

Spring Training

Major League Complex Address: Cleveland Indians Player Development Complex, 2601 S. Wood Blvd., Goodyear, AZ 85338. **Telephone:** (623) 302-5678. **Fax:** (623) 302-5670. **Seating Capacity:** 8,000.

Hotel Address: Quality Inn, 950 North Dysart Road, Goodyear, AZ 85338. **Telephone:** (623) 932-9191. **Telephone:** (863) 294-4451.

Minor League Clubs

Complex Address/Hotel: Same as major league club.

2009 SCHEDULE

PROGRESSIVE FIELD

Standard Game Times: 7:05 p.m.; Sun. 1:05.

APRIL

6-9 . . . at Texas
10-12 . . . Toronto
13-15 . . . at Kansas City
16-10 . . . at Yankees
21-23 . . . Kansas City
24-26 . . . Minnesota
27-29 . . . Boston

MAY

1-3 . . . at Detroit
4-5 . . . at Toronto
6-7 . . . at Boston
8-10 . . . Detroit
11-13 . . . White Sox
14-17 . . . at Tampa Bay
19-21 . . . at Kansas City
22-24 . . . at Cincinnati
25-28 . . . Tampa Bay
29-31 . . . Yankees

JUNE

1 . . . Yankees
2-4 . . . at Minnesota
5-7 . . . at White Sox
9-11 . . . Kansas City
12-14 . . . St. Louis
15-17 . . . Milwaukee
19-21 . . . at Cubs
23-25 . . . at Pittsburgh
26-28 . . . Cincinnati
29-30 . . . White Sox

JULY

1 . . . White Sox
3-5 . . . Oakland
7-9 . . . at White Sox
10-12 . . . at Detroit
16-19 . . . Seattle
21-23 . . . at Toronto
24-26 . . . at Seattle
27-29 . . . at Angels
31 . . . Detroit

AUGUST

1-2 . . . Detroit
4-6 . . . Minnesota
7-9 . . . at White Sox
11-13 . . . Texas
14-16 . . . at Minnesota
18-20 . . . Los Angels
21-23 . . . Seattle
24-26 . . . at Kansas City
27-30 . . . at Baltimore

SEPTEMBER

1-3 . . . at Detroit
4-6 . . . Minnesota
7-9 . . . Texas
11-13 . . . Kansas City
14-16 . . . at Minnesota
17-20 . . . at Oakland
22-24 . . . Detroit
25-27 . . . Baltimore
28-30 . . . White Sox

OCTOBER

1-4 . . . at Boston

Colorado Rockies

Office Address: 2001 Blake St., Denver, CO 80205.
Telephone: (303) 292-0200. **Fax:** (303) 312-2116.
Website: www.coloradorockies.com.

Ownership

Operated by: Colorado Rockies Baseball Club Ltd.

Vice Chairman/CEO: Charles Monfort. **Vice Chairman:** Richard Monfort. **Executive Assistant to Vice Chairmen:** Patricia Penfold.

BUSINESS OPERATIONS

Charles Monfort

President: Keli McGregor. **Executive Assistant to President:** Terry Douglass. **Senior Vice President, Business Operations:** Greg Feasel. **VP, Human Resources:** Elizabeth Stecklein.

Finance

Senior Vice President/CFO: Hal Roth. **VP, Finance:** Michael Kent. **Senior Director, Purchasing:** Gary Lawrence. **Purchasing Assistant:** Gloria Giraldi. **Director, Accounting:** Phil Emerson. **Accountants:** Joel Binfet, Laine Campbell. **Payroll Administrator:** Juli Daedelow.

Marketing/Sales

Senior Director, Corporate Sales: Marcy English-Glasser. **Director, New Partner Development:** Brendan Falvey. **Director, Promotions/Special Events:** Jason Fleming. **Coordinator, Promotions/Special Events:** Liz Coates. **Assistant Director, In-Game Entertainment/Broadcasting:** Kent Krosbakken.

Vice President, Community/Retail Operations: Jim Kellogg. **Managers, Community Affairs:** Dallas Davis, Antigone Vigil. **Manager, Community Fields Program/Historian:** Paul Parker. **Director, Retail Operations:** Aaron Heinrich. **Director, Information Systems:** Bill Stephani. **Senior Director, Advertising/Marketing:** Jill Campbell. **Coordinator, Advertising/Marketing:** Sarah Topf. **Assistant, Advertising/Marketing:** Marisol Villagomez. **Assistant Editor, Publications:** Paul Swydan.

Public Relations/Communications

Telephone: (303) 312-2325. **Fax:** (303) 312-2319.

Vice President, Communications/Public Relations: Jay Alves. **Assistant to the VP, Communications/Public Relations:** Irma Thumim. **Manager, Communications/Public Relations:** Charlie Hepp. **Coordinator, Communications/Public Relations:** Nick Piburn.

Stadium Operations

Senior Director, Food Service Operations/Development: Albert Valdes. **Vice President, Ballpark Operations:** Kevin Kahn. **Manager, Ballpark Services:** Mary Beth Benner. **Senior Director, Guest Services:** Steven Burke. **Director, Security:** Don Lyon. **Senior Director, Engineering/Facilities:** James Wiener. **Director, Engineering:** Randy Carlill. **Director, Facilities:** Oly Olsen. **Head Groundskeeper:** Mark Razum. **Assistant Head Groundskeeper:** Jose Gonzalez. **PA Announcer:** Reed Saunders. **Official Scorers:** Dave Einspahr, Dave Plati.

Ticketing

Telephone: (303) 762-5437, (800) 388-7625. **Fax:** (303) 312-2115.

Vice President, Ticket Operations/Sales: Sue Ann McClaren. **Senior Director, Ticket Operations/Development:** Kevin Fenton. **Assistant Director, New Business Development:** Todd Thomas. **Director, Ticket Operations/Finances:** Kent Hakes. **Assistant Director, Ticket Operations:** Scott Donaldson. **Manager, Ticket Operations:** Kevin Flood. **Coordinator, Ticket Operations:** Mandy Stecklein. **Representative, Ticket Ops/Spring Training Promotions/Group Sales:** Andy Finley. **Director, Season Tickets/Group Sales:** Jeff Benner. **Manager, Season Tickets:** Farrah Magee. **Supervisor, Outbound Sales:** Matt Haddad. **Account Representatives, Ticket Sales:** Grayson Beatty, Ryan Dillon, Jason Regan. **Client Services Representative, Season Tickets:** Bobby Dicroce. **Account Executives, Group Sales:** Kristy Hermann, Evelyn Rockett. **Senior Account Executive, Suites:** Scott Amerman. **Manager, Party Facilities/Premier Services:** Fred Graf. **Coordinator, Party Facilities/Premiere Services:** Traci Sauerteig. **Director, Ticket Services/Spring Training Business Operations:** Chuck Javernick. **Supervisor, Ticket Services:** James Valdez.

Travel/Clubhouse

Director, Major League Operations: Paul Egins.

Director, Clubhouse Operations: Keith Schulz. **Assistant to Director, Clubhouse Operations:** Joe Diaz. **Visiting Clubhouse Manager:** Alan Bossart.

GENERAL INFORMATION

Stadium (year opened): Coors Field (1995).
Home Dugout: First base. **Playing Surface:** Grass.
Team Colors: Purple, black and silver.
Player Representative: Unavailable.
Driving Directions: I-70 to I-25 South to exit 213 (Park Avenue) or 212C (20th Street); I-25 to 20th Street, east to park.

Dan O'Dowd

BASEBALL OPERATIONS

Telephone: (303) 292-0200. **Fax:** (303) 312-2320.

Executive Vice President/General Manager: Dan O'Dowd. **Assistant to Executive VP/GM:** Adele Armagost.

VP/Assistant GM: Bill Geivett. **Director, Baseball Operations:** Jeff Bridich. **Manager, Baseball Operations:** Matt Vinnola. **Assistant, Baseball Operations/General Counsel:** Zack Rosenthal.

Special Assistants to GM: Pat Daugherty (Aurora, CO), Dave Holliday (Tulsa, OK), Marcel Lachemann (Penryn, CA), Kasey McKeon (Stoney Creek, NC).

Major League Staff

Manager: Clint Hurdle.

Coaches: Bench—Jim Tracy; Pitching—Bob Apodaca; Hitting—Don Baylor; First Base—Glenallen Hill; Third Base—Rich Dauer; Bullpen—Jim Wright; Bullpen Catcher—Mark Strittmatter; Strength/Conditioning Coach—Brian Jordan; Video—Brian Jones.

Medical/Training

Director, Medical Operations: Tom Probst. **Medical Director:** Dr. Thomas Noonan. **Club Physicians:** Dr. Allen Schreiber, Dr. Douglas Wyland. **Head Trainer:** Keith Dugger.

Player Development

Telephone: (303) 292-0200. **Fax:** (303) 312-2320.

Director, Player Development: Marc Gustafson.

Assistant, Player Development: Walter Sylvester. **Field Coordinator:** Ron Gideon. **Roving Instructors:** Scott Fletcher (infield), Marv Foley (catching), Trenidad Hubbard (outfield/baserunning), Jim Johnson (hitting), Bo McLaughlin (pitching). **Special Assistant, Baseball Operations:** Rick Mathews. **Senior Advisor, Player Development:** Bobby Knoop. **Video Coordinator:** Jimmy Hartley. **Mental Skills Coach:** Ronn Svetich. **Equipment Manager:** Jerry Bass.

Farm System

Class	Club (League)	Manager	Coach	Pitching Coach
Triple-A	Colorado Springs (PCL)	Tom Runnells	Rene Lachemann	Chuck Kniffin
Double-A	Tulsa (TL)	Stu Cole	Dave Hajek	Bryan Harvey
High A	Modesto (CL)	Jerry Weinstein	Duane Espy	Doug Linton
Low A	Asheville (SAL)	Joe Mikulik	Houston Jimenez	Dave Schuler
Short-season	Tri-City (NWL)	Fred Ocasio	Anthony Sanders	Darryl Scott
Rookie	Casper (PIO)	Tony Diaz	Kevin Riggs	Craig Bjornson.
Rookie	Rockies (DSL)	Mauricio Gonzalez	F. Nunez/E. Jose	Edison Lora.

Scouting

Telephone: (303) 292-0200. **Fax:** (303) 312-2320.

Vice President, Scouting: Bill Schmidt. **Assistant Director, Scouting:** Danny Montgomery. **Manager, Scouting:** Zach Wilson. **Manager, Pro Scouting:** Jon Weil. **Advance Scout:** Chris Warren. **Major League Scouts:** Will George (Woolwich Township, NJ). **Pro Scouts:** Jack Gillis (Sarasota, FL), Mike Hamilton (Dallas, TX), Mike Paul (Tucson, AZ). **Special Assignment Scout:** Terry Wetzel (Overland Park, KS).

National Crosschecker: Ty Coslow (Louisville, KY). **Scouting Adviser:** Dave Snow (Seal Beach, CA).

Area Scouts: John Cedarburg (Fort Myers, FL), Scott Corman (Lexington, KY), Dar Cox (Frisco, TX), Jeff Edwards (Humble, TX), Mike Ericson (Glendale, AZ), Chris Forbes (Bellevue, WA), Mike Garlatti (Edison, NJ), Mark Germann (Atkins, IA), Matt Hattabaugh (Westminster, CA), Damon Iannelli (Brandon, MS), Jon Lukens (La Jolla, CA), Alan Matthews (Decatur, GA), Jay Matthews (Concord, NC), Jorge de Posada (Rio Piedras, PR), Ed Santa (Powell, OH), Gary Wilson (Sacramento, CA). **Part-Time Scouts:** Greg Booker (Elon, NC), Norm DeBriyn (Fayetteville, AR), Jeff Hipps (Millbrae, CA), Marc Johnson (Centennial, CO), Dave McQueen (Bossier City, LA), Greg Pullia (Plymouth, MA).

Director, International Operations: Rolando Fernandez. **Director, Venezuelan Operations:** Francisco Cartaya. **Manager, Dominican Operations:** Jhonathan Leyba. **Manager, Pacific Rim Operations:** Ming Harbor. **International Scouts:** Phil Allen (Australia), Martin Cabrera (Dominican Republic), Claudino Hernadez (Panama), Carlos Gomez (Venezuela), Orlando Medina (Venezuela), Frank Roa (Dominican Republic), Chi-Sheng Tsai (Taiwán).

Spring Training

Major League Complex Address: Hi Corbett Field, 3400 E. Camino Campestre, Tucson, AZ 85716. **Telephone:** (520) 322-4500. **Seating Capacity:** 8,655. **Location:** I-10 to Broadway exit, east on Broadway to Randolph Park. **Hotel Address:** Hilton Tucson East, 7600 Broadway, Tucson, AZ 85710.

Minor League Clubs

Complex Address: Same as major league club. **Hotel Address:** Randolph Park Hotel & Suites, 102 N. Alvernon, Tucson, AZ 85711. **Telephone:** (520) 795-0330.

2009 SCHEDULE

COORS FIELD

Standard Game Times: 7:05 p.m.; Sat. 6:05; Sun. 1:05.

APRIL

6-8 . . . at Arizona
10-12 . . . Philadelphia
13 . . . at Cubs
15 . . . at Cubs
17-19 . . . at Dodgers
20-22 . . . at Arizona
24-26 . . . Dodgers
27-29 . . . San Diego

MAY

1-3 . . . at San Francisco
4-5 . . . at San Diego
6-7 . . . San Francisco
8-10 . . . Florida
12-14 . . . Houston
15-17 . . . at Pittsburgh
18-21 . . . at Atlanta
22-24 . . . at Detroit
25-27 . . . Dodgers
29-31 . . . San Diego

JUNE

1-4 . . . at Houston
5-8 . . . at St. Louis
9-11 . . . at Milwaukee
12-14 . . . Seattle
16-18 . . . Tampa Bay
19-21 . . . Pittsburgh
22-24 . . . at Angels
26-28 . . . at Oakland
29-30 . . . at Dodgers

JULY

1 . . . at Dodgers
3-5 . . . Arizona
6-8 . . . Washington
9-12 . . . Atlanta
16-19 . . . at San Diego
20-22 . . . Arizona
24-26 . . . San Francisco
27-30 . . . at Mets
31 . . . at Cincinnati

AUGUST

1-2 . . . at Cincinnati
4-6 . . . at Philadelphia
7-10 . . . Cubs
11-13 . . . Pittsburgh
14-16 . . . at Florida
18-20 . . . at Washington
21-24 . . . San Francisco
25-27 . . . Dodgers
28-30 . . . at San Francisco

SEPTEMBER

1-3 . . . Mets
4-6 . . . Arizona
7-10 . . . Cincinnati
11-13 . . . at San Diego
14-16 . . . at San Francisco
18-20 . . . at Arizona
22-24 . . . San Diego
25-27 . . . St. Louis
29-30 . . . Milwaukee

OCTOBER

1 . . . Milwaukee
2-4 . . . at Dodgers

Detroit Tigers

Office Address: 2100 Woodward Ave, Detroit, MI 48201.
Telephone: (313) 471-2000. **Fax:** (313) 471-2138.
Website: www.tigers.com

Ownership

Operated By: Detroit Tigers Inc. **Owner:** Michael Ilitch.

President, CEO/General Manager: David Dombrowski. **Special Assistant to President:** Al Kaline, Willie Horton. **Executive Assistant to President/CEO/GM:** Marty Lyon. **Senior Vice President:** Jim Devellano.

Mike Ilitch

BUSINESS OPERATIONS

Senior Vice President, Business Operations: Duane McLean.
Executive Assistant to Senior VP, Business Operations: Peggy Bacarella.

Finance

Vice President/CFO: Stephen Quinn.

Senior Director, Finance: Kelli Kollman. **Director, Purchasing/Supplier Diversity:** DeAndre Berry. **Accounting Manager:** Sheila Robine. **Financial Analyst:** Kristin Jorgensen. **Accounts Payable Coordinator:** Debbie Sword. **Accounts Receivable Coordinator:** Sharon Szkarlat. **Administrative Assistant:** Tracy Rice. **Director, Human Resources:** Karen Gruca. **Senior Manager, Payroll Administration:** Maureen Kraatz. **Director, Information Technology:** Scott Wruble.

Public, Community Affairs

Vice President, Community/Public Affairs: Elaine Lewis.

Manager, Player Relations, Sports/Youth Programs: Sam Abrams. **Director, Tigers Foundation:** Jordan Field. **Manager, Community Affairs:** Alexandrea Thrubis. **Community Affairs Coordinator:** Kristen Joe. **Administrative Assistant:** Audrey Zielinski.

Sales, Marketing

Vice President, Corporate Partnerships/Ticket Sales: Steve Harms. **Senior Director, Corporate Sales:** Kurt Buhler. **Corporate Sales Manager:** Zach Wagner, John Wolski. **Sponsorship Services Manager:** Amy Peterson. **Sponsorship Services Coordinator:** Mallory Seide.

Vice President, Marketing: Ellen Hill Zeringue. **Marketing Manager:** Ron Wade. **Director, Promotions/In-Game Entertainment:** Eli Bayless. **Promotions Coordinator:** Jared Karner. **Vice President, Suite Sales/Services:** Scot Pett.

Media Relations, Communications

Telephone: (313) 471-2114. **Fax:** (313) 471-2138.

Vice President, Communications: Ron Colangelo. **Director, Baseball Media Relations:** Brian Britten. **Manager, Baseball Media Relations:** Rick Thompson. **Coordinator, Baseball Media Relations:** Russell Carlton. **Director, Broadcasting:** Molly Light.

Ballpark Operations

Vice President, Park Operations: Michael Healy.

Director, Park Operations: Michael Churchill. **Head Groundskeeper:** Heather Nabozny. **Assistant Groundskeeper:** Gail DeGennaro. **Senior Manager, Park Operations:** Ed Goward. **Manager, Event/Guest Services:** Jill Baran. **Park Operations Manager:** Allan Carrise. **Scoreboard Operations Manager:** Robb Wilson. **Security Manager:** Gary Zulinski. **Event Services Coordinator:** Rofeal Daniels. **Administrative Coordinator:** Eryka Cheatham. **Ballpark Operations Assistants:** Kiril Bayoff, Derek Okrie, Brandon Weingartz.

Ticketing

Telephone: (313) 471-2255.

Director, Ticket Sales: Steve Fox. **Director, Group Sales:** Dwain Lewis. **Senior Director, Ticket Services:** Victor Gonzalez.

Travel, Clubhouse

Traveling Secretary: Bill Brown. **Manager, Home Clubhouse:** Jim Schmakel. **Assistant Manager, Visiting Clubhouse:** John Nelson. **Clubhouse Assistant:** Tyson Steele. **Baseball Video Operations:** Jeremy Kelch. **Assistant, Baseball Video Operations:** Andy Bjornstad, Tim Janicki.

GENERAL INFORMATION

Stadium (year opened): Comerica Park (2000).
Home Dugout: Third Base. **Playing Surface:** Grass.
Team Colors: Navy blue, orange and white.
Player Representative: Curtis Granderson.
Driving Directions: I-75 to Grand River exit, follow service drive east to stadium, located off Woodward Avenue.

Dave Dombrowski

BASEBALL OPERATIONS

Telephone: (313) 471-2000. **Fax:** (313) 471-2099.

General Manager: David Dombrowski.

Vice President/Assistant GM: Al Avila. **VP/Baseball Legal Counsel:** John Westhoff. **VP, Player Personnel:** Scott Reid. **VP, Amateur Scouting:** David Chadd. **Special Assistant:** Dick Egan. **Director, Baseball Operations:** Mike Smith. **Assistant Director, Amateur Scouting:** James Orr. **Executive Assistant:** Eileen Surma.

Major League Staff

Manager: Jim Leyland.

Coaches: Pitching—Rick Knapp; Batting—Lloyd McClendon; Infield—Rafael Belliard; First Base—Andy Van Slyke; Third Base—Gene Lamont; Bullpen—Jeff Jones.

Medical, Training

Director, Medical Services/Head Athletic Trainer: Kevin Rand. **Assistant Athletic Trainers:** Steve Carter, Doug Teter. **Strength/Conditioning Coach:** Javair Gillett. **Team Physician:** Dr. Michael Workings. **Team Physician:** Dr. Stephen Lemos. **Team Physician (Florida):** Dr. Louis Saco.

Player Development

Telephone: (863) 686-8075. **Fax:** (863) 688-9589.

Director, Minor League Operations: Dan Lunetta. **Director, Player Development:** Glenn Ezell. **Director, Minor League/Scouting Administration:** Cheryl Evans.

Director, Latin American Scouting: Miguel Garcia. **Director, Dominican Republic Operations:** Ramon Perez. **Director, International Operations:** Tom Moore. **Pacific Rim Coordinator:** Kevin Hooker. **Director, Latin American Player Development:** Manny Crespo.

Minor League Operations Coordinator: Avi Becher. **Minor League Operations Administrative Assistant:** Marilyn Acevedo. **Minor League Field Coordinator:** Mike Rojas. **Minor League Medical Coordinator:** Dustin Campbell. **Minor League Strength/Conditioning Coordinator:** Chris Walter. **Assistant Minor League Strength/Conditioning Coordinator:** Steve Chase.

Roving Instructors: Toby Harrah (hitting), Jon Matlack (pitching), Kevin Bradshaw (infield), Gene Roof (outfield/baserunning), Brian Peterson (performance enhancement).

Farm System

Class	Club	Manager	Coach	Pitching Coach
Triple-A	Toledo (IL)	Larry Parrish	Leon Durham	A.J. Sager
Double-A	Erie (EL)	Tom Brookens	Glenn Adams	Ray Burris
High A	Lakeland (FSL)	Andy Barkett	Larry Herndon	Joe Coleman
Low A	West Michigan (MWL)	Joe DePastino	Benny Distefano	Mark Johnson
Short-season	Oneonta (NYP)	Howard Bushong	Luis Quinones	Jorge Cordova
Rookie	Tigers (GCL)	Basilio Cabrera	Garrett Guest	Greg Sabat
Rookie	Tigers (DSL)	Frey Peniche	Pedruin Bautista	R. Martinez/ J. Parra
Rookie	Tigers (VSL)	Josman Robles	Jesus Garces	Unavailable

Scouting

Telephone: (863) 413-4112. **Fax:** (863) 413-1954.

Vice President, Amateur Scouting: David Chadd.

Assistant Director, Amateur Scouting: James Orr. **Major League Scouts:** Scott Bream (Phoenix, AZ), Jim Olander (Vail, AZ), Mike Russell (Gulf Breeze, FL), Bruce Tanner (New Castle, PA), Jeff Wetherby (Wesley Chapel, FL).

National Crosscheckers: Ray Crone (Cedar Hill, TX), Scott Pleis (Lake St. Louis, MO). **Regional Crosscheckers:** East—Murray Cook (Orlando, FL); Central—Bob Cummings (Oak Lawn, IL); Midwest—Mike Hankins (Lee's Summit, MO); West—Tim McWilliam (San Diego, CA).

Area Scouts: Grant Brittain (Hickory, NC), Bill Buck (Manassas, VA), Rolando Casanova (Miami, FL), Scott Cerny (Rocklin, CA), Tim Grieve (New Braunfels, TX), Garrett Guest (University Park, FL), Phil Huttmann (Studio City, CA), Ryan Johnson (Auburn, WA), Marty Miller (Chicago, IL), Steve Nichols (Mount Dora, FL), Tom Osowski (Franklin, WI), Brian Reid (Laveen, AZ), Jim Rough (Chelsea, AL), Chris Wimmer (Yukon, OK), Harold Zonder (Louisville, KY).

Director, International Scouting: Tom Moore. **Director, Latin American Development:** Manny Crespo. **Director, Latin American Scouting:** Miguel Garcia.

Major League Club

Complex Address: Joker Marchant Stadium, 2301 Lakeland Hills Blvd., Lakeland, FL 33805. **Telephone:** (863) 686-8075. **Seating Capacity:** 9,000. **Location:** I-4 to exit 19 (Lakeland Hills Boulevard). **Hotel Address:** Holiday Inn Lakeland Hotel and Conference Center, 3260 Hwy. 98 N., Lakeland, FL 33805. **Telephone:** (863) 688-8280.

Minor League Clubs

Complex/Hotel Address: Tigertown, 2125 N. Lake Ave., Lakeland, FL 33805. **Telephone:** (863) 686-8075.

2009 SCHEDULE

COMERICA PARK

Standard Game Times: 7:05 p.m.; Sun. 1:05.

APRIL

4-9 . . . . at Toronto
10-12 . . . . Texas
13-15 . . . . White Sox
17-19 . . . . at Seattle
21-23 . . . . at Los Angeles
24-26 . . . . . at Kansas City
27-29 . . . . Yankees

MAY

1-3 . . . . Cleveland
4-5 . . . . .Minnesota
6-7 . . . . at White Sox
8-10 . . . . at Cleveland
12-14 . . . . . . at Minnesota
15-17 . . . . Oakland
19-21 . . . . Texas
22-24 . . . . .Colorado
25-27 . . . . . at Kansas City
28-31 . . . . . . .at Baltimore

JUNE

2-4 . . . . Boston
5-7 . . . . Angels
8-11 . . . . at White Sox
12-14 . . . . . . at Pittsburgh
16-18 . . . . .at St. Louis
19-21 . . . . Milwaukee
23-25 . . . . Cubs
26-28 . . . . at Houston
29-30 . . . . at Oakland

JULY

1 . . . . .atOakland
3-5 . . . . at Minnesota
6-8 . . . . Kansas City
10-12 . . . . Cleveland
17-19 . . . . .at Yankees
21-23 . . . . Seattle
24-26 . . . . White Sox
27-29 . . . . at Texas
31 . . . . at Cleveland

AUGUST

1-2 . . . . at Cleveland
3-6 . . . . Baltimore
7-9 . . . . .Minnesota
10-13 . . . . at Boston
14-16 . . . . Kansas City
18-20 . . . . Seattle
21-23 . . . . at Oakland
24-26 . . . . at Angels
28-30 . . . . Tampa Bay

SEPTEMBER

1-3 . . . . Cleveland
4-6 . . . . .at Tampa Bay
8-10 . . . . Kansas City
11-14 . . . . Toronto
15-17 . . . . Kansas City
18-20 . . . . . . at Minnesota
22-24 . . . . . . at Cleveland
25-27 . . . . . . at White Sox
28-30 . . . . .Minnesota

OCTOBER

1 . . . . .Minnesota
2-4 . . . . White Sox

Florida Marlins

Office Address: Dolphin Stadium, 2267 Dan Marino Blvd. Miami, FL 33056.
Telephone: (305) 626-7400. **Fax:** (305) 626-7302.
Website: www.marlins.com.

Ownership

Owner/CEO: Jeffrey Loria. **Vice Chairman:** Joel Mael.

President: David Samson. **Special Assistants to President:** Jeff Conine, Andre Dawson, Tony Perez. **Special Assistant to Owner:** Jack McKeon. **Executive Assistant to Owner, Vice Chairman/President:** Beth McConville.

Jeffrey Loria

BUSINESS OPERATIONS

Executive Vice President/CFO: Michel Bussiere. **Executive Assistant to the Executive V.P./CFO:** Lisa Milk. **Senior Vice President, Stadium Development:** Claude Delorme. **Executive Assistant to the Senior V.P. Stadium Development:** Ingrid Rodriguez. **Manager, Game Services:** Antonio Torres-Roman. **Coordinator, World Baseball Classic:** Victoria Mathias. **Director, Human Resources:** Ana Hernandez. **Coordinator, Human Resources:** Brian Estes. **Benefits:** Ruby Mattei. **Supervisor, Office Services:** Karl Heard. **Assistant, Office Services:** Donna Kirton. **Senior Receptionist:** Kathy Lanza. **Receptionist:** Dianette Oliva.

Finance

Senior Vice President, Finance: Susan Jaison. **Controller:** Alina Trigo. **Administrator, Payroll:** Carolina Calderon. **Staff Accountant:** Alina Quiros. **Coordinator, Accounts Payable:** Marva Alexander. **Coordinator, Finance:** Diana Jorge.

Director, Information Technology: David Enriquez. **Manager, Technical Support:** David Kuan. **Network Engineer:** Ozzie Macias. **Manager, Telecommunications:** Sam Mora. **IT Help Desk Technician:** Alexis Farres.

Marketing

Vice President, Marketing: Sean Flynn. **Manager, Retail Operations:** Robyn Feinstein. **Manager, Hispanic Sales/Marketing:** Juan Martinez. **Manager, Promotions:** Matt Britten. **Coordinator, Marketing:** Boris Menier. **Coordinator, Promotions:** Rafael Capdevila. **Coordinator, Mermaids:** Jose Guerrero. **Coordinator, Marlins en Miami:** Danny Vargas.

Sales

Vice President, New Business Development: Dale Hendricks. **Vice President, Corporate Sales:** Brendan Cunningham. **Manager, Corporate Sales:** Tony Tome. **Manager, Broadcast Sales:** Brian Schutz. **Corporate Sales Executives:** David Goldberg, Peter Kahn. **Coordinators, Corporate Sales:** Sheri Talerico, Christina Brito. **Executive Assistant, Corporate Sales:** Judy Cavanagh. **Director, Season/Group Sales:** William Makris. **Director, Customer Service:** Spencer Linden.

Senior Account Executive, Groups: Mario Signorello. **Supervisor, Group Sales:** Charles Sano. **Account Executive, Groups:** Bray LaDow. **Senior Account Executives:** Sean Flood, Orestes Hernandez.

Media Relations, Communications

Telephone: (305) 626-7492. **Fax:** (305) 626-7302.

Senior Vice President, Communications/Broadcasting: P.J. Loyello. **Director, Media Relations:** Matthew Roebuck. **Manager, Media Relations:** Marty Sewell. **Administrative Assistant, Media Relations:** Maria Armella. **Director, Broadcasting:** Emmanuel Munoz. **Manager, Broadcasting:** Karen Deery. **Manager, Community Affairs:** Angela Smith. **Coordinator, Player Relations:** Alex Morin.

Executive Director, Marlins Community Foundation: Nancy Olson. **Coordinators, Marlins Community Foundation:** Kelly Schnackenberg, Jeremy Stern.

In-Game Entertainment

Director, Game Presentation/Events: Larry Blocker. **Manager, Game Presentation/Events:** Eric Ramirez. **Assistants, Presentation/Events:** Andrew Resnick, Luis Dones, Gabe Gacharna. **Director, Creative Services:** Alfred Hernandez. **Manager, Creative Services:** Robert Vigon. **Mascot:** John DeCicco. **PA Announcer:** Dick Sanford.

Travel, Clubhouse

Senior Director, Team Travel: Bill Beck. **Equipment Manager:** John Silverman. **Visiting Clubhouse Manager:** Bryan Greenberg. **Assistant, Clubhouse/Umpire's Room:** Michael "Rock" Hughes.

GENERAL INFORMATION

Stadium (year opened): Dolphin Stadium (1993).
Home Dugout: First Base. **Playing Surface:** Grass.
Team Colors: Teal, black, white and silver.
Player Representative: Unavailable.
Driving Directions: From south, Florida Turnpike extension to stadium exit; From north, I-95 to I-595 West to Florida Turnpike to stadium exit; From west, I-75 to I-595 to Florida Turnpike to stadium exit; From east, Highway 826 West to NW 27th Avenue, north to Dan Marino Blvd., right to stadium.

BEN VAN HOUTEN

Jack Zduriencik

BASEBALL OPERATIONS

President, Baseball Operations: Larry Beinfest.

Vice President/General Manager: Michael Hill. **Vice President, Player Personnel/Assistant GM:** Dan Jennings. **Special Assistant to GM/Pro Scout:** Orrin Freeman. **Vice President/General Counsel:** Derek Jackson. **Video Coordinator:** Cullen McRae. **Executive Assistant to the EVP/GM:** Rita Filbert. **Executive Assistant to the VP/General Counsel:** Marie Thomas.

Major League Staff

Manager: Fredi Gonzalez.

Coaches: Bench—Carlos Tosca; Pitching—Mark Wiley; Hitting—Jim Presley; First Base/Infield—Andy Fox; Third Base—Bo Porter; Bullpen—Steve Foster; Bullpen Coordinator—Pierre Arsenault.

Medical, Training

Head Trainer: Sean Cunningham. **Assistant Trainer:** Mike Kozak. **Director, Strength/Conditioning:** Paul Fournier.

Player Development

Vice President, Player Development/Scouting/Assistant GM: Jim Fleming. **Director, Player Development:** Brian Chattin. **Assistant, Player Development:** Manny Colon. **Assistant, Baseball Operations:** Marc Lippman. **Assistant, Player Development/Scouting:** Michael Youngberg.

Field Coordinator: John Pierson. **Coordinators:** Gene Basham (training/rehabilitation), Tarrik Brock (outfield/baserunning), Tim Cossins (catching), John Mallee (hitting), Wayne Rosenthal (pitching), Josh Seligman (Strength/conditioning), Josue Espada (infield).

Minor League Equipment Manager: Mark Brown. **Minor League Clubhouse Manager:** Lou Assalone.

Farm System

Class	Club (League)	Manager	Coach	Pitching Coach
Triple-A	New Orleans (PCL)	Edwin Rodriguez	Steve Phillips	Scott Mitchell
Double-A	Jacksonville (SL)	Brandon Hyde	Theron Todd	Reid Cornelius
High A	Jupiter (FSL)	Tim Leiper	Anthony Iapoce	John Duffy
Low A	Greensboro (SAL)	Darin Everson	Robert Bell	Charlie Corbell Jr.
Short-season	Jamestown (NYP)	Andy Haines	Frank Moore	Doc Watson
Rookie	Jupiter (GCL)	Jorge Hernandez	Angel Espada	Jeff Schwarz
Rookie	Marlins (DSL)	Ray Nunez	Luis Brito	Edison Santana

Scouting

Telephone: (561) 630-1816/Pro (305) 626-7400.

Director, Scouting: Stan Meek. **Assistant Director, Scouting:** Gregg Leonard. **Assistant, Pro Scouting:** Dan Noffsinger. **Player Development/Scouting Assistant:** Michael Youngberg.

Advance Scout: Joel Moeller (San Clemente, CA). **Pro Scouts:** Roger Jongewaard (Fallbrook, CA), Dave Roberts (Fort Worth, TX), Phil Rossi (Jessup, PA), Tommy Thompson (Greenville, NC), Michael White (Lakewood Ranch, FL).

National Crosschecker: David Crowson (College Station, TX). **Regional Supervisors:** East—Matt Haas (Cincinnati, OH); Central—Ray Hayward (Norman, OK); West—Scott Goldby (Yuba City, CA); Canada—Steve Payne (Barrington, RI).

Area Scouts: Matt Anderson (Williamsport, PA), Carlos Berroa (Caguas, PR), Carmen Carcone (Canton, GA), Dennis Cardoza Boyd, TX), Robby Corsaro (Victorville, CA), John Hughes (Walnut Creek, CA), Kevin Ibach (Arlington Heights, IL), Brian Kraft (Auburndale, FL), Joel Matthews (Concord, NC), Tim McDonnell (Westminster, CA), Nick Zumsande (Fairfax, IA), Gabe Sandy (Gresham, OR), Scott Stanley (Peoria, AZ), Ryan Wardinsky (Edmond, OK), Mark Willoughby (Hammond, LA).

Director, International Operations: Albert Gonzalez.

International Supervisors: Sandy Nin (Santo Domingo, Dominican Republic)Wilmer Castillo (Maracay, VZ). **International Scouts:** Luis Cordoba (Panama), Willie Marrugo (Cartagena, Colombia), Alix Martinez (Santo Domingo, DR), Victor Montoya (Caracas, VZ), Domingo Ortega (Santo Domingo, DR), Jaime Torres (Barcelona, VZ), Robin Torres (Zulia, VZ).

Spring Training

Complex Address (first year): Roger Dean Stadium (1998), 4751 Main St., Jupiter, FL 33458. **Telephone:** (561) 775-1818.

Seating Capacity: 7,000.

Location: I-95 to exit 83, east on Donald Ross Road for one mile to Central Blvd, left at light, follow Central Boulevard to circle and take Main Street to Roger Dean Stadium.

Hotel Address: Hampton Inn, 401 RCA Blvd., Palm Beach Gardens, FL 33410. **Telephone:** (561) 625-8880. **FAX:** (561) 625-6766.

Minor League Clubs

Complex Address: Same as major league club. **Hotel Address:** Fairfield Inn, 6748 W. Indiantown Rd., Jupiter, FL 33458. **Telephone:** (561) 748-5252.

2009 SCHEDULE

DOLPHINS STADIUM

Standard Game Times:
7:05 p.m.; Sun. 1:05

APRIL

6-8 . . . . Washington
10-12 . . . . Mets
14-16 . . . . at Atlanta
17-19 . . . . . at Washington
20-22 . . . . . . at Pittsburgh
24-26 . . . . . . Philadelphia
27-29 . . . . at Mets
30 . . . . at Cubs

MAY

1-3 . . . . at Cubs
4-5 . . . . Cincinnati
6-7 . . . . Atlanta
8-10 . . . . at Colorado
12-14 . . . . . at Milwaukee
15-17 . . . . Dodgers
18-21 . . . . Arizona
22-24 . . . . Tampa Bay
25-27 . . . . at Philadelphia
29-31 . . . . at Mets

JUNE

1-4 . . . . Milwaukee
5-8 . . . . San Francisco
9-11 . . . . St. Louis
12-14 . . . . at Toronto
16-18 . . . . at Boston
19-21 . . . . Yankees
23-25 . . . . Baltimore
26-28 . . . . . at Tampa Bay
29-30 . . . . . . Washington

JULY

1 . . . . Washington
3-5 . . . . Pittsburgh
6-8 . . . . . . at San Francisco
9-12 . . . . at Arizona
17-19 . . . . . . Philadelphia
20-22 . . . . at San Diego
24-26 . . . . at Dodgers
28-30 . . . . Atlanta
31 . . . . Cubs

AUGUST

1-2 . . . . Cubs
4-6 . . . . at Washington
7-9 . . . . . . at Philadelphia
10-13 . . . . Houston
14-16 . . . . Colorado
18-20 . . . . at Houston
21-23 . . . . at Atlanta
25-27 . . . . Mets
28-30 . . . . San Diego
31 . . . . Atlanta

SEPTEMBER

1-3 . . . . Atlanta
4-6 . . . . at Washington
8-10 . . . . at Mets
11-13 . . . . Washington
14-16 . . . . at St. Louis
17-20 . . . . . . at Cincinnati
21-23 . . . . . . Philadelphia
25-27 . . . . Mets
28-30 . . . . at Atlanta

OCTOBER

2-4 . . . . . . at Philadelphia

Houston Astros

Office Address: Minute Maid Park, Union Station, 501 Crawford, Suite 400, Houston, TX 77002.
Mailing Address: P.O. Box 288, Houston, TX 77001.
Telephone: (713) 259-8000. **Fax:** (713) 259-8981.
E-mail Address: fanfeedback@astros.mlb.com. **Website:** www.astros.com.

Ownership

Operated By: McLane Group LP.
Chairman/CEO: Drayton McLane.
Board of Directors: Bob McClaren, G.W. Sanford, Webb Stickney.

Drayton McLane

BUSINESS OPERATIONS

President, Business Operations: Pam Gardner. **Executive Assistant:** Eileen Colgin.

Senior Vice President, Finance/Administration: Jackie Traywick. **Controller:** Jonathan Germer. **Director, Treasury/Office Services:** Damian Babin. **Senior Accountant:** Abby Price. **Accounts Payable Coordinator:** Monique Sam. **Vice President, Human Resources:** Larry Stokes. **Human Resources Coordinator:** Chanda Lawdermilk. **Director, Payroll/Employee Benefits:** Ruth Kelly. **Manager, Payroll:** Jessica Horton. **Benefits Coordinator:** Cyndi Campbell.

Marketing/Sales

Senior Vice President, Premium Sponsorships: Jamie Hildreth. **Vice President, Sponsorships/Business Development:** John Sorrentino. **Vice President, Market Development:** Rosi Hernandez. **Vice President, Marketing:** Jennifer Randall. **Director, Marketing/Promotions:** Clint Pasche. **Marketing Manager:** Mallory Conger. **Assistant Director, Sponsorship Sales:** Shane Hildreth. **Sponsorship Accounts Manager:** Marisa Lopez. **Market Development Manager:** Chris Hunsaker. **Graphics Designer:** Chris Garcia.

Public Relations/Communications

Telephone: (713) 259-8900. **Fax:** (713) 259-8981.

Senior Vice President, Communications: Jay Lucas. **Director, Media Relations:** Gene Dias. **Assistant Director, Media Relations:** Sally Gunter. **Media Relations Coordinator:** Stephen Grande. **VP, Foundation Development:** Marian Harper. **Director, Community Affairs:** Shawn Bertani. **Director, Procurement:** Seth Courtney. **Director, Information Technology:** Steve Reese. **Network Administrator:** Michael Hovan.

Stadium Operations

Vice President, Ballpark Operations: Bobby Forrest. **VP, Special Events:** Kala Sorenson. **Assistant Director, Engineering:** David McKenzie. **Audio-Visual Coordinator:** James Sorenson. **Director, Ballpark Entertainment:** Kirby Kander. **Assistant Director, Ballpark Entertainment:** Brock Jessel. **Production Coordinator:** Joey Graham. **Director, Affiliate Relations:** Mike Cannon. **Radio Broadcast Engineer:** Lowell Matheny. **Director, Telecommunications/Executive Assistant:** Tracy Faucette. **Director, Guest Services:** Michael Kenny. **Guest Services Manager:** Cedrick Edwards. **Guest Services Coordinator:** Morgan Gower. **Assistant Sales Director, Special Events/Conference Center:** Leigh Ann Dawson. **Sales Manager, Special Events:** Valerie Eissler. **Minute Maid Park Tour Manager:** Steven Kelly. **Director, Major League Field Operations:** Dan Bergstrom. **Groundskeeper:** Willie Berry. **First Assistant Groundskeeper:** Kyle Lewis. **Second Assistant Groundskeeper:** Joe Johannsen. **Third Assistant Groundskeeper:** Eric Jaramillo.

PA Announcer: Bob Ford. **Official Scorers:** Rick Blount, Ivy McLemore, Greg Porzucek, Trey Wilkinson.

Ticketing

Telephone: (713) 259-8500. **Fax:** (713) 259-8326.

Senior Director, Ticket Sales: Bill Goren. **Senior Director, Ticket Services:** Brooke Ellenberger. **Director, Ticket Operations:** Marcia Coronado. **Director, Box Office Operations:** Bill Cannon. **Manager, Premium Sales:** Clay Kowalski. **Manager, Ticket Services:** Adam Eiseman. **Manager, Ticket Sales:** Jolene Krause. **Administrative Assistant, Ticket Sales:** Joannie Cobb. **Senior Account Executive:** Brent Broussard. **Ticket Production Coordinator:** Sandy Luna.

Travel/Clubhouse

Director, Team Travel: Barry Waters.

Equipment Manager: Dennis Liborio. **Assistant Equipment Managers:** Carl Schneider. **Visiting Clubhouse Manager:** Steve Perry. **Umpire/Clubhouse Assistant:** Chuck New.

GENERAL INFORMATION

Stadium (year opened): Minute Maid Park (2000).
Home Dugout: First Base. **Playing Surface:** Grass.
Team Colors: Brick red, sand beige and black.
Player Representative: Unavailable.
Driving Directions: From I-10 East, take Smith Street (exit 769A), left at Texas Ave., 0.6 miles to park at corner of Texas Ave. and Crawford St.; from I-10 West, take San Jacinto St. (exit 769B), right on Fannin St., left on Texas Ave., 0.3 miles to park; From Hwy. 59 North: take Gray Ave./Pierce Ave. exit, 0.3 miles on Gray St. to Crawford St., one mile to park.

Ed Wade

BASEBALL OPERATIONS

Telephone: (713) 259-8000. **Fax:** (713) 259-8600.

President, Baseball Operations: Tal Smith.

General Manager: Ed Wade. **Assistant GM/Player Relations:** David Gottfried. **Director, Research/Analysis:** Charlie Norton. **Assistant Director, Baseball Operations:** Jay Edmiston. **Coordinator, Player Development:** Allen Rowin. **Coordinator, Scouting:** Mike Burns. **Executive Assistant:** Traci Dearing. **Video Coordinator:** Jim Summers.

Major League Staff

Manger: Cecil Cooper.

Coaches: Bench—Ed Romero; Pitching—Dewey Robinson; Hitting—Sean Berry; First Base—Jose Cruz, Sr.; Third Base—Dave Clark; Bullpen—Mark Bailey.

Medical, Training

Medical Director: Dr. David Lintner. **Team Physicians:** Dr. Tom Mehlhoff, Dr. Jim Muntz.

Head Trainer: Nathan Lucero. **Assistant Trainer:** Rex Jones. **Strength/Conditioning Coaches:** Dr. Gene Coleman.

Player Development

Telephone: (713) 259-8922. **Fax:** (713) 259-8600.

Assistant GM/Director, Player Development: Ricky Bennett.

Field Coordinator: Al Pedrique. **Minor League Coordinators:** Mike Barnett (hitting), Britt Burns (pitching), Jaime Garcia (assistant pitching), Gary Redus (outfield/baserunning), Danny Sheaffer (catching), Pete Fagan (training/rehabilitation), Mike Smith (strength/conditioning).

Farm System

Class	Club	Manager	Hitting Coach	Pitching Coach
Triple-A	Round Rock (PCL)	Marc Bombard	Ron Jackson	Burt Hooton
Double-A	Corpus Christi (TL)	Luis Pujols	Keith Bodie	Stan Boroski
High A	Lancaster (CAL)	Wes Clements	Darryl Robinson	Don Alexander
Low A	Lexington (SAL)	Tom Lawless	Pete Rancont	Charley Taylor
Short-season	Tri-City (NYP)	Jim Pankovits	Joel Chimelis	Gary Ruby
Rookie	Greeneville (APP)	Rodney Linares	Stubby Clapp	Travis Driskill
Rookie	Astros (GCL)	Omar Lopez	D.J. Boston	Rick Aponte
Rookie	Astros (DSL)	Luis Martinez	Luis Mateo	Hector Eduardo

Scouting

Telephone: (713) 259-8921. **Fax:** (713) 259-8600.

Assistant GM, Amateur Scouting: Bobby Heck. **Director, Latin American Scouting:** Felix Francisco. **Director, Pacific Rim Scouting:** Glen Barker. **Director, Major League Scouting:** Fred Nelson. **Major League Scouts:** Gene DeBoer (Brandon, WI), Jack Lind (Mesa, AZ), Walt Matthews (Texarkana, TX), Paul Ricciarini (Pittsfield, MA), Bob Skinner (San Diego, CA), Fred Nelson, Ken Califano, Matt Galante, Lee Thomas. **Professional Scouts:** Jeff McAvoy (Palmer, MA), Scipio Spinks (Missouri City, TX), Tad Slowik (Arlington Heights, IL), Hank Allen, Gerry Craft, Tom Weidenbauer.

National Crosschecker: David Post (Canton, GA). **Regional Supervisors:** Midwest—Ralph Bratton (Dripping Springs, TX); West—Mark Ross (Tucson, AZ); East—Clarence Johns (Tallahassee, FL). **Area Scouts:** J.D. Alleva (Charlotte, NC), Keith Bogan (Ridgeland, MS), Greg Brown, Brad Budzinski, Tim Costic, Dough Deutsch, Ed Fastaia, Paul Gale (Keizer, OR), Joe Graham (Rocklin, CA), Troy Hoerner, Jesse Kapellusch, John Kosciak, Lincoln Martin (Douglasview, GA), Tom McCormack (University City, MO), Rusty Pendergrass (Missouri City, TX), Mark Randall (Edmonton, Alberta, Canada), Joey Sola (Caguas, PR), Jim Stevenson (Tulsa, OK), Everett Stull, Nick Venuto (Massillon, OH).

Senior Advising Scouts: Bob King (La Mesa, CA), Bob Poole (Redwood City, CA), Gene Wellman (Danville, CA).

International Scouts: Venezuela: Daniel Acuna, Oscar Alvarado, Miguel Chacoa, Joan Fernandez, Johan Maya, Luimac Quero, Wolfgang Ramos, Luis Yanez. **Dominican Republic:** Rafael Belen, Jose Lima, Andres Lopez, Francis Mojica. **Colombia:** Carlos Martinez. **Europe:** Mauro Mazzotti. **Mexico:** Maxinimo Leon. **Panama:** Jose Luis Santos. **Nicaragua:** Leocadio Guevara. **Curacao:** Wellington Herrera.

Spring Training

Complex Address (first year): Osceola County Stadium (1985), 631 Heritage Park Way, Kissimmee, FL 34744. **Telephone:** (321) 697-3150. **Fax:** (321) 697-3199. **Seating Capacity:** 5,300. **Location:** From Florida Turnpike South, take exit 244, west on U.S. 192, right on Bill Beck Blvd..

Hotel Address: Reunion Resort & Club, 1000 Reunion Way, Reunion, Florida 34747. **Telephone:** 407-662-1000.

Minor League Clubs

Complex Address: 1000 Bill Beck Blvd., Kissimmee, FL 34744. **Telephone:** (321) 697-3100. **Hotel Address:** Same as major league club.

2009 SCHEDULE

MINUTE MAID PARK

Standard Game Times:
7:05 p.m.; Sat. 6:05; Sun. 1:05.

APRIL

6-8 . . . . . . Cubs
10-12 . . . . . . at St. Louis
13 . . . . . . at Pittsburgh
15-16 . . . . . . at Pittsburgh
17-20 . . . . . . Cincinnati
21-23 . . . . . . Dodgers
24-26 . . . . . . Milwaukee
27-30 . . . . . . at Cincinnati

MAY

1-3 . . . . . . at Atlanta
4-5 . . . . . . at Washington
6-7 . . . . . . Cubs
8-10 . . . . . . San Diego
12-14 . . . . . . at Colorado
15-17 . . . . . . at Cubs
19-21 . . . . . . Milwaukee
22-24 . . . . . . Texas
25-27 . . . . . . at Cincinnati
29-31 . . . . . . at Pittsburgh

JUNE

1-4 . . . . . . Colorado
5-7 . . . . . . Pittsburgh
9-11 . . . . . . Cubs
12-14 . . . . . . at Arizona
16-18 . . . . . . at Texas
19-21 . . . . . . at Minnesota
23-25 . . . . . . Kansas City
26-28 . . . . . . Detroit
29-30 . . . . . . at San Diego

JULY

1-2 . . . . . . at San Diego
3-5 . . . . . . at San Francisco
6-8 . . . . . . Pittsburgh
9-12 . . . . . . Washington
16-19 . . . . . . at Dodgers
20-22 . . . . . . St. Louis
24-26 . . . . . . Mets
27-29 . . . . . . at Cubs
31 . . . . . . at St. Louis

AUGUST

1-2 . . . . . . at St. Louis
3-5 . . . . . . San Francisco
7-9 . . . . . . Milwaukee
10-13 . . . . . . at Florida
14-16 . . . . . . at Milwaukee
18-20 . . . . . . Florida
21-23 . . . . . . Arizona
25-27 . . . . . . at St. Louis
28-30 . . . . . . at Arizona
31 . . . . . . at Cubs

SEPTEMBER

1-2 . . . . . . at Cubs
4-7 . . . . . . Philadelphia
8-10 . . . . . . Atlanta
11-13 . . . . . . Pittsburgh
14-16 . . . . . . at Cincinnati
18-20 . . . . . . at Milwaukee
21-23 . . . . . . St. Louis
25-27 . . . . . . Cincinnati
28-30 . . . . . . at Philadelphia

OCTOBER

1 . . . . . . at Philadelphia
2-4 . . . . . . at Mets

Kansas City Royals

Office Address: One Royal Way, Kansas City, MO 64129.
Mailing Address: P.O. Box 419969, Kansas City, MO 64141.
Telephone: (816) 921-8000. **Fax:** (816) 924-0347.
Website: www.royals.com

Ownership

Operated By: Kansas City Royals Baseball Club Inc.

Chairman/CEO: David Glass. **President:** Dan Glass. **Board of Directors:** Ruth Glass, Don Glass, Dayna Martz, Julia Kauffman, Herk Robinson. **Executive Administrative Assistant (Executive Staff):** Ginger Salem.

David Glass

BUSINESS OPERATIONS

Senior Vice President/Business Operations: Kevin Uhlich. **Executive Administrative Assistant:** Cindy Hamilton.

Finance/Administration

Director, Finance: Joe Kurtzman. **Director, Renovation Accounting/Risk Management:** Patrick Fleischmann. **Senior Director, Payroll/Benefits/Human Resources:** Tom Pfannenstiel. **Senior Director, Information Systems:** Jim Edwards.

Senior Director, Ticket Operations: Rick Amos. **Director, Ticket Operations:** Chris Darr.

Communications/Broadcasting

Vice President, Communications/Broadcasting: Mike Swanson. **Director, Broadcast Services/Royals Alumni:** Fred White. **Manager, Radio Network Operations:** Don Free.

Media Relations

Director, Media Relations: David Holtzman. **Coordinator, Media Services:** Dina Wathan. **Coordinator, Communications/Broadcasting:** Colby Curry.

Publicity/Community Relations

Vice President, Community Affairs/Publicity: Toby Cook. **Senior Director, Community Relations:** Ben Aken. **Senior Director, Publicity:** Lora Grosshans. **Senior Director, Royals Charities:** Joy Sedlacek. **Director, Community Outreach:** Betty Kaegel.

Ballpark Operations

Vice President, Ballpark Operations/Development: Bob Rice. **Director, Event Operations:** Renee VanLaningham. **Director, Fan Experience/Hospitality:** Carrie Bligh. **Director, Groundskeeping/Landscaping:** Trevor Vance. **Director, Stadium Services:** Johnny Williams. **Director, Stadium Engineering/Maintenance:** Todd Burrow.

Sales/Marketing

Vice President, Sales/Marketing: Mark Tilson. **Director, Marketing:** Debi Teter. **Senior Director, Entertainment/Production:** Don Costante. **Director, Game Entertainment:** Chris DeRuyscher.

Senior Director, Sales/Service: Dawson Hughes. **Director, Sales:** Theo Hodges. **Director, Ticket Services:** Scott Wadsworth.

Business Development

Vice President, Corporate Alliance: Neil Harwell.

Senior Director, Corporate Sales: Mitch Wheeler. **Senior Director, Corporate Sponsorship Marketing:** Kim Hillix-Burgess. **Senior Director, Corporate Sponsorship Relations:** Michelle Kammerer.

GENERAL INFORMATION

Stadium (year opened): Ewing M. Kauffman Stadium (1973).
Home Dugout: First Base. **Playing Surface:** Grass.
Team Colors: Royal blue and white.
Team Representative: Unavailable.
Driving Directions: From north or south, take I-435 to stadium exits. From east or west, take I-70 to stadium exits.

Dayton Moore

BASEBALL OPERATIONS

Telephone: (816) 921-8000. **Fax:** (816) 924-0347.

Senior Vice President, Baseball Operations/General Manager: Dayton Moore.

VP, Baseball Operations/Assistant GM: Dean Taylor. **Assistant GM, Scouting/Player Development:** J.J. Picollo. **Senior Advisor to GM/Scouting Player Development:** Mike Arbuckle. **Director, Baseball Administration:** Jin Wong. **Director, Baseball Operations:** Lonnie Goldberg. **Baseball Operations Assistant:** Kyle Vena. **Coordinator, Pro Scouting:** Gene Watson. **Senior Advisors:** Art Stewart, Donnie Williams. **Assistant to GM:** Brian Murphy. **Special Assistant to GM, International Operations:** Rene Francisco. **Special Assistant/Player Personnel:** Louie Medina. **VP, Baseball Operations:** George Brett. **Video Coordinator:** Mark Topping. **Team Travel:** Jeff Davenport.

Major League Staff

Manager: Trey Hillman.

Coaches: Bench—John Gibbons; Pitching—Bob McClure; Batting—Kevin Seitzer; First Base—Rusty Kuntz; Third Base—Dave Owen; Bullpen—John Mizerock; Special Assignment Coach—Eddie Rodriguez

Medical/Training

Team Physician: Dr. Steven Joyce. **Athletic Trainer:** Nick Swartz.

Player Development

Telephone: (816) 921-8000. **Fax:** (816) 924-0347.

Director, Minor League Operations: Scott Sharp. **Special Assistant:** Jack Maloof. **Special Assistant to Player Development/Scouting:** John Wathan. **Coordinators:** Bill Fischer (pitching), Doug Sisson (field), Tony Tijerina (catching), Andre David (hitting), Mark Harris (infield), Quilvio Veras (baserunning). **Roving Pitching Coach:** Doug Henry.

Farm System

Class	Club (League)	Manager	Coach	Pitching Coach
Triple-A	Omaha (PCL)	Mike Jirschele	Tommy Gregg	Tom Burgmeier
Double-A	N-West Arkansas (TL)	Brian Poldberg	Terry Bradshaw	Larry Carter
High A	Wilmington (CL)	Brian Rupp	Justin Gemoll	Steve Luebber
Low A	Burlington (MWL)	Jim Gabella	Pookie Wilson	Jerry Nyman
Rookie	Idaho Falls (PIO)	Darryl Kennedy	Jon Williams	Carlos Martinez
Rookie	Burlington (APP)	Nelson Liriano	Omar Ramirez	Bobby St. Pierre
Rookie	Royals (AZL)	Julio Bruno	Kenny Munoz	C. Reyes, M. Davis
Rookie	Royals (DSL)	Jose Mejia	Larry Sutton	Rafael Roque

Scouting

Telephone: (816) 921-8000. **Fax:** (816) 924-0347.

Assistant Director, Scouting: Steve Williams. **Manager, Scouting Operations:** Linda Smith.

Major League Scouts: Charles Bolton (Indianapolisl, IN), Tom McDevitt (Charleston, ILL), Matt Price (Atlanta, GA), Mike Pazik (Bethesda, MD). **Advance Scout:** Kelly Heath (Palm Harbor, FL).

National Supervisors: Marty Maier (Chesterfield, MO), Junior Vizcaino (Raleigh, NC), Dennis Woody (Danville, AR). **Regional Supervisors:** John Flannery (Austin, TX), Sean Rooney (Pompton Lake, NJ), Gregg Kilby (Tampa, Florida).

Area Scouts: Jason Bryans (Windsor, Canada), Steve Connelly (Wilson, NC), Casey Fahy (Clayton, NJ), Sean Gibbs (Canton, GA), Colin Gonzales (Northern Florida), Steve Gossett (Fremont, NE), Ben Jones (Ft. Wayne, IN), Scott Melvin (Quincy, IL), Alex Mesa (Miami, FL), Ken Munoz (Scottsdale, AZ), Scott Nichols (Richland, MS), Dan Ontiveros (Laguna Niguel, CA), Wes Penick (Clive, IA), John Ramey (Wildomar, CA), Johnny Ramos (Carolina, PR), Scott Ramsay (Valley, WA), Brian Rhees (Live Oak, TX), Rick Schroeder (Pleasanton, CA), Dennis Sheehan (Glasco, NY), Lloyd Simmons (Oklahoma City, OK).

Latin America Supervisor: Orlando Estevez. **International Scouts:** Salvador Donadelli (Venezuela), Juan Indriago (Venezuela), Joelvis Gonzalez (Venezuela), Juan Lopez (Nicaragua), Rafael Miranda (Colombia), Fausto Morel (Dominican), Daurys Nin (Dominican), Ricardo Ortiz (Panama), Edis Perez (Dominican), Hector Pineda (Dominican), Mike Randall (South Africa), Pedro Silverio (Dominican), Rafael Vasquez (Dominican), Franco Wawoe (Curacao), Louis Yu (Taiwan).

Spring Training

Complex Address (first year): Surprise Stadium (2003), 15946 N. Bullard Ave., Surprise, AZ 85374. **Telephone:** (623) 266-8800. **Seating Capacity:** 10,700. **Location:** I-10 West to Route 101 North, 101 North to Bell Road, left on Bell for five miles, stadium on left.

Hotel Address: Wingate Inn & Suites, 1188 N. Dysart Rd., Avondale, AZ 85323. **Telephone:** (623) 547-1313.

Minor League Clubs

Complex: Same as Major League club. **Hotel Address:** Quality Inn, 16741 N. Greasewood St., Surprise, AZ 85374. **Telephone:** (623) 583-3500.

2009 SCHEDULE

KAUFFMAN STADIUM

Standard Game Times: 7:10 p.m.; Sat. 6:10; Sun. 1:10.

APRIL
6-9 . . . . at White Sox
10-12 . . . . Yankees
13-15 . . . . Cleveland
17-19 . . . . at Texas
21-23 . . . . . . at Cleveland
24-26 . . . . Detroit
27-30 . . . . Toronto

MAY
1-3 . . . . at Minnesota
4-5 . . . . White Sox
6-7 . . . . Seattle
8-10 . . . . at Angels
12-13 . . . . at Oakland
14-17 . . . . Baltimore
19-21 . . . . Cleveland
22-24 . . . . .at St. Louis
25-27 . . . . Detroit
29-31 . . . . White Sox

JUNE
2-4 . . . . at Tampa Bay
5-7 . . . . at Toronto
9-11 . . . . at Cleveland
12-14 . . . . Cincinnati
16-18 . . . . .Arizona
10-21 . . . . St. Louis
23-25 . . . . at Houston
26-28 . . . . . . at Pittsburgh
29-30 . . . . .Minnesota

JULY
1 . . . . .Minnesota
2-5 . . . . White Sox
6-8 . . . . at Detroit
9-12 . . . . at Boston
17-19 . . . . Tampa Bay
20-22 . . . . Angels
24-26 . . . . Texas
27-30 . . . . .at Baltimore
31 . . . . Tampa Bay

AUGUST
1-3 . . . . at Tampa Bay
4-6 . . . . Seattle
7-9 . . . . Oakland
11-13 . . . . . . at Minnesota
14-16 . . . . at Detroit
17-19 . . . . at White Sox
21-23 . . . . .Minnesota
24-26 . . . . Cleveland
27-30 . . . . at Seattle
31 . . . . at Oakland

SEPTEMBER
1-2 . . . . at Oakland
4-7 . . . . Angels
8-10 . . . . Detroit
11-13 . . . . at Cleveland
15-17 . . . . at Detroit
18-20 . . . . at White Sox
21-24 . . . . Boston
25-27 . . . . .Minnesota
28-30 . . . . .at Yankees

OCTOBER
2-4 . . . . at Twins

Los Angeles Angels

Office Address: Angel Stadium of Anaheim, 2000 Gene Autry Way, Anaheim, CA 92806.
Mailing Address: P.O. Box 2000, Anaheim, CA 92803.
Telephone: (714) 940-2000. **Fax:** (714) 940-2205.
Website: www.angelsbaseball.com.

Ownership

Owner: Arturo Moreno.
President: Dennis Kuhl.

BUSINESS OPERATIONS

Arte Moreno

Chief Financial Officer: Bill Beverage. **Vice President, Finance/Administration:** Molly Taylor Jolly. **Controller:** Cris Fisher. **Accountants:** Lorelei Largey, Kylie McManus, Jennifer Whynott. **Assistant, Accounting:** Linda Chubak. **Director, Human Resources:** Jenny Price. **Benefits Coordinator:** Tracie Key. **Human Resources Representative:** Arianna Fernandez. **Manager, Recruitment/Training:** Brittany Johnson. **Manager, Information Services:** Al Castro. **Senior Network Engineer:** Neil Farris. **Senior Customer Support Analyst:** David Yun. **Assistant Network Administrator:** Paramjit Singh. **Travel Account Manager:** Chantelle Bell.

Marketing/Corporate Sales

Senior Vice President, Sales/Marketing: John Carpino. **VP, Corporate Sales:** Richard McClemmy. **Corporate Account Executives:** Pennie Contos, Joe Furmanski, Mike Gullo, Jennifer Soliman, Scott Adams, Rick Turner, Sabrina Warner. **Spanish Radio Account Executives:** Carla Enriquez, Rob Aylesworth. **Sponsorship Services Manager:** Cesar Sanchez. **Senior Sponsorship Services Coordinator:** Maria Dinh. **Sponsorship Services Coordinators:** Derek Ohta, Jackie Perkins.

Vice President, Marketing/Ticket Sales: Robert Alvarado. **Marketing Associates:** Matt Artin, Elaine Lombardi, Ernie Prukner, John Rozak. **Marketing Coordinator/Graphic Designer:** Jeff Lee. **Ticket Sales Manager:** Tom DeTemple. **Client Services Manager:** Brian Sanders. **Event Manager:** Manny Almaraz. **Client Services Representatives:** Arthur Felix, Ashley Green, Justin Hallenbeck, Amanda Gurney, Brandon Joffe, Alisa Moreno, Matt Swanson, Kellie Wardecki. **Group Sales Account Executive:** Angel Rodriguez. **Premium Sales/Service Representative:** Brian Lawrence. **Ticket Sales Account Executives:** Clint Blevins, Jeff Leuenberger, Jasmin Matthews, Scott Tarlo. **Administrative Assistant, Marketing:** Monica Campanis. **Administrative Assistant, Sales:** Pat Lissy.

Public/Media Relations/Communications

Telephone: (714) 940-2014. **Fax:** (714) 940-2205.

Vice President, Communications: Tim Mead. **Director, Communications:** Nancy Mazmanian. **Communications Manager:** Eric Kay. **Administrative Assistant, Communications:** Jennifer Hoyer. **Manager, Community Relations:** Matt Bennett. **Community Relations Coordinator:** Lindsay McHolm. **Publications Manager:** Doug Ward. **Traveling Secretary:** Tom Taylor. **Club Photographers:** Debora Robinson, John Cordes, Bob Binder.

Ballpark Operations/Facilities

Director, Ballpark Operations: Sam Maida. **Director, Facility Services:** Mike McCay. **Event Manager:** Calvin Ching. **Manager, Security:** Keith Cleary. **Maintenance Manager, Field/Ground:** Barney Lopas. **Assistant Manager, Facility Services:** Linda Fitzgerald. **Maintenance Supervisor:** David Tamblyn. **Purchasing Manager:** Ron Sparks. **Purchasing Assistant:** Suzanne Peters. **Receptionists:** Sandy Sanford, Margie Walsh. **Manager, Entertainment/Production:** Peter Bull. **Producer, Video Operations:** David Tsuruda. Associate Producer: Danny Pitts. **Entertainment Supervisor:** Heather Capizzi. **PA Announcer:** David Courtney.

Ticketing

Manager, Ticket Operations: Sheila Brazelton. **Assistant Ticket Manager:** Susan Weiss. **Ticketing Supervisor:** Ryan Vance. **Ticketing Representatives:** Cyndi Nguyen, Clancy Holligan, Kim Weaver.

Travel/Clubhouse

Clubhouse Manager: Ken Higdon.

Assistant Clubhouse Manager: Keith Tarter. **Visiting Clubhouse Manager:** Brian Harkins. **Senior Video Coordinator:** Diego Lopez. **Video Coordinator:** Ruben Montano.

GENERAL INFORMATION

Stadium (year opened): Angel Stadium of Anaheim (2004).
Home Dugout: Third Base. **Playing Surface:** Grass.
Team Colors: Red, dark red, blue and silver.
Player Representative: Unavailable.
Driving Directions: Highway 57 (Orange Freeway) to Orangewood exit, west on Orangewood, stadium on west side of Orange Freeway.

Tony Reagins

BASEBALL OPERATIONS

General Manager: Tony Reagins.

Assistant GM: Ken Forsch. **Special Advisor:** Bill Stoneman. **Special Assistant to GM:** Gary Sutherland. **Manager, Baseball Operations:** Tory Hernandez.

Major League Staff

Manager: Mike Scioscia. **Coaches:** Bench—Ron Roenicke; Pitching—Mike Butcher; Batting—Mickey Hatcher; First Base—Alfredo Griffin; Third Base—Dino Ebel; Bullpen—Orlando Mercado; Bullpen Catcher—Steve Soliz.

Medical/Training

Medical Director: Dr. Lewis Yocum. **Team Physician:** Dr. Craig Milhouse.

Head Athletic Trainer: Ned Bergert. **Athletic Trainer:** Rick Smith. **Assistant Athletic Trainer:** Adam Nevala. **Physical Therapist:** David Hogarth. **Strength/Conditioning Coach:** T.J. Harrington. **Director, Legal Affairs/Risk Management:** David Cohen. **Administrative Assistant, Trainers:** Chris Titchenal.

Player Development

Director, Player Development: Abe Flores. **Assistant, Player Development/Scouting:** Justin Hollander. **Administrative Assistant:** Terri Shambaugh. **Administration Manager, Arizona:** Eric Blum.

Field Coordinator/Hitting Instructor: Todd Takayoshi. **Roving Instructors:** Tom Gregorio (catching), Geoff Hostetter (training coordinator), Bill Lachemann (catching/special assignment), Rob Picciolo (infield), Kernan Ronan (pitching).

Farm System

Class	Club	Manager	Coach	Pitching Coach
Triple-A	Salt Lake (PCL)	Bobby Mitchell	Jim Eppard	Erik Bennett
Double-A	Arkansas (TL)	Bobby Magallanes	Francisco Matos	Ken Patterson
High A	R. Cucamonga (CAL)	Keith Johnson	Damon Mashore	Daniel Ricabal
Low A	Cedar Rapids (MWL)	Bill Mosiello	Brent Del Chiaro	Brandon Emanuel
Rookie	Orem (PIO)	Tom Kotchman	Mike Eylward	Zeke Zimmerman
Rookie	Angels (AZL)	Ty Boykin	Dick Schofield	Trevor Wilson
Rookie	Angels (DSL)	Charlie Romero	Edgal Rodriguez	Santos Alcala

Scouting

Telephone: (714) 940-2038. **Fax:** (714) 940-2203.

Director, Amateur Scouting: Eddie Bane.

Major League Scouts: Marc Russo (Clearwater, FL), Rich Schlenker (Walnut Creek, CA), Jeff Schugel (Denver, CO), Brad Sloan (Brimfield, IL), Dale Sutherland (La Crescenta, CA).

National Crosscheckers: Jeff Malinoff (Lopez, WA), Ric Wilson (Chandler, AZ). **Regional Supervisors:** East—Mike Silvestri (Davie, FL); Midwest—Ron Marigny (New Orleans, LA); West—Bo Hughes (Sherman Oaks, CA).

Area Scouts: Arnold Brathwaite (Grand Prairie, TX), Jim Bryant (Mobile, AL), John Burden (Fairfield, OH), Tim Corcoran (Le Verne, CA), Bobby DeJardin (San Clemente, CA), Demetrius Figgins (Deerfield Beach, FL), John Gracio (Mesa, AZ), Kevin Ham (El Paso, TX), Casey Harvie (Lake Stevens, WA), Tom Kotchman (Seminole, FL), Chris McAlpin (Norman Park, GA), Greg Morhardt (So. Windsor, CT), Joel Murrie (Evergreen, CO), Dan Radcliff (Palmyra, VA), Scott Richardson (Elk Grove, CA), Jeff Scholzen (Santa Clara, UT), Rob Wilfong (San Dimas, CA).

International Supervisor: Clay Daniel (Jacksonville, FL).

International Scouts: Felipe Gutierrez (Mexico), Alex Messier (Canada), Jose Ortiz (Dominican Republic), Leo Perez (Dominican Republic), Carlos Porte (Venezuela), Roberto Reynoso (Dominican Republic), Freddy Rodriguez (Dominican Republic), Dennys Suarez (Venezuela), Mitsuo Sumi (Japan), Ramon Valenzuela (Dominican Republic), Cesar Velasquez (Venezuela), Grant Weir (Australia).

Major League Club

Complex Address (first year): Tempe Diablo Stadium (1993), 2200 W. Alameda, Tempe, AZ 85282. **Telephone:** (480) 858-7500. **FAX:** (480) 438-7583. **Seating Capacity:** 9,785. **Location:** I-10 to exit 153B (48th Street), south one mile on 48th Street to Alameda Drive, left on Alameda.

Minor League Clubs

Complex Address: Tempe Diablo Minor League Complex, 2225 W. Westcourt Way, Tempe, AZ 85282. **Telephone:** (480) 858-7555.

Hotel Address: Extended Stay America, 3421 E. Elwood Street, Phoenix, AZ 85040. **Telephone:** (602) 438-2900.

2009 SCHEDULE

ANGEL STADIUM

Standard Game Times: 7:05 p.m.; Sun. 12:35.

APRIL

6-9 . . . Oakland
10-12 . . . Boston
14-16 . . . at Seattle
17-19 . . . at Minnesota
21-23 . . . Detroit
24-26 . . . Seattle
28-29 . . . at Baltimore
30 . . . at Yankees

MAY

1-3 . . . at Yankees
4-5 . . . at Oakland
6-7 . . . Toronto
8-10 . . . Kansas City
12-14 . . . Boston
15-17 . . . at Texas
18-21 . . . at Seattle
22-24 . . . at Dodgers
25-27 . . . White Sox
29-31 . . . Seattle

JUNE

2-4 . . . at Toronto
5-7 . . . at Detroit
9-11 . . . at Tampa Bay
12-14 . . . San Diego
15-17 . . . at San Francisco
19-21 . . . Dodgers
22-24 . . . Colorado
26-28 . . . at Arizona
29-30 . . . Texas

JULY

1 . . . at Texas
2-5 . . . Baltimore
6-8 . . . Texas
10-12 . . . Yankees
16-19 . . . at Oakland
20-22 . . . at Kansas City
23-26 . . . Minnesota
27-29 . . . Cleveland
31 . . . at Minnesota
1-2 . . . at Minnesota
4-6 . . . at White Sox
7-9 . . . Texas
10-12 . . . Tampa Bay
14-17 . . . at Baltimore
18-20 . . . at Cleveland
21-23 . . . at Toronto
24-26 . . . Detroit
28-30 . . . Oakland
31 . . . at Seattle

SEPTEMBER

1-2 . . . at Seattle
4-7 . . . at Kansas City
8-10 . . . Seattle
11-13 . . . White Sox
15-17 . . . at Boston
18-20 . . . at Texas
21-23 . . . Yankees
25-27 . . . Oakland
28-30 . . . Texas

OCTOBER

1 . . . Texas
2-4 . . . at Oakland

Los Angeles Dodgers

Office Address: 1000 Elysian Park Ave, Los Angeles, CA 90012.
Telephone: (323) 224-1500. **Fax:** (323) 224-1269.
Website: www.dodgers.com

Ownership

Owner and Chairman: Frank McCourt. **President:** Jamie McCourt. **Special Advisor to Chairman:** Tommy Lasorda. **Special Advisor to Chairman:** Dr. Frank Jobe.

BUSINESS OPERATIONS

Frank McCourt

Executive Vice President, COO: Dennis Mannion. **Executive VP, CMO:** Dr. Charles Steinberg. **Senior VP, General Counsel:** Sam Fernandez.

Finance

CFO: Peter Wilhelm. **VP Finance/Accounting:** Marlo Vandemore.

Sales/Advertising/Client Services

Vice President, Partnership Management: Steve Spartin. **Director, Group/Season Ticket Sales:** David Siegel.

Communications

VP, Communications: Josh Rawitch. **Assistant Director, Public Relations:** Joe Jareck. **Assistant Director, Media Relations:** Mark Rogoff. **Assistant Director, Business/Multicultural PR:** Yvonne Carrasco. **Assistant Director, Business/Entertainment Public Relations:** Drew Merle. **Director, Publications:** Jorge Martin. **Director, Administration/Marketing/Public Relations:** Vanessa Leyvas. **Director, Community Relations:** Don Newcombe.

Stadium Operations

Vice President, Stadium Operations: Lon Rosenberg. **Vice President, Security:** Ray Maytorena. **Director, Security/ Guest Services:** Shahram Ariane. **Facilities Manager:** Mike Grove. **Assistant Director, Turf/Grounds:** Eric Hansen. **PA Announcer:** Eric Smith. **Official Scorers:** Don Hartack, Ed Munson. **Organist:** Nancy Bea Hefley.

Ticketing

Telephone: (323) 224-1471. **Fax:** (323) 224-2609.

Vice President, Ticket Operations: Billy Hunter. **Assistant Director, Ticket Operations:** Seth Bluman.

Travel, Clubhouse

Manager, Team Travel: Scott Akasaki.

Home Clubhouse Manager: Mitch Poole. **Visiting Clubhouse Manager:** Jerry Turner. **Advisor, Team Travel:** Billy DeLury.

GENERAL INFORMATION

Stadium (year opened): Dodger Stadium (1962).
Home Dugout: Third Base. **Playing Surface:** Grass.
Team Colors: Dodger blue and white.
Player Representative: Unavailable.
Driving Directions: I-5 to Stadium Way exit, left on Stadium Way, right on Academy Road, left to Stadium Way to Elysian Park Avenue, left to stadium; I-110 to Dodger Stadium exit, left on Stadium Way, right on Elysian Park Avenue; US 101 to Alvarado exit, right on Sunset, left on Elysian Park Avenue.

Ned Colletti

BASEBALL OPERATIONS

Telephone: (323) 224-1500. **Fax:** (323) 224-1463.

General Manager: Ned Colletti.

Vice President/Assistant GM: Kim Ng. **Special Assistant, Baseball Operations:** Jose Vizcaino. **Director, Baseball Operations:** Ellen Harrigan. **Director, Asian Operations:** Acey Kohrogi. **Director, International Operations:** Joseph Reaves. **Manager, Team Travel:** Scott Akasaki.

Major League Staff

Manager: Joe Torre.

Coaches: Bench—Bob Schaefer; Pitching—Rick Honeycutt; Hitting—Don Mattingly; First Base—Mariano Duncan; Third Base—Larry Bowa; Bullpen—Ken Howell; Coach--Manny Mota; Major League Hitting Instructor-Jeff Pentland.

Medical/Training

Team Physicians: Dr. Neal ElAttrache, Dr. Ken Landis.

Director, Medical Services/Head Trainer: Stan Conte. **Assistant Athletic Trainers:** Todd Tomczyk, Rick Lembo. **Strength/Conditioning Coach:** Brendon Huttmann. **Physical Therapist:** Sue Falsone. **Massage Therapist:** Ichiro Tani. **Minor League Strength Coordinator:** Mike Winkler. **Minor League Physical Therapist:** David Rivera. **Minor League Medical Coordinator:** Jim Young.

Player Development

Telephone: (323) 224-1431. **Fax:** (323) 224-1359.

Assistant GM, Player Development: De Jon Watson. **Assistant Director, Player Development:** Chris Haydock.

Field Coordinator: Mike Brumley. **Hitting Coordinator:** Gene Clines. **Pitching Coordinator:** Rafael Chaves. **Outfield/Baserunning Coordinator:** Rodney McCray. **Infield Coordinator:** Matt Martin. **Catching Coordinator:** Travis Barbary. **Director, Operations, Campo Las Palmas:** Jose Castellanos. **Field Coordinator, Campo Las Palmas:** Antonio Bautista.

Farm System

Class	Club (League)	Manager	Coach	Pitching Coach
Triple-A	Albuquerque (PCL)	Tim Wallach	John Moses	Jim Slaton
Double-A	Chattanooga (SL)	John Valentin	Luis Salazar	Glenn Dishman
High A	Inland Empire (CAL)	Carlos Subero	Franklin Stubbs	Charlie Hough
Low A	Great Lakes (MWL)	Juan Bustabad	Michael Boughton	Danny Darwin
Rookie	Ogden (PIO)	Damon Berryhill	Hector Cruz	Chuck Crim
Rookie	Dodgers (AZL)	Jeff Carter	Leo Garcia	Casey Deskins
Rookie	Dodgers (DL)	Pedro Mega	Tony Mota	Kremlin Martinez

Scouting

Assistant GM, Scouting: Logan White. **Director, Amateur Scouting:** Tim Hallgren.

Special Advisor, Amateur Scouting/National Crosschecker: Gib Bodet (San Clemente, CA). **National Crosscheckers:** Paul Fryer (Calabasas, CA), Larry Barton (Leona Valley, CA). **Manager, Scouting:** Jane Capobianco. **Scouting Coordinator:** Trey Magnuson.

East Coast Supervisor: John Green (Tucson, AZ). **Midwest Supervisor:** Gary Nickels (Naperville, IL). **West Coast Supervisor:** Tom Thomas (Phoenix, AZ).

Major League Scouts: Al La Macchia, Carl Loewenstine, Ron Rizzi, Mitch Webster.

Area Scouts: Fred Costello (Livermore, CA), Chuck Crim (Santa Clarita, CA), Bobby Darwin (Cerritos, CA), Manny Estrada (Longwood, FL), Scott Hennessey (Ponte Vedra, FL), Calvin Jones (Highland Village, TX), Henry Jones (Vancouver, WA), Lon Joyce (Spartanburg, SC), Dennis Moeller (Birmingham, AL), Matthew Paul (Hermitage, TN), Clair Rierson (Frederick, MD), Chet Sergo (Stoughton, WI), Chris Smith (Montgomery, TX), Brian Stephenson (Chandler, AZ), Scott Little (Jackson, MO), Marty Lamb (Nicholasville, KY).

International Scouts: Ralph Avila (Dominican), Elvio Jimenez (Dominican), Gustavo Zapata (Central America), Rolando Chirino (Curacao), Ezequiel Sepulveda (Dominican), Rafael Rijo (Dominican), Bienvenido Tavarez (Dominican), Wilton Guerrero (Dominican), Keiichi Kojima (Japan), Byung-Hwan An (Korea), Mike Brito (Mexico), Camilo Pascual (Venezuela), Bernardo Torres (Venezuela), Oswaldo Villalobos (Venezuela), Maximo Gross (Dominican).

Part-Time Scouts: George Genovese, Artie Harris, Luis Faccio, Greg Goodwin.

Major League Club

Major League Club

Complex Address: Camelback Ranch, 10710 West Camelback Rd., Phoenix, AZ 85037. **Seating Capacity:** 10,000. **Location:** I-10 or I-17 to Loop 101 West or North, Take Exit 5 (Camelback Road West to ballpark. **Telephone:** (623) 877-8585. **Hotel:** Unavailable.

Minor League Clubs

Complex/Hotel Address: Same as major league club.

2009 SCHEDULE

DODGER STADIUM

Standard Game Times: 7:10 p.m.; Fri. 7:40

APRIL

6 . . . . at San Diego
8-9. . . . . at San Diego
10-12 . . . . at Arizona
13 . . . . San Francisco
15-16 . . . . . San Francisco
17-19 . . . . Colorado
21-23 . . . . at Houston
24-26 . . . . at Colorado
27-29 . . . . at San Francisco
30 . . . . San Diego

MAY

1-3. . . . . San Diego
4-5. . . . . Arizona
6-7. . . . . Washington
8-10. . . . . . San Francisco
12-14 . . . . at Philadelphia
15-17 . . . . at Florida
18-20 . . . . Mets
22-24 . . . . Angels
25-27 . . . . at Colorado
28-31 . . . . at Cubs

JUNE

1-3. . . . . Arizona
4-7. . . . . Philadelphia
9-10. . . . . San Diego
12-14 . . . . at Texas
16-18 . . . . Oakland
19-21 . . . . at Angels
23-25 . . . . . . at White Sox
26-28 . . . . Seattle
29-30 . . . . Colorado

JULY

1 . . . . Colorado
3-5. . . . . at San Diego
7-9. . . . . at Mets
10-12 . . . . . at Milwaukee
16-19 . . . . Houston
20-22 . . . . Cincinnati
24-26 . . . . Florida
27-30 . . . . at St. Louis
31 . . . . at Atlanta

AUGUST

1-2. . . . . at Atlanta
3-5. . . . . Milwaukee
6-9. . . . . Atlanta
10-12 . . . . at San Francisco
14-16 . . . . at Arizona
17-19 . . . . St. Louis
20-23 . . . . Cubs
25-27 . . . . at Colorado
28-30 . . . . . . at Cincinnati
31 . . . . Arizona

SEPTEMBER

1-3. . . . . Arizona
4-6. . . . . San Diego
7-9. . . . . at Arizona
11-13 . . . . at San Francisco
14-16 . . . . Pittsburgh
18-20 . . . . . San Francisco
22-24 . . . . . at Washington
25-28 . . . . . . at Pittsburgh
29-30 . . . . . . at San Diego

OCTOBER

1 . . . . at San Diego
2-4. . . . . Colorado

Milwaukee Brewers

Office Address: Miller Park, One Brewers Way, Milwaukee, WI 53214.
Telephone: (414) 902-4400. **Fax:** (414) 902-4053.
Website: www.brewers.com.

Ownership

Operated By: Milwaukee Brewers Baseball Club.
Chairman/Principal Owner: Mark Attanasio.

BUSINESS OPERATIONS

Mark Attanasio

Executive Vice President, Business Operations: Rick Schlesinger. **Executive VP, Finance/ Administration:** Bob Quinn. **VP, General Counsel:** Marti Wronski. **Director, Business Operations:** Teddy Werner. **Executive Assistant, Business Operations:** Adela Reeve. **Executive Assistant, Ownership Group:** Samantha Ernest.

Finance/Accounting

Vice President, Controller: Joe Zidanic. **Director, Reporting/Special Projects:** Steve O'Connell. **Business Manager/Financial Analyst:** Tom Stocco. **Accounting Manager:** Vicki Wise. **Staff Accountant:** Meredith Zaffrann.

Vice President, Human Resources/Office Management: Sally Andrist. **Human Resources Assistant:** Zandie Hernandez.

Vice President, Technology/Information Systems: John Winborn. **Network Administrator:** Corey Kmichik. **Application Developer:** Tod Johnson. **Systems Support Specialist:** Adam Bauer.

Marketing/Corporate Sponsorships

Vice President, Corporate Marketing: Tom Hecht. **Senior Director, Corporate Marketing:** Greg Hilt. **Directors, Corporate Marketing:** Andrew Pauls, Dave Tamburrino. **Vice President, Consumer Marketing:** Todd Taylor. **Senior Director, Marketing:** Kathy Schwab. **Director, Merchandise Branding:** Jill Aronoff. **Director, Corporate Suite Services:** Shaunna Richardson.

Senior Director, Broadcasting/Entertainment: Aleta Mercer. **Director, Audio/Video Productions:** Deron Anderson. **Manager, Entertainment/Broadcasting:** Andrew Olson. **Coordinator, Audio/Video Production:** Cory Wilson.

Media Relations/Communications

Telephone: (414) 902-4500. **Fax:** (414) 902-4053.

Vice President, Communications: Tyler Barnes. **Director, Media Relations:** Mike Vassallo. **Manager, Media Relations:** John Steinmiller. **Coordinator, Media Relations:** Ken Spindler.

Director, Community Relations: Katina Shaw. **Community Relations Assistant:** Erica Bowring. **Manager, Youth Outreach:** Larry Hisle. **President, Brewers Charities:** Lynn Sprangers.

Stadium Operations

Director, Stadium Operations: Bob Hallas. **Director, Event Services:** Matt Kenny. **Director, Grounds:** Gary Vanden Berg. **Landscape Manager:** Miranda Bintley. **Supervisor, Warehouse:** Patrick Rogo. **Vice President, Brewers Enterprises:** Jason Hartlund. **Manager, Event Services:** Jennacy Cruz. **Receptionists:** Willa Oden, Jody McBee.

Ticketing

Telephone: (414) 902-4000. **Fax:** (414) 902-4100.

Senior Director, Ticket Sales: Jim Bathey. **Director, Group Sales:** Chris Barlow. **Director, Season Ticket Sales:** Billy Freiss. **Director, Ticket Operations:** Regis Bane. **Administrative Assistant:** Irene Bolton. **Assistant Director, Ticket Services:** Nancy Jorgensen. **Manager, Ticket Operations:** Chad Olson.

GENERAL INFORMATION

Stadium (year opened): Miller Park (2001).
Home Dugout: First Base. **Playing Surface:** Grass.
Team Colors: Navy blue, gold and white.
Player Representative: Chris Capuano.
Driving Directions: From airport/south, I-94 West to Madison exit, to stadium.

Doug Melvin

BASEBALL OPERATIONS

Telephone: (414) 902-4400. **Fax:** (414) 902-4059.

Executive Vice President/General Manager: Doug Melvin.

VP, Assistant GM: Gord Ash. **Special Assistant to GM/Baseball Operations:** Dan O'Brien.

Director, Administration/Player Development/Scouting: Tom Flanagan. **Manager, Advance Scouting/Baseball Research:** Karl Mueller. **Coordinator, Baseball Research/Special Projects:** Mike Schwartz. **Coordinator, Professional Scouting:** Zack Minasian. **Coaching Assistant/Digital Media Coordinator:** Joe Crawford. **Senior Administrator, Baseball Operations:** Barb Stark.

Major League Staff

Manager: Ken Macha.

Coaches: Bench—Willie Randolph; Pitching—Bill Castro; Hitting—Dale Sveum; First Base—Ed Sedar; Third Base—Brad Fischer; Bullpen—Stan Kyles.

Medical, Training

Head Team Physician: Dr. William Raasch. **Head Athletic Trainer:** Roger Caplinger. **Assistant Athletic Trainer/Strength and Conditioning Coordinator:** Dan Wright.

Player Development

Special Assistant to GM/Director, Player Development: Reid Nichols (Phoenix, AZ).

Business Manager: Scott Martens. **Assistant Director, Player Development:** Tony Diggs. **Coordinator, Administration/Player Development:** Mark Mueller. **Field/Catching Coordinator:** Charlie Greene. **Coordinators:** Frank Neville (medical), Lee Tunnell (pitching), Mike Lum (hitting). **Roving Instructors:** Garth Iorg (roving infield), Ken Berry (roving outfield).

Farm System

Class	Club (League)	Manager	Coach	Pitching Coach
Triple-A	Nashville (PCL)	Don Money	Sandy Guerrero	Chris Bosio
Double-A	Huntsville (SL)	Bob Miscik	Jim Lett	John Curtis
High A	Brevard County (FSL)	Mike Guerrero	Corey Hart	Fred Dabney
Low A	Beloit (MWL)	Jeff Isom	Matt Erickson	Chris Hook
Rookie	Helena (PIO)	Rene Gonzales	Ned Yost IV	Elvin Nina
Rookie	Brewers (AZL)	Tony Diggs	Kenny Dominguez	S. Cline/J. Nunez

Scouting

Telephone: (414) 902-4400. **Fax:** (414) 902-4059.

Special Assistant to GM/Director, Professional Scouting: Dick Groch (Marysville, MI).

Director, Amateur Scouting: Bruce Seid. **Assistant Director, Amateur Scouting:** Ray Montgomery. **Manager/Coordinator, Scouting:** Zack Minasian. **Coordinator, Amateur Scouting:** Amanda Kropp.

Professional Scouts: Lary Aaron (Atlanta, GA), Chris Bourjos (Scottsdale, AZ), Scott Campbell (Milwaukee, WI), Brad Del Barba (Ft. Mitchell, KY), Bryan Gale (Jupiter, FL), Ben McLure (Hummelstown, PA), Cory Melvin (Tampa, FL), Tom Mooney (Pittsfield, MA), Marv Thompson (West Jordan, UT), Tom Wheeler (Martinez, CA), Leon Wurth (Nashville, TN). **Roving Crosschecker:** Jim Rooney (Scottsdale, AZ). **Regional Supervisors:** West—Corey Rodriguez (Hermosa Beach, CA); Midwest—Ray Montgomery (Pearland, TX); East—Doug Reynolds (Tallahassee, FL).

Area Scouts: Josh Belovsky (Orange, CA), Jeremy Booth (Houston, TX), Kevin Clouser (Phoenix, AZ), Tim Collinsworth (Rowlett, TX), Mike Farrell (Indianapolis, IN), Manolo Hernandez (Puerto Rico), Dan Huston (Thousand Oaks, CA), Harvey Kuenn, Jr. (New Berlin, WI), Jay Lapp (London, Ontario, Canada), Marty Lehn (White Rock, British Columbia, Canada), Joe Mason (Millbrook, AL), Justin McCray (Davis, CA), Tim McIlvaine (Tampa, FL), Dan Nellum (Crofton, MD), Brandon Newell (Bellingham, WA), Ryan Robinson (Tallahassee, FL), Brian Sankey (Yarmouth Port, MA), Charles Sullivan (Weston, FL). **Part-Time Scouts:** John Bushart (West Hills, CA), Richard Colpaert (Shelby Township, MI), Don Fontana (Pittsburgh, PA), John Haar (Burnaby, British Columbia, Canada), Joe Hodges (Rockwood, TN), Roger Janeway (Englewood, OH), Mike LaBossiere (Brandon, Manitoba, Canada), Johnny Logan (Milwaukee, WI), J.P. Roy (Saint Nicolas, Quebec, Canada), J.R. Salinas (Houston, TX), Lee Seid (Las Vegas, NV), Brad Stoll (Lawrence, KS), Nathan Trosky (Carmel, CA).

Latin American Supervisor: Fernando Arango (Davie, FL).

International Scouts: Fausto Sosa Pena (Dominican Republic), Freddy Torres (Venezuela), Rafael Espinal (Dominican Republic), Jose Guarache (Venezuela), Jose Zambrano (Venezuela).

Major League Club

Complex Address: Maryvale Baseball Park, 3600 N. 51st Ave., Phoenix, AZ 85031. **Telephone:** (623) 245-5555. **Seating Capacity:** 9,000. **Location:** I-10 to 51st Ave., north on 51st Ave.

Hotel Address: Holiday Inn Express-Tempe, 5300 S. **Priest Dr., Tempe, AZ 85283. Telephone:** (480) 820-7500.

Minor Leage Teams

Complex Address: Maryvale Baseball Complex, 3805 N. 53rd Ave., Phoenix, AZ 85031. **Telephone:** (623) 245-5600. **Hotel Address:** Same as major league club.

2009 SCHEDULE

MILLER PARK

Standard Game Times: 7:05 p.m.; Sat. 6:05; Sun. 1:05.

APRIL

7-9 . . . . . at San Francisco
10-12 . . . . Chicago
13-15 . . . . Cincinnati
17-19 . . . . at Mets
21-23 . . . . at Philadelphia
24-26 . . . . at Houston
27-29 . . . . Pittsburgh
30 . . . . Arizona

MAY

1-3 . . . . Arizona
4-5 . . . . at Pittsburgh
6-7 . . . . at Cincinnati
8-10 . . . . Cubs
12-14 . . . . Florida
15-17 . . . . at St. Louis
19-21 . . . . at Houston
22-24 . . . . . . at Minnesota
25-27 . . . . St. Louis
29-31 . . . . Cincinnati

JUNE

1-4 . . . . at Florida
5-7 . . . . at Atlanta
9-11 . . . . Colorado
12-14 . . . . White Sox
15-17 . . . . . . at Cleveland
19-21 . . . . at Detroit
23-25 . . . . Minnesota
26-28 . . . . . San Francisco
29-30 . . . . Mets

JULY

1 . . . . Mets
2-5 . . . . at Cubs
7-9 . . . . St. Louis
10-12 . . . . Dodgers
16-19 . . . . . . at Cincinnati
20-22 . . . . . . at Pittsburgh
24-26 . . . . Atlanta
27-30 . . . . . . Washington
31 . . . . at San Diego

AUGUST

1-2 . . . . at San Diego
3-5 . . . . at Dodgers
7-9 . . . . at Houston
11-13 . . . . San Diego
14-16 . . . . Houston
17-19 . . . . . . at Pittsburgh
21-24 . . . . . at Washington
25-27 . . . . Cincinnati
28-30 . . . . Pittsburgh

SEPTEMBER

1-3 . . . . at St. Louis
4-6 . . . . San Francisco
7-9 . . . . St. Louis
11-13 . . . . at Arizona
14-17 . . . . at Cubs
18-20 . . . . Houston
21-23 . . . . Cubs
24-27 . . . . . . Philadelphia
29-30 . . . . at Colorado

OCTOBER

1 . . . . at Colorado
2-4 . . . . at St. Louis

Minnesota Twins

Office Address: 34 Kirby Puckett Place, Minneapolis, MN 55415.
Telephone: (612) 375-1366. **Fax:** (612) 375-7480.
Website: www.twinsbaseball.com.

Ownership

Operated By: The Minnesota Twins.
Chief Executive Officer: Jim Pohlad.
Chairman, Executive Committee: Howard Fox. **Executive Board:** James Pohlad, Robert Pohlad, William Pohlad, Dave St. Peter.

Carl Pohlad

BUSINESS OPERATIONS

President, Minnesota Twins: Dave St. Peter. **President, Twins Sports Inc.:** Jerry Bell. **Senior Vice President, Business Development:** Laura Day. **Senior Vice President, Business Administration/CFO:** Kip Elliott

New Ballpark Development

Construction Consultant: Dick Strassburg. **Project Manager:** Paul Johnson. **Director, New Ballpark Development:** Scott O'Connell. **Development, Finance/Accounting:** Dan Starkey.

Human Resources/Finance/Technology

Vice President, Human Resources/Diversity: Raenell Dorn. **Payroll Manager:** Lori Beasley. **Benefits Manager:** Leticia Silva. **Human Resources Generalist:** Holly Corbin. **Human Resources Assistant:** Jane Neumann.

Director, Finance: Andy Weinstein. **Manager, Ticket Accounting:** Jerry McLaughlin. **Accountant:** Lyndsey Taylor. **Manager, Finance Planning/Analysis:** Amy Fong-Christianson. **Manager, Accounting:** Lori Windschitl. **Director, Purchasing:** Bud Hanley. **Administrative Assistant:** Ka Her. **Vice President, Technology:** John Avenson. **Director, Technology:** Wade Navratil. **Manager, Technology Infrastructure:** Tony Persio.

Marketing/Broadcasting

VP, Marketing: Patrick Klinger. **Director, Advertising:** Nancy O'Brien. **Director, Event Marketing:** Heidi Sammon. **Promotions Coordinator:** Julie Rohloff. **Manager, Emerging Markets:** Miguel Ramos. **Director, Broadcasting/Game Presentation:** Andy Price. **Radio Network Producer:** Mark Genosky.

Corporate Partnerships

VP, Corporate Partnerships: Eric Curry. **Senior Manager, Client Services:** Bodie Forsling. **Manager, Corporate Client Services:** Katie Beaulieu. **Coordinator, Corporate Client Services:** Paulette Cheatham. **Coordinator, Traffic/Service:** Amy Johnson.

Communications

Telephone: (612) 375-7471. **Fax:** (612) 375-7473.

Director, Baseball Communications: Mike Herman. **Manager, Publications/Media Services:** Molly Gallatin. **Manager, Baseball Communications:** Dustin Morse. **Coordinator, Baseball Communications:** Mitch Hestad.

Public Affairs

Executive Director, Public Affairs/Twins Community Fund: Kevin Smith. **Director, Community Affairs:** Bryan Donaldson. **Manager, Corporate Communications:** Chris Iles.

Ticketing

Telephone: (612) 338-9467. **Fax:** (612) 375-7464.

VP, Ticket Sales/Service: Steve Smith. **Manager, Ticket Sales/Service:** Eric Hudson. **Manager, Group Ticket Sales:** Rob Malec. **Manager, Communications/Support:** Beth Vail. **Database Marketing Coordinator:** Brandon Johnson. **Director, Ticket Operations:** Paul Froehle. **Manager, Box Office:** Mike Stiles. **Supervisor, Ticket Office:** Karl Dadenbach. **Group Ticket Coordinator:** Robyn McQuillan. **Manager, Call Center/New Ballpark Migration:** Patrick Forsland.

Stadium Operations

VP, Operations: Matt Hoy. **Director, Stadium Operations:** Dave Horsman. **Manager, Stadium Operations:** Dan Smoliak. **Manager, Security:** Dick Dugan. **Manager, Merchandise:** Matt Noll. **PA Announcer:** Adam Abrams. **Equipment Manager:** Rod McCormick. **Visitors Clubhouse:** Troy Matchan. **Manager, Major League Video:** Sean Harlin.

GENERAL INFORMATION

Stadium (year opened): Hubert H. Humphrey Metrodome (1982).
Home Dugout: Third Base. Playing Surface: Field Turf.
Team Colors: Burgundy, navy blue and white.
Team Representative: Unavailable.
Driving Directions: I-35W south to Washington Avenue exit or I-35W north to Third Street exit. I-94 East to I-35W north to Third Street exit or I-94 West to Fifth Street exit.

Bill Smith

BASEBALL OPERATIONS

Telephone: (612) 375-7484. **Fax:** (612) 375-7417.

Senior Vice President/General Manager: Bill Smith.

Vice President, Player Personnel: Mike Radcliff. **Assistant GM:** Rob Antony. **Senior Advisor to GM:** Terry Ryan. **Special Assistants to GM:** Joe McIlvaine, Tom Kelly. **Director, Baseball Operations:** Brad Steil. **Baseball Operations Assistant:** Joe Pohlad. **Administrative Assistant to GM:** Jack Goin. **Director, Team Travel:** Remzi Kiratli.

Major League Staff

Manager: Ron Gardenhire.

Coaches: Bench—Steve Liddle; Pitching—Rick Anderson; Batting—Joe Varva; First Base—Jerry White; Third Base—Scott Ullger; Bullpen—Rick Stelmaszek.

Medical, Training

Club Physicians: Dr. Dan Buss, Dr. Vijay Eyunni, Dr. Tom Jetzer, Dr. John Steubs, Dr. Jon Hallberg, Dr. Gustavo Navarrete.

Head Trainer: Rick McWane. **Assistant Trainer:** Dave Pruemer. **Strength/Conditioning Coach:** Perry Castellano.

Player Development

Telephone: (612) 375-7488. **Fax:** (612) 375-7417.

Director, Minor Leagues: Jim Rantz.

Administrative Assistant, Minor Leagues: Kate Townley. **Minor League Coordinators:** Joel Lepel (field), Eric Rasmussen (pitching), Bill Springman (hitting), Paul Molitor (infield/baserunning).

Farm System

Class	Club	Manager	Coach	Pitching Coach
Triple-A	Rochester (IL)	Stan Cliburn	Riccardo Ingram	Bobby Cuellar
Double-A	New Britain (EL)	Tom Nieto	Floyd Rayford	Stu Cliburn
High A	Fort Myers (FSL)	Jeff Smith	Jim Dwyer	Steve Mintz
Low A	Beloit (MWL)	Nelson Prada	Rich Miller	Gary Lucas
Rookie	Elizabethton (APP)	Ray Smith	Jeff Reed	Jim Shellenback
Rookie	Twins (GCL)	Jake Mauer	Milt Cuyler	R. Hernandez/ I. Arteaga
Rookie	Twins (DSL)	Julio Paula	Pablo Frias	Jose Leger
Rookie	Twins (VSL)	Asdrubal Estrada	Ramon Borrego	Luis Ramirez

Scouting

Telephone: (612) 375-7525. **Fax:** (612) 375-7417.

Director, Scouting: Deron Johnson (Sacramento, CA). **Administrative Assistant:** Amanda Daley.

Major League Scouts: Ken Compton (Cypress, CA), Earl Frishman (Tampa, FL), Bob Hegman (Lee's Summit, MO).

Coordinator, Professional Scouting: Vern Followell (Buena Park, CA). **Pro Scout:** Bill Milos (Crown Point, IN).

Scouting Supervisors: East—Mark Quimuyog (Lynn Haven, FL), West—Sean Johnson (Chandler, AZ), South—Tim O'Neil (Lexington, KY), Midwest—Mike Ruth (Lee's Summit, MO).

Area Scouts: Trevor Brown (Oregon City, OR), Billy Corrigan (Tampa, FL), JR DiMercurio (Kansas City, MO), Mike Eaglin (Los Angeles, CA), Marty Esposito (Robinson, TX), John Leavitt (Garden Grove, CA), Hector Otero (Miami, FL/Puerto Rico), Jeff Pohl (Evansville, IN), Jack Powell (Sweetwater, TN), Elliott Strankman (San Ramon, CA), Ricky Taylor (Hickory, NC), Jay Weitzel (Salamanca, NY), Ted Williams (Peoria, AZ), John Wilson (Blairstown, NJ), Mark Wilson (Lindstrom, MN), Earl Winn (Bowling Green, KY).

Coordinator, International Scouting: Howard Norsetter (Australia).

Coordinator, Latin American Scouting: Jose Marzan.

International Scouts: Cary Broder (Taiwan), John Cortese (Italy), Glenn Godwin (Europe, Africa), Fred Guerrero (Dominican Republic), Andy Johnson (Europe), David Kim (South Korea), Jose Leon (Venezuela, Panama), Kenny Su (Taiwan), Koji Takahashi (Japan).

Major League Club

Complex Address (first year): Lee County Sports Complex/Hammond Stadium (1991), 14100 Six Mile Cypress Pkwy., Fort Myers, FL 33912. **Telephone:** (239) 768-4282. **Seating Capacity:** 7,905. **Location:** Exit 21 off I-75, west on Daniels Parkway, left on Six Mile Cypress Parkway.

Hotel Address: Clarion Hotel, 12635 Cleveland Ave., Fort Myers, FL 33907. **Telephone:** (239) 936-4300.

Minor League Clubs

Complex Address/Hotel: Same as major league club.

2009 SCHEDULE

HUBERT H. HUMPHREY METRODOME

Standard Game Times: 7:10 p.m.; Sat. 6:10; Sun 1:10.

APRIL
6-9 . . . . . Seattle
10-12 . . . . . at White Sox
13-16 . . . . . Toronto
17-19 . . . . . Angels
21-22 . . . . . at Boston
24-26 . . . . . at Cleveland
27-29 . . . . . Tampa Bay

MAY
1-3 . . . . . Kansas City
4-5 . . . . . at Detroit
6-7 . . . . . at Baltimore
8-10 . . . . . Seattle
12-14 . . . . . Detroit
15-18 . . . . . at Yankees
19-21 . . . . . at White Sox
22-24 . . . . . Milwaukee
25-28 . . . . . Boston
29-31 . . . . . at Tampa Bay

JUNE
2-4 . . . . . Cleveland
5-7 . . . . . at Seattle
8-11 . . . . . at Oakland
12-14 . . . . . at Cubs
16-18 . . . . . Pittsburgh
19-21 . . . . . Houston
23-25 . . . . . at Milwaukee
26-28 . . . . . at St. Louis
29-30 . . . . . at Kansas City

JULY
1 . . . . . at Kansas City
3-5 . . . . . Detroit
7-9 . . . . . Yankees
10-12 . . . . . White Sox
17-19 . . . . . at Texas
20-23 . . . . . at Athletics
23-26 . . . . . at Angels
27-29 . . . . . White Sox
31 . . . . . Angels

AUGUST
1-2 . . . . . Angels
4-6 . . . . . at Cleveland
7-9 . . . . . at Detroit
11-13 . . . . . Kansas City
14-16 . . . . . Cleveland
17-20 . . . . . at Texas
21-23 . . . . . at Kansas City
24-26 . . . . . Baltimore
28-30 . . . . . Texas
31 . . . . . White Sox

SEPTEMBER
1-2 . . . . . White Sox
4-6 . . . . . at Cleveland
7-10 . . . . . at Toronto
11-13 . . . . . Oakland
14-16 . . . . . Cleveland
18-20 . . . . . Detroit
21-23 . . . . . at White Sox
25-27 . . . . . at Kansas City
28-30 . . . . . at Detroit

AUGUST
1 . . . . . at Detroit
2-4 . . . . . Kansas City

New York Mets

Office Address: Citi Field, Flushing, NY 11368.
Telephone: (718) 507-6387. **Fax:** (718) 507-6395.
Website: www.mets.com, www.losmets.com.

Ownership

Operated By: Sterling Mets LP.

Chairman/Chief Executive Officer: Fred Wilpon. **President:** Saul Katz. **Chief Operating Officer:** Jeff Wilpon. **Board of Directors:** Fred Wilpon, Saul Katz, Jeff Wilpon, Richard Wilpon, Michael Katz, David Katz, Tom Osterman, Arthur Friedman, Steve Greenberg, Stuart Sucherman.

Fred Wilpon

BUSINESS OPERATIONS

Executive Vice President, Business Operations: David Howard. **Executive Vice President/General Counsel:** David Cohen.

Finance

CFO: Mark Peskin. **Vice President/Controller:** Len Labita. **Assistant Controller/Director:** Rebecca Landau-Mahadeva. **Director, Baseball Accounting:** Robert Gerbe.

Marketing, Sales

Senior Vice President, Marketing/Communications: David Newman. **Senior Director, Marketing:** Tina Mannix. **Senior Director, Marketing Productions:** Tim Gunkel. **Director, Broadcasting/Special Events:** Lorraine Hamilton.

Director, Marketing Communications: Jill Grabill. **Director, Community Outreach:** Jill Knee. **Senior Vice President, Corporate Sales/Services:** Tom Murphy. **Vice President, Corporate Sales/Services:** Paul Asencio. **Vice President, Venue Services:** Mike Landeen. **Director, Corporate Sales/Partnerships:** Pete Helfer. **Director, Corporate Sales/Partnerships:** Matthew Soloff. **Director, Suite Sales/Services:** Patrick Jones.

Media Relations

Telephone: (718) 565-4330. **Fax:** (718) 639-3619.

Vice President, Media Relations: Jay Horwitz.

Director, Media Relations: Shannon Forde. **Manager, Media Relations:** Ethan Wilson. **Media Relations Coordinator:** Billy Harner.

Ballpark Operations

Vice President, Facilities: Karl Smolarz.

Vice President, Operations: Pat McGovern.

Director, Ballpark Operations: Sue Lucchi. **Assistant Ballpark Manager:** Mike Dohnert. **Manager, Field Operations:** Bill Deacon.

Senior Director, Information Technology: Joe Milone. **Director, Information Technology:** Robert Gradante. **PA Announcer:** Alex Anthony. **Official Scorers:** Bill Shannon, Howie Karpin, Jordan Sprechman, David Freeman, Billy Altman.

Ticketing

Telephone: (718) 507-8499. **Fax:** (718) 507-6369.

Vice President, Ticket Sales/Services: Bill Ianniciello. **Senior Director, Ticket Operations:** Joan Sullivan. **Senior Director, Group Sales/Ticket Sales Services:** Tom Fersch. **Director, Ticket Sales Development:** Jamie Ozure. **Director, Ticket Operations:** John Giglio.

Guest Experience

Vice President, Guest Experience: Craig Marino.

Venue Services

Vice President, Venue Services: Mike Landeen. **Director, Venue Services:** Paul Schwartz. **Director, Hospitality/Catering Events:** Heather Collamore.

Travel, Clubhouse

Clubhouse Manager, Associate Travel Director: Charlie Samuels. **Assistant Equipment Manager:** Dave Berni. **Visiting Clubhouse Manager:** Tony Carullo. **Video Editor:** Joe Scarola.

GENERAL INFORMATION

Stadium (year opened): Citi Field (2009).

Home Dugout: First Base. **Playing Surface:** Grass.

Team Colors: Blue and orange.

Player Representative: David Wright.

Driving Directions: From Bronx and Westchester, take Cross Bronx Expressway to Bronx-Whitestone Bridge, then take bridge to Whitestone Expressway to Northern Boulevard/Shea Stadium exit. From Brooklyn, take Eastbound BQE to Eastbound Grand Central Parkway.

Omar Minaya

BASEBALL OPERATIONS

Telephone: (718) 565-4315. **Fax:** (718) 507-6391.

Executive Vice President/General Manager: Omar Minaya.

Assistant GM: John Ricco. **VP, Player Development:** Tony Bernazard. **VP, Scouting:** Sandy Johnson. **Special Assistants to GM:** Bryan Lambe, Ramon Pena. **Executive Assistant to GM:** Leonor Barua. **Coordinator, Baseball Operations:** Adam Fisher. **Statistical Analyst:** Ben Baumer.

Major League Staff

Manger: Jerry Manuel.

Coaches: Bench—Sandy Alomar, Sr.; Pitching—Dan Warthen; Batting—Howard Johnson; First Base—Luis Alicea; Third Base—Razor Shines; Bullpen—Randy Niemann.

Medical, Training

Medical Director: Dr. David Altchek. **Physician:** Dr. Struan Coleman. **Trainer:** Ray Ramirez.

Player Development

Telephone: (718) 565-4302. **Fax:** (718) 205-7920.

Director, Minor League Operations: Adam Wogan. **Coordinator, Minor League Operations:** Jon Miller. **Assistant, Player Development:** Michelle Holmes. **Field Coordinator:** Luis Aguayo. **Coordinator, Instruction/Infield:** Kevin Morgan. **Hitting Coordinator:** Lamar Johnson. **Pitching Coordinator:** Rick Waits. **Catching Coordinator:** Bob Natal. **Outfield/Baserunning/Bunting Coordinator:** Sonny Jackson. **Coordinator, Strength/Conditioning:** Jason Craig.

Farm System

Class	Club	Manager	Coach(es)	Pitching Coach
Triple-A	Buffalo (IL)	Ken Oberkfell	Luis Natera	Ricky Bones
Double-A	Binghamton (EL)	Mako Oliveras	B. Malek/D. Mitchell	Hector Berrios
High A	St. Lucie (FSL)	Tim Teufel	G. Jabalera/J. Morales	Rob Ellis
Low A	Savannah (SAL)	Edgar Alfonzo	J. Carrero/G. Greer	Marc Valdez
Short-season	Brooklyn (NYP)	Pedro Lopez	Jack Voight	Rick Tomlin
Rookie	Kingsport (APP)	Mike DeFelice	J. Lopez/R. Ellis	Frank Fultz
Rookie	Mets (GCL)	Julio Franco	L. Rojas/T. McCraw	Jonathan Hurst
Rookie	Mets (DSL)	Liliano Castro	J. Váldez/F. Martinez	Benjamin Marte
Rookie	Mets (VSL)	Leo Hernandez	Yunir Garcia	Rafael Lazo

Scouting

Telephone: (718) 565-4311. **Fax:** (718) 205-7920.

Director, Amateur Scouting: Rudy Terrasas. **Assistant, Amateur Scouting:** Elizabeth Gadsden. **Coordinator, Amateur Scouting:** Ian Levin. **Assistant, Professional/International Scouting:** Anne Fairbanks. **Advance Scout:** Bob Johnson (University Park, FL).

Pro Scouts: Mack Babitt (Richmond, CA), Russ Bove (Longwood, FL), Doug Gassaway (Blum, TX), Roland Johnson (Newington, CT), Jerry Krause (Highland Park, IL), Duane Larson (Knoxville, TN), Harry Minor (Long Beach, CA), Jim Thompson (Wallingford, PA). **National Crosschecker:** David Lakey (Kingwood, TX). **Regional Supervisors:** East—Steve Barningham (Land O'Lakes, FL), West—Tim Fortugno (Elk Grove, CA). **Area Supervisors:** Mike Brown (Chandler, AZ), Erwin Bryant (Lexington, KY), Larry Chase (Pearcy, AR), Ray Corbett (College Station, TX), Spencer Graham (Yorktown, VA), Scott Hunter (Mount Laurel, NJ), Larry Izzo, Jr. (Deer Park, NY), Tommy Jackson (Jupiter, FL), Steve Leavitt (Huntington Beach, CA), Fred Mazuca (Tustin, CA), Marlin McPhail (Irmo, SC), Les Parker (Hudson, FL), Claude Pelletier (St. Lazare, Quebec), Art Pontarelli (Lincoln, RI), Jim Reeves (Camas, WA), Junior Roman (San Sebastian, Puerto Rico), Max Semler (Lake City, FL), Marc Siebert (Cantonment, FL), Doug Thurman (San Jose, CA), Scott Trcka (Hobart, IN).

Director, Pacific Rim Scouting: Isao O'Jimi. **Director, International Scouting:** Ismael Cruz. **Area Supervisors, Venezuela:** Robert Alfonzo. **International Scouts:** Modesto Abreu (Dominican Republic), Marciano Alvarez (Dominican Republic), Claudio Brito (Dominican Republic), Lionel Chattelle (Germany), David Davalillo (Venezuela), Tony Harris (Australia), Harold Herrera (Colombia), Ivanosky Wong Hurtado (Venezuela), Rafael Arturo Jimenez (Venezuela), Luis Marquez (Venezuela), Kevin Park (S. Korea), Eduardo Urdaneta Reverol (Venezuela), Pablo Garcia Rodriguez (Venezuela), Felix Nivar (Dominican Republic), Franklin Taveras (Dominican Republic), Jose Sandy Rosario Valdez (Dominican Republic), Marcelino Vallejo (Dominican Republic), Caryl Van Zanten (Netherland Antilles), Victor Hugo Vasquez (Venezuela), Alex Zapata (Panama).

Spring Training

Complex Address: St. Lucie Sports Complex/Tradition Field, 525 NW Peacock Blvd., Port St. Lucie, FL 34986. **Telephone:** (772) 871-2100. **Seating Capacity:** 7,000. **Location:** Exit 121C (St. Lucie West Blvd) off I-95 , east 1/4 mile, left onto NW Peacock.

Hotel Address: Spring Hill Suites, 2000 NW Courtyard Circle, Port St. Lucie, FL 34986. **Telephone:** (772) 871-2929.

Minor League Clubs

Complex Address: Same as major league club. **Hotel Address:** Holiday Inn, 10120 South Federal Hwy., Port St. Lucie, FL 34952. **Telephone:** (772) 337-2200.

2009 SCHEDULE

SHEA STADIUM

Standard Game Times:
7:10 p.m.; Sun. 1:10.

APRIL

6	at Cincinnati
8-9	at Cincinnati
10-12	at Florida
13	San Diego
15-16	San Diego
17-19	Milwaukee
21-23	at St. Louis
24-26	Washington
27-29	Florida

MAY

1-3	at Philadelphia
4-5	at Atlanta
6-7	Philadelphia
8-10	Pittsburgh
11-13	Atlanta
14-17	at San Francisco
18-20	at Dodgers
22-24	at Boston
25-27	Washington
29-31	Florida

JUNE

1-4	at Pittsburgh
5-7	at Washington
9-11	Philadelphia
12-14	at Yankees
16-18	at Baltimore
19-21	Tampa Bay
22-25	St. Louis
26-28	Yankees
29-30	at Milwaukee

JULY

1	at Milwaukee
3-5	at Philadelphia
7-9	Dodgers
10-12	Cincinnati
16-19	at Atlanta
20-22	at Washington
24-26	at Houston
27-30	Colorado
31	Arizona

AUGUST

1-3	Arizona
4-5	St. Louis
6-9	at San Diego
10-12	at Arizona
14-17	San Francisco
18-20	Atlanta
21-24	Philadelphia
25-27	at Florida
28-30	at Cubs

SEPTEMBER

1-3	at Colorado
4-6	Cubs
8-10	Florida
11-13	at Philadelphia
15-17	at Atlanta
18-20	Washington
21-23	Atlanta
25-27	at Florida
28-30	at Washington

OCTOBER

2-4	Houston

New York Yankees

Office Address: Yankee Stadium, One East 161st Street, Bronx, NY 10451.
Telephone: (718) 293-4300. **Fax:** (718) 293-8431.
Website: www.yankees.com ; www.yankeesbeisbol.com.

OWNERSHIP

Principal Owner/Chairperson: George M. Steinbrenner III.

Managing General Partner/Co-Chairperson: Harold Z. Steinbrenner.

General Partner/Co-Chairperson: Henry G. Steinbrenner. **General Partner/Vice Chairperson:** Jennifer Steinbrenner Swindal. **General Partner/Vice Chairperson:** Jessica Steinbrenner. **Vice Chairperson:** Joan Steinbrenner. **Senior Vice President:** Felix Lopez.

George Steinbrenner

BUSINESS OPERATIONS

President: Randy Levine, Esq.

COO: Lonn A. Trost, Esq.

Senior VP, Strategic Ventures: Marty Greenspun. **Senior VP, Chief Security Officer:** Sonny Hight. **Senior VP, Business Development:** Jim Ross. **Senior VP, Corporate/Community Relations:** Brian Smith. **Senior VP, Corporate Sales/Sponsorship:** Michael Tusiani. **Senior Vice President, Marketing:** Deborah Tymon. **Vice President/CFO, Accounting:** Robert Brown. **CFO/VP, Financial Operations:** Scott Krug. **Deputy General Counsel/VP, Legal Affairs:** Alan Chang.

Business Development

Executive Director, Premium Sales: Rob Chibbaro. **Director, Premium Services:** Harvey Winston.

CORPORATE/COMMUNITY RELATIONS

Director, Latino Affairs: Manny Garcia, Esq.

Corporate Sales/Sponsorships

Directors, Corporate Sales/Sponsorships: Brian Calka, John Penhollow.

Media Relations/Publicity

Telephone: (718) 579-4460. **Fax:** (718) 293-8414.

Director, Media Relations/Publicity: Jason Zillo. **Managers, Media Relations/Publicity:** Jason Latimer, Michael Margolis. **Coordinators, Media Relations/Publicity:** Loran Moran, Connie Schwab. **Assistant, Media Relations:** Kenny Leandry. **Media Advisor, Pacific Rim:** Isao Hirooka. **Administrative Assistant, Media Relations:** Dolores Hernandez.

Office Operations

Director, Human Resources: Betsy Peluso. **Senior Director, Technology:** Mike Lane. **Director, Archives/Records Management:** Tom Barbagallo.

Scoreboard/Broadcasting

Senior Producer, Scoreboard/Video Production: Nima Ghandforoush. **Producer, Scoreboard/Video Production:** Gregory Colello.

Security/Stadium Operations

Executive Director, Team Security: Edward Fastook. **Executive Director, Stadium Security:** Todd Lechter. **Senior Director, Stadium Operations:** Doug Behar. **Senior Director, Scoreboard/Broadcasting:** Michael Bonner. **Stadium Superintendent:** Pete Pullara. **Head Groundskeeper:** Dan Cunningham. **Museum Curator:** Brian Richards.

Ticket Operations

Telephone: (718) 293-6000. **Fax:** (718) 293-4841.

Senior Director, Ticket Operations: Irfan Kirimca. **Executive Director, Ticket Operations:** Kevin Dart.

Travel, Clubhouse

Traveling Secretary: Ben Tuliebitz.

Home Clubhouse Manager: Rob Cucuzza. **Visiting Clubhouse Manager:** Lou Cucuzza Jr. **Video Operations, Batting Practice Pitcher:** Charlie Wonsowicz. **Bullpen Catcher:** Roman Rodriguez.

GENERAL INFORMATION

Stadium (year opened): Yankee Stadium (2009).
Home Dugout: First Base. **Playing Surface:** Grass.
Team Colors: Navy blue and white.
Player Representative: Mike Mussina.
Driving Directions: From I-95 North, George Washington Bridge to Cross Bronx Expressway to exit 1C; Major Deegan South (I-87) to exit G (161st Street); I-87 North to 149th or 155th Streets; I-87 South to 161st Street.

Brian Cashman

BASEBALL OPERATIONS

Telephone: (718) 293-4300. **Fax:** (718) 293-0015.

Senior Vice President/General Manager: Brian Cashman.

Senior VP, Special Advisor: Gene Michael.

VP/Assistant GM: Jean Afterman, Esq.

Special Assistants: Gordon Blakeley, Tino Martinez, Stump Merrill.

Director, Quantitative Analysis: Michael Fishman. **Director, Mental Conditioning:** Chad Bohling. **Coordinator, Major League Operations:** Anthony Flynn. **Assistant, Baseball Operations:** Steve Martone.

Major League Staff

Manager: Joe Girardi.

Coaches: Bench—Tony Pena; Pitching—Dave Eiland; Batting—Kevin Long; First Base—Mick Kelleher; Third Base—Rob Thomson; Bullpen—Mike Harkey.

Medical/Training

Team Physician, New York: Dr. Chris Ahmad. **Team Physician, Tampa:** Dr. Andrew Boyer.

Head Trainer: Gene Monahan. **Assistant Trainer:** Steve Donohue. **Strength/Conditioning Coordinator:** Dana Cavalea.

Player Development

Telephone: (813) 875-7569. **Fax:** (813) 873-2302.

Senior Vice President, Baseball Operations: Mark Newman. **Vice President, Player Personnel:** Billy Connors. **Director, Player Development:** Pat Roessler. **Special Assistant to Player Development/Scouting:** Pat McMahon. **Assistant Director, Baseball Operations:** Eric Schmitt. **Administrative Assistant:** Jackie Williams. **Minor League Coordinators:** Nardi Contreras (pitching), James Rowson (hitting), Jody Reed (defensive), Julio Mosquera (Catching), Jack Hubbard (outfield).

Farm System

Class	Club	Manager	Hitting Coach	Pitching Coach
Triple-A	Scranton/WB (IL)	Dave Miley	Butch Wynegar	Scott Aldred
Double-A	Trenton (EL)	Tony Franklin	Frank Menechino	Tom Phelps
High A	Tampa (FSL)	Luis Sojo	Julius Matos	Greg Pavlick
Low A	Charleston (SAL)	Torre Tyson	Greg Colbrunn	Jeff Ware
Short-season	Staten Island (NYP)	Josh Paul	Ty Hawkins	Pat Daneker
Rookie	Tampa (GCL)	Tom Slater	Derek Shumpert	Carlos Chantres
Rookie	Yankees I (DSL)	Carlos Mota	Freddie Tiburcio	Wilfredo Cordova
Rookie	Yankees II (DSL)	Raul Dominguez	Roy Gomez	Jose Duran

Scouting

Telephone: (813) 875-7569. **Fax:** (813) 873-2302.

Vice President, Amateur Scouting: Damon Oppenheimer. **Assistant Director, Amateur Scouting:** John Kremer.

Director, Professional Scouting: Billy Eppler. **Assistant Director, Professional Scouting:** Will Kuntz. **Professional Scouts:** Ron Brand (Plano, TX), Joe Caro (Tampa, FL), Jay Darnell (San Diego, CA), Bill Emslie (Trinity, FL), Dan Freed (Livingston, FL), Bill Livesey (St. Petersburg, FL), Bill Mele (Pittsfield, MA), Tim Naehring (Cincinnati, OH), Greg Orr (Sacramento, CA), Kevin Reese (Sterling, VA), Rick Williams (Tampa, FL), Tom Wilson (Lake Havasu, AZ), Bob Miske (part-time, Amherst, NY). **National Crosscheckers:** Kendall Carter, Donny Rowland. **Regional Crosscheckers:** East—Brian Barber (Winter Garden, FL); Midwest—Tim Kelly (Pickerington, OH); West—Jeff Patterson (Yorba Linda, CA).

Area Scouts: Mark Batchko (Arlington, TX), Steve Boros (Kingwood, TX), Jeff Deardorff (Clermont, FL), Mike Gibbons (Liberty Township, OH), Matt Hyde (Canton, MA.), David Keith (Anaheim, CA), Steve Kmetko (Phoenix, AZ), Steve Lemke (Geneva, IL), Scott Lovekamp (Lynchburg, VA), Darryl Monroe (Decatur, GA), Cesar Presbott (Bronx, NY), Dennis Twombley (Redondo Beach, CA), D.J. Svihlik (Birmingham, AL), Mike Thurman (West Linn, OR).

Assistant Director, International Operations: Alex Cotto. **Director, Latin American Scouting:** Victor Mata. .

Dominican Scouts: Angel Ovalles, Juan Rosario, Jose Sabino. **Venezuelan Scouts:** Darwin Bracho, Jose Gavidea, Hector Rincones, Cesar Suarez. **International Scouts:** Luis Sierra (Colombia), Lee Sigman (Mexico), Edgar Rodriguez (Nicaragua), Carlos Levy (Panama), Chairon Isenia (Curacao), Ken Su (Pacific Rim), John Wadsworth (Austrailia).

Major League Club

Complex Address: George M. Steinbrenner Field, One Steinbrenner Dr., Tampa, FL 33614. **Telephone:** (813) 875-7753. **Seating Capacity:** 11,076. .

Hotel: Unavailable.

Minor League Clubs

Complex Address: Yankees Player Development/Scouting Complex, 3102 N. Himes Ave., Tampa, FL 33607. **Telephone:** (813) 875-7569. **Hotel:** Unavailable.

2009 SCHEDULE

YANKEE STADIUM

Standard Game Times: 7:05 p.m.; Sat.-Sun. 1:05.

APRIL

6-9 . . . . at Baltimore
10-12 . . . . . at Kansas City
13-15 . . . . . . at Tampa Bay
16-19 . . . . Cleveland
20-22 . . . . Oakland
24-26 . . . . at Boston
27-29 . . . . at Detroit
30 . . . . Angels

MAY

1-3 . . . . Angels
4-5 . . . . Boston
6-7 . . . . Tampa Bay
8-10 . . . . at Baltimore
12-14 . . . . at Toronto
15-18 . . . . Minnesota
19-21 . . . . Baltimore
22-24 . . . . . . Philadelphia
25-27 . . . . at Texas
20-31 . . . . . . at Cleveland

JUNE

1 . . . . at Cleveland
2-4 . . . . Texas
5-8 . . . . Tampa Bay
9-11 . . . . at Boston
12-14 . . . . Mets
16-18 . . . . Washington
19-21 . . . . at Florida
23-25 . . . . at Atlanta
26-28 . . . . at Mets
30 . . . . Seattle

JULY

1-2 . . . . Seattle
3-6 . . . . Toronto
7-9 . . . . at Minnesota
10-12 . . . . . at Los Angeles
17-19 . . . . Detroit
20-22 . . . . Baltimore
24-26 . . . . Oakland
27-29 . . . . . . at Tampa Bay
30 . . . . at White Sox

AUGUST

1-2 . . . . at White Sox
4-5 . . . . at Toronto
6-9 . . . . Boston
10-12 . . . . Toronto
13-16 . . . . at Seattle
17-19 . . . . at Oakland
21-23 . . . . at Boston
25-27 . . . . Texas
28-30 . . . . White Sox
31 . . . . at Baltimore
1-2 . . . . at Baltimore
3-6 . . . . at Toronto
7-9 . . . . Tampa Bay
11-13 . . . . Baltimore
15-16 . . . . Toronto
18-20 . . . . at Seattle
21-23 . . . . . . at Los Angeles
25-27 . . . . Boston
28-30 . . . . Kansas City

OCTOBER

2-4 . . . . at Tampa Bay

Oakland Athletics

Office Address: 7000 Coliseum Way, Oakland, CA 94621.
Telephone: (510) 638-4900. **Fax:** (510) 562-1633.
Website: www.oaklandathletics.com

Ownership

Co-Owner, Managing Partner: Lewis Wolff.
Owner-Partner: John Fisher.

Lew Wolff

BUSINESS OPERATIONS

President: Michael Crowley. **Executive Assistant to President:** Carolyn Jones.
General Counsel: Steve Johnston. **Senior Counsel:** Neil Kraetsch.

Finance/Administration

Vice President, Finance: Paul Wong.

Director, Finance: Kasey Miraglia. **Payroll Manager:** Kathy Leviege. **Senior Accountant:** Isabelle Mahaffey. **Accounting Analyst:** Ling Ding. **Specialist, Accounts Receivable:** David Bunnell. **Ticket Accountant:** Scott Zumsteg. **Staff Accountant:** John Anki. **Manager, Human Resources:** Kim Kubo. **Assistant, Human Resources:** Heather Gregg. **Manager, Information Systems Manager:** Nathan Hayes. **Assistant, Information Systems:** David Friedberg. **Coordinator, Office Services:** Julie Vasconcellos. Executive Office Receptionist: Maggie Baptist. Travel Specialist: Colleen Osterberg.

Sales/Marketing

Vice President, Sales/Marketing: Jim Leahey. **Assistant, Sales/Marketing:** Breanne Pund. **Director, Corporate Sales:** Franklin Lowe. **Corporate Account Managers:** Matthew Gallagher, Jill Golden, Susan Weiglein. **Manager, Marketing/Advertising:** Zachary Glare. **Manager, Creative Services:** Mike Ono. **Advertising Coordinator:** Amy MacEwen. **Manager, Promotions/Special Events:** Heather Rajeski. **Special Events Assistants:** Katie Fagundes, Caroline Griggs, Jenna Zito. **Director, Merchandise:** Kaye Kennedy. **Manager, Retail Operations:** Austin Rancadore.

Public Relations/Communications

Telephone: (510) 563-2207. **Fax:** (510) 562-1633.

Vice President, Broadcasting/Communications: Ken Pries. **Manager, Broadcast Services:** Warren Chu. **Director, Public Relations:** Bob Rose. **Manager, Baseball Information:** Mike Selleck. **Manager, Media/Player Relations:** Kristy Fick. **Manager, Media Services:** Debbie Gallas. **Team Photographer:** Michael Zagaris. **Director, Community Relations:** Detra Paige. **Assistant, Community Relations:** Erik Farrell.

Senior Director, In-Stadium Entertainment: Troy Smith. **Director, Multimedia Services:** David Don.

Stadium Operations

Vice President, Stadium Operations: David Rinetti. **Sr. Manager, Stadium Operations:** Paul LeVeau. **Manager, Stadium Services:** Randy Duran. **Manager, Stadium Operations Events:** Kristy Ledbetter. **Manager, Stadium Operations:** Tara O'Connor. **Coordinator, Stadium Operations:** Peter Young. **Stadium Operations Scheduler:** Gabrielle Weems. **Head Groundskeeper:** Clay Wood. **Arizona Groundskeeper:** Chad Huss.

Ticketing

Director, Ticket Sales: Todd Santino. **Manager, Luxury Suite Sales:** Parker Newton. **Senior Account Managers, Season Ticket Sales:** Phil Chapman, Christopher Terwoord. **Manager, Premium Seating/Business Development:** Sean O'Keefe. **Manager, Season Ticket Sales:** Brian DiTucci. **Manager Group Sales:** Kati Westcott. **Account Managers, Season Group Sales:** Adam Clar, Debbie Pratt, Jessica Scott. **Supervisor, Inside Sales and CRM:** Aaron Dragomir.

Director, Ticket Operations: Steve Fanelli. **Senior Manager, Ticket Services:** Josh Ziegenbusch. **Manager, Ticket Operations:** David Adame. **Manager, Box Office:** Anthony Silva. **Coordinator, Ticket Operations:** Anthony Blue. **Manager, Spring Operations/Ticket Services:** Travis LaDolce. **Supervisor, Ticket Services:** Catherine Glazer. **Ticket Services Representatives:** John Austin, Adam Clark, Anuj Patel, Matt Weiss. **Senior Manager, Premium Seating Services:** Susie Weiss. **Coordinator, Premium Seating:** Moti Bycel. **.**

Travel/Clubhouse

Director, Team Travel: Mickey Morabito. **Equipment Manager:** Steve Vucinich. **Visitors Clubhouse Attendant:** Mike Thalblum. **Assistant Equipment Manager:** Brian Davis. **Umpires Assistant:** Matt Weiss. **Clubhouse Assistant:** William Angel.

GENERAL INFORMATION

Stadium (year opened): McAfee Coliseum (1968).
Home Dugout: Third Base. **Playing Surface:** Grass.
Team Colors: Kelly green and gold.
Player Representative: Unavailable.
Driving Directions: From I-880, take either the 66th Avenue or Hegenberger Road exit.

Billy Beane

BASEBALL OPERATIONS

Vice President/General Manager: Billy Beane.

Assistant GM: David Forst. **Director, Player Personnel:** Billy Owens. **Special Assistant to GM:** Randy Johnson. **Executive Assistant:** Betty Shinoda. **Director, Baseball Administration:** Pamela Pitts. **Baseball Operations Analyst:** Farhan Zaidi. **Video Coordinator:** Adam Rhoden.

Major League Staff

Manager: Bob Geren.

Coaches: Bench—Tye Waller; Pitching—Curt Young; Batting—Jim Skaalen; First Base—Todd Steverson; Third Base—Mike Gallego; Bullpen—Ron Romanick. **Bullpen Catcher:** Casey Chavez.

Medical, Training

Head Athletic Trainer: Steve Sayles. **Assistant Athletic Trainer:** Walt Horn. **Director, Strength/Conditioning:** Bob Alejo. **Major League Massage Therapist:** Yoshihiro Nishio. **Coordinator, Medical Services:** Larry Davis. **Team Physicians:** Dr. Allan Pont, Dr. Robert Napoles, Dr. Elliot Schwartz. **Team Orthopedist:** Dr. John Frazier. **Consulting Orthopedists:** Dr. Thomas Peatman, Dr. Lewis Yocum, Dr. Stephen Viess.

Arizona Team Physicians: Dr. Fred Dicke, Dr. Doug Freedberg.

Player Development

Telephone: (510) 638-4900. **Fax:** (510) 563-2376.

Director, Player Development: Keith Lieppman. **Director, Minor League Operations:** Ted Polakowski. **Administrative Assistant, Player Development:** Cheryl Polakowski.

Minor League Roving Instructors: Juan Navarrete (infield), Ron Plaza (infield), Gil Patterson (pitching), Greg Sparks (hitting). **Special Instructor for Scouting/Player Development:** Ruben Escalera. **Minor League Video Coordinator:** Mark Smith.

Minor League Medical Coordinator: Jeff Collins. **Coordinator, Medical Services:** Larry Davis. **Minor League Coordinator, Strength/Conditioning:** Judd Hawkins. **Coordinator, Minor League Pitching Rehab:** Garvin Alston. **Supervisor, Arizona Clubhouse:** Jesse Sotomayor. **Manager, Arizona Clubhouse:** James Gibson. **Staff, Arizona Clubhouse:** Chad Yaconetti.

Farm System

Class	Club (League)	Manager	Coach	Pitching Coach
Triple-A	Sacramento (PCL)	Tony DeFrancesco	Brian McArn	R. Rodriguez/B. La Rosa
Double-A	Midland (TL)	Darren Bush	Webster Garrison	Scott Emerson
High A	Stockton (CL)	Aaron Nieckula	Tim Garland	Don Schulze
Low A	Kane County (MWL)	Steve Scarsone	Haas Pratt	Jimmy Escalante
Short-season	Vancouver (NWL)	Rick Magnante	Casey Myers	Craig Lefferts
Rookie	Phoenix (AZL)	Marcus Jensen	Juan Dilone	Ariel Prieto

Scouting

Telephone: (510) 638-4900. **Fax:** (510) 563-2376.

Director, Scouting: Eric Kubota (Rocklin, CA).

Assistant Director, Scouting: Michael Holmes. **Director, Pro Scouting:** Chris Pittaro (Hamilton, NJ). **Major League Advance Scout:** Joe Sparks (Phoenix, AZ). **National Crosschecker:** Ron Vaughn (Corona, CA). **Western Crosschecker:** Scott Kidd (Los Altos, CA). **Midwest Crosschecker:** Steve Bowden (Houston, TX). **Pro Scouts:** Bryn Alderson (San Francisco, CA), Jeff Bittiger (Saylorsburg, PA), Will Schock (Oakland, CA), Craig Weissmann (San Diego, CA), Mike Ziegler (Orlando, FL). **Area Scouts:** Neil Avent (Greensboro, NC), Yancy Ayres (Topeka, KS), Armann Brown (Houston, TX), Jermaine Clark (Livermore, CA), Jim Coffman (Portland, OR), Matt Higginson (Oakville, ON), Leland Maddox (TBA), Rick Magnante (Van Nuys, CA), Eric Martins (Diamond Bar, CA), Kevin Mello (Champaign, IL), Kelcey Mucker (Baton Rouge, LA), Matt Ranson (Nicholasville, KY), Marc Sauer (Cliffwood Beach, NJ), Trevor Schaffer (Belleair, FL), Jeremy Schied (Phoenix, AZ), Rich Sparks (Sterling Heights, MI), J.T. Stotts (Moorpark, CA).

Director, Latin American Operations: Raymond Abreu (Santo Domingo, DR). **Coordinator, Latin American Scouting:** Julio Franco (Caracas, VZ).

International Scouts: Ruben Barradas (VZ), Juan Carlos De La Cruz (DR), Angel Eusebio (DR), Andri Garcia (VZ), Pablo Marmol (DR), Amaury Reyes (DR), Russell Spear (AU), Oswaldo Troconis (VZ), Juan Villanueva (VZ), Adam Hislop (Taiwan).

Spring Training

Complex Address: Phoenix Municipal Stadium, 5999 E. Van Buren, Phoenix, AZ 85008. **Telephone:** (602) 225-9400. **Seating Capacity:** 8,500. **Location:** I-10 to exit 153 (48th Street), HoHoKam Expressway to Van Buren Street (U.S. Highway 60), right on Van Buren. **Hotel Address:** Doubletree Suites Hotel, 320 N. 44th St., Phoenix, AZ 85008. **Telephone:** (602) 225-0500.

Minor League Clubs

Complex Address: Papago Park Baseball Complex, 1802 N. 64th St., Phoenix, AZ 85008. **Telephone:** (480) 949-5951. **Hotel Address:** Extended Stay America, 4357 East Oak Street, Phoenix, AZ 85008. **Telephone:** (602) 225-2998.

2009 SCHEDULE

McAFEE COLISEUM

Standard Game Times:
7:05 p.m.; Sat.-Sun. 1:05.

APRIL

6-9 . . . . at Angels
10-12 . . . . Seattle
13-15 . . . . Boston
17-19 . . . . at Toronto
20-22 . . . . at Yankees
24-26 . . . . Tampa Bay
28-30 . . . . at Texas

MAY

1-3 . . . . at Seattle
4-5 . . . . Angels
6-7 . . . . Texas
8-10 . . . . Toronto
12-13 . . . . Kansas City
15-17 . . . . at Detroit
18-21 . . . . . . at Tampa Bay
22-24 . . . . Arizona
25-27 . . . . Seattle
29-31 . . . . at Texas

JUNE

1-4 . . . . at White Sox
5-7 . . . . Baltimore
8-11 . . . . Minnesota
12-14 . . . . at San Francisco
16-18 . . . . at Dodgers
19-21 . . . . . . at San Diego
22-24 . . . . . . San Francisco
26-28 . . . . Colorado
29-30 . . . . Detroit

JULY

1 . . . . Detroit
3-5 . . . . at Cleveland
6-8 . . . . at Boston
10-12 . . . . . . at Tampa Bay
16-19 . . . . Angels
20-22 . . . . Minnesota
24-26 . . . . at Yankees
27-30 . . . . at Boston
31 . . . . Toronto

AUGUST

1-2 . . . . Toronto
3-6 . . . . Texas
7-9 . . . . at Kansas City
10-12 . . . . at Baltimore
14-16 . . . . White Sox
17-19 . . . . Yankees
21-23 . . . . Detroit
24-26 . . . . at Seattle
28-30 . . . . at Angels
31 . . . . Kansas City

SEPTEMBER

1-2 . . . . Kansas City
3-6 . . . . Seattle
8-9 . . . . at White Sox
11-13 . . . . . . at Minnesota
14-16 . . . . at Texas
17-20 . . . . Cleveland
21-24 . . . . Texas
25-27 . . . . at Angels
29-30 . . . . at Seattle

OCTOBER

1 . . . . at Seattle
2-4 . . . . Angels

Philadelphia Phillies

Office Address: Citizens Bank Park, One Citizens Bank Way, Philadelphia, PA 19148.
Telephone: (215) 463-6000. **Website:** www.phillies.com.

Ownership

Operated By: The Phillies.
President/CEO: David Montgomery. **Chairman:** Bill Giles.

BUSINESS OPERATIONS

Senior Vice President/General Counsel: Bill Webb. **Vice President, Employee/Customer Services:** Kathy Killian. **Director, Business Development:** Joe Giles.

David Montgomery

Finance

Senior Vice President, Business/Finance: Jerry Clothier. **VP, CFO:** John Nickolas. **Director, Payroll Services:** Karen Wright. **Director, Information Systems:** Brian Lamoreaux.

Marketing/Promotions

Senior Vice President, Marketing/Sales: David Buck. **Manager, Client Services/Alumni Relations:** Debbie Nocito. **Director, Corporate Partnerships:** Rob MacPherson. **Managers, Advertising Sales:** Scott Nickle, Tom Sullivan. **Director, Advertising Sales:** Brian Mahoney. **Director, Marketing Programs/Events:** Kurt Funk. **Director, Entertainment:** Chris Long. **Manager, Broadcasting:** Rob Brooks. **Manager, Advertising/Internet Services:** Jo-Anne Levy-Lamoreaux.

Public Relations/Communications

Telephone: (215) 463-6000. **Fax:** (215) 389-3050.

Vice President, Public Relations: Bonnie Clark. **Director, Public Relations:** Leigh Tobin. **Manager, Media Relations:** Greg Casterioto. **Media Relations Assistant:** Kevin Gregg.

Ballpark Operations

Senior Vice President, Operations/Administration: Michael Stiles. **Director, Ballpark Operations:** Mike DiMuzio. **Director, Event Operations:** Eric Tobin. **Manager, Concessions Development:** Bruce Leith. **Head Groundskeeper:** Mike Boekholder. **PA Announcer:** Dan Baker. **Official Scorers:** Jay Dunn, Joseph Bellina, Mike Maconi.

Ticketing

Telephone: (215) 463-1000. **Fax:** (215) 463-9878.

Vice President, Sales/Ticket Operations: John Weber. **Director, Ticket Department:** Dan Goroff. **Director, Ticket Technology/Development:** Chris Pohl. **Manager, Suite Sales/Services:** Tom Mashek. **Manager, Phone Center:** Phil Feather. **Manager, Club Sales/Services:** Derek Schuster. **Manager, Season Ticket Services:** Mike Holdren.

Travel/Clubhouse

Director, Team Travel/Clubhouse Services: Frank Coppenbarger.

Manager, Visiting Clubhouse: Kevin Steinhour. **Assistant, Home Clubhouse:** Phil Sheridan. **Manager, Equipment/Umpire Services:** Dan O'Rourke.

GENERAL INFORMATION

Stadium (year opened): Citizens Bank Park (2004).
Home Dugout: First Base. **Playing Surface:** Natural Grass.
Team Colors: Red, white and blue.
Player Representative: Unavailable.
Driving Directions: From I-95 or I-76, take the Broad Street exit. The ballpark is on on the north side of Pattison Avenue, between 11th and Darien Streets.

Ruben Amaro, Jr.

BASEBALL OPERATIONS

Senior Vice President/General Manager: Ruben Amaro Jr. **Assistant GM, Player Development/Scouting:** Chuck LaMar. **Assistant GM, Player Personnel:** Benny Looper. **Assistant GM:** Scott Proefrock. **Director, Baseball Administration:** Susan Ingersoll Papaneri. **Baseball Information Analyst:** Jay McLaughlin. **Senior Advisor to GM:** Dallas Green. **Special Assistant to GM:** Charley Kerfeld.

Major League Staff

Manager: Charlie Manuel.

Coaches: Bench—Pete Mackanin; Pitching—Rich Dubee; Batting—Milt Thompson; First Base—Davey Lopes; Third Base—Sam Perlozzo; Bullpen Coach—Mick Billmeyer; Bullpen Catcher—Tim Gradoville.

Medical/Training

Director, Medical Services: Dr. Michael Ciccotti. **Head Trainer:** Scott Sheridan. **Assistant Trainer:** Mark Andersen. **Conditioning Coordinator:** Doug Lien.

Player Development

Telephone: (215) 463-6000. **Fax:** (215) 755-9324.

Assitant GM, Player Personnel: Benny Looper. **Assistant GM. Player Development/Scouting:** Chuck LaMar. **Director, Minor League Operations:** Steve Noworyta. **Assistant Director, Minor League Operations:** Lee McDaniel. **Director, Latin American Operations:** Sal Artiaga. **Director, Florida Operations:** John Timberlake.

Field Coordinator: Mike Compton. **Coordinators:** Brian Cammarota (trainer), Mike Compton (catching), Gorman Heimueller (pitching), Shawn Fcasni (conditioning), Sal Rende (hitting), Jerry Martin (outfield/baserunning), Doug Mansolino (infield).

Farm System

Class	Club (League)	Manager	Coach	Pitching Coach
Triple-A	Lehigh Valley (IL)	Dave Huppert	Gregg Gross	Rod Nichols
Double-A	Reading (EL)	Steve Roadcap	Frank Cacciatore	Steve Schrenk
High A	Clearwater (FSL)	Razor Shines	Ernie Whitt	Kevin Jordan
Low A	Lakewood (SAL)	Dusty Wathan	Greg Legg	Bob Milacki
Short-season	Williamsport (NYP)	Chris Truby	Bobby Meacham	Tom Filer
Rookie	Clearwater(GCL)	Roly DeArmas	Luis Melendez	Aris Tirado
Rookie	Phillies (DSL)	Manny Amador	Domingo Brito	C. Henriquez
Rookie	Phillies (VSL)	Rafael DeLima	S. Navas/J. Tiamo	L. Straker

Scouting

Director, Scouting: Marti Wolever (Papillion, NE). **Assistant Director, Scouting:** Rob Holiday.

Coordinators, Scouting: Mike Ledna (Arlington Heights, ILL), Bill Moore (Alta Loma, CA).

Regional Supervisors: Gene Schall (East/Harleysville, Pa.), **Brian Kohlscheen (Central/Norman, OK), Darrell Conner (West/Riverside, CA).**

Area Scouts: Steve Cohen (Spring, TX), Joey Davis (Ranco Murrieta, CA), Nate Dion (West Chester, OH), Ellis Dungan (Charlotte, NC), Mike Garcia (Moreno Valley CA), Brad Holland (Gilbert AZ), Tim Kissner (Kirkland WA), Chip Lawrence (Palmetto, FL), Paul Murphy (Wilmington, DE), Demerius Pittman (Corona CA), Paul Scott (Rockwall, TX), David Seifert (Evansville IN), Mike Stauffer (Ridgeland, MS), Eric Valent (Wernersville PA).

International Supervisor: Sal Agostinelli (Kings Park (NY).

International Scouts: Alex Agostino (Canada), Roque Bernardina (Curacao), Omar Cisneros (Nicaragua), Tomas Herrera (Mexico), Eric Jacques (Europe), Allan Lewis (Panama, Central America), Jesus Mendez (Venezuela), Koby Perez (Dominican Republic).

Director, Major League Scouting: Gordon Lakey (Barker, TX). **Advance Scout:** Craig Colbert. **Major League Scouts:** Jim Fregosi Jr. (Murrieta, CA), Howie Frieling. **Professional Scouts:** Sonny Bowers (Hewitt, TX), Hank King (Limerick, PA), Dean Jongewaard (Fountain Valley, CA), Jerry Lafferty (Kansas City, MO), Jon Mercurio (Coraopolis, PA), Roy Tanner (North Charleston, SC), Del Unser (Scottsdale, AZ).

Independent League Coordinator: Mal Fichman (Boise, ID).

Spring Training

Complex Address: Bright House Networks Field, 601 N. Old Coachman Rd., Clearwater, FL 33765. **Telephone:** (727) 467-4457. **FAX:** (727) 712-4498. **Seating Capacity:** 8,500. **Location:** Route 60 West, right on Old Coachman Road, ballpark on right after Drew Street.

Hotel: None.

Minor League Clubs

Complex Address: Carpenter Complex, 651 N. Old Coachman Rd., Clearwater, FL 33765. **Telephone:** (727) 799-0503. **FAX:** (727) 726-1793. **Hotel Addresses:** Hampton Inn, 21030 U.S. Highway 19 North, Clearwater, FL 34625. **Telephone:** (727) 797-8173; Econolodge, 21252 U.S. Hwy. 19, Clearwater, FL 34625. **Telephone:** (727) 799-1569.

2009 SCHEDULE

CITIZENS BANK PARK

Standard Game Times:
7:10 p.m.; Fri. 7:40

APRIL	
5	Atlanta
7-8	Atlanta
10-12	at Colorado
13	at Washington
15-16	at Washington
17-20	San Diego
21-23	Milwaukee
24-26	at Florida
27-29	Washington

MAY	
1-3	Mets
4-5	at St. Louis
6-7	at Mets
8-10	Atlanta
12-14	Dodgers
15-17	at Washington
19-21	at Cincinnati
22-24	at Yankees
25-27	Florida
29-31	Washington

JUNE	
1-3	at San Diego
4-7	at Dodgers
9-11	at Mets
12-14	Boston
16-18	Toronto
19-21	Baltimore
23-25	at Tampa Bay
26-28	at Toronto
30	at Atlanta

JULY	
1-2	at Atlanta
3-5	Mets
6-9	Cincinnati
10-12	Pittsburgh
17-19	at Florida
20-22	Cubs
24-26	St. Louis
27-29	at Arizona
30-31	at San Francisco

AUGUST	
1-2	at San Francisco
4-6	Colorado
7-9	Florida
11-13	at Cubs
14-16	at Atlanta
18-20	Arizona
21-24	at Mets
25-27	at Pittsburgh
28-30	Atlanta

SEPTEMBER	
1-3	San Francisco
4-7	at Houston
8-10	at Washington
11-13	Mets
15-17	Washington
18-20	at Atlanta
21-23	at Florida
24-27	at Milwaukee
28-30	Houston

OCTOBER	
1	Houston
2-4	Florida

Pittsburgh Pirates

Office Address: PNC Park at North Shore, 115 Federal St, Pittsburgh, PA 15212.
Mailing Address: P.O. Box 7000, Pittsburgh, PA 15212.
Telephone: (412) 323-5000. **Fax:** (412) 325-4412.
Website: www.pirates.com

Ownership

Chairman of the Board: Robert Nutting.
Board of Directors: Donald Beaver, G. Ogden Nutting, Robert Nutting, William Nutting, Duane Wittman.

Executive

President: Frank Coonelly.
Executive Vice President/CFO: Jim Plake. **Executive VP/Chief Marketing Officer:** Lou DePaoli. **Senior VP/Baseball Legal Counsel:** Larry Silverman

GEORGE GOJKOVICH
Frank Coonelly

BUSINESS OPERATIONS

Finance

Controller: David Bowman. **Senior Director, Human Resources:** Pam Nelson Minter. **Senior Director, Information Technology:** Terry Zeigler. **Director, Office Services:** Patti Mistick.

Communications

Fax: (412) 325-4413.
Senior Director, Communications: Brian Warecki. **Director, Media Relations:** Jim Trdinich. **Director, Broadcasting:** Marc Garda. **Manager, Media Services:** Dan Hart. **Manager, Business Communications:** Matt Nordby.

Community Relations

Vice President, Community/Public Affairs: Patty Paytas.
Director, Development of Pirates Charitie : Denise Balkovec. **Manager, Community Relations:** Michelle Mejia.

Marketing/Sales

Senior Director, Marketing, Advertising/Branding: Brian Chiera. **Senior Director, Corporate Partnerships:** Mike Egan.
Director, Alumni Affairs, Promotions/Licensing: Joe Billetdeaux. **Director, Advertising:** Kiley Cauvel.
Manager, Special Events: Christine Serkoch, Dan Millar. **Manager, In-Game Entertainment:** Eric Wolff. **Media Producer:** Ken Brown. **Manager, Promotions/Licensing:** Megan Morris. **Manager, Non-Gameday Event Sales:** Ann Elder.

Stadium Operations

Senior Director, Ballpark Operations: Chris Hunter. **Senior Director, Security/Contract Services:** Jeff Podobnik. **Manager, Security/Service Operations:** Mark Weaver. **Manager, Field Maintenance:** Manny Lopez.

Ticketing

Telephone: (800) 289-2827. **Fax:** (412) 325-4404.
Senior Director, Ticket Sales/Services: Christopher Zaber. **Senior Director, Analytics/Business Development:** Jim Alexander
Manager, Ticket Services: Dave Wysocki. **Director, Season Sales/Fan Experience:** Terri Smith. **Director, Ticket Development:** Jim Popovich. **Director, Premium Sales/Suite Services:** Joan Schmitt. **Manager, Group Services/Gold Club:** Charlene Cheroke. **Manager, Client Relations:** Jared Kramer. **Manager, Group Ticket Sales:** Mike Thompson. **Manager, Inside Sales:** Justin Gurney.

Travel/Clubhouse

Traveling Secretary: Greg Johnson.
Equipment Manager/Home Clubhouse Operations: Scott Bonnett. **Visitors Clubhouse Manager:** Kevin Conrad.

GENERAL INFORMATION

Stadium (year opened): PNC Stadium (2001).
Home Dugout: Third Base. **Playing Surface:** Grass.
Team Colors: Black, gold, red and white.
Player Representative: Paul Maholm.
Driving Directions: From south, I-279 through Fort Pitt Tunnel, make left off bridge to Fort Duquesne Bridge, cross Fort Duquesne Bridge, follow signs to PNC Park. From north, I-279 to PNC Park (exit 12, left lane), follow directions to parking.

Neal Huntington

BASEBALL OPERATIONS

Senior VP/General Manager: Neal Huntington.

Director, Baseball Operations: Bryan Minniti. **Director, Baseball Systems Development:** Dan Fox. **Special Assistants to GM:** Jim Benedict, Keith Champion, Larry Corrigan, Marc DelPiano, Joe Ferrone, Jax Robertson, Doug Strange, Pete Vuckovich.

Major League Staff

Manager: John Russell.

Coaches: Bench—Gary Varsho; Pitching— Joe Kerrigan ; Hitting—Don Long; First Base— Perry Hill ; Third Base—Tony Beasley; Bullpen—Luis Dorante.

Medical/Training

Medical Director: Dr. Patrick DeMeo. **Team Physician:** Dr. Edward Snell. **Head Athletic Trainer:** Brad Henderson. **Assistant Athletic Trainer:** Mike Sandoval. **Strength/Conditioning Coordinator:** Frank Velasquez. **Latin American Strength/Conditioning Coordinator:** Kiyoshi Momose. **Physical Therapist/Rehab Coordinator:** Erwin Valencia.

Minor Leagues

Director, Player Development: Kyle Stark.

Minor League Field Coordinator: Jeff Banister. **Advisor, Player Development:** Rich Donnelly. **Outfield/Baserunning Coordinator:** Kimera Bartee. **Pitching Coordinator:** Troy Buckley. **Infield Coordinator:** Carlos Garcia. **Hitting Coordinator:** Gregg Ritchie. **Athletic Training Coordinator:** Carl Randolph. **Strength/Conditioning Coordinator:** Chris Dunaway. **Rehab Coordinator:** Marc Oceguera. **Latin American Field Coordinator:** Euclides Rojas. **Minor League Administrator:** Diane DePasquale.

Farm System

Class	Club (League)	Manager	Coach(es)	Pitching Coach
Triple-A	Indianapolis (IL)	Frank Kremblas	Jeff Branson	Ray Searage
Double-A	Altoona (EL)	Matt Walbeck	Ryan Long	Dean Treanor
High A	Lynchburg (CL)	P.J. Forbes	Dave Howard	Wally Whitehurst
Low A	West Virginia (SAL)	Gary Green	Edgar Varela	Jeff Johnson
Short-season	State College (NYP)	Gary Robinson	Brandon Moore	Mike Steele
Rookie	Bradenton (GCL)	Tom Prince	R. Pena /W. Huyke	Miguel Bonilla
Rookie	Pirates (DSL)	Ramon Zapata	Cecilio Beltre	R. Carrion/H. Corniel
Rookie	Pirates (VSL)	Osmin Melendez	Ivan Colmenares	J. Prieto/D. Urbina

Scouting

Fax: (412) 325-4414.

Director, Scouting: Greg Smith.

Assistant Director, Scouting: Joe Delli Carri. **Scouting Administrator:** Jim Asher.

National Supervisors: Jack Bowen (Los Angeles, CA), Jimmy Lester (Columbus, GA).

Regional Supervisors: Jesse Flores (Long Beach, CA), Rob Guzik (Latrobe, PA), Rodney Henderson (Lexington, KY), Everett Russell (Thibodaux, LA)

Area Scouts: Rick Allen (Agoura Hills, CA), Matt Bimeal (Overland Park, KS), Sean Campbell (Newport Beach, CA), Jerome Cochran (Slidell, LA), Steve Fleming (Louisa, VA), Trevor Haley (Montgomery, TX), Greg Hopkins (Beaverton, OR), Chris Kline (Allentown, PA), Mike Leuzinger (Canton, TX), Darren Mazeroski (Panama City Beach, FL), Bump Merriweather (Glendale, AZ), Hal Morris (Munster, IN), Greg Schliz (Greenville, SC) , Josh Shaffer (Sacramento, CA), Brian Tracy (Mason, OH), Matt Wondolowski (Ft. Lauderdale, FL).

Part-Time Scouts: Elmer Gray (Pittsburgh, PA), William Price (Austin, TX), Jose Rosario (Bayamon, PR), Bill Sizemore (Sacramento, CA), Troy Williams (Europe).

Director, Latin American Scouting: Rene Gayo.

Supervisors, Dominican Republic: Josue Herrera, Nelson Llenas. **Full-Time Scouts:** Orlando Covo (Colombia), Nelson Llenas (Dominican Republic), Ellis Pena (Dominican Republic), Rodolfo Petit (Venezuela), Cristino Valdez (Dominican Republic), Chino Valdez (Mexico). **Supervisor, Venezuela:** Rodolfo Petit. **Supervisor, Mexico:** Chino Valdez.

International Scouts: Wilfredo Blanco (Nicaragua), Fu-Chun Chiang (Taiwan), Orlando Covo (Colombia), Luis Cuthbert (Nicaragua), Daniel Garcia (Colombia), Tony Harris (Australia), Jose Pineda (Panama), Tom Randolph (International), Marc Van Zanten (Netherlands Antilles), Darryl Yrausquin (Aruba), Domingo Zabala (Guatemala).

Spring Training

Stadium Address (first year): McKechnie Field (1969), 17th Ave. West and Ninth Street West, Bradenton, FL 34205. **Seating Capacity:** 6,562. **Location:** U.S. 41 to 17th Ave, west to 9th Street.

Complex/Hotel Address: Pirate City, 1701 27th St. E., Bradenton, FL 34208. **Telephone:** (941) 747-3031. **FAX:** (941) 747-9549.

Minor League Clubs

Complex/Hotel Address: Same as major league club..

2009 SCHEDULE

PNC PARK

Standard Game Times: 7:05 p.m.; Sun. 1:35.

APRIL

6-9 . . . . at St. Louis
10-12 . . . . . . at Cincinnati
13 . . . . Houston
15-16 . . . . Houston
17-19 . . . . Atlanta
20-22 . . . . Florida
24-26 . . . . . . at San Diego
27-29 . . . . . at Milwaukee

MAY

1-3 . . . . Cincinnati
4-5 . . . . Milwaukee
6-7 . . . . at St. Louis
8-10 . . . . at Mets
12-14 . . . . St. Louis
15-17 . . . . Colorado
18-21 . . . . at Washington
22-24 . . . . . . at White Sox
25-27 . . . . at Cubs
29-31 . . . . Houston

JUNE

1-4 . . . . Mets
5-7 . . . . at Houston
8-11 . . . . at Atlanta
12-14 . . . . Detroit
16-18 . . . . . . at Minnesota
19-21 . . . . at Colorado
23-25 . . . . Cleveland
26-28 . . . . Kansas City
29-30 . . . . Cubs

JULY

1 . . . . Cubs
3-5 . . . . at Florida
6-8 . . . . at Houston
10-12 . . . . at Philadelphia
17-19 . . . . . San Francisco
20-22 . . . . Milwaukee
23-26 . . . . at Arizona
27-29 . . . . at San Francisco
31 . . . . Washington

AUGUST

1-3 . . . . Washington
4-6 . . . . Arizona
7-9 . . . . St. Louis
11-13 . . . . at Colorado
14-16 . . . . at Cubs
17-19 . . . . Milwaukee
21-23 . . . . Cincinnati
25-27 . . . . Philadelphia
28-30 . . . . . . at Milwaukee
31 . . . . at Cincinnati

SEPTEMBER

1-2 . . . . at Cincinnati
4-6 . . . . St. Louis
7-9 . . . . Cubs
11-13 . . . . at Houston
14-16 . . . . at Dodgers
18-21 . . . . San Diego
22-24 . . . . Cincinnati
25-28 . . . . Dodgers
29-30 . . . . at Cubs

OCTOBER

1 . . . . at Cubs
2-4 . . . . at Cincinnati

St. Louis Cardinals

Office Address: 700 Clark Street, St. Louis MO 63102.
Telephone: (314) 345-9600. **Fax:** (314) 345-9523.
Website: www.stlcardinals.com.

Ownership

Operated By: St. Louis Cardinals, LLC.

Chairman: Bill Dewitt, Jr.

Vice Chairman: Fred Hanser. **Secretary/Treasurer:** Andrew Baur. **President:** Bill DeWitt III. **Senior Administrative Assistant to Chairman:** Grace Pak. **Senior Administrative Assistant to President:** Julie Laningham.

BUSINESS OPERATIONS

Mark Lamping

Vice President, Event Services: Vicki Bryant. **Manager, Event Services:** Missy Tobey. **Director, Government Affairs/Special Projects:** Ron Watermon. **Director, Human Resources:** Christine Nelson. **Manager, Office Administration/Human Resources Specialist:** Karen Brown.

Finance

Fax: (314) 345-9520.

Senior Vice President/Chief Financial Officer: Brad Wood. **Director, Finance:** Rex Carter. **Supervisor, Ticket Accounting/Reporting:** Michelle Flach. **Senior Accountant:** Tracey Sessions. **Accounting Manager:** John Lowry. **Manager, Payroll/Compliance Reporting:** Shellie Ward. **Director, Purchasing/Cost Analysis:** Mark Murray.

Marketing/Sales

Fax: (314) 345-9529

Senior Vice President, Sales/Marketing: Dan Farrell. **Administrative Assistant, Corporate Sales:** Gail Ruhling. **Vice President, Corporate Sales/Marketing/Stadium Entertainment:** Thane van Breusegen. **Senior Account Executive, Corporate Sales:** Jeff Floerke. **Director, Scoreboard Operations/Senior Account Executive:** Tony Simokaitis.

Media Relations/Community Relations

Fax: (314) 345-9530

Director, Media Relations: Brian Bartow. **Assistant Directors, Media Relations:** Melody Yount/Jim Anderson. **Director, Publications:** Steve Zesch. **Publication Assistants:** Lauren Anderson, Larry State. **Vice President, Cardinals Care/Community Relations:** Michael Hall. **Administrative Assistant:** Mary Ellen Edmiston. **Director, Target Marketing:** Ted Savage. **Youth Baseball Commissioner, Cardinals Care:** Keith Brooks. **Coordinator, Cardinals Care:** Lucretia Payne. **Supervisor, Community Relations:** Jessica Illert. **Community Relations Specialist:** Mark Taylor.

Stadium Operations

Fax: (314) 345-9535

Vice President, Stadium Operations: Joe Abernathy. **Administrative Assistant:** Hope Baker. **Director, Stadium Operations:** Mike Bertani. **Director, Security/Special Services:** Joe Walsh. **Director, Quality Assurance/Guest Services:** Mike Ball. **Manager, Stadium Operations:** Cindy Richards. **Head Groundskeeper:** Bill Findley. **Assistant Head Groundskeeper:** Chad Casella. **PA Announcer:** John Ulett. **Official Scorers:** Gary Muller, Jeff Durbin, Mike Smith.

Ticketing

Fax: (314) 345-9522

Vice President, Ticket Sales/Service: Joe Strohm. **Director, Ticket Services:** Derek Thornburg. **Manager, Ticket Services:** Brady Bruhn. **Manager, Premium Ticket Sales:** Delores Scanlon. **Manager, Season Ticket Sales/Services:** Jamie Brickler. **Manager, Ticket Technology:** Jennifer Needham. **Manager, Small Groups:** Mary Clare Bena. **Director, Fan Development/Alumni Relations:** Martin Coco. **Supervisor, Receptionist:** Marilyn Mathews.

Travel, Clubhouse

Fax: (314) 345-9523

Traveling Secretary: C.J. Cherre. **Equipment Manager:** Rip Rowan. **Assistant Equipment Manager:** Ernie Moore. **Visiting Clubhouse Manger:** Jerry Risch. **Video Coordinator:** Chad Blair.

GENERAL INFORMATION

Stadium (year opened): Busch Stadium (2006).

Home Dugout: First Base. **Playing Surface:** Grass.

Team Colors: Red and white.

Player Representative: Braden Looper.

Driving Directions: From Illinois, take I-55 South, I-64 West, I-70 West or US 40 West across the Mississippi River (Poplar Street Bridge) to Busch Stadium exit. In Missouri, take I-55 North, I-64 East, I-70 East, I-44 East or US 40 East to downtown St. Louis and Busch Stadium exit.

John Mozeliak

BASEBALL OPERATIONS

Fax: (314) 345-9525

Vice President, General Manager: John Mozeliak.

Assistant GM: John Abbamondi. **Executive Assistant to GM:** Linda Brauer. **Special Assistants to GM:** Gary LaRocque, Mike Jorgensen, Matt Slater, Alan Benes, Cal Eldred. **Director, Baseball Development:** Mike Girsch. **Director, Major League Administration:** Judy Carpenter-Barada. **Coordinator, Baseball Operations/Professional Scouting:** Matt Carroll. **Coordinator, Asian Development:** Robert Fidler. **Administrative Assistant, Baseball Operations:** Ellen Gingles.

Player Development

Fax: (314) 345-9519

Vice President, Amateur Scouting/Player Development: Jeff Luhnow. **Director, Minor League Operations:** John Vuch. **Coordinators:** Dyar Miller (Pitching), Brent Strom (Pitching Instruction), Dann Bilardello (Roving Catching), Dan Radison (Roving Hitting), Adam Olsen (Strength/Conditioning), Keith Joynt (Strength/Conditioning Assistant).

Minor League Equipment Manager: Buddy Bates.

Major League Staff

Telephone: (314) 345-9600.

Manager: Tony La Russa.

Coaches: Bench—Joe Pettini; Pitching—Dave Duncan; Batting—Hal McRae; First Base—Dave McKay; Third Base—Jose Oquendo; Bullpen—Marty Mason

Medical/Training

Medical Advisor: Dr. George Paletta. **Head Trainer:** Barry Weinberg. **Assistant Trainer:** Greg Hauck.

Class	Club (League)	Manager	Coach	Pitching Coach
Triple-A	Memphis (PCL)	Chris Maloney	Mark Budaska	Blaise Ilsley
Double-A	Springfield (TL)	Ron Warner	Derrick May	Bryan Eversgerd
High A	Palm Beach (FSL)	Tom Spencer	Jeff Albert	Dennis Martinez
Low A	Quad Cities (MWL)	Steve Dillard	Joe Kruzel	Arthur Adams
Short-season	Batavia (NYP)	Mark DeJohn	Ramon Ortiz	Tim Leveque
Rookie	Johnson City (APP)	Mike Shildt	Johnny Rodriguez	Doug White
Rookie	Cardinals (GCL)	Steve Turco	Javier Meza	Dernier Orozco
Rookie	Cardinals (DSL)	Claudio Almonte	Rene Rojas	Bill Villanueva
Rookie	Cardinals (VSL)	Enrique Brito	Unavailable	Henderson Lugo

Scouting

Telephone: (314) 345-9358. **Fax:** (314) 345-9525.

Assistant Scouting Director: Jaron Madison (Vallejo, CA). **Coordinator, Pro Scouting:** Matt Carroll (St. Louis, MO).

Professional Scouts: Bruce Benedict (Atlanta, GA), Alan Benes (Town & Country, MO); Chuck Fick (Newbury Park, CA), Mike Jorgensen (Fenton, MO), Marty Keough (Scottsdale, AZ), Gary LaRocque (Browns Summit, NC), Deric McKamey (Buffton, OH), Joe Rigoli (Parsippany, NJ), Matt Slater (Stevenson Ranch, CA),

National/Regional Supervisors: Joe Almaraz (San Antonio, TX), Mike Roberts (Hot Springs, AR), Roger Smith (Eastman, GA).

Area Supervisors: Matt Blood (New Orleans, LA), Jay Catalano (Joelton, TN), Mike Elias (Oakton, VA), Ralph Garr, Jr. (Houston, TX), Charlie Gonzalez (Weston, FL), Brian Hopkins (Brunswick, OH), Jeff Ishii (Chino, CA), Mike Juhl (Indian Trail, NC), Aaron Krawiec (Gilbert, AZ), Aaron Looper (Shawnee, OK), Scott Melvin (Quincy, IL), Sean Moran (Levittown, PA), Jamal Strong (Surprise, AZ), Matt Swanson (Ripon, CA).

Director, International Operations: Moises Rodriguez. **Latin American Supervisor:** Juan Mercado.

International Scouts: Domingo Garcia (Dominican Republic), Jose Gregorio Gonzalez (Venezuela), Carlos Heron (Panama), Neder Horta (Colombia), Carlos Lugo (Dominican Republic), Rene Rojas (Dominican Republic), Crysthiam Blanco (Nicaragua), Fermin Coronel (Curacao).

Major League Club

Complex Address (first year): Roger Dean Stadium (1998), 4795 University Dr., Jupiter, FL 33458. **Telephone:** (561) 775-1818. **FAX:** (561) 799-1380. **Seating Capacity:** 6,864. **Location:** I-95 to exit 58, east on Donald Ross Road for 1/4 mile.

Hotel Address: Embassy Suites, 4350 PGA Blvd., Palm Beach Gardens, FL 33410. **Telephone:** (561) 622-1000.

Minor League Clubs

Complex: Same as major league club. **Hotel:** West Palm Beach Marriott, 630 Clearwater Rd., West Palm Beach, FL 33401. **Telephone:** (561) 833-1234.

2009 SCHEDULE

BUSCH STADIUM

Standard Game Times: 7:10 p.m.; Sun. 1:15.

APRIL

6-9 . . . . Pittsburgh
10-12 . . . . Houston
13-15 . . . . at Arizona
16-19 . . . . at Cubs
21-23 . . . . Mets
24-26 . . . . Cubs
27-29 . . . . at Atlanta
30 . . . . at Washington

MAY

1-3 . . . . . . at Washington
4-5 . . . . Philadelphia
6-7 . . . . Pittsburgh
8-10 . . . . at Cincinnati
12-14 . . . . . . at Pittsburgh
15-17 . . . . Milwaukee
19-21 . . . . Cubs
22-24 . . . . Kansas City
25-27 . . . . . at Milwaukee
29-31 . . . . at San Francisco

JUNE

1-4 . . . . Cincinnati
5-8 . . . . Colorado
9-11 . . . . at Florida
12-14 . . . . . . at Cleveland
16-18 . . . . Detroit
19-21 . . . . . at Kansas City
22-25 . . . . at Mets
26-28 . . . . Minnesota
29-30 . . . . . San Francisco

JULY

1-2 . . . . San Francisco
3-5 . . . . at Cincinnati
7-9 . . . . at Milwaukee
10-12 . . . . at Cubs
17-19 . . . . Arizona
20-22 . . . . at Houston
24-26 . . . . at Philadelphia
27-30 . . . . Dodgers
31 . . . . Houston

AUGUST

1-2 . . . . Houston
4-5 . . . . at Mets
7-9 . . . . at Pittsburgh
10-12 . . . . Cincinnati
14-16 . . . . San Diego
17-19 . . . . at Dodgers
20-23 . . . . . . at San Diego
25-27 . . . . Houston
28-30 . . . . Washington

SEPTEMBER

1-3 . . . . Milwaukee
4-6 . . . . at Pittsburgh
7-9 . . . . at Milwaukee
11-13 . . . . Atlanta
14-16 . . . . Florida
18-20 . . . . Cubs
21-23 . . . . at Houston
25-27 . . . . at Colorado
29-30 . . . . . . at Cincinnati

OCTOBER

1 . . . . at Cincinnati
2-4 . . . . Milwaukee

San Diego Padres

Office Address: PETCO Park, 100 Park Blvd, San Diego, CA 92101.
Mailing Address: P.O. Box 122000, San Diego, CA 92112.
Telephone: (619) 795-5000.
E-mail address: comments@padres.com. **Website:** www.padres.com.

Ownership

Operated By: Padres LP.
Chairman: John Moores. **Co-Vice Chairmen:** Glenn Doshay, Charles Noell.

CEO: Sandy Alderson.

Sandy Alderson

BUSINESS OPERATIONS

Executive Vice President/Business Operations: Jeff Overton. **Executive VP/General Counsel:** Katie Pothier. **Executive VP/Senior Advisor:** Dave Winfield.

Finance

Executive Vice President/CFO: Fred Gerson. **VP/Sales:** Jim Ballweg. **Director, Corporate Sales:** Marty Gorsich. **Director, Information Systems:** Joe Lewis.

Media Relations/Community Relations

Telephone: (619) 795-5265. **Fax:** (619) 795-5266.

Director, Media Relations: Warren Miller. **Manager, Media Relations:** Leah Tobin. **Coordinator, Media Relations:** Bret Picciolo. **Assistant, Media Relations:** Ben Coughlan. **Club Photographer:** Chris Hardy.

Vice President, Community Relations: Michele Anderson. **Director, Padres Foundation:** Sue Botos. **Manager, Community Relations:** Nhu Tran.

Stadium Operations

Executive Vice President, Ballpark Management/General Manager, PETCO Park: Richard Andersen. **VP, Ballpark Operations:** Mark Guglielmo.

Director, Security/Transportation: Ken Kawachi. **Director, Landscape/Field Maintenance:** Luke Yoder. **PA Announcer:** Frank Anthony. **Official Scorers:** Bill Zavestoski, Jack Murray, Tim Powers.

Ticketing

Telephone: (619) 795-5005. **Fax:** (619) 795-5034.

Executive Director, Ticket Operations: Jim Kiersnowski.

Manager, Ticket Sales: Ryan Ross. **Director, Ticket Customer Services:** Laura Evans.

Travel, Clubhouse

Director, Team Travel/Equipment Manager: Brian Prilaman.

Assistant Clubhouse Manager: Tony Petricca. **Assistant to the Equipment Manager:** Spencer Dallin. **Visiting Clubhouse Manager:** David Bacharach.

GENERAL INFORMATION

Stadium (year opened): Petco Park (2004).
Home Dugout: First Base. **Playing Surface:** Grass.
Team Colors: Padres sand, navy blue and sky blue.
Player Representative: Unavailable.
Driving Directions: Four major thoroughfares feed into and out of downtown in all directions: Pacific Highway, I-5, State Route 163 and State Route 94/Martin Luther King Freeway. Eight freeway interchanges service the area around the ballpark.

Kevin Towers

BASEBALL OPERATIONS

Telephone: (619) 795-5076. **Fax:** (619) 795-5361.

Executive Vice President/General Manager: Kevin Towers.

Executive Vice President: Paul DePodesta. **Vice President/Assistant GM:** Fred Uhlman Jr. **Special Assistants to GM/Major League Scouts:** Ken Bracey, Bill Bryk. **Director, Baseball Operations:** Jeff Kingston. **Assistant:** Ryan Isaac.

Major League Staff

Manager: Bud Black.

Coaches: Bench—Ted Simmons; Pitching—Darren Balsley; Hitting—Jim Lefebvre; First Base—Rick Renteria; Third Base—Glenn Hoffman; Bullpen—Darrel Akerfelds.

Medical/Training

Club Physician: Scripps Clinic Medical staff.

Head Athletic Trainer: Todd Hutcheson. **Assistant Athletic Trainer:** Paul Navarro.

Strength/Conditioning Coach: Jim Malone.

Player Development

Telephone: (619) 795-5343. **Fax:** (619) 795-5036.

Vice President, Scouting/Player Development: Grady Fuson.

Director, Minor League Operations: Mike Wickham. **Coordinator, Latin American Operations:** Juan Lara. **Administrator, Dominican Republic Operations:** Cesar Rizik. **Administrative Assistant, Scouting/Player Development:** Ilana Miller.

Roving Instructors: Mike Couchee (pitching), Tony Muser (hitting), Tom Gamboa (field coordinator), Duffy Dyer (catching), Gary Jones (infield), John Maxwell (trainer coordinator), Dan Morrison (strength/conditioning).

Farm System

Class	Farm Club (League)	Manager	Coach	Pitching Coach
Triple-A	Portland (PCL)	Randy Ready	Max Venable	Glenn Abott
Double-A	San Antonio (TL)	Terry Kennedy	Orv Franchuck	Steve Webber
High A	Lake Elsinore (CAL)	Carlos Lezcano	Shane Spencer	Dave Rajsich
Low A	Fort Wayne (MWL)	Doug Dascenzo	Tom Tonincasa	Tom Bradley
Short-season	Eugene (NW)	Greg Riddoch	Eric Peyton	Bronswell Patrick
Rookie	Padres (AZL)	Jose Flores	Bob Skube	Jimmy Jones
Rookie	Padres (DSL)	Evaristo Lantigua	Jose Amancio	Carlos Hernandez

Scouting

Telephone: (619) 795-5343. **Fax:** (619) 795-5036.

Director, Scouting: Bill Gayton.

Director, International Scouting/Major League Scout: Randy Smith.

Assistant to the Director, Scouting: Pete DeYoung.

Major League Scouts: Ken Bracey (Dunlap, IL), Ray Crone (Waxahachie, TX), Bill Bryk (Schereville, IL).

Professional Scouts: Chris Gwynn (Alta Loma, CA), Van Smith (Belleville, IL), Joe Bochy (Plant City, FL).

National Crosscheckers: Bob Filotei (Mobile, AL), Scott Littlefield (Long Beach, CA).

Amateur Scouts: Adam Bourassa (Raleigh, NC), Jim Bretz (South Windsor, CT), Lane Decker (Piedmont, OK), Pete DeYoung (La Jolla, CA), David Francia (Dickinson, AL), Brendan Hause (Carlsbad, CA), Tim Holt (Allen, TX), Noah Jackson (Mill Valley, CA), Ash Lawson (Athens, TN), Dave Lottsfeldt (Castle Rock, CO), Andrew Salvo (Everett, WA), Rob Sidwell (Windermere, FL), Jeff Stewart (Normal, IL). **Part-Time Scouts:** Robert Gutierrez (Carol City, FL), Hank Krause (Akron, IA), Willie Ronda (Las Lomas Rio Piedras, Puerto Rico), Cam Walker (Centerville, IA), Murray Zuk (Souris, Manitoba).

International Scouting Supervisors: Coordinator, Latin American Scouting: Felix Feliz, Trevor Schumm (Pacific Rim), Yfrain Linares (Venezuela), Robert Rowley (Mexico, Central/South America).

International Scouts: Antonio Alejos (Venezuela), Milton Croes (Aruba), Marcial Del Valle (Colombia), Emenejildo Diaz (Dominican Republic), Elvin Jarquin (Nicaragua), Martin Jose (Dominican Republic), Victor Magdaleno (Venezuela), Ricardo Montenegro (Panama), Luis Prieto (Venezuela), Ysreal Rojas (Dominican Republic), Jose Salado (Dominican Republic).

Spring Training

Complex Address (first year): Peoria Sports Complex (1994), 8131 W. Paradise Lane, Peoria, AZ 85382. **Telephone:** (623) 486-7000. **FAX:** (623) 486-7154. **Seating Capacity:** 10,000. **Location:** I-17 to Bell Road exit, west on Bell to 83rd Ave.

Hotel Address: La Quinta Inns and Suites, 16321 N. 83rd Avenue Peoria, AZ 85382. **Telephone:** (623) 487-1900

Minor League Teams:

Complex/Hotel: Same as major league club..

2009 SCHEDULE

PETCO PARK

Standard Game Times:
7:05 p.m.; Sun. 1:05

APRIL
6 . . . . Dodgers
8-9 . . . . Dodgers
10-12 . . . . . San Francisco
13 . . . . at Mets
15-16 . . . . at Mets
17-20 . . . . at Philadelphia
21-22 . . . . at San Francisco
24-26 . . . . Pittsburgh
27-29 . . . . at Colorado
30 . . . . at Dodgers

MAY
1-3 . . . . at Dodgers
4-5 . . . . Colorado
6-7 . . . . Arizona
8-10 . . . . at Houston
12-14 . . . . at Cubs
15-17 . . . . Cincinnati
19-21 . . . . . San Francisco
22-24 . . . . Cubs
25-27 . . . . at Arizona
29-31 . . . . at Colorado

JUNE
1-3 . . . . Philadelphia
5-8 . . . . Arizona
9-10 . . . . at Dodgers
12-14 . . . . at Angels
16-18 . . . . Seattle
19-21 . . . . Oakland
23-25 . . . . at Seattle
26-28 . . . . at Texas
29-30 . . . . Houston

JULY
1-2 . . . . Houston
3-5 . . . . Dodgers
6-8 . . . . at Arizona
9-12 . . . . . at San Francisco
16-19 . . . . Colorado
20-22 . . . . Florida
24 . . . . at Washington
27-30 . . . . . . at Cincinnati
31 . . . . Milwaukee

AUGUST
1-2 . . . . Milwaukee
3-5 . . . . Atlanta
6-9 . . . . Mets
11-13 . . . . . at Milwaukee
14-16 . . . . at St. Louis
17-19 . . . . Cubs
20-23 . . . . St. Louis
25-27 . . . . at Atlanta
28-30 . . . . at Florida
31 . . . . Washington

SEPTEMBER
1-2 . . . . Washington
4-6 . . . . at Dodgers
7-9 . . . . . . at San Francisco
11-13 . . . . Colorado
14-16 . . . . Arizona
18-21 . . . . . . at Pittsburgh
22-24 . . . . at Colorado
25-27 . . . . at Arizona
29-30 . . . . Dodgers

OCTOBER
1 . . . . Dodgers
2-4 . . . . San Francisco

San Francisco Giants

Office Address: AT&T Park, 24 Willie Mays Plaza, San Francisco, CA 94107.
Telephone: (415) 972-2000. **Fax:** (415) 947-2800.
Website: sfgiants.com, sfgigantes.com.

Ownership

Operated by: San Francisco Baseball Associates L.P.

Chief Executive Officer: William H. Neukom. **Senior General Partner:** Sue Burns. **President Emeritus:** Peter A. Magowan. **Special Assistant:** Willie Mays. **Senior Advisor:** Willie McCovey.

BUSINESS OPERATIONS

Peter Magowan

President/Chief Operating Officer: Laurence M. **Baer. Senior Vice President/General Counsel:** Jack F. **Bair. Vice President, Human Resources:** Joyce Thomas.

Finance

Senior Vice President/Chief Financial Officer: John F. Yee. **Senior Vice President/Chief Information Officer:** Bill Schlough. **Senior Director, Information Technology:** Ken Logan. **Senior Vice President, Facilities:** Alfonso G. Felder. **Vice President, Finance:** Lisa Pantages.

Marketing/Sales

Senior Vice President, Corporate Marketing: Mario Alioto. **Vice President, Corporate Sponsorship:** Jason Pearl. **Director, Special Events:** Valerie McGuire. **Senior Vice President, Consumer Marketing:** Tom McDonald. **Senior Director, Marketing/Entertainment:** Chris Gargano. **Vice President, Client Relations:** Annemarie Hastings. **Vice President, Sales:** Jeff Tucker. **Manager, Season Ticket Sales:** Craig Solomon. **General Manager, Retail:** Dave Martinez. **Director, Retail Operations:** Bonnie MacInnes.

Media Relations/Community Relations

Telephone: (415) 972-2445. **Fax:** (415) 947-2800.

Senior Vice President, Communications: Staci Slaughter. **Senior Director, Broadcast Services:** Maria Jacinto. **Senior Director, Media Relations:** Jim Moorehead. **Senior Media Relations Coordinator:** Matt Chisholm. **Hispanic Media Relations Coordinator/Spanish Language Broadcaster:** Erwin Higueros. **Media Relations Assistant:** Eric Smith. **Vice President, Print Publications/Creative Services:** Nancy Donati. **Director, Public Affairs/Community Relations:** Shana Daum. **Director, Photography/Archives:** Missy Mikulecky.

Ballpark Operations

Senior Vice President, Ballpark Operations: Jorge Costa. **Vice President, Guest Services:** Rick Mears. **Senior Director, Ballpark Operations:** Gene Telucci. **Senior Director, Security:** Tinie Roberson. **Head Groundskeeper:** Greg Elliott. **PA Announcer:** Renel Brooks-Moon. **Official Scorers:** Chuck Dybdal, Art Santo Domingo, Michael Duca.

Ticketing

Telephone: (415) 972-2000. **Fax:** (415) 972-2500.

Managing Vice President, Ticket Services/Client Relations: Russ Stanley. **Director, Ticket Services:** Devin Lutes. **Senior Ticket Accounting Manager:** Kem Easley. **Senior Ticket Operations Manager:** Anita Sprinkles. **Senior Box Office Manager:** Todd Pierce.

Travel/Clubhouse

Coordinator, Team Travel: Michael King. **Coordinator, Organizational Travel:** Mike Scardino. **Giants Equipment Manager:** Miguel Murphy. **Visitors Clubhouse Manager:** Harvey Hodgerney. **Assistant Equipment Managers:** Rob Dean, Ron Garcia.

GENERAL INFORMATION

Stadium (year opened): AT&T Park (2000).
Home Dugout: Third Base. **Playing Surface:** Grass.
Team Colors: Black, orange and cream.
Player Representative: Randy Winn.
Driving Directions: From Peninsula/South Bay, I-280 north (or U.S. 101 north to I-280 north) to Mariposa Street exit, right on Mariposa, left on Third Street. From East Bay (Bay Bridge), I-80/Bay Bridge to Fifth Street exit, right on Fifth Street, right on Folsom Street, right on Fourth Street, continue on Fourth Street to parking lots (across bridge).

Brian Sabean

BASEBALL OPERATIONS

Telephone: (415) 972-1922. **Fax:** (415) 947-2737.

Senior Vice President/General Manager: Brian R. Sabean.

Vice President, Player Personnel: Dick Tidrow. **Vice President, Baseball Operations:** Bobby Evans. **Special Assistant to the General Manager:** Felipe Alou. **Senior Advisor, Baseball Operations:** Tony Siegle. **Senior Director, Baseball Operations/Pro Scouting:** Jeremy Shelley. **Coordinator, Baseball Operations/Quantitative Analysis:** Yeshayah Goldfarb. **Executive Assistant to the General Manager:** Karen Sweeney. **Coordinator, Video Operations:** Danny Martin.

Major League Staff

Manager: Bruce Bochy

Coaches: Bench—Ron Wotus; Pitching—Dave Righetti; Hitting—Carney Lansford; First Base—Roberto Kelly; Third Base—Tim Flannery; Bullpen—Mark Gardner, Bill Hayes

Medical Training

Team Physicians: Dr. Robert Murray, Dr. Ken Akizuki, Dr. Anthony Saglimbeni. **Head Trainer:** Dave Groeschner. **Assistant Trainers:** Mark Gruesbeck, Ben Potenziano. **Coordinator, Medical Administration:** Chrissy Yuen.

Player Development

Director, Player Development: Fred Stanley.

Senior Consultants, Player Personnel: Jack Hiatt, Ron Perranoski. **Special Assistants:** Joe Amalfitano, Jim Davenport. **Director, Arizona Operations:** Alan Lee. **Senior Advisor, Player Personnel:** Rock Down. **Minor League Operations Assistant:** Eric Flemming. **Coordinator, Player Personnel:** Clara Ho. **Minor League Operations Assistant:** Gabriel Alvarez. **Coordinator, Instruction:** Shane Turner. **Coordinator, Minor League Pitching:** Bert Bradley.

Farm System

Class	Farm Club (League)	Manager	Coach	Pitching Coach
Triple-A	Fresno (PCL)	Dan Rohn	Hensley Meulens	Pat Rice
Double-A	Connecticut (EL)	Steve Decker	Garey Ingram	Ross Grimsley
High A	San Jose (CAL)	Andy Skeels	Gary Davenport	Jerry Cram
Low A	Augusta (SAL)	Dave Machemer	Lipso Nava	Steve Kline
Short-season	Salem-Keizer (NWL)	Tom Trebelhorn	Ricky Ward	Brian Cooper
Rookie	Giants (AZL)	Mike Goff	Victor Torres	Mike Caldwell
Rookie	Giants (DSL)	Jesus Tavarez	Carlos Valderrama	Marcos Aguasvivas

Scouting

Telephone: (415) 972-1922. **Fax:** (415) 972-2737.

Special Assistant to General Manager, Scouting: John Barr (Haddonfield, NJ).

Senior Advisor, Scouting: Ed Creech (Moultrie, GA). **Coordinator, Amateur Scouting:** Doug Mapson (Chandler, AZ).

Special Assistants, Scouting: Matt Nerland (Clayton, CA), Ted Uhlaender (Parshall, CO). **Special Assignment Scout:** Darren Wittcke (Gresham, OR). **Senior Consultants, Scouting:** Dick Cole (Costa Mesa, CA), Bo Osborne (Woodstock, CA). **Assistant, Scouting:** Adam Nieting.

Major League Scouts: Steve Balboni (Murray Hill, NJ), Lee Elder (Augusta, GA), Stan Saleski (Dayton, OH), Rudy Santin (Miami, FL), Paul Turco, Sr. (Sarasota, FL), Tom Zimmer (St. Pete, FL).

Supervisors: Northeast—John Castleberry (Tacoma, WA); West—Doug Mapson (Chandler, AZ); Midwest—Joe Strain (Englewood, CO); East Coast—Paul Turco, Jr. (Tampa, FL).

Territorial Scouts: Northeast Region—Brad Barth (Williamstown, NJ), Kevin Christman (Noblesville, IN), John DiCarlo (Glenwood, NJ), Pat Portugal (Wake Forest, NC), Glenn Tufts (Bridgewater, MA). Southeast Region—Andrew Jefferson (Mobile, AL), Ron Merrill (Danville, VA), Mike Metcalf (Sarasota, FL), Sean O'Connor (Cartersville, GA), Felix Negron (Bayamon, PR), Tim Rock (Orlando, FL). Midwest Region—Ray Callari (Cote St. Luc, Quebec), Lou Colletti (Elk Grove Village, IL) , Chuck Hensley (Erie, CO), Tom Korenek (Houston, TX), Todd Thomas (Dallas, TX), Hugh Walker (Jonesboro, AR). Western Region—Brad Cameron (Los Alamitos, CA), Jim Chapman (Langley, BC), Michael Kendall (Rancho Palos Verde, CA), John Shafer (Portland, OR), Keith Snider (Stockton, CA), Matt Woodward (Vancouver, WA).

Director, Dominican Operations: Pablo Peguero. **Venezuela Supervisor:** Ciro Villalobos.

Major League Club

Complex Address (first year): Scottsdale Stadium (1981), 7408 E. Osborn Rd., Scottsdale, AZ 85251. **Telephone:** (480) 990-7972. **FAX:** (480) 990-2643. **Seating Capacity:** 11,500. **Location:** Scottsdale Road to Osborne Road, east on Osborne 1/2 mile.

Hotel Address: Hilton Garden Inn Scottsdale Old Town, 7324 East Indian School Rd., Scottsdale, AZ 85251. **Telephone:** (480) 481-0400.

Minor League Clubs

Complex Address: Indian School Park, 4415 N. Hayden Road at Camelback Road, Scottsdale, AZ 85251. **Telephone:** (480) 990-0052. **FAX:** (480) 990-2349.

2009 SCHEDULE

AT&T PARK

Standard Game Times:
7:15 p.m.; Sun. 1:05

APRIL

7-9	Milwaukee
10-12	at San Diego
13	at Dodgers
15-16	at Dodgers
17-19	Arizona
21-22	San Diego
24-26	at Arizona
27-29	Dodgers

MAY

1-3	Colorado
4-5	at Cubs
6-7	at Colorado
8-10	at Dodgers
11-13	Washington
14-17	Mets
19-21	at San Diego
22-24	at Seattle
25-27	Atlanta
29-31	St. Louis

JUNE

2-4	at Washington
5-8	at Florida
9-11	at Arizona
12-14	Oakland
15-17	Angels
19-21	Texas
22-24	at Oakland
26-28	at Milwaukee
29-30	at St. Louis

JULY

1-2	at St. Louis
3-5	Houston
6-8	Florida
9-12	San Diego
17-19	at Pittsburgh
20-23	at Atlanta
24-26	at Colorado
27-29	Pittsburgh
30-31	Philadelphia

AUGUST

1-2	Philadelphia
3-5	at Houston
7-9	Cincinnati
10-12	Dodgers
14-17	at Mets
18-20	at Cincinnati
21-24	at Colorado
25-27	Arizona
28-30	Colorado

SEPTEMBER

1-3	at Philadelphia
4-6	at Milwaukee
7-9	San Diego
11-13	Dodgers
14-16	Colorado
18-20	at Dodgers
21-23	at Arizona
24-27	Cubs
29-30	Arizona

OCTOBER

1	Arizona
2-4	at San Diego

Seattle Mariners

Office Address: 1250 First Avenue South, Seattle, WA 98134.
Mailing Address: P.O. Box 4100, Seattle, WA 98194.
Telephone: (206) 346-4000. **Fax:** (206) 346-4400.
Website: www.mariners.com.

Ownership

Board of Directors: Minoru Arakawa, John Ellis, Chris Larson, Howard Lincoln, Wayne Perry, Frank Shrontz, Craig Watjen.

Chair and CEO: Howard Lincoln

President, Chief Operating Officer: Chuck Armstrong.

Chuck Armstrong

BUSINESS OPERATIONS

Finance

Executive Vice President, Finance/Ballpark Operations: Kevin Mather. **VP, Finance:** Tim Kornegay. **Controller:** Greg Massey. **VP, Human Resources:** Marianne Short.

Marketing, Sales

Executive Vice President, Business/Operations: Bob Aylward. **VP, Corporate Business/Community Relations:** Joe Chard. **Director, Corporate Business:** Ingrid Russell-Narcisse. **VP, Marketing:** Kevin Martinez. **Director, Marketing:** Gregg Greene. **Senior Director, Merchandise:** Jim La Shell.

Vice President, Sales: Frances Traisman. **Director, Group/Season Ticket Sales:** Bob Hellinger. **Director, Private Suite Sales:** Steve Camp. **Suite Sales:** Moose Clausen, Jill Dahlen.

Baseball Information, Communications

Telephone: (206) 346-4000. **Fax:** (206) 346-4400.

Vice President, Communications: Randy Adamack.

Director, Baseball Information: Tim Hevly. **Manager, Baseball Information:** Jeff Evans. **Coordinator, Baseball Information:** Kelly Munro. **Assistant, Baseball Information:** Fernando Alcala.

Director, Public Information: Rebecca Hale. **Director, Graphic Design:** Carl Morton. **Director, Community Relations:** Gina Hasson. **Manager, Community Programs:** Sean Grindley.

Ticketing

Telephone: (206) 346-4001. **Fax:** (206) 346-4100.

Director, Ticketing/Parking Operations: Malcolm Rogel. **Director, Ticket Services:** Jennifer Sweigert. **Manager, Group/Suite Ticket Services:** Steve Belling. **Manager, Box Office:** Malcolm Rogel.

Stadium Operations

Vice President, Ballpark Operations: Scott Jenkins. **Senior Director, Safeco Field Operations:** Tony Pereira. **Director, Security:** Jason Weaving. **Director, Events:** Jill Hashimoto.

Vice President, Information Services: Dave Curry. **Director, PBX/Retail Systems:** Oliver Roy. **Director, Procurement:** Sandy Fielder.

Head Groundskeeper: Bob Christofferson. **Assistant Head Groundskeepers:** Tim Wilson, Leo Liebert. **PA Announcer:** Tom Hutyler. **Official Scorer:** Eric Radovich.

Travel, Clubhouse

Director, Team Travel: Ron Spellecy.

Clubhouse Manager: Ted Walsh. **Visiting Clubhouse Manager:** Henry Genzale. **Video Coordinator:** Carl Hamilton.

GENERAL INFORMATION

Stadium (year opened): Safeco Field (1999).
Home Dugout: First Base. **Playing Surface:** Grass.
Team Colors: Northwest green, silver and navy blue.
Player Representative: Unavailable.
Driving Directions: I-5 or I-90 to Fourth Avenue South exit.

Bill Bavasi

BASEBALL OPERATIONS

Executive Vice President/General Manager: Jack Zduriencik.

VP/Associate GM: Lee Pelekoudas. **Special Assistants:** Tony Blengino, John Boles, Ken Madeja, Dave Wallace. **Director, Baseball Administration:** Jim Na. **Administrator, Baseball Operations:** Debbie Larsen.

Major League Staff

Manager: Don Wakamatsu.

Coaches: Bench—Ty Van Burkleo; Pitching— Rick Adair; Batting—Alan Cockrell; First Base—Lee Tinsley; Third Base—Bruce Hines; Bullpen—John Wetteland.

Medical, Training

Medical Director: Dr. Edward Khalfayan. **Club Physician:** Dr. **Mitchel Storey. Head Trainer:** Rick Griffin. **Assistant Trainers:** Rob Nodine, Takayoshi Morimoto. **Stength/Conditioning:** Allen Wirtala.

Player Development

Telephone: (206) 346-4313. **Fax:** (206) 346-4300.

Director, Player Development: Pedro Grifol. **Director, Minor League/Scouting Operations:** Hide Sueyoshi. **Administrator, Player Development:** Jan Plein.

Coordinator, Minor League Instruction: Tim Tollman. **Trainer Coordinator:** Mickey Clarizio. **Roving Instructors:** James Clifford (strength/conditioning), Darrin Garner (infield), Roger Hansen (catching), Jose Castro (hitting), Dave Wallace (pitching).

Farm System

Class	Club (League)	Manager	Coach	Pitching Coach
Triple-A	Tacoma (PCL)	Darren Brown	Alonzo Powell	Dwight Bernard
Double-A	West Tenn (EL)	Philip Plantier	Terry Pollreisz	Thomas Dettore
High A	High Desert (CAL)	Jim Horner	Tommy Cruz	Lance Painter
Low A	Clinton (MWL)	Scott Steinmann	Eddie Menchaca	Lance Painter
Short-season	Everett (NWL)	John Tamargo	R. Santo Domingo	Unavailable
Rookie	Pulaski (APP)	Rob Mummau	Nasusel Cabrera	Jesus Azuaje
Rookie	Peoria (AZL)	Jose Moreno	Andy Bottin	Gary Wheelock
Rookie	Mariners (DSL)	Jose Guillen	F. Gerez/J. Guerrero	Danielin Acevedo
Rookie	Mariners (VSL)	Russell Vasquez	W. Oropeza/H. Espinoza	Johnny Molina

Scouting

Telephone: (206) 346-4000. **Fax:** (206) 346-4300.

Director, Amateur Scouting: Tom McNamara. **Director, Pro Scouting:** Carmen Fusco Administrator, Scouting: Hallie Larson.

Major League Scouts: Bob Harrison (Long Beach, CA), Greg Hunter (Seattle, WA), Steve Jongewaard (Napa, CA), Bill Kearns (Milton, MA), John McMichen (Treasure Island, FL), Frank Mattox (Peoria, AZ), Wayne Morgan (Pebble Beach, CA), Steve Pope (Asheville, NC).

National Coordinators: Mike Cadahia, Paul Gibson (Center Moriches, NY), Ron Tostenson (El Dorado Hills, CA). **Territorial Coordinators:** West—Tom Davis (Ripon, CA); Midwest—Mark Lummus (Cleburne, TX)

Territorial Supervisors: Dave Alexander (Lafayette, IN), Garrett Ball (Sandy Springs, GA), Chuck Carlson (Treasure Island, FL), Jim Fitzgerald (Woodinville, WA), Phil Geisler (Mount Horeb, WI), David May (Wilmington, DE), Rob Mummau (Stephens City, VA), Brian Nichols (Taunton, MA), Chris Pelekoudas (Goodyear, AZ), Stacey Pettis (Antioch, CA), Tim Reynolds (Irvine, CA), Alvin Rittman (Memphis, TN), Mike Tosar (Miami, FL), Kyle Van Hook (Brenham, TX), Greg Whitworth (Los Angeles, CA), Brian Williams (Cincinnati, OH), Dan Wright (Cave Springs, AR).

Vice President, International Operations: Bob Engle (Tampa, FL).

Coordinator, Special Projects International: Ted Heid (Glendale, AZ). **Coordinator, Pacific Rim:** Pat Kelly. **Coordinator, Canada/Europe:** Wayne Norton (Port Moody, British Columbia).

Supervisors, International Scouting: Emilio Carrasquel (Venezuela), Patrick Guerrero (Dominican Republic), Jamey Storvick (Taiwan), Curtis Wallace (Colombia), Yasushi Yamamoto (Japan).

Spring Training

Complex Address (first year): Peoria Sports Complex (1993), 15707 N. 83rd Ave., Peoria, AZ 85382. **Telephone:** (623) 776-4800. **Fax:** (623) 776-4829. **Seating Capacity:** 10,000. **Location:** I-17 to Bell Road exit, west on Bell to 83rd Ave.

Hotel Address: LaQuinta Inn & Suites, 16321 N. 83rd Ave., Peoria, AZ 85382. **Telephone:** (623) 487-1900.

Minor League Clubs

Complex Address: Peoria Sports Complex (1993), 15707 N. 83rd Ave., Peoria, AZ 85382. **Telephone:** (602) 412-9000. **Fax:** (602) 412-9382. **Hotel Address:** Hampton Inn, 8408 W. Paradise Lane, Peoria, AZ 85382. **Telephone:** (623) 486-9918.

2009 SCHEDULE

SAFECO FIELD

Standard Game Times:
7:05 p.m.; Sun. 1:05.

APRIL

6-9	at Minnesota
10-12	at Oakland
14-16	Angels
17-19	Tigers
21-23	Tampa Bay
24-26	at Los Angeles
27-29	at White Sox

MAY

1-3	Oakland
4-5	Texas
6-7	at Kansas City
8-10	at Minnesota
12-14	at Texas
15-17	Boston
18-21	Angels
22-24	San Francisco
25-27	at Oakland
29-31	at Angels

JUNE

1-3	Baltimore
5-7	Minnesota
9-11	at Baltimore
12-14	at Colorado
16-18	at San Diego
19-21	Arizona
23-25	San Diego
26-28	at Dodgers
30	at Yankees

JULY

1-2	at Yankees
3-5	at Boston
6-8	Baltimore
9-12	Texas
16-19	at Cleveland
21-23	at Detroit
24-26	Cleveland
27-29	Toronto
30-31	at Texas

AUGUST

1-2	at Texas
4-6	at Kansas City
7-9	at Kansas City
10-12	White Sox
13-16	Yankees
18-20	at Detroit
21-23	at Cleveland
24-26	Oakland
27-30	Kansas City
31	Angels

SEPTEMBER

1-2	Angels
3-6	at Oakland
8-10	at Angels
11-3	at Texas
15-17	White Sox
18-20	Yankees
22-23	at Tampa Bay
24-27	at Toronto
29-30	Oakland

OCTOBER

1	Oakland
2-4	Texas

Tampa Bay Rays

Office Address: Tropicana Field, One Tropicana Drive, St. Petersburg, FL 33705.
Telephone: (727) 825-3137. **Fax:** (727) 825-3111.
Website: www.raysbaseball.com

Ownership

Principal Owner: Stuart Sternberg. **President:** Matt Silverman.

BUSINESS OPERATIONS

Stuart Sternberg

Senior Vice President, Administration/General Counsel: John Higgins. **Senior VP, Business Operations:** Brian Auld. **Senior VP/Chief Sales Officer:** Mark Fernandez. **Senior VP, Development/Business Affairs:** Michael Kalt. **VP, Development:** Melanie Lenz. **Director, Development:** William Walsh. **Senior Director, Information Technology:** Juan Ramirez. **Senior Director, Procurement/Business Services:** Bill Wiener, Jr. **Senior Manager, Human Resources:** Jennifer Tran. **Director, Partner/VIP Relations:** Cass Halpin.

Finance

Vice President, Finance: Rob Gagliardi. **Controller:** Patrick Smith. **Supervisor, Accounting:** Sandra Faulkner. **Supervisor, Payroll:** Brenda Richardson. **Coordinator, Accounting:** Jill Baetz. **Coordinator, Accounts Payable:** Sam Reams. **Financial Analyst:** Jason Gray.

Marketing/Community Relations

Vice President, Marketing/Community Relations: Tom Hoof. **Senior Director, Marketing:** Brian Killingsworth. **Director, Community Relations:** Suzanne Murchland. **Senior Manager, Community Relations:** Leslie Tieszen. **Manager, Community Relations:** Beth Bohnsack. **Manager, Advertising:** Carey Cox.

Communications/Broadcasting

Phone: (727) 825-3242.

Vice President, Communications: Rick Vaughn. **Director, Communications:** Chris Costello. **Manager, Communications:** Carmen Molina. **Coordinator, Communications:** Dave Haller. **Manager, Print/Graphics:** Erik Ruiz.

Senior Director, Broadcasting: Larry McCabe. **Director, Radio Operations:** Rich Herrera. **Manager, Broadcast Traffic:** Erin Buscemi.

Corporate Partnerships

Directors, Corporate Partnerships: Aaron Cohn, Wes Engram. **Director, Corporate Partnership Services:** Jason Wilmoth. **Managers, Corporate Partnerships:** Scott Ester, Sarah Helman, Brett Torrence.

Ticket Sales

Phone: (888) FAN-RAYS.

Vice President, Sales/Service: Brian Richeson. **Senior Director, Group/Suite Sales:** Clark Beacom. **Director, Season Ticket Sales/Service:** Jeff Tanzer. **Manager, Group Sales:** Chad Collard.

Director, Ticket Operations: Robert Bennett. **Assistant Director, Ticket Operations:** Ken Mallory. **Manager, Box Office/Phone Center:** Tim Burke. **Manager, Home Plate Club:** Craig Champagne. **Manager, Luxury Suite Services:** Kendall Roberts. **Manager, Inside Sales:** Derek Cheung.

Stadium Operations

Vice President, Operations/Facilities: Rick Nafe. **Senior Director, Building Operations:** Scott Kelyman. **Director, Event Operations:** Tom Karac. **Director, Building Operations:** Chris Raineri. **Manager, Events:** Todd Hardy. **Director, Audio/Visual Services:** Ron Golick. **Manager, Security:** Michael Griffith. **Manager, Systems:** Eric Kampfmann. **Booking Coordinator:** Caren Dana. **Head Groundskeeper:** Dan Moeller.

Vice President, Branding/Fan Experience: Darcy Raymond. **Director, In-Game Entertainment:** Lou Costanza. **Manager, In-Game Entertainment:** Courtney Jantz. **Senior Manager, Customer Service:** Eric Weisberg. **Senior Coordinators, Video:** Jeff Cederbaum, Jon Dougherty. **Senior Coordinator, Entertainment:** Jamie Patterson. **Senior Coordinator, Fan Experience:** Stephen Thomas.

Travel, Clubhouse

Director, Team Travel: Jeff Ziegler. **Equipment Manager, Home Clubhouse:** Chris Westmoreland. **Assistant Manager, Home Clubhouse:** Jose Fernandez. **Manager, Visiting Clubhouse:** Guy Gallagher. **Assistant Manager, Visiting Clubhouse:** Brandon Richesin. **Video Coordinator:** Chris Fernandez.

GENERAL INFORMATION

Stadium (year opened): Tropicana Field (1998).
Home Dugout: First Base. **Playing Surface:** FieldTurf Duofilament.
Team Colors: Dark blue, light blue, yellow.
Player Representative: Evan Longoria.
Driving Directions: I-275 South to St. Petersburg, exit 11, left onto Fifth Avenue, right onto 16th Street.

Andrew Friedman

BASEBALL OPERATIONS

Executive Vice President, Baseball Operations: Andrew Friedman. **Senior VP, Baseball Operations:** Gerry Hunsicker.

Director, Baseball Operations: Dan Feinstein. **Director, International Operations:** Carlos Alfonso. **Director, Major League Administration:** Sandy Dengler. **Senior Baseball Advisor:** Don Zimmer. **Senior Programmer:** Brian Plexico. **Coordinator, Baseball Operations:** James Click. **Assistant, Baseball Operations:** Erik Neander. **Assistant, Baseball Operations Systems:** Matt Hahn.

Major League Staff

Manager: Joe Maddon.

Coaches: Bench—Dave Martinez; Pitching—Jim Hickey; Hitting—Steve Henderson; First Base—George Hendrick; Third Base—Tom Foley; Bullpen—Bobby Ramos; Quality Assurance—Todd Greene.

Medical/Training

Medical Director: Dr. James Andrews. **Medical Team Physician:** Dr. Michael Reilly. **Orthopedic Team Physician:** Dr. Koco Eaton. **Head Athletic Trainer:** Ron Porterfield. **Assistant Athletic Trainers:** Paul Harker, Nick Paparesta. **Strength/Conditioning Coach:** Kevin Barr.

Minor Leagues

Telephone: (727) 825-3267. **Fax:** (727) 825-3493.

Director, Minor League Operations: Mitch Lukevics. **Assistant Director, Minor League Operations:** Chaim Bloom. **Administrator, Player Development:** Giovanna Rodriguez.

Field Coordinator: Jim Hoff. **Minor League Coordinators:** Skeeter Barnes (outfield/baserunning), Dick Bosman (pitching), Steve Livesey (hitting), Jamie Nelson (catching), Mark Vinson (medical training), Joel Smith (rehabilitation/athletic training), Trung Cao (strength/conditioning). **Equipment Manager:** Tim McKechney. **Assistant Equipment Manager:** Shane Rossetti.

Farm System

Class	Club(League)	Manager	Coach	Pitching Coach
Triple-A	Durham (IL)	Charlie Montoyo	Dave Myers	Xavier Hernandez
Double-A	Montgomery (SL)	Billy Gardner Jr.	O. Timmons	Neil Allen
High A	Charlotte (FSL)	Jim Morrison	Joe Szekely	Bill Moloney
Low A	Bowling Green (SAL)	Matt Quatraro	Hector Torres	R.C. Lichtenstein
Short-season	Hud. Valley (NYP)	Brady Williams	M. Castillo/M. Johns	Rafael Montalvo
Rookie	Princeton (APP)	Jared Sandberg	R. Deleon/D. DeMent	Marty DeMerritt
Rookie	Rays (GCL)	Joe Alvarez	B. Oglivie/R. Ruiz	Darwin Peguero
Rookie	Rays (DSL)	Julio Zorrilla	Eddy De los Santos	Manuel Esquivia
Rookie	Rays (VSL)	Wuarner Rincones	Esteban Gonzalez	Jorge Moncada

Scouting

Telephone: (727) 825-3241. **Fax:** (727) 825-3493.

Director, Scouting: R.J. Harrison (Phoenix, AZ).

Administrator, Scouting: Nancy Berry. **Assistant, Scouting/Minor League Operations:** Rob Metzler.

Professional Scouts: Matt Arnold (Taylor Mill, KY), Bart Braun (Vallejo, CA), Mike Cubbage (Keswick, VA), Larry Doughty (Leawood, KS), Bill Evers (New Port Richey, FL), Gene Glynn (Weseca, MN), Gail Henley (La Verne, CA), Brian Keegan (Matthews, NC), John McLaren (Peoria, AZ), Jim Pransky (Davenport, IA), Elanis Westbrooks (Houston, TX).

National Crosscheckers: Jeff Cornell (Lee's Summitt, MO), Tim Huff (Cave Creek, AZ). **East Coast Crosschecker:** Kevin Elfering (Wesley Chapel, FL). **Midwest Crosschecker:** Ken Stauffer (Katy, TX). **West Coast Crosschecker:** Fred Repke (Carson City, NV).

Area Scouts: James Bonnici (Davison, MI), Evan Brannon (St. Petersburg, FL), John Ceprini (Massapequa, NY), Tom Couston (Chicago, IL), Rickey Drexler (New Iberia, LA), Jayson Durocher (Cave Creek, AZ), Brian Hickman (Sapulpa, OK), Milt Hill (Cumming, GA), Paul Kirsch (Sherwood, OR), Brad Matthews (Concord, NC), Rob Moen (Playa del Rey, CA), Brian Morrison (Fairfield, CA), Pat Murphy (Marble Falls, TX), Jake Wilson (Carlsbad, CA), Doug Witt (Brooklyn, MD).

Part-Time Area Scouts: Tom Delong (Ocala, FL), Jose Hernandez (Miami, FL), Jim Lief (Wellington, FL), Graig Merritt (Pitts Meadow, Canada), Gil Martinez (San Juan, PR), Casey Onaga (Aiea, HI), Paul Robles (Loomis, CA), Tony Russo (Fayetteville, NC), Donald Turley (Spring, TX).

Director, Dominican Republic Operations: Eddy Toledo. **Director, Venezuelan Operations:** Ronnie Blanco. **Coordinator, Colombia:** Carlos Ramirez. **Pacific Rim Coordinator:** Tim Ireland.

Spring Training

Stadium Address: Charlotte Sports Park, 2300 El Jobean Road, Port Charlotte, FL, 33948. **Telephone:** (888) 326-7297. **Seating Capacity:** 5,000. **Location:** I-75 to US -17 to US 41, turn left onto El Jobean Rd. **Hotel Address:** Unavailable

Minor League Clubs

Complex/Hotel Address: Same as major league club.

2009 SCHEDULE

TROPICANA FIELD

Standard Game Times:
7:10 p.m.; Sun. 1:40.

APRIL

6-9 . . . . at Boston
10-12 . . . . . . .at Baltimore
13-15 . . . . Yankees
16-19 . . . . White Sox
21-23 . . . . at Mariners
24-26 . . . . at Oakland
27-29 . . . . . . at Minnesota
30 . . . . Boston

MAY

1-3 . . . . Boston
4-5 . . . . Baltimore
6-7 . . . . .at Yankees
8-10 . . . . at Boston
12-13 . . . . at Baltimore
14-17 . . . . Cleceland
18-21 . . . . Oakland
22-24 . . . . at Florida
25-28 . . . . at Cleveland
20-31 . . . . .Minnesota

JUNE

2-4 . . . . Kansas City
5-8 . . . . .at Yankees
9-11 . . . . Angels
12-14 . . . . .Washington
16-18 . . . . at Colorado
19-21 . . . . .at Mets
23-25 . . . . . . Philadelphia
26-28 . . . . Florida
29-30 . . . . at Toronto

JULY

1 . . . . at Toronto
3-5 . . . . at Texas
7-9 . . . . Toronto
10-12 . . . . Oakland
17-19 . . . . . at Kansas City
20-23 . . . . . . at White Sox
24-26 . . . . at Toronto
27-29 . . . . Yankees
31 . . . . Kansas City

AUGUST

1-3 . . . . Kansas City
4-5 . . . . Boston
7-9 . . . . at Seattle
10-12 . . . . at Angels
14-16 . . . . Toronto
18-20 . . . . Baltimore
21-23 . . . . Texas
24-26 . . . . at Toronto
28-31 . . . . at Detroit

SEPTEMBER

1-3 . . . . Boston
4-6 . . . . Detroit
7-9 . . . . .at Yankees
11-13 . . . . at Boston
14-17 . . . . .at Baltimore
18-20 . . . . Toronto
22-23 . . . . Seattle
25-27 . . . . at Texas
28-30 . . . . Baltimore

OCTOBER

1 . . . . Baltimore
2-4 . . . . Yankees

Texas Rangers

Office Address: 1000 Ballpark Way, Arlington, TX 76011.
Mailing Address: P.O. Box 90111, Arlington, TX 76011.
Telephone: (817) 273-5222. **Fax:** (817) 273-5110.
Website: www.texasrangers.com.

Ownership

Owner: Hicks Holdings.
Chairman of the Board: Tom Hicks.

BUSINESS OPERATIONS

Tom Hicks

Senior Executive VP: Jim Sundberg. **Executive VP, Hicks Holdings LLC:** Casey Shilts. **Executive VP, Sales:** Andy Silverman. **Executive VP, Ballpark Operations:** Rob Matwick. **Executive VP, Marketing/Community Development:** Dale Petroskey. **Executive VP, Communications:** John Blake. **Executive VP, Finance:** Kellie Fischer. **VP, Hicks Holdings LLC:** Thomas Hicks Jr. **Assistant VP, Rangers:** Alex Hicks.

Finance/Accounting

Assistant VP, Controller: Starr Pritchard. **Assistant Controller:** Donna Kee. **Payroll Manager:** Donna Ebersole.

Human Resources/Legal/Information Technology

VP, Human Resources: Terry Turner. **Associate Counsel:** Kate Jett. **Manager, Benefits/Compensation:** Carla Clack. **Supervisor, Staffing/Development:** Shannon Cain.

Assistant Vice President, Information Technology: Mike Bullock. **Manager, Application Systems:** Bill Edevane.

Business/Event Operations

VP, Event Operations/Security: John Hardin. **Senior Director, Customer Service:** Donnie Pordash. **Director, Event Operations:** Danielle Cornwell.

Communications/Community Relations

Phone: (817) 273-5203. **Fax:** (817) 273-5110.

Senior Director, Media Relations: Rich Rice. **Senior Director, Player/Community Relations:** Taunee Taylor. **Assistant Director, Player/Community Relations:** Jenny Martin. **Director, Publications:** Matthew Postins. **Director, Broadcasting:** Angie Swint. **Assistant, Media Relations:** Court Berry-Tripp. **Assistant, Community Relations:** Ashleigh Greathouse. **Coordinator, Media Relations:** Brian SanFilippo. **Coordinator, Communications:** Deanna Damon.

Facilities

Assistant VP, Facilities Operations: Gib Searight. **Director, Grounds:** Dennis Klein. **Director, Maintenance/MEP:** Mike Call.

Marketing/Community Development

Assistant VP, Marketing: Kelly Calvert. **Senior Creative Director, Graphic Design:** Rainer Uhlir. **Director, Media:** Heidi Benoit. **Creative Director, Media:** Rush Olson. **Manager, Marketing:** Kaylan Eastepp. **VP, Community Development:** Norm Lyons. **Executive Director, Foundation/Hispanic Marketing:** Karin Morris.

Merchandising

Assistant VP, Merchandising: Diane Atkinson. **Director, Merchandising:** Stephen Moore. **Manager, Dallas Merchandise Store:** Chris LeBlanc. **Manager, Warehouse Operations:** Sean Parent. **Retail Manager:** Eric Garcia. **Assistant Retail Manager:** Randy Wolveck. **Grand Slam Store Manager:** John Reneau.

Ticket Sales

VP, Suite Sales: Paige Farragut. **Vice President, Dallas Sales:** Dan Fine. **Senior Director, Baseball Programs/Youth Ballpark/Corporate Clinics:** Breon Dennis. **Director, Inside Sales:** Chip Kisabeth. **Director, Dallas Sales:** Monroe Good. **Director, Fort Worth Sales:** Coty Kaptain. **Manager, Group Sales:** Pat Harvey. **Manager, Season Tickets:** Troy King.

Ticket Operations

Director, Ticket Operations: Mike Lentz. **Manager, Ticket Operations:** Jordan Jackson. **Coordinator, Season Tickets:** Ben Rogers. **Coordinator, Group Tickets:** Cale Vennum. **Coordinator, Ticket Accounting Administration:** Ranae Lewis.

GENERAL INFORMATION

Stadium (year opened): Rangers Ballpark in Arlington (1994).
Home Dugout: First Base. **Playing Surface:** Grass.
Team Colors: Royal blue and red.
Player Representative: C.J. Wilson.
Driving Directions: From I-30, take Ballpark Way exit, south on Ballpark Way; From Route 360, take Randol Mill exit, west on Randol Mill.

Jon Daniels

BASEBALL OPERATIONS

Telephone: (817) 273-5222. **Fax:** (817) 273-5285.

General Manager: Jon Daniels.

Assistant GM: Thad Levine. **Senior Advisor to the GM:** John Hart. **Senior Director, Baseball Operations:** Don Welke. **Special Assistant to GM:** Jay Robertson. **Senior Advisor to GM:** Tom Giordano. **Senior Advisor, Arizona Operations/Pro Scouting:** Mel Didier. **Executive Assistant to GM:** Barbara Pappenfus.

Major League Staff

Manager: Ron Washington.

Coaches: Bench—Jackie Moore; Pitching—Mike Maddux; Batting—Rudy Jaramillo; First Base—Gary Pettis; Third Base—Dave Anderson; Bullpen—Andy Hawkins; Special Assignment Coach--Johnny Narron.

Medical, Training

Team Physician: Dr. Keith Meister. **Team Internist:** Dr. David Hunter. **Spine Consultant:** Dr. Andrew Dossett. **Head Trainer/Medical Director:** Jamie Reed. **Assistant Trainer:** Kevin Harmon. **Director, Strength/Conditioning:** Jose Vazquez.

Player Development

Telephone: (817) 273-5224. **Fax:** (817) 273-5285.

Director, Player Development: Scott Servais.

Director, Minor League Operations: John Lombardo.

Assistant, Player Development/Scouting: Todd Walther. **Manager, Cultural Enhancement:** Bill McLaughlin.

Roving Instructors: Danny Clark (pitching), Spike Owen (infield), Mike Boulanger (hitting), Keith Comstock (rehab pitching coach), Wayne Kirby (baserunning/outfield), Napoleon Pichardo (strength), Matthew Lucero (medical coordinator), Brian Bobier (rehab coordinator).

Manager, Minor League Complex Operations: Chris Guth. **Assistant Equipment Manager:** Brandon Boyd. **Arizona Clubhouse Manager:** Garret Kohler.

Farm System

Class	Club (League)	Manager	Coach	Pitching Coach
Triple-A	Oklahoma (PCL)	Bobby Jones	Scott Coolbaugh	Terry Clark
Double-A	Frisco (TL)	Mike Micucci	Brant Brown	Joe Slusarski
High A	Bakersfield (CAL)	Steve Buechele	Jason Wood	Dave Chavarria
Low A	Hickory (SAL)	Hector Ortiz	Brian Dayett	TBD
Short-season	Spokane (NWL)	Tim Hulett	Jason Hart	Jeff Andrews
Rookie	Rangers (AZL)	Bill Richardson	Josue Perez	J. Burgos/C. Pulido
Rookie	Rangers (DSL)	Jayce Tingler	Guillermo Mercedes	P. Blanco/J. Jaimes

Scouting

Telephone: (817) 273-5277. **Fax:** (817) 273-5285.

Director, Scouting: Ron Hopkins (Seattle, WA).

Director, Pro/International Scouting: A.J. **Preller. Assistant Director, International Scouting:** Mike Daly. **Assistant Director, Pro Scouting:** Josh Boyd. **Manager, Amateur Scouting:** Bobby Crook. **Assistant, Pro Scouting:** Matt Klotsche.

Professional Scouts: Mike Anderson (Austin, TX), Russ Ardolina (Rockville, MD), Keith Boeck (Chandler, AZ), Scot Engler (Montgomery, IL), Gary Rajsich (Arlington, TX).

National Crosschecker: Kip Fagg (Gilbert, AZ). **Central Crosschecker:** Mike Grouse (Olathe, KS). **Eastern Crosschecker:** Jake Krug. **Western Crosschecker:** Kevin Bootay (Sacramento, CA).

Area Scouts: Juan Alvarez (Miami, FL), Roger Coryell (Ypsilanti, MI), Jim Cuthbert (Chapel Hill, NC), Guy DeMutis (Windermere, FL), Jay Eddings (Sperry, OK), Steve Flores (Temecula, CA), Todd Guggiana (Long Beach, CA), Jay Heafner (Morris Plain, NJ), Derek Lee (Frankfurt, IL), Rick Matsko (New Brunswick, NJ), Gary McGraw (Gaston, OR), Butch Metzger (Sacramento, CA), John Poloni (Tarpon Springs, FL), Andy Pratt (Scottsdale, AZ), Dustin Smith (Emporia, KS), Randy Taylor (Katy, TX), Frankie Thon (Guaynabo, Puerto Rico), Jeff Wood (Birmingham, AL).

Director, Pacific Rim Operations: Jim Colborn. **Latin Coordinator:** Manny Batista. **Dominican Program Coordinator:** Danilo Troncosco. **International Scouts:** Rafic Saab (Venezuela), Pedro Avila (Venezuela), Chu Halabi (Curacao), Danilo Troncoso (Dominican Republic), Rodolfo Rosario (Dominican Republic), Eduardo Thomas (Panama), Joel Ronda (Puerto Rico).

Major League Club

Complex Address: Surprise Stadium, 15754 N. Bullard Ave., Surprise, AZ 85374. **Telephone:** (623) 266-8100. **Seating Capacity:** 10,714. **Location:** I-10 West to Route 101 North, 101 North to Bell Road, left at Bell for seven miles, stadium on left. **Hotel Address:** Windmill Suites at Sun City West, 12545 W. Bell Rd., Surprise, AZ 85374. **Telephone:** (623) 583-0133.

Minor League Clubs

Complex Address: Same as major league club.

Hotel Address: Hampton Inn, 2000 N. Litchfield Rd., Goodyear, AZ 85338. **Telephone:** (623) 536-1313; Holiday Inn Express, 1313 N. Litchfield Rd., Goodyear, AZ 85338.

2009 SCHEDULE

RANGERS BALLPARK

Standard Game Times: 7:05 p.m.; Sun. 1:05.

APRIL

6-9 . . . . Cleveland
10-12 . . . . at Detroit
13-15 . . . . Baltimore
17-19 . . . . Kansas City
21-23 . . . . at Toronto
24-27 . . . . . . .at Baltimore
28-30 . . . . Oakland

MAY

1-3 . . . . White Sox
4-7 . . . . at Oakland
8-10 . . . . at White Sx
12-14 . . . . Seattle
15-17 . . . . Angels
19-21 . . . . at Detroit
22-24 . . . . at Houston
25-27 . . . . Yankees
29-31 . . . . Oakland

JUNE

2-4 . . . . .at Yankees
5-7 . . . . at Boston
8-11 . . . . Toronto
12-14 . . . . Dodgers
16-18 . . . . Houston
19-21 . . . . at San Francisco
23-25 . . . . at Arizona
26-28 . . . . San Diego
29-30 . . . . Angels

JULY

1 . . . . Angels
3-5 . . . . Tampa Bay
6-8 . . . . at Angels
9-12 . . . . at Seattle
17-19 . . . . .Minnesota
20-22 . . . . Boston
24-26 . . . . . at Kansas City
27-29 . . . . Detroit
30-31 . . . . Seattle

AUGUST

1-2 . . . . Seattle
3-6 . . . . at Oakland
7-9 . . . . at Angels
11-13 . . . . at Cleveland
14-16 . . . . Boston
17-20 . . . . .Minnesota
21-23 . . . . . . .at Tampa Bay
25-27 . . . . .at Yankees
28-30 . . . . . . at Minnesota
31 . . . . Toronto

SEPTEMBER

1-2 . . . . Toronto
4-6 . . . . .at Baltimore
7-9 . . . . at Cleveland
11-13 . . . . Seattle
14-16 . . . . Oakland
18-20 . . . . Angels
21-24 . . . . at Oakland
25-27 . . . . Tampa Bay
28-30 . . . . at Angels

OCTOBER

1 . . . . at Angels
2-4 . . . . at Seattle

Toronto Blue Jays

Office/Mailing Address: 1 Blue Jays Way, Suite 3200, Toronto, Ontario M5V 1J1.

Telephone: (416) 341-1000. **Fax:** (416) 341-1250.

Website: www.bluejays.com.

Ownership

Operated by: Toronto Blue Jays Baseball Club.

Principal Owner: Rogers Communications Inc.

BUSINESS OPERATIONS

Paul Godfrey

President/CEO: Tony Viner.

Senior Vice President, Stadium Operations: Richard Wong. **VP, Special Projects:** Howard Starkman.

Finance

Vice President, Finance/Administration: John Boots. **Executive Administrative Assistant:** Donna Kuzoff. **Controller:** Lynda Kolody. **Director, Payroll/Benefits:** Brenda Dimmer. **Director, Risk Management:** Suzanne Joncas. **Financial Business Managers:** Leslie Galant-Gardiner, Tanya Proctor. **Manager, Ticket Receipts/Vault Services:** Joseph Roach. **Manager, Financial Planning:** Ciaran Keegan. **Manager, Stadium Payroll:** Sharon Dykstra. **Director, Human Resources:** Michelle Carter. **Coordinator, Human Resources:** Gurpreet Singh. **Director, Information Technology:** Jacques Farand. IT Project Manager: Anthony Miranda.

Marketing/Community Relations

Vice President, Marketing: Laurel Lindsay.

Executive Director, Jays Care Foundation: Danielle Silverstein. **Director, Community Relations:** Michael Volpatti. **Director, Player/Alumni Relations:** Jennifer Santamaria. **Executive Producer, Game Entertainment:** Deb Belinsky.

Vice President, Sales: Gary Murphy. **Director, Business Development:** John Griffin. **Director, Corporate Partnerships:** Robert Mackay. **Directors, Partnership Marketing:** Kelly Gianopoulos. **Krista Semotiuk.**

Communications

Telephone: (416) 341-1301/1302/1303. **Fax:** (416) 341-1250.

Vice President, Communications: Jay Stenhouse.

Manager, Baseball Information: Mal Romanin. **Manager, Communications:** Nadia Flaim. **Coordinator, Baseball Information:** Erik Grosman. **Coordinators, Communications:** Kendra Hunter, Sue Mallabon.

Stadium Operations

Vice President, Stadium Operations/Security: Mario Coutinho. **Executive Assistant, Stadium Operations/Security:** June Sym. **Head Groundskeeper:** Tom Farrell.

Ticketing

Telephone: (416) 341-1234. **Fax:** (416) 341-1177.

Vice President, Ticket Sales/Service: Jason Diplock. **Senior Adviser/Director, Special Projects:** Sheila Stella. **Director, Ticket Operations:** Doug Barr. **Director, Ticket Sales/Service:** Franc Rota.

Travel/Clubhouse

Manager, Team Travel: Mike Shaw.

Equipment Manager: Jeff Ross. **Clubhouse Manager:** Kevin Malloy. **Visiting Clubhouse Manager:** Len Frejlich. **Video Operations:** Robert Baumander. **Video Operations Assistant:** Brian Abraham.

GENERAL INFORMATION

Stadium (year opened): Rogers Centre (1989).

Home Dugout: Third base. **Playing Surface:** Field turf.

Team Colors: Blue, silver, graphite, black and white.

Player Representative: Unavailable.

Driving Directions: From west, take QEW/Gardiner Expressway eastbound and exit at Spadina Avenue, north on Spadina one block, right on Bremner Boulevard. From east, take Gardiner Expressway westbound and exit at Spadina Avenue, north on Spadina one block, right on Bremner Boulevard.

J.P. Ricciardi

BASEBALL OPERATIONS

Senior Vice President, Baseball Operations/General Manager: J.P. Ricciardi.

VP, Baseball Operations/Assistant GM: Alex Anthopoulos. **Assistant GM, Player Personnel:** Tony LaCava. **Special Assistant to GM:** Sal Butera. **Executive Assistant to GM:** Ainsley Doyle. **Executive Assistant, Major League Operations:** Heather Connolly. **Special Assistant:** Sal Butera.

Major League Staff

Manager: Cito Gaston.

Coaches: Bench—Brian Butterfield; Pitching—Brad Arnsberg; Hitting—Gene Tenace; First Base—Dwayne Murphy; Third Base—Nick Leyva; Bullpen—Bruce Walton.

Medical, Training

Medical Advisor: Dr. Bernie Gosevitz. **Team Physician:** Dr. Ron Taylor.

Head Trainer: George Poulis. **Assistant Trainer:** Dave Abraham. **Strength/Conditioning Coordinator:** Bryan King. **Director, Team Safety:** Ron Sandelli.

Player Development

Telephone: (727) 734-8007. **Fax:** (727) 734-8162.

Director, Player Development: Dick Scott.

Director, Employee Assistance Program: Ray Karesky.

Manager, Minor League Operations: Charlie Wilson. **Assistant, Latin American Operations:** Jeff Roemer. **Coordinator, Minor League Administration:** Joanna Nelson. **Administrative Assistant:** Kim Marsh.

Roving Instructors: Dane Johnson (pitching), Rick Langford (Rehab/Pitching Instruction), Chad Mottola (hitting), Mel Queen. **Minor League Coordinators:** Mike Frostad (training/rehab), Donovan Santas (strength/conditioning), Billy Wardlow (equipment).

Farm System

Class	Club (League)	Manager	Coach	Pitching Coach
Triple-A	Las Vegas (PCL)	Mike Basso	Ken Joyce	Dave LaRoche
Double-A	New Hampshire (EL)	Gary Cathcart	Paul Elliott	Tom Signore
High A	Dunedin (FSL)	Omar Malave	Al LeBoeuf	Darold Knowles
Low A	Lansing (MWL)	Clayton McCullough	Justin Mashore	Antonio Caceres
Short-season	Auburn (NYP)	Dennis Holmberg	Charlie Poe	Vince Horsman
Rookie	Blue Jays (GCL)	John Schneider	D. Pano/D. Solano	Pete Walker
Rookie	Blue Jays (DSL)	Miguel Bernard	Emilio De Los Santos	Oswaldo Peraza

Scouting

Telephone: (416) 341-1115. **Fax:** (416) 341-1245.

Director, Scouting: Jon Lalonde.

Assistant Director, Scouting: Andrew Tinnish. **Scouting Advisor:** Smoke Laval. **Scouting Coordinator:** Ryan Mittleman.

Professional Scouts: Tom Clark, Kimball Crossley, Jim D'Aloia, Rob Ducey, Steve Springer, Marc Tramuta. **Major League Scouts:** Mike Berger, Perry Minasian, Roy Smith.

National Crosscheckers: Bob Fontaine, Billy Gasparino, Mike Mangan, Tommy Tanous. **Area Scouts:** Chris Becerra (San Francisco, CA), Matt Briggs (Charlotte, NC), Tom Burns (Harrisburg, PA), Dan Cholowsky (Queen Creek, AZ), Joel Grampietro (Tampa, FL), Rick Ingalls (Long Beach, CA), Aaron Jersild (Houston, TX), Steve Miller (Chicago, IL), Ty Nichols (Broken Arrow, OK), Jorge Rivera (Puerto Nuevo, PR), Carlos Rodriguez (Miami, FL), Tim Rooney (Los Angeles, CA), Rob St. Julien (Lafayette, LA).

Director, Canadian Scouting: Kevin Briand. **Canadian Scouts:** Don Cowan (Delta, BC), Sean McCann (Toronto, ON), Jean Marc Mercier (Charlesbourg, PQ).

Director, Latin American Operations: Marco Paddy. **International Scouts:** Miguel Bernard (Dominican Republic), Robinson Garces (Venezuela), Rafael Moncada (Venezuela), Lorenzo Perez (Dominican Republic), Luis Rodriquez (Panama), Hilario Soriano (Dominican Republic), Greg Wade (Australia).

Spring Training

Stadium Address (first year): Knology Park (1977), 373 Douglas Ave. #A, Dunedin, FL 34698. **Telephone:** (727) 733-9302. **Seating Capacity:** 5,509. **Location:** From I-275, north on Highway 19, left on Sunset Point Road for 4 miles, right on Douglas Avenue, stadium one mile on right.

Minor League Clubs

Complex Address: Bobby Mattick Training Center at Englebert Complex, 1700 Solon Ave., Dunedin, FL 34698. **Telephone:** (727) 743-8007. **Hotel Address:** Red Roof Inn, 3200 U.S. 19 N., Clearwater, FL 34684. **Telephone:** (727) 786-2529.

2009 SCHEDULE

ROGERS CENTRE

Standard Game Times:
7:07 p.m.; Sun. 1:07.

APRIL

6-9 . . . . Detroit
10-12 . . . . . . at Cleveland
13-16 . . . . . . at Minnesota
17-19 . . . . Oakland
21-23 . . . . Texas
24-26 . . . . . . at White Sox
27-30 . . . . . at Kansas City

MAY

1-3 . . . . Baltimore
4-5 . . . . Cleveland
6-7 . . . . at Angels
8-10 . . . . at Oakland
12-14 . . . . Yankees
15-18 . . . . White Sox
19-21 . . . . at Boston
22-24 . . . . at Atlanta
25-27 . . . . at Baltimore
29-31 . . . . Boston

JUNE

2-4 . . . . Angels
5-7 . . . . Kansas City
8-11 . . . . at Rangers
12-14 . . . . Marlins
16-18 . . . . . at Philadelphia
19-21 . . . . . at Washington
23-25 . . . . Cincinnati
26-28 . . . . Philadelphia
29-30 . . . . Tampa Bay

JULY

1 . . . . Tampa Bay
3-6 . . . . Yankees
7-9 . . . . at Tampa Bay
10-12 . . . . at Baltimore
17-19 . . . . Boston
21-23 . . . . Cleveland
24-26 . . . . Tampa Bay
27-29 . . . . at Seattle
31 . . . . at Oakland

AUGUST

1-2 . . . . at Oakland
4-5 . . . . Yankees
7-9 . . . . Baltimore
10-12 . . . . at Yankees
14-16 . . . . at Tampa Bay
18-20 . . . . Boston
21-23 . . . . Angels
24-26 . . . . Tampa Bay
28-30 . . . . at Boston
31 . . . . at Texas

SEPTEMBER

1-2 . . . . at Texas
3-6 . . . . Yankees
7-10 . . . . Minnesota
11-14 . . . . at Detroit
15-16 . . . . at Yankees
18-20 . . . . at Tampa Bay
21-23 . . . . Baltimore
24-27 . . . . Seattle
28-30 . . . . at Boston

OCTOBER

2-4 . . . . at Baltimore

Washington Nationals

Office Address: 1500 South Capitol St. SE, Washington, DC 20003.
Telephone: (202) 640-7000. **Fax:** (202) 547-0025.
Website: www.nationals.com

Ownership

Managing Principal Owner: Theodore Lerner.

Principal Owners: Annette Lerner, Mark Lerner, Marla Lerner Tanenbaum, Debra Lerner Cohen, Robert Tanenbaum, Edward Cohen, Judy Lenkin Lerner.

Business Operations

President: Stan Kasten. **Executive Vice President:** Bob Wolfe.

Executive Assistant to President/Executive Vice President: Cheryl Stevens. **MLB Executive Associate:** Ramin Tabib.

Stan Kasten

Legal/Business Affairs

Senior Director, Business Development: Catherine Silver. **Director, Ballpark Enterprises:** Heather Westrom. **Vice President, Club Counsel:** Damon Jones. **Assistant Counsel:** Amy Inlander.

Finance/Human Resources

Chief Financial Officer: Lori Creasy. **Controller:** Ted Towne. **Director, Accounting:** Kelly Pitchford. **Senior Accountants:** Ross Hollander, Rachel Proctor. **Manager, Payroll:** Mario Munoz. **Baseball Analyst:** Michael Page. **Vice President, Human Resources:** Bettina Deynes, Benefits Administrator: Stephanie Giroux, Assistant, Human Resources: Alan Gromest.

Media Relations/Communications

Senior Director, Baseball Media Relations: John Dever. **Director, Baseball Media Relations:** Mike Gazda. **Coordinator, Baseball Media Relations:** Bill Gluvna. **Vice President, Communications:** Chartese Burnett. **Manager, Communications:** Lisa Pagano. **Assistant Communications:** Christina Miller.

Community Relations

Director, Community Relations: Barbra Silva. **Senior Vice President, External Affairs:** Alphonso Maldon, Jr. **Vice President, Ballpark District:** Gregory McCarthy. **Coordinator, Community Relations:** Nadia Wajid. **Chair, Washington Nationals Dream Foundation:** Marla Lerner Tanenbaum.

Sales/Marketing

Vice President, Marketing/Broadcasting: John Guagliano. **Senior Director, Production/Entertainment:** Jacqueline Coleman. **Manager, Creative Services/Broadcasting:** Daniel Kasper. **Manager, Promotions/Activation:** Lauren Prober. **Manager, Special Events:** Christine O'Connor. **Scoreboard Producer:** Dave Lundin. **Associate Producer:** Benjamin Smith. **Production Coordinator:** Kellee Mickens, Graphic Designer: Eric Soderberg. **Coordinator, Entertainment:** Thomas Davis.

Vice President, Corporate Partnerships: Tod Rosensweig. **Director, Partner Service:** Allison Grinham.

Ticketing

Executive Director, Sales: Chris Gargani. **Director, Ticket Sales:** Brian Lowe. **Senior Director, Client Services:** Stacey Marthaler. **Manager, Customer Service:** Andy Burns. **Manager, Ticket Services:** Dave Wredberg. **Director, Ticket Operations:** Derek Younger. **Manager, Ticket Operations:** Peter Wallace. **Manager, Box Office:** Tyler Hubbard.

Ballpark Operations

Director, Ballpark Operations: Matthew Blush. **Director, Security:** Robert Campbell. **Manager, Guest Services:** Kynneth Sutton. **Manager, Premium Client Relations:** Jonathan Stahl. **Manager, Premium Event Services:** Gabrielle Thibodeau. **Coordinators, Ballpark Operations:** Reemberto Rodriguez, Adam Lasky. **Director, Florida Operations:** Thomas Bell. **Manager, Facility:** Philip Laws. **Head Groundskeeper:** Larry DiVito. **Manager, Shipping/Receiving:** Javier Ferreira.

Travel/Clubhouse

Director, Team Travel: Rob McDonald. **Clubhouse Manager:** Mike Wallace. **Visiting Clubhouse Manager:** Matt Rosenthal.

GENERAL INFORMATION

Stadium (year opened): Nationals Park (2008).
Home Dugout: First Base. **Playing Surface:** Grass.
Team Colors: Red, white and blue.
Player Representative: Unavailable.
Driving Directions: From Maryland, use the Beltway, take 295 southbound to the Howard Road exit (3B). Go across the South Capitol Street bridge (north). Turn right on either Potomac Avenue, N Street or M Street (east) toward designated lots and garages. From Virginia, take the 14th Street bridge and merge onto I-395 northbound to the Maine Avenue exit. Follow Maine Avenue until it becomes M Street. Follow M Street across South Capitol Street and turn right on either Van Street or 1st Street SE toward the lots and garages.

Jim Bowden

BASEBALL OPERATIONS

Senior Vice President/General Manager: Jim Bowden. **Assistant GM/VP, Baseball Operations:** Mike Rizzo. **Assistant GM/VP, Player Development:** Bob Boone. **Director, Baseball Operations:** Brian Parker. **Assistant Director, Baseball Operations:** Adam Cromie. **Assistant GM, Baseball Administration:** Squire Galbreath. **Executive Assistant to GM:** Harolyn Cardozo. **Special Assistants to GM:** Jose Rijo, Pat Corrales, Moose Stubing.

Major League Staff

Manager: Manny Acta.

Coaches: Bench—Jim Riggleman; Pitching—Randy St. Claire; Hitting—Rick Eckstein; First Base—Marquis Grissom; Third Base—Pat Listach; Bullpen—Randy Knorr.

Medical, Training

Team Medical Director: Dr. Wiemi Duoghui. **Head Trainer:** Lee Kuntz. **Assistant Trainer:** Mike McGowen. **Strength/Conditioning Coach:** John Philbin.

Player Development

Director, Player Development: Bobby Williams. **Assistant Director, Player Development:** Mark Scialabba. **Special Assistant, Player Development:** Devon White. **Coordinator, Scouting/Player Development:** Jason Choi. **Coordinator, Minor League Operations:** Ryan Thomas.

Field Coordinator: Jeff Garber. **Roving Coordinators:** Ralph Dickeson (hitting), Spin Williams (pitching), Mark Grater (rehab pitching coordinator), Jose Cardenal (outfield/baserunning), Bobby Grater (catching), Landon Randes (strength/conditioning), Jose Baez (Dominican). **Minor league equipment/clubhouse:** John Mullin.

Farm System

Class	Club	Manager	Coach(es)	Pitching Coach
Triple-A	Syracuse (IL)	Tim Foli	Darnell Coles	Steve McCatty
Double-A	Harrisburg (EL)	John Stearns	Troy Gingrich	Randy Tomlin
High A	Potomac (CL)	Trent Jewett	Jerry Browne	Paul Menhart
Low A	Hagerstown (SAL)	Matt LeCroy	T. Tarasco/R. Aviles	Rich Gale
Short-season	Vermont (NYP)	Jeff Garber	Unavailable	Franklyn Bravo
Rookie	Nationals (GCL)	Bobby Henley	Paul Sanagorski	Joel Sanchez

Scouting

Director, Scouting: Dana Brown. **Assistant Director, Scouting/National Crosschecker:** Kris Kline (Clearwater, FL). **Assistant, Scouting:** Reed Dunn. **Special Assignment/Pro Scouts:** Bill Singer (Osprey, FL), Jeff Zona (Mechanicsville, VA).

Advance Scout: Wade Taylor (Orlando, FL).

National Crosschecker: Deric Ladnier (Pensacola, FL). **Regional Crosscheckers:** East—Marteese Robinson (Mechanicsville, VA); Midwest—Jimmy Gonzales (San Antonio, TX); West—Kris Kline (Anthem, AZ).

Area Scouts: Mike Alberts (Worcester, MA), Tony Arango (Davie, FL), Steve Arnieri (Barrington, IL), Marc Baca (Temecula, CA), Denis Boucher (Montreal, QC), Ryan Fox (Broken Arrow, OK), Bob Hamelin (Concord, NC), Kerrick Jackson (Kirkwood, MO), Craig Kornfield (Rancho Santa Margarita, CA), Bob Laurie (Plano, TX), Eric Robinson (Hiram, GA), Alex Smith (Abingdon, MD), Mitch Sokol (Phoenix, AZ), Paul Tinnel (Bradenton, FL), Tyler Wilt (Montgomery, TX).

Part-Time Scout: Wilmer Reid (Philadelphia, PA).

International Scouts: Delvy Santiago (Puerto Rico), Moises De La Mota (Dominican Republic), Bernadino Valera (Dominican Republican), Angel Ozuna (Dominican Republic).

Spring Training

Complex Address (first year): Space Coast Stadium (2003), 5800 Stadium Pkwy., Viera, FL 32940. **Telephone:** (321) 633-9200. **Seating Capacity:** 8,100. **Location:** I-95 southbound to Fiske Blvd. (exit 74), south on Fiske/Stadium Parkway to stadium; I-95 northbound to State Road #509/Wickham Road (exit 73), left off exit, right on Lake Andrew Drive; turn right on Stadium Parkway, stadium is 1/2 mile on left.

Hotel Address: Melbourne Airport Hilton, 200 Rialto Place, Melbourne, FL 32901. **Telephone:** (321) 768-0200.

Minor League Clubs

Complex Address: Carl Barger Complex, 5600 Stadium Pkwy., Viera, FL 32940. **Telephone:** (321) 633-8119. **Hotel Address:** Imperial Hotel & Conference Center, 8298 N. Wickman Rd., Viera, FL 32940. **Telephone:** (321) 255-0077.

2009 SCHEDULE

NATIONALS PARK

Standard Game Times:
7:05 p.m.; Sun. 1:35

APRIL

6-8 . . . . at Florida
10-12 . . . . at Atlanta
13 . . . . Philadelphia
15-16 . . . . . . Philadelphia
17-19 . . . . Florida
20-22 . . . . Atlanta
24-26 . . . . at Mets
27-29 . . . . at Philadelphia
30 . . . . St. Louis

MAY

1-3 . . . . St. Louis
4-5 . . . . Houston
6-7 . . . . at Dodgers
8-10 . . . . at Arizona
11-13 . . . . at San Francisco
15-17 . . . . . . Philadelphia
18-21 . . . . Pittsburgh
22-24 . . . . Baltimore
25-27 . . . . at Mets
29-31 . . . . at Philadelphia

JUNE

2-4 . . . . San Francisco
5-7 . . . . Mets
9-11 . . . . Cincinnati
12-14 . . . . . at Tampa Bay
16-18 . . . . at Yankees
19-21 . . . . Toronto
23-25 . . . . Boston
26-28 . . . . . . at Baltimore
29-30 . . . . at Florida

JULY

1 . . . . at Florida
3-5 . . . . Atlanta
6-8 . . . . at Colorado
9-12 . . . . at Houston
16-19 . . . . Cubs
20-22 . . . . Mets
24-26 . . . . San Diego
27-30 . . . . . at Milwaukee
31 . . . . at Pittsburgh

AUGUST

1-3 . . . . at Pittsburgh
4-6 . . . . Florida
7-9 . . . . Arizona
11-12 . . . . at Atlanta
13-16 . . . . . . at Cincinnati
18-20 . . . . Colorado
21-24 . . . . Milwaukee
25-27 . . . . at Cubs
28-30 . . . . at St. Louis
31 . . . . at San Diego

SEPTEMBER

1-2 . . . . at San Diego
4-6 . . . . Florida
8-10 . . . . Philadelphia
11-13 . . . . at Florida
15-17 . . . . at Philadelphia
18-20 . . . . at Mets
22-24 . . . . Dodgers
25-27 . . . . Atlanta
28-30 . . . . Mets

OCTOBER

1-4 . . . . at Atlanta

MEDIA INFORMATION

LOCAL MEDIA INFORMATION

AMERICAN LEAGUE

BALTIMORE ORIOLES

Radio Announcers: Joe Angel, Fred Manfra. **Flagship Station:** WHFS-FM (105.7).

TV Announcers: Jim Hunter, Jim Palmer, Buck Martinez, Gary Thorne. **Flagship Station:** Mid-Atlantic Sports Network (MASN).

Newspapers, Daily Coverage (*national/beat writers): Baltimore Sun (*Dan Connolly, Jeff Zerbiec), Washington Post (Marc Carig, *Dave Sheinin), Frederick News Post (Stan Goldberg), Carroll County Times (Josh Land). **MLB.com:** Spencer Fordin.

BOSTON RED SOX

Radio Announcers: Joe Castiglione, Dave O'Brien. **Flagship Station:** WRKO (680 AM).

TV Announcers: Don Orsillo, Jerry Remy. **Flagship Station:** New England Sports Network (regional cable).

Spanish Radio Announcers: Uri Berenguer, Juan Carlos Baez. **Flagship Station:** WROL (950 AM)

Newspapers, Daily Coverage (*national/beat writers): Boston Globe (Amalie Benjamin, *Nick Cafardo), Boston Herald (Rob Bradford, Jeff Horrigan, Michael Silverman), Providence Journal (Steve Krasner, Sean McAdam), Worcester Telegram & Gazette (Bill Ballou, Phil O'Neill), Hartford Courant (Jeff Goldberg, Paul Doyle). **MLB.com:** Ian Browne.

CHICAGO WHITE SOX

Radio Announcers: Steve Stone, Ed Farmer. **Flagship Station:** WMVP/ESPN Radio 1000-AM.

TV Announcers: Ken Harrelson, Darrin Jackson. **Flagship Stations:** WGN TV-9, WCIU-TV, Comcast Sports Net (regional cable).

Newspapers, Daily Coverage (*national/beat writers): Chicago Sun-Times (Joe Cowley), Chicago Tribune (Mark Gonzales), Daily Herald (Scot Gregor). **MLB.com:** Scott Merkin.

CLEVELAND INDIANS

Radio Announcers: Tom Hamilton, Mike Hegan. **Flagship Station:** WTAM 1100-AM.

TV Announcers: Rick Manning, Matt Underwood. **Flagship Station:** SportsTime Ohio.

Newspapers, Daily Coverage (beat writers): Cleveland Plain Dealer (Paul Hoynes), Lake County News-Herald (Jim Ingraham), Akron Beacon-Journal (Sheldon Ocker). **MLB.com:** Anthony Castrovince.

DETROIT TIGERS

Radio Announcers: Dan Dickerson, Jim Price. **Flagship Station:** WXYT 1270-AM.

TV Announcers: Rod Allen, Mario Impemba. **Flagship Station:** Fox Sports Net Detroit (regional cable).

Newspapers, Daily Coverage (beat writers): Detroit Free Press (John Lowe, Jon Paul Morosi), Detroit News (Tom Gage), Oakland Press (Jim Hawkins), Booth Group (Danny Knobler). **MLB.com:** Jason Beck.

KANSAS CITY ROYALS

Radio Announcers: Denny Matthews, Bob Davis. **Kansas City affiliate:** KCSP 610-AM.

TV Announcers: Ryan Lefebvre, Paul Splittorff. **Flagship Stations:** Royals Sports Television Network.

Newspapers, Daily Coverage (beat writers): Kansas City Star (Bob Dutton). **MLB.com:** Dick Kaegel.

LOS ANGELES ANGELS

Radio Announcers: Rory Markas, Terry Smith. **Spanish**— Jose Mota. **Flagship Station:** ESPN Radio 710-AM, AM 830 (Spanish).

TV Announcers: Rex Hudler, Steve Physioc, Mark Gubicza. **Flagship Stations:** FSN West (regional cable).

Newspapers, Daily Coverage (*national/beat writers): Los Angeles Times (Kevin Baxter, Mike DiGiovanna), Orange County Register (Bill Plunkett), Riverside Press Enterprise (Matt Hurst), San Gabriel Valley Tribune/LA News Group (Doug Padilla). **MLB.com:** Lyle Spencer.

MINNESOTA TWINS

Radio Announcers: John Gordon, Dan Gladden, Kris Atteberry. **Flagship Station:** KSTP-1500.

TV Announcers: Bert Blyleven, Dick Bremer. **Flagship Station:** Fox Sports Net North.

Newspapers, Daily Coverage (beat writers): St. Paul Pioneer Press (Phil Miller), Minneapolis Star Tribune (LaVelle Neal, Joe Christensen). **MLB.com:** Kelly Thesier.

NEW YORK YANKEES

Radio Announcers: John Sterling, Suzyn Waldman.

Flagship Station: WCBS 880-AM.

TV Announcers: Michael Kay, Paul O'Neill, Ken Singleton.

Flagship Stations: YES Network (Yankees Entertainment & Sports).

Newspapers, Daily Coverage (beat writers): New York Daily News (Mark Feinsand), New York Post (George King), New York Times (Tyler Kepner), Newark Star-Ledger (Ed Price), The Bergen Record (Pete Caldera), Newsday (Kat O'Brien), Hartford Courant (Dom Amore), The Journal News (Pete Abraham). **MLB.com:** Brian Hoch.

OAKLAND ATHLETICS

Radio Announcers: Vince Cotroneo, Ray Fosse, Ken Korach. **Flagship Station:** FREE FM 106.9, KYCY AM 1550

TV Announcers: Ray Fosse, Glen Kuiper. **Flagship Stations:** KICU, FOX Sports Net Bay Area (regional cable).

Newspapers, Daily Coverage (*national/beat writers): San Francisco Chronicle (*John Shea, Susan Slusser), Oakland Tribune (Josh Suchon), Contra Costa Times (*Rick Hurd), San Jose Mercury News (*Dan Brown), Sacramento Bee (Paul

Gutierrez), Santa Rosa Press Democrat (Jeff Fletcher). **MLB.com:** Mychael Urban.

SEATTLE MARINERS

TV/Radio Announcers: Mike Blowers, Dave Niehaus, Rick Rizzs, Dave Simms

Flagship Stations: KOMO 1000-AM (radio), FOX Sports Net Northwest (TV).

Newspapers, Daily Coverage (*national/beat writers): Seattle Times (Geoff Baker, *Larry Stone), Seattle Post-Intelligencer (John Hickey), Tacoma News Tribune (Ryan Divish, Larry Larue), The Everett Herald (Kirby Arnold), Kyodo News (Keizo Konishi), Daily Sports (Nobuyuki Kobayashi). **MLB.com:** Jim Street.

TAMPA BAY RAYS

Radio Announcers: Andy Freed, Dave Wills. **Flagship Station:** WHNZ 1250 AM.

TV Announcers: Dewayne Staats, Todd Kalas. **Flagship Stations:** FSN FLORIDA (regional cable), PAX-TV.

Spanish Radio Announcers: Enrique Oliu, Ricardo Taveras. **Flagship Station:** WGES (680 AM)

Newspapers, Daily Coverage (beat writers): St. Petersburg Times (Marc Topkin, Ed Encina), Tampa Tribune (Marc Lancaster, Carter Gaddis), Bradenton Herald (Roger Mooney), Port Charlotte Sun-Herald (John Fineran), Lakeland Ledger (Dick Scanlon), Sarasota Herald-Tribune (Dennis Maffezoli). **MLB.com:** Bill Chastain.

TEXAS RANGERS

Radio Announcers: Eric Nadel, Victor Rojas; Spanish—Eleno Ornelas, Jose Guzman. **Flagship Station:** KRLD 1080-AM, KESS 1270-AM (Spanish).

TV Announcers: Josh Lewin, Tom Grieve. **Flagship Stations:** KDFI, KDFW, Fox Sports Southwest (regional cable).

Newspapers, Daily Coverage (beat writers): Fort Worth Star-Telegram (Jeff Wilson). **MLB.com:** T.R. Sullivan.

TORONTO BLUE JAYS

Radio Announcers: Jerry Howarth, Mike Wilner, Alan Ashby. **Flagship Station:** THE FAN 590-AM.

TV Announcers: Rogers SportsNet—Jamie Campbell, Pat Tabler, Rance Mulliniks, Darrin Fletcher. TSN—Rod Black, Pat Tabler. **Flagship Stations:** Rogers SportsNet, The Sports Network.

Newspapers, Daily Coverage (*national/beat writers): Toronto Sun (Mike Rutsey, *Bob Elliott, Mike Ganter), Toronto Star (*Richard Griffin, Cathal Kelly, Alan Ryan, Mark Zwolinski), Globe and Mail (Robert MacLeod), National Post (John Lott, Jeremy Sandler). **MLB.com:** Jordan Bastian.

NATIONAL LEAGUE

ARIZONA DIAMONDBACKS

Radio Announcers: Greg Schulte, Tom Candiotti, Jeff Munn, Spanish—Miguel Quintana, Oscar Soria, Richard Saenz, Arturo Ochoa. **Flagship Stations:** KTAR 620-AM, KSUN 1400-AM (Spanish).

TV Announcers: Daron Sutton, Mark Grace, Greg Schulte, Joe Garagiola. **Flagship Stations:** KTVK-TV 3, FSN Arizona (regional cable).

Newspapers, Daily Coverage (beat writers): Arizona Republic (Nick Piecoro), East Valley Tribune (Jack Magruder), Arizona Daily Star, Tucson Citizen (Ken Brazzle). **MLB.com:** Steve Gilbert.

ATLANTA BRAVES

Radio Announcers: Pete Van Wieren.

Flagship Station: WGST 640-AM & 94.9 FM The Bull. **Spanish:** Pete Manzano, Fernando Palacios.

TV Announcers: FSN South and SportsSouth—Joe Simpson, Jon "Boog" Sciambi.

Fox Sports Net South and SportSouth -Joe Simpson and Jon Sciambi.

Flagship Stations: TBS (national cable); Fox Sports Net South, SportSouth (regional cable).

Newspapers, Daily Coverage (*national/beat writers): Atlanta Journal-Constitution (*Carroll Rogers, Dave O'Brien), Morris News Service (*Travis Haney). **MLB.com:** Mark Bowman.

CHICAGO CUBS

Radio Announcers: Pat Hughes, Ron Santo. **Flagship Station:** WGN 720-AM.

TV Announcers: Len Kasper, Bob Brenly. **Flagship Stations:** WGN Channel 9 (national cable), Comcast Sports Net Chicago (regional cable), WCIU-TV Channel 26.

Newspapers, Daily Coverage (*national/beat writers): Chicago Tribune (*Phil Rogers, *Dave Van Dyck, Paul Sullivan), Chicago Sun-Times (*Chris De Luca, Gordon Wittenmyer), Arlington Heights Daily Herald (Bruce Miles). **MLB.com:** Carrie Muskat.

CINCINNATI REDS

Radio Announcers: Marty Brennaman, Thom Brennaman, Jeff Brantley. **Flagship Station:** WLW 700-AM.

TV Announcers: George Grande, Chris Welsh, Thom Brennaman, Jeff Brantley. **Flagship Station:** FSN Ohio (regional cable).

Newspapers, Daily Coverage (beat writers): Cincinnati Enquirer (John Fay), Cincinnati Post (C. Trent Rosecrans), Dayton Daily News (Hal McCoy), Columbus Dispatch (Jim Massie). **MLB.com:** Mark Sheldon.

COLORADO ROCKIES

Radio Announcers: Jack Corrigan, Jeff Kingery. **Flagship Station:** KOA 850-AM.

Spanish Radio Announcers : Tony Guevara.

TV Announcers: Drew Goodman, George Frazier, Jeff Huson. **Flagship Stations:** KWGN, 2, WB, FSN Rocky Mountain (regional cable).

Newspapers, Daily Coverage (beat writers): Rocky Mountain News (*Tracy Ringolsby, Jack Etkin), Denver Post (Troy Renck, Patrick Saunders). **MLB.com:** Thomas Harding.

FLORIDA MARLINS

Radio Announcers: Dave Van Horne, Glenn Geffner. **Flagship Stations:** WQAM 560-AM, WQBA 1140-AM (Spanish).

Spanish Radio Announcers: Felo Ramirez, Yiky Quintana.

TV Announcers: Tommy Hutton, Rich Waltz. **Spanish TV Announcers:** Cookie Rojas, Raul Striker Jr.

Flagship Stations: FSN Florida, Sun Sports (regional cable).

Newspapers, Daily Coverage (*national/beat writers): Miami Herald (Clark Spencer, Mike Phillips), Fort Lauderdale Sun-Sentinel (Mike Berardino, Juan Rodriguez), Palm Beach Post (Joe Capozzi). **MLB.com:** Joe Frisaro

HOUSTON ASTROS

Radio Announcers: Brett Dolan, Milo Hamilton, Dave Raymond. **Spanish:** Alex Trevino, Francisco Romero. **Flagship Stations:** KTRH 740-AM, KLAT 1010-AM (Spanish).

TV Announcers: Bill Brown, Jim Deshaies. **Flagship Station:** Fox Sports Net (regional cable).

Newspapers, Daily Coverage (beat writers): Houston Chronicle (*Jesus Ortiz, Brian McTaggart), The Herald Coaster (Bill Hartman). **MLB.com:** Alyson Footer, Jim Molony.

LOS ANGELES DODGERS

Radio Announcers: Vin Scully, Rick Monday, Charley Steiner, Jerry Reuss; Spanish—Jaime Jarrin, Fernando Valenzuela, Pepe Yniguez. **Flagship Stations:** KFWB 980-AM, KWKW 1330-AM (Spanish).

TV Announcers: Vin Scully, Steve Lyons, Charley Steiner. **Flagship Stations:** KCAL 9, Fox Sports Net Prime Ticket (regional cable).

Newspapers, Daily Coverage (*national/beat writers): Los Angeles Times (Kevin Baxter, Dylan Hernandez), South Bay Daily Breeze (Bill Cizek), Los Angeles Daily News (Tony Jackson), Orange County Register (Al Balderas), Riverside Press-Enterprise (Diamond Leung). Spanish—La Opinion (Carlos Alvarado). **MLB.com:** Ken Gurnick.

MILWAUKEE BREWERS

Radio Announcers: Bob Uecker. **Flagship Station:** WTMJ 620-AM.

TV Announcers: Bill Schroeder, Brian Anderson. **Flagship Station:** Fox Sports Net North.

Newspapers, Daily Coverage (beat writers): Milwaukee Journal Sentinel (Tom Haudricourt), Wisconsin State Journal (Vic Feuerherd), Capital Times (Dennis Semrau). **MLB.com:** Adam McCalvy.

NEW YORK METS

Radio Announcers: Howie Rose, Ed Coleman. **Flagship Station:** WFAN 660-AM.

TV Announcers: Gary Cohen, Keith Hernandez, Ron Darling, Ralph Kiner, Kevin Burkhardt. **Flagship Stations:** CW11-TV, Sports Net New York (regional cable).

Newspapers, Daily Coverage (*national/beat writers): New York Times (*Jack Curry, Ben Shpigel), New York Daily News (*Bill Madden, *John Harper, *Anthony McCarron, Adam Rubin), New York Post (*Joel Sherman), Newsday (*Ken Davidoff, Dave Lennon), Newark Star-Ledger (*Dan Graziano), The Bergen Record (*Bob Klapisch, Steve Popper), The Journal News (John Delcos). **MLB.com:** Marty Noble.

PHILADELPHIA PHILLIES

Radio Announcers: Larry Andersen, Scott Franzke, Harry Kalas, Gary Matthews. **Flagship Stations:** WPHT 1210-AM.

TV Announcers: Larry Andersen, Harry Kalas, Gary Matthews, Chris Wheeler. **Flagship Stations:** WPSG CW 57, Comcast SportsNet (regional cable).

Newspapers, Daily Coverage (*national/beat writers): Philadelphia Inquirer (Todd Zolecki, *Jim Salisbury), Philadelphia Daily News (*Paul Hagen), Bucks County Courier Times (Randy Miller), Delaware County Times (Ryan Lawrence), Wilmington News-Journal (Scott Lauber), The Morning Call (Stephen Miller). **MLB.com:** Ken Mandel.

PITTSBURGH PIRATES

Radio Announcers: Steve Blass, Greg Brown, Bob Walk, John Wehner. **Flagship Station:** WPGB 104.7 FM.

TV Announcers: Tim Neverett, Steve Blass, Greg Brown, Bob Walk, John Wehner. **Flagship Station:** Fox Sports Net Pittsburgh (regional cable).

Newspapers, Daily Coverage (beat writers): Pittsburgh Post-Gazette (Dejan Kovacevic), Pittsburgh Tribune-Review (Rob Biertempfel), Beaver County Times (John Perrotto). **MLB.com:** Jenifer Langosch.

ST. LOUIS CARDINALS

Radio Announcers: Mike Shannon, John Rooney. **Flagship Station:** KTRS 550-AM.

TV Announcers: Al Hrabosky, Dan McLaughlin, Rick Horton, Jay Randolph. **Flagship Stations:** KSDK Channel 5, Fox Sports Midwest (regional cable).

Newspapers, Daily Coverage (beat writers): St. Louis Post-Dispatch (Joe Strauss, Rick Hummel, Derrick Goold), Belleville, Ill., News-Democrat (David Wilhelm). **MLB.com:** Matthew Leach.

SAN DIEGO PADRES

Radio Announcers: Ted Leitner, Jerry Coleman Flagship Station: XX Sports Radio 105.7 FM /1090-AM.

TV Announcers: Mark Grant, Tony Gwynn. **Flagship Station:** Channel 4 San Diego (cable).

Newspapers, Daily Coverage (beat writers): San Diego Union-Tribune (Tom Krasovic, Bill Center), North County Times (Dan Hayes, John Maffei). **MLB.com:** Corey Brock.

SAN FRANCISCO GIANTS

Radio Announcers: Mike Krukow, Duane Kuiper, Jon Miller, Greg Papa, Dave Flemming. **Spanish:** Erwin Higueros. **Flagship Station:** KNBR 680-AM (English); KLOK-1170 AM (Spanish).

TV Announcers: FSN Bay Area—Mike Krukow, Duane Kuiper; KTVU-FOX 2—Jon Miller, Mike Krukow, Duane Kuiper,

Greg Papa. **Spanish:** Tito Fuentes. **Flagship Stations:** KTVU-FOX 2, FSN Bay Area (regional cable).

Newspapers, Daily Coverage (*national/beat writers): San Francisco Chronicle (Henry Schulman, *John Shea), San Jose Mercury News (Andrew Baggarly, *Dan Brown), Santa Rosa Press Democrat (Jeff Fletcher), Contra Costa Times (*Rick Hurd). **MLB.com:** Chris Haft.

WASHINGTON NATIONALS

Radio Announcers: Charlie Slowes, Dave Jageler. **Flagship Station:** Washington Post Radio (WTOP 1500-AM, 107.7 FM).

TV Announcers: Bob Carpenter, Rob Dibble. **Flagship Station:** Mid-Atlantic Sports Network (MASN).

Newspapers, Daily Coverage (beat writers): Baltimore Sun (*Dan Connolly), The Free-Lance Star (Rich Campbell), Washington Post (Barry Svrluga, *Dave Sheinin), Washington Times (Mark Zuckerman). Washington Examiner (Rick Snider). **MLB.com:** Bill Ladson.

NATIONAL MEDIA INFORMATION

BASEBALL STATISTICS

ELIAS SPORTS BUREAU INC.

Official Major League Statistician

Mailing Address: 500 Fifth Ave., **Suite 2140, New York, NY 10110. Telephone:** (212) 869-1530. **Fax:** (212) 354-0980. **Website:** www.esb.com.

President: Seymour Siwoff.

Executive Vice President: Steve Hirdt. **Vice President:** Peter Hirdt. **Data Processing Manager:** Chris Thorn.

MAJOR LEAGUE BASEBALL ADVANCED MEDIA

Official Minor League Statistician

Mailing Address: 75 Ninth Ave., **New York, NY 10011. Telephone:** (212) 485-3444. **Fax:** (212) 485-3456.

Director: Misann Ellmaker. **Deputy Project Manager:** Nathan Blackmon. **Senior Project Manager:** Sammy Arena. **Senior Editorial Producer:** Jason Ratliff. **Senior Manager, Statistics Operations:** Chris Lentine. **Senior Reporter:** Jonathan Mayo. **Reporters:** Kevin Czerwinski, Lisa Winston.

STATS Inc.

Mailing Address: 8130 Lehigh Ave., **Morton Grove, IL 60053. Telephone:** (847) 583-2100. **Fax:** (847) 470-9140. **Website:** biz.stats.com.

CEO: Gary Walrath. **Executive Vice Presidents:** Steve Byrd, Robert Schur. **Directors, Sales:** Jim Capuano, Vin Bagnaturo, Eric Kutzin, Greg Kirkorsky. **Director, Marketing:** Walter Lis. **Director, Sports Operations:** Allan Spear. **Manager, Baseball Operations:** Jeff Chernow.

TELEVISION NETWORKS

ESPN/ESPN2

- **Sunday Night Baseball**
- **Monday Night Baseball**
- **Wednesday Night Baseball**
- **Opening Day, Holiday Games**
- **Spring Training Games**
- **Baseball Tonight**
- **Home Run Derby, All-Star Game Programming**

Mailing Address, ESPN Connecticut: ESPN Plaza, Bristol, CT 06010. **Telephone:** (860) 766-2000. **Fax:** (860) 766-2213.

Mailing Address, ESPN New York Executive Offices: 77 W. **66th St., New York, NY, 10023. Telephone:** (212) 456-7777. **Fax:** (212) 456-2930.

President, ESPN/ABC Sports: George Bodenheimer.

Executive Vice President, Administration: Ed Durso.

Executive VP, Content: John Skipper. **Executive VP, Studio/Remote Production:** Norby Williamson.

Senior VP, Programming/Acquisitions: Len DeLuca. **VP, Programming:** Mike Ryan.

Senior VP/Executive Producer, Remote Production: Jed Drake. **Senior Coordinating Producer, Remote Production:** Tim Scanlan. **Coordinating Producer, Remote Production:** Matt Sandulli.

Senior VP/Managing Editor, Studio Production: Mark Gross. **Senior Coordinating Producer, Baseball Tonight:** Jay Levy.

Senior VP, Communications: Chris LaPlaca. **VP, Communications:** Mike Soltys. **VP, Communications:** Diane Lamb. **Associate Manager:** Nate Smeltz.

ESPN CLASSIC, ESPNEWS

Vice President, Programming/Acquisitions: John Papa.

ESPN INTERNATIONAL, ESPN DEPORTES

Executive Vice President/Managing Director, ESPN International: Russell Wolff.

Senior VP, ESPN Radio/ESPN Deportes: Traug Keller.

General Manager, ESPN Deportes: Lino Garcia.

Senior VP, International Production, ESPN Classic/ESPNEWS: Jodi Markley. **Vice President, International Production/Operations:** Chris Calcinari.

FOX SPORTS

- **Saturday Game of the Week**
- **All-Star Game**
- **National League Championship Series**
- **World Series**

Mailing Address, Los Angeles: Fox Network Center, Building 101, Fifth floor, 10201 West Pico Blvd., **Los Angeles, CA 90035. Telephone:** (310) 369-6000. **Fax:** (310) 969-6700.

Mailing Address, New York: 1211 Avenue of the Americas, 20th Floor, New York, NY 10036. **Telephone:** (212) 556-2500. **Fax:** (212) 354-6902. **Website:** www.foxsports.com.

Chairman, Chief Executive Officer, Fox Sports Television Group: David Hill. **President/Executive Producer:** Ed Goren. **Executive Vice President, Production/Coordinating Studio Producer:** Scott Ackerson. **Executive VP, Production/Field Operations:** Bill Brown. **Executive VP, Programming/Production:** George Greenberg. **Senior VP, Research/Programming:** Bill Wanger. **Coordinating Producer, MLB on Fox:** Pete Macheska. **Lead Game Director:** Bill Webb. **Studio Producer, MLB on Fox:** Gary Lang. **Studio Director, MLB on Fox:** Bob Levy.

Senior VP, Communcations: Lou D'Ermilio. **VP, Communications:** Dan Bell. **Director, Communications:** Tim Buckman. **Communications Manager:** Ileana Pena.

Broadcasters: Kenny Albert, Thom Brennaman, Joe Buck, Mark Grace, Eric Karros, Kevin Kennedy, Josh Lewin, Tim McCarver, Matt Vasgersian, Jeanne Zelasko.

MLB NETWORK

- **MLB Tonight**
- **Hot Stove**
- **Regular Season Games**
- **Spring Training**
- **World Baseball Classic**
- **Caribbean World Series**
- **All-Time Games**
- **Prime 9**
- **Baseball's Seasons**

Mailing Address: 1 MLB Network Plaza, Secaucus, NJ 07094. **Telephone:** (201) 520-6400.

President/CEO: Tony Petitti. **Senior Vice President, Production:** John Entz. **Senior VP, Programming/Business Affairs:** Rob McGlarry. **Vice President, Programming:** Andy Butters. **Coordinating Producers:** Marc Caiafa, Michael Konner, Dave Patterson, Mike Santini. **News Assignment:** Doug Jaclin.

TURNER SPORTS

- **American League/National League Division Series**
- **American League Championship Series**
- **Sunday Game of the Week**

Mailing Address: 1015 Techwood Drive, Atlanta, GA 30318. **Telephone:** (404) 827-1700. **Fax:** (404) 827-1339. **Website:** www.tbs.com.

President: David Levy. **Senior Producer:** Glenn Diamond. **Directors:** Tom Cox, Tom Sahara. **Executive Producer:** Jeff Behnke. **Senior Producer:** Howard Zalkowitz.

FOX SPORTS NET

- **Regional Coverage**

Mailing Address: 10201 W. **Pico Blvd., Building 103, Los Angeles, CA 90035. Telephone:** (310) 369-1000. **Fax:** (310) 969-6049.

President/CEO, Fox Sports Television Group: David Hill. **President, Fox National Cable Networks:** Bob Thompson. **President, Fox Regional Cable Sports Networks:** Randy Freer. **President, Advertising Sales:** Lou LaTorre. **Executive VP, Programming/Production:** George Greenberg. **Senior VP, Production/Executive Producer, Event Coverage:** Doug Sellers. **Director, Communications:** Justin Simon. **Senior Publicist:** Emily Corliss.

OTHER TELEVISION NETWORKS

ABC SPORTS

Mailing Address: 47 W. **66th St., New York, NY 10023. Telephone:** (212) 456-7777. **Fax:** (212) 456-4317.

President, ABC Sports: George Bodenheimer. **President:** George Bodenheimer. **Senior Vice President, Programming:** Loren Matthews.

CBS SPORTS

Mailing Address: 51 W. **52nd St., New York, NY 10019. Telephone:** (212) 975-5230. **Fax:** (212) 975-4063.

President, CBS Sports: Sean McManus. **Senior Vice Presidents, Programming:** Mike Aresco, Rob Correa. **Vice President, Communications:** Leslie Anne Wade.

CNN SPORTS

Mailing Address: One CNN Center, Atlanta, GA 30303. **Telephone:** (404) 878-1600. **Fax:** (404) 878-0011.

Vice President, Production: Jeffrey Green.

HBO SPORTS

Mailing Address: 1100 Avenue of the Americas, New York, NY 10036. **Telephone:** (212) 512-1000. **Fax:** (212) 512-1751.

President, HBO Sports: Ross Greenburg.

NBC SPORTS

Mailing Address: 30 Rockefeller Plaza, Suite 1558, New York, NY 10112. **Telephone:** (212) 664-2014. **Fax:** (212) 664-6365.

Chairman, NBC Sports: Dick Ebersol. **President, NBC Sports:** Ken Schanzer.

Vice President, Sports Communications: Mike McCarley.

ROGERS SPORTSNET (Canada)

Mailing Address: 333 Bloor St. **East, Toronto Ontario M4W 1G9. Telephone:** (416) 332-5600. **Fax:** (416) 332-5629. **Website:** www.sportsnet.ca.

President, Rogers Media: Tony Viner. **President, Rogers Sportsnet:** Doug Beeforth. **Vice President, Communications:** Jan Innes. **Director, Communications/Promotions:** Dave Rashford.

THE SPORTS NETWORK (Canada)

Mailing Address: Bell Globemedia Inc., **9 Channel Nine Court, Scarborough, Ontario M1S 4B5. Telephone:** (416) 332-5000. **Fax:** (416) 332-4337. **Website:** www.tsn.ca

Executive Producer, News: Marc Milliere. **President, TSN:** Phil King. **Executive Producer:** Jim Marshall. **VP, Programming and Production:** Rick Chisholm, VP, Marketing: Adam Ashton. **Communications Director:** Andrea Goldstein. **Executive Producer, tsn.ca:** Mike Day.

RADIO NETWORKS

ESPN RADIO

- **Game of the Week**
- **Sunday Night Baseball**
- **All-Star Game**
- **Division Series**
- **League Championship Series**
- **World Series**

Address: ESPN Plaza, 935 Middle St., **Bristol, CT 06010. Telephone:** (860) 766-2000, (800) 999-9985. **Fax:** (860) 589-5523. **Website:** espnradio.espn.go.com/espnradio/index.

General Manager, ESPN Radio Network: Mo Davenport. **Senior Director, Operations:** Scott Masteller. **Senior Director, Programming:** Peter Gianesini. **Senior Director, Marketing/Integration:** Freddy Rolon. **Executive Producer, Remote Broadcasts:** John Martin. **News Editor:** Peter Ciccone. **Program Directors:** Justin Craig, Louise Cornetta, Larry Gifford, David Zaslowsky. **Chief Engineer:** Tom Evans. **Administrative Coordinator:** Janet Alden. **VP, Sports, ABC Radio Network and VP/Affiliate Relations:** T.J. **Lambert.**

Executive Producer, Major League Baseball on ESPN Radio: John Martin.

Commentators: Dan Shulman, Dave Campbell, Jim Durham, Dave Barnett, Jon Miller, Joe Morgan, Joe D'Ambrosio.

MLB ADVANCED MEDIA MULTIMEDIA

Mailing Address: 75 Ninth Ave., **New York, NY 10011. Telephone:** (212) 485-3444. **Fax:** (212) 485-3456. **E-Mail Address:** radio@mlb.com. **Website:** www.mlb.com.

Senior Vice President, Multimedia/Distribution: Joe Inzerillo. **VP/Executive Producer, Content:** Jim Jenks. **Senior Director, Production:** Daria Debuono. **Director, Remote Programming:** Mike Siano. **Director, Studio Programming:** Richard Bush. **Video Acquisition:** Stephanie Gentile. **Audio Acquisition:** Scott Majeska.

Talent: John Marzano, Billy Sample, Hal Bodley, Seth Everett, Vinny Micucci, Casey Stern, Ed Randall, Jim Salisbury, Peter McCarthy, Noah Coslov.

XM SATELLITE RADIO

- **24-hour MLB Home Plate channel (baseball talk)**
- **MLB live play-by-play for spring training, regular season, playoffs, World Series**
- **MLB En Espanol channel (Spanish language play-by-play and baseball talk)**

Mailing Address: 1500 Eckington Place NE, Washington, DC 20002. **Telephone:** (202) 380-4000. **Fax:** 202-380-4500. **E-Mail Address:** mlb@xmradio.com. **Website:** www.xmradio.com.

Executive Vice President, Programming: Eric Logan. **Vice President, Talk Programming:** Kevin Straley. **Senior VP, Corporate Communications:** Nathaniel Brown. **VP, Corporate Affairs:** Chance Patterson. **Director, MLB Programming:** Chuck Dickemann. **Executive Producer, MLB Home Plate Channel:** Matt Fishman. **Commentators:** Joe Castellano, Rob Dibble, Kevin Kennedy, Ronnie Lane, Buck Martinez, Mark Patrick, Billy Ripken, Cal Ripken Jr., **Charley Steiner, Chuck Wilson.**

SPORTING NEWS RADIO NETWORK

Mailing Address: 6900 E Camelback Rd, Ste 610. **Telephone:** (602) 635-4177. **Producers Line:** (800) 224-2004. **Fax:** (480) 945-0177. **Website:** www.sportingnewsradio.com.

President: Clancy Woods. **SVP, Business Development:** Shawn Pastor. **VP, Sales:** Lee Rosenthal. **VP, Sales & Marketing:** Paul Talbot. **Senior Programming Manager:** Craig Larson.

SPORTS BYLINE USA

Mailing Address: 300 Broadway, Suite 8, San Francisco, CA 94133. **Telephone:** (415) 434-8300. **Guest Line:** (800) 358-4457. **Studio Line:** (800) 878-7529. **Fax:** (415) 391-2569. **E-Mail Address:** questions@sportsbyline.com. **Website:**

www.sportsbyline.com.

President: Darren Peck. **Executive Producer:** Alex Murillo.

NEWS ORGANIZATIONS

ASSOCIATED PRESS

Mailing Address: 450 W. **33rd St., New York, NY 10010. Telephone:** (212) 621-1630. **Fax:** (212) 621-1639. **Website:** www.ap.org.

Sports Editor: Terry Taylor. **Deputy Sports Editor:** Ben Walker. **Sports Photo Editor:** Mike Feldman. **Baseball Writers:** Ron Blum, Mike Fitzpatrick. **BLOOMBERG SPORTS**

Address: 731 Lexington Ave., **New York, NY 10022. Telephone:** (212) 617-2301. **Fax:** (917) 369-5633.

Sports Managing Editor: Jay Beberman. **Sports Editor:** Larry Siddons, Vince Golle, Danielle Sessa. **Writers:** Mike Buteau, Dan Bollerman, Larry DiTore, Mason Levinson, Erik Matuszewski.

CANADIAN PRESS

Mailing Address, Toronto: 36 King St. **Mailing Address, Montreal:** 215 Saint-Jacques St., **Suite 100, Montreal, Quebec H2Y 1M6. Telephone:** (416) 507-2154 (Toronto), (514) 985-7240 (Montreal). **Fax:** (416) 507-2074 (Toronto), (514) 282-6915 (Montreal). **E-Mail Address:** sports@cp.org.

Sports Editor: Neil Davidson. **Baseball Writer, Toronto:** Shi Davidi. **Baseball Writer, Montreal:** Bill Beacon.

CBS SPORTSLINE.com

Mailing Address: 2200 W. **Cypress Creek, Fort Lauderdale, FL 33309. Website:** cbs.sportsline.com.

Senior Writer: Scott Miller.

ESPN.com

Mailing Address: ESPN Plaza, Bristol, CT 06010. **Telephone:** (860) 766-2000.

Vice President/Executive Editor: Patrick Stiegman. **Deputy Editor:** David Kull.

ESPN/SPORTSTICKER

Mailing Address: ESPN Plaza, Building B, Fourth Floor, Bristol, CT 06010. **Telephone:** (860) 766-1899. **Fax:** (800) 336-0383. **E-Mail Address:** newsroom@sportsticker.com.

General Manager: Jim Morganthaler. **News Director:** Chris Bernucca. **Baseball Editor:** Jim Keller. **Manager, Customer Marketing/Communications:** Lou Monaco.

Senior Bureau Manager: Michael Walczak. **Bureau Managers:** Tom Diorio. **Associate Bureau Manager:** Ian Anderson. **Programmer Analysts:** John Foley, Walter Kent. **Historical Consultant:** Bill Weiss.

FOX SPORTS.com

Mailing Address: 1440 Sepulveda Blvd., **Los Angeles, CA. Telephone:** (310) 444-8000. **Fax:** (310) 444-8180. **Website:** www.msn.foxsports.com.

Senior Vice President/General Manager: Ross Levinsohn.

MLB ADVANCED MEDIA (MLB.COM)

Office Address: 75 Ninth Ave., **5th Floor, New York, NY 10011. Telephone:** (212) 485-3444. **Fax:** (212) 485-3456.

Chief Executive Officer: Bob Bowman.

Vice President, Marketing: Kristen Fergason. **VP, Ticketing:** Heather Benz. **VP, Human Resources:** Leslie Knickerbocker. **Senior VP/Chief Technical Officer:** Joe Choti. **Senior VP, Corporate Communications:** Jim Gallagher. **Executive VP, E-Commerce and Sponsorships:** Noah Garden. **Executive VP/Editor-In-Chief, mlb.com:** Dinn Mann. **VP, Design:** Deck Rees.

Senior VP/General Counsel: Michael Mellis, Executive VP, Business: George Kliavkoff.

SI.com

Mailing Address: 1271 Avenue of the Americas, 32nd Floor, New York, NY 10020. **Telephone:** (212) 522-1212. **Fax:** (212) 467-0339.

Managing Editor: Paul Fichtenbaum.

PRESS ASSOCIATIONS

BASEBALL WRITERS' ASSOCIATION OF AMERICA

Mailing Address: P.O. **Box 610611, Bayside, NY 11361. Telephone:** (718) 767-2582. **Fax:** (718) 767-2583. **E-Mail Address:** bbwaa@aol.com.

President: David O'Brien (Atlanta Journal-Constitution). **Vice President:** John Lowe (Detroit Free Press). **Secretary/ Treasurer:** Jack O'Connell (BBWAA). **Board of Directors:** Bob Dutton (Kansas City Star), Scott Miller (CBS Sports.com), John Shea (San Francisco Chronicle), David Sheinin (Washington Post).

NATIONAL COLLEGIATE BASEBALL WRITERS ASSOCIATION

Mailing Address: 5201 N. **O'Connor Blvd., Suite 300, Irving, TX 75039. Telephone:** (214) 774-1351. **Fax:** (214) 496-0055. **E-Mail Address:** rdanderson@c-usa.org

Executive Director: Bo Carter (National Football Foundation), Associate Executive Director: Russell Anderson (Conference USA).

NEWSPAPERS/PERIODICALS

USA TODAY

Mailing Address: 7950 Jones Branch Dr., **McLean, VA 22108. Telephones/Baseball Desk:** (703) 854-5286, 854-5954,

854-3706, 854-3744, 854-3746. **Fax:** (703) 854-2072. **Website:** www.usatoday.com.

Publishing Frequency: Daily (Monday-Friday).

Baseball Editors: Peter Barzilai, Gabe Lacques, Matt Cimento, John Tkach. **Baseball Writers:** Mel Antonen, Mike Dodd, Gabe Lacques, Seth Livingston, Bob Nightengale, Jorge Ortiz, Paul White.

THE SPORTING NEWS

Mailing Address: 10176 Corporate Square Dr., **Suite 200, St. Louis, MO 63132. Telephone:** (314) 997-7111. **Fax:** (314) 993-7726. **Website:** www.sportingnews.com.

Publishing Frequency: Weekly.

Senior Vice President/Editorial Director: John Rawlings. **Executive Editor:** Bob Hille. **Managing Editor:** Stan McNeal. **Senior Editor:** Tom Gatto. **Senior Photo Editor:** Paul Nisely.

SPORTS ILLUSTRATED

Mailing Address: 1271 Avenue of the Americas, New York, NY 10020. **Telephone:** (212) 522-1212. **Fax, Editorial:** (212) 522-4543. **Fax, Public Relations:** (212) 522-0747. **Website:** www.si.com.

Publishing Frequency: Weekly.

Managing Editor: Terry McDonnell. **Senior Editor:** Christian Stone. **Associate Editor:** David Sabino. **Senior Writers:** Tom Verducci, Danny Habib, Jon Heyman. **Staff Writer:** Chris Ballard. **Writers/Reporters:** Albert Chen, Melissa Segura, Andrea Woo, Ben Reiter. **Photo Editor:** Nate Gordon. **Vice President, Communications:** Art Berke.

USA TODAY SPORTS WEEKLY

Mailing Address: 7950 Jones Branch Dr., **McLean, VA 22108. Telephone:** (800) 872-1415, (703) 854-3340. **Fax:** (703) 854-2034. **Website:** www.usatoday.com.

Publishing Frequency: Weekly.

Publisher: Craig Moon. **Managing Editor:** Monte Lorell. **Senior Editor:** Lee Ivory. **Senior Assignment Editor:** Tim McQuay. **Baseball Editors:** Peter Barzilai, Steve Borelli, Gabe Laques. **Baseball Writers:** Steve DiMeglio, Bob Nightengale, Paul White.

STREET AND SMITH'S SPORTS BUSINESS JOURNAL

Mailing Address: 120 W. **Morehead St., Suite 310, Charlotte, NC 28202. Telephone:** (704) 973-1400. **Fax:** (704) 973-1401. **Website:** www.sportsbusinessjournal.com.

Publishing Frequency: Weekly.

Publisher: Richard Weiss. **Editor-in-chief:** Abraham Madkour. **Managing Editor:** Ross Nethery.

ESPN THE MAGAZINE

Mailing Address: 19 E. **34th St., Seventh Floor, New York, NY 10016. Telephone:** (212) 515-1000. **Fax:** (212) 515-1290. **Website:** www.espn.com.

Publishing Frequency: Bi-weekly.

Executive Editors: Steve Wulf, Sue Hovey. **Senior Editors:** Jon Scher, Ed McGregor. **Senior Writers:** Jorge Arangure Jr., **Jeff Bradley, Tim Keown, Tim Kurkjian, Buster Olney. Associate Editors:** Ian Gordon, Matt Meyers. **Writer/Reporter:** Amy Nelson. **Photo Editor:** Catriona Ni Aolain. **Photo Operations Coordinator:** Tricia Reed. **Manager, Communications:** Ellie Seifert.

BASEBALL AMERICA

Address: 4319 S. **Alston Ave., Suite 103, Durham, NC 27713. Mailing Address:** P.O. **Box 12877, Durham, NC 27709. Telephone:** (919) 682-9635. **Fax:** (919) 682-2880.

Publishing Frequency: Bi-weekly.

President/Publisher: Lee Folger. **Editors In Chief:** Will Lingo, John Manuel. **Managing Editor:** J.J. **Cooper. Executive Editor:** Jim Callis.

BASEBALL DIGEST

Mailing Address: 990 Grove St., **Evanston, IL 60201. Telephone:** (847) 491-6440. **Fax:** (847) 491-6203. **E-Mail Address:** bkuenster@centurysports.net. **Website:** www.centurysports.net/baseball.

Publishing Frequency: Monthly, April through January.

Publisher: Norman Jacobs. **Editor:** John Kuenster. **Managing Editor:** Bob Kuenster.

COLLEGIATE BASEBALL

Mailing Address: P.O. **Box 50566, Tucson, AZ 85703. Telephone:** (520) 623-4530. **Fax:** (520) 624-5501. **E-Mail Address:** editor@baseballnews.com. **Website:** www.baseballnews.com.

Publishing Frequency: Bi-weekly, January-June; September, October.

Publisher: Lou Pavlovich. **Editor:** Lou Pavlovich Jr.

JUNIOR BASEBALL MAGAZINE

Mailing Address: P.O. **Box 3059, Langhorne, PA 19047. Telephone:** (203) 210-5726. **Customer Service:** (888) 487-2448. **Fax:** (480) 275-3055. **E-Mail Address:** editor@juniorbaseball.com. **Website:** www.juniorbaseball.com.

Publishing Frequency: Bi-monthly.

Publisher/Editor: Jim Beecher.

SPORTS ILLUSTRATED FOR KIDS

Mailing Address: 1271 Avenue of the Americas, Third Floor, New York, NY 10020. **Telephone:** (212) 522-1212. **Fax:** (212) 522-0120. **Website:** www.sikids.com.

Publishing Frequency: Monthly.

Publisher: Dave Watt. **Managing Editor:** Bob Der. **Baseball Editor:** Michael Northrop. **Online Editors:** Justin Tejada.

GENERAL INFORMATION

MAJOR LEAGUE BASEBALL PLAYERS ASSOCIATION

Mailing Address: 12 E. 49th St., 24th Floor, New York, NY 10017. **Telephone:** (212) 826-0808. **FAX:** (212) 752-4378. **E-Mail Address:** feedback@mlbpa.org. **Website:** www.mlbplayers.com.

Year Founded: 1966.

Executive Director: Donald Fehr.

Chief Operating Officer: Gene Orza. **General Counsel:** Michael Weiner. **Assistant General Counsel:** Doyle Pryor, Robert Lenaghan, Jeff Fannell.

Special Assistants to Executive Director: Bobby Bonilla, Phil Bradley, Steve Rogers, Allyne Price.

Managing Officer: Martha Child. **Manager, Financial Operations:** Marietta DiCamillo. **Contract Administrator:** Cindy Abercrombie. **Accounting Assistants:** Terri Hinkley, Yolanda Largo. **Administrative Assistants:** Virginia Carballo, Aisha Hope, Melba Markowitz, Sharon O'Donnell, Lisa Pepin. **Receptionist:** Rebecca Rivera.

Director, Business Affairs/Licensing: Judy Heeter. **General Manager, Licensing:** Richard White. **Director, Communications:** Greg Bouris. **Assistant General Counsel, Licensing:** Evie Goldstein. **Category Director, Interactive Games:** John Olshan. **Communications Manager:** Chris Dahl. **Category Director, Trading Cards/Collectibles:** Evan Kaplan. **Category Manager, Apparel/Novelties:** Nancy Willis. **Manager, Player Trust:** Melissa Persaud. **Administrative Manager:** Heather Gould. **Program Coordinator:** Hillary Falk. **Licensing Assistant:** Eric Rivera. Manager, Office Services: Victor Lugo. Executive Secretary/Licensing: Sheila Peters.

Executive Board: Player representatives of the 30 major league clubs.

MLBPA Representatives: Tony Clark, Mark Loretta. **MLBPA Alternate Representatives:** Ray King, Craig Counsell.

SCOUTING

MAJOR LEAGUE BASEBALL SCOUTING BUREAU

Mailing Address: 3500 Porsche Way, Suite 100, Ontario, CA 91764. **Telephone:** (909) 980-1881. **FAX:** (909) 980-7794.

Year Founded: 1974.

Director: Frank Marcos. **Assistant Director:** Rick Oliver. **Office Coordinator:** Debbie Keedy. **Administrative Assistant:** Ana Melendez.

Board of Directors: Ed Burns (Major League Baseball), Dave Dombrowski (Tigers), Bob Gebhard (Diamondbacks), Roland Hemond (White Sox), Frank Marcos (MLBSB), Omar Minaya (Mets), Randy Smith (Padres), Art Stewart (Royals), Kevin Towers (Padres).

Scouts: Rick Arnold (Spring Mills, PA), Matt Barnicle (Huntington Beach, CA), Andy Campbell (Chandler, AZ), Mike Childers (Lexington, KY), Craig Conklin (Cayucos, CA), Dan Dixon (Temecula, CA), Jim Elliott (Winston-Salem, NC), Brad Fidler (Douglassville, PA), Art Gardner (Walnut Grove, MS), Rusty Gerhardt (New London, TX), Dennis Haren (San Diego, CA), Chris Heidt (Cherry Valley, IL), Don Jacoby (Winter Haven, FL), Don Kohler (Asbury, NJ), Mike Larson (Waseca, MN), Johnny Martinez (Overland Park, KS), Wayne Mathis (Cuero, TX), Junie Melendez (Toledo, OH), Paul Mirocke (Lutz, FL), Carl Moesche (Gresham, OR), Tim Osborne (Woodstock, GA), Gary Randall (Rock Hill, SC), Willie Romay (Miami Springs, FL), Kevin Saucier (Pensacola, FL), Harry Shelton (Ocoee, FL), Pat Shortt (South Hempstead, NY), Craig Smajstrla (Pearland, TX), Christie Stancil (Raleigh, NC), Ed Sukla (Irvine, CA), Doug Takarawa (Fountain Valley, CA), Jim Walton (Shattuck, OK).

Supervisor, Canada: Walt Burrows (Brentwood Bay, B.C.). **Canadian Scouts:** Curtis Bailey (Red Deer, Alberta), Jason Chee-Aloy (Toronto, Ontario), Bill Green (Vancouver, B.C.), Andrew Halpenny (Winnipeg, Manitoba), Ian Jordan (Kirkland, Quebec), Ken Lenihan (Bedford, Nova Scotia), Dan Mendham (Dorchester, Ontario), Todd Plaxton (Saskatoon, Sask.), Jasmin Roy (Longueuil, Quebec), Bob Smyth (Ladysmith, B.C.), Tony Wylie (Anchorage, AK).

Supervisor, Puerto Rico: Pepito Centeno (Cidra, PR).

PROFESSIONAL BASEBALL SCOUTS FOUNDATION

Mailing Address: 9665 Wilshire Blvd., Suite 801, Beverly Hills, CA 90212. **Telephone:** (310) 858 1935. **FAX:** (310) 246-4862. **E-Mail Address:** hitter19@aol.com. **Website:** www.professionalbaseballscoutsfoundation.com.

Chairman: Dennis Gilbert. **Director:** Cindy Picerni.

Board of Directors: Bill Gayton, Pat Gillick, Derrick Hall, Roland Hemond, Gary Hughes, Lisa Jackson, Tommy Lasorda, J.J. Lally, Roberta Mazur, Harry Minor, Bob Nightengale, Tracy Ringolsby, Dale Sutherland, Kevin Towers, Dave Yoakum, John Young.

SCOUT OF THE YEAR FOUNDATION

Mailing Address: P.O. Box 211585, West Palm Beach, FL 33421. **Telephone:** (561) 798-5897, (561) 818-4329. **FAX:** (561) 798-4644. **E-Mail Address:** bertmazur@aol.com.

President: Roberta Mazur. **Vice President:** Tracy Ringolsby. **Treasurer:** Ron Mazur II.

Board of Advisers: Joe L. Brown, Bob Fontaine, Pat Gillick, Roland Hemond, Gary Hughes, Tommy Lasorda, Allan Simpson, Ron Shapiro, Ted Spencer, Bob Watson.

UMPIRES

WORLD UMPIRES ASSOCIATION

Mailing Address: P.O. Box 394, Neenah, WI 54957. **Telephone:** (920) 969-1580. **FAX:** (920) 969-1892. **E-Mail Address:** worldumpiresassn@aol.com. **Website:** www.worldumpires.com.

Year Founded: 2000.

President: John Hirschbeck. **Vice President:** Tim Welke. **Secretary/Treasurer:** Jeff Nelson. **Labor Counsel:** Joel Smith. **Administrator:** Phil Janssen.

PROFESSIONAL BASEBALL UMPIRE CORPORATION

Office Address: 201 Bayshore Dr. SE, St. Petersburg, FL 33701. **Mailing Address:** P.O. Box A, St. Petersburg, FL 33731. **Telephone:** (727) 822-6937. **Fax:** (727) 821-5819.

President: Pat O'Conner. **Treasurer/Executive Vice President:** Tim Purpura. **Secretary/VP, Legal Affairs/General Counsel:** Scott Poley. **Special Assistant, PBUC:** Lillian Patterson. **Special Assistant to President:** Mike Fitzpatrick.

Executive Director, PBUC: Justin Klemm (Branchburg, NJ). **Chief, Instruction/Field Evaluator:** Mike Felt (Lansing, MI). **Field Evaluators/Instructors:** Jorge Bauza (San Juan, PR), Dennis Cregg (Webster, MA), Larry Reveal (Chesapeake, VA), Andy Shultz (Philadelphia).

HARRY WENDELSTEDT UMPIRE SCHOOL

Mailing Address: 88 S. St. Andrews Dr., Ormond Beach, FL 32174. **Telephone:** (386) 672-4879. **FAX:** (386) 672-3212. **E-Mail Address:** admin@umpireschool.com. **Website:** www.umpireschool.com.

Operators: Harry Wendelstedt, Hunter Wendelstedt.

JIM EVANS ACADEMY OF PROFESSIONAL UMPIRING

Mailing Address: 200 South Wilcox St., #508, Castle Rock, CO 80104. **Telephone:** (303) 290-7411. **E-Mail Address:** jimsacademy@earthlink.net. **Website:** www.umpireacademy.com.

Operator: Jim Evans.

TRAINERS

PROFESSIONAL BASEBALL ATHLETIC TRAINERS SOCIETY

Mailing Address: 400 Colony Square, Suite 1750, 1201 Peachtree St., Atlanta, GA 30361. **Telephone:** (404) 875-4000. **FAX:** (404) 892-8560. **E-Mail Address:** rmallernee@mallernee-branch.com. **Website:** www.pbats.com.

Year Founded: 1983.

President: Jamie Reed (Texas Rangers). **Secretary:** Richie Bancells (Baltimore Orioles). **Treasurer:** Jeff Porter (Atlanta Braves). **American League Head Athletic Trainer Representative:** Kevin Rand (Detroit Tigers). **American League Assistant Athletic Trainer Representative:** Steve Carter (Detroit Tigers). **National League Head Athletic Trainer Representative:** Roger Caplinger (Milwaukee Brewers). **National League Assistant Athletic Trainer Representative:** Rex Jones (Houston Astros).

General Counsel: Rollin Mallernee.

MUSEUMS

BABE RUTH BIRTHPLACE

Office Address: 216 Emory St., Baltimore, MD 21230. **Telephone:** (410) 727-1539. **FAX:** (410) 727-1652. **E-Mail Address:** info@baberuthmuseum.com. **Website:** www.baberuthmuseum.com.

Year Founded: 1973.

Executive Director: Mike Gibbons. **Curator:** Shawn Herne.

Museum Hours: April-September, 10 a.m.-6 p.m (10 a.m.-7:30 p.m. for Baltimore Orioles home games); October-March, Tuesday-Sunday, 10 a.m.-5 p.m. (10a.m.-8 p.m. for Baltimore Ravens home games).

CANADIAN BASEBALL HALL OF FAME AND MUSEUM

Museum Address: 386 Church St., St. Marys, Ontario N4X 1C2. **Mailing Address:** P.O. Box 1838, St. Marys, Ontario N4X 1C2. **Telephone:** (519) 284-1838. **FAX:** (519) 284-1234. **E-Mail Address:** baseball@baseballhalloffame.ca. **Website:** www.baseballhalloffame.ca.

Year Founded: 1983.

President/CEO: Tom Valcke. **Director, Operations:** Scott Crawford. **Curator:** Carl McCoomb.

Museum Hours: May—weekends only; June 1-Oct. 8—Daily, 10:30-4p.m.

FIELD OF DREAMS MOVIE SITE

Address: 28963 Lansing Rd., Dyersville, IA 52040. **Telephone:** (888) 875-8404. **FAX:** (319) 875-7253. **E-Mail Address:** shoelessjoe@fieldofdreamsmoviesite.com. **Website:** www.fieldofdreamsmoviesite.com.

Year Founded: 1989.

Manager, Business/Marketing: Betty Boeckenstedt.

Hours: April-November, 9 a.m.-6 p.m.

LEGENDS OF THE GAME BASEBALL MUSEUM

Address: 1000 Ballpark Way, Suite 400, Arlington, TX 76011. **Telephone:** (817) 273-5600. **FAX:** (817) 273-5093. **E-Mail Address:** museum@texasrangers.com. **Website:** http://museum.texasrangers.com.

Director: Amy Polley.

Hours: April-September, game days/Texas Rangers, 9 a.m.-7:30 p.m.; non-game days, Mon.-Sat., 9 a.m.-4 p.m., Sunday 11 a.m.-4 p.m.; October-March, Tues.-Sat., 10 a.m.-4 p.m.

LITTLE LEAGUE BASEBALL MUSEUM

Office Address: 525 Route 15 S., Williamsport, PA 17701. **Mailing Address:** P.O. Box 3485, Williamsport, PA 17701. **Telephone:** (570) 326-3607. **FAX:** (570) 326-2267. **E-Mail Address:** museum@littleleague.org. **Website:** www.littleleague.org/museum.

Year Founded: 1982.

Director: Janice Ogurcak. **Administrative Assistant:** Adam Thompson.

Museum Hours: Memorial Day-Labor Day, 10 a.m.-7 p.m. (Sun., noon-7 p.m.); Labor Day-Memorial Day, Mon., Thurs. and Fri., 10 a.m.-5 p.m., Sat. noon-5 p.m., Sun. noon-4 p.m.

LOUISVILLE SLUGGER MUSEUM AND FACTORY

Office Address: 800 W. Main St., Louisville, KY 40202. **Telephone:** (502) 588-7228. **FAX:** (502) 585-1179. **Website:** www.sluggermuseum.org.

Year Founded: 1996.

Executive Director: Anne Jewell.

Museum Hours: Mon.-Sat., Jan. 2-Dec. 23, 9 a.m.-5 p.m,; Sunday (April-November), noon-5p.m.

THE NATIONAL PASTIME: MUSEUM OF MINOR LEAGUE BASEBALL

(Under Development)

Museum Address: 175 Toyota Plaza, Suite 300, Memphis, TN 38103. **Telephone:** (901) 722-0207. **FAX:** (901) 527-1642. **E-Mail Address:** dchase@memphisredbirds.com. **Website:** www.memphisredbirds.com/autozone_park/museum.html.

Founders: Dean Jernigan, Kristi Jernigan.

Executive Director: Dave Chase.

NATIONAL BASEBALL HALL OF FAME AND MUSEUM

Address: 25 Main St., Cooperstown, NY 13326. **Telephone:** (888) 425-5633, (607) 547-7200. **FAX:** (607) 547-2044. **E-Mail Address:** info@baseballhalloffame.org. **Website:** www.baseballhalloffame.org.

Year Founded: 1939.

Chairman: Jane Forbes Clark. **Vice Chairman:** Joe Morgan. **President:** Jeff Idelson.

Museum Hours: Memorial Day Weekend-Labor Day, 9 a.m.-9 p.m.; remainder of year, 9 a.m.-5 p.m. Open daily except Thanksgiving, Christmas, New Year's Day.

2009 Hall of Fame Induction Ceremonies: July 26.

NEGRO LEAGUES BASEBALL MUSEUM

Mailing Address: 1616 E. 18th St., Kansas City, MO 64108. **Telephone:** (816) 221-1920. **FAX:** (816) 221-8424. **E-Mail Address:** nlmuseum@hotmail.com. **Website:** www.nlbm.com.

Year Founded: 1990.

Executive Director: Don Motley. **Marketing Director:** Bob Kendrick. **Curator:** Raymond Doswell.

Museum Hours: Tues.-Sat. 9 a.m.-6 p.m.; Sun. noon-6 p.m. Closed Monday.

NOLAN RYAN FOUNDATION AND EXHIBIT CENTER

Mailing Address: 2925 S. Bypass 35, Alvin, TX 77511. **Telephone:** (281) 388-1134. **FAX:** (281) 388-1135. **Website:** www.nolanryanfoundation.org.

Hours: Mon.-Sat. 9 a.m.-4 p.m.

TED WILLIAMS MUSEUM and HITTERS HALL OF FAME

Mailing Address: 2455 N. Citrus Hills Blvd., Hernando, FL 34442. **Telephone:** (352) 527-6566. **FAX:** (352) 527-4163. **E-Mail Address:** twm@tedwilliamsmuseum.com. **Website:** twmuseum.com.

Executive Director: Dave McCarthy. **Director, Operation:** Mike Colabelli.

Museum Hours: Tues.-Sun., 10 a.m.-4 p.m.

RESEARCH

SOCIETY FOR AMERICAN BASEBALL RESEARCH

Mailing Address: 812 Huron Rd. **E., Suite 719, Cleveland, OH 44115. Telephone:** (216) 575-0500. **FAX:** (216) 575-0502. **Website:** www.sabr.org.

Year Founded: 1971.

President: Dick Beverage. **Vice President:** Bill Nowlin. **Secretary:** Neil Traven. **Treasurer:** F.X. **Flinn. Directors:** Fred Ivor-Campbell, Tom Hufford, Paul Hirsch, Andy McCue.

Executive Director: John Zajc. **Membership Services Associate:** Eileen Canepari. **Director, Publications:** Jim Charlton.

ALUMNI ASSOCIATIONS

MAJOR LEAGUE BASEBALL PLAYERS ALUMNI ASSOCIATION

Mailing Address: 1631 Mesa Ave., Suite B, Colorado Springs, CO 80906. **Telephone:** (719) 477-1870. **FAX:** (719) 477-1875. **E-Mail Address:** postoffice@mlbpaa.com. **Website:** www.baseballalumni.com.

President: Brooks Robinson. **Chief Executive Officer:** Dan Foster. **Board of Directors:** Sandy Alderson, John Doherty, Denny Doyle, Brian Fisher, Jim "Mudcat" Grant, Rich Hand, Jim Hannan (chairman), Jim Poole, Steve Rogers, Will Royster, Jose Valdivielso, Fred Valentine (vice chairman).

Legal Counsel: Sam Moore. **Vice President, Player Appearances:** Chris Torgusen. **VP, Special Events:** Geoffrey Hixson. **Director, Administration:** Blaze Bautista. **Special Events Coordinator:** Mike Groll. **Youth Baseball Coordinator:** Derek Mayfield.

ASSOCIATION OF PROFESSIONAL BALL PLAYERS OF AMERICA

Mailing Address: 1820 W. Orangewood Ave., Suite 206, Orange, CA 92868. **Telephone:** (714) 935-9993. **FAX:** (714) 935-0431. **E-Mail Address:** ballplayersassn@aol.com. **Website:** www.apbpa.org.

Year Founded: 1924.

President: Roland Hemond. **First Vice President:** Tal Smith. **Second VP:** Dick Wagner. **Secretary/Treasurer:** Dick Beverage. **Administrative Assistant:** Patty Helmsworth.

Directors: Sparky Anderson, Mark Grace, Tony Gwynn, Orel Hershiser, Whitey Herzog, Tony La Russa, Tom Lasorda, Brooks Robinson, Nolan Ryan, Tom Seaver.

BASEBALL ASSISTANCE TEAM (BAT)

Mailing Address: 245 Park Ave., 31st Floor, New York, NY 10167. **Telephone:** (212) 931-7822, (212) 931-7823. **FAX:** (212) 949-5433.

Year Founded: 1986.

President, Chief Executive Officer: Ted Sizemore. **Vice Presidents:** Frank Torre, Greg Wilcox, Earl Wilson. **Chairman:** Bobby Murcer.

Executive Director: James Martin. **Secretary:** Thomas Ostertag. **Treasurer:** Jonathan Mariner. **Consultant:** Sam McDowell.

MINOR LEAGUE BASEBALL ALUMNI ASSOCIATION

Mailing Address: P.O. Box A, St. Petersburg, FL 33731. **Telephone:** (727) 822-6937. **FAX:** (727) 821-5819. **E-Mail Address:** alumni@minorleaguebaseball.com. **Website:** www.milb.com.

Manager, Exhibiton Services/Alumni Association: Noreen Brantner.

MINISTRY

BASEBALL CHAPEL

Mailing Address: P.O. Box 302, Springfield, PA 19064. **Telephone:** (610) 690-2477. **E-Mail Address:** office@baseballchapel.org. **Website:** www.baseballchapel.org.

Year Founded: 1973.

President: Vince Nauss.

Director, Hispanic Ministry: Rich Sparling. **Director, Ministry Operations:** Rob Crose. **Director, Player Relations:** Steve Sisco.

Board of Directors: Don Christenson, Greg Groh, Dave Howard, Vince Nauss, Bill Sampen, Walt Wiley.

TRADE/EMPLOYMENT

BASEBALL WINTER MEETINGS/THE BASEBALL TRADE SHOW

Mailing Address: P.O. Box A, St. Petersburg, FL 33731. **Telephone:** (727) 822-6937, (727) 456-1718. **FAX:** (727) 825-3785. **Website:** www.baseballtradeshow.com

Manager, Exhibition Services: Noreen Brantner.

2008 Convention: Dec. 8-11, Las Vegas.

PROFESSIONAL BASEBALL EMPLOYMENT OPPORTUNITIES

Mailing Address: P.O. Box A, St. Petersburg, FL 33731. **Telephone:** (866) 937-7236. **FAX:** (727) 821-5819. **E-Mail Address:** info@pbeo.com. **Website:** www.pbeo.com.

Contact: Scott Kravchuk.

BASEBALL CARD MANUFACTURERS

DONRUSS/PLAYOFF

Mailing Address: 2300 E. Randol Mill, Arlington, TX 76011. **Telephone:** (817) 983-0300. **FAX:** (817) 983-0400. **Website:** www.donruss.com.

Marketing Manager: Scott Prusha.

GRANDSTAND CARDS

Mailing Address: 22647 Ventura Blvd., #192, Woodland Hills, CA 91364. **Telephone:** (818) 992-5642. **FAX:** (818) 348-9122. **E-Mail Address:** gscards1@pacbell.net. **Website:** www.grandstandcards.com.

MULTIAD SPORTS

Mailing Address: 1720 W. Detweiller Dr., Peoria, IL 61615. **Telephone:** (800) 348-6485, ext. **5111. FAX:** (309) 692-8378. **E-Mail Address:** bjeske@multiad.com. **Website:** www.multiad.com/sports.

TOPPS

Mailing Address: One Whitehall St., New York, NY 10004. **Telephone:** (212) 376-0300. **FAX:** (212) 376-0573. **Website:** www.topps.com.

UPPER DECK

Mailing Address: 5909 Sea Otter Place, Carlsbad, CA 92008. **Telephone:** (800) 873-7332. **FAX:** (760) 929-6548. **E-Mail Address:** customer_service@upperdeck.com. **Website:** www.upperdeck.com.

MINOR LEAGUES

MINOR LEAGUE BASEBALL

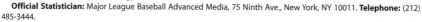

NATIONAL ASSOCIATION OF PROFESSIONAL BASEBALL LEAGUES

MINOR LEAGUE BASEBALL™

Office Address: 201 Bayshore Dr. SE, St. Petersburg, FL 33701.
Mailing Address: P.O. Box A, St. Petersburg, FL 33731. **Telephone:** (727) 822-6937. **Fax:** (727) 821-5819. **Website:** www.milb.com.
Year Founded: 1901.
President, Chief Executive Officer: Pat O'Conner.
Vice President: Stan Brand (Washington, D.C.).
Executive VP/Chief Operating Officer: Tim Purpura.
Manager, Baseball Operations/Executive Assistant to President: Mary Wooters.

Pat O'Conner

Senior Vice President, Business Operations: John Cook.
Vice President Legal Affairs/General Counsel: D. Scott Poley. **Assistant Director, Legal Affairs:** Sandie Hebert. **Special Counsel:** George Yund (Cincinnati, OH).
Executive Director, Baseball Operations: Tim Brunswick.
Director, Media Relations: Steve Densa.
Director, Accounting: Jonathan Shipman. **Director, Security/Facility Operations:** John Skinner. **Assistant Director, Accounting:** James Dispanet. **Manager, Accounting:** Jeff Carrier.
Director, Information Technology: Rob Colamarino.
Official Statistician: Major League Baseball Advanced Media, 75 Ninth Ave., New York, NY 10011. **Telephone:** (212) 485-3444.
2009 Winter Meetings: Indianapolis, December 7-10.

AFFILIATED MEMBERS/COUNCIL OF LEAGUE PRESIDENTS

Triple-A

League	President	Telephone	Fax Number
International	Randy Mobley	(614) 791-9300	(614) 791-9009
Mexican	Plinio Escalante	011-52-555-557-1007	011-52-555-557-1007
Pacific Coast	Branch Rickey	(719) 636-3399	(719) 636-1199

Double-A

League	President	Telephone	Fax Number
Eastern	Joe McEacharn	(207) 761-2700	(207) 761-7064
Southern	Don Mincher	(770) 321-0400	(770) 321-0037
Texas	Tom Kayser	(210) 545-5297	(210) 545-5298

High Class A

League	President	Telephone	Fax Number
California	Joe Gagliardi	(408) 369-8038	(408) 369-1409
Carolina	John Hopkins	(336) 691-9030	(336) 691-9070
Florida State	Chuck Murphy	(386) 252-7479	(386) 252-7495

Low Class A

League	President	Telephone	Fax Number
Midwest	George Spelius	(608) 364-1188	(608) 364-1913
South Atlantic	Eric Krupa	(727) 456-1420	(727) 499-6853

Short-Season

League	President	Telephone	Fax Number
New York-Penn	Ben Hayes	(727) 821-7000	(727) 822-3768
Northwest	Bob Richmond	(208) 429-1511	(208) 429-1525

Rookie Advanced

League	President	Telephone	Fax Number
Appalachian	Lee Landers	(704) 873-5300	(704) 873-4333
Pioneer	Jim McCurdy	(509) 456-7615	(509) 456-0136

Rookie

League	President	Telephone	Fax Number
Arizona	Bob Richmond	(208) 429-1511	(208) 429-1525
Dominican Summer	Orlando Diaz	(809) 532-3619	(809) 532-3619
Gulf Coast	Tom Saffell	(941) 966-6407	(941) 966-6872
Venezuela Summer	Saul Gonzalez	011-58-41-24-0321	011-58-41-24-0705

NATIONAL ASSOCIATION BOARD OF TRUSTEES

TRIPLE-A

At-large: Ken Young (Norfolk). **International League:** Mike Tamburro (Pawtucket). **Pacific Coast League:** Sam Bernabe, Chairman (Iowa). **Mexican League:** Gabriel Escalante (Campeche).

DOUBLE-A

Eastern League: Joe Finley, (Trenton). **Southern League:** Frank Burke (Chattanooga). **Texas League:** Bill Valentine (Arkansas).

CLASS A

California League: Tom Volpe (Stockton). **Carolina League:** Chuck Greenberg (Myrtle Beach). **Florida State League:** Ken Carson, secretary (Dunedin). **Midwest League:** Dave Walker (Burlington). **South Atlantic League:** Chip Moore (Rome).

SHORT-SEASON

New York-Penn League: Bill Gladstone (Tri-City). **Northwest League:** Bob Beban (Eugene).

ROOKIE

Appalachian League: Mitch Lukevics (Princeton). **Pioneer League:** Dave Baggott, vice chairman (Ogden). **Gulf Coast League:** Bill Smith (Twins).

PROFESSIONAL BASEBALL PROMOTION CORPORATION

Office Address: 201 Bayshore Dr. SE, St. Petersburg, FL 33701. **Mailing Address:** P.O. Box A, St. Petersburg, FL 33731. **Telephone:** (727) 822-6937. **Fax/Marketing:** (727) 894-4227. **Fax/Licensing:** (727) 825-3785.

President: Pat O'Conner.

Executive VP/Chief Operating Officer: Tim Purpura.

Senior Vice President, Business Operations: John Cook. **Vice President, Legal Affairs/General Counsel:** D. Scott Poley. **Executive Director, Baseball Operations:** Tim Brunswick. **Executive Director, Branded Properties:** Brian Earle. **Executive Director, Sales/Marketing:** Rod Meadows. **Director, Information Technology:** Rob Colamarino. **Director, Media Relations:** Steve Densa.

Director, Licensing: Tina Gust. **Director, Accounting:** Jonathan Shipman. **Director, Security/Facility Operations:** John Skinner. **Senior Assistant Director, Special Operations:** Kelly Ryan. **Assistant Director, Licensing:** Carrie Adams. **Assistant Director, Special Operations:** Scott Kravchuk. **Senior Manager, Sales/Marketing Operations:** Melissa Keilen. **Manager, Special Operations:** Casey Boudrot. **Manager, Exhibition Services:** Noreen Brantner. **Manager, Accounting:** Jeff Carrier. **Manager, Sponsor Relations:** Nicole Ferro. **Manager, Contracts:** Jeannette Machicote. **Manager, Team Relations:** Mary Marandi. **DAP Manager, Durham Operations/Alumni Association/Charities:** Jill Rusinko. **Manager, Trademarks:** Bryan Sayre. **Assistant to Marketing Director, Sponsorship Development:** Heather Raburn. **Assistant/Special Operations:** Darryl Henderson.

PROFESSIONAL BASEBALL UMPIRE CORPORATION

Office Address: 201 Bayshore Dr. SE, St. Petersburg, FL 33701. **Mailing Address:** P.O. Box A, St. Petersburg, FL 33731. **Telephone:** (727) 822-6937. **Fax:** (727) 821-5819.

President: Pat O'Conner. **Treasurer/Vice President Administration:** Tim Purpura. **Secretary/Vice President, Legal Affairs/General Counsel:** D. Scott Poley. **Executive Director, PBUC:** Justin Klemm (Branchburg, NJ). **Chief, Instruction/Field Evaluator:** Mike Felt (Lansing, MI).

Field Evaluators/Instructors: Jorge Bauza (San Juan, PR), Larry Reveal (Chesapeake, VA), Andy Shultz (Philadelphia). **Evaluator:** Dusty Dellinger (China Grove, NC). **Special Assistant, PBUC:** Lillian Patterson.

GENERAL INFORMATION

	Regular Season				All-Star Games	
	Teams	Games	Opening Day	Closing Day	Date	Host
International	14	144	April 9	Sept. 7	*July 15	Portland
Pacific Coast	16	144	April 9	Sept. 7	*July 15	Portland
Eastern	12	142	April 8	Sept. 7	July 15	Trenton
Southern	10	140	April 9	Sept. 7	July 13	Birmingham
Texas	8	140	April 9	Sept. 7	July 1	Frisco
California	10	140	April 9	Sept. 7	#June 23	Lake Elsinore
Carolina	8	140	April 9	Sept. 7	#June 23	Lake Elsinore
Florida State	12	140	April 9	Sept. 6	June 20	Ft. Myers
Midwest	14	140	April 9	Sept. 7	June 23	Clinton
South Atlantic	16	140	April 9	Sept. 7	June 23	Charleston, WV
New York-Penn	14	76	June 19	Sept. 6	Aug. 18	State College
Northwest	8	76	June 20	Sept. 6	None	
Appalachian	10	68	June 23	Sept. 1	None	
Pioneer	8	76	June 23	Sept. 11	None	
Arizona	9	56	June 22	Aug. 31	None	
Gulf Coast	16	56/60	June 17	Aug. 27	None	

*Triple-A All-Star Game. #California League vs. Carolina League

INTERNATIONAL LEAGUE

TRIPLE-A

Office Address: 55 South High St., Suite 202, Dublin, Ohio 43017.
Telephone: (614) 791-9300. **Fax:** (614) 791-9009.
E-Mail Address: office@ilbaseball.com. **Website:** www.ilbaseball.com.

Randy Mobley

Years League Active: 1884-

President/Treasurer: Randy Mobley

Vice Presidents: Harold Cooper, Dave Rosenfield, Tex Simone.

Assistant to the President: Chris Sprague. **Corporate Secretary:** Max Schumacher.

Directors: Bruce Baldwin (Gwinnett), Don Beaver (Charlotte), Joe Finley (Lehigh Valley), George Habel (Durham), Joe Napoli (Toledo), Bob Rich Jr. (Buffalo), Dave Rosenfield (Norfolk), Jeremy Ruby (Scranton/Wilkes-Barre), Ken Schnacke (Columbus), Max Schumacher (Indianapolis), Naomi Silver (Rochester), John Simone (Syracuse), Mike Tamburro (Pawtucket), Gary Ulmer (Louisville).

Office Manager: Gretchen Addison.

Division Structure: North-Buffalo, Lehigh Valley, Pawtucket, Rochester, Scranton/Wilkes-Barre, Syracuse. **West-**Columbus, Indianapolis, Louisville, Toledo. **South-**Charlotte, Durham, Gwinnett, Norfolk.

Regular Season: 144. **2009 Opening Date:** April 9. **Closing Date:** Sept. 7.

All-Star Game: July 15 at Portland, OR (IL vs. Pacific Coast League).

Playoff Format: South winner meets West winner in best of five series; wild card (non-division winner with best winning percentage) meets North winner in best of five series. Winners meet in best of five series for Governors' Cup championship.

Triple-A Championship Game: Sept. 22, Oklahoma City (IL vs. Pacific Coast League).

Roster Limit: 24. **Player Eligibility:** No restrictions.

Official Baseball: Rawlings ROM-INT.

Umpires: Chris Bakke (Fargo, ND), Lance Barrett (Burleson, TX), Scott Barry (Quincy, MI), Damien Beal (Birmingham, AL), Jason Bradley (Blackshear, GA), Fran Burke, Charlotte, NC), Kevin Causey (Chesterfield, VA), Chris Conroy (North Adams, MA), Mike Estabrook (Boynton Beach, FL), Chad Fairchild (Parrish, FL), Manny Gonzalez (Venezuela), Rob Healey (Warwick, RI), James Hoye (North Royalton, OH), Adrian Johnson (Houston, TX), Jason Klein (Orange, CT), Mark Lollo (New Lexington, OH), Alan Porter (Warminster, PA), Bobby Price (Marlton, NY), David Rackley (Seabrook, TX), Brian Reilly (Lansing, MI), Art Thigpen (Lakeland, FL), R.J. Thompson (Jonesborough, TN), David Uyl (Shorewood, IL), Justin Vogel (Jacksonville, FL).

STADIUM INFORMATION

			Dimensions				
Club	**Stadium**	**Opened**	**LF**	**CF**	**RF**	**Capacity**	**2008 Att.**
Buffalo	Coca-Cola Field	1988	325	404	325	18,150	590,386
Charlotte	Knights Stadium	1990	325	400	325	10,002	312,290
Columbus	Huntington Park	2009	325	400	330	15,000	537,889
Durham	Durham Bulls Athletic Park	1995	305	400	327	10,000	514,281
*Gwinnett	Gwinnett Stadium	2009	325	400	325	10,000	289,570*
Indianapolis	Victory Field	1996	320	402	320	14,500	606,166
Lehigh Valley	Coca-Cola Park	2008	336	400	325	10,000	602,033
Louisville	Louisville Slugger Field	2000	325	400	340	13,131	638,777
Norfolk	Harbor Park	1993	333	410	338	12,067	433,767
Pawtucket	McCoy Stadium	1946	325	400	325	10,031	643,049
Rochester	Frontier Field	1997	335	402	325	10,840	490,806
Scranton/WB	PNC Field	1989	330	408	330	10,982	496,658
Syracuse	Alliance Bank Stadium	1997	330	400	330	11,671	392,028
Toledo	Fifth Third Field	2002	320	412	315	8,943	584,596

*Franchise played in Richmond last year.

BUFFALO BISONS

Office Address: Coca-Cola Field, One James D. Griffin Plaza, Buffalo, NY 14203.
Telephone: (716) 846-2000. **Fax:** (716) 852-6530.
E-Mail address: info@bisons.com. **Website:** www.bisons.com.

Affiliation (first year): New York Mets (2009). **Years in League:** 1886-90, 1912-70, 1998-

OWNERSHIP, MANAGEMENT

Operated By: Rich Products Corp.

Principal Owner/President: Robert Rich Jr. **President, Rich Entertainment Group:** Melinda Rich. **President, Rich Baseball Operations:** Jon Dandes. **Vice President/Treasurer:** David Rich. **VP/Secretary:** William Gisel.

VP/General Manager: Mike Buczkowski. **VP, Finance:** Joseph Segarra. **Corporate Counsel:** Jill K. Bond, William

Grieshober. **Director, Sales:** Christopher Hill. **Director, Stadium Operations:** Tom Sciarrino. **Controller:** Kevin Parkinson. **Senior Accountants:** Rita Clark, Nicole Winiarski. **Accountant:** Amy Delaney. **Director, Ticket Operations:** Mike Poreda. **Director, Public Relations:** Brad Bisbing. **Director, Game Day Entertainment/Promotions Coordinator:** Matt LaSota. **Sales Coordinator:** Cindy Smith. **Account Executives:** Mark Gordon, Jim Harrington, Robert Kates, Amanda Kolin, Geoff Lundquist, Margaret Martello, Burt Mirti, Frank Mooney, Anthony Sprague. **Manager, Merchandise:** Kathleen Wind. **Manager, Office Services:** Margaret Russo. **Executive Assistant:** Tina Lesher. **Community Relations:** Gail Hodges. **Director, Food Services:** Robert Free. **Assistant Concessions Manager:** Roger Buczek. **Head Groundskeeper:** Dan Blank. **Chief Engineer:** Pat Chella. **Home Clubhouse/Baseball Operations Coordinator:** Scott Lesher. **Visiting Clubhouse Manager:** Dan Brick.

FIELD STAFF

Manager: Ken Oberkfell. **Coach:** Luis Natera. **Pitching Coach:** Ricky Bones. **Trainer:** Brian Chicklo.

GAME INFORMATION

Radio Announcers: Ben Wagner, Duke McGuire. **No of Games Broadcast:** Home-72, Road-72. **Flagship Station:** WWKB-1520.

PA Announcer: Unavailable. **Official Scorers:** Mike Kelly, Kevin Lester.

Stadium Name: Coca-Cola Field. **Location:** From north, take I-190 to Elm Street exit, left onto Swan Street. From east, take I-190 West to exit 51 (Route 33) to end, exit at Oak Street, right onto Swan Street. From west, take I-190 East, exit 53 to I-90 North, exit at Elm Street, left onto Swan Street. **Standard Game Times:** 7:05 p.m., 1:05 Sunday Ticket Price Range: $5-18.

Visiting Club Hotel: Adams Mark Hotel, 120 Church St, Buffalo, NY 14202. **Telephone:** (716) 845-5100. Hyatt Hotel, 2 Fountain Plaza, Buffalo, NY 14202. **Telephone:** (716) 856-1234.

CHARLOTTE KNIGHTS

Office Address: 2280 Deerfield Dr., Fort Mill, SC 29715.
Telephone: (704) 357-8071. **Fax:** (704) 329-2155.
E-Mail address: knights@charlotteknights.com. **Website:** www.charlotteknights.com.
Affiliation (first year): Chicago White Sox (1999). **Years in League:** 1993-

OWNERSHIP, MANAGEMENT

Operated by: Knights Baseball, LLC.

Principal Owners: Bill Allen, Don Beaver.

Vice President/General Manager: Dan Rajkowski. **Director, Group Sales:** Thomas Lee. **Director, Media Relations:** John Agresti. **Director, Creative Services:** Mike Riviello. **Director, Broadcasting/Team Travel:** Matt Swierad. **Director, Corporate Accounts:** Chris Semmens. **Operations Manager:** Mark McKinnon. **Business Manager:** Michael Sanger. **Sales Executive:** Heath Dillard. **Group Event Coordinators:** Chris Petot, Jacob Giles. **Box Office Coordinator:** Meredith Storrie. **Director, Merchandise:** Becka Leveille. **Head Groundskeeper:** Eddie Busque. **Assistant Groundskeeper:** Mike Headd. **Clubhouse Manager:** Dan Morphis. **Manager, Media Relations:** Patrick Starck. **Director, Community Relations:** Tim O'Reilly. **Community/Public Relations Asst.:** Nate Hill. **Corporate Sales Account Executives:** Brett Butler. **Marketing Assistant:** Chris Inklebarger. **Executive Assistant to the General Manager:** Julie Clark. **Office Manager:** Jastina Patterson.

FIELD STAFF

Manager: Chris Chambliss. **Coach:** Gary Ward. **Pitching Coach:** Richard Dotson. **Trainer:** Scott Johnson. **Strength/ Conditioning:** Chad Efron.

GAME INFORMATION

Radio Announcer: Mike Pacheco, Matt Swierad. **No. of Games Broadcast:** Home-72 Road-72. **Flagship Station:** WFNA 1660-AM.

PA Announcer: Ken Conrad. **Official Scorers:** Sam Copeland, Bill Walker.

Stadium Name: Knights Stadium. **Location:** Exit 88 off I-77, east on Gold Hill Road. **Ticket Price Range:** $8-13.

Visiting Club Hotel: Comfort Suites, 10415 Centrum Parkway, Pineville, NC 28134. **Telephone:** 704-540-0559.

COLUMBUS CLIPPERS

Office Address: 330 Huntington Park Lane, Columbus, OH 43215.
Telephone: (614) 462-5250. **Fax:** (614) 462-3271.
E-Mail address: info@clippersbaseball.com. **Website:** www.clippersbaseball.com.
Affiliation (first year): Cleveland Indians (2009). **Years in League:** 1955-70, 1977-

OWNERSHIP, MANAGEMENT

Operated By: Columbus Baseball Team Inc.

Principal Owner: Franklin County, Ohio. **Board of Directors:** Steven Francis, Tom Fries, Wayne Harer, Thomas Katzenmeyer, David Leland, Cathy Lyttle, Bob Milbourne, Richard Smith, McCullough Williams.

President/General Manager: Ken Schnacke. **Assistant GM:** Mark Warren. **Director, Stadium Operations:** Steve Dalin. **Director, Ticket Operations:** Scott Ziegler. **Assistant Director, Ticket Operations:** Eddie Langhenry. **Director, Marketing:** Mark Galuska. **Assistant Director, Marketing:** Ty Debevoise. **Director, Broadcasting:** Scott Leo. **Director,**

Communications/Media Relations: Joe Santry. **Assistant Director, Media Relations:** Anthony Slosser. **Director, Merchandising:** Krista Oberlander. **Assistant Director, Merchandising:** Brittany White. **Director, Finance:** Bonnie Badgley. **Director, Group Sales:** Ben Keller. **Assistant Director, Group Sales:** Brett Patton. **Director, Corporate/Special Events:** Anna Larimer. **Assistant to GM:** Kelly Ryther. **Administrative Assistant, Tickets:** Ashley Alexander. **Administrative Assistants, Marketing:** Kyle Blizzard, Paula Knudsen. **Director, Multimedia:** Yoshi Ando. **Director, Clubhouse Operations:** George Robinson. **Home Clubhouse Manager:** Jeremy Delewski. **Visiting Clubhouse Manager:** John White. **Administrative Assistants:** Alex Gleitman, Gabe Norris.

FIELD STAFF

Manager: Torey Lovullo. **Hitting Coach:** Jon Nunnally. **Pitching Coach:** Scott Radinsky. **Trainer:** Jeff Desjardins. **Strength/Conditioning Coach:** Brendan Verner.

GAME INFORMATION

Radio Announcer: Scott Leo. **No of Games Broadcast:** Home-72, Road-72. **Flagship Station:** WMNI 920AM.

PA Announcer: Colin Smith. **Official Scorer:** Jim Habermehl.

Stadium Name: Huntington Park. **Location: From north:** South on I-71 to I-670 west. Exit at Neil Avenue. Turn left at intersection onto Neil Avenue. **From south:** North on I-71. Exit at Front St. (#100A). Turn left at intersection onto Front Street. Turn left onto Nationwide Blvd. **From east:** West on I-70. Exit at Fourth Street. Continue on Fulton Street to Front Street. Turn right onto Front Street. Turn left onto Nationwide Blvd. **From west:** East on I-70. Exit at Fourth Street. Continue on Fulton Street to Front Street. Turn right onto Front Street. Turn left onto Nationwide Blvd.

Ticket Price Range: $6-15.

Visiting Club Hotel: Crowne Plaza, 33 E. Nationwide Blvd., Columbus, OH 43215. **Telephone:** 877-348-2424. Drury Hotels Columbus Convention Center, 88 E. Nationwide Blvd., Columbus, OH 43215. **Telephone:** 614-221-7008. Hyatt Regency Downtown, 350 N. High St., Columbus, OH 43215. **Telephone:** 614-463-1234.

DURHAM BULLS

Office Address: 409 Blackwell St., Durham, NC 27701.
Mailing Address: P.O. Box 507, Durham, NC 27702.
Telephone: (919) 687-6500. **Fax:** (919) 687-6560.
Website: www.durhambulls.com
Affiliation (first year): Tampa Bay Rays (1998). **Years in League:** 1998-

OWNERSHIP, MANAGEMENT

Operated By: Capitol Broadcasting Company, Inc.

President, CEO: Jim Goodmon.

Vice President: George Habel.

General Manager: Mike Birling. **Assistant GM:** Jon Bishop. **Account Executive, Sponsorships:** Cameron Knowles, Chris Overby, Neil Solondz, Gregg Van Leuven. **Coordinator, Sponsorship Services:** Allison Phillips. **Director, Media Relations/Promotions:** Matt DeMargel. **Coordinator, Multimedia:** Ari Ecker. **Coordinator, Mascot/Community Relations:** Nicholas Tennant. **Assistant, Media Relations/Promotions:** Wes Skipwith. **Director, Ticketing:** Tim Season. **Business Development Coordinators:** Rich Brady, Lindsey Dawson, Mike Miller, Mary Beth Warfford, Clay White. **GM, Concessions:** Jamie Jenkins. **Assistant GM, Concessions:** Tammy Scott. **Head Groundskeeper:** Scott Strickland. **Manager, Business:** Rhonda Carlile. **Supervisor, Accounting:** Theresa Stocking. **Accountant:** Emily Farlow. **Security:** Ed Sarvis. **Box Office Sales:** Jerry Mach. **Manager, Home Clubhouse:** Colin Saunders. **Visiting/Umpires Clubhouses:** Aaron Kuehner. **Team Ambassador:** Bill Law.

FIELD STAFF

Manager: Charlie Montoyo. **Coach:** Unavailable. **Pitching Coach:** Xavier Hernandez. **Trainer:** Unavailable.

GAME INFORMATION

Radio Announcers: Steve Barnes, Neil Solondz, Ken Tanner. **No. of Games Broadcast:** Home-72, Road-72. **Flagship Station:** 99.9 FM The Fan.

PA Announcer: Tony Riggsbee. **Official Scorer:** Brent Belvin.

Stadium Name: Durham Bulls Athletic Park. **Location:** From Raleigh, I-40 West to Highway 147 North, exit 12B to Willard, two blocks on Willard to stadium. From I-85, Gregson Street exit to downtown, left on Chapel Hill Street, right on Mangum Street. **Standard Game Times:** 7 p.m., Sunday 5 p.m. **Ticket Price Range:** $6-9.

Visiting Club Hotel: Durham Marriot at the Civic Center, 201 Foster St., Durham, NC 27701. **Telephone:** (919) 768-6000.

GWINNETT BRAVES

Office Address: One Braves Ave, Lawrenceville, GA 30043.
Mailing Address: One Braves Ave, Lawrenceville, GA 30043.
Telephone: (678) 277-0300. **Fax:** (678) 277-0338
E-Mail Address: gwinnettinfo@braves.com. **Website:** www.gwinnettbraves.com
Affiliation (first year): Atlanta Braves (1966). **Years in League:** 1884, 1915-17, 1954-64, 1966-

OWNERSHIP, MANAGEMENT

General Manager: Bruce Baldwin. **Assistant General Managers:** Bill Blackwell, Toby Wyman. **Office Manager:** Deanne Proud. **Manager, Stadium Operations:** Ryan Stoltenberg. **Manager, Field Maintenance:** Gerry Huppman. **Manager, Public/Community Affairs:** Courtney Lawson. **Manager, Corporate Sales:** Samantha Dunn. **Manager, Ticket Operations:** Mike Castle. **Coordinator, Marketing/Promotions:** Lisa Howell. **Coordinator, Public Affairs:** Chris Downey. **Ticket/Corporate Sales Representatives:** Jerry Pennington, Lindsay Harmon.

FIELD STAFF

Manager: Dave Brundage. **Coach:** Jamie Dismuke. **Pitching Coach:** Derek Botelho. **Trainer:** Mike Graus.

GAME INFORMATION

Radio Announcers: Tony Schiavone, Judd Hickinbotham. **No of Games Broadcast:** Home-72 Road-72. **Flagship Station:** WDUN 550-AM.

PA Announcer: TBD. **Official Scorers:** Tim Gaines, Frank Barnett, James Roberts, Jamie Britt.

Stadium Name: Gwinnett Stadium. **Location:** I-85 (at Exit 115, S.R. 20 West) and I-985 (at Exit 4), follow signs to park. **Ticket Price Range:** $5-30.

Visiting Club Hotel: Courtyard by Marriott Buford/Mall of Georgia, 1405 Mall of Georgia Boulevard, Buford, GA 30519 (678) 215-8007

INDIANAPOLIS INDIANS

Office Address: 501 W. Maryland Street, Indianapolis, IN 46225.
Telephone: (317) 269-3542. **Fax:** (317) 269-3541.
E-Mail address: indians@indyindians.com. **Website:** www.indyindians.com.
Affiliation (first year): Pittsburgh Pirates (2005). **Years in League:** 1963, 1998-.

OWNERSHIP, MANAGEMENT

Operated By: Indians Inc.

President/Chairman of the Board: Max Schumacher.

Vice President/General Manager: Cal Burleson. **Assistant General Manager:** Randy Lewandowski. **Director, Marketing/Communications:** Chris Herndon. **Director, Facilities:** Tim Hughes. **Director, Business Operations:** Brad Morris. **Director, Tickets:** Matt Guay. **Manager, Corporate Partnerships:** Joel Zawacki. **Director, Merchandising:** Mark Schumacher. **Director, Broadcasting:** Howard Kellman. **Event Operations Manager:** Mark Anderson. **Stadium Operations Manager:** Steve Bray. **Stadium Maintenance Manager:** Allan Danehy. **Office Manager:** Julie Fischer. **Administrative Assistant:** Angela Kendall. **Assistant Director, Facilities:** Bill Sampson. **Marketing Coordinator/Designer:** Diana Biette. **Media Relations Manager:** Brian Bosma. **Community Relations Manager:** Ryan Bowman. **Marketing Manager:** Autumn Gasior. **Merchandising Assistant:** Stu Tobias. **Ticket Services Manager:** Bryan Spisak. **Senior Ticket/Premium Services Manager:** Kerry Vick. **Ticket Sales Executives:** Ryan Barrett, Drew Heincker, Jonathan Howard, Keri Oberting. **Mascot Coordinator:** Chris Goldfarb. **Ticket Services Assistants:** Cris Haro, Kyle Fisher, Bradley Vitale. **Media Relations Assistant:** Andrew Jennings. **Community Relations Assistant:** Molly Madtson. **Merchandise Assistant:** Ryan Dyer. **Promotions Assistant:** Adam Pitt. **Head Groundskeeper:** Joey Stevenson. **Assistant Groundskeeper:** Evan Buckley. **Home Clubhouse Manager:** Bob Martin. **Visiting Clubhouse Managers:** Jeremy Martin.

FIELD STAFF

Manager: Frank Kremblas. **Hitting Coach:** Jeff Branson. **Pitching Coach:** Ray Searage. **Trainer:** Jose Ministral. **Strength/Conditioning Coach:** Mubarak Malik.

GAME INFORMATION

Radio Announcer: Howard Kellman, Scott McCauley. **No. of Games Broadcast:** Home-72, Road-72. **Flagship Station:** WXLW 950-AM.

PA Announcer: Bruce Schumacher. **Official Scorers:** Bill McAfee, Gary Johnson, Kim Rogers.

Stadium Name: Victory Field. **Location:** I-70 to West Street exit, north on West Street to ballpark. I-65 to Martin Luther King and West Street exit, south on West Street to ballpark. **Standard Game Times:** 7 p.m. on Mon/Tues/Thur/Sat., 1 p.m. on Wed., 7:15 p.m. on Fri., 2 p.m. on Sun. **Ticket Price Range:** $9-13.

Visiting Club Hotel: Holiday Inn Express, 410 South Missouri Street, Indianapolis, IN 46225. **Telephone:** (317) 822-6400. Comfort Suites, 515 S. West Street., Indianapolis, IN 46225. **Telephone:** (317) 631-9000.

LEHIGH VALLEY IRONPIGS

Office Address: 1050 IronPigs Way, Allentown, PA 18109.
Telephone: (610) 841-7447. **Fax:** (610) 841-1509.
E-Mail address: info@ironpigsbaseball.com. **Website:** www.ironpigsbaseball.com.
Affiliation (first year): Philadelphia Phillies (2008). **Years in League:** 2008-

OWNERSHIP, MANAGEMENT

Ownership: Gracie Baseball LP,

President: Chuck Domino.

General Manager: Kurt Landes. **Assistant GM, Marketing:** Danny Tetzlaff. **Assistant GM, Ticketing:** Howard Scharf.

Director, Media Relations: Matt Provence. **Manager, Media Relations:** Jon Schaeffer. **Director, Community Relations:** Sarah Marten. **Director, Merchandise:** Janine Kurpiel. **Manager, Merchandise:** Julie Rowan. **Director, Ticket Sales:** Scott Hodge. **Director, Ticket Operations:** Amy Schoch. **Director, Group Sales:** Don Wilson. **Director, Marketing:** Ron Rushe. **Director, Marketing Services:** Christa Linzey. **Director, Creative Services:** Matt Zidik. **Director, Promotions:** Lindsey Knupp. **Director, Special Events:** Mary Nixon. **Event Coordinator:** Kristen Cooper. **Director, Concessions:** Alex Rivera. **Manager, Concessions:** Brock Hartranft. **Executive Chef:** John Ponist. **Director, Finance:** Deb Landes. **Manager, Finance:** Michelle Perl. **Stadium Operations Managers:** Paul Cashin, Jason Kiesel. **Marketing Managers:** Corey Bugno, Matt Glass, Josh LaBarba. **Manager, Ticket Operations:** Erin Owens. **Tickets/Group Representatives:** Mark Anderson, Ryan Contento, Scott Evans, Katrina Lerch, Bryan Schuster, Brandon Smith, Katie Ward. **Field Operations:** Bill Butler. **Receptionist:** Ashley Bielec.

FIELD STAFF

Manager: Dave Huppert. **Hitting Coach:** Greg Gross. **Pitching Coach:** Rod Nichols. **Trainer:** Jason Kirkman.

GAME INFORMATION

Radio Announcers: Matt Provence, Jon Schaeffer. **No. Games Broadcast:** 144 (72 Home; 72 Away). **Flagship Radio Station:** ESPN 1240/1320 AM. **Television Station:** TV2. **Television Announcers:** Mike Zambelli, Ricky Bottalico, Matt Provence. **No. Games Televised:** 72 Home. **PA Announcer:** Tim Chorones. **Official Scorers:** Jack Logic, David Sheriff.

Stadium Name: Coca-Cola Park.

Location: Take U.S. 22 to exit for Airport Road South. Head south, make right on American Parkway. Left into stadium. **Standard Game Times:** 7:05 p.m.; Sun. 1:35 p.m. (April-May), 5:35 p.m. (June-August).

Visiting Club Hotel: Hotel Bethlehem (437 Main Street, Bethlehem, PA 18018). **Telephone:** (610) 625-5000

LOUISVILLE BATS

Office Address: 401 E. Main St, Louisville, KY 40202.
Telephone: (502) 212-2287. **Fax:** (502) 515-2255.
E-Mail address: info@batsbaseball.com. **Website:** www.batsbaseball.com.
Affiliation (first year): Cincinnati Reds (2000). **Years in League:** 1998-

OWNERSHIP, MANAGEMENT

Chariman: Dan Ulmer Jr. **Board of Directors:** Edward Glasscock, Gary Ulmer, Roberts Stallings, Kenny Huber, Steve Trager, J. Michael Brown.

Vice President/GM: Dale Owens. **Assistant GM/Director, Marketing:** Greg Galiette. **Director, Stadium Operations:** Scott Shoemaker. **Director, Ticket Sales:** James Breeding. **Director, Baseball Operations:** Earl Stubblefield. **Controller:** Michele Anderson. **Manager, Tickets:** George Veith. **Director, Ticket Operations:** Kyle Reh. **Director, Public Relations:** Megan Dimond. **Director, Group Sales:** Bryan McBride. **Director, Broadcasting:** Jim Kelch. **Director, Suite Level Services:** Kerri Ferrell. **Senior Account Executives:** Hal Norwood, Jason Abraham, Josh Hargreaves. **Assistant Director, Public Relations:** Nick Evans. **Assistant Director, Stadium Operations:** Brian Tabler. **Account Executive/Radio Broadcaster:** Matt Andrews. **Account Executives:** Evan Patrick, Curtis Cunningham, Sarah Nordman, Tony Brown, Patrick Crush. **Community Relations:** Jodi Tischendorf. **Groundskeeper:** Tom Nielsen.

FIELD STAFF

Manager: Rick Sweet. **Hitting Coach:** Adrian "Smokey" Garrett. **Pitching Coach:** Ted Power. **Trainer:** Chris Lapole.

GAME INFORMATION

Radio Announcers: Jim Kelch, Matt Andrews. **No. of Games Broadcast:** Home-72, Road-72. **Flagship Station:** WKRD 790-AM.

PA Announcer: Charles Gazaway. **Official Scorer:** Ken Horn. **Organist:** Bob Ramsey.

Stadium Name: Louisville Slugger Field. **Location:** I-64 and I-71 to I-65 South/North to Brook Street exit, right on Market Street, left on Jackson Street; stadium on Main Street between Jackson and Preston. **Ticket Price Range:** $5-10.

Visiting Club Hotel: Galt House Hotel, 140 North Fourth Street, Louisville, KY 40202. **Telephone:** (502) 589-5200.

NORFOLK TIDES

Office Address: 150 Park Ave, Norfolk, VA 23510.
Telephone: (757) 622-2222. **Fax:** (757) 624-9090.
E-Mail Address: receptionist@norfolktides.com. **Website:** www.norfolktides.com.
Affiliation (first year): Baltimore Orioles (2007). **Years in League:** 1969-

OWNERSHIP, MANAGEMENT

Operated By: Tides Baseball Club Inc.

President: Ken Young.

General Manager: Dave Rosenfield. **Assistant GM:** Ben Giancola. **Business Manager:** Mike Giedlin. **Director, Media Relations:** Ian Locke. **Director, Community Relations:** Heather McKeating. **Director, Ticket Operations:** Gretchen Todd. **Business Manager:** Mike Giedlin. **Director, Group Sales:** Stephanie Brammer. **Director, Stadium Operations:** Mike Zeman. **Manager, Merchandising:** Mandy Cormier. **Corporate Sponsorships, Promotions:** Jonathan Mensink, Mike Watkins. **Director, Corporate Development/Military Affairs:** H.M. "Bones" Reynolds. **Assistant Director, Stadium Operations:** Mike Cardwell. **Box Office Manager:** Linda Waisanen. **Event Staff Manager:** Kayla Seil. **Ticket Office**

Assistant: Sze Fong. **Administrative Assistant:** Stefanie Cola. **Group Sales Assistants:** Sara Keyzers, Christina Dewey. **Head Groundskeeper:** Kenny Magner. **Assistant Groundskeeper:** Keith Collins. **Home Clubhouse Manager:** Kevin Casey. **Visiting Clubhouse Manager:** Mark Bunge.

FIELD STAFF

Manager: Gary Allenson. **Coach:** Dallas Williams. **Pitching Coach:** Mike Griffin. **Trainer:** Mark Shires.

GAME INFORMATION

Radio Announcers: Bob Socci, Pete Michaud. **No. of Games Broadcast:** Home-72, Road-72. **Flagship Station:** ESPN 1310-AM.

PA Announcers: John Lewis, Jack Ankerson. **Official Scorers:** Dave Lewis, Mike Holtzclaw.

Stadium Name: Harbor Park. **Location:** Exit 9, 11A or 11B off I-264, adjacent to the Elizabeth River in downtown Norfolk. **Ticket Price Range:** $9.50-11.

Visiting Club Hotel: Sheraton Waterside, 777 Waterside Dr, Norfolk, VA 23510. **Telephone:** (757) 622-6664.

PAWTUCKET RED SOX

Office Address: One Ben Mondor Way, Pawtucket, RI 02860.
Mailing Address: P.O. Box 2365, Pawtucket, RI 02861.
Telephone: (401) 724-7300. **Fax:** (401) 724-2140.
E-Mail Address: info@pawsox.com. **Website:** www.pawsox.com.
Affiliation (first year): Boston Red Sox (1973). **Years in League:** 1973-

OWNERSHIP, MANAGEMENT

Operated by: Pawtucket Red Sox Baseball Club, Inc.

Chairman: Ben Mondor. **President:** Mike Tamburro.

Vice President/General Manager: Lou Schwechheimer. **VP, Chief Financial Officer:** Matt White. **VP, Sales/Marketing:** Michael Gwynn. **VP, Stadium Operations:** Mick Tedesco. **VP, Public Relations:** Bill Wanless. **Director, Community Relations:** Jeff Bradley. **Manager, Sales:** Augusto Rojas. **Manager, Finance:** Kathryn Tingley. **Director, Merchandising:** Eric Petterson. **Director, Media Creation:** Kevin Galligan. **Director, Concession Services:** Jim Hogan. **Director, Corporate Sales:** Mike Abramson. **Director, Warehouse Operations:** Dave Johnson. **Director, Group Sales:** Bill Crawford. **Asst. Director, Community Relations:** Becky Berta. **Account Executive:** Ben Bradley. **Head Groundskeeper:** Matt McKinnon. **Director, Security:** Rick Medeiros. **Director, Clubhouse Operations:** Carl Goodreau. **Executive Chef:** Ken Bowdish.

FIELD STAFF

Manager: Ron Johnson. **Coach:** Russ Morman. **Pitching Coach:** Rich Sauveur. **Trainer:** Greg Barajas.

GAME INFORMATION

Radio Announcer: Dan Hoard, Steve Hyder. **No. of Games Broadcast:** Home-72, Away-72. **Flagship Station:** WHJJ 920-AM.

PA Announcer: Jim Martin. **Official Scorer:** Bruce Guindon.

Stadium Name: McCoy Stadium. **Location:** From north, 95 South to exit 2A in Massachusetts (Newport Ave.), follow Newport Ave. for 2 miles, right on Columbus Ave., follow one mile, stadium on right. From south, 95 North to exit 28 (School Street), right at bottom of exit ramp, through two sets of lights, left onto Pond Street, right on Columbus Ave., stadium entrance on left. From west (Worcester), 295 North to 95 South and follow directions from north. From east (Fall River), 195 West to 95 North and follow directions from south. **Standard Game Times:** 7 p.m.; Sat. 6, Sun. 1. **Ticket Price Range:** $6-10.

Visiting Club Hotel: Comfort Inn, 2 George St., Pawtucket, RI 02860. **Telephone:** (401) 723-6700.

ROCHESTER RED WINGS

Office Address: One Morrie Silver Way, Rochester, NY 14608.
Telephone: (585) 454-1001. **Fax:** (585) 454-1056, (585) 454-1057.
E-Mail Address: info@redwingsbaseball.com. **Website:** www.redwingsbaseball.com.
Affiliation (first year): Minnesota Twins (2003). **Years in League:** 1885-89, 1891-92, 1895-

OWNERSHIP, MANAGEMENT

Operated by: Rochester Community Baseball.

Chairman, Chief Operating Officer: Naomi Silver. **President:** Gary Larder.

General Manager: Dan Mason. **Assistant GM:** Will Rumbold. **Controller:** Darlene Giardina. **Head Groundskeeper:** Gene Buonomo. **Director, Media/Public Relations:** Chuck Hinkel. **Director, Corporate Development:** Nick Sciarratta. **Group/Picnic Director:** Parker Allen. **Director, Promotions:** Matt Cipro. **Director, Ticket Operations:** Rob Dermody. **Director, Production:** Jeff Coltoniak. **Director, Merchandising:** Barbara Moore. **Director, Human Resources:** Paula LoVerde. **Account Executive:** Jeff Cogan, Bob Craig. **Assistant Director, Groups/Picnics:** Zach Holmes. **Executive Secretary:** Ginny Colbert. **Director, Food Services:** Jeff Dodge. **Manager, Catering:** Courtney Trawitz. **Manager, Concessions:** Jeff DeSantis. **Business Manager, Concessions:** Dave Bills. **Clubhouse Operations:** Terry Costello.

FIELD STAFF

Manager: Stan Cliburn. **Coach:** Ricardo Ingram. **Pitching Coach:** Bobby Cuellar. **Trainer:** Tony Leo.

GAME INFORMATION

Radio Announcers: Joe Altobelli, Josh Whetzel. **No. of Games Broadcast:** Home-72, Away-72. **Flagship Stations:** WHTK 1280-AM, WYSL 1040-AM.

PA Announcer: Kevin Spears. **Official Scorer:** Warren Kozereski.

Stadium Name: Frontier Field. **Location:** I-490 East to exit 12 (Brown/Broad Street) and follow signs. I-490 West to exit 14 (Plymouth Ave.) and follow signs. **Standard Game Times:** 7:05 p.m., Sun 1:35. **Ticket Price Range:** $6.50-10.50

Visiting Club Hotel: Crown Plaza, 70 State St., **Rochester, NY 14608. Telephone:** (585) 546-3450.

SCRANTON/WILKES-BARRE YANKEES

Office Address: 235 Montage Mountain Rd, Moosic, PA 18507.

Telephone: (570) 969-2255. **Fax:** (570) 963-6564.

E-Mail address: info@swbyankees.com. **Website:** www.swbyankees.com.

Affiliation (first year): New York Yankees (2007). **Years in League:** 1989-

OWNERSHIP, MANAGEMENT

Operated By: Mandalay Baseball Properties.

President: Kristen Rose.

Executive Vice President/General Manager: Jeremy Ruby. **VP, Marketing Services:** Jon Stephenson. **VP, Corporate Partnerships:** Jason Tribbet. **VP, Accounting/Finance:** Paul Chilek. **VP, Ticket Sales:** Ryan Limburg. **VP, Stadium Operations:** Curt Camoni. **Accounting Manager:** Billy Steiner. **Vice President, Corporate Partnerships:** Jason Tribbet. **Director, Corporate Partnerships:** Mike Trudnak. **Play Ball/Sponsor Service Manager:** Mike Cummings. **Sponsor Service Manager:** Kristina Knight. **Sponsor Service Manager:** Jeff Verklan. **Suite/Sponsor Service Manager:** Angela Wright. **Sales, Marketing Manager:** Josh Katyl. **Corporate Marketing Managers:** Tim Connell, Dave Walsh. **Senior Group Sales Manager:** Raquel Bonventre. **Group Sales Coordinators:** Blake Burgess, Brandon Lawrence, Robert McLane, Chris Muhlberg, Andrew Reichert. **Customer Account Managers:** Janice Matacic, Steve Vasilenko. **Director, Ticket Operations:** Jeff Weinhold. **Box Office Manager:** Ann Marie Nocera. **Director, Merchandise:** Sarah Phillips. **Head Groundskeeper:** Steve Horne. **Assistant Groundskeeper:** Bill Casterline. **Director, Facility Operations:** Joe Villano. **Office Manager:** Kelly Byron. **Director, Broadcasting/Media Relations:** Mike Vander Woude. **Director, Game Entertainment:** Barry Snyder.

FIELD STAFF

Manager: Dave Miley. **Coach:** Butch Wynegar. **Pitching Coach:** Scott Aldred. **Coach:** Aaron Ledesma. **Trainer:** Darren London. **Strength/Conditioning Coach:** Lee Tressel.

GAME INFORMATION

Radio Announcer: Mike Vander Woude. **No of Games Broadcast:** Home-72 Road-72. **Flagship Station:** WICK 1340-1400 AM.

PA Announcer: Johnny Davies. **Official Scorers:** Jeep Fanucci, Bob McGoff.

Stadium Name: PNC Field. **Location:** I-81 to exit 182 (Davis Street/Montage Mountain Road), take Montage Mountain Road one mile to stadium. **Ticket Price Range:** $8-10.

Visiting Club Hotel: Radisson at Lackawanna Stadium, 700 Lackawanna Ave, Scranton, PA 18503. **Telephone:** (570) 342-8300.

SYRACUSE CHIEFS

Office Address: One Tex Simone Dr., Syracuse, NY 13208.

Telephone: (315) 474-7833. **Fax:** (315) 474-2658.

E-Mail Address: baseball@syracusechiefs.com. **Website:** www.syracusechiefs.com.

Affiliation (first year): Washington Nationals (2009). **Years in League:** 1885-89, 1891-92, 1894-1901, 1918, 1920-27, 1934-55, 1961-.

OWNERSHIP, MANAGEMENT

Operated by: Community Owned Baseball Club of Central New York, Inc.

Chairman: Charles Rich. **President:** Ron Gersbacher. **Executive Vice President/COO:** Anthony "Tex" Simone. **General Manager:** John Simone. **Assistant General Manager/Director, Marketing/Promotions:** Mike Voutsinas. **Assistant General Manager, Business:** Don Lehtonen. **Director, Sales:** Paul Fairbanks. **Director, Group Sales:** Victor Gallucci. **Director, Broadcasting/Public Relations:** Bob McElligott. **Director, Merchandising:** Wendy Shoen. **Director, Ticket Office:** Erin Shappell. **Director, Operations:** H.J. Refici. **Administrative Assistant:** Priscilla Venditti. **Turf Manager:** Wes Ganobcik. **Team Historian:** Ron Gersbacher.

FIELD STAFF

Manager: Tim Foli. **Coach:** Darnell Coles. **Pitching Coach:** Steve McCatty. **Trainer:** Unavailable.

GAME INFORMATION

Radio Announcer: Bob McElligott. **No. of Games Broadcast:** Home-72, Away-72. **Flagship Station:** WHEN Sportsradio 620-AM, NOVA 105.1-FM.

PA Announcer: Brent Axe. **Official Scorer:** Tom Leo.

Stadium Name: Alliance Bank Stadium. **Location:** New York State Thruway to exit 36 (I-81 South), to 7th North Street exit, left on 7th North, right on Hiawatha Boulevard. **Standard Game Times:** 7 p.m., Sun. 6. **Ticket Price Range:** $6-10.

Visiting Club Hotel: Ramada Inn, 1305 Buckley Rd., Syracuse, NY 13212. **Telephone:** (315) 457-8670.

TOLEDO MUD HENS

Office Address: 406 Washington St, Toledo, OH 43604.
Telephone: (419) 725-4367. **Fax:** (419) 725-4368.
E-Mail address: mudhens@mudhens.com. **Website:** www.mudhens.com.
Affiliation (first year): Detroit Tigers (1987). **Years in League:** 1889, 1965-

OWNERSHIP, MANAGEMENT

Operated By: Toledo Mud Hens Baseball Club, Inc.

Chairman of the Board: Michael Miller.

Vice President: David Huey. **Secretary/Treasurer:** Charles Bracken.

President/General Manager: Joseph Napoli.

Assistant GM/Director, Marketing, Advertising, Sales: Scott Jeffer. **Assistant GM/Director, Corporate Partnerships:** Neil Neukam. **Assistant GM, Ticket Sales/Operations:** Erik Ibsen. **CFO:** Pam Alspach. **Manager, Promotions:** JaMay Edwards. **Director, Media/Public Relations:** Jason Griffin. **Director, Ticket Sales/Services:** Thom Townley. **Accounting:** Sheri Kelly, Brian Leverenz. **Manager, Gameday Operations:** Greg Setola. **Manager, Box Office Sales:** Justin Morelli. **Manager, Community Relations:** Cheri Pastula. **Corporate Sales Associate:** Ed Sintic, Todd Yunker. **Season Ticket/ Group Sales Associates:** Chris Hole, Mike Keedy, Frank Kristie, Kyle Moll, John Mulka, Eric Tomaszewski. **Manager, Online Marketing:** Nathan Steinmetz. **Season Ticket Service Coordinator:** Jessica Aten. **Manager, Video Board Operations:** Mike Ramirez. **Graphic Designer:** Dan Royer. **Manager, Souvenir Sales:** Craig Katz. **Assistant Manager, Souvenir Sales:** Heidi Srock. **Manager, Ballpark Operations:** Ken Westenkirchner. **Office Manager:** Carol Hamilton. **Executive Assistant:** Tracy Evans. **Turf Manager:** Jake Tyler. **Assistant Turf Manager:** Kyle Leppelmeier. **Clubhouse Manager:** Joe Sarkisian. **Team Historian:** John Husman.

FIELD STAFF

Manager: Larry Parrish. **Coach:** Leon Durham. **Pitching Coach:** A.J. Sager. **Trainer:** Matt Rankin.

GAME INFORMATION

Radio Announcers: Frank Gilhooley, Jim Weber, Jason Griffin. **No of Games Broadcast:** Home-72 Road-72. **Flagship Station:** WCWA 1230 AM

PA Announcer: Kevin Mullan. **Official Scorers:** Jeff Businger, Ron Klenfelter, Guy Lammers, Jay Wagner.

Stadium Name: Fifth Third Field. **Location:** From Ohio Turnpike 80/90, exit 54 (4A) to I-75 North, follow I-75 North to exit 201-B, left onto Erie Street, right onto Washington Street. From Detroit, I-75 South to exit 202-A, right onto Washington Street. From Dayton, I-75 North to exit 201-B, left onto Erie Street, right on Washington Street. From Ann Arbor, Route 23 South to I-475 East, I-475 east to I-75 South, I-75 South to exit 202-A, right onto Washington Street. **Ticket Price Range:** $9.

Visiting Club Hotel: Park Inn, 101 North Summit, Toledo, OH 43604. **Telephone:** (419) 241-3000.

PACIFIC COAST LEAGE

PACIFIC COAST LEAGUE

TRIPLE-A

Mailing Address: 630 Southpointe Court, Suite 106, Colorado Springs, CO 80906.
Telephone: (719) 636-3399. **Fax:** (719) 636-1199.
E-Mail Address: office@pclbaseball.com. **Website:** www.pclbaseball.com.
President: Branch B. Rickey.
Vice President: Don Logan (Las Vegas).

Branch Rickey

Directors: Don Beaver (New Orleans), Sam Bernabe (Iowa), Dave Chase (Memphis), Chris Cummings (Fresno), Dave Elmore (Colorado Springs), Kirby Schlegel (Tacoma), Don Logan (Las Vegas), Jay Miller (Round Rock), Greg Miller (Salt Lake), Bill Shea (Omaha), Scott Pruitt (Oklahoma), Merritt Paulson (Portland), Art Savage (Sacramento), John Traub (Albuquerque), Glenn Yaeger (Nashville), Stuart Katzoff (Reno).

Vice President, Business Operations: George King. **Director, Administration:** Melanie Fiore. **Director, Media/Operations:** John Meyer.

Division Structure: American Conference—Northern: Iowa, Memphis, Nashville, Omaha. **Southern:** Albuquerque, New Orleans, Oklahoma, Round Rock. **Pacific Conference—Northern:** Colorado Springs, Portland, Salt Lake, Tacoma. **Southern:** Fresno, Las Vegas, Sacramento, Reno.

Regular Season: 144 games. **2009 Opening Date:** April 9. **Closing Date:** Sept. 7.

All-Star Game: July 15 at Portland, OR (PCL vs. International League).

Playoff Format: Pacific Conference/Northern winner meets Southern winner, and American Conference/Northern winner meets Southern winner in best-of-five semifinal series. Winners meet in best-of-five series for league championship.

Triple-A Championship Game: Sept. 22, Oklahoma City (PCL vs. International League).

Roster Limit: 24. **Player Eligibility Rule:** No restrictions.

Brand of Baseball: Rawlings ROM.

Umpires: Dan Bellino (Crystal Lake, IL), Cory Blaser (Westminster, CO), Angel Campos (San Bernadino, CA), Delfin Colon (San Juan, Puerto Rico), Robert Drake (Mesa, AZ), Stephen Fritzoni (Hesperio, CA), Chris Guccione (Brighton, CO), Jason Kiser (Columbia, MO), Brian Knight (Helena, MT), Barry Larson (Hayden, ID), Jeff Latter (Gresham, OR), Eric Loveless (Layton, UT), Jeff Macias (Phoenix, AZ), Jonathan Merry (Dahlonega, GA), Casey Moser (Iowa Park, TX), Michael Muchlinski (Ephrata, WA), Shawn Rakos (Orting, WA), D.J. Reyburn (Nashville, TN), Mark Ripperger (Carlsbad, CA), Will Robinson (Savannah, GA), Todd Tichenor (Holcomb, KS), Chris Tiller (Bullard, TX), Jake Uhlenhopp (Phoenix, AZ), Jason Dunn (Savannah, TN), John Brammer (Benbrook, TX), John Tumpane (Oak Lawn, IL), Vic Carapazza (Nashville, TN), Tyler Funneman (Wildwood, IL).

			Dimensions				
Club	Stadium	Opened	LF	CF	RF	Capacity	2008 Att.
Albuquerque	Isotopes Park	2003	340	400	340	13,279	593,606
Colorado Springs	Security Service Field	1988	350	410	350	8,400	303,048
Fresno	Chukchansi Park	2002	324	402	335	12,500	526,754
Iowa	Principal Park	1992	335	400	335	11,000	487,348
Las Vegas	Cashman Field	1983	328	433	328	9,334	374,780
Memphis	AutoZone Park	2000	319	400	322	14,200	569,172
Nashville	Herschel Greer Stadium	1978	327	400	327	10,700	354,662
New Orleans	Zephyr Field	1997	333	405	332	10,000	349,500
Oklahoma	AT&T Bricktown Ballpark	1998	325	400	325	13,066	470,140
Omaha	Johnny Rosenblatt Stadium	1948	332	408	332	24,000	349,376
Portland	PGE Park	1926	319	405	321	19,810	392,512
*Reno	Aces Ballpark	2009	339	410	340	9,000	245,121
Round Rock	The Dell Diamond	2000	330	400	325	10,000	668,623
Sacramento	Raley Field	2000	330	405	325	14,111	700,168
Salt Lake	Franklin Covey Field	1994	345	420	315	15,500	500,780
Tacoma	Cheney Stadium	1960	325	425	325	9,600	327,871

* Franchise played in Tucson in 2008.

ALBUQUERQUE ISOTOPES

Office Address: 1601 Avenida Cesar Chavez SE, Albuquerque, NM 87106.
Telephone: (505) 924-2255. **Fax:** (505) 242-8899.
E-Mail address: info@albuquerquebaseball.com.
Website: www.albuquerquebaseball.com.
Affiliation (first year): Los Angeles Dodgers (2009). **Years in League:** 1972-2000, 2003-

OWNERSHIP, MANAGEMENT

President: Ken Young. **Secretary/Treasurer:** Emmett Hammond. **General Manager:** John Traub. **Assistant General Manager, Sales/Marketing:** Nick LoBue. **Director, Box Office/Retail Operations:** Chrissy Baines. **Director,**

Sales/Promotions: Adam Beggs. **Director, Media Relations:** Steve Hurlbert. **Director, Stadium Operations:** Bobby Atencio. **Manager, Suite Relations:** Paul Hartenberger. **Manager, Marketing/Promotions:** Lauren Farris. **Season Ticket/Group Sales Representatives:** Eddie Enriquez, Jordan Gillum, Joe Rugo, Jason Buchta. **Community Relations Coordinator:** Melissa Lee. **Director, Accounting:** Cynthia DiFrancesco. **Assistant Director, Retail Operations:** Kara Hayes. **Assistant Director, Box Office Operations:** Ben Zalewski. **Director, Field Operations:** Jarad Alley. **Assistant Director, Field Operations:** Shawn Moore. **Home Clubhouse Manager:** Jonathan Sanchez. **Visiting Clubhouse Manager:** Rick Pollack. **Office Manager:** Susan Martindale. **Ovations Foodservice General Manager:** Jay Satenspiel. **Ovations Foodservice Concession Manager:** Shannon Sanchez. **Ovations Foodservice Catering Manager:** Jamie Yoder.

FIELD STAFF

Manager: Tim Wallach. **Coach:** John Moses. **Pitching Coach:** Jim Slaton. **Trainer:** Greg Harrel.

GAME INFORMATION

Radio Announcer: Robert Portnoy. **No. of Games Broadcast:** Home-72 Road-72. **Flagship Station:** KNML 610-AM.

PA Announcer: Stu Walker. **Official Scorers:** Gary Herron, John Miller.

Stadium Name: Isotopes Park. **Location:** From 1-25, exit east on Avenida Cesar Chavez SE to University Boulevard. From I-40, exit south on University Boulevard SE to Avenida Cesar Chavez. **Standard Game Times:** 7:05 p.m., 6:05 Sunday. **Ticket Price Range:** $6-24.

Visiting Club Hotel: MCM Elegante, 2020 Menaul NE, Albuquerque, NM 87107. **Telephone:** (505) 884-2511.

COLORADO SPRINGS SKY SOX

Office Address: 4385 Tutt Blvd, Colorado Springs, CO 80922.
Telephone: (719) 597-1449. **Fax:** (719) 597-2491.
E-Mail address: info@skysox.com. **Website:** www.skysox.com.
Affiliation (first year): Colorado Rockies (1993). **Years in League:** 1988-

OWNERSHIP, MANAGEMENT

Operated By: Colorado Springs Sky Sox Inc.

Principal Owner: David Elmore.

President/General Manager: Tony Ensor. **Senior Vice President, Marketing:** Rai Henniger. **Asst. GM/Director, Sales:** Jeff Windle. **Asst. GM/Director, Public Relations:** Mike Hobson. **Asst. GM/Director, Promotions:** Matt Person. **Director, Broadcast Operations:** Dan Karcher. **Accountant:** Kelly Hanlon. **Director, Ticket Sales:** Whitney Shellem. **Director, Stadium Operations:** Matt Pribbernow. **Director, Group Sales:** Adam Sciorsci. **Assistant Director, Group Sales:** Keith Hodges. **Group Sales Manager:** Brien Smith. **Groups Sales Manager:** Ryan Stos. **Group Sales Manager:** Philip McMullen. **General Manager/Diamond Creations:** Don Giuliano. **Director, Catering:** Roberto Gutierrez. **Community Relations Coordinator:** Jon Eddy. **Graphics Manager:** Erin Eads. **Head Groundskeeper:** Steve DeLeon. **Administrative Assistant:** Marianne Paine. **Home Clubhouse Manager:** Ricky Grima. **Visiting Clubhouse Manager:** Steve Martin.

FIELD STAFF

Manager: Tom Runnells. **Coach:** Rene Lachemann. **Pitching Coach:** Chuck Kniffin. **Trainer:** Heath Townsend.

GAME INFORMATION

Radio Announcer: Dan Karcher. **No. of Games Broadcast:** Home-72 Road-72. **Flagship Station:** KZNT 1460-AM.

PA Announcer: Unavailable. **Official Scorer:** Marty Grantz, Rich Wastler.

Stadium Name: Security Service Field. **Location:** I-25 South to Woodmen Road exit, east on Woodmen to Powers Boulevard, right on Powers to Barnes Road. **Standard Game Times:** 7:05 p.m.; Sun. 1:05. **Ticket Price Range:** $5-11.

Visiting Club Hotel: La Quinta Inn, Garden of the Gods, 4385 Sinton Rd., Colorado Springs, CO 80907. **Telephone:** (719) 528-5060.

FRESNO GRIZZLIES

Office Address: 1800 Tulare St, Fresno, CA 93721.
Telephone: (559) 320-4487. **Fax:** (559) 264-0795.
E-Mail address: info@fresnogrizzlies.com. **Website:** www.fresnogrizzlies.com.
Affiliation (first year): San Francisco Giants (1998). **Years in League:** 1998-

OWNERSHIP, MANAGEMENT

Operated By: Fresno Baseball Club, LLC.

Executive Vice President/General Manager: Andrew Stuebner. **Senior VP, Operations:** Garret Fahrmann. **Senior**

VP, Marketing: Scott Carter. **VP, Tickets:** Shaun Northup. **VP, Corporate Partnerships:** Josh Phanco. **VP, Finance:** SuSin Correa. **Director, Media/Public Relations:** Paul Kennedy. **Director, Entertainment/Publications:** Krista Boyd. **Director, Marketing:** Walmer Medina. **Director, Mascot Relations:** Brad Collins. **Director, Merchandise:** Stephanie Hartman. **Director, Community Relations:** Danielle Witt. **Community Relations Coordinator:** Daniel Newman. **Director, Client Services:** Andrew Melrose. **Corporate Partnerships Manager:** Meredith Hartery. **Client Services Executives:** Laura Pimentel, Taylor Woods. **Director, Sales:** Derek Franks. **Director, Tickets:** Jason Hannold. **Box Office Manager:** Paul Giambalvo. **Group Sales Manager:** Freddie Dominguez, Jr. **Inside Sales Manager:** Pat Wallach. **Senior Account Executive:** Ray Ortiz. **Group Sales Account Executives:** Jonathan Gilbert, Adam Gleich. **Director, Stadium Operations:** Harvey Kawasaki. **Director, Event Operations:** Matt Studwell. **Manager, Operations:** Ira Calvin. **Head Groundskeeper:** David Jacinto. **Director, Human Resources:** Ashley Tennell. **Finance Managers:** Monica Delacerda, Becky DeOchoa, Murray Shamp. **Receptionist:** DeeAnn Hernandez. **GM, Ovations Concessions:** Ron Hassett.

FIELD STAFF

Manager: Dan Rohn. **Hitting Coach:** Hensley Meulens. **Pitching Coach:** Pat Rice. **Athletic Trainer:** Anthony Reyes.

GAME INFORMATION

Radio Announcers: Doug Greenwald, Guy Haberman. **No of Games Broadcast:** Home-72 Road-72. **Flagship Station:** ESPN Radio 790-AM.

Official Scorer: Darrell Copeland. **MLBAM Stringer:** Jim Nelson

Stadium Name: Chukchansi Park. **Location:** 1800 Tulare St, Fresno, CA 93721. **Directions:** From 99 North, take Fresno Street exit, left on Fresno Street, left on Inyo or Tulare to stadium. From 99 South, take Fresno Street exit, left on Fresno Street, right on Broadway to H Street. From 41 North, take Van Ness exit toward Fresno, left on Van Ness, left on Inyo or Tulare, stadium is straight ahead. From 41 South, take Tulare exit, stadium is located at Tulare and H Streets, or take Van Ness exit, right on Van Ness, left on Inyo or Tulare, stadium is straight ahead. **Ticket Price Range:** $9-17.

Visiting Club Hotel: Radisson Hotel Fresno, 2233 Ventura St, Fresno, CA 93721. **Telephone:** (559) 441-2931.

IOWA CUBS

Office Address: One Line Dr, Des Moines, IA 50309.
Telephone: (515) 243-6111. **Fax:** (515) 243-5152.
E-Mail address: info@iowacubs.com. **Website:** www.iowacubs.com
Affiliation (first year): Chicago Cubs (1981). **Years in League:** 1969-

OWNERSHIP, MANAGEMENT

Operated By: Raccoon Baseball Inc.

Chairman, Principal Owner: Michael Gartner. **Executive Vice President:** Michael Giudicessi.

President, General Manager: Sam Bernabe. **Vice President/Assistant GM:** Jim Nahas. **VP, CFO:** Sue Tollefson. **VP/Director, Stadium Operations:** Tom Greene. **VP/Director, Broadcast Operations:** Deene Ehlis. **Media Relations Manager:** Andrea Breen. **Director, Logistics:** Scott Sailor. **Group Sales Coordinators:** Kenny Houser, Lindsay Cox, Mark Dempsey. **Director, Sales:** Rich Gilman. **Director, Luxury Suites:** Brent Conkel. **Ticket Office Manager:** Katie Hogan. **Manager, Stadium Operations:** Jeff Tilley. **Assistant Manager, Stadium Operations:** Janelle Videgar. **Corporate Sales Executives:** Melanie Doser, Nate Teut, Randy Wehofer. **Corporate Relations:** Red Hollis. **Head Groundskeeper:** Chris Schlosser. **Director, Merchandise:** Rick Giudicessi. **Coordinator, Merchandise:** Amber Gartner. **Accountant:** Lori Auten. **Manager, Cub Club:** Bob Thormeier. **Director, Information Systems:** Larry Schunk. **Director, Video Operations:** Aaron Johnson. **Office Manager:** Betsy Duncan. **Landscape Coordinator:** Shari Kramer.

FIELD STAFF

Manager: Bobby Dickerson. **Hitting Coach:** Von Joshua. **Pitching Coach:** Mike Mason. **Trainer:** Matt Johnson.

GAME INFORMATION

Radio Announcer: Deene Ehlis. **No of Games Broadcast:** Home-72 Road-72.

Flagship Station: AM 940 KPSZ. **PA Announcers:** Geoff Conn, Mark Pierce, Corey Coon. **Official Scorers:** Dirk Brinkmeyer, Brian Gibson.

Stadium Name: Principal Park. **Location:** I-80 or I-35 to I-235, to Third Street exit, south on Third Street, left on Line Drive. **Standard Game Times:** 7:05 p.m.; 12:05; 1:05 Sundays. **Ticket Price Range:** $6-11.

Visiting Club Hotel: Valley West Inn, 3535 Westown Pkwy, West Des Moines, IA 50266. **Telephone:** (515) 225-2524.

LAS VEGAS 51S

Office Address: 850 Las Vegas Blvd. North, Las Vegas, NV 89101.
Telephone: (702) 386-7200. **Fax:** (702) 386-7214.
E-Mail address: info@lv51.com. **Website:** http://www.lv51.com.
Affiliation (first year): Toronto Blue Jays (2009). **Years in League:** 1983-.

OWNERSHIP, MANAGEMENT

Operated By: Stevens Family Trust.

President/General Manager: Don Logan. **Assistant GM/Vice President, Marketing:** Chuck Johnson. **VP, Sales/Marketing:** Mike Hollister. **VP, Ticket Operations:** Mike Rodriguez. **VP, Operations/Security:** Nick Fitzenreider. **Special Assistant to GM:** Bob Blum. **Controller:** Jeff Buchman. **Director, Business Development:** Derek Eige. **Director, Broadcasting:** Russ Langer. **Manager, Community Relations:** Larry Brown. **Manager, Baseball Administration:** Denise Korach. **Media Relations Director:** Jim Gemma. **Ticket Operations Assistant:** Michelle Taggart. **Administrative Assistants:** Jan Dillard, Pat Dressel. **Managers, Corporate Marketing:** Erik Eisenberg, Isaiah Flynn, Melissa Harkavy, Bruce Simons. **Merchandise Coordinator:** Ashley Reese. **Sponsorship Services Manager:** William Graham. **Operations Manager:** Chip Vespe. **Interns:** Lisa Gulick, Michael Savio.

FIELD STAFF

Manager: Mike Basso. **Hitting Coach:** Ken Joyce. **Pitching Coach:** Dave LaRoche. **Trainer:** Jon Woodworth. **Strength/Conditioning Coach:** Rob Helmick.

GAME INFORMATION

Radio Announcer: Russ Langer. **No. of Games Broadcast:** Home-72 Road-72. **Flagship Station:** Fox Sports Radio 920-AM.

PA Announcer: Dan Bickmore. **Official Scorers:** Mark Wasik, Gary Arlitz.

Stadium Name: Cashman Field. **Location:** I-15 to U.S. 95 exit (downtown), east to Las Vegas Boulevard North exit, one-half mile north to stadium. **Standard Game Time:** 7:05 p.m. **Ticket Price Range:** $9-14.

Visiting Club Hotel: Golden Nugget Hotel & Casino, 129 Fremont Street, Las Vegas, NV 89101. **Telephone:** (702) 385-7111.

MEMPHIS REDBIRDS

Office Address: 175 Toyota Plaza, Suite 300, Memphis, TN 38103.
Telephone: (901) 721-6000. **Fax:** (901) 842-1222.
Website: www.memphisredbirds.com
Affiliation (first year): St. Louis Cardinals (1998). **Years in League:** 1998-

OWNERSHIP, MANAGEMENT

Operated By: Memphis Redbirds Baseball Foundation, Inc.

Founders: Dean Jernigan, Kristi Jernigan.

President, Baseball Operations/General Manager: Dave Chase. **President, Business Operations:** Bill Harter. **Senior Vice President, Sales:** Pete Rizzo. **Vice President, Community Relations:** Reggie Williams. **Accounting Manager:** Art Davis. **Director, Ticket Sales:** Ryan Thompson. **Director, Communications:** Kyle Parkinson. **Director, Operations:** Dusty Kilgour. **Manager, Ticket Operations:** Mark Anderson. **Marketing/Promotions Manager:** Harrison Lampley. **Group Sales Coordinator:** Devyn Parkinson. **Graphics Coordinator:** Allison Rhoades. **Game Entertainment Coordinator:** Jessica McDaniel. **Coordinator, Premium Seats/Foundation Services:** Kela Jones. **Programs Coordinator:** Corey Gillum. **Retail Supervisor:** Starr Taiani. **Senior Account Executive:** Lisa Shurden. **Account Executive:** Ronnie Russell. **Sales Coordinator:** Katie Reid. **Executive Assistant:** Cindy Compton. Ticket Sales Executives: Adam Shelton, Valerie Hight, Daniel Shaffer. **Office Coordinator:** Linda Smith. **Head Groundskeeper:** Ed Collins. **Chief Engineer:** Danny Abbott. **Maintenance:** Spencer Shields.

FIELD STAFF

Manager: Chris Maloney. **Coach:** Mark Budaska. **Pitching Coach:** Blaise Ilsley. **Trainer:** Chris Conroy.

GAME INFORMATION

Radio Announcer: Steve Selby. **No of Games Broadcast:** Home-72 Road-72. **Flagship Station:** WHBQ 560-AM.

PA Announcer: Tim Van Horn. **Official Scorer:** J.J. Guinozzo.

Stadium Name: AutoZone Park. **Location:** North on I-240, exit at Union Avenue West, one and half mile to park. **Standard Game Times:** 7:05 p.m.; Saturday 6:05; Sunday 2:05. **Ticket Price Range:** $5-17.

Visiting Club Hotel: Sleep Inn at Court Square, 40 N. Front, Memphis, TN 38103. **Telephone:** (901) 522-9700.

NASHVILLE SOUNDS

Office Address: 534 Chestnut Street, Nashville, TN 37203.
Telephone: (615) 242-4371. **Fax:** (615) 256-5684.
E-Mail address: info@nashvillesounds.com. **Website:** www.nashvillesounds.com
Affiliation (first year): Milwaukee Brewers (2005). **Years in League:** 1998-

OWNERSHIP, MANAGEMENT

Operated By: AmeriSports LLC.

President/Owner: Al Gordon.

Chief Operating Officer: Glenn Yaeger. **Executive Director, Business Operations:** Brandon Vonderharr. **Assistant GM, Communications/Baseball Operations:** Doug Scopel. **Assistant GM, Sponsorship Sales:** Jason Bennett. **Director, Accounting:** Barb Walker. **Director, Sales:** Drew Himsworth. **Director, Stadium Operations:** Ken Thomas. **Director, Broadcasting:** Chuck Valenches. **Manager, Community Relations:** Becky Davis. **Manager,**

Entertainment: Buddy Yelton. **Managers, Sales:** Eric Adams, Dustin Skilbred. **Manager, Ticketing:** Eric Laue. **Director, Faith Nights:** Ryan Bennett. **Office Manager:** Sharon Ridley. **Head Groundskeeper:** Peter Lockwood. **Clubhouse Manager:** J.R. Rinaldi, Thomas Miller, Peter Thomashefski.

FIELD STAFF

Manager: Don Money. **Coach:** Sandy Guerrero. **Pitching Coach:** Chris Bosio. **Trainer:** Jeff Paxson. **Strength/Conditioning Coach:** Tom Reynolds.

GAME INFORMATION

Radio Announcer: Chuck Valenches. **No of Games Broadcast:** Home-72 Road-72. **Flagship Station:** WNSR 560-AM.

PA Announcers: Eric Berner, Jim Kiser. **Official Scorers:** Eric Jones, Trevor Garrett.

Stadium Name: Herschel Greer Stadium. **Location:** I-65 to Wedgewood exit, west to Eighth Avenue, right on Eighth to Chestnut Street, right on Chestnut. **Standard Game Times:** 6 p.m. (April, Aug.), 7 p.m. (May-July); Wed. noon; Sat. 6, Sun. 2 (April-May), 6 (June-Sept.). **Ticket Price Range:** $6-10.

Visiting Club Hotel: Holiday Inn Select, 2613 West End Ave, Nashville, TN 37203. **Telephone:** (615) 327-4707.

NEW ORLEANS ZEPHYRS

Office Address: 6000 Airline Dr, Metairie, LA 70003.

Telephone: (504) 734-5155. **Fax:** (504) 734-5118.

E-Mail address: zephyrs@zephyrsbaseball.com. **Website:** www.zephyrsbaseball.com.

Affiliation (first year): Florida Marlins (2009). **Years in League:** 1998-

OWNERSHIP, MANAGEMENT

Operated By: New Orleans Zephyrs Baseball Club, LLC.

Managing Partner/President: Don Beaver. **COO/Executive Director:** Ron Maestri. **General Manager:** Mike Schline. **Director, Community Relations:** Marc Allen. **Director, Broadcasting/Team Travel:** Tim Grubbs. **Director, Operations:** Todd Wilson. **Director, Marketing/Special Events:** Jaime Burchfield. **Director, Ticket Operations:** Kathy Kaleta. **Director, Finance:** Donna Verdun. **Promotions, Director:** Jessica DeOro. **Director, Media Relations:** Dave Sachs. **Group Sales Director:** Leah Rigby. **Group Sales Representatives:** Kevin Ferguson, Jordan Price, Lindsey Rall. **Corporate Sales Executive:** Melissa Mahony. **Merchandise Manager:** Dan Zajac. **Head Groundskeeper:** Thomas Marks. **Assistant Groundskeeper:** Craig Shaffer. **Maintenance Coordinator:** Bill Rowell. **Ticket Operations Assistant:** Katie Bonaccorso. **Receptionist:** Susan Hirar. **Director of Operations, Messina's Inc.:** George Messina. **Administrative Assistant, Messina's Inc.:** Priscilla Arbello. **Catering Manager, Messina's Inc.:** Kristen Wahl. **Conncessions Manager, Messina's Inc.:** Darin Yuratich.

FIELD STAFF

Manager: Edwin Rodriguez. **Coach:** Steve Phillips. **Pitching Coach:** Scott Mitchell. **Trainer:** Steve Miller.

GAME INFORMATION

Radio Announcers: Tim Grubbs, Ron Swoboda. **Color Analyst/Speakers Bureau:** Ron Swoboda. **No. of Games Broadcast:** Home-72 Road-72. **Flagship Station:** WIST 690-AM.

PA Announcer: Doug Moreau. **Official Scorer:** J.L. Vangilder.

Stadium Name: Zephyr Field. **Location:** I-10 West toward Baton Rouge, exit at Clearview Pkwy (exit 226) and continues south, right on Airline Drive (U.S. 61 North) for 1 mile, stadium on left. From airport, take Airline Drive (U.S. 61) east for 4 miles, stadium on right. **Standard Game Times:** 7 p.m.; **Sat. 6; Sun. 2. Ticket Price Range:** $6-10.

Visiting Club Hotel: Best Western-St. Christopher, 114 Magazine St., New Orleans, LA 70130. **Telephone:** (504) 648-0444.

OKLAHOMA CITY REDHAWKS

Office Address: 2 S. Mickey Mantle Dr, Oklahoma City, OK 73104.

Telephone: (405) 218-1000. **Fax:** (405) 218-1001.

E-Mail address: info@oklahomaredhawks.com. **Website:** www.oklahomaredhawks.com.

Affiliation (first year): Texas Rangers (1983). **Years in League:** 1963-1968, 1998-

OWNERSHIP, MANAGEMENT

Operated By: Oklahoma Baseball Club LLC.

Principal Owner: Robert Funk. **Managing General Partner:** Scott Pruitt.

Executive Director: John Allgood. **CFO:** Steve McEwen. **Director, Public Relations/Assistant to Managing General Partner:** Holly McGowen. **Director, Facility Operations:** Harlan Budde. **Director, Operations:** Mike Prange. **Director, Sponsorships:** Mark Pritchard. **Director, Multimedia Sales:** David Patterson. **Director, Special Events:** Mary Ramsey. **Senior Accountant:** Nicole Wise. **Corporate Sponsorship:** Brandon Baker. **Ticket Operations Manager:** Armando Reyes. **Director, Ticket Sales:** Randy Walker, Account Executives: Jason Black, Paul Arebalo, Jeff Hawkins. **Group Sales Account Executives:** Megan Morgan. **Office Manager/Administrative Coordinator:** Kellie Mayberry. **Clubhouse Manager:** Russ Oliver. **Head Groundskeeper:** Monte McCoy.

FIELD STAFF

Manager: Bobby Jones. **Pitching Coach:** Terry Clark. **Coach:** Scott Coolbaugh. **Trainer:** Unavailable.

GAME INFORMATION

Radio Announcer: Jim Byers. **No of Games Broadcast:** Home-72 Road-72. **Flagship Station:** KEBC 1340 AM.

PA Announcer: Matt Gierat. **Official Scorers:** Mike Treps, Justin Tinder.

Stadium Name: AT&T Bricktown Ballpark. **Location:** Near interchange of I-235 and I-40, take Lincoln exit off I-40 to Reno, west on Reno to ballpark. **Standard Game Times:** 7:05 p.m.; Sunday 2:05 (April-May), 7:05 (June-August). **Ticket Price Range:** $6-15.

Visiting Club Hotel: Courtyard Oklahoma City Downtown/Bricktown, 2 West Reno Ave., Oklahoma City, OK 73102. **Telephone:** (405) 235-2780.

OMAHA ROYALS

Office Address: Rosenblatt Stadium, 1202 Bert Murphy Ave., Omaha, NE 68107.

Administrative Office Phone: (402) 734-2550. **Ticket Office Phone:** (402) 738-5100. **Fax:** (402) 734-7166.

E-Mail Address: info@oroyals.com. **Website:** www.oroyals.com.

Affiliation (first year): Kansas City Royals (1969). **Years in League:** 1998-

OWNERSHIP, MANAGEMENT

Operated by: Omaha Royals Limited Partnership.

Principal Owners: William Shea, Warren Buffett, Walter Scott. **President:** Alan Stein.

Vice President/General Manager: Martie Cordaro. **VP/Baseball Operations:** Kyle Fisher. **Assistant GM/Marketing:** Rob Crain. **Director, Broadcasting:** Mark Nasser. **Director, Media Relations:** Kevin McNabb. **Director, Community Relations:** Lesley Crutcher. **Director, Ticketing:** Dave Endress. **Merchandising Manager:** Jason Kinney. **Ticket Operations Manager:** Paul Hammes. **Ticket Sales Executives:** James Jensen, Adam Kelly, Andrea Stava. **Corporate Sales Executive:** Diann Spataro. **Controller:** Laurie Schlender. **Administrative Assistants:** Kay Besta, Lois Biggs. **Head Groundskeeper:** Jesse Cuevas. **General Manager, Concessions:** Ryan Slane.

Field Staff

Manager: Mike Jirschele. **Pitching Coach:** Tom Burgmeier. **Hitting Coach:** Tommy Gregg. **Trainer:** Drew Van Dam.

GAME INFORMATION

Radio Announcers: Mark Nasser, Kevin McNabb. **No. of Games Broadcast:** Home-72, Away-72. **Flagship Station:** KOIL-AM 1180. **PA Announcer:** Bill Jensen, Paul Cohen, Craig Evans. **Official Scorer:** Frank Adkisson, Steve Pivovar, Kent Poncelow, Ryan White.

Stadium Name: Rosenblatt Stadium. **Location:** south of I-80 on 13th St.

Standard Game Times: 6:35 p.m. Mon-Thu. (April-May); 7:05 p.m. Mon.-Thu. (June-August); 7:05 p.m. Fri. and Sat.; 1:35 p.m. Sun. (11:05 a.m. and 12:05 p.m. selected weekdays)

Visiting Club Hotel: Holiday Inn at Ameristar, 2202 River Road, Council Bluffs, IA 51501. **Phone:** (712) 322-5050; Fax: (712) 322-9232.

PORTLAND BEAVERS

Office Address: 1844 SW Morrison, Portland, OR 97205.

Telephone: (503) 553-5400. **Fax:** (505) 553-5405.

E-Mail address: info@pgepark.com. **Website:** www.portlandbeavers.com.

Affiliation (first year): San Diego Padres (2001). **Years in League:** 1903-1917, 1919-72, 1978-1993, 2001-

OWNERSHIP, MANAGEMENT

Operated By: Shortstop, LLC.

President/General Manager: Merritt Paulson. **Senior Vice President, Business Development/Broadcasting:** Ryan Brach. **Senior VP, Operations:** Ken Puckett. **VP, Ticket Sales:** Joe Cote. **VP, Business Operations/Marketing:** Cory Dolich. **VP, Baseball Operations/Communications:** Chris Metz. **Senior Advisor:** Jack Cain. **Finance/Human Resources:** Martin Harvey. **Director, Group Sales:** Ashley Bedford. **Director, Ticket Operations:** Ben Hoel. **Director, Partner Services:** Suzy Stride. **Senior Manager, Creative Services:** Ryan Wantland. **Senior Manager, Season Ticket Accounts:** Dan Zusman. **Manager, Partner Services:** Rachel Faires. **Managers, Corporate Partnerships:** Matt Kolasinski, Nate Liberman. **Manager, Housekeeping:** Brian Kennedy. **Manager, Media Relations:** Marc Kostic. **Manager, Community Outreach:** Sierra Smith. **Manager, Promotions:** Jennifer Smoral. **Manager, Facility Maintenance:** Dave Tankersley. **Manager, Guest Services:** Andrea Tolonen. **Senior Coordinator, Marketing:** Emily Berlin. **Ticket Sales Coordinator/Executive Assistant:** Patti Peters. **Corporate Ticket Sales Account Executives:** Tim Hagerty, Neil Moore, Brian Pollard, Sara Wiggins. **Account Executives, Group Ticket Sales:** Katie Hoffner, Alison Mathes, Kyle Veach. **Accounts Receivable:** Penny Bishop. **Accounts Payable:** Mary Cate Preston. **Receptionist/Office Manager:** Jeanne Nichols. **Head Groundskeeper:** Jesse Smith. **Home Clubhouse Manager:** Shane Hickenbottom. **Visiting Clubhouse Manager:** Tyler Neves. **Supervisor, Maintenance:** Ryan Utterback.

Operations/Systems Coordinator: John Burchim.

FIELD STAFF

Manager: Randy Ready. **Coach:** Max Venable. **Pitching Coach:** Glenn Abbott. **Trainer:** Wade Yamasaki.

GAME INFORMATION

Radio Announcers: Rich Burk, Tim Hagerty. **No. of Games Broadcast:** Home-72 Road-72. **Flagship Station:** KKAD 1550-AM.

PA Announcer: Kevin Flink. **Official Scorer:** Blair Cash.

Stadium Name: PGE Park. **Location:** I-450 to West Burnside exit, SW 20th Street to park. **Standard Game Times:** 7:05 p.m.; Sun. 2:05. **Ticket Price Range:** $5-14.50.

Visiting Club Hotel: Doubletree Hotel-Portland Lloyd Center, 1000 NE Multnomah, Portland, OR 97232. **Telephone:** (503) 281-6111.

RENO ACES

Office Address: 50 W. Liberty St., Reno, NV 89501
Telephone: (775) 334-4700. **Fax:** (775) 334-4701
Website: www.renoaces.com
Affiliation (first year): Arizona Diamondbacks (2009). **Years in League:** 2009-

OWNERSHIP, MANAGEMENT

President/Managing Partner: Stuart Katzoff. **Partners:** Jerry Katzoff, Herb Simon. **General Counsel:** Brett Beecham.

General Manager: Rick Parr. **Vice President, Sales/Marketing:** Justin Piper. **VP, Special Projects:** Tracy Berrey. **VP, Operations:** David Avila. **Director, Ticketing:** Brian Moss. **Director, Media Relations:** T.J. **Lasita. Director, Marketing/Promotions:** Brett McGinness. **Director, Corporate Partnership:** Dwight Dortch. **Director, Box Office:** Charles Lucas. **Director, Merchandise:** Jessica Berry. **Manager, Client Services:** Andrei Losche. **Client Services/ Tickets:** Adam Kincaid. **Consultant:** Lou Scheinfeld. **Manager, Box Office:** Brooke Noel. **Coordinator, Promotions:** Amanda Alling. **Account Executives, Corporate Partnership:** Brady Raggio, Kelle Venezia. **Account Executives, Hospitality:** Stephanie Dolan, Dan Izzo. **Account Executive, Hospitality/Non-Profits:** Jenni Dawson. **Executive Assistant:** Jan Baldeo. **Associates:** Ari Grey, Marshall Berman. **Director, Broadcasting:** Ryan Radtke.

FIELD STAFF

Manager: Brett Butler. **Coach:** Rick Burleson. **Pitching Coach:** Mike Parrott. **Trainer:** James Ready. **Strength/ Conditioning Coordinator:** Brian Melton.

GAME INFORMATION

Radio Announcer: Ryan Radtke. **No. of Games Broadcast:** Home-72, Away-72. **Flagship Station:** TBA.

PA Announcer: Unavailable. **Official Scorers:** Unavailable.

Stadium Name: Aces Ballpark. **Location:** From Carson City (south of Reno): 395 North to exit 66 (Mill Street), left at Mill Street, right at S. Park Street, left at Kuenzll Street, right at East 2nd Street to ballpark. From East: I-80 West to exit 14 (Wells Avenue), left on Wells, right on Kuenzll, right at East 2nd Street.

Standard Game Times: 7:05 pm; Sun., 1:05 pm/5:05 pm. **Ticket Price Range:** $7-29.

Visiting Club Hotel: Siena Hotel Spa Casino. **Telephone:** (775) 321-5831.

ROUND ROCK EXPRESS

Office Address: 3400 East Palm Valley Blvd., Round Rock, TX 78665.
Telephone: (512) 255-2255. **Fax:** (512) 255-1558.
E-Mail Address: info@rrexpress.com. **Website:** www.roundrockexpress.com
Affiliation (first year): Houston Astros (2005). **Year in League:** 2005-

OWNERSHIP, MANAGEMENT

Operated By: Ryan Sanders Baseball, LP.

Principal Owners: Nolan Ryan, Reid Ryan, Don Sanders, Jay Miller, Eddie Maloney, Brad Sanders, Bret Sanders.

President: Jay Miller. **General Manager:** Dave Fendrick. **Controller:** Debbie Coughlin. **Director, Communications:** Avery Holton. **Director, Community Relations:** Heather Tantimonaco. **Director, Ballpark Entertainment:** Clint Musslewhite. **Director, Merchandising (Ryan Sanders Baseball):** Brooke Milam. **Director, Ticket Operations:** Ross Scott. **Director, United Heritage Center:** Scott Allen. **Director, Special Events:** Laura Whatley. **Director, Group Sales:** Henry Green. **Director, Sales:** Gary Franke. **Director, Marketing Development:** Gregg Miller. **Account Executives:** Brent Green, Richard Tapia, Kyle Hutchens. **Receptionist:** Wendy Gordon. **Field Superintendent:** Brad Detmore. **Director, Broadcasting:** Mike Capps. **Clubhouse Manager:** Kenny Bufton. **Visiting Clubhouse Manager:** Kevin Taylor. **Assistant Manager, The Railyard Retail Store:** Debbie Goodman. **Director, Stadium Operations:** Khalil Coltrain. **Director, Stadium Maintenance:** Aurelio Martinez. **Housekeeping:** Ofelia Gonzalez.

FIELD STAFF

Manager: Marc Bombard. **Pitching Coach:** Burt Hooton. **Coach:** Ron Jackson. **Trainer:** Mike Freer.

GAME INFORMATION

Radio Announcer: Mike Capps. **No. of Games Broadcast:** Home-72 Road-72. **Flagship Station:** 1530 AM.

PA Announcer: Clint Musslewhite. **Official Scorer:** Tommy Tate, Avery Holton.

Stadium Name: The Dell Diamond. **Location:** Take I-35 North to Exit 253 (Highway 79 East/Taylor). Highway 79 east for 3½ miles. Stadium on left. **Standard Game Times:** 7:05 p.m., 2:05. **Ticket Price Range:** $5-12.

Visiting Club Hotel: Hilton Garden Inn, 2310 N IH-35, Round Rock, TX 78681. **Telephone:** (512) 341-8200.

SACRAMENTO RIVER CATS

Office Address: 400 Ballpark Dr, West Sacramento, CA 95691.

Telephone: (916) 376-4700. **Fax:** (916) 376-4710.

E-Mail address: info@rivercats.com. **Website:** www.rivercats.com.

Affiliation (first year): Oakland Athletics (2000). **Years in League:** 1903, 1909-11, 1918-60, 1974-76, 2000-

OWNERSHIP, MANAGEMENT

Operated By: Sacramento River Cats Baseball Club, LLC.

Chief Executive Officer: Art Savage. **President, General Manager/COO:** Alan Ledford. **Executive Vice Presidents:** Bob Hemond. **Vice President, Finance/Project Development:** Jeff Savage. **General Counsel:** Matthew Re. **Senior Manager, Administrative Services:** Gay Caputo. **Executive VP/CFO:** Dan Vistica. **Director, Finance:** Jess Olivares. **Accounting Clerk:** Madeline Forma. **Vice President, Media Relations/Assistant GM:** Gabe Ross. **Senior Vice President, Business Development:** Darrin Gross. **Director, Corporate Services:** Jennifer Maiwald. **Manager, Luxury Suites:** Ryan Von Sossan. **VP, Ticket Sales:** Ripper Hatch. **Director, Ticket Sales:** Chad Collins. **Director, Ticket Operations:** Steve Hill. **Senior Manager, Ticket Operations:** Jennifer Tokuyama. **Manager, Group Sales:** Creighton Kahoalii. **Manager, Inside Sales:** Chris Dreesman. **Managers, Ticket Packages:** Scott Kemp, Christi Lorenson, Matt Togami. **Seninor Account Executive, Corporate Sales:** Bryan Iredell. **Account Executives, Corporate Sales:** Steve Gracio, Tonya Mcelwee. **Senior Group Event Executive:** Melanie Levy. **Group Event Executives:** Mike Luevano, Andrew Halford, Ross Johnson, Marie Maita. **Coordinator, Group Sales/Service:** Ashley Auld. **Vice President, Marketing:** Bryan Srabian. **Senior Manager, Marketing:** Danna Bubalo. **Senior Manager, Promotions:** Jeremy Neisser. **Coordinator, Website/Research:** Brent Savage. **Graphic Artist, Creative Department:** Mike Villareal. **Vice President, Community Relations:** Tony Asaro. **Vice President, Operations:** Matt Larose. **Senior Director, Operations:** Matt Thomas. **Coordinator, Grounds:** Marcello Clamar. **Clubhouse Manager:** Rod Garcia. **Manager, Guest Services:** Carla Mosher. **Manager, Operations:** Mario Constancio. **Coordinator, Guest Services/Operations:** Shannon Roland. **Receptionist:** Rae Matheny. **Chief Engineer:** Shaun Meyer. **Engineer:** Javier Navarro. **Day Porter:** Alexandra Ortiz. **Manager, Field Events/Entertainment:** Stephanie Spees. .

FIELD STAFF

Manager: Tony DeFrancesco. **Hitting Coach:** Brian McArn. **Pitching Coach:** Rick Rodriguez. **Trainer:** Brad LaRosa.

GAME INFORMATION

Radio Announcers: Johnny Doskow. **No. of Games Broadcast:** Home-72 Road-72. **Flagship Station:** KHITS 92.1 FM.

PA Announcer: Mark Standriff. **Official Scorers:** Brian Berger, Brian Bjork, Mark Honbo.

Stadium Name: Raley Field. **Location:** I-5 to Business-80 West, exit at Jefferson Boulevard. **Standard Game Time:** 7:05 p.m. **Ticket Price Range:** $5-18.

Visiting Club Hotel: Holiday Inn, Capitol Plaza, 300 J St., Sacramento, CA 95814. **Telephone:** (916) 446-0100.

SALT LAKE BEES

Office Address: 77 W. 1300 South, Salt Lake City, UT 84115.

Mailing Address: P.O. Box 4108, Salt Lake City, UT 84110.

Telephone: (801) 325-2337. **Fax:** (801) 485-6818.

E-Mail Address: info@slbees.com. **Website:** www.slbees.com.

Affiliation (first year): Los Angeles Angels (2001). **Years in League:** 1915-25, 1958-65, 1970-84, 1994-.

OWNERSHIP, MANAGEMENT

Operated by: Larry H. Miller Baseball Inc.

Principal Owner: Larry Miller.

President: Randy Rigby. **Senior Vice President, Business Operations/CFO:** Robert Hyde. **Senior VP, Broadcasting:** Chris Baum. **Senior VP, Facilities:** Scott Williams. **Vice President/General Manager:** Marc Amicone. **Vice President, Finance:** John Larson. **Senior VP, Sales/Marketing:** Jim Olson. **VP, Communications:** Linda Luchetti. **VP, Marketing:** Eric Schulz. **Senior VP, Strategic Partnerships/Advertising:** Mike Snarr. **Assistant GM/Director, Corporate Sales:** Brad Tammen. **Controller:** McKay Smith. **Director, Ticket Sales:** Casey Patterson. **Director, Broadcasting:** Steve Klauke. **Communications Coordinator:** Hannah Lee. **Box Office Manager:** Laura Russell. **Corporate Sponsorship Executive:** Wes Brown. **Ticket/Group Sales Manager:** Brian Prutch. **Ticket Sales Executives:** Bobby Aragon, Tyler Beauchamp, Dennis Carter, Vince Costanzo, Brad Jacoway, Joshua James, Eric Woodbury, Ben Leonhardt. **Team Photographer:** Brent Asay. **Director, Events/Booking:** Mark Powell. **Vice**

President, Public Safety: Jim Bell. **Vice President, Food Services:** Mark Stedman. **Concession Manager:** Dave Dalton. **Head Groundskeeper:** Ryan Kaspitzke. **Assistant Groundskeepers:** Kevin Asay, Chris Coleman, Ryan Heiner. **Clubhouse Manager:** Eli Rice.

FIELD STAFF

Manager: Bobby Mitchell. **Hitting Coach:** Jim Eppard. **Pitching Coach:** Eric Bennett. **Trainer:** Brian Reinker.

GAME INFORMATION

Radio Announcer: Steve Klauke. **No. of Games Broadcast:** Home-72, Away-72. **Flagship Station:** ESPN 1230-AM.

PA Announcer: Jeff Reeves. **Official Scorers:** Howard Nakagama, Terry Harward.

Stadium name: Franklin Covey Field. **Location:** I-15 North/South to 1300 South exit, east to ballpark at West Temple. **Standard Game Times:** 7 p.m., 6:30 (April-May); Sun. 2. **Ticket Price Range:** $7-22.

Visiting Club Hotel: Sheraton City Centre, 150 W. 500 South, Salt Lake City, UT 84101. **Telephone:** (801) 401-2000.

TACOMA RAINIERS

Stadium Address: 2502 South Tyler St., Tacoma, WA 98405.

Office Address: 3560 Bridgeport Way West, Suite 3E, University Place, WA 98466.

Telephone: (253) 752-7707. **Fax:** (253) 752-7135

Website: www.tacomarainiers.com

Affiliation: Seattle Mariners (1995). **Years in League:** 1904-1905, 1960-

OWNERSHIP, MANAGEMENT

Owners: Bob Schlegel, Kirby Schlegel, Nick Lachey.

President: Aaron Artman.

Vice President: Jocelyn Hill. **Vice President, Corporate Partnerships:** Brian Simpson. **Vice President, Ticket Sales:** Chip Maxson. **General Manager, Food and Beverage:** Corey Brandt. **Director, Corporate Partnerships:** Josie Wilkes. **Director, Marketing/Community Development:** Annie Shultz. **Director, Special Events:** Alyson Jones. **Director, Game Entertainment:** Danah Wietry. **Director, Media Development:** Geoff Corkum. **Director, Facilities/Head Groundskeeper:** Ryan Schutt. **Director, Ticket Sales:** Shane Santman. **Director, Merchandise:** Kacy Roe. **Director, Operations:** Ashley Roth. **Director, Administration:** Patti Stacy. **Corporate Partner Services Manager:** Kari Hockett. **Production Artist:** Ashley Rimgale. **Controller:** Jacquie Sonnenfeld. **Ticket Operations Manager:** Geoff Weatherbie. **Senior Corporate Sales Manager:** Josh Baker. **Corporate Sales Managers:** Adam Baker, Matt Barron, Brett Breece, Brian Casper. **Group Sales Managers:** Chris Aubertin, Nicole Eaton, Lindsay Enger, Beth Mager. **Clubhouse Manager:** Alex Muller. **Assistant Clubhouse Manager:** Rich Arneson.

FIELD STAFF

Manager: Daren Brown. **Coach:** Alonzo Powell. **Pitching Coach:** Dwight Bernard. **Trainer:** Tom Newberg. **Strength/Conditioning Coach:** Chad Uihlein.

GAME INFORMATION

Radio Broadcaster: Mike Curto. **No. of Games Broadcast:** Home-72, Away-72. **Flagship Station:** KHHO 850-AM.

PA Announcer: Steve Manning. **Official Scorekeepers:** Gary Brooks, Micahel Jessee.

Stadium Name: Cheney Stadium. **Location:** From I-5, take exit 132 (Highway 16 West) for 1.2 miles to 19th Street East exit, right on Tyler St for 1/3 mile. **Standard Game Times:** 7 p.m.; Sun., 1:35. **Ticket Price Range:** $6-9.

Visiting Club Hotel: La Quinta, 1425 E. 27th St., Tacoma, WA 98421. **Telephone:** (253) 383-0146.

EASTERN LEAGUE

DOUBLE-A

Office Address: 30 Danforth St., Suite 208, Portland, ME 04101.
Telephone: (207) 761-2700. **Fax:** (207) 761-7064.
E-Mail Address: elpb@easternleague.com. **Website:** www.easternleague.com.
Years League Active: 1923-.
President, Treasurer: Joe McEacharn.

Joe McEacharn

Vice President, Secretary: Charles Eshbach. **Vice President:** Chuck Domino. **Assistant to President:** Bill Rosario.

Directors: Greg Agganis (Akron), Lou DiBella (Connecticut), Bill Dowling (New Britain), Charles Eshbach (Portland), Joe Finley (Trenton), Chuck Greenberg (Altoona), Art Matin (Erie), Michael Reinsdorf (Harrisburg), Arthur Solomon (New Hampshire), Craig Stein (Reading), Mike Urda (Binghamton), Ken Young (Bowie).

Division Structure: Northern—Binghamton, Connecticut, New Britain, New Hampshire, Portland, Trenton. **Southern**—Akron, Altoona, Bowie, Erie, Harrisburg, Reading.

Regular Season: 142 games. **2009 Opening Date:** April 8. **Closing Date:** Sept. 7.

All-Star Game: July 15 at Trenton.

Playoff Format: Top two teams in each division meet in best-of-five series. Winners meet in best-of-five series for league championship.

Roster Limit: 24. **Player Eligibility Rule:** No restrictions. **Brand of Baseball:** Rawlings .

Umpires: Matthew Abbott (Zanesville, OH), Jason Arends (Cedar Rapids, IA), Mark Buchanan (Phoenix, AZ), Darren Budahn (Milwaukee, WI), Jon Byrne (Thornlie, WA), John Conrad (Phoenix, AZ), Derek Crabill (Wonder Lake, IL), Shaun Francis (Cohoes, NY), Chris Hamner (Richmond, VA), Matt Hensel (Monroe, CT), Cory Hinga (Schoolcraft, MI), Joel Hospodka (Omaha, NE), Doug Levy (Sharon, MA), Scott Mahoney (Livermore, CA), Grant Menke (North Bethesda, MD), Brad Purdom (Bend, OR), David Soucy (Brighton, MA), Chad Whitson (Dublin, OH).

STADIUM INFORMATION

			Dimensions				
Club	**Stadium**	**Opened**	**LF**	**CF**	**RF**	**Capacity**	**2008 Att.**
Akron	Canal Park	1997	331	400	337	9,097	342,816
Altoona	Blair County Ballpark	1999	325	405	325	7,210	346,973
Binghamton	NYSEG Stadium	1992	330	400	330	6,012	220,638
Bowie	Prince George's Stadium	1993	309	405	309	10,000	261,459
Connecticut	Thomas J. Dodd Memorial Stadium	1995	309	401	309	6,695	202,004
Erie	Jerry Uht Park	1995	312	400	328	6,000	234,955
Harrisburg	Commerce Bank Park	1987	335	400	335	6,300	164,182
New Britain	New Britain Stadium	1996	330	400	330	6,146	365,756
New Hampshire	MerchantsAuto.com Stadium	2005	326	400	306	6,500	373,227
Portland	Hadlock Field	1994	315	400	330	7,368	412,403
Reading	FirstEnergy Stadium	1951	330	400	330	9,000	436,789
Trenton	Mercer County Waterfront Park	1994	330	407	330	6,440	409,131

AKRON AEROS

Office Address: 300 S Main St, Akron, OH 44308.
Telephone: (330) 253-5151. **Fax:** (330) 253-3300.
E-Mail address: info@akronaeros.com. **Website:** www.akronaeros.com.
Affiliation (first year): Cleveland Indians (1989). **Years in League:** 1989-

OWNERSHIP, MANAGEMENT

Operated By: Akron Professional Baseball, Inc.

Principal Owners: Mike Agganis, Greg Agganis.

Executive Vice President/General Manager: Jeff Auman. **Vice President:** Kevin Brodzinski. **Assistant General Manager:** Ken Fogel. **Director, Corporate/Suite Sales:** Calvin Funkhouser. **Director, Ticket Operations:** Kim Fogel. **Director, Ticket Sales:** Keith Solar. **Senior Account Representative, Group Sales:** Thomas Craven. **Account Representative, Ticket Sales:** Ross Swaldo. **Director, Field/Facility Operations:** Matt Duncan. **Office Manager:** Arlene Spahn. **Media Relations Coordinator:** Rob Sinclair. **Merchandising Coordinator:** Aaron Baxter. **Video Operations/Game Entertainment Coordinator:** Mark Greathouse. **Financial Consultant:** Bob Larkins. **Clubhouse/Equipment Manager:** Shad Gross. **Aerofare General Manager:** Bob Jankowski. **Aerofare Assistant General Manager:** Brad Strobl. **Aerofare Suites/Picnics Supervisor:** Molly Taylor.

FIELD STAFF

Manager: Mike Sarbaugh. **Coach:** Lee May Jr. **Pitching Coach:** Ruben Niebla. **Trainer:** Mike Salazar.

GAME INFORMATION

Radio Announcers: Jim Clark, Rob Sinclair. **No of Games Broadcast:** Home-71 Road-71. **Flagship Station:**

Sports Radio 1350-AM. **PA Announcer:** Joe Jastrzemski, Joe Dunn. **Official Scorer:** Roger Grecni.

Stadium Name: Canal Park. **Location:** From I-76 East or I-77 South, exit onto Route 59 East, exit at Exchange/Cedar, right onto Cedar, left at Main Street. From I-76 West or I-77 North, exit at Main Street/Downtown, follow exit onto Broadway Street, left onto Exchange Street, right at Main Street. **Ticket Price Range:** $8-10.

Visiting Club Hotel: Radisson Hotel Akron Centre, 20 W. Mill St, Akron, OH 44308. **Telephone:** (330) 384-1500.

ALTOONA CURVE

Office Address: Blair County Ballpark, 1000 Park Avenue, Altoona, PA 16602.

Mailing Address: P.O. Box 1029, Altoona, PA 16603.

Telephone: (814) 943-5400. **Fax:** (814) 942-9132.

E-Mail Address: frontoffice@altoonacurve.com. **Website:** www.altoonacurve.com.

Affiliation (first year): Pittsburgh Pirates (1999). **Years in League:** 1999-

OWNERSHIP, MANAGEMENT

Operated By: Lozinak Professional Baseball.

Managing Member: Bob Lozinak. **COO:** David Lozinak. **CFO:** Mike Lozinak. **Chief Administrative Officer:** Steve Lozinak. **General Manager:** Rob Egan. **Senior Advisor:** Sal Baglieri. **Director, Communications:** Dan Zangrilli. **Director, Broadcasting:** Ron Potesta. **Director, Community Relations:** Elsie Zengel. **Director, Merchandising:** Ben Rothrock. **Director, Ballpark Operations:** Kirk Stiffler. **Director, Promotions:** Matt Hoover. **Executive Producer, In-Game Entertainment:** John Foreman. **Director, Ticket Sales:** Denny Watson. **Ticket Sales Associates:** Chris Keefer, Mike Pence, Colin Scott. **Administrative Assistant:** Carol Schmittle. **Accounting Specialist:** Tara Figard. **Sponsorship Sales Account Executive:** Katie Hammaker. **Director, Catering/Concessions:** Barbara Newsom. **Team Physician:** Dr. Joshua Port.

FIELD STAFF

Manager: Matt Walbeck. **Coach:** Ryan Long. **Pitching Coach:** Dean Treanor. **Trainer:** Thomas Pribyl.

GAME INFORMATION

Radio Announcer: Dan Zangrilli, Ron Potesta. **No. of Games Broadcast:** Home-71 Road-71. **Flagship Station:** TBA

PA Announcer: Rich DeLeo. **Official Scorer:** Ted Beam.

Stadium Name: Blair County Ballpark. **Location:** Located just off the Frankstown Road Exit of I-99. **Standard Game Times:** 7:05 p.m., 6:35 (April-May); Sun. 6:05, 3:05 (April-May). **Ticket Price Range:** $5-12.

Visiting Club Hotel: Ramada Altoona, Route 220 and Plank Road, Altoona, PA 16602. **Telephone:** (814) 946-1631.

BINGHAMTON METS

Office Address: 211 Henry St, Binghamton, NY 13901.

Mailing Address: P.O. Box 598, Binghamton, NY 13902.

Telephone: (607) 723-6387. **Fax:** (607) 723-7779.

E-Mail address: bmets@bmets.com. **Website:** www.bmets.com.

Affiliation (first year): New York Mets (1992). **Years in League:** 1923-37, 1940-63, 1966-68, 1992-

OWNERSHIP, MANAGEMENT

Principal Owners: Bill Maines, David Maines, George Scherer, Michael Urda.

General Manager: Scott Brown. **Assistant GM:** Jim Weed. **Director, Stadium Operations:** Richard Tylicki. **Director, Ticket Operations:** Casey Both. **Director, Video Productions:** Jon Cofer. **Director, Marketing:** Heith Tracy. **Special Event Coordinators:** Connor Gates, Erica Mincher, Bob Urda. **Ticket Office Manager:** Casey Both. **Scholastic Programs Coordinator:** Lou Ferraro. **Community Relations Coordinator:** Amy Fancher. **Office Manager:** Rebecca Brown. **Merchandising Manager:** Lisa Shattuck. **Broadcasting Director:** Robert Ford. **Sports Turf Manager:** Stephen Wiseman. **Home Clubhouse Manager:** Pete Stasio. **Visiting Clubhouse Manager:** Jim Coughlin.

FIELD STAFF

Manager: Mako Oliveras. **Coaches:** Bobby Malek/Donovan Mitchell. **Pitching Coach:** Hector Berrios.

GAME INFORMATION

Radio Announcer: Robert Ford. **No. of Games Broadcast:** Home-71 Road-71. **Flagship Station:** WNBF 1290-AM.

PA Announcer: Unavailable. **Official Scorer:** Steve Kraly.

Stadium Name: NYSEG Stadium. **Location:** I-81 to exit 4S (Binghamton), Route 11 exit to Henry Street. **Standard Game Times:** 7:05 p.m., 6:35 (April-May); Sun. 1:05. **Ticket Price Range:** $9-10.

Visiting Club Hotel: Best Western, 569 Harry L Drive, Johnson City, NY 13790. **Telephone:** (607) 729-9194.

BOWIE BAYSOX

Office Address: Prince George's Stadium, 4101 NE Crain Hwy, Bowie, MD 20716.
Telephone: (301) 805-6000. **Fax:** (301) 464-4911.
E-Mail address: info@baysox.com. **Website:** www.baysox.com.
Affiliation (first year): Baltimore Orioles (1993). **Years in League:** 1993-

OWNERSHIP, MANAGEMENT

Owned By: Bowie Baysox Baseball Club LLC.

President: Ken Young.

General Manager: Brian Shallcross. **Assistant GM:** Phil Wrye. **Director, Marketing:** Brandan Kaiser. **Director, Field/Facility Operations:** Matt Parrott. **Director, Ticket Operations:** Charlene Fewer. **Director, Sponsorships:** Matt McLaughlin. **Director, Promotions:** Lauren Phillips. **Promotions Manager:** Chris Rogers. **Communications Manager:** Tom Sedlacek. **Communications Assistant:** Andrew Zelinski. **Community Programs Manager:** Dana DeFilippo. **Marketing Assistant:** Dale Eustler. **Marketing Assistant/Mascot Operations:** Fred Love. **Assistant Director, Sales:** Kari Fredriksen. **Account Executive:** Aaron Gunter. **Group Events Managers:** Vince Riggs, Janna Green. **Manager, Stadium Operations:** Rick Wade. **Director, Gameday Personnel:** Darlene Mingioli. **Clubhouse Manager:** Andy Maalouf. **Visiting Clubhouse Manager:** Mark Conrad. **Office Manager:** Karen Marcher. **Bookkeeper:** Carol Terwilliger.

FIELD STAFF

Manager: Brad Komminsk. **Coach:** Moe Hill. **Pitching Coach:** Unavailable. **Trainer:** Joe Benge.

GAME INFORMATION

Radio Announcer: Unavailable. **No. of Games Broadcast:** Unavailable. **Flagship Station:** Unavailable.

PA Announcer: Adrienne Roberson. **Official Scorer:** Bill Hay, Carl Smith

Stadium Name: Prince George's Stadium. **Location:** ¼ mile south of U.S. 50/RT. 301 Interchange in Bowie.

Standard Game Times: 7:05 p.m; Sun. 2:05 (April-May), 6:05 (June-Sept.) **Ticket Price Range:** $6-14.

Visiting Club Hotel: Best Western Annapolis, 2520 Riva Rd, Annapolis, MD 21401. **Telephone:** (410) 224-2800.

CONNECTICUT DEFENDERS

Office Address: 14 Stott Ave, Norwich, CT 06360.
Telephone: (860) 887-7962. **Fax:** (860) 886-5996.
E-Mail address: info@ctdefenders.com. **Website:** www.ctdefenders.com.
Affiliation (first year): San Francisco Giants (2003). **Years in League:** 1995-

OWNERSHIP, MANAGEMENT

Operated By: Navigators Baseball LP.

President/Managing Partner: Lou DiBella.

General Manager: Charlie Dowd. **Controller:** John Cunningham. **Corporate Sales:** Steve Kunsey. **Director, Group Sales:** Steve Given. **Group Sales Representative:** Lindsay Carroll. **Director, Ticket Sales:** Brendon Porter. **Director, Merchandise/Concessions:** Shannon Johnson. **Assistant Merchandise/Concessions:** Heather Bartlett. **Director, Media/Broadcasting:** Brian Irizarry. **Assistant Media/Broadcasting:** Matt Martinez. **Head Groundskeeper:** Paul Lopez. **Assistant Groundskeeper:** Mike Foley. **Account Executive:** Nick Lampasona. **Operations Assistant:** Ryan Lefler. **Accounts Payable:** Tammy Nolin. **Office Manager:** Dale Firmin.

FIELD STAFF

Manager: Steve Decker. **Coach:** Garey Ingram. **Pitching Coach:** Ross Grimsley. **Trainer:** Eric Ortega.

GAME INFORMATION

Radio Announcers: Brian Irizarry, Matt Martinez. **No of Games Broadcast:** Home-71 Road-71. **Flagship Station:** WICH 1310-AM.

PA Announcer: Ed Weyant. **Official Scorer:** TBA.

Stadium Name: Sen. Thomas J. Dodd Memorial Stadium. **Location:** I-395 to exit 82, follow signs for Dodd Stadium. **Standard Game Times:** 6:35 p.m.; Sunday, 1:05. **Ticket Price Range:** $7-10.

Visiting Club Hotel: Comfort Inn Mystic, 48 Whitehall Avenue, Mystic, CT 6355. **Telephone:** (860) 572-8531.

ERIE SEA WOLVES

Office Address: 110 E. 10th St, Erie, PA 16501.
Telephone: (814) 456-1300. **Fax:** (814) 456-7520.
E-Mail address: seawolves@seawolves.com. **Website:** www.seawolves.com.
Affiliation (first year): Detroit Tigers (2001). **Years in League:** 1999-

OWNERSHIP, MANAGEMENT

Principal Owners: Mandalay Baseball Properties, LLC.

General Manager: John Frey. **Assistant GM, Sales:** Mike Uden. **Assistant GM, Marketing:** Rob Magee. **Senior Ticket Sales Executive/Suite Coordinator:** Becky Obradovic. **Director, Finance:** Bernadette Mulvihill. **Director, Media Relations:** Greg Gania. **Box Office Manager:** Mark Pirrello. **Manager, Marketing/Promotions:** Carol Trumbo. **Director, Operations/Concessions:** Eric Phillips. **Operations Manager:** Ryan Stephenson.

FIELD STAFF

Manager: Tom Brookens. **Coach:** Glen Adams. **Pitching Coach:** Ray Burris. **Trainer:** Chris McDonald.

GAME INFORMATION

Radio Announcer: Greg Gania. **No. of Games Broadcast:** Home-71 Road-71. **Flagship Station:** Fox Sports Radio WFNN 1330-AM.

PA Announcer: Bob Shreve. **Official Scorer:** Les Caldwell.

Stadium Name: Jerry Uht Park. **Location:** U.S. 79 North to East 12th Street exit, left on State Street, right on 10th Street. **Standard Game Times:** 7:05 p.m., 6:35 (April-May); Sun. 1:05. **Ticket Price Range:** $5-12.

Visiting Club Hotel: Avalon Hotel, 16 W. 10th St, Erie, PA 16501. **Telephone:** (814) 459-2220.

HARRISBURG SENATORS

Office Address: Commerce Bank Park, City Island, Harrisburg, PA 17101.
Mailing Address: P.O. Box 15757, Harrisburg, PA 17105.
Telephone: (717) 231-4444. **Fax:** (717) 231-4445.
E-Mail address: information@senatorsbaseball.com. **Website:** www.senatorsbaseball.com.
Affiliation (first year): Washington Nationals (2005). **Years in League:** 1924-35, 1987-

OWNERSHIP, MANAGEMENT

Operated By: Senators Partners, LLC.

Chairman: Michael Reinsdorf. **CEO:** Bill Davidson. **President:** Kevin Kulp.

General Manager: Randy Whitaker. **Director, Picnic Operations:** Melissa Altemose. **Director, Broadcasting/ Media Relations:** Terry Byrom. **Director, Creative Services:** Brianna Dubel. **Director, Stadium Operations:** Tim Foreman. **Director, Game Entertainment:** Aaron Margolis. **Director, Group Sales:** Mac Simmons. **Director, Community Relations:** Emily Winslow. **Ticket Sales Manager:** Jon Tapper. **Box Office Manager:** Andy Brooks. **Corporate Sales Executive:** Jessica Snader. **Ticket Sales Executives:** Jon Boles, Jessica Kauffman, Drew Praster. **Sales Executive:** Sarah Keel. **Head Groundskeeper:** Brandon Forsburg. **Bookkeeper:** Donna Demczak.

FIELD STAFF

Manager: John Stearns. **Coach:** Tony Gingrich. **Pitching Coach:** Randy Tomlin. **Trainer:** Beth Jarrett.

GAME INFORMATION

Radio Announcer: Terry Byrom. **No. of Games Broadcast:** Home-71 Road-71. **Flagship Station:** 1460-AM.

PA Announcer: Chris Andre. **Official Scorer:** Unavailable.

Stadium Name: Commerce Bank Park. **Location:** I-83, exit 23 (Second Street) to Market Street, bridge to City Island. **Ticket Price Range:** $3-10.

Visiting Club Hotel: Holiday Inn West, 5401 Carlisle Pike, Mechanicsburg, PA 17050. **Telephone:** (800) 772-7829.

NEW BRITAIN ROCK CATS

Office Address: 230 John Karbonic Way, New Britain, CT 06051.
Mailing Address: P.O. Box 1718, New Britain, CT 06050.
Telephone: (860) 224-8383. **Fax:** (860) 225-6267.
E-Mail address: rockcats@rockcats.com. **Website:** www.rockcats.com.
Affiliation (first year): Minnesota Twins (1995). **Years in League:** 1983-

OWNERSHIP, MANAGEMENT

Operated By: New Britain Baseball Club Inc.

Principal Owners: Bill Dowling, Coleman Levy. **President, CEO:** Bill Dowling. **Chairman of the Board:** Coleman Levy.

Vice President/General Manager: John Willi. **Vice President:** Evan Levy. **Assistant GM/Sales:** Ricky Ferrell.

Director, Broadcasting: Jeff Dooley. **Director, Ticket Operations:** Mike DiMartini. **Director, Group Sales:** Jonathan Lissitchuck. **Director, Promotions:** Kim Pizighelli. **Director, Media Relations:** Robert Dowling. **Director, Corporate Sales:** Andres Levy. **Group Sales Manager:** Evan Paradis. **Stadium Operations Coordinator:** Mike Mariano. **Marketing Coordinator:** Lori Soltis. **Corporate Sales Manager:** Kate Baumann. **Controller:** Paula Perdelwitz. **Concessionaire:** Centerplate/Chris Coonrad.

FIELD STAFF

Manager: Tom Nieto. **Coach:** Floyd Rayford. **Pitching Coach:** Stu Cliburn. **Trainer:** Chad Jackson.

GAME INFORMATION

Radio Announcer: Jeff Dooley. **No. of Games Broadcast:** Home-71 Road-71. **Flagship Station:** WTIC 1080-AM/96.5-FM, WMRD 1150-AM.

PA Announcer: Don Steele. **Official Scorer:** Ed Smith.

Stadium Name: New Britain Stadium. **Location:** From I-84, take Route 72 East (exit 35 of Route 9 South (exit 39A), left at Ellis Street (exit 25), left at South Main Street, stadium one mile on right. From Route 91 or Route 5, take Route 9 North to Route 71 (exit 24), first exit. **Ticket Price Range:** $5-12.

Visiting Club Hotel: Holiday Inn Express, 120 Laning St, Southington, CT 06489. **Telephone:** (860) 276-0736.

NEW HAMPSHIRE FISHER CATS

Office Address: 1 Line Dr., Manchester, NH 03101.
Telephone: (603) 641-2005. **Fax:** (603) 641-2055.
E-Mail address: info@nhfishercats.com. **Website:** www.nhfishercats.com.
Affiliation (first year): Toronto Blue Jays (2004). **Years in League:** 2004-

OWNERSHIP, MANAGEMENT

Operated By: Triple Play LLC.

Owner: Art Solomon.

President/General Manager: Rick Brenner. **Vice President, Business Operations:** Tim Restall. **VP, Sales:** Mike Ramshaw. **VP, Marketing:** Loren Foxx. **Corporate Controller:** Cindy Garron. **Director, Public Affairs:** Danielle Matteau. **Director, Media Relations:** Mike Murphy. **Director, Ticket Sales:** Dennis Meehan. **Director, Group Sales:** Erik Lesniak. **Head Turf Manager:** Eric Blanton. **Manager, Stadium Operations:** Matt Moore. **Merchandise Manager:** Kaitlyn Tomasello. **Community Relations Manager/Ticket Sales Account Executive:** Morgan Crandall. **Marketing Manager:** Liam Roberge. **Production Manager:** Jake Charleston. **Box Office Manager:** Pat Lewis. **Ticket Sales Account Executives:** Stephanie Livoli, Mike Murphy, Jeremy Roop, Gregg Tadgell, Joel Leroy, Tim Hough. **Office Manager/Ticket Sales Account Executive:** Kathryn Mitchell.

FIELD STAFF

Manager: Gary Cathcart. **Hitting Coach:** Paul Elliott. **Pitching Coach:** Tom Signore. **Trainer:** Voon Chong.

GAME INFORMATION

Radio Announcers: Mike Murphy, Bob Lipman. **No of Games Broadcast:** Home-71 Road-71. **Flagship Station:** WGIR 610-AM.

PA Announcer: John Zahr. **Official Scorers:** Chick Smith, Lenny Parker, Greg Royce.

Stadium Name: Merchantsauto.com Stadium. **Location:** From I-93 North, take I-293 North to exit 5 (Granite Street), right on Granite Street, right on South Commercial Street, right on Line Drive. **Ticket Price Range:** $6-12.

Visiting Club Hotel: Comfort Inn, 298 Queen City Ave, Manchester, NH 03102. **Telephone:** (603) 668-2600.

PORTLAND SEA DOGS

Office Address: 271 Park Ave, Portland, ME 04102.
Mailing Address: P.O. Box 636, Portland, ME 04104.
Telephone: (207) 874-9300. **Fax:** (207) 780-0317.
E-Mail address: seadogs@seadogs.com. **Website:** www.seadogs.com.
Affiliation (first year): Boston Red Sox (2003). **Years in League:** 1994-

OWNERSHIP, MANAGEMENT

Operated By: Portland, Maine Baseball, Inc.

Principal Owner, Chairman: Daniel Burke.

President, General Manager: Charles Eshbach. **Executive Vice President:** John Kameisha. **VP:** Jim Heffley. **Assistant GM, Media Relations:** Chris Cameron. **Assistant GM, Sales/Promotions:** Geoff Iacuessa. **Director, Group Sales:** Liz Riley. **Director, Ticketing:** Dave Strong. **Assistant Director, Ticketing:** Sarah Connolly. **Director, Video Operations:** Todd Jamison. **Director, Broadcasting:** Mike Antonellis. **Director, Food Services:** Mike Scorza. **Asstistant Director, Food Services:** Greg Moyes. **Clubhouse Managers:** Craig Candage Sr., Craig Candage Jr. **Head Groundskeeper:** Rick Anderson.

FIELD STAFF

Manager: Arnie Beyeler. **Coach:** Dave Joppie. **Pitching Coach:** Mike Cather. **Trainer:** Jon Jochim.

GAME INFORMATION

Radio Announcer: Mike Antonellis. **No. of Games Broadcast:** Home-71 Road-71. **Flagship Station:** WBAE 1490-AM.

PA Announcer: Dean Rogers. **Official Scorer:** Thom Hinton.

Stadium Name: Hadlock Field. **Location:** From South, I-295 to exit 5, merge onto Congress Street, left at St. John Street, merge right onto Park Ave. From North, I-295 to exit 6A, right onto Park Ave. **Ticket Price Range:** $4-9.

Visiting Club Hotel: Wyndham Hotel, 363 Maine Mall Rd, South Portland, ME 04106. **Telephone:** (207) 775-6161.

READING PHILLIES

Office Address: Route 61 South/1900 Centre Ave., Reading, PA 19605.
Mailing Address: P.O. Box 15050, Reading, PA 19612.
Telephone: (610) 375-8469. **Fax:** (610) 373-5868.
E-Mail Address: info@readingphillies.com. **Website:** www.readingphillies.com.
Affiliation (first year): Philadelphia Phillies (1967). **Years in League:** 1933-35, 1952-61, 1963-65, 1967-.

OWNERSHIP, MANAGEMENT

Operated By: E&J Baseball Club, Inc.
Principal Owner: Reading Baseball LP
President: Chuck Domino.

General Manager: Scott Hunsicker. **Assistant GM:** Ashley Forlini. **Director, Stadium Operations/Concessions:** Andy Bortz. **Director, Sales:** Joe Bialek. **Director, Baseball Operations/Merchandise:** Kevin Sklenarik. **Director, Communications:** Rob Hackash. **Director, Ticket Operations:** Mike Becker. **Director, Group Sales:** Mike Robinson. **Controller:** Kristyne Haver. **Corporate Sales/Graphic Artist/Game Entertainment:** Matt Jackson. **Group Sales Managers:** Brian Babik, Holly Frymyer. **Client Relationship Managers:** Curtis Burns, Ryan Contento, Chris McConney, Matt Hoffmaster. **Group Sales Manager:** Tim McGee. **Operations/Concessions Assistant:** Tim Martino. **Head Groundskeeper:** Dan Douglas. **Office Manager:** Deneen Giesen. **Video Director:** Andy Kauffman.

FIELD STAFF

Manager: Steve Roadcap. **Coach:** Frank Cacciatore. **Pitching Coach:** Steve Schrenk. **Trainers:** Chris Mudd, Justin Zabrosky

GAME INFORMATION

Radio Announcers: Steve Degler, Kale Beers. **No. of Games Broadcast:** Home-71, Away-71. **Flagship Station:** ESPN 1240-AM.

PA Announcer: Dave Bauman. **Official Scorers:** John Gump, Paul Jones, Brian Kopetsky, Josh Leiboff, Dick Shute.

Stadium Name: FirstEnergy Stadium. **Location:** From east, take Pennsylvania Turnpike West to Morgantown exit, to 176 North, to 422 West, to Route 12 East, to Route 61 South exit. From west, take 422 East to Route 12 East, to Route 61 South exit. From north, take 222 South to Route 12 exit, to Route 61 South exit. From south, take 222 North to 422 West, to Route 12 East exit at Route 61 South. **Standard Game Times:** 7:05 p.m., Mon.-Thurs. (April-May) 6:35; Sun. 1:05. **Ticket Price Range:** $6-11

Visiting Club Hotel: Days Inn, 910 Woodland Ave., Wyomissing PA 19610. **Telephone:** (610) 375-1500.

TRENTON THUNDER

Office Address: One Thunder Road, Trenton, NJ 08611.
Telephone: (609) 394-3300. **Fax:** (609) 394-9666.
E-Mail address: fun@trentonthunder.com. **Website:** www.trentonthunder.com.
Affiliation (first year): New York Yankees (2003). **Years in League:** 1994-

OWNERSHIP, MANAGEMENT

Operated By: Garden State Baseball, LLP.
General Manager/COO: Will Smith.
Vice President, Marketing: Eric Lipsman. **Director, Ticket Operations:** Matt Pentima. **Director, Public Relations:** Bill Cook. **Director, Merchandising:** Joe Pappalardo. **Executive Director, Ticket Sales:** Jason Schubert. **Director, Stadium Operations:** Ryan Crammer. **Director, Broadcasting:** Steve Rudenstein. **Director, Food/ Beverages:** Kevin O'Byrne. **Concourse Supervisor, Food Service America:** Chris Champion. **Assistant Director, Ticket Sales:** Patience Purdy. **Office Manager:** Kathy Gallagher. **Production Manager:** Greg Lavin. **Baseball Operations/Accounting Manager:** Jeff Hurley. **Stadium Operations Manager:** Steve Brokowsky. **Merchandise Manager:** Caitlin Hyde. **Group Sales Account Executives:** Kelsey Albair, Krysten Hardifer, Chad Heidel, Dave Kuhn, Matt Schwartz. **Ticket Sales Account Executive:** Erin Leigh. **Marketing and All Star Game Coordinator:** Rachel Wolf. **Home Clubhouse Manager:** Tom Kackley. **Visiting Clubhouse Manager:** John Annis. **Head Groundskeeper:** Ryan Hills.

FIELD STAFF

Manager: Tony Franklin. **Hitting Coach:** Frank Menechino. **Pitching Coach:** Tommy Phelps. **Coach:** Vic Valencia. **Trainer:** Tim Lentych.

GAME INFORMATION

Radio Announcer: Steve Rudenstein. **No. of Games Broadcast:** Home-71 Road 71. **Flagship Station:** Unavailable.
PA Announcer: Bill Bromberg. **Official Scorers:** Jay Dunn, Greg Zak.
Stadium Name: Samuel L. Plumeri Sr. Field at Mercer County Waterfront Park. **Location:** From I-95, take Route 1 North to Route 29 South, stadium entrance just before tunnel. From NJ Turnpike, take Exit 7A and follow I-195 West. Road will become Rte. 29. Follow through tunnel and ballpark is on left. **Standard Game Times:** 7:05 p.m.; Sat. 1:05 (April); Sun 1:05. **Ticket Price Range:** $9-12.
Visiting Club Hotel: Trenton Marriott, 1 West Lafayette Street, Trenton, NJ 08608. **Telephone:** (609) 421-4000.

SOUTHERN LEAGUE

DOUBLE-A

Mailing Address: 2551 Roswell Rd., Suite 330, Marietta, GA 30062.
Telephone: (770) 321-0400. **Fax:** (770) 321-0037.
E-Mail Address: soleague@earthlink.net. **Website:** www.southernleague.com.

Years League Active: 1964-.

President: Don Mincher.

Vice President: Steve DeSalvo.

Directors: Peter Bragan Jr. (Jacksonville), Steve Bryant (Carolina), Frank Burke (Chattanooga), Steve DeSalvo (Mississippi), Tom Dickson (Montgomery), Doug Kirchhofer (Tennessee), Tom Hanson (West Tenn), Jonathan Nelson (Birmingham), Miles Prentice (Huntsville), Bill Shanahan (Mobile).

Vice President, Operations: Lori Webb. **Media Relations Director:** Nate Beardsley.

Division Structure: North—Carolina, Chattanooga, Huntsville, Tennessee, West Tenn. **South**—Birmingham, Jacksonville, Mississippi, Mobile, Montgomery.

Regular Season: 140 games (split schedule). **2009 Opening Date:** April 9. **Closing Date:** Sept. 7.

All-Star Game: July 13 at Birmingham.

Playoff Format: First-half division winners meet second-half division winners in best-of-five series. Winners meet in best-of-five series for league championship.

Roster Limit: 24. **Player Eligibility Rule:** No restrictions.

Brand of Baseball: Rawlings.

Umpires: Unavailable.

Don Mincher

STADIUM INFORMATION

			Dimensions				
Club	**Stadium**	**Opened**	**LF**	**CF**	**RF**	**Capacity**	**2008 Att.**
Birmingham	Regions Park	1988	340	405	340	10,800	302,979
Carolina	Five County Stadium	1991	330	400	330	6,500	281,012
Chattanooga	AT&T Field	2000	325	400	330	6,362	236,639
Huntsville	Joe W. Davis Municipal Stadium	1985	345	405	330	10,200	160,080
Jacksonville	Baseball Grounds of Jacksonville	2003	321	420	317	11,000	364,365
Mississippi	Trustmark Park	2005	337	332	400	7,416	212,107
Mobile	Hank Aaron Stadium	1997	325	400	310	6,000	220,821
Montgomery	Montgomery Riverwalk Stadium	2004	335	402	332	7,000	292,181
Tennessee	Smokies Park	2000	330	400	330	6,000	250,209
West Tenn	Pringles Park	1998	310	395	320	6,000	140,445

BIRMINGHAM BARONS

Office Address: 100 Ben Chapman Dr., Hoover, AL 35244.
Mailing Address: P.O. Box 360007, Birmingham, AL 35236.
Telephone: (205) 988-3200. **Fax:** (205) 988-9698.
E-Mail Address: barons@barons.com. **Website:** www.barons.com
Affiliation (first year): Chicago White Sox (1986). **Years in League:** 1964-65, 1967-75, 1981-

OWNERSHIP, MANAGEMENT

Principal Owners: Don Logan, Jeff Logan, Stan Logan.

General Manager: Jonathan Nelson. **Assistant GM:** Michael Pepper. **Director, Stadium Operations:** James Young. **Director, Broadcasting:** Curt Bloom. **Director, Media Relations:** Justin Firesheets. **Director, Sales:** Bill Adema. **Director, Tickets/Retail:** Charlie Santiago. **Director, Group Sales:** Brad Hudson. **Director, Promotions/Community Relations:** Kyle Krebs. **Corporate Event Planners:** Dusty Lewis, Elizabeth Taylor. **Community Group Ticket Representative:** Shawn Pharo. **General Manager, Grand Slam Catering:** Eric Crook. **Director, Catering:** Taylor Youngson. **Office Manager:** Jennifer Dillard. **Accountant:** Jo Ann Bragan. **Intern:** Zane Davitz. **Head Groundskeeper:** Daniel Ruggiero. **Assistant Groundskeeper:** Josh Hyde. **Interns:** Zane Davitz, Brian Johnson, John Mason-Smith, Craig Phillips, John Roberts, Justin Vollenweider.

FIELD STAFF

Manager: Ever Magallanes. **Hitting Coach:** Andy Tomberlin. **Pitching Coach:** J.R. Pedrew. **Trainer:** Joe Geck. **Strength/Conditioning:** Raymond Smith.

GAME INFORMATION

Radio Announcer: Curt Bloom. **No of Games Broadcast:** Home-70 Road-70. **Flagship Station:** Unavailable.

PA Announcer: Jacob Allison. **Official Scorer:** Grant Martin.

Stadium Name: Regions Park. **Location:** I-459 to Highway 150 (exit 10) in Hoover. **Standard Game Times:** 7:05 p.m.; Sun. 2:05 (First Half), 5:05 (Second Half). **Ticket Price Range:** $7-12.

Visiting Club Hotel: Days Inn at the Galleria, 1800 Riverchase Dr, Birmingham, AL 35244. **Telephone:** (205) 985-7500.

CAROLINA MUDCATS

Office Address: 1501 N.C. Hwy. 39, Zebulon, NC 27597.
Mailing Address: P.O. Drawer 1218, Zebulon, NC 27597.
Telephone: (919) 269-2287. **Fax:** (919) 269-4910.
E-Mail Address: muddy@gomudcats.com. **Website:** www.gomudcats.com.
Affiliation (first year): Cincinnati Reds (2009). **Years in League:** 1991-

OWNERSHIP, MANAGEMENT

Operated by: Carolina Mudcats Professional Baseball Club Inc.

Principal Owner: Steve Bryant.

General Manager: Joe Kremer. **Assistant GM:** Eric Gardner. **Office Manager:** Jackie DiPrimo. **Director, Broadcasting:** Patrick Kinas. **Directors, Stadium Operations:** Eric Morgan, Sandy Newsome. **Director, Marketing:** Alexandra Briley. **Director, Food/Beverage:** Zia Torabian. **Assistant Director, Food/Beverage:** Alan Hinnant. **Director, Community Relations:** Lindsay Wiener. **Merchandise Manager:** LuAnne Reynolds. **Coordinator, Multi-Media Productions:** Aaron Bayles. **Director, Tickets:** Jon Clemmons. **Corporate Sales Representative:** Ricky Ray. **Director, Group Sales:** Haig Lea. **Group Sales Associates:** Adrain Bridges, Chris Signorelli, Josh Bridges. **Director, Fundraising:** Macy Dykema. **Head Groundskeeper:** John Packer. **Director, Special Events:** Nathan Priddy.

FIELD STAFF

Manager: David Bell. **Coach:** Ryan Jackson. **Pitching Coach:** Unavailable. **Trainer:** Jimmy Mattocks.

GAME INFORMATION

Radio Announcer: Patrick Kinas. **No. of Games Broadcast:** Home-70, Away-70. **Flagship Stations:** WDOX-AM 570; WKXU-FM 102.5.

PA Announcer: Dave Slade. **Official Scorer:** TBA.

Stadium Name: Five County Stadium. **Location:** From Raleigh, U.S. 64 East to 264 East, exit at Highway 39 in Zebulon. **Standard Game Times:** 7:15 p.m.; Sat. 6:15; Sun. 2. **Ticket Price Range:** $5-9.

Visiting Club Hotel: Best Western Raleigh North, 2715 Capital Blvd., Raleigh, NC 27604. **Telephone:** (919) 872-5000.

CHATTANOOGA LOOKOUTS

Office Address: 201 Power Alley, Chattanooga, TN 37402.
Mailing Address: P.O. Box 11002, Chattanooga, TN 37401.
Telephone: (423) 267-2208. **Fax:** (423) 267-4258.
E-Mail Address: lookouts@lookouts.com. **Website:** www.lookouts.com.
Affiliation (first year): Los Angeles Dodgers (2009). **Years in League:** 1964-65, 1976-

OWNERSHIP, MANAGEMENT

Operated By: Scenic City Baseball LLC.

Principal Owner: Daniel Burke, Frank Burke, Charles Eshbach.

President/General Manager: Frank Burke. **Assistant GM:** John Maedel. **Director, Business Administration/Executive Assistant:** Debby Kennedy. **Director, Group Sales:** Bill Wheeler. **Director, Merchandising/Marketing:** Chrysta Jorgensen. **Director, Media Relations:** Peter Intza. **Director, Ticketing Operations:** Luis Gonzalez. **Director, Concessions:** Steve Sullivan. **Director, Broadcasting:** Larry Ward. **Head Groundskeeper:** Bo Henley. **Director, Stadium Operations:** Alex Vaughn. **Director, Business Administration/Accounting:** Brian Eshbach. **Assistant Director, Broadcasting:** Will Poindexter. **Assistant Director, Concessions:** John Quirk. **Ticketing Assistant:** Gavin Cox. **Ticketing Assistant:** Matt St. Charles.

FIELD STAFF

Manager: John Valentin . **Hitting Coach:** Luis Salazar. **Pitching Coach:** Glenn Dishman. **Trainer:** Yosuke Nakajima.

GAME INFORMATION

Radio Announcers: Larry Ward, Will Poindexter. **No. of Games Broadcast:** Home-70 Road-70. **Flagship Station:** WDOD 1310-AM.

PA Announcer: John Maedel. **Official Scorers:** Wirt Gammon, Andy Paul, Laird Leathers .

Stadium Name: AT&T Field. **Location:** From I-24, take U.S. 27 North to exit 1C (4th Street), first left onto Chestnut Street, left onto Third Street. **Ticket Price Range:** $4-8.

Visiting Club Hotel: Clarion Inn & Suites , 2345 Shallowford Rd, Chattanooga, TN 37412. **Telephone:** (423) 855-2898.

HUNTSVILLE STARS

Office Address: 3125 Leeman Ferry Rd., Huntsville, AL 35801.
Mailing Address: 3125 Leeman Ferry Rd., Huntsville, AL 35801.
Telephone: (256) 882-2562. **Fax:** (256) 880-0801.
E-Mail Address: info@huntsvillestars.com. **Website:** www.huntsvillestars.com.
Affiliation (first year): Milwaukee Brewers (1999). **Years in League:** 1985-

OWNERSHIP, MANAGEMENT

Operated By: Huntsville Stars LLC.
President: Miles Prentice.
General Manager: Buck Rogers. **Director, Broadcasting:** Brett Pollock. **Office Manager:** Earl Grilliot. **Director, Field Maintenance:** Jamie Hill. **Director, Media/Public Relations:** Brian Massey. **Director, Merchandising:** Kylee Hanish. **Director, Stadium Operations:** Paul Westbrook. **Director, Ticketing/Group Sales:** Babs Rogers. **Director, Concessions:** Scott Tolmach.

FIELD STAFF

Manager: Bob Miscik. **Coach:** Jim Lett. **Pitching Coach:** John Curtis. **Athletic Trainer:** Dave Yeager.

GAME INFORMATION

Announcer: Brett Pollock. **Flagship station:** All games webcast only.
PA Announcers: Todd Blass, J.J. Lewis. **Official Scorer:** Don Rizzardi.
Stadium Name: Joe W. Davis Municipal Stadium. **Location:** I-65 to I-565 East, south on Memorial Parkway to Drake Avenue exit, right on Don Mincher Drive. **Ticket Price Range:** $8-$20, depending on food packages. **Visiting Club Hotel:** Microtel Inn & Suites, 1820 Chase Creek Row, Huntsville, AL 35811. **Tel:** 256-859-6655.

JACKSONVILLE SUNS

Office Address: 301 A. Philip Randolph Blvd., Jacksonville, FL 32202.
Mailing Address: P.O. Box 4756, Jacksonville, FL 32201.
Telephone: (904) 358-2846. **Fax:** (904) 358-2845.
E-Mail Address: info@jaxsuns.com. **Website:** www.jaxsuns.com.
Affiliation (first year): Florida Marlins (2009). **Years In League:** 1970-

OWNERSHIP, MANAGEMENT

Operated by: Baseball Jax Inc.
Principal Owner, Chairman of the Board: Peter Bragan Sr. **Madame Chairman:** Mary Frances Bragan.
President/General Manager: Peter Bragan Jr. **Assistant GM:** Brad Rodriguez. **Director, Ticket Operations:** Jane Carole Bunting. **Director, Broadcasting/Media Relations:** J.P. Shadrick. **Director, Community Relations:** Katherine Jeschke. **Director, Field Operations:** Ed Attalla. **Director, Sponsorship Sales:** Chris Peters. **Director, Merchandise:** Victoria Eure. **Director, Sales/Promotions:** Casey Nichols. **Director, Stadium Operations:** Matt Glancy. **Office Manager:** Barbara O'Berry. **Director, Video Services:** David Scheldorf. **Manager, Box Office:** Amy DeLettre. **Director, Group Sales:** Meghan Clark. **Group Sales Associate:** Kathleen Parker. **General Manager, Ballpark Foods:** Jamie Davis. **Assistant GM, Ballpark Foods/Finance:** Mitch Buska. **Administrative Assistants:** Sarah Foster, J.D. Metrie, January Putt, Josh Rudd. **Administrative Receptionist:** Theresa Viets.

FIELD STAFF

Manager: Brandon Hyde. **Hitting Coach:** Theron Todd. **Pitching Coach:** Reid Cornelius. **Trainer:** Dustin Luepker.

GAME INFORMATION

Radio Announcer: J.P. Shadrick. **No. of Games Broadcast:** Home-70, Away-70. **Flagship Station:** WFXJ 930-AM.
PA Announcer: John Leard. **Official Scorer:** Jason Eliopulos. **Press Box Assistant:** Brian DeLettre
Stadium Name: The Baseball Grounds of Jacksonville. **Location:** I-95 South to Martin Luther King Parkway exit, follow Gator Bowl Blvd. around Alltel Stadium; I-95 North to Exit 347 (Emerson Street), go right to Hart Bridge Expressway, take Sports Complex exit, left at light to stop sign, take left and follow around Alltel Stadium; From Mathews Bridge, take A. Philip Randolph exit, right on A. Philip Randolph, straight to stadium. **Standard Game Times:** 7:05 p.m., Wed. 1:05, Sun. 3:05/5:05. **Ticket Price Range:** $5.50-19.50.
Visiting Club Hotel: Hyatt Regency Jacksonville Riverfront, 225 Coastline Dr., Jacksonville, FL 32202. **Telephone:** (904) 633-9095.

MISSISSIPPI BRAVES

Office Address: Trustmark Park, 1 Braves Way, Pearl, MS 39208.
Mailing Address: P.O. Box 97389, Pearl, MS 39288.
Telephone: (601) 932-8788. **Fax:** (601) 936-3567.
E-Mail Address: mississippi.braves@braves.com. **Website:** www.mississippibraves.com.
Affiliation (first year): Atlanta Braves (2005). **Years in League:** 2005-

OWNERSHIP, MANAGEMENT

Operated By: Atlanta National League Baseball Club Inc.

General Manager: Steve DeSalvo. **Assistant GM:** Jim Bishop. **Ticket Manager:** Bob Askin. **Merchandise Manager:** Sarah Banta. **Advertising/Design Manager:** Brian Byrd. **Facility Maintenance Manager:** Greg Craddock. **Community Relations Manager:** Lisa Dunn. **Sales Associate:** Matt McCoy. **Head Chef:** Tina Funches. **Sales Associate:** Sean Guillotte. **Suites/Catering Manager:** Debbie Herrington. **Stadium Operations Manager:** Brian Parker. **Special Events Manager:** Georganna Keenum. **Assistant Restaurant Manager:** Jack McGill. **Promotions/Entertainment Manager:** Brian Prochilo. **Concessions Manager:** Felicia Thompson. **Office Administrator:** Christy Shaw. **Public Relations Manager:** Nicholas Skinner. **Restaurant Manager:** Gene Slaughter.

Director, Field/Facility Operations: Matt Taylor.

FIELD STAFF

Manager: Phillip Wellman. **Coach:** Roosevelt Brown. **Pitching Coach:** Marty Reed. **Trainer:** Ricky Alcantara.

GAME INFORMATION

Radio Announcer: Ben Ingram. **No. of Games Broadcast:** Home-70 Road-70. **Flagship Station:** WYAB 103.9 FM.

PA Announcer: Derrel Palmer. **Official Scorer:** Butch Raley. **Stadium Name:** Trustmark Park.

Location: I-20 to exit 48/Pearl (Pearson Road). **Ticket Price Range:** $5-12.

Visiting Club Hotel: Holiday Inn Trustmark Park, 110 Bass Pro Drive, Pearl, MS 39208. **Telephone:** (601) 939-5238.

MOBILE BAYBEARS

Office Address: Hank Aaron Stadium, 755 Bolling Bros. Blvd., Mobile, AL 36606.
Telephone: (251) 479-2327. **Fax:** (251) 476-1147.
E-Mail Address: baybears@mobilebaybears.com. **Website:** www.mobilebaybears.com
Affiliation (first year): Arizona Diamondbacks (2007). **Years in League:** 1966, 1970, 1997-

OWNERSHIP, MANAGEMENT

Operated by: HWS Baseball Group.

Principal Owner: Mike Savit.

President/COO: Bill Shanahan. **Assistant General Manager, Finance:** Betty Adams. **Assistant GM, Ticket Operations:** Jeff Long. **Assistant GM, Promotions/Corporate Sales:** Mike Callahan. **Assistant GM, Director, Operations:** John Hilliard. **Head Groundskeeper:** Unavailable. **Director, Community Relations/Merchandising:** Cindy Bunn. **Audio/Visual Director:** Ari Rosenbaum. **Sales/Director, Youth Programs:** Lloyd Meyers. **Broadcaster/Media Relations:** Wayne Randazzo. **Sales Representatives:** Sarah Martin, Garrett Wolf. **Clubhouse Manager:** Rick Schweitzer. **Stadium Operations Assistant:** Wade Vadakin. **Internet Liaison/Team Chaplain:** Lorin Barr.

FIELD STAFF

Manager: Hector De La Cruz. **Coach:** Turner Ward. **Pitching Coach:** Jeff Pico. **Trainer:** Ryan DiPanfilo. **Strength/Conditioning:** Josh Cuffe.

GAME INFORMATION

Radio Announcer: Wayne Randazzo. **No. of Games Broadcast:** Home-70, Away-70. **Flagship Station:** Comcast Channel 19, www.baybearsradio.com.

PA Announcer: Mike Callahan. **Official Scorers:** Randy Peters.

Stadium Name: Hank Aaron Stadium. **Location:** I-65 to exit 1 (Government Blvd. East), right at Satchel Paige Drive, right at Bolling Bros. Boulevard. **Standard Game Times:** 7:05 p.m.; **Sun. 6:**05, 2:05 (April-May). **Ticket Price Range:** $5-10.

Visiting Club Hotel: Riverview Plaza, 64 S. Water St., Mobile, AL 36602. **Telephone:** (251) 438-4000.

MONTGOMERY BISCUITS

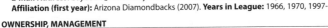

Office Address: 200 Coosa St., Montgomery, AL 36104.
Telephone: (334) 323-2255. **Fax:** (334) 323-2225.
E-Mail address: info@biscuitsbaseball.com. **Website:** www.biscuitsbaseball.com.
Affiliation (first year): Tampa Bay Rays (2004). **Years in League:** 1965-1980, 2004-

OWNERSHIP, MANAGEMENT

Operated By: Montgomery Professional Baseball LLC.

Principal Owners: Tom Dickson, Sherrie Myers.

General Manager: Greg Rauch. **Assistant GM:** Marla Terranova. **Director, Operations:** Steve Blackwell. **Group Sales Manager:** Michael Davis. **Director, Fan Entertainment:** April Catarella. **Box Office Manager:** Alyson Smith. **Group Sales Manager:** Michael Davis. **Retail Manager:** Monte Meyers. **Director, Food Service:** Jason Wilson. **Business Manager:** Linda Fast.

FIELD STAFF

Manager: Billy Gardner Jr. **Coach:** Ozzie Timmons. **Pitching Coach:** Neil Allen. **Trainer:** Lea Slagle.

GAME INFORMATION

Radio Announcer: Jim Tocco. **No of Games Broadcast:** Home-70 Road-70. **Flagship Station:** WLWI 1440-AM.

PA Announcer: Rick Hendrick. **Official Scorer:** Kyle Kreutzer.

Stadium Name: Montgomery Riverwalk Stadium. **Location:** I-65 to exit 172, east on Herron Street, left on Coosa Street. **Ticket Price Range:** $7-11.

Visiting Club Hotel: La Quinta Inn, 128 Eastern Blvd, Montgomery, AL 36117. **Telephone:** (334) 271-1260.

TENNESSEE SMOKIES

Office Address: 3540 Line Drive, Kodak, TN 37764.
Telephone: (865) 286-2300. **Fax:** (865) 523-9913.
E-Mail Address: info@smokiesbaseball.com. **Website:** www.smokiesbaseball.com.
Affiliation (first year): Chicago Cubs (2007). **Years in League:** 1964-67, 1972-

OWNERSHIP, MANAGEMENT

Operated By: SPBC LLC.

President: Doug Kirchhofer.

General Manager: Brian Cox. **Assistant GM:** Jeff Shoaf. **Director, Stadium Operations:** Bryan Webster. **Director, Community Relations:** Lauren Chesney. **Director, Food/Beverage:** Tony DaSilveira. **Director, Marketing/Communications:** Rennie Leon. **Director, Entertainment/Client Services:** Ryan Cox. **Director, Video Production:** Carl Mandell. **Director, Ticket/Retail Operations:** Robby Scheuermann. **Director, Field Operations:** Bob Shoemaker. **Director, Group Sales:** Ryan Koehler. **Corporate Sales Executives:** Dan Blue, Andy Kroeger. **Group Sales Representatives:** Dan Blue, Matt Strutner, Tim Volk, Steve Winfree, Amanda Ocel. **Business Manager:** Suzanne French. **Administrative Assistants:** Tolena Trout, Dixie Nichols.

FIELD STAFF

Manager: Ryne Sandberg. **Hitting Coach:** Tom Beyers. **Pitching Coach:** Dennis Lewallyn. **Trainer:** Nick Frangella.

GAME INFORMATION

Radio Announcer: Mick Gillispie. **No. of Games Broadcast:** Home-70 Road-70. **Flagship Station:** WNML 99.1-FM/990-AM.

PA Announcer: George Yardley. **Official Scorers:** Jeff Muir, Jack Tate , Bernie Reimer .

Stadium Name: Smokies Park. **Location:** I-40 to exit 407, Highway 66 North. **Standard Game Times:** 7:15 p.m., Sun. 2 or 5. **Ticket Price Range:** $5-10.

Visiting Club Hotel: Days Inn-Exit 407, 3402 Winfield Dunn Pkwy, Kodak, TN 37764. **Telephone:** (865) 933-4500.

WEST TENN DIAMOND JAXX

Office Address: 4 Fun Place, Jackson, TN 38305.
Telephone: (731) 988-5299. **Fax:** (731) 988-5246.
E-Mail Address: fun@diamondjaxx.com. **Website:** www.diamondjaxx.com.
Affiliation (third year): Seattle Mariners (2007). **Years in League:** 1998-

OWNERSHIP, MANAGEMENT

Operated by: Diamond Jaxx Baseball Club LLC.

Chairman: David Freeman. **President:** Reese Smith.

General Manager: Tom Hanson. **Assistant GM:** Jason Compton. **Vice President, Operations:** Josh Beard. **Director, Operations:** Robert Jones. **Manager, Media Relations/Broadcasting:** Chris Harris. **Director, Promotions/Merchandise:** David Madison. **Manager, Ticketing/Sales:** Andrew Lambert. **Manager, Game Day Entertainment/Sales:** Dustin Warren. **Manager, Community Relations/Sales:** Mickey Goodwin. **Turf Manager:** Ben Canovan. **Manager, Catering/Concessions:** Kurt Brown. **Supervisor, Suite/Picnic Catering:** Julie Moore. **Executive Assistant:** Aaron White. **Clubhouse Manager:** Bradley Arnold. **Ticketing/Merchandise Intern:** Whitney Strawn. **Operations Intern:** Matthew Brown. **Sales/Marketing Interns:** CJ Fedewa, Chris Coll, Brittany Pearce, Elon Porter, John Whithead. **Press Box Interns:** Sam Woods, Jake Hanson.

FIELD STAFF

Manager: Phil Plantier. **Hitting Coach:** Terry Pollreisz. **Pitching Coach:** Tom Dettore. **Trainer:** Matt Toth .

GAME INFORMATION

Radio Announcer: Chris Harris. **No. of Games Broadcast:** Home-70, Away-70. **Flagship Station:** Unavailable.

PA Announcer: Unavailable. **Official Scorer:** Tracy Brewer.

Stadium Name: Pringles Park. **Location:** From I-40, take exit 85 South on F.E. Wright Drive, left onto Ridgecrest Road. **Standard Game Times:** 7:05 p.m.; Sun 2:05. **Ticket Price Range:** $6-9.

Visiting Club Hotel: Doubletree Hotel, 1770 Hwy. 45 Bypass, Jackson, TN 38305. **Telephone:** (731) 664-6900.

TEXAS LEAGUE

TEXAS LEAGUE OF PROFESSIONAL BASEBALL CLUBS

DOUBLE-A

Mailing Address: 2442 Facet Oak, San Antonio, TX 78232.

Telephone: (210) 545-5297. **Fax:** (210) 545-5298.

E-Mail Address: texasleague@sbcglobal.net. **Website:** www.texas-league.com.

Years League Active: 1888-1890, 1892, 1895-1899, 1902-1942, 1946-.

President, Treasurer: Tom Kayser.

Tom Kayser

Vice President: Ken Schrom. **Corporate Secretary:** Pete Laven.

Directors: Jon Dandes (Northwest Arkansas), Ken Schrom (Corpus Christi), William DeWitt III (Springfield), Chuck Lamson (Tulsa), Scott Sonju (Frisco), Miles Prentice (Midland), Bill Valentine (Arkansas), Burl Yarbrough (San Antonio).

Division Structure: North—Arkansas, Northwest Arkansas, Springfield, Tulsa. **South**—Corpus Christi, Frisco, Midland, San Antonio.

Regular Season: 140 games (split schedule). **2009 Opening Date:** April 9. **Closing Date:** Sept. 7. **All-Star Game:** July 1 at Frisco, TX.

Playoff Format: First-half division winners play second-half division winners in best-of-five series. Winners meet in best-of-five series for league championship.

Roster Limit: 24. **Player Eligibility Rule:** No restrictions.

Brand of Baseball: Rawlings.

Umpires: Stephen Barga (Castle Rock, CO), Clint Fagan (Tomball, TX), Jeff Gosney (Newark, OH), Mike Jarboe (La Crescenta, CA), Jason Kaminsky (El Cajon, CA), Kellen Levy (Portland, OR), Mike Lusky (Baldwin Park, CA), Brad Myers (Holland, OH), Dan Oliver (Seattle, WA), Brett Robson (Cannington, West Australia, AU), Brian Sinclair (San Antonio, TX), Dixon Stureman (Morgan Hill, CA).

STADIUM INFORMATION

			Dimensions				
Club	**Stadium**	**Opened**	**LF**	**CF**	**RF**	**Capacity**	**2008 Att.**
Arkansas	Dickey-Stephens Park	2007	332	400	330	5,842	377,997
Corpus Christi	Whataburger Field	2005	325	400	315	5,362	479,651
Frisco	Dr Pepper Ballpark	2003	335	409	355	10,000	562,166
Midland	Citibank Ballpark	2002	330	410	322	4,669	292,563
NW Arkansas	Arvest Ballpark	2008	325	400	325	6,500	358,792
San Antonio	Nelson Wolff Municipal Stadium	1994	310	407	340	6,200	300,267
Springfield	John Q. Hammons Field	2003	315	400	330	6,750	461,020
Tulsa	Drillers Stadium	1981	335	390	340	10,997	297,409

ARKANSAS TRAVELERS

Office Address: Dickey-Stephens Park, 400 West Broadway, North Little Rock, AR 72114.

Mailing Address: P.O. Box 55066, Little Rock, AR 72215.

Telephone: (501) 664-1555. **Fax:** (501) 664-1834.

E-Mail address: travs@travs.com. **Website:** www.travs.com.

Affiliation (first year): Los Angeles Angels (2001). **Years in League:** 1966-

OWNERSHIP, MANAGEMENT

President: Bert Parke.

Executive Vice President/COO: Bill Valentine. **General Manager:** Pete Laven. **Director, Media Relations:** Phil Elson. **Assistant GM, Groups:** Paul Allen. **Assistant GM, Tickets:** David Kay. **Director, Food/Beverage:** Chris McLean. **Director, In-Game Entertainment:** Tommy Adam. **Account Executive:** Billy Stinnette. **Director, Suite Operations:** Heather Massey. **Director, Merchandise:** Debra Wingfield. **Park Superintendent:** Greg Johnston. **Assistant Park Superintendent:** Reggie Temple. **Turf Manager:** Noah Simmons. **Bookkeeper:** Nena Valentine. **Office Manager:** Jared Schein.

FIELD STAFF

Manager: Bobby Magallanes. **Batting Coach:** Francisco Matos. **Pitching Coach:** Ken Patterson. **Trainer:** Eric Munson.

GAME INFORMATION

Radio Announcer: Phil Elson. **No. of Games Broadcast:** Home-70 Road-70. **Flagship Station:** Unavailable.

PA Announcer: Unavailable. **Official Scorers:** Tim Cooper, Doug Crise, Mike Garrity.

Stadium Name: Dickey-Stephens Park. **Location:** I-30 to Broadway exit. Proceed west to ballpark, located at Broadway Avenue and the Broadway Bridge. **Standard Game Time:** 7:10 p.m. **Ticket Price Range:** $3-10.

Visiting Club Hotel: LaQuinta-North Little Rock, 4100 E. McCain Blvd., North Little Rock, AR 72117. **Telephone:** (501) 758-8888.

CORPUS CHRISTI HOOKS

Office Address: 734 East Port Ave, Corpus Christi, TX 78401.
Telephone: (361) 561-4665. **Fax:** (361) 561-4666.
E-Mail Address: info@cchooks.com. **Website:** www.cchooks.com.
Affiliation (fourth year): Houston Astros (2005). **Years in League:** 1958-59, 2005-

OWNERSHIP, MANAGEMENT

Operated By: Ryan-Sanders Baseball.

Principal Owners: Eddie Maloney, Reese Ryan, Reid Ryan, Nolan Ryan, Brad Sanders, Bret Sanders, Don Sanders. **CEO:** Reid Ryan. **CFO:** Reese Ryan. **COO:** Jay Miller.

Executive Vice President: JJ Gottsch. **President:** Ken Schrom. **General Manager:** Michael Wood. **Vice President, Sales:** Adam Nuse. **Director, Sponsor Services:** Elisa Macias. **Director, Retail:** Brooke Milam. **Controller:** Christy Lockard. **Director, Communications:** Matt Rogers. **Director, Broadcasting:** Matt Hicks. **Director, Stadium Operations:** Tina Athans. **Promotions Coordinator:** Seamus Gallivan. **Director, Group Sales:** Andy Steavens. **Director, Ballpark Entertainment:** Steve Richards. **Box Office Manager:** Spencer Moore. **Field Superintendent:** Garrett Reddehase. **Ballpark Entertainment:** Shayla Andreas, Gil Perez. **Media Relations:** Michael Coffin.

FIELD STAFF

Manager: Luis Pujols. **Hitting Coach:** Keith Bodie. **Pitching Coach:** Stan Boroski. **Athletic Trainer:** Jamey Snodgrass.

GAME INFORMATION

Radio Announcers: Matt Hicks. **No. of Games Broadcast:** Home-70 Road-70. **Flagship Station:** KKTX-AM 1360.

PA Announcer: Scott Johnson. **Official Scorer:** Unavailable.

Stadium Name: Whataburger Field. **Location:** I-37 to end of interstate, left at Chaparral, left at Hirsh Ave. **Ticket Price Range:** $5-12.

Visiting Club Hotel: Omni Hotel, 900 N. Shoreline Dr., Corpus Christi, TX 78401. **Telephone:** (361) 886-3553.

FRISCO ROUGHRIDERS

Office Address: 7300 RoughRiders Trail, Frisco, TX 75034.
Telephone: (972) 731-9200. **Fax:** (972) 731-5355.
E-Mail Address: info@ridersbaseball.com. **Website:** www.ridersbaseball.com.
Affiliation (first year): Texas Rangers (2003). **Years in League:** 2003-

OWNERSHIP, MANAGEMENT

Operated by: Mandalay Sports Entertainment.

President/General Manager: Scott Sonju. **Executive Assistant/Office Manager:** Penny Martin. **Accounting/HR Manager:** Dustin Alban. **Senior Vice President:** Michael Byrnes. **VP, Business Development:** Andrew Kahn. **Director, Corporate Partnerships:** Steven Nelson. **Director, Business Development:** Katie Maguffee. **Senior Director, Partner Services:** Scott Burchett. **Partner/Event Services Coordinator:** Kristin Russell. **Graphic Design Coordinator:** Erik Davila. **Partner Services Coordinator:** Matt Ratliff. **Director, Community Development:** Mara Simon-Meyer. **VP, Ticket Sales:** Matt Goodman. **Senior Director, Group Sales:** Jenna Byrnes. **Ticket Operations Managers:** Mac Amin, Shannon Muller. **Sales/Marketing Coordinator:** Morgan Denton. **Sennior Corporate Marketing Manager:** Justin Ramquist. **Director, Inside Sales/Customer Service:** Jay Lockett. **Inside Sales Manager:** Chris Sorrels. **Senior Group Sales Coordinator:** Ryan Bippert. **Director, Game Entertainment:** Gabriel Wilhelm. **VP, Operations:** Michael Poole. **Director, Maintenance:** Alfonso Bailon. **Head Groundskeeper:** David Bicknell.

FIELD STAFF

Manager: Mike Micucci. **Coach:** Brant Brown. **Pitching Coach:** Joe Slusarski. **Trainer:** Chris Gorosics. **Strength/ Conditioning:** Luke Chichetto

GAME INFORMATION

Broadcaster: Scott Garner. **No. of Games Broadcast:** Home-70, Away-70. **Flagship Station:** Unavailable.

PA Announcer: John Clemens. **Official Scorers:** Kenny King, Larry Bump.

Stadium Name: Dr Pepper Ballpark. **Location:** Dallas North Tollway to State Highway 121. **Standard Game Times:** 7 p.m., Sun. 6.

Visiting Club Hotel: ExtendedStay Deluxe Plano, 2900 North Dallas Tollway. **Telephone:** (972) 378-9978.

MIDLAND ROCKHOUNDS

Office Address: 5514 Champions Dr., Midland, TX 79706.
Telephone: (432) 520-2255. **Fax:** (432) 520-8326.
Website: www.midlandrockhounds.org.
Affiliation (first year): Oakland Athletics (1999). **Years in League:** 1972-

OWNERSHIP, MANAGEMENT

Operated By: Midland Sports, Inc.

Principal Owners: Miles Prentice, Bob Richmond. **President:** Miles Prentice.

Executive Vice President: Bob Richmond. **General Manager:** Monty Hoppel. **Assistant GM:** Jeff VonHolle. **Assistant GM, Marketing/Tickets:** Jamie Richardson. **Assistant GM, Merchandise/Facilities:** Ray Fieldhouse. **Assistant GM, Media Relations:** Greg Bergman. **Director, Broadcasting/Publications:** Bob Hards. **Director, Business Operations:** Eloisa Galvan. **Director, Ticket Operations:** Michael Richardson. **Director, Group Sales:** Jeremy Lukas. **Head Groundskeeper:** Eric Ferland. **Director, Community Relations/Promotions:** Jon Conners. **Director, Advertising:** David Hutfles. **Account Executive:** Wren Nance. **Office Manager:** Frances Warner. **Director, Team Operations/Clubhouse:** Randy Christian. **Assistant Director, Stadium Operations:** Kurt Rininger.

FIELD STAFF

Manager: Darren Bush. **Hitting Coach:** Webster Garrison. **Pitching Coach:** Scott Emerson. **Trainer:** Justin Whitehouse.

GAME INFORMATION

Radio Announcer: Bob Hards. **No. of Games Broadcast:** Home-70, Away-70. **Flagship Station:** Unavailable.

PA Announcer: Wes Coles. **Official Scorer:** Paul Burnett/Steve Marcum.

Stadium Name: Citibank Ballpark. **Location:** From I-20, exit Loop 250 North to Highway 191 intersection. **Standard Game Times:** 7 p.m., 6:30 (April-May, August); Sun. 4, 6 (June-Aug.). **Ticket Price Range:** $5-9.

Visiting Club Hotel: Sleep Inn and Suites, 5612 Deauville Blvd, Midland, TX 79706. **Telephone:** (432) 694-4200.

NORTHWEST ARKANSAS NATURALS

Office Address: 3000 S. 56th Street, Springdale, AR 72762.

Telephone: (479) 927-4900. **Fax:** (479) 756-8088.

E-Mail Address: info@nwanaturals.com. **Website:** www.nwanaturals.com.

Affiliation (first year): Kansas City Royals (1995). **Years in League:** 1987-

OWNERSHIP, MANAGEMENT

Principal Owner: Rich Products Corp.

Chairman: Robert Rich Jr. **President, Rich Entertainment:** Melinda Rich. **President, Rich Baseball:** Jon Dandes.

General Manager: Eric Edelstein. **Assistant GM:** Justin Cole. **Business Manager:** Anna Whitham. **Manager, Marketing/PR:** Frank Novak. **Stadium Operations Manager:** Monty Sowell. **Operations Coordinator:** Andrea Campbell. **Merchandise Coordinator:** Morgan Smith. **Ticket Office Coordinator:** Brian Nickerson. **Baseball Operations Coordinator:** Steven Davis. **Sales Coordinator:** Amanda Potter. **Ticket Sales Coordinator:** Dustin Dethlefs. **Clubhouse Manager:** Danny Helmer.

FIELD STAFF

Manager: Brian Poldberg. **Hitting Coach:** Terry Bradshaw. **Pitching Coach:** Larry Carter. **Trainer:** Chris DeLucia

GAME INFORMATION

Radio Announcers: Steven Davis. **No. of Games Broadcast:** Home-70, Away-70. **Flagship:** KURM 790-AM.

PA Announcer: Bill Rogers. **Official Scorer:** Chris Ledeker.

Stadium Name: Arvest Ballpark. **Location:** I-540 to U.S. 412 West (Sunset Ave). Left on 56th St. **Ticket Price Range:** $6-12. **Standard Game Times:** 7 p.m.; Fri. 7:30; Sun. 4.

Visiting Club Hotel: Holiday Inn Springdale; 1500 S. 48th St., Springdale, AR 72762. **Telephone:** (479) 751-8300.

SAN ANTONIO MISSIONS

Office Address: 5757 Hwy. 90 W, San Antonio, TX 78227.

Telephone: (210) 675-7275. **Fax:** (210) 670-0001.

E-Mail address: sainfo@samissions.com. **Website:** www.samissions.com.

Affiliation (first year): San Diego Padres (2007). **Years in League:** 1888, 1892, 1895-99, 1907-42, 1946-64, 1968-

OWNERSHIP, MANAGEMENT

Operated By: Elmore Sports Group.

Principal Owner: David Elmore.

President: Burl Yarbrough. **General Manager:** David Gasaway. **Assistant GMs:** Mickey Holt, Bill Gerlt. **Director, Accounting:** Ivan Molina-Meraz. **Field Superintendent:** Karsten Blackwelder. **Assistant Field Superintendent:** Andy Day. **Director, Media Relations:** Noah Frank. **Director, Corporate Sales:** Gary Taylor. **Director, Sales/Marketing:** Rick Polster. **Director, Box Office:** Tiffany Johnson.

FIELD STAFF

Manager: Terry Kennedy. **Coach:** Orv Franchuk. **Pitching Coach:** Steve Webber. **Trainer:** JoJo Tarantino.

GAME INFORMATION

Radio Announcers: Roy Acuff, Stu Paul. **No of Games Broadcast:** Home-70 Road-70. **Flagship Station:** KKYX 680-AM.

PA Announcer: Stan Kelly. **Official Scorer:** David Humphrey.

Stadium Name: Nelson W. Wolff Municipal Stadium. **Location:** From I-10, I-35, or I-37, take U.S. 90 West to Callaghan Road exit, stadium on right. **Ticket Price Range:** $5-10.

Visiting Club Hotel: Quality Inn and Suites, 9522 Brimhall Rd, San Antonio, TX 78254. **Telephone:** (210) 372-9900.

SPRINGFIELD CARDINALS

Office Address: 955 East Trafficway, Springfield, MO 65802.
Telephone: (417) 863-0395. **Fax:** (417) 863-0388.
E-Mail address: springfield@stlcardinals.com. **Website:** www.springfieldcardinals.com.
Affiliation (first year): St. Louis Cardinals (2005). **Years in League:** 2005-

OWNERSHIP, MANAGEMENT

Operated By: St. Louis Cardinals.

Vice President/General Manager: Matt Gifford. **VP, Baseball/Business Operations:** Scott Smulczenski. **VP, Sales/Marketing:** Kirk Elmquist. **VP, Facility Operations:** Bill Fischer. **Director, Ticket Operations:** Angela Deke. **Public Relations Manager/Broadcaster:** Mike Lindskog. **Corporate Sales Manager:** Dan Reiter. **Visual Marketing Specialist:** Jacob Neimeyer. **Ticket Sales:** Jared Nevins, Christine Weyler. **Head Groundskeeper:** Brock Phipps. **Assistant Groundskeeper:** Aaron Lowrey.

FIELD STAFF

Manager: Ron Warner. **Hitting Coach:** Derrick May. **Pitching Coach:** Bryan Eversgerd. **Trainer:** Jay Pierson.

GAME INFORMATION

Radio Announcer: Mike Lindskog, Rob Evans. **No of Games Broadcast:** Home-70 Road-70. **Flagship Station:** JOCK 98.7-FM.

PA Announcer: Kevin Howard. **Official Scorers:** Mark Stillwell, Tim Tourville.

Stadium Name: Hammons Field. **Location:** Highway 65 to Chestnut Expressway exit, west to National, south on National, west on Trafficway. **Standard Game Time:** 7:10 p.m. **Ticket Price Range:** $6-24.50.

Visiting Club Hotel: University Plaza Hotel, 333 John Q. Hammons Parkway, Springfield, MO 65806. **Telephone:** (417) 864-7333.

TULSA DRILLERS

Office Address: 4802 E. 15th St, Tulsa, OK 74112.
Telephone: (918) 744-5998. **Fax:** (918) 747-3267.
E-Mail Address: mail@tulsadrillers.com. **Website:** www.tulsadrillers.com.
Affiliation (first year): Colorado Rockies (2003). **Years in League:** 1933-42, 1946-65, 1977-

OWNERSHIP, MANAGEMENT

Operated By: Tulsa Baseball Inc.

Principal Owner/President: Chuck Lamson. **Vice President:** Went Hubbard.

General Manager: Mike Melega. **Assistant GM:** Jason George. **Bookkeeper:** Cheryll Couey. **Office Manager:** Cheryl Northness. **Director, Ticket Sales:** Mark Hilliard. **Director, Operations:** Peter McAdams. **Director, Media Relations:** Brian Carroll. **Manager, Promotions/Merchandise:** Tom Jones. **Manager, Ticket Sales:** Rob Gardenhire. **Manager, Group Ticket Sales:** Brandon Shiers. **Head Groundskeeper:** Gary Shepherd. **Assistant Groundskeeper:** Logan Medlock.

FIELD STAFF

Manager: Stu Cole. **Coach:** Dave Hajek. **Pitching Coach:** Bryan Harvey. **Trainer:** Austin O'Shea.

GAME INFORMATION

Radio Announcer: Unavailable. **No. of Games Broadcast:** Home-70 Road-70. **Flagship Station:** KTBZ 1430-AM.

PA Announcer: Kirk McAnany. **Official Scorers:** Bruce Howard, Duane DaPron, Larry Lewis.

Stadium Name: Drillers Stadium. **Location:** Three miles north of I-44 and 1.5 miles south of I-244 at East 15th Street and South Yale Avenue. **Standard Game Times:** 7:05 p.m.; Sun. 2:05. **Ticket Price Range:** $6-12.50.

Visiting Club Hotel: Southern Hills Marriott, 1902 E. 71st St., Tulsa, OK 74136. **Telephone:** (918) 493-7000.

CALIFORNIA LEAGUE

Office Address: 2380 South Bascom Avenue, Suite 200, Campbell, CA 95008.
Telephone: (408) 369-8038. **Fax:** (408) 369-1409.
Website: www.californialeague.com.
E-Mail: cabaseball@aol.com.
Years League Active: 1941-1942, 1946-

Joe Gagliardi

President/Treasurer: Joseph M. Gagliardi.

Vice President: David Elmore. **Secretary:** John Oldham.

Directors: Bobby Brett (High Desert), Michael Savit (Modesto), Jeff Katofsky (Lancaster), Gary Jacobs (Lake Elsinore), David Elmore (Inland Empire), Tom Seidler (Visalia), Jim Weyermann (San Jose), Hank Stickney (Rancho Cucamonga), Tom Volpe (Stockton), D.G. Elmore (Bakersfield).

League Administrator: Kathleen Kelly. **Chief Legal Counsel:** Gayle Green. **Supervisor, Umpire Development:** John Oldham.

Division Structure: North—Bakersfield, Modesto, San Jose, Stockton, Visalia. **South**—High Desert, Inland Empire, Lake Elsinore, Lancaster, Rancho Cucamonga.

Regular Season: 140 games (split schedule). **Opening Date:** April 9. **Closing Date:** Sept 7.

Playoff Format: Playoff Format: Six teams. First-half winners in each division earn first-round bye; second-half winners meet wild cards with next best overall records in best-of-three quarterfinals. Winners meet first-half champions in best-of-five semifinals. Winners meet in best-of-five series for league championship.

All-Star Game: June 23 at Lake Elsinore.

Roster Limit: 25 active (35 under control).

Player Eligibility: No more than two players and one player/coach on active list may have more than six years experience.

Brand of Baseball: Rawlings.

Umpires: Unavailable.

STADIUM INFORMATION

			Dimensions				
Club	**Stadium**	**Opened**	**LF**	**CF**	**RF**	**Capacity**	**2008 Att.**
Bakersfield	Sam Lynn Ballpark	1941	328	354	328	4,200	67,377
High Desert	Mavericks Stadium	1991	340	401	340	3,808	117,594
Inland Empire	Arrowhead Credit Union Park	1996	330	410	330	5,000	183,845
Lake Elsinore	The Diamond	1994	330	400	310	7,866	224,069
Lancaster	Clear Channel Stadium	1996	350	410	350	4,500	124,934
Modesto	John Thurman Field	1952	312	400	319	4,000	164,306
R. Cucamonga	The Epicenter	1993	335	400	335	6,615	286,290
San Jose	Municipal Stadium	1942	340	390	340	4,000	183,788
Stockton	Banner Island Ballpark	2005	300	399	326	5,200	214,080
Visalia	Recreation Park	1946	320	405	320	1,647	67,045

BAKERSFIELD BLAZE

Office Address: 4009 Chester Ave., Bakersfield, CA 93301.
Mailing Address: P.O. Box 10031, Bakersfield, CA 93389.
Telephone: (661) 716-4487. **Fax:** (661) 322-6199.
E-Mail Address: blaze@bakersfieldblaze.com. **Website:** www.bakersfieldblaze.com.
Affiliation: Texas Rangers (2005). **Years In League:** 1941-42, 1946-75, 1978-79, 1982-

OWNERSHIP, MANAGEMENT

Principal Owner: Bakersfield Baseball Club LLC.

President: D.G. Elmore.

General Manager: Shawn Schoolcraft. **Director, Food/Beverage:** Brandon Caudill. **Director, Community Relations:** Alicja Burnette. **Director, Field Operations:** Bill Gentry. **Clubhouse Manager:** Kevin Johnson.

FIELD STAFF

Manager: Steve Beuchele. **Coach:** Jason Wood. **Pitching Coach:** Dave Chavarria. **Trainer:** Jacob Newburn.

GAME INFORMATION

Radio: None.

PA Announcer: Mike Cushine. **Official Scorer:** Tim Wheeler.

Stadium Name: Sam Lynn Ballpark. **Location:** Highway 99 to California Avenue, east three miles to Chester Avenue, north two miles to stadium. **Standard Game Time:** 7:30 p.m. **Ticket Price Range:** $5-9.

Visiting Club Hotel: Days Inn, 818 Real Road, Bakersfield, CA 93309. **Telephone:** (661) 324-6666.

HIGH DESERT MAVERICKS

Stadium/Office Address: 12000 Stadium Way, Adelanto, CA 92301.
Telephone: (760) 246-6287. **Fax:** (760) 246-3197.
Website: www.hdmavs.com.
Affiliation (first year): Seattle Mariners (2007). **Years in League:** 1991-

OWNERSHIP, MANAGEMENT

Operated By: High Desert Mavericks Inc.

Principal Owner: Bobby Brett. **Brett Sports COO.:** Andy Billig. **President:** Brent Miles. **General Manager:** Tim Altier. **Assistant General Manager/Ticket Sales:** CJ Loper. **Assistant General Manager/Operations:** Eric Jensen. **Sponsorship Coordinator:** Makenzie Schiller. **Account Executive:** Joshua Montinieri. **Controller:** Robin Buckles.

FIELD STAFF

Manager: Jim Horner. **Hitting Coach:** Tommy Cruz. **Pitching Coach:** Jaime Navarro. **Athletic Trainer:** Jeremy Clipperton.

GAME INFORMATION

Radio Announcer: Alex Freedman. **No. of Games Broadcast:** Home-70 Road-70. **Flagship Station:** KIXW 960 AM.

PA Announcer: Ernie Escajeda. **Official Scorer:** Bob Witt.

Stadium Name: Stater Bros. **Stadium. Location:** I-15 North to Highway 395 to Adelanto Road. **Ticket Price Range:** $6-8.

Visiting Club Hotel: Motel 6, 9757 Cataba Rd. Hesperia, CA 92395. **Telephone:** (760) 947-0094.

INLAND EMPIRE 66ERS

Office Address: 280 South E St., San Bernardino, CA 92401.
Telephone: (909) 888-9922. **Fax:** (909) 888-5251.
Website: www.ie66ers.com.
Affiliation (first year): Los Angeles Dodgers (2007). **Years in League:** 1941, 1987-

OWNERSHIP, MANAGEMENT

Operated by: Inland Empire 66ers Baseball Club of San Bernardino.

Principal Owners: David Elmore, Donna Tuttle.

Owner/President: Dave Elmore. **Owner/Chairman:** Donna Tuttle. **Vice President:** Paul Stiritz. **Vice President, Business Development:** Dave Oldham. **CFO:** John Fonseca. **Director, Broadcasting:** Mike Saeger. **Director, Corporate Communications:** Laura Tolbirt. **Director, Food/Beverage:** Joe Hudson. **Manager, Stadium Operations:** Ryan English. **Director, Group Sales:** Raj Narayanan. **Corporate Sales Manager:** Adam Turner. **Community Groups Manager:** Jillian Pena. **Assistant Director, Broadcasting:** Matt Pedersen. **Group Events Planner:** Tom Baxter. **Assistant Director, Food/ Beverage:** Michael Lindal. **Account Executive/Administrative Assistant:** Angie Rodriguez. **Head Groundskeeper:** Dan Mudd.

FIELD STAFF

Manager: Carlos Subero. **Hitting Coach:** Unavailable. **Pitching Coach:** Charlie Hough.

GAME INFORMATION

Radio Announcer: Mike Saeger, Matt Pedersen. **Flagship Station:** KCAA 1050-AM.

PA Announcer: J.J. Gould. **Official Scorer:** Les Canterbury.

Stadium Name: Arrowhead Credit Union Park. **Location:** From south, I-215 to 2nd Street exit, east on 2nd, right on G Street; from north, I-215 to 3rd Street exit, left on Rialto, right on G Street. **Standard Game Times:** 7:05 p.m.; Sun. 1:05 (April-June), (July-Aug.) 6:05. **Ticket Price Range:** $5-10.

Visiting Club Hotel: Hilton San Bernardino, 285 East Hospitality Lane, San Bernardino, CA 92408. **Telephone:** (909) 889-0133.

LAKE ELSINORE STORM

Office Address: 500 Diamond Dr, Lake Elsinore, CA 92530.
Mailing Address: P.O. Box 535, Lake Elsinore, CA 92531.
Telephone: (951) 245-4487. **Fax:** (951) 245-0305.
E-Mail Address: info@stormbaseball.com. **Website:** www.stormbaseball.com.
Affiliation (first year): San Diego Padres (2001). **Years in League:** 1994-

OWNERSHIP, MANAGEMENT

Operated By: Lake Elsinore Storm LP.

Owner: Gary Jacobs, Len Simon.

President: Dave Oster. **Vice President/General Manager:** Chris Jones. **Assistant GM, Community Relations:** Tracy Kessman. **Assistant GM, Corporate Sales:** Allan Benavides. **Director, Broadcasting:** Sean McCall. **Director, New**

Business: Jhmichea Snyder. **Director, Merchandising:** Donna Grunow. **Graphic Designer:** Mark Beskid. **Director, Food/Beverage:** Arjun Suresh. **Executive Chef:** Steve Bearse. **Director, Ticket Operations:** Ruli Garcia. **Director, Mascot Operations:** Patrick Gardenier. **Director, Finance:** Rick Riegler. **Account Executives:** Dave McCrory, Joe Martinez, Bob Gillett. **Assistant Director, Business Operations:** Christina Conlon. **Office Manager:** Jennifer Trammell. **Director, Grounds/Maintenance:** Chris Ralston. **Grounds Supervisor:** Peter Hayes. **Maintenance Supervisor:** Roberto Cabrera. **Director, Media Relations:** Steve Smaldone. **Assistant Director, Marketin**g: Courtney Kessler. **Assistant Director, Food/Beverage:** Mark Labban. **Assistant Director, Ticket Operations:** J.T. Onyett. **Assistant Director, Merchandising:** Hanam Tran. **Assistant Director, Stadium Operations:** Colin Cook.

FIELD STAFF

Manager: Carlos Lezcano. **Coach:** Shane Spencer. **Pitching Coach:** Dave Rajsich. **Trainer:** Will Sinon.

GAME INFORMATION

Radio Announcer: Sean McCall. **No. of Games Broadcast:** Home-70 Road-70. **Flagship Station:** San Diego 1700-AM.

PA Announcer: Joe Martinez. **Official Scorer:** Lloyd Nixon.

Stadium Name: The Diamond. **Location:** From I-15, exit at Diamond Drive, west one mile to stadium. **Standard Game Times:** 7:05 p.m.; Wed. 6:05; Sun. 2:08 (first half), 6:08 (second half). **Ticket Price Range:** $7-10.

Visiting Club Hotel: Lake Elsinore Hotel and Casino, 20930 Malaga St, Lake Elsniore, CA 92530. **Telephone:** (951) 674-3101.

LANCASTER JETHAWKS

Office Address: 45116 Valley Central Way, Lancaster, CA 93536.
Telephone: (661) 726-5400. **Fax:** (661) 726-5406.
E-Mail Address: info@jethawks.com. **Website:** www.jethawks.com.
Affiliation (first year): Houston Astros (2009). **Years in League:** 1996-

OWNERSHIP, MANAGEMENT

Operated By: Hawks Nest LLC.

President: Peter Carfagna. **Senior Vice President:** Pete Carfagna.

Vice President: Brad Seymour. **General Manager:** Larry Thornhill. **Assistant GM:** Derek Sharp. **Director, Stadium Operations:** John Laferney. **Director, Promotions:** Jeremy Castillo. **Director, Broadcasting/Media Relations:** Jeff Lasky. **Director, Community Relations:** Will Murphy. **Director, Food/Beverage:** Stephen Toth. **Ticket Operations Manager:** Trent Wondra. **Ticket Account Executive:** Larry Brady. **Office Administrator:** Alexis Whitman.

FIELD STAFF

Manager: Wes Clements. **Coach:** Darryl Robinson. **Pitching Coach:** Don Alexander. **Trainer:** Eric Montague.

GAME INFORMATION

Radio Announcer: Jeff Lasky. **No. of Games Broadcast:** Home-70, Away-70. **Flagship Station:** Unavailable.

PA Announcer: Fred Jaramillo. **Official Scorer:** David Guenther.

Stadium Name: Clear Channel Stadium. **Location:** Highway 14 in Lancaster to Avenue I exit, west one block to stadium. **Standard Game Times:** 7 p.m.; Sun. 2 (April–June), 5 (July-Sept.). **Ticket Price Range:** $6-12.

Visiting Club Hotel: Best Western Antelope Valley Inn, 44055 North Sierra Hwy., Lancaster, CA 93534. **Telephone:** (661) 948-4651.

MODESTO NUTS

Office Address: 601 Neece Dr., Modesto, CA 95351.
Mailing Address: P.O. Box 883, Modesto, CA 95353.
Telephone: (209) 572-4487. **Fax:** (209) 572-4490.
E-Mail Address: fun@modestonuts.com. **Website:** www.modestonuts.com.
Affiliation (first year): Colorado Rockies (2005). **Years in League:** 1946-64, 1966-

OWNERSHIP, MANAGEMENT

Operated by: HWS Group IV.

Principal Owner: Mike Savit.

President: Bill Shanahan. **Vice President/GM:** Michael Gorrasi. **Director, Tickets:** Tyler Richardson. **Accounting/HR Manager:** Debra Baucom. **Director, Media Services:** David Umfleet. **Director. Group Sales:** Eric Rauber. **Director, Food/Beverage:** Ed Mack. **Director, Stadium Operations:** Tony DeGrande. **Account Executive:** Zach Brockman.

FIELD STAFF

Manager: Jerry Weinstein. **Coach:** Duane Espy. **Pitching Coach:** Doug Linton. **Trainer:** Chris Dovey.

GAME INFORMATION

Radio Announcer: Greg Young. **No. of Games Broadcast:** Home-50, Away-50. **Flagship Station:** KESP 970-AM.

PA Announcer: Unavailable. **Official Scorer:** Unavailable.

Stadium Name: John Thurman Field. **Location:** Highway 99 in southwest Modesto to Tuolomne Boulevard exit, west on Tuolomne for one block to Neece Drive, left for 1/4 mile to stadium. **Standard Game Times:** 7:05 p.m.; Sun. 1:05 (April-

June), 6:05 (July-Aug.). **Ticket Price Range:** $5-10.

Visiting Club Hotel: Ramada Inn, 2001 W. Orangeburg Ave., Modesto, CA 95350. **Telephone:** (209) 521-9000.

RANCHO CUCAMONGA QUAKES

Office Address: 8408 Rochester Ave., Rancho Cucamonga, CA 91730.
Mailing Address: P.O. Box 4139, Rancho Cucamonga, CA 91729.
Telephone: (909) 481-5000. **Fax:** (909) 481-5005.
E-Mail Address: moreinfo@rcquakes.com. **Website:** www.rcquakes.com.
Affiliation (first year): Los Angeles Angels (2001). **Years in League:** 1993-

OWNERSHIP, MANAGEMENT

Operated By: Valley Baseball Inc.

Owners: Henry Stickney, Scott Ostlund, Charles Buquet.

Executive Vice President/General Manager: Gerard McKearny. **Assistant GM/VP, Ticket Operations:** Kyle Schoonover. **Director, Operations:** Ryan Eifler. **Director, Entertainment/Promotions:** Jonathan Mercier. **Director, Broadcasting/Media Relations:** Jeff Levering. **Director, Group Services/Guest Relations:** Linda Rathfon. **Director, Marketing:** Kevin Shaw. **Accounting Manager:** Garret Nelson. **Ticket Office Manager:** Rachel Barker. **Director, Inside Sales:** Matt Bumpass. **Food Operations Manager:** Mike Liotta. **Group Sales Representatives:** Kyle Burleson, Matt Dedeluk, Shannon Easter. **Graphic Designer:** Alison Dahlgren. **Office Manager:** Shelley Scebbi.

FIELD STAFF

Manager: Eric Owens. **Coach:** Damon Mashore. **Pitching Coach:** Dan Ricabal. **Trainer:** Mike Metcalfe.

GAME INFORMATION

Radio Announcer: Jeff Levering

PA Announcer: Unavailable. **Official Scorer:** Unavailable.

Stadium Name: The Epicenter. **Location:** I-10 to I-15 North, exit at Foothill Boulevard, left on Foothill, left on Rochester to Stadium. **Standard Game Times:** 7:05 p.m.; 7:35 (home Fridays), Sun. 2:05 (April-July), 5:05 (July-Sept.). **Ticket Price Range:** $8-12.

Visiting Club Hotel: Best Western Heritage Inn, 8179 Spruce Ave, Rancho Cucamonga, CA 91730. **Telephone:** (909) 466-1111.

SAN JOSE GIANTS

Office Address: 588 E. Alma Ave., San Jose, CA 95112.
Mailing Address: P.O. Box 21727, San Jose, CA 95151.
Telephone: (408) 297-1435. **Fax:** (408) 297-1453.
E-Mail Address: info@sjgiants.com. **Website:** www.sjgiants.com.
Affiliation (first year): San Francisco Giants (1988). **Years in League:** 1942, 1947-58, 1962-76, 1979-

OWNERSHIP, MANAGEMENT

Operated by: Progress Sports Management.

Principal Owners: Heidi Stamas, Richard Beahrs, Rich Kelley.

President/CEO: Jim Weyermann.

Vice President/General Manager: Mark Wilson. **VP, Marketing/Public Affairs:** Juliana Paoli. **Assistant GM:** Zach Walter. **Director, Player Relations:** Linda Pereira. **Director, Stadium Operations:** Lance Motch. **Director, Group Sales:** Ainslie Reynolds. **Controller:** Cami Yuasa. **Manager, Marketing/Public Affairs:** Mandy Stone. **Manager, Ticket Services:** Marilena Mahan. **Sales Managers:** Taylor Haynes, Adam Hensleigh. **Radio Broadcaster/Baseball Operations:** Joe Ritzo. **International Relations Executive:** Kaz Sekine. **Assistant Special Projects Coordinator:** Tyler Weyermann. **Marketing Intern:** Ben Guerrero.

FIELD STAFF

Manager: Andy Skeels. **Hitting Coach:** Gary Davenport. **Pitching Coach:** Jerry Cram. **Trainer:** Yukiya Oba.

GAME INFORMATION

Radio Broadcaster: Joe Ritzo. **No. of Games Broadcast:** Home-70, Away-70. **Flagship:** www.sjgiants.com.

PA Announcer: Russ Call. **Official Scorers:** Michael Melligan, Luke Fortier, Brian Burkett.

Stadium Name: Municipal Stadium. **Location:** South on I-280, Take 10th/11th Street Exit. Turn right on 10th Street. Turn left on Alma Ave. North on I-280: Take the 10th/11th Street Exit. Turn left on 10th Street. Turn Left on Alma Ave. Standard Game Times: 7 p.m.; Sat. 6; Sun. 2 (5 after June 14). **Ticket Price Range:** $7-15.

Visiting Club Hotel: Pruneyard Plaza, 1995 S. Bascom Ave., Campbell, CA 95008. **Telephone:** (408) 559-4300.

STOCKTON PORTS

Office Address: 404 W. Fremont St, Stockton, CA 95203.
Telephone: (209) 644-1900. **Fax:** (209) 644-1931.
E-Mail Address: info@stocktonports.com. **Website:** www.stocktonports.com.
Affiliation (first year): Oakland Athletics (2005). **Years in League:** 1941, 1946-72, 1978-

OWNERSHIP, MANAGEMENT

Operated By: 7th Inning Stretch LLC.

President/General Manager: Pat Filippone. **Assistant GM:** Luke Reiff. **Manager, Media Relations:** Kristin Pratt. **Director, Marketing:** Justin Gray. **Director, Group Sales:** Ben Carr. **Director, Finance:** Terri Bailey. **Director, Corporate Sales:** Zach Sharkey. **Senior Account Executive:** John Watts. **Community Relations Manager:** Danielle Alt. **Stadium Operations Manager:** Ethan Bagen. **Box Office Manager:** Kyle Osgood. **Account Executives:** Sam Harold, Tim Pasisz. **Special Events Account Executive:** Kyle DeWitt. **Corporate Sponsorships Account Executive:** Mark Mendes. **Food/Beverage Service Provider:** Ovations. **Front Desk:** Deborah Auditor.

FIELD STAFF

Manager: Aaron Nieckula. **Coach:** Tim Garland. **Pitching Coach:** Don Schulze. **Trainer:** Brian Thorson.

GAME INFORMATION

Radio Announcer: Zack Bayrouty. **No of Games Broadcast:** Home-70, Away-70. **Flagship Station:** Unavailable.

PA Announcer: Mike Conway. **Official Scorer:** Paul Muyskens.

Stadium Name: Banner Island Ballpark. **Location:** From I-5/99, take Crosstown Freeway (Highway 4) exit El Dorado Street, north on El Dorado to Freemont Street, left on Freemont. **Standard Game Times:** 7:05 p.m.; Sun. 2:05 first half, 6:05 second half. **Ticket Price Range:** $6-20.

Visiting Club Hotel: Best Western Waterloo, 4219 East Waterloo Road, Stockton CA 95215. **Telephone:** (209) 931-3131.

VISALIA RAWHIDE

Office Address: 300 N. Giddings St, Visalia, CA 93291.
Telephone: (559) 732-4433. **Fax:** (559) 739-7732.
E-Mail Address: info@rawhidebaseball.com. **Website:** www.rawhide-baseball.com.
Affiliation (first year): Arizona Diamondbacks (2007). **Years in League:** 1946-62, 1968-75, 1977-

OWNERSHIP, MANAGEMENT

Operated By: Top of the Third Inc.

Principal Owners: Kevin O'Malley, Tom Seidler.

President/General Manager: Tom Seidler. **Assistant GM:** Jennifer Pendergraft. **Assistant GM/Legal Counsel:** Liz Martin. **Director, Ticketing:** Mike Candela. **Director, Broadcasting:** Donny Baarns. **Manager, Media Relations:** Mark Freeman. **Head Groundskeeper:** Chris Mills. **Ballpark Operations Manager:** Jim Flavin. **Director, Concessions:** Ryan Mumford. **Client Servicing Representative:** Adam Martin. **Group Coordinator:** Heather Haak. **Assistant Group Coordinator:** Jamie Woychek. **Community Relations Coordinator:** Alanna Snedigar. **Event Coordinator:** Jacquie Walker. **Merchandise Coordinator:** Brittany Sackmann. **Assistant Manager, Ballpark Operations:** Lee Gansky. **Clubhouse Manager:** Brad Chang.

FIELD STAFF

Manager: Mike Bell. **Coach:** Alan Zinter. **Pitching Coach:** Wellington Cepeda. **Trainer:** Nick Oldroyd. **Strength/Conditioning:** Jason Downing.

GAME INFORMATION

Radio Announcers: Donny Baarns, Mark Freeman. **No. of Games Broadcast:** Home-70, Away-70. **Flagship Station:** KJUG 1270-AM.

PA Announcer: Unavailable. **Official Scorers:** Harry Kargenian, Chuck Knox.

Stadium Name: Recreation Ballpark. **Location:** From Highway 99, take 198 East to Mooney Boulevard exit, left at second signal on Giddings; four blocks to ballpark. **Standard Game Times:** Mon.-Sat. **7:**05 p.m.; **Sun. 1:**05 (first half), 6:05 (second half). **Ticket Price Range:** $5-15.

Visiting Club Hotel: Lamp Liter Inn, 3300 W Mineral King Ave, Visalia, CA 93291. **Telephone:** (559) 732-4511.

CAROLINA LEAGUE

HIGH CLASS A

Office Address: 1806 Pembroke Rd., Greensboro, NC 27408.
Mailing Address: P.O. Box 9503, Greensboro, NC 27429.
Telephone: (336) 691-9030. **Fax:** (336) 691-9070.
E-Mail Address: office@carolinaleague.com.
Website: www.carolinaleague.com
Years League Active: 1945-.
President/Treasurer: John Hopkins.

John Hopkins

Vice Presidents: Art Silber (Potomac), Calvin Falwell (Lynchburg). **Corporate Secretary:** Ken Young (Frederick). **Directors:** Mike Dee (Salem), Calvin Falwell (Lynchburg), Chuck Greenberg (Myrtle Beach), Dave Ziedelis (Frederick), Cam McRae (Kinston), Jack Minker (Wilmington), Billy Prim (Winston-Salem), Art Silber (Potomac).

Administrative Assistant: Marnee Larkins.

Division Structure: North—Frederick, Lynchburg, Potomac, Wilmington. **South**—Kinston, Myrtle Beach, Salem, Winston-Salem.

Regular Season: 140 games (split schedule). **2009 Opening Date:** April 9. **Closing Date:** Sept. 7.

All-Star Game: June 23 at Lake Elsinore. (Carolina League vs. California League).

Playoff Format: First-half division winners play second-half division winners in best-of-five series; if a team wins both halves, it plays a wild card (team with next-best record). Division series winners meet in best-of-five series for Mills Cup.

Roster Limit: 25 active. **Player Eligibility Rule:** No age limit. No more than two players and one player/coach on active list may have six or more years of prior minor league service.

Brand of Baseball: Rawlings.

Umpires: Matt Arcovio (Fairport, NY), Drew Ashcraft (Lexington, KY), Jeremy Crowe (Hartford, KY), Andy Dudones (Uniontown, OH), Kolin Kline (Arvada, CO), Will Little (Jonesboro, TN), Jon Saphire (Centerville, OH), Stu Scheurwater (Regina, SK).

STADIUM INFORMATION

			Dimensions				
Club	**Stadium**	**Opened**	**LF**	**CF**	**RF**	**Capacity**	**2008 Att.**
Frederick	Harry Grove Stadium	1990	325	400	325	5,400	295,656
Kinston	Grainger Stadium	1949	335	390	335	4,100	130,406
Lynchburg	City Stadium	1940	325	390	325	4,000	162,131
Myrtle Beach	BB&T Coastal Federal Field	1999	325	405	328	4,324	242,397
Potomac	Pfitzner Stadium	1984	315	400	315	6,000	177,760
Salem	Salem Memorial Stadium	1995	325	401	325	6,300	235,823
Wilmington	Frawley Stadium	1993	325	400	325	6,532	312,375
Winston-Salem	Ernie Shore Field	1956	325	400	325	6,000	169,963

FREDERICK KEYS

Office Address: 21 Stadium Dr, Frederick, MD 21703.
Telephone: (301) 662-0013. **Fax:** (301) 662-0018.
E-Mail address: info@frederickkeys.com. **Website:** www.frederickkeys.com.
Affiliation (first year): Baltimore Orioles (1989). **Years in League:** 1989-

OWNERSHIP, MANAGEMENT

Ownership: Maryland Baseball Holding LLC.

President: Ken Young. **General Manager:** Dave Ziedelis. **Assistant General Manager:** Branden McGee. **Sponsorship Manager:** Christian Amorosi. **Director, Public Relations:** Adam Pohl. **Box Office Manager:** Adam Weaver. **Director, Marketing:** Katy Fincham. **Group Sales Manager:** Quinn Williams. **Ticket Sales Manager:** Jeff Wiggins. **Finance Manager:** Tami Hetrick. **Office Manager:** Barb Freund. **Account Managers:** Dave Burdette, Towney Godfrey. **Head Groundskeeper:** Kyle Slaton. **Stadium Operations Manager:** Nick Kefauver. **Stadium Operations Intern:** Mitch Strakonsky. **Public Relations Assistant:** Margaret Sacchet. **Marketing Assistants:** Donal McRae, Heather Young. **Group Sales Assistant:** Ralph McIntyre. **Ticket Sales Assistant:** Matt Cherry. **Box Office Assistant:** Elizabeth Walther. **Ovations General Manager:** Anita Clarke.

FIELD STAFF

Manager: Richie Hebner. **Coach:** J.J. Cannon. **Pitching Coach:** Kennie Steenstra. **Trainer:** Patrick Wesley.

GAME INFORMATION

Radio Announcers: Adam Pohl, Towney Godfrey.

PA Announcer: Andy Redmond. **Official Scorers:** Bob Roberson, Dennis Hetrick, Dave Musil.

Stadium Name: Harry Grove Stadium. **Location:** From I-70, take exit 54 (Market Street), left at light. From I-270, take exit

32 (I-70 Baltimore/Hagerstown) towards Baltimore (I-70), to exit 54 at Market Street. **Ticket Price Range:** $8-11.

Visiting Club Hotel: Comfort Inn, 7300 Executive Way, Frederick, MD 21701. **Telephone:** (301) 668-7272.

KINSTON INDIANS

Office Address: 400 East Grainger Avenue, Kinston, NC 28501.
Mailing Address: P.O. Box 3542, Kinston, NC 28502.
Telephone: (252) 527-9111. **Fax:** (252) 527-0498.
E-Mail Address: info@kinstonindians.com. **Website:** www.kinstonindians.com.
Affiliation (first year): Cleveland Indians (1987). **Years in League:** 1956-57, 1962-74, 1978-

OWNERSHIP, MANAGEMENT

Operated by: Slugger Partners LP.

Principal Owner/Chairman: Cam McRae.

General Manager: Shari Massengill. **Assistant GM:** Janell Bullock. **Director, Broadcasting/Public Relations:** Chris Hemeyer. **Director, Food/Beverage:** Tony Patterson. **Head Groundskeeper:** Steven Watson. **Clubhouse Operations:** Robert Smeraldo. **Team Photographer:** Carl Kline.

FIELD STAFF

Manager: Chris Tremie. **Coach:** Rouglas Odor. **Pitching Coach:** Greg Hibbard. **Trainer:** Chad Wolfe.

GAME INFORMATION

Radio Announcer: Chris Hemeyer. **No. of Games Broadcast:** Home-70, Away-70. **Flagship Station:** WWNB 1490 AM.

PA Announcer: Nathan Perry. **Official Scorer:** Steve Oliver.

Stadium Name: Grainger Stadium. **Location:** From west, take U.S. 70 Business (Vernon Avenue), left on East Street; from east, take U.S. 70 West, right on Highway 58, right on Vernon Avenue, right on East Street. **Standard Game Times:** 7 p.m., Sun. 2. **Ticket Price Range:** $4-7.

Visiting Club Hotel: Hampton Inn, Highway 70 Bypass, Kinston NC 28504. **Telephone:** (252) 523-1400.

LYNCHBURG HILLCATS

Office Address: Lynchburg City Stadium, 3180 Fort Ave, Lynchburg, VA 24501.
Mailing Address: P.O. Box 10213, Lynchburg, VA 24506.
Telephone: (434) 528-1144. **Fax:** (434) 846-0768.
E-Mail address: info@lynchburg-hillcats.com. **Website:** www.lynchburg-hillcats.com.
Affiliation (first year): Pittsburgh Pirates (1995). **Years in League:** 1966-

OWNERSHIP, MANAGEMENT

Operated By: Lynchburg Baseball Corp.

President: Calvin Falwell.

General Manager: Paul Sunwall. **Assistant GM:** Ronnie Roberts. **Head Groundskeeper/Sales:** Darren Johnson. **Director, Broadcasting/Publications:** Scott Bacon. **Director, Food/Beverage:** Jason Wells. **Ticket Manager:** Zach Willis. **Director, Information Technology:** Andrew Chesser. **Office Manager:** Diane Tucker.

FIELD STAFF

Manager: P.J. Forbes. **Coach:** Dave Howard. **Pitching Coach:** Wally Whitehurst. **Trainer:** Bryan Housand. **Strength/Conditioning Coach:** Derek Frankllin.

GAME INFORMATION

Radio Announcer: Scott Bacon, Scott Blusiewicz. **No. of Games Broadcast:** Home-70 Road-70. **Flagship Station:** WKDE 105.5-FM.

PA Announcer: Chuck Young. **Official Scorers:** Malcolm Haley, Chuck Young.

Stadium Name: Calvin Falwell Field at Lynchburg City Stadium. **Location:** U.S. 29 Business South to Lynchburg City Stadium (exit 6). U.S. 29 Business North to Lynchburg City Stadium (exit 4). **Ticket Price Range:** $5-9.

Visiting Club Hotel: Best Western, 2815 Candlers Mountain Rd, Lynchburg, VA 24502. **Telephone:** (434) 237-2986.

MYRTLE BEACH PELICANS

Office Address: 1251 21st Ave. N, Myrtle Beach, SC 29577.
Telephone: (843) 918-6002. **Fax:** (843) 918-6001.
E-Mail Address: info@myrtlebeachpelicans.com. **Website:** www.myrtlebeachpelicans.com.
Affiliation (first year): Atlanta Braves (1999). **Years in League:** 1999-

OWNERSHIP, MANAGEMENT

Operated By: Myrtle Beach Pelicans LP.

Managing Partner: Chuck Greenberg.

President: Todd Parnell. **General Manager:** North Johnson. **Senior Director, Business Development:** Guy Schuman. **Senior Director, Sports Turf Management/Ballpark Operations:** Chris Ball. **Director, Broadcasting/Communications:** Jon Laaser. **Assistant Director, Broadcasting/Communications:** Tommy Thrall. **Director, Promotions:** Maggie Neil. **Box Office Manager:** Josh Holley. **Ticket Sales Associates:** Ryan Moore, Derrick Nunziante, Brian Stefan. **Director, Community Relations:** Julie Borshak. **Facility Operations Manager:** Mike Snow. **Executive Producer, In-Game Entertainment:** Jake White. **Director, Merchandising:** Claire Martin. **GM/Ovations Catering:** Brad Leininger. **Accounting Assistant:** Karen Ulyicsni. **Administrative Assistant:** Shellene May. **Clubhouse Manager:** Stan Hunter. **Visiting Clubhouse Manager:** Bob Leber.

FIELD STAFF

Manager: Rocket Wheeler. **Hitting Coach:** Rick Albert. **Pitching Coach:** Guy Hanson. **Trainer:** Chas Miller.

GAME INFORMATION

Radio Announcers: Jon Laaser, Tommy Thrall. **No. of Games Broadcast:** Home-70, Road-70. **Flagship Station:** ESPN Radio 93.9-FM/93.7-FM/1050-AM.

PA Announcer: Unavailable. **Official Scorer:** Steve Walsch.

Stadium Name: BB&T Coastal Federal Field. **Location:** U.S. Highway 17 Bypass to 21st Avenue North, 1/2 mile to stadium. **Standard Game Times:** 7:05 p.m.; Sun. 3:05/6:05. **Ticket Price Range:** $7-11.

Visiting Club Hotel: Holiday Inn Express-Broadway at the Beach, U.S. Highway 17 Bypass & 29th Avenue North, Myrtle Beach, SC 29578. **Telephone:** (843) 916-4993.

POTOMAC NATIONALS

Office Address: 7 County Complex Ct., Woodbridge, VA 22192.
Mailing Address: P.O. Box 2148, Woodbridge, VA 22195.
Telephone: (703) 590-2311. **Fax:** (703) 590-5716.
E-Mail Address: info@potomacnationals.com. **Website:** www.potomacnationals.com.
Affiliation (first year): Washington Nationals (2005). **Years in League:** 1978-

OWNERSHIP, MANAGEMENT

Operated By: Potomac Baseball LLC.

Principal Owner: Art Silber. **President:** Lani Silber Weiss.

General Manager: Jonathan Griffith. **Assistant GM, Marketing/Media:** Anthony Oppermann. **Assistant GM, Corporate Sales:** Ben Terry. **Assistant GM, Stadium Operations:** Carter Buschman. **Director, Ticket Operations:** Peter Frikker. **Corporate Sales Executive:** Ryan Johnston. **Group Sales Account Executive:** Andrew Stinson.

FIELD STAFF

Manager: Trent Jewett. **Coach:** Jery Browne. **Pitching Coach:** Paul Menhart. **Trainer:** Atsushi Toriida.

GAME INFORMATION

Radio Announcer: Anthony Oppermann, Anthony Masterson. **No. of Games Broadcast:** Home-70 Road-70. **Flagship:** www.potomacnationals.com.

PA Announcer: Anthony Masterson. **Official Scorer:** David Vincent, Ben Trittipoe.

Stadium Name: G. Richard Pfitzner Stadium. **Location:** From I-95, take exit 158B and continue on Prince William Parkway for five miles, right into County Complex Court. **Standard Game Times:** 7:05 p.m.; Sat. 6:35; Sun. 1:05. **Ticket Price Range:** $7-13.

Visiting Club Hotel: Holiday Inn Quantico Center, 3901 Fettler Park Dr., Dumfries, VA 22026. **Telephone:** (703) 441-9001.

SALEM RED SOX

Office Address: 1004 Texas St., Salem, VA 24153.
Mailing Address: P.O. Box 842, Salem, VA 24153.
Telephone: (540) 389-3333. **Fax:** (540) 389-9710.
E-Mail Address: info@salemsox.com. **Website:** www.salemsox.com
Affiliation (first year): Boston Red Sox (2009). **Years in League:** 1968-

OWNERSHIP, MANAGEMENT

Operated By: Carolina Baseball LLC/Fenway Sports Group.

President: Mike Dee.

Vice President/General Manager: John Katz. **VP/Director, Finance:** Brian Bowles. **Senior Assistant GM:** Allen Lawrence. **Assistant GM:** Jeremy Auker. **Director, Food/Beverage:** Scott Burton. **Head Groundskeeper:** Tracy Schneweis. **Director, Ticket Operations/Special Events:** Jeanne Boester. **Assistant Director, Group Sales:** Jeremy Long. **Food Service Manager:** Giles Cochran. **Director, Broadcasting:** Jason Benetti. **Media/Community Relations Manager:** Dave Cawley. **Ticket Manager:** Steven Elovich. **Merchandise Manager:** Erin Hanson. **Account Executives:** Evan Christian, Ryan Kirwan, Andrew Goetz, Tom Waugaman. **Clubhouse Manager:** Tom Wagner.

FIELD STAFF

Manager: Chad Epperson. **Coach:** Carlos Febles. **Pitching Coach:** Dick Such. **Trainer:** Paul Buchheit.

GAME INFORMATION

Radio Announcer: Jason Benetti. **No. of Games Broadcast:** Home-70 Road-70. **Flagship Station:** WFIR 960-AM.

PA Announcer: Unavailable. **Official Scorer:** Billy Wells.

Stadium Name: Lewis-Gale Medical Center Field at Salem Memorial Baseball Stadium. **Location:** I-81 to exit 141 (Route 419), follow signs to Salem Civic Center Complex. **Standard Game Times:** 7:07 p.m.; Sat. 6:07; Sun. 2:07 (April-June 15), 6:07 (June 16-Sept.) **Ticket Price Range:** $7-9.

Visiting Club Hotel: Comfort Inn Airport, 5070 Valley View Blvd, Roanoke, VA 24012. **Telephone:** (540) 527-2020.

WILMINGTON BLUE ROCKS

Office Address: 801 Shipyard Dr., Wilmington, DE 19801.
Telephone: (302) 888-2015. **Fax:** (302) 888-2032.
E-Mail Address: info@bluerocks.com. **Website:** www.bluerocks.com.
Affiliation (first year): Kansas City Royals (2007). **Years in League:** 1993-

OWNERSHIP, MANAGEMENT

Operated by: Wilmington Blue Rocks LP.

Honorary President: Matt Minker. **President:** Tom Palmer.

General Manager: Chris Kemple. **Assistant GM:** Andrew Layman. **Director, Broadcasting/Media Relations:** John Sadak. **Assistant Director, Broadcasting/Media Relations:** Matt Janus. **Director, Merchandise:** Jim Beck. **Merchandise Assistant:** Marie Graney. **Director, Promotions:** Kevin Linton. **Director, Marketing:** Mark VanderHaar. **Marketing Assistants:** Anton Kolodziej, Patrick McVey. **Director, Community Relations:** Dave Arthur. **Community Relations Assistant:** Jacob Schrum. **Director, Sales/Ticket Operations:** Jared Forma. **Ticket Manager:** Mike Miller. **Group Sales Associates:** Stefani DiChiara-Rash, Joe Valenti. **Group Sales Assistant:** Greg Mathews. **Ticket Office Assistants:** A.J, Aleman, Gabe Gigliotti. **Director, Field Operations:** Steve Gold. **Director, Finance:** Denis Weigert. **Video Production/ Game Entertainment Manager:** Kyle Love. **Office Manager:** Lauren Hainey.

FIELD STAFF

Manager: Brian Rupp. **Coach:** Justin Gemoll. **Pitching Coach:** Steve Luebber. **Athletic Trainer:** Dave Iannicca.

GAME INFORMATION

Radio Announcers: John Sadak, Matt Janus. **No. of Games Broadcast:** Home-70, Away-70. **Flagship Station:** WWTX 1290-AM.

PA Announcer: Kevin Linton. **Official Scorers:** Dick Shute, Adam Kamras, E.J. Casey.

Stadium Name: Judy Johnson Field at Daniel S. Frawley Stadium. **Location:** I-95 North to Maryland Ave. (exit 6), right on Maryland Ave., and through traffic light onto Martin Luther King Blvd., right at traffic light on Justison St., follow to Shipyard Dr.; I-95 South to Maryland Ave. (exit 6), left at fourth light on Martin Luther King Blvd., right at fourth light on Justison St., follow to Shipyard Dr. **Standard Game Times:** 7:05 p.m., 6:35 (April-May); Sat. 6:05; Sun. 1:35. **Ticket Price Range:** $4-10.

Visiting Club Hotel: Quality Inn-Skyways, 147 N. DuPont Hwy., New Castle, DE 19720. **Telephone:** (302) 328-6666.

WIINSTON-SALEM DASH

Office Address: 926 Brookstown Ave, Winston-Salem, NC 27101.
Telephone: (336) 759-2233. **Fax:** (336) 759-2233.
E-Mail Address: info@wsdash.com. **Website:** www.wsdash.com.
Affiliation (first year): Chicago White Sox (1997). **Years in League:** 1945-

OWNERSHIP, MANAGEMENT

Operated by: Sports Menagerie.

Principal Owners: Billy Prim and Andrew "Flip" Flipowski. **President:** Guy Schuman.

General Manager: Ryan Manuel. **CFO:** Kurt Gehsmann. **Director, Broadcasting and Media Relations:** Ed Collari. **Office Manager:** Amanda Ebert. **Head Groundskeeper:** Doug Tanis. **Media Relations Assistant:** David Roach. **Director, Group Sales:** Jerry Shadley. **Account Executives:** Sarcanda Bellissimo, Shaun McElhinny. **Director, Tickets:** Brian Shollenberger. **Director, Merchandise:** Amy Newman. **Director, Community Relations:** Trey Halny. **Director, Stadium Operations:** Cass Ferguson. **Concessions Director:** David Evans. **Assistant to GM:** David Beal.

FIELD STAFF

Manager: Tim Blackwell. **Coach:** Robert Sasser. **Pitching Coach:** Brian Drahman. **Athletic Trainer:** Josh Fallin.

GAME INFORMATION

Radio Announcer: Ed Collari. **No. of Games Broadcast:** Home-70, Away-70. **Flagship Station:** WSJS 600/1200-AM.

PA Announcer: Larry Barry. **Official Scorer:** Larry Hoover.

Stadium Name: Not Available. **Location:** I-40 Business to Cherry Street exit, north through downtown to Deacon Blvd., right to park. **Standard Game Times:** 7 pm. Wed: Noon. Sat: 6 pm. Sun: 2 pm.

Visiting Club Hotel: Quality Inn at Hanes Mall, 2008 S Hawthorne Rd, Winston-Salem, NC 27103. **Telephone:** (336) 765-6670.

FLORIDA STATE LEAGUE

HIGH CLASS A

Office Address: 115 E. Orange Ave., Daytona Beach, FL 32114.
Mailing Address: P.O. Box 349, Daytona Beach, FL 32115.
Telephone: (386) 252-7479. **Fax:** (386) 252-7495.
E-Mail Address: fslbaseball@cfl.rr.com. **Website:** www.floridastateleague.com.

Chuck Murphy

Years League Active: 1919-1927, 1936-1941, 1946-.

President/Treasurer: Chuck Murphy.

Vice Presidents: Ken Carson (Dunedin), Paul Taglieri (St. Lucie).

Corporate Secretary: David Hood.

Directors: Brian Barnes (Jupiter), Ken Carson (Dunedin), Jeff Eiseman (Port Charlotte), Shawn Gelnett (Palm Beach), Marvin Goldklang (Fort Myers), Dan Wolfert (Sarasota), Ron Myers (Lakeland), Bill Papierniak (Daytona), Kyle Smith (Brevard County), Vance Smith (Tampa), Paul Taglieri (St. Lucie), John Timberlake (Clearwater).

Office Secretary: Laura LeCras.

Division Structure: North—Brevard County, Clearwater, Daytona, Dunedin, Lakeland, Tampa. **South**—Fort Myers, Jupiter, Palm Beach, Port Charlotte, St. Lucie, Sarasota.

Regular Season: 140 games (split schedule). **2009 Opening Date:** April 9. **Closing Date:** Sept. 6.

All-Star Game: June 20 at Fort Myers.

Playoff Format: First-half division winners meet second-half winners in best-of-three series. Winners meet in best-of-five series for league championship.

Roster Limit: 25. **Player Eligibility Rule:** No age limit. No more than two players and one player-coach on active list may have six or more years of prior minor league service.

Brand of Baseball: Rawlings.

Umpires: Sean M. Barber (Lakeland, FL), Kelvin Bultron (Canovanas, PR), Travis D. Carlson (Tampa, FL.), Matthew A. Cunningham (Carmel, IN), Jordan S. Ferrell (Clarksville, TN.), James M. Guyll (Ft. Wayne, In.), Joseph M. Hannigan (Westmont, Il.), Anthony A. Johnson (McComb, MS), Roberto M. Medina (Toa Baja, PR), Brandon A. Misun (Edmond, OK), Matthew S. Pridemore (Douglas, GA.), Joe A. Rackley (Seabrook, TX).

STADIUM INFORMATION

			Dimensions				
Club	Stadium	Opened	LF	CF	RF	Capacity	2008 Att.
Brevard County	Space Coast Stadium	1994	340	404	340	7,500	66,256
Clearwater	Bright House Networks Field	2004	330	400	330	8,500	168,637
*Charlotte	Charlotte Sports Park	2009	N/A	N/A	N/A	N/A	47,944
Daytona	Jackie Robinson Ballpark	1930	317	400	325	4,000	164,007
Dunedin	Knology Park	1977	335	400	315	6,106	48,321
Fort Myers	William H. Hammond Stadium	1991	330	405	330	7,500	124,749
Jupiter	Roger Dean Stadium	1998	330	400	325	6,871	68,585
Lakeland	Joker Marchant Stadium	1966	340	420	340	7,100	52,305
Palm Beach	Roger Dean Stadium	1998	330	400	325	6,871	66,073
St. Lucie	Tradition Field	1988	338	410	338	7,500	93,626
Sarasota	Ed Smith Stadium	1989	340	400	340	7,500	43,088
Tampa	Legends Field	1996	318	408	314	10,386	86,870

*Played in Vero Beach in 2008

BREVARD COUNTY MANATEES

Office Address: 5800 Stadium Pkwy., Suite 101, Viera, FL 32940.
Telephone: (321) 633-9200. **Fax:** (321) 633-4418.
E-Mail Address: info@spacecoaststadium.com. **Website:** www.manateesbaseball.com.
Affiliation (first year): Milwaukee Brewers (2005). **Years in League:** 1994-

OWNERSHIP, MANAGEMENT

Operated By: Central Florida Baseball Group LLC.

Chairman: Dr. Tom Winters. **Vice Chairman:** Dewight Titus. **President:** Charlie Baumann.

General Manager: Kyle Smith. **Business Operations Manager:** Kelley Wheeler. **Director, Group Sales:** Meghan Cornett. **Director, Sales:** Dan Covey.

FIELD STAFF

Manager: Mike Guerrero. **Coach:** Corey Hart. **Pitching Coach:** Fred Dabney. **Trainer:** Tommy Craig. **Strength/ Conditioning:** Unavailable.

GAME INFORMATION

PA Announcer: J.C. Meyerholz. **Radio:** None.

Official Scorer: Ron Jernick.

Stadium Name: Space Coast Stadium. **Location:** I-95 North to Wickham Rd. (exit 191), left onto Wickham, right at traffic circle onto Lake Andrew Drive for 1 1/2 miles through the Brevard County government office complex to the four-way stop, right on Stadium Parkway. Space Coast Stadium 1/2 mile on the left. I-95 South to Rockledge exit (exit 195), left onto Stadium Parkway. Space Coast Stadium is 3 miles on right. Standard Game Times: 7 pm.; Sat. 7; Sun. 1. **Ticket Price Range:** $7.

Visiting Club Hotel: Holiday Inn Hotel & Conference Center, 8928 N. Wickham Rd, Viera, FL 32940. **Telephone:** (321) 255-0077.

CHARLOTTE STONE CRABS

Office Address: 2300 El Jobean Rd., Port Charlotte, FL 33948.

Mailing Address: 2300 El Jobean Rd., Building A, Port Charlotte, FL 33948.

Telephone: (941) 206-4487. **Fax:** (941) 206-3599.

E-Mail Address: info@stonecrabsbaseball.com. **Website:** www.stonecrabsbaseball.com.

Affiliation (first year): Tampa Bay Rays (2009). **Years in League:** 2009-

OWNERSHIP, MANAGEMENT

Operated By: Ripken Baseball.

General Manager: Joe Hart. **Marketing Manager:** Jonathan Gantt. **Director, Food/Beverage:** Nick Barkley. **Director, Operations:** Sean Sawyer. **Director, Ticket Sales:** Scott Moudry. **Box Office Manager:** Nick Jones. **Corporate Partnerships Manager:** Patrick McMaster. **Bookkeeper:** Tamera Figueroa. **Ticket Sales Manager:** Adam English. **Account Executives:** Andy Beuster, Dante Plassio, Brad Schoem, Peter Walsifer.

FIELD STAFF

Manager: Jim Morrison. **Coach:** Joe Szekely. **Pitching Coach:** Bill Moloney. **Trainer:** Chris Tomashoff.

GAME INFORMATION

PA Announcer: Josh Grant. **Official Scorer:** Not Available.

Stadium Name: Charlotte Sports Park. **Location:** I-75 to Exit 179, turn left onto Toldeo Blade Blvd. then right on El Jobean Rd. **Ticket Price Range:** $6-11.

Visiting Club Hotel: Days Inn, 1941 Tamiami Trail, Port Charlotte, FL 33948. **Telephone:** 941-627-8900.

CLEARWATER THRESHERS

Office Address: 601 N. Old Coachman Rd, Clearwater, FL 33765.

Telephone: (727) 712-4300. **Fax:** (727) 712-4498.

Website: www.threshersbaseball.com.

Affiliation (first year): Philadelphia Phillies (1985). **Years in League:** 1985-

OWNERSHIP, MANAGEMENT

Operated by: Philadelphia Phillies.

Chairman: Bill Giles. **President:** David Montgomery.

Director, Florida Operations/General Manager: John Timberlake. **Assistant Director, Florida Operations:** Lee McDaniel. **Business Manager:** Dianne Gonzalez. **Assistant GM/Director, Sales:** Dan McDonough. **Assistant GM/Ticketing:** Jason Adams. **Group Sales:** Dan Madden, Bobby Mitchell. **Ballpark Operations:** Jay Warren. **Maintenance Coordinator:** Cory Sipe. **Manager, Food/Beverage:** Brad Dudash. **Community Relations:** Amanda Warner. **Ticket Manager:** Mike Nash. **Office Manager:** De De Angelillis. **Head Groundskeeper:** Opie Cheek.

FIELD STAFF

Manager: Ernie Whitt. **Coach:** Kevin Jordan, Ramon Hernandez. **Pitching Coach:** Dave Lundquist. **Trainer:** Ichiro Kitano.

GAME INFORMATION

Radio: None.

PA Announcer: Don Guckian. **Official Scorer:** Larry Wiederecht.

Stadium Name: Bright House Field. **Location:** U.S. 19 North and Drew Street in Clearwater. **Standard Game Times:** 7 p.m.; Sun. 1. **Ticket Price Range:** $4-9.

Visiting Club Hotel: LaQuinta Inn, 21338 U.S. 19 N., Clearwater, FL 33765. **Telephone:** (727) 799-1565.

DAYTONA CUBS

Office Address: 105 E. Orange Ave, Daytona Beach, FL 32114.

Telephone: (386) 257-3172. **Fax:** (386) 257-3382.

E-Mail Address: info@daytonacubs.com. **Website:** www.daytonacubs.com.

Affiliation (first year): Chicago Cubs (1993). **Years in League:** 1920-24, 1928, 1936-41, 1946-73, 1977-87, 1993-

OWNERSHIP, MANAGEMENT

Operated By: Big Game Florida LLC.

Principal Owner/President: Andrew Rayburn.

General Manager: Bill Papierniak. **Assistant GMs:** Brady Ballard, Tom Denlinger. **Director, Broadcasting/Media Relations:** Christian Bruey. **Director, Stadium Operations:** J.R. Laub. **Director, Tickets:** Eric Freeman. **Director, Groups:** Brandon Greene. **Director, Food/Beverage:** Josh Lawther. **Manager, Special Events/Group Sales:** Laura Landry. **Box Office Manager:** Amanda Earnest. **Manager, Client Services/Community Relations:** Christina Shisler. **Office Manager:** Tammy Devine.

FIELD STAFF

Manager: Buddy Bailey. **Coach:** Richie Zisk. **Pitching Coach:** Tom Pratt. **Trainer:** Bob Grimes.

GAME INFORMATION

Radio Announcer: Christian Bruey. **No. of Games Broadcast:** Home-70, Road-70. **Flagship Station:** Not Available.

PA Announcer: Tim Lecras. **Official Scorer:** Don Roberts.

Stadium Name: Jackie Robinson Ballpark. **Location:** I-95 to International Speedway Blvd. Exit (Route 92), east to Beach Street, south to Magnolia Ave., east to ballpark; A1A North/South to Orange Ave., west to ballpark. **Standard Game Time:** 7:05 p.m. **Ticket Price Range:** $6-12.

Visiting Club Hotel: Acapulco Hotel & Resort, 2505 S. Atlantic Ave., Daytona Beach Shores, FL 32218. **Telephone:** (386) 761-2210.

DUNEDIN BLUE JAYS

Office Address: 373-A Douglas Ave., Dunedin, FL 34698.

Telephone: (727) 733-9302. **Fax:** (727) 734-7661.

E-Mail Address: feedback@dunedinbluejays.com. **Website:** www.dunedinbluejays.com.

Affiliation (first year): Toronto Blue Jays (1987). **Years in League:** 1978-79, 1987-

OWNERSHIP, MANAGEMENT

Operated by: Toronto Blue Jays.

General Manager: Shelby Nelson. **Assistant GM:** Janette Donoghue. **Senior Consultant:** Ken Carson. **Manager, Ticket Operations:** Michael Nielsen. **Administrative Assistant:** Cile Fullerton. **Account Executives:** Kevin Schildt, Cameron O'Connell, Kathi Wiegand. **Office Manager:** Karen Howell. **Interns:** Jeff Probst, Tim Livingston, Ian Shollenberger, Garrett Konrad. **Head Groundskeeper:** Budgie Clark. **Assistant Groundskeeper:** Patrick Skunda. **Clubhouse Managers:** Adelis Barious, Freddy Mcdina.

FIELD STAFF

Manager: Omar Malave. **Hitting Coach:** Al Lebeouf. **Pitching Coach:** Darold Knowles. **Trainer:** Bob Tarpey.

GAME INFORMATION

Radio: None.

PA Announcer: Dave Bell. **Official Scorer:** Josh Huff.

Stadium Name: Dunedin Stadium. **Location:** From I-275, north on Highway 19, left on Sunset Point Rd. for 4 1/2 miles, right on Douglas Ave., stadium is 1/2 mile on right. **Standard Game Times:** 7 p.m.; Sun. 1. **Ticket Price Range:** $6.

Visiting Club Hotel: Comfort Inn Countryside, 26508 U.S. 19 N., Clearwater, FL 33761. **Telephone:** (727) 796-1234.

FORT MYERS MIRACLE

Office Address: 14400 Six Mile Cypress Pkwy, Fort Myers, FL 33912.

Telephone: (239) 768-4210. **Fax:** (239) 768-4211.

E-Mail Address: miracle@miraclebaseball.com. **Website:** www.miraclebaseball.com.

Affiliation (first year): Minnesota Twins (1993). **Years in League:** 1926, 1978-87, 1991-

OWNERSHIP, MANAGEMENT

Operated By: Greater Miami Baseball Club LP.

Principal Owner/Chairman: Marvin Goldklang. **CEO:** Mike Veeck. **President:** Linda McNabb. **General Manager:** Steve Gliner. **Assistant General Manager:** Kris Koch. **Director, Business Operations:** Suzanne Reaves. **Director, Sales/Marketing:** Terry Simon. **Director, Promotions/Media Relations:** Gary Sharp. **Director, Ticket Sales:** Matt Bomberg. **Manager, Food/Beverage:** Rory Broome. **Account Executive:** Travis Easton. **Community Relations Coordinator:** Joy Donahue. **Ticket Sales Representative:** Joe Livingston. **Administrative Assistants:** Josh Baumer, Natalie Platt. **Customer Relations Associates:** Nikki Greer, Sue Pinola. **Head Groundskeeper:** Keith Blasingim.

FIELD STAFF

Manager: Jeff Smith. **Coach:** Jim Dwyer. **Pitching Coach:** Steve Mintz. **Trainer:** Larry Bennese.

GAME INFORMATION

Radio Announcer: Unavailable. **No. of Games Broadcast:** Home-70, Road-70. **Flagship Station:** ESPN 770-AM.

PA Announcer: Gary Sharp. **Official Scorer:** Scott Pederson.

Stadium Name: William H. **Hammond Stadium. Location:** Exit 131 off I-75, west on Daniels Parkway, left on Six Mile Cypress Parkway. **Standard Game Times:** 7:05 p.m.; Sun. 1:05. **Ticket Price Range:** $5-7.

Visiting Club Hotel: Fairfield Inn by Marriot, 7090 Cypress Terrace, Fort Myers, FL 33907. **Telephone:** (239) 437-5600.

JUPITER HAMMERHEADS

Office Address: 4751 Main Street, Jupiter, FL 33458.
Telephone: (561) 775-1818. **Fax:** (561) 691-6886.
E-Mail Address: f.desk@rogerdeanstadium.com. **Website:** www.jupiterhammerheads.com.
Affiliation (first year): Florida Marlins (2002). **Years in League:** 1998-

OWNERSHIP, MANAGEMENT

Owned By: Florida Marlins. **Operated By:** Jupiter Stadium Ltd.

General Manager, JSL: Joe Pinto. **Executive Assistant:** Carol McAteer.

GM, Jupiter Hammerheads: Brian Barnes. **Assistant GM, Jupiter Hammerheads:** Shawn Gelnett. **Marketing Manager:** Selena Samios. **Merchandise Manager:** Stephanie Glavin. **Stadium Building Manager:** Jorge Toro. **Facility Operations Manager:** Marshall Jennings. **Assistant Facility Operations Managers:** Matt Eggerman, Jordan Treadway. **Assistant Ticket Manager:** Bethany Sims. **Ticket Manager:** Noel Ruiz-Castaneda. **Stadium/Event Operations Manager:** Bryan Knapp. **Corporate Partnership Representatives:** Barb Zorn, Katie Thompson. **Group Events Coordinator:** Lisa Fegley. **Office Manager:** Chris Tunno.

FIELD STAFF

Manager: Tim Leiper. **Coach:** Anthony Iapoce. **Pitching Coach:** John Duffy. **Trainer:** Cesar Roman.

GAME INFORMATION

Radio: None.

PA Announcers: John Frost, Dick Sanford. **Official Scorer:** Brennan McDonald.

Stadium Name: Roger Dean Stadium. **Location:** I-95 to exit 83, east on Donald Ross Road for 1/4 mile. **Standard Game Times:** 7:05 p.m.; Sat. 6:05; Sun. 5:05. **Ticket Price Range:** $6.50-8.50.

Visiting Club Hotel: Comfort Inn & Suites Jupiter, 6752 West Indiantown Rd, Jupiter, FL 33458. **Telephone:** (561) 745-7997.

LAKELAND FLYING TIGERS

Office Address: 2125 N Lake Ave, Lakeland, FL 33805.
Mailing Address: PO Box 90187, Lakeland, FL 33804.
Telephone: (863) 686-8075. **Fax:** (863) 688-9589.
Website: www.lakelandflyingtigers.com.
Affiliation (first year): Detroit Tigers (1967). **Years in League:** 1919-26, 1953-55, 1960, 1962-64, 1967-.

OWNERSHIP, MANAGEMENT

Owned By: Detroit Tigers, Inc.

Principal Owner: Mike Ilitch. **President:** David Dombrowski. **Director, Florida Operations:** Ron Myers.

General Manager: Zack Burek. **Manager, Administration/Operations:** Shannon Follett. **Ticket Manager:** Ryan Eason. **Group Sales Manager:** Megan Menesale. **Executive Chef:** David Hailey. **Receptionist:** Maria Walls.

FIELD STAFF

Manager: Andy Barkett. **Coach:** Larry Herndon. **Pitching Coach:** Joe Coleman.

GAME INFORMATION

Radio: None.

PA Announcers: Shari Szabo. **Official Scorer:** Sandy Shaw.

Stadium Name: Joker Marchant Stadium. **Location:** Exit 33 on I-4 to 33 South, 1 1/2 miles on left. **Standard Game Times:** 7 pm; Sat 6; Sun 1 (April), 6 (May-Aug). **Ticket Price Range:** $4-6.

Visiting Club Hotel: Howard Johnson Inn ExecutiveCenter, 3311 US Highway 98 North, Lakeland, FL 33805. **Telephone:** (863) 688-7972.

PALM BEACH CARDINALS

Office Address: 4751 Main Street, Jupiter, FL 33458.
Telephone: (561) 775-1818. **Fax:** (561) 691-6886.
E-Mail address: f.desk@rogerdeanstadium.com. **Website:** www.palmbeachcardinals.com.
Affiliation (first year): St. Louis Cardinals (2003). **Years in League:** 2003-

OWNERSHIP, MANAGEMENT

Owned By: St. Louis Cardinals. **Operated By:** Jupiter Stadium Ltd.

General Manager, JSL: Joe Pinto. **Executive Assistant:** Carol McAteer.

GM, Palm Beach Cardinals: Chris Easom. **Assistant GM:** Brian Barnes. **Marketing Manager:** Selena Samios. **Merchandise Manager:** Stephanie Glavin. **Stadium Building Manager:** Jorge Toro. **Assistant Facility Operations**

Managers: Matt Eggerman, Jordan Treadway. **Office Manager:** Chris Tunno. **Ticket Manager:** Noel Ruiz-Castaneda. **Stadium/Event Operations Manager:** Bryan Knapp. **Corporate Partnership Representatives:** Barb Zorn, Katie Thompson. **Group Events Coordinator:** Lisa Fegley. **Assistant Ticket Manager:** Bethany Sims.

FIELD STAFF

Manager: Tom Spencer. **Coach:** Jeff Albert. **Pitching Coach:** Derek Lilliquist. **Trainer:** Allen Thompson.

GAME INFORMATION

Radio: None.

PA Announcers: John Frost, Dick Sanford. **Official Scorer:** Lou Villano.

Stadium Name: Roger Dean Stadium. **Location:** I-95 to exit 83, east on Donald Ross Road for 1/4 mile. **Standard Game Times:** 7:05 p.m.; Sat. 6:05; Sun. 5:05. **Ticket Price Range:** $6.50-8.50.

Visiting Club Hotel: Comfort Inn & Suites Jupiter, 6752 West Indiantown Rd, Jupiter, FL 33458. **Telephone:** (561) 745-7997.

ST. LUCIE METS

Office Address: 525 NW Peacock Blvd., Port St. Lucie, FL 34986.
Telephone: (772) 871-2100. **Fax:** (772) 878-9802.
Website: www.traditionfield.com.
Affiliation (first year): New York Mets (1988). **Years in League:** 1988-

OWNERSHIP, MANAGEMENT

Operated by: Sterling Mets LP.

Chairman: Fred Wilpon. **President:** Saul Katz. **Senior Executive Vice President/COO:** Jeff Wilpon.

Director, Florida Operations/General Manager: Paul Taglieri. **Assistant Director, Florida Operations/Assistant General Manager:** Traer Van Allen. **Manager, Food/Beverage Operations:** Brian Paupeck. **Manager, Sales/Ballpark Operations:** Ryan Strickland. **Group Sales/Community Relations Coordinator:** Katie Hatch. **Executive Assistant:** Cynthia Gaumond. **Staff Accountant:** Paula Andreozzi. **Administrative Assistants:** Matt Gagnon, Clinton Van Allen. **Head Groundskeeper:** Tommy Bowes. **Clubhouse Manager:** Jack Brenner.

FIELD STAFF

Manager: Tim Teufel. **Coach:** G. Jabalera/J. Morales**. Pitching Coach:** Rob Ellis.

GAME INFORMATION

Radio: None.

PA Announcer: Matt Gagnon. **Official Scorer:** Bob Adams.

Stadium Name: Tradition Field. **Location:** Exit 121 (St. Lucie West Blvd.) off I-95, east 1/2 mile, left on NW Peacock Blvd. Standard Game Times: 7 p.m.; Sat. 6; Sun. 2. **Ticket Price Range:** $4-6.

Visiting Club Hotel: Springhill Suites, 2000 NW Courtyard Circle., Port St. Lucie, FL 34956. **Telephone:** (772) 879-2929.

SARASOTA REDS

Mailing Address: 1090 N. Euclid Ave, Sarasota, FL 34237.
Telephone: (941) 365-4460. **Fax:** (941) 365-4217.
E-Mail Address: sarasotaredsinfo@reds.com. **Website:** www.sarasotareds.com.
Affiliation (first year): Cincinnati Reds (2005). **Years in League:** 1927, 1961-65, 1989-

OWNERSHIP, MANAGEMENT

Operated By: Cincinnati Reds LLP.

General Manager, Florida Operations/Sarasota Reds: Dan Wolfert. **Assistant GM:** Mike Rebok. **Manager, Sales/Marketing:** Gary Saunders. **Ticket Manager:** Barbara Robinson. **Coordinator, Florida Baseball Operations:** Eric Jordan. **Administrative Assistants:** Matt Fuchs, Drew Greathouse, Steve Pulcinella. **Equipment Manager:** Jon Snyder. **Head Groundskeeper:** Gene Egan. **Clubhouse Manager:** TBD.

FIELD STAFF

Manager: Joe Ayrault. **Coach:** Jorge Orta. **Pitching Coach:** Tom Brown. **Athletic Trainer:** Tomas Vera.

GAME INFORMATION

Radio: None.

PA Announcer: Alex Topp. **Official Scorers:** David Taylor, Phil Denis.

Stadium Name: Ed Smith Stadium. **Location:** I-75 to exit 210, three miles west to Tuttle Ave., right on Tuttle 1/2 mile to 12th Street, stadium on left. **Standard Game Times:** 7 p.m.; Sat. 6; Sun. 1. **Ticket Price Range:** $5-6.

Visiting Club Hotel: AmericInn and Suites, 5931 Fruitville Rd, Sarasota, FL 34232. **Telephone:** (941) 342-8778.

TAMPA YANKEES

Office Address: One Steinbrenner Dr., Tampa, FL 33614.
Telephone: (813) 875-7753. **Fax:** (813) 673-3174.
E-Mail Address: vsmith@yankees.com. **Website:** tybaseball.com.
Affiliation (first year): New York Yankees (1994). **Years in League:** 1919-27, 1957-1988, 1994-

OWNERSHIP, MANAGEMENT

Operated by: New York Yankees LP.
Principal Owner: George Steinbrenner.
General Manager: Vance Smith. **Assistant GM:** Julie Kremer. **Director, Stadium Operations:** Dean Holbert. **Director, Sales/Marketing:** Howard Grosswirth. **Director, Ticket Sales:** Brian Valdez. **Head Groundskeeper:** Ritchie Anderson.

FIELD STAFF

Manager: Luis Sojo. **Hitting Coach:** Julius Matos. **Pitching Coach:** Greg Pavlick. **Coach:** Tim McIntosh. **Trainer:** Kris Russell. **Strength/Conditioning:** Jay Signorelli.

GAME INFORMATION

Radio: None.
PA Announcer: Steve Hague. **Official Scorer:** Unavailable.
Stadium Name: Steinbrenner Field. **Location:** I-275 to Martin Luther King, west on Martin Luther King to Dale Mabry. **Standard Game Times:** 7 p.m.; Sun. 1. **Ticket Price Range:** $4-6.
Visiting Club Hotel: Sheraton Suites Tampa Airport, 4400 W. Cypress St., Tampa, FL 33607. **Telephone:** (813) 873-8675.

MIDWEST LEAGUE

LOW CLASS A

Office Address: 1118 Cranston Rd., Beloit, WI 53511.
Mailing Address: P.O. Box 936, Beloit, WI 53512.

Telephone: (608) 364-1188. **Fax:** (608) 364-1913.

E-Mail Address: mwl@midwestleague.com. **Website:** www.midwestleague.com.

Years League Active: 1947-.

President, Treasurer: George H. Spelius.

George Spelius

Vice Presidents: Ed Larson, Richard A. Nussbaum II. **Legal Counsel/Secretary:** Richard A. Nussbaum II.

Directors: Jason Freier (Fort Wayne), Tom Barbee (Cedar Rapids), Lew Chamberlin (West Michigan), Dennis Conerton (Beloit), Tom Dickson (Lansing), David Heller (Quad Cities), Joe Kernan (South Bend), Gary Mayse (Dayton), Paul Schnack (Clinton), William Stavropoulos (Great Lakes), Rocky Vonachen (Peoria), Dave Walker (Burlington), Mike Woleben (Kane County), Rob Zerjav (Wisconsin).

League Administrator: Holly Voss.

Division Structure: East—Dayton, Fort Wayne, Lansing, South Bend, Great Lakes, West Michigan. **West**—Beloit, Burlington, Cedar Rapids, Clinton, Kane County, Peoria, Quad Cities, Wisconsin.

Regular Season: 140 games (split schedule). **2009 Opening Date:** April 9. **Closing Date:** Sept. 7.

All-Star Game: June 23 at Clinton.

Playoff Format: Eight teams qualify. First-half and second-half division winners and wild-card teams meet in best-of-three quarterfinal series. Winners meet in best-of-three series for division championships. Division champions meet in best-of-five final for league championship.

Roster Limit: 25 active. **Player Eligibility Rule:** No age limit. No more than two players and one player-coach on active list may have more than five years experience.

Brand of Baseball: Rawlings ROM-MID.

Umpires: Unavailable.

STADIUM INFORMATION

			Dimensions				
Club	**Stadium**	**Opened**	**LF**	**CF**	**RF**	**Capacity**	**2008 Att.**
Beloit	Pohlman Field	1982	325	380	325	3,500	82,546
Burlington	Community Field	1947	338	403	318	3,200	68,313
Cedar Rapids	Veterans Memorial Stadium	2000	315	400	325	5,300	164,568
Clinton	Alliant Energy Field	1937	335	390	325	4,000	114,662
Dayton	Fifth Third Field	2000	338	402	338	7,230	586,417
Fort Wayne	Parkview Field	2009	336	400	318	Unavailable	237,966
Great Lakes	Dow Diamond	2007	332	400	325	5,200	299,416
Kane County	Philip B. Elfstrom Stadium	1991	335	400	335	7,400	472,596
Lansing	Oldsmobile Park	1996	305	412	305	11,000	353,571
Peoria	O'Brien Field	2002	310	400	310	7,500	275,673
Quad Cities	John O'Donnell Stadium	1931	343	400	318	4,024	207,048
South Bend	Coveleski Regional Stadium	1987	336	405	336	5,000	163,479
West Michigan	Fifth Third Ballpark	1994	317	402	327	10,051	367,532
Wisconsin	Fox Cities Stadium	1995	325	400	325	5,500	190,263

BELOIT SNAPPERS

Office Address: 2301 Skyline Dr., Beloit, WI 53511.

Mailing Address: P.O. Box 855, Beloit, WI 53512.

Telephone: (608) 362-2272. **Fax:** (608) 362-0418.

E-Mail Address: snappy@snappersbaseball.com. **Website:** www.snappersbaseball.com.

Affiliation (first year): Minnesota Twins (2005). **Years in League:** 1982-.

OWNERSHIP, MANAGEMENT

Operated by: Beloit Professional Baseball Association Inc.

Chairman: Dennis Conerton. **President:** Marcy Olsen.

General Manager: Jeff Vohs. **Assistant General Manager:** Riley Gostisha. **Director, Media/Community Relations/Marketing:** Marcus Jacobs. **Director, Ticket Operations/Merchandise:** Matt Bosen. **Director, Corporate Sales/Promotions:** Tom Gross.

GAME INFORMATION

Radio Announcer: Jason Lamar. **No. of Games Broadcast:** 22. **Flagship Station:** WTJK 1380-AM.

PA Announcer: Unavailable. **Official Scorer:** Unavailable.

Stadium Name: Pohlman Field. **Location:** I-90 to exit 185-A, right at Cranston Road for 1 1/2 miles; I-43 to Wisconsin 81 to Cranston Road, right at Cranston for 1 1/2 miles.

Standard Game Times: 7 p.m., **6:**30 (April-May); Sun. 2. **Ticket Price Range:** $6-8.

Visiting Club Hotel: Econo Lodge, 2956 Milwaukee Rd., Beloit, WI 53511. **Telephone:** (608) 364-4000.

BURLINGTON BEES

Office Address: 2712 Mt. Pleasant St, Burlington, IA 52601.

Mailing Address: P.O. Box 824, Burlington, IA 52601.

Telephone: (319) 754-5705. **Fax:** (319) 754-5882.

E-Mail Address: staff@gobees.com. **Website:** www.gobees.com.

Affiliation (first year): Kansas City Royals (2001). **Years in League:** 1962-

OWNERSHIP, MANAGEMENT

Operated By: Burlington Baseball Association Inc.

President: Dave Walker.

General Manager: Chuck Brockett. **Assistant GM, Sales/Marketing:** Jared Schjei. **Director, Media Relations/Broadcaster:** Matt Pauley. **Director, Group Outings:** Whitney Henderson. **Groundskeeper:** T.J. Brewer.

FIELD STAFF

Manager: Jim Gabella. **Coach:** Pookie Wilson. **Pitching Coach:** Jerry Nyman. **Athletic Trainer:** Yoshi Kitaura.

GAME INFORMATION

Radio Announcer: Matt Pauley. **No. of Games Broadcast:** Home-70, Away-70. **Flagship Station:** NewsRadio KBUR 1490-AM.

PA Announcer: Nathan McCoy. **Official Scorer:** Ted Gutman.

Stadium Name: Community Field. **Location:** From U.S. 34, take U.S. 61 North to Mt. Pleasant Street, east 1/8 mile. **Standard Game Times:** 6:30 p.m., Sun. 2. **Ticket Price Range:** $4-7.

Visiting Club Hotel: Pzazz Best Western FunCity, 3001 Winegard Dr, Burlington, IA 52601. **Telephone:** (319) 753-2223.

CEDAR RAPIDS KERNELS

Office Address: 950 Rockford Rd. SW, Cedar Rapids, IA 52404.

Mailing Address: P.O. Box 2001, Cedar Rapids, IA 52406.

Telephone: (319) 363-3887. **Fax:** (319) 363-5631.

E-Mail Address: kernels@kernels.com. **Website:** www.kernels.com.

Affiliation (first year): Los Angeles Angels (1993). **Years in League:** 1962-

OWNERSHIP, MANAGEMENT

Operated by: Cedar Rapids Ball Club Inc.

President: Tom Barbee.

General Manager: Jack Roeder. **CFO:** Doug Nelson. **Director, Operations:** Scott Wilson. **Director, Broadcasting:** John Rodgers. **Director, Communications:** Andrew Pantini. **Sports Turf Manager:** Jesse Roeder. **Director, Ticket/Group Sales:** Andrea Murphy. **Director, Finance/Human Resources:** Charlie Patrick. **Director, Entertainment:** Sonya Masse. **Stadium Operations Manager:** Seth Dohrn. **Director, Marketing/Community Relations:** Jessica Fergesen. **Director, Food/Beverage:** Dave Soper. **Receptionist:** Marcia Moran.

FIELD STAFF

Manager: Keith Johnson. **Hitting Coach:** Brent Del Chiaro. **Pitching Coach:** Brandon Emanuel. **Trainer:** Dan Nichols.

GAME INFORMATION

Radio Announcer: John Rodgers. **No. of Games Broadcast:** Home-70, Away-70. **Flagship Station:** KMRY 1450-AM.

PA Announcer: Dale Brodt. **Official Scorer:** Unavailable.

Stadium Name: Veterans Memorial Stadium. **Location:** From I-380 North, take the Wilson Ave. exit, turn left on Wilson Ave. After the railroad tracks, turn right on Rockford Road. Proceed .8 miles, stadium is on left. From I-380 South, exit at First Avenue. Proceed to Eighth Avenue (first stop sign) and turn left. Stadium entrance is .1 miles on right (before tennis courts). **Standard Game Times:** 6:35 p.m., **Sat.-Sun.:** 2:05. **Ticket Price Range:** $7-10.

Visiting Club Hotel: Best Western Cooper's Mill, 100 F Ave. NW, Cedar Rapids, IA 52405. **Telephone:** (319) 366-5323.

CLINTON LUMBERKINGS

Office Address: Alliant Energy Field, 537 Ball Park Drive, Clinton, IA 52732.
Mailing Address: P.O. Box 1295, Clinton, IA 52733.
Telephone: (563) 242-0727. **Fax:** (563) 242-1433.
E-Mail Address: lumberkings@lumberkings.com. **Website:** www.lumberkings.com.
Affiliation (first year): Seattle Mariners (2009). **Years in League:** 1956-

OWNERSHIP, MANAGEMENT

Operated By: Clinton Baseball Club Inc.

Chairman: Don Roode. **President:** Paul Schnack. **General Manager:** Ted Tornow. **Assistant GM:** Nate Kreinbrink. **Director, Operations:** Justin Sampson. **Director, Media Relations:** Dave Lezotte.

FIELD STAFF

Manager: Scott Steinmann. **Coach:** Jesus Azuaje. **Pitching Coach:** Lance Painter. **Trainer:** Eduardo Tamez. **Equipment Manager:** Tyler Hildreth.

GAME INFORMATION

Radio: None.

PA Announcer: Brad Seward. **Official Scorer:** Tom Whaley.

Stadium Name: Alliant Energy Field. **Location:** Highway 67 North to Sixth Avenue North, right on Sixth, cross railroad tracks, stadium on right. **Standard Game Times:** 6:30 p.m. (April-May, Sept.), 7 (June-Aug.); Sun. 2. **Ticket Price Range:** $5-7.

Visiting Club Hotel: Super 8 Motel, 1711 Lincoln Way, Clinton, IA 52732. **Telephone:** (563) 242-8870.

DAYTON DRAGONS

Office Address: Fifth Third Field, 220 N. Patterson Blvd, Dayton, OH 45402.
Mailing Address: P.O. 2107, Dayton, OH 45401.
Telephone: (937) 228-2287. **Fax:** (937) 228-2284.
E-Mail Address: dragons@daytondragons.com. **Website:** www.daytondragons.com.
Affiliation (first year): Cincinnati Reds (2000). **Years in League:** 2000-

OWNERSHIP, MANAGEMENT

Operated By: Dayton Professional Baseball LLC./Mandalay Baseball Properties. **Owners:** Mandalay Baseball Properties, Earvin "Magic" Johnson, Archie Griffin.

President: Robert Murphy. **Executive Vice President:** Eric Deutsch. **Executive VP/General Manager:** Gary Mayse. **Accounting/Finance:** Mark Schlein. **VP, Sponsorships:** Jeff Webb. **VP, Ticket Sales:** Jeff Stewart. **Director, Sponsor Services:** Brad Eaton. **Director, Entertainment:** Shari Sharkins. **Director, Marketing:** Jim Francis. **Director, Media Relations:** Tom Nichols. **Senior Ticketing Agent:** Sally Ledford. **Ticketing Coordinator:** Mike Muncy. **Marketing Managers:** Brandy Abney, Nicole Becker, Brian Botos, Chris Hart, Laura Rose, Clint Taylor. **Senior Ticket Sales Managers:** Andrew Aldenderfer, Mike Vujea. **Corporate Marketing Managers:** Viterio Jones, Phil Salwan, Ryan York. **Event Operations Manager:** Chad Adams. **Senior Operations Director:** Joe Eaglowski. **Facilities Operations Manager:** Joe Elking. **Baseball Operations Manager:** John Wallace. **Director, Operations:** Andrew Ottmar. **Office Manager:** Leslie Stuck. **Staff Accountant:** Dorothy Day. **Administrative Assistant:** Lisa Rike. **Administrative Secretary:** Barbara Van Schaik.

FIELD STAFF

Manager: Todd Benzinger. **Hitting Coach:** Tony Jaramillo. **Pitching Coach:** Rigo Beltran. **Trainer:** Alfonso Flores.

GAME INFORMATION

Radio Announcer: Tom Nichols. **No. of Games Broadcast:** Home-70, Away-70. **Flagship Station:** WING 1410-AM ESPN Radio.

PA Announcers: Ben Oburn, Kim Parker. **Official Scorers:** Roy Cassidy, Matt Lindsay.

Stadium Name: Fifth Third Field. **Location:** I-75 South to downtown Dayton, left at First Street; I-75 North, right at First Street exit. **Ticket Price Range:** $7-13.25.

Visiting Club Hotel: Comfort Inn, 7125 Miller Lane, Dayton, OH 45414. **Telephone:** (937) 890-9995.

FORT WAYNE TINCAPS

Office Address: 1301 Ewing St. Fort Wayne, IN 46802.
Telephone: (260) 482-6400. **Fax:** (260) 471-4678.
E-Mail Address: info@tincaps.com. **Website:** www.tincaps.com.
Affiliation (first year): San Diego Padres (1999). **Years in League:** 1993-.

OWNERSHIP, MANAGEMENT

Operated By: Hardball Capital.

Owners: Jason Freier, Chris Schoen.

President/General Manager: Mike Nutter. **Vice President/Assistant General Manager, Sales/Finance:** Brian Schackow. **Vice President/Senior Assistant General Manager, Corporate Parnerships:** David Lorenz. **Vice President/Assistant General Manager, Marketing/Entertainment/Promotions Michael Limmer. Director, Group Sales:** Brad Shank. **Assistant Director, Group Sales:** Jared Parcell. **Director, Ticketing:** Pat Ventura. **Director, Concessions:** Bill Lehn. **Director, Facilities:** Tim Burkhart. **Assistant Director, Facilities:** Chris Watson. **Director, Field Maintenance:** Mitch McClary. **Manager, Graphic Design:** Tony Desplaines. **Manager, Video Production:** Allen Wertheimer. **Manager, Ticket Sales:** Tyler Baker, Brent Harring, Ryan Ledman, Justin Shurley. **Manager, Corporate Partnerships:** Chris Snyder. **Director, Broadcasting:** Dan Watson. **Office Manager:** Cathy Tinney. **Manager, Merchandise:** Karen Schieber. **Manager, Promotions:** Abigail Naas.

FIELD STAFF

Manager: Doug Dascenzo. **Hitting Coach:** Tom Tornincasa. **Pitching Coach:** Tom Bradley. **Trainer:** Ernesto Vega.

GAME INFORMATION

Radio Announcer: Dan Watson, Mike Maahs. **No. of Games Broadcast:** Home-70, Away-70. **Flagship Station:** WKJG 1380-AM.

PA Announcer: Jim Shovlin. **Official Scorer:** Unavailable.

Stadium Name: Parkview Field. **Location:** Downtown Fort Wayne off of Jefferson Blvd.

Ticket Price Range: $5-12.50.

Visiting Club Hotel: Quality Inn, 1734 W. Washington Center Road, Fort Wayne, IN 46818. **Telephone:** (260) 489-5554.

GREAT LAKES LOONS

Office Address: 825 East Main St., Midland, MI 48640.

Mailing Address: P.O. Box 365, Midland, MI 48640.

Telephone: (989) 837-2255. **Fax:** (989) 837-8780.

E-Mail Address: info@loons.com. **Website:** www.loons.com.

Affiliation (first year): Los Angeles Dodgers (2007). **Years in League:** 2007-.

OWNERSHIP, MANAGEMENT

Operated By: Michigan Baseball Operations.

Stadium Ownership: Michigan Baseball Foundation.

Founder/Foundation President: William Stavropoulos.

President/General Manager: Paul Barbeau. **Assistant GM, Finance:** Tammy Brinkman. **Assistant GM, Retail/Guest Services:** Ann Craig. **Assistant GM, Ticket Sales:** Scott Litle. **Assistant GM, Marketing/Promotions:** Chris Mundhenk. **Director, Special Events:** Dave Gomola. **Director, Communications:** Brad Golder. **Director, Food/Beverage:** Nick Kavalauskas. **Director, Production:** Chris Lones. **Director, Facilities/Operations:** Matt McQuaid. **Director, Ticket Operations:** Jason Osterberg. **Director, Sponsorships:** Karrie Sells. **Director, Business Operations:** Patti Tuma. **Head Groundskeeper:** Keith Winter. **Catering/Kitchen Services Manager:** Shantel Johnson-Lawson. **HR/Business Manager, Food/Beverage:** Alyson Schafer. **Promotions Manager:** Linda Uliano. **Group Sales Coordinators:** Heather Jones, Tiffany Seward. **Account Executives:** Korrey Shoup, Matt Simcox. **Ticket Accountant:** Jamie Simpson. **Catering Supervisor:** Mike Koski. **Concessions/Warehouse Supervisor:** Nick Barton.

FIELD STAFF

Manager: Juan Bustabad. **Pitching Coach:** Danny Darwin. **Hitting Coach:** Michael Boughton. **Trainer:** Zachary Hoffman.

GAME INFORMATION

Radio Announcer: Brad Golder. **No. of Games Broadcast:** Home-70, Away-70. **Flagship Station:** ESPN 100.9-FM (WLUN)

PA Announcer: Jerry O'Donnell. **Official Scorer:** Terry Wilczek.

Stadium Name: Dow Diamond. **Location:** I-75 to US-10 W. Take the M-20/US10 Business exit on the left toward downtown Midland. Merge onto US-10 W/MI-20 W (also known as Indian Street). Turn left onto State Street. The entrance to the stadium is at the intersection of Ellsworth and State Streets.

Standard Game Times: Mon.-Sat.: 6:05 p.m. (April), 7:05 (May-Sept.); Sun. 3:05.

Ticket Price Range: $6-9.

Visiting Club Hotel: Holiday Inn of Midland, 1500 W. Wackerly Street, Midland, MI 48640. **Telephone:** (989) 631-4220.

KANE COUNTY COUGARS

Office Address: 34W002 Cherry Lane, Geneva, IL 60134.

Telephone: (630) 232-8811. **Fax:** (630) 232-8815.

E-Mail Address: info@kanecountycougars.com. **Website:** www.kccougars.com.

Affiliation (first year): Oakland Athletics (2003). **Years in League:** 1991-

OWNERSHIP, MANAGEMENT

Operated By: Cougars Baseball Partnership/American Sports Enterprises, Inc.

President: Mike Woleben.

Vice President: Mike Murtaugh. **Vice President/General Manager:** Jeff Sedivy. **Assistant GM/Sales Director:** Curtis Haug. **Assistant GM, Media/Promotions:** Jeff Ney. **Special Assistant to GM:** Rich Essegian. **Director, Food/Beverage:** Mike Klafehn. **Luxury Suite Level Manager:** Lydia Boone. **Catering Manager:** Sheila Savage. **Assistant Catering Manager:** Liz Pabst. **Concessions Supervisor:** Jon Williams. **Personnel Manager:** Robin Newlin. **Director, Ticket Sales:** Joe Wagoner. **Senior Ticket Sales Representatives:** Alex Miller, Patti Savage. **Account Executives:** Christy Gallagher, Matt Hayden, Jeff Lapansky, Camden Linstead, Kyle Manigold, Ray Sohl. **Director, Ticket Operations:** Erin Wiencek. **Ticket Operations:** Dana Kelly, Rob Koskosky, Gary Olson, Anjeanette Yates. **Director, Community Relation Programming:** Amy Mason. **Media Relations Coordinator:** Shawn Touney. **Manager, Advertising Placement:** Bill Baker. **Client Services Representative:** Jenn McArthur. **Design/Graphics:** Emmet Broderick, Nick Braglia. **Webmaster/PA Announcer:** Kevin Sullivan. **Business Manager:** Mary Almlie. **Controller:** Doug Czurylo. **Finance/Accounting Manager:** Lance Buhmann. **Accounting Clerk/Merchandise Manager:** Katie Doyle. **Director, Security:** Dan Klinkhamer. **Stadium Operations/Account Executive:** David Edison. **Stadium Operations Assistant:** Steve Moravecek. **Stadium Maintenance Supervisor:** Jeff Snyder. **Stadium Maintenance:** Steve Azzaro. **Head Groundskeeper:** Matt Ramirez.

FIELD STAFF

Manager: Steve Scarsone. **Hitting Coach:** Haas Pratt. **Pitching Coach:** Jimmy Escalante. **Trainer:** Nate Brooks.

GAME INFORMATION

Radio Announcer: Jeff Hem. **No. of Games Broadcast:** Home-70, Away-70. **Flagship Station:** WBIG 1280-AM.

PA Announcer: Kevin Sullivan. **Official Scorer:** Bill Baker.

Stadium Name: Philip B. **Elfstrom Stadium. Location:** From east or west, I-88 (Ronald Reagan Memorial Tollway) to Farnsworth Avenue North exit, north five miles to Cherry Lane, left into stadium complex; from northwest, I-90 (Jane Addams Memorial Tollway) to Randall Road South exit, south to Fabyan Parkway, east to Kirk Road, north to Cherry Lane, left into stadium complex. **Standard Game Times:** 6:30 p.m.; Sat. 6; Sun. 2. **Ticket Price Range:** $8-14.

Visiting Club Hotel: Best Western Naperville, 1617 Naperville Rd., Naperville, IL 60563. **Telephone:** (630) 505-0200.

LANSING LUGNUTS

Lansing Lugnuts™

Office Address: 505 E. Michigan Ave, Lansing, MI 48912.

Telephone: (517) 485-4500. **Fax:** (517) 485-4518.

E-Mail Address: info@lansinglugnuts.com. **Website:** www.lansinglugnuts.com.

Affiliation (first year): Toronto Blue Jays (2005). **Years in League:** 1996-

OWNERSHIP, MANAGEMENT

Operated By: Take Me Out to the Ballgame LLC.

Principal Owners: Tom Dickson, Sherrie Myers.

General Manager: Pat Day. **Assistant GM:** Nick Grueser. **Director, Food/Beverage:** Brett Telder. **Business Manager:** Heather Viele. **Director, Ticketing/Marketing Operations:** Jeff Jaworski. **Director, Operations/Head Groundskeeper:** Matt Anderson. **Group Sales Manager:** Greg Kruger. **Corporate Sales Manager:** Nick Brzezinski. **Retail Manager:** Matt Hicks. **Concessions Manager:** Alex Terranova. **Catering Manager:** Jenny Smart. **Assistant Business Manager:** Rebekah Butler. **Administrative Assistant:** Angela Sees. **Marketing Manager:** Julia Janssen. **Marketing Assistant:** Lauren Truax. **Corporate Account Executive:** Kevin Novack. **Group Sales Representative:** Kohl Tyrrell. **Sponsorship Service Representatives:** Jill Niemi, Michaela McAnany. **Stadium Operations:** Dennis Busse. **Assistant Box Office Manager:** Brian Burita.

FIELD STAFF

Manager: Clayton McCullough. **Coach:** Justin Mashore. **Pitching Coach:** Antonio Caceres. **Trainer:** Bob Tarpey.

GAME INFORMATION

Radio Announcer: Jesse Goldberg-Srassler. **No of Games Broadcast:** Home-70, Away-70. **Flagship Station:** WQTX 92.1-FM.

Official Scorer: Seth Van Hoven, Dave Schaberg.

Stadium Name: Oldsmobile Park. **Location:** I-96 East/West to U.S. 496, exit at Larch Street, north of Larch, stadium on left. **Ticket Price Range:** $7-9.

Visiting Club Hotel: Lexington Lansing Grand Hotel, 925 South Creyts Road, Lansing MI 48917. **Telephone:** (517) 323-7100.

PEORIA CHIEFS

Peoria Chiefs™

Office Address: 730 SW Jefferson, Peoria, IL 61602.

Telephone: (309) 680-4000. **Fax:** (309) 680-4080.

E-Mail Address: feedback@chiefsnet.com. **Website:** www.peoriachiefs.com.

Affiliation (first year): Chicago Cubs (2005). **Years in League:** 1983-

OWNERSHIP, MANAGEMENT

Operated By: Peoria Chiefs Community Baseball Club LLC.

President: Rocky Vonachen. **Vice President/General Manager:** Ralph Converse. **Director, Ticket Sales:** Eric Obalil. **VP, Corporate Sales:** Justin Reckamp. **Broadcast/Media Manager:** Nathan Baliva. **Director, Guest Services/Account Executive:** Howard Yates. **Manager, Box Office:** Ryan Sivori. **Entertainment/Events Manager:** Sarah Grady. **Account Executives:** Luke Cross, Amanda Curtis, Joel Merrill, Jack Schmitz, Kyle Wicks. **Head Groundskeeper:** Noel Brusius.

FIELD STAFF

Manager: Marty Pevey. **Hitting Coach:** Barbaro Garbey. **Pitching Coach:** Rich Bombard. **Trainer:** Kelly Vanhove.

GAME INFORMATION

Radio Announcer: Nathan Baliva. **No. of Games Broadcast:** Home-70, Away-70. **Flagship Station:** 96.5-FM ESPN Radio

PA Announcer: Unavailable. **Official Scorer:** Brandon Thome.

Stadium Name: O'Brien Field. **Location:** From South/East, I-74 to exit 93 (Jefferson Street), continue one mile, stadium is one block on left. From North/West, I-74 to Glen Oak Exit. Turn right on Glendale which turns into Kumpf Blvd. Turn right on Jefferson, stadium on left. **Standard Game Times:** 7 p.m., 6:30 (April-May, after Aug. 22); Sat. 6:30; Sun. 2. **Ticket Price Range:** $6-10.

Visiting Club Hotel: Super 8-Peoria, 1816 W. War Memorial Dr., Peoria, IL 61614. **Telephone:** (309) 698-8074.

QUAD CITIES RIVER BANDITS

Office Address: 209 S. Gaines St., Davenport, IA 52802.
Telephone: (563) 322-6348. **Fax:** (563) 324-3109.
E-Mail Address: bandit@riverbandits.com. **Website:** www.riverbandits.com.
Affiliation (first year): St. Louis Cardinals (2005). **Years in League:** 1960-.

OWNERSHIP, MANAGEMENT

Operated by: Main Street Iowa.

Vice President/General Manager: Kirk Goodman. **Vice President/Chief Marketing Officer:** Cory Howerton. **Assistant General Manager:** Stefanie Brown. **Director, Broadcasting/Media Relations:** Ben Chiswick. **Director, Sales/Service:** Joe Loncarich. **Director, Ticket Operations:** Nick Harvey. **Director, Baseball Operations:** Bob Evans. **Production Manager:** Shane Huff. **Head Groundskeeper/Stadium Operations:** Ben Kratz. **Account Executives:** Justin Jacobs, Matt Tangen. **Director, Food Service:** Ben Blankenship.

FIELD STAFF

Manager: Steve Dillard. **Hitting Coach:** Joe Kruzel. **Pitching Coach:** Arthur "Ace" Adams. **Trainer:** Brian Puchalski.

GAME INFORMATION

Radio Announcer: Ben Chiswick. **No. of Games Broadcast:** Home-70, Away-70. **Flagship Station:** WYEC 93.9 FM.

PA Announcer: Unavailable. **Official Scorer:** Unavailable.

Stadium Name: Modern Woodmen Park. **Location:** From I-74, take Grant Street exit left, west onto River Drive, left on South Gaines Street; from I-80, take Brady Street exit south, right on River Drive, left on South Gaines Street. **Standard Game Times:** 7 p.m., 6:30 (April); Sun. 5. **Ticket Prices:** $5-12.

Visiting Club Hotel: AmericInn, 301 Jason Way Court, Davenport, IA 52806. **Telephone:** (563) 323-3303.

SOUTH BEND SILVER HAWKS

Office Address: 501 W. South St, South Bend, IN 46601.
Mailing Address: P.O. Box 4218, South Bend, IN 46634.
Telephone: (574) 235-9988. **Fax:** (574) 235-9950.
E-Mail Address: hawks@silverhawks.com. **Website:** www.silverhawks.com.
Affiliation (first year): Arizona Diamondbacks (1997). **Years in League:** 1988-.

OWNERSHIP, MANAGEMENT

Operated By: South Bend Professional Baseball Club LLC.

President: Joe Kernan.

Vice President, Baseball Operations: John Baxter. **Director, Finance:** Cheryl Carlson. **Director, Sales/Marketing:** Amy Hill. **Director, Stadium Operations:** Peter Argueta. **Marketing Manager:** Jeff Scholfield. **Group Sales Manager:** James McAvoy. **Box Office Manager:** Kirk Venderlic. **Sales Manager:** Terry Coleman. **Senior Account Executive:** Jon Lies. **Account Executive:** Jackie Batteast. **Corporate Sales:** Rita Baxter. **Head Groundskeeper:** Joel Reinebold.

FIELD STAFF

Manager: Mark Haley. **Hitting Coach:** Francisco Morales. **Pitching Coach:** Erik Sabel. **Trainer:** Brian Czachowski. **Strength Coach:** Vaughn Robinson.

GAME INFORMATION

Radio: None.

Stadium Name: Stanley Coveleski Regional Stadium. **Location:** I-80/90 toll road to exit 77, take US 31/33 south to South Bend to downtown (Main Street), to Western Avenue, right on Western, left on Taylor. **Ticket Price Range:** $5-7.

Visiting Club Hotel: Quality Inn, 515 Dixie Way North, South Bend, IN 46637. **Telephone:** (574) 272-6600.

WEST MICHIGAN WHITECAPS

Office Address: 4500 West River Dr., Comstock Park, MI 49321.
Mailing Address: P.O. Box 428, Comstock Park, MI 49321.
Telephone: (616) 784-4131. **Fax:** (616) 784-4911.
E-Mail Address: playball@whitecaps-baseball.com. **Website:** www.whitecapsbaseball.com.
Affiliation (first year): Detroit Tigers (1997). **Years in League:** 1994-

OWNERSHIP, MANAGEMENT

Operated By: Whitecaps Professional Baseball Corp.

Principal Owners: Denny Baxter, Lew Chamberlin.

President: Scott Lane. **Vice President, Whitecaps Professional Baseball:** Jim Jarecki. **VP, Sales:** Steve McCarthy. **Director, Outside Events:** Matt Costello. **Director, Food/Beverage:** Matt Timon. **Director, New Business Development:** Dan McCrath. **Community Relations Coordinator:** Anna Peterson. **Manager, Marketing/Media:** Mickey Graham. **Promotions Coordinator:** Brian Oropallo. **Box Office Manager:** Meghan Brennan. **Groundskeeper:** Greg Salyer. **Manager, Facility Maintenance:** John Passarelli. **Director, Ticket Sales:** Chad Sayen.

FIELD STAFF

Manager: Joe DePastino. **Hitting Coach:** Benny Distefano. **Pitching Coach:** Mark Johnson. **Trainer:** Corey Tremble.

GAME INFORMATION

Radio Announcer: Unavailable. **No. of Games Broadcast:** Home-70, Away-70. **Flagship Station:** WBBL 1340-AM.

PA Announcers: Mike Newell, Bob Wells. **Official Scorers:** Mike Dean, Don Thomas.

Stadium Name: Fifth Third Ballpark. **Location:** U.S. 131 North from Grand Rapids to exit 91 (West River Drive). **Ticket Price Range:** $5-10.

Visiting Club Hotel: Holiday Inn Express-GR North, 358 River Ridge Dr. NW, Walker, MI 49544. **Telephone:** (616) 647-4100.

WISCONSIN TIMBER RATTLERS

Office Address: 2400 N. Casaloma Dr, Appleton, WI 54913.
Mailing Address: P.O. Box 7464, Appleton, WI 54912.
Telephone: (920) 733-4152. **Fax:** (920) 733-8032.
E-Mail Address: info@timberrattlers.com. **Website:** www.timberrattlers.com.
Affiliation (first year): Milwaukee Brewers (2009). **Years in League:** 1962-

OWNERSHIP, MANAGEMENT

Operated By: Appleton Baseball Club Inc.

Chairman: Craig Dickman.

President/General Manager: Rob Zerjav. **Stadium Operations Manager:** Jeron Schmidt. **Team Operations:** Bob Estes. **Controller:** Cathy Spanbauer. **VP, Communications/Community/Media Relations:** Nikki Becker. **VP, Marketing/Promotions:** Angie Ceranski. **Manager, Merchandise/Internet:** Jay Grusznski. **Assistant GM/Director, Ticket Sales:** Aaron Hahn. **Group Sales:** Isaac Bray, Brandon Goebel, Dayna Haddock. **Box Office Manager:** Darren Shimanski. **Corporate Sales:** Sarah Heth, Chris Mehring. **Groundskeeper:** Eddie Warczak.

FIELD STAFF

Manager: Jeff Isom. **Coach:** Matt Erikson. **Pitching Coach:** Chris Hook. **Trainer:** Aaron Hoback.

GAME INFORMATION

Radio Announcer: Chris Mehring. **No. of Games Broadcast:** Home-70, Away-70. **Flagship Station:** WNAM 1280-AM.

PA Announcer: Joe Dotterweich. **Official Scorer:** Jay Grusznski.

Stadium Name: Time Warner Cable Field Fox Cities Stadium. **Location:** Highway 41 to Highway 15 (00) exit, west to Casaloma Drive, left to stadium. **Standard Game Times:** 7:05 p.m., 6:35 (April-May); Sat. 6:35; Sun. 1:05. **Ticket Price Range:** $5-8.50.

Visiting Club Hotel: Microtel Inn & Suites, 321 Metro Dr, Appleton, WI 54913. **Telephone:** (920) 997-3121.

SOUTH ATLANTIC LEAGUE

LOW CLASS A

Eric Krupa

Office Address: 111 Second Avenue NE, Suite 335, St. Petersburg, FL 33701.

Telephone: (727) 456-1240. **Fax:** (727) 499-6853.

E-Mail Address: office@saloffice.com. **Website:** www.southatlanticleague.com.

Years League Active: 1904-1964, 1979-.

President/Secretary-Treasurer: Eric Krupa.

First Vice President: Chip Moore (Rome). **Second Vice President:** Craig Brown (Greenville).

Directors: Don Beaver (Hickory), Cooper Brantley (Greensboro), Craig Brown (Greenville), Peter Carfagna (Lake County), Joseph Finley (Lakewood), Marvin Goldklang (Charleston), Art Solomon (Bowling Green), Alan Ostfield (Asheville), Alan Levin (West Virginia), Tom Volpe (Delmarva), Chip Moore (Rome), Art Matin (Hagerstown), Chris Flannery (Augusta), Jason Freier (Savannah), Brad Smith (Kannapolis), Alan Stein (Lexington).

Division Structure: North—Delmarva, Greensboro, Hagerstown, Hickory, Lake County, Lakewood, Kannapolis, West Virginia. **South**—Asheville, Augusta, Bowling Green, Charleston, Greenville, Lexington, Rome, Savannah.

Regular Season: 140 games (split schedule). **2009 Opening Date:** April 9. **Closing Date:** Sept. 7.

All-Star Game: June 23 at West Virginia.

Playoff Format: First-half and second-half division winners meet in best-of-three semifinal series. Winners meet in best-of-five series for league championship.

Roster Limit: 25 active. **Player Eligibility Rule:** No age limit. No more than two players and one player-coach on active list may have more than five years of experience.

Brand of Baseball: Rawlings.

Umpires: Unavailable.

STADIUM INFORMATION

			Dimensions				
Club	**Stadium**	**Opened**	**LF**	**CF**	**RF**	**Capacity**	**2008 Att.**
Asheville	McCormick Field	1992	328	402	300	4,000	175,892
Augusta	Lake Olmstead Stadium	1995	330	400	330	4,322	200,222
*Bowling Green	Bowling Green Ballpark	2009	312	401	325	4,559	61,290
Charleston	Joseph P. Riley Jr. Ballpark	1997	306	386	336	5,800	279,606
Delmarva	Arthur W. Perdue Stadium	1996	309	402	309	5,200	226,754
Greensboro	NewBridge Bank Park	2005	322	400	320	7,599	440,787
Greenville	West End Field	2006	310	400	302	5,000	349,116
Hagerstown	Municipal Stadium	1931	335	400	330	4,600	137,283
Hickory	L.P. Frans Stadium	1993	330	401	330	5,062	133,512
Kannapolis	Fieldcrest Cannon Stadium	1995	330	400	310	4,700	119,668
Lake County	Classic Park	2003	320	400	320	7,273	316,572
Lakewood	FirstEnergy Park	2001	325	400	325	6,588	425,166
Lexington	Applebee's Park	2001	320	401	318	6,033	370,570
Rome	State Mutual Stadium	2003	335	400	330	5,100	222,168
Savannah	Historic Grayson Stadium	1941	290	410	310	8,000	105,537
West Virginia	Appalachian Power Park	2005	330	400	320	4,300	213,030

*Franchise played in Columbus, Ga., last year.

ASHEVILLE TOURISTS

Office Address: McCormick Field, 30 Buchanan Place, Asheville, NC 28801.

Telephone: (828) 258-0428. **Fax:** (828) 258-0320.

E-Mail Address: info@theashevilletourists.com. **Website:** www.theashevilletourists.com.

Affiliation (first year): Colorado Rockies (1994). **Years in League:** 1976-

OWNERSHIP, MANAGEMENT

Operated By: Palace Baseball.

Executive Director: Mike Bauer. **General Manager:** Larry Hawkins. **Assistant GMs:** Jodee Ciszewski, Chris Smith. **Box Office Manager:** Patrick Spence. **GM Centerplate, Concessions:** Brian Candler. **Office Manager:** Ryan Doyle. **Director, Broadcasting:** Jay Burnham. **Corporate Sales Managers:** Jason Kane, Mike Kish, Brian Rodgers. **Outside Sales:** Bob Jones. **Publications/Website:** Bill Ballew.

FIELD STAFF

Manager: Joe Mikulik. **Coach:** Houston Jimenez. **Pitching Coach:** Dave Schuler. **Trainer:** Billy Whitehead.

GAME INFORMATION

Radio Announcer: Jay Burnham. **No. of Games Broadcast:** Home-70 Road-70. **Flagship Station:** WRES 100.7 FM.

PA Announcer: Rick Diggler. **Official Scorer:** Mike Gore.

Stadium Name: McCormick Field. **Location:** I-240 to Charlotte Street South exit, south one mile on Charlotte, left on McCormick Place. **Ticket Price Range:** $6-10.

Visiting Club Hotel: Quality Inn, 1 Skyline Drive, Arden, NC 28704. **Telephone:** (828) 684-6688.

AUGUSTA GREENJACKETS

Office Address: 78 Milledge Rd., Augusta, GA 30904.

Mailing Address: P.O. Box 3746, Augusta, GA 30914.

Telephone: (706) 736-7889. **Fax:** (706) 736-1122.

E-Mail Address: info@greenjacketsbaseball.com. **Website:** www.greenjacketsbaseball.com.

Affiliation (first year): San Francisco Giants (2005). **Years in League:** 1988-

OWNERSHIP, MANAGEMENT

Owners: Baseball Enterprises, LCC.

Operated By: Ripken Professional Baseball.

General Manager: Nick Brown. **Assistant GM:** Tom D'Abruzzo. **Director, Stadium Operations:** David Ryther, Jr. **Director, Ticket Sales:** Jonathan Pribble. **Corporate Partnership Manager:** Aaron Fiet. **Account Executives:** Kyle Coppess, Danielle Jackson, Chris Lieberman, Chris Norwood, Stacia Pomeroy, Adam Schmansky. **Entertainment Coordinator:** Stephanie Fish Bindewald. **Marketing Coordinator:** Lauren Christie. **Box Office Coordinator:** Bryan Gerber. **Bookkeeper:** Debbie Whisenant.

FIELD STAFF

Manager: Dave Machemer. **Hitting Coach:** Lipso Nava. **Pitching Coach:** Steve Kline. **Trainer:** James Petra.

GAME INFORMATION

Radio Announcer: Unavailable. **No. of Games Broadcast:** Home-70 Road-70. **Flagship Station:** WRDW 1630-AM.

PA Announcer: Scott Skadan. **Official Scorer:** Ted Miller.

Stadium Name: Lake Olmstead Stadium. **Location:** I-20 to Washington Road exit, east to Broad Street exit, left on Milledge Road. **Standard Game Times:** Mon.-Sat.: **7:**05 p.m.; **Sun. 2:**05/5:35. **Ticket Price Range:** $6-11.

Visiting Club Hotel: Quality Inn, 1455 Walton Way, Augusta, GA 30901. **Telephone:** (706) 722-2224.

BOWLING GREEN HOT RODS

Office Address: Bowling Green Ballpark, 300 8th Avenue, Bowling Green, KY 42104.

Telephone: (270) 901-2121. **Fax:** (270) 901-2165.

E-Mail Address: fun@bghotrods.com. **Website:** www.bghotrods.com.

Affiliation (first year): Tampa Bay Rays (2009). **Years in League:** 2009-

OWNERSHIP, MANAGEMENT

Operated By: Triple Play, LLC.

Owner: Art Solomon.

President: Rick Brenner. **General Manager/CEO:** Brad Taylor. **Assistant General Manager/Sales:** Greg Coleman. **Assistant General Manager/Operations:** Ken Clary. **Controller:** Leigh Witty. **Director, Administration:** Sally Lancaster. **Director, Broadcast/Media Relations:** Tom Gauthier. **Director, Merchandise:** Kyle Hanrahan. **Head Turf Manager:** Ray Sayre. **Stadium Operations Assistant:** Chase Elliott. **Production Manager:** Atlee McHeffey. **Ticket Operations Manager:** Whitney McKeon. **Box Office Manager:** Paul Reynolds. **Account Executives:** Keith Hetzer, Bailey Rolfs, Leslie Sanderfur. **Merchandise Assistant:** Ryan Renick. **Production Assistant:** Cameron Wengrzyn. **Marketing/Sales Assistant:** Shari Krakauer.

FIELD STAFF

Manager: Matt Quatraro. **Coach:** Hector Torres. **Pitching Coach:** R.C. Lichtenstein. **Trainer:** Nick Medina.

GAME INFORMATION

Radio Announcer: Tom Gauthier. **No. of Games Broadcast:** Home-70, Away-70. **Flagship Station:** WBGN 1340-AM.

PA Announcer: Unavailable. **Official Scorer:** Unavailable.

Stadium Name: Bowling Green Ballpark. **Location:** From I-65, take Exit 26 (KY-234/Cemetery Road) into Bowling Green for 3.2 miles, Left onto South Kentucky Street for 0.2 miles, Left onto 8th Avenue. **Standard Game Times:** Mon.-Thurs.: 6:35 p.m. (April, Aug.), 7:05 (May-July); Fri. 7:05; Sat. 1:05 (April), 7:05 (May-Sept.); Sun. 1:05. **Ticket Prices:** $5-10.

Visiting Club Hotel: Candlewood Suites, 540 Wall Street, Bowling Green, KY 42104. **Telephone:** (270) 843-5505.

CHARLESTON RIVERDOGS

Office Address: 360 Fishburne St., Charleston, SC 29403.
Mailing Address: P.O. Box 20849, Charleston, SC 29413.
Telephone: (843) 723-7241. **Fax:** (843) 723-2641.
E-Mail Address: admin@riverdogs.com. **Website:** www.riverdogs.com.
Affiliation (first year): New York Yankees (2005). **Years in League:** 1973-78, 1980-.

OWNERSHIP, MANAGEMENT

Operated by: The Goldklang Group/South Carolina Baseball Club LP.

Chairman: Marv Goldklang. **President:** Mike Veeck. **Director of Fun:** Bill Murray. **Co-Owner:** Dr. Gene Budig.

General Manager: Dave Echols. **Assistant GMs:** Andy Lange, Jim Pfander. **Director, Sales/Operations:** Harold Craw. **Director, Media Relations:** Andy Solomon. **Business Manager:** Dale Stickney. **Director, Special Events:** Melissa McCants. **Assistant Director, Special Events:** Megan Chambers. **Director, Food/Beverage:** Wil Lindsay. **Assistant Director, Food/Beverage:** Mike DeNicola. **Sales Managers:** Jake Terrell, Mike Petrini, Night Train Veeck. **Office Manager:** Kristal Lessington. **Director, Mascot Development:** Jamie Ballentine. **Payroll:** Aubra Carlton. **Director, Community Relations:** Lavon Alls. **Director, Merchandise:** Mike DeAntonio. **Box Office Manager:** Noel Blaha. **Head Groundskeeper:** Mike Williams.

FIELD STAFF

Manager: Torre Tyson. **Hitting Coach:** Greg Colbrunn. **Pitching Coach:** Jeff Ware. **First-Base Coach:** Sherman Obando. **Trainer:** Scott DiFrancesco.

GAME INFORMATION

Radio Announcer: Danny Reed. **No. of Games Broadcast:** Home-70, Away-70. **Flagship Station:** WTMZ 910-AM.

PA Announcer: Ken Carrington. **Official Scorer:** Chuck Manka.

Stadium Name: Joseph P. Riley Jr. Ballpark. **Location:** From U.S. 17, take Lockwood Drive North, right on Fishburne Street. **Standard Game Times:** 7:05 p.m., Sun. 5:05. **Ticket Price Range:** $5-12.

Visiting Club Hotel: Best Western, 250 Spring St., Charleston, SC 29403.
Telephone: (843) 722-4000.

DELMARVA SHOREBIRDS

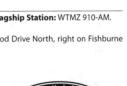

Office Address: 6400 Hobbs Rd, Salisbury, MD 21804.
Mailing Address: P.O. Box 1557, Salisbury, MD 21802.
Telephone: (410) 219-3112. **Fax:** (410) 219-9164.
E-Mail Address: information@theshorebirds.com. **Website:** www.theshorebirds.com.
Affiliation (first year): Baltimore Orioles (1997). **Years in League:** 1996-.

OWNERSHIP, MANAGEMENT

Operated By: 7th Inning Stretch, LLP.

Directors: Tom Volpe, Pat Filippone.

General Manager: Chris Bitters. **Assistant GM/Director, Corporate Sales:** Jimmy Sweet. **Director, Community Relations:** Aubrey Pfau. **Ticket Office Manager:** Brandon Berns. **Director, Stadium Operations:** Aaron Becker. **Head Groundskeeper:** Dave Super. **Assistant Groundskeeper:** Caroline Beauchamp. **Director, Marketing:** Brian Patey. **Director, Ticket Operations:** Randy Atkinson. **Group Sales Manager:** Evan Wagner. **Group/Ticket Sales Managers:** David Bledsoe, Emily Horlacher, Jonathan Patrick. **Corporate Sales Manager:** Nick Hearn. **Accounting Manager:** Gail Potts. **Office Manager:** Audrey Vane.

FIELD STAFF

Manager: Orlando Gomez. **Coach:** Ryan Minor. **Pitching Coach:** Blaine Beatty. **Trainer:** Aaron Scott.

GAME INFORMATION

Radio Announcer: Randy Scott. **No of Games Broadcast:** Home-70 Road-70. **Flagship Station:** WTGM 960-AM.

PA Announcer: Jim Whittemore. **Official Scorer:** Gary Hicks.

Stadium Name: Arthur W. Perdue Stadium. **Location:** From U.S. 50 East, right on Hobbs Road; From U.S. 50 West, left on Hobbs Road. **Standard Game Times:** 7:05 p.m. **Ticket Price Range:** $4-12.

Visiting Club Hotel: Hampton Inn & Suites, 304 Prosperity Lane, Fruitland, MD 21826. **Telephone:** (410) 548-1282.

GREENSBORO GRASSHOPPERS

Office Address: 408 Bellemeade St., Greensboro, NC 27401.
Telephone: (336) 268-2255. **Fax:** (336) 273-7350.
E-Mail Address: info@gsohoppers.com. **Website:** www.gsohoppers.com.
Affiliation (first year): Florida Marlins (2003). **Years in League:** 1979-.

OWNERSHIP, MANAGEMENT

Operated By: Greensboro Baseball LLC.

Principal Owners: Cooper Brantley, Wes Elingburg, Len White.

President/General Manager: Donald Moore. **Vice President, Baseball Operations:** Katie Dannemiller. **CFO:** Jimmy Kesler. **Assistant GM/Head Groundskeeper:** Jake Holloway. **Assistant GM, Sales/Marketing:** Tim Vangel. **Director, Ticketing:** Kate Barnhill. **Executive Assistant:** Rosalee Brewer. **Director, Community Relations/Promotions:** Laura Damico. **Assistant Director, Stadium Operations:** Chad Green. **Assistant Groundskeeper:** Kaid Musgrave. **Director, Merchandise:** Yunhui Harris. **Director, Group Sales:** Brian Lee. **Group Sales Associates:** Travis Kerstetter, Todd Olson. **Director, Special Events/Hoppin' Fun:** Allison Moore. **Director, Creative Services:** Amanda Williams.

FIELD STAFF

Manager: Darin Everson. **Hitting Coach:** Charlie Corbell. **Pitching Coach:** Bobby Bell. **Trainer:** Julio Hernandez.

GAME INFORMATION

Radio Announcer: Andy Durham. **No. of Games Broadcast:** Home-70, Away-0. **Flagship Station:** WPET 950-AM.

PA Announcer: Jim Scott. **Official Scorer:** Unavailable.

Stadium Name: NewBridge Bank Park. **Location:** From I-85, take Highway 220 South (exit 36) to Coliseum Blvd, continue on Edgeworth Street, ballpark at corner of Edgeworth and Bellemeade Streets. **Ticket Price Range:** $6-9.

Visiting Club Hotel: Ramada Inn Conference Center/Coliseum, 2003 Athena Ct., Greensboro, NC 27407. **Telephone:** (336) 294-9922.

GREENVILLE DRIVE

Office Address: 945 South Main St, Greenville, SC 29601.

Telephone: (864) 240-4500. **Fax:** (864) 240-4501.

E-Mail Address: info@greenvilledrive.com. **Website:** www.greenvilledrive.com.

Affiliation (first year): Boston Red Sox (2005). **Years in League:** 2005-

OWNERSHIP, MANAGEMENT

Operated By: RB3 LLC.

Co-Owner/President: Craig Brown.

General Manager: Mike deMaine. **Senior Vice President:** Nate Lipscomb. **Director, Finance:** Cathy Boortz. **Director, Ticket Operations:** Paul Ortenzo. **Director, Group Sales:** Andy Paul. **Director, Marketing Services:** Mike Bonasia. **Director, Ballpark Operations:** Blake Wilson. **Operations Manager:** Justin Miller. **Director, Media Relations:** Eric Jarinko. **Director, Merchandise:** Renee Allen. **Director, Food/Beverage:** Jeff Cirelli. **Producer, Game Entertainment:** Jeremiah Dew. **Entertainment Production Manager:** Jon Eckert. **Corporate Marketing Managers:** Tosh Anderson, Jordan Kinder, Stacy Morgan, Derick Stewart. **Head Groundskeeper:** Greg Burgess.

FIELD STAFF

Manager: Kevin Boles. **Hitting Coach:** Billy McMillon. **Pitching Coach:** Bob Kipper. **Trainer:** Brandon Henry.

GAME INFORMATION

Radio: None.

PA Announcer: Joe Trusty. **Official Scorer:** Sanford Rogers.

Stadium Name: Fluor Field. **Location:** From south: I-85N to exit 42 toward downtown Greenville, turn left onto Augusta Road, stadium is two miles on the left. **From north:** I-85S to I-385 toward Greenville, turn left onto Church Street, turn right onto University Ridge. **Standard Game Times:** 7 p.m.; Sun. 2. **Ticket Price Range:** $5-8.

Visiting Club Hotel: Confort Inn & Suites, 831 Congaree Road, Greenville, SC 29607. **Telephone:** (864) 288-6221.

HAGERSTOWN SUNS

Office Address: 274 E. Memorial Blvd., Hagerstown, MD 21740.

Telephone: (301) 791-6266. **Fax:** (301) 791-6066.

E-Mail Address: info@hagerstownsuns.com. **Website:** www.hagerstownsuns.com.

Affiliation (first year): Washington Nationals (2007). **Years in League:** 1993-

OWNERSHIP, MANAGEMENT

Principal Owner/Operated by: Mandalay Baseball Properties LLC.

President/General Manager: Bob Flannery. **Director, Business Operations:** Carol Gehr. **Director, Corporate Partnerships:** Joel Pagliaro. **Director, Stadium Operations/Head Groundskeeper:** Blake Bostelman. **Director, Food/Beverage:** Nick Bilski. **Director, Promotions/Special Events:** Reed Hunley. **Director, Ticket Sales/Merchandise:** Jason Bucur. **Director, Media Relations/Broadcasting:** Ryan Mock. **Interns:** Karl Micka-Foos, Eric Rosenwach. **Clubhouse Manager:** Lance Dunblazier.

FIELD STAFF

Manager: Matt LeCroy. **Hitting Coach:** Tony Tarasco. **Pitching Coach:** Rich Gale. **Coach:** Ramon Aviles. **Trainer:** Jeff Allred.

GAME INFORMATION

Radio Announcer: Ryan Mock. **No. of Games Broadcast:** Home-70, Away-70. **Flagship Station:** Unavailable.

PA Announcer: Karl Micka-Foos. **Official Scorer:** Chris Spaid.

Stadium Name: Municipal Stadium. **Location:** Exit 32B (U.S. 40 West) on I-70 West, left at Eastern Boulevard; Exit 6A (U.S. 40 East) on I-81, right at Eastern Boulevard. **Standard Game Times:** 7:05 p.m., 6:35 (April-May); Sun. 1:35, 5:35 (July-Sept.). **Ticket Price Range:** $5-13.

Visiting Club Hotel: Clarion Hotel & Conference Center, 901 Dual Hwy., Hagerstown, MD 21740. **Telephone:** (301) 733-5100.

HICKORY CRAWDADS

Office Address: 2500 Clement Blvd. NW, Hickory, NC 28601.
Mailing Address: P.O. Box 1268, Hickory, NC 28603.
Telephone: (828) 322-3000. **Fax:** (828) 322-6137.
E-Mail Address: crawdad@hickorycrawdads.com. **Website:** www.hickorycrawdads.com.
Affiliation (first year): Texas Rangers (2009). **Years in League:** 1952, 1960, 1993-

OWNERSHIP, MANAGEMENT

Operated by: Hickory Baseball Inc.

Principal Owners: Don Beaver, Luther Beaver, Charles Young.

President: Don Beaver. **General Manager:** Mark Seaman. **Assistant GM:** Charlie Downs. **Sales Account Executive:** Mark Parker. **Director, Ticket Operations:** Beth Stauffer. **Director, Promotions:** Brett Koch. **Director, Community Relations:** Ashby Knack. **Head Groundskeeper:** Stuart Morris. **Director, Stadium Operations:** Tony Iliano. **Director, Food/Beverage:** Erik Bernard. **Sales Representatives:** Kathryn Bobel, Blake Boswell, Michael Beshears, Kyle Koch.

FIELD STAFF

Manager: Hector Ortiz. **Hitting Coach:** Brian Dayett. **Pitching Coach:** Unavailable. **Trainer:** Jeff Bodenheimer. **Strength/Conditioning:** Ryan McNeal.

GAME INFORMATION

Radio Announcer: Unavailable. **No. of Games Broadcast:** Home-70, Away-70. **Flagship Station:** WMNC 92.1-FM.

PA Announcers: JuJu Phillips, Ralph Mangum, Jason Savage. **Official Scorer:** Gary Olinger.

Stadium Name: L.P. Frans Stadium. **Location:** I-40 to exit 123 (Lenoir North), 321 North to Clement Blvd., left for 1/2 mile. **Standard Game Times:** 7 p.m.; Sun. 3.

Visiting Club Hotel: Crowne Plaza, 1385 Lenior-Rhyne Boulevard SE, Hickory, NC 28602. **Telephone:** (828) 323-1000.

KANNAPOLIS INTIMIDATORS

Office Address: 2888 Moose Rd., Kannapolis, NC 28083.
Mailing Address: P.O. Box 64, Kannapolis, NC 28082.
Telephone: (704) 932-3267. **Fax:** (704) 938-7040.
E-Mail Address: info@intimidatorsbaseball.com. **Website:** www.intimidatorsbaseball.com.
Affiliation (first year): Chicago White Sox (2001). **Years in League:** 1995-

OWNERSHIP, MANAGEMENT

Operated by: Smith Family Baseball Inc.

President: Brad Smith.

Vice President: Tim Mueller. **General Manager:** Randy Long. **Director, Head Groundskeeper/Stadium Operations:** Billy Ball. **Director, Ticket Sales:** Jason Bright. **Director, Group Sales:** Greg Pizzuto. **Director, Broadcasting/Media Relations:** Alex Gyr. **Director, Operations/Sales Executive:** Michael Childers. **Interns:** Kara Bremer, Heath Dickes, Fran Faulkner, Tyler Kasischke, Tim Qua.

FIELD STAFF

Manager: Ernie Young. **Hitting Coach:** Greg Briley. **Pitching Coach:** Larry Owens. **Trainer:** Kevin Pillifant. **Strength/Conditioning Coach:** Tim Rodmaker.

GAME INFORMATION

Radio Announcer: Alex Gyr. **No. of Games Broadcast:** Home-70, Away-70. **Flagship Station:** www.intimidators-baseball.com.

PA Announcer: Shea Griffin. **Official Scorer:** Unavailable.

Stadium Name: Fieldcrest Cannon Stadium. **Location:** Exit 63 on I-85, west on Lane Street to Stadium Drive. **Standard Game Times:** 7:05 p.m., Sun. 5:05. **Ticket Price Range:** $3-8.

Visiting Club Hotel: Fairfield Inn by Marriott, 3033 Cloverleaf Pkwy., Kannapolis, NC 28083. **Telephone:** (704) 795-4888.

LAKE COUNTY CAPTAINS

Office Address: Classic Park, 35300 Vine Street, Eastlake, OH 44095-3142.
Telephone: (440) 975-8085. **Fax:** (440) 975-8958.
E-Mail Address: bseymour@captainsbaseball.com. **Website:** www.captainsbaseball.com.
Affiliation (first year): Cleveland Indians (2003). **Years in League:** 2003-

OWNERSHIP, MANAGEMENT

Operated By: Cascia, LLC.
Owners: Peter & Rita Carfagna, Ray & Katie Murphy.
Chairman/Secretary/Treasurer: Peter Carfagna. **Vice Chairman:** Rita Carfagna. **Vice President:** Ray Murphy. **Senior Vice President:** Pete E. Carfagna. **Vice President/General Manager:** Brad Seymour. **Assistant General Manager, Sales:** Neil Stein. **Senior Director, Media/Community Relations:** Craig Deas. **Director, Promotions:** Jonathan Levey. **Director, Captains Concessions:** John Klein. **Manager, Stadium Operations/Merchandise:** Aaron Levi. **Director, Turf Management/Stadium Operations:** Jared Olson. **Director, Finance:** Rob Demko. **Manager, Ticket Operations:** Jen Yorko. **Manager, Corporate Sales:** Alex Cvijetinovic. **Manager, Group Sales:** Amy Gladieux. **Account Representative, Group Sales:** Andrew Grover. **Account Representative, Group Sales:** Jeff Gates. **Account Representative, Group Sales:** Shannon O'Boyle. **Office Assistant:** Jim Carfagna.

FIELD STAFF

Manager: Aaron Holbert. **Hitting Coach:** Jim Rickon. **Pitching Coach:** Tony Arnold. **Trainer:** Jeremy Heller.

GAME INFORMATION.

Radio Announcer: Unavailable. **No. of Games Broadcast:** Home-70, Away-70. **Flagship Station:** WREO 97.1-FM.
PA Announcer: Ray Milavec. **Official Scorer:** Unavailable.
Stadium Name: Classic Park. **Location:** From Ohio State Route 2 East, exit at Ohio 91, go left and the stadium is 1/4 mile north on your right. From Ohio State Route 90 East, exit at Ohio 91, go right and the stadium in approximately five miles north on your right. **Standard Game Times:** 7 p.m., 6:30 (April-May), Sun. **1.**
Visiting Club Hotel: Comfort Inn & Suites, 7701 Reynolds Road, Mentor, OH 44060. **Telephone:** (440) 951-7333.

LAKEWOOD BLUECLAWS

Office Address: 2 Stadium Way, Lakewood, NJ 08701.
Telephone: (732) 901-7000. **Fax:** (732) 901-3967.
Email Address: info@blueclaws.com. **Website:** www.blueclaws.com.
Affiliation (first year): Philadelphia Phillies (2001). **Years in League:** 2001-

OWNERSHIP, MANAGEMENT

Operated By: American Baseball Company, LLC.
President: Joseph Finley. **Partners:** Joseph Caruso, Lewis Eisenberg, Joseph Plumeri, Craig Stein.
General Manager: Geoff Brown. **Assistant GM, Operations:** Brandon Marano. **Assistant GM, Sales:** Rich Mozingo. **Accounting Controller:** Bob Halsey. **Director, Community Relations:** Jim DeAngelis. **Director, Promotions:** Hal Hansen. **Director, Marketing:** Mike Ryan. **Director, Group Sales:** Jim McNamara. **Director, New Client Development:** Mike Van Hise. **Director, Business Development:** Dan DeYoung. **Director, Inside Sales:** Joe Harrington. **Director, Ticket Operations:** Rebecca Ramos. **Director, Food/Beverage Services:** Chris Tafrow. **Executive Chef:** Sandy Cohen. **Front Office Manager:** Jaimie Smith. **Marketing Manager:** Zack Rosenberg. **Special Events Manager:** Lisa Carone. **Special Events Manager:** Steve Farago. **Corporate Sales Manager:** Joe Pilon. **Ticket Sales Manager:** Ross Pibal. **Ticket Sales Manager:** Ryan Strzalka. **Ticket Sales Manager:** Jon Muldowney. **Group Sales Manager:** Tracy Davis. **Group Sales Coordinator:** Julie Goldberg. **Merchandise Manager:** Tom Frye. **Concessions Manager:** Brendan Geary. **Media/Public Relations Manager:** Greg Giombarrese. **Head Groundskeeper:** Ryan Radcliffe. **Home Clubhouse Manager:** Russ Schaeffer. **Visiting Clubhouse Manager:** Tom Germano. **Assistants:** Layli Ameri, John Bailey, Ryan Bigler, Casey Coppinger, Josh Ellis, Josh Feinberg, Kevin Fenstermacher, Thomas Gibat, Kristin Kocielski, Andrew Halle, Kyle Lindquist, Diane Nadramia, Pierson Smythe, Alex Varone, Mark Zaiger, Brad Ziegler.

FIELD STAFF

Manager: Dusty Wathan. **Hitting Coach:** Greg Legg. **Pitching Coach:** Bob Milacki. **Trainer:** Mickey Kozack.

GAME INFORMATION

Radio Announcers: Greg Giombarrese, Josh Ellis. **No. of Games Broadcast:** Home-70, Road-70. **Flagship Station:** WOBM 1160-AM.
PA Announcers: Kevin Clark, Mike Gavin. **Official Scorer:** Joe Bellina.
Stadium Name: FirstEnergy Park. **Location:** Route 70 to New Hampshire Ave., north on New Hampshire for 2 1/2 miles to ballpark. **Standard Game Times:** 7:05 p.m., 6:35 (April-May); Sun. 1:05, 5:05 (July-Aug.). **Ticket Prices:** $6-11.
Visiting Team Hotel: Quality Inn of Toms River, 815 Route 37 West, Toms River, NJ 08755. **Telephone:** (732) 341-3400.

LEXINGTON LEGENDS

Office Address: 207 Legends Lane, Lexington, KY 40505.
Telephone: (859) 252-4487. **Fax:** (859) 252-0747.
E-Mail Address: webmaster@lexingtonlegends.com. **Website:** www.lexington-legends.com.
Affiliation (first year): Houston Astros (2001). **Years in League:** 2001-

OWNERSHIP, MANAGEMENT

Operated By: Ivy Walls Management Co.

Principal Owner: Bill Shea. **President/COO:** Alan Stein.

General Manager: Andy Shea. **Assistant GM:** Luke Kuboushek. **Vice President, Facilities:** Gary Durbin. **Director, Stadium Operations/Human Resource Manager:** Shannon Kidd. **Business Manager:** Jeff Black. **Financial Assistant:** Tina Wright. **Director, Marketing:** Seth Poteat. **Box Office Manager:** David Barry. **Director, Broadcasting/Media Relations:** Keith Elkins. **Account Executive:** Ron Borkowski. **Senior Sales Executives:** Justin Ball, Scott Tenney. **Executive Assistant/Community Relations:** Emily Crumrine. **Promotions Coordinator:** Mario Anderson. **Head Groundskeeper:** Chris Pearl. **Facility Specialist:** Steve Moore. **Receptionist:** Beverly Howard.

FIELD STAFF

Manager: Tom Lawless. **Coach:** Pete Rincon. **Pitching Coach:** Charley Taylor. **Trainer:** Jon Patton.

GAME INFORMATION

Radio Announcer: Keith Elkins. **No of Games Broadcast:** Home-70 Road-70. **Flagship Station:** WLXG 1300-AM.

PA Announcer: Unavailable. **Official Scorer:** Travis Weber.

Stadium Name: Applebee's Park. **Location:** From I-64/75, take exit 113, right onto North Broadway toward downtown Lexington for 1.2 miles, past New Circle Road (Highway 4), right into stadium, located adjacent to Northland Shopping Center. **Standard Game Times:** 7:05 p.m., 6:35 (April-May); Sun. 2:05 (April-May), 6:05 (June-Aug.). **Ticket Price Range:** $4-16.50.

Visiting Club Hotel: Ramada Inn and Conference Center, 2143 N. Broadway, Lexington, KY 40505. **Telephone:** (859) 299-1261.

ROME BRAVES

Office Address: State Mutual Stadium, 755 Braves Blvd., Rome, GA 30161.
Mailing Address: P.O. Box 5515, Rome, GA 30162.
Telephone: (706) 368-9388. **Fax:** (706) 368-6525.
E-Mail Address: rome.braves@braves.com. **Website:** www.romebraves.com.
Affiliation (first year): Atlanta Braves (2003). **Years in League:** 2003-.

OWNERSHIP, MANAGEMENT

Operated By: Atlanta National League Baseball Club Inc.

General Manager: Michael Dunn. **Assistant GM:** Jim Jones. **Director, Stadium Operations:** Eric Allman. **Director, Ticket Manager:** Doug Bryller. **Director, Food/Beverage:** Dave Atwood. **Manager, Special Projects:** Erin White. **Administrative Manager:** Libby Simonds. **Account Representatives:** John Layng, Robert Sturdivant. **Head Groundskeeper:** Mike Geiger. **Retail Manager:** Starla Roden. **Warehouse Operations Manager:** Terry Morgan. **Neighborhood Outreach Coordinator:** Laura Harrison.

FIELD STAFF

Manager: Randy Ingle. **Coach:** Bobby Moore. **Pitching Coach:** Jim Czajkowski. **Trainer:** Allan Chase.

GAME INFORMATION

Radio Announcer: Unavailable. **No. of Games Broadcast:** Home-70, Away-70. **Flagship Station:** WLAQ 1410-AM.

PA Announcer: Eddie Brock. **Official Scorer:** Ron Taylor.

Stadium Name: State Mutual Stadium. **Location:** I-75 North to exit 190 (Rome/Canton), left off exit and follow Highway 411/Highway 20 to Rome, right at intersection on Highway 411 and Highway 1 (Veterans Memorial Highway), stadium is at intersection of Veterans Memorial Highway and Riverside Parkway. **Ticket Price Range:** $4-10.

Visiting Club Hotel: Days Inn, 840 Turner McCall Blvd., Rome, GA 30161. **Telephone:** (706) 295-0400.

SAVANNAH SAND GNATS

Office Address: 1401 E. Victory Dr., Savannah, GA 31404.
Mailing Address: P.O. Box 3783, Savannah, GA 31414.
Telephone: (912) 351-9150. **Fax:** (912) 352-9722.
E-Mail Address: info@sandgnats.com. **Website:** www.sandgnats.com.
Affiliation (firt year): New York Mets (2007). **Years in League:** 1904-1915, 1936-1960, 1962, 1984-.

OWNERSHIP, MANAGEMENT

Operated By: Hardball Capital, LLC.

President: R.C. Reuteman.

General Manager: Bradley Dodson. **Director, Media Relations/Creative Services:** Mike Passanisi. **Director, Sales:** Ric Sisler. **Director, Tickets:** Dave Wellenzohn. **Senior Account Executive:** Jeff Bierly. **Director, Promotions:** Cristina Faiella. **Account Executive:** Chase Polhemus. **Director, Finance:** Tasha Drain. **Head Groundskeeper:** Andy Rock.

FIELD STAFF

Manager: Edgar Alfonzo. **Coaches:** J. Carrero/G. Greer. **Pitching Coach:** Marc Valdez.

GAME INFORMATION

Radio Announcer: Mike Passanisi. **No. of Games Broadcast:** Home-70, Away-0. **Flagship Station:** www.sandgnats.com.

PA Announcer: Unavailable. **Official Scorer:** Michael MacEachern.

Stadium Name: Historic Grayson Stadium. **Location:** I-16 to 37th Street exit, left on 37th, right on Abercorn Street, left on Victory Drive; From I-95 to exit 16, east on 204, right on Victory Drive, Stadium is on right in Daffin Park. **Standard Game Times:** 7 p.m., Sun. 2. **Ticket Price Range:** $7-10.

Visiting Club Hotel: Unavailable.

WEST VIRGINIA POWER

Office Address: 601 Morris St, Suite 201, Charlestown, WV 25301.
Telephone: (304) 344-2287. **Fax:** (304) 344-0083.
E-Mail Address: team@wvpower.com. **Website:** www.wvpower.com.
Affiliation (first year): Pittsburgh Pirates (2009). **Years in League:** 1987-

OWNERSHIP, MANAGEMENT

Operated By: Palisades Baseball.

Principal Owner: Alan Levin.

Executive Vice President: Andy Milovich. **General Manager:** Joe Payne. **Director, Group Sales:** Jeremy Taylor. **Director, Tickets:** Mike Link. **Director, Marketing:** Kristin Call. **Director, Promotions:** Dan Helm. **Director, Client Services:** Alex Harris. **Director, Concessions:** Jeff Meehan. **Accountant:** Kim Hill. **Receptionist:** Terri Byrd. **Director, Catering:** Shawn Huffman. **Box Office Manager:** Dan Cudoc. **Groundskeeper:** Brian Eiche. **Director, Broadcast/Media Relations:** Andy Barch.

FIELD STAFF

Manager: Gary Green. **Coach:** Edgar Varela. **Pitching Coach:** Jeff Johnson. **Trainer:** Unavailable.

GAME INFORMATION

Radio Announcer: Andy Barch. **No. of Games Broadcast:** Home-70, Away-70. **Flagship Station:** WSWW 1490-AM.

PA Announcer: Donald Cook. **Official Scorer:** Lee France.

Stadium Name: Appalachian Power Park. **Location:** I-77 South to Capitol Street exit, left on Lee Street, left on Brooks Street. **Standard Game Times:** 7:05 p.m., Sun. 2:05 (April-May); 5:05 (June-Sept.). **Ticket Price Range:** $6-8.

Visiting Club Hotel: Ramada Plaza Hotel, 400 Second Avenue, South Charleston, WV 25303. **Telephone:** (304) 744-4641.

NEW YORK-PENN LEAGUE

SHORT-SEASON

Mailing Address: 6161 MLK Street North, Suite 205, St. Petersburg, FL 33703.
Telephone: (727) 289-7112. **Fax:** (727) 683-9691.

Website: www.newyork-pennleague.com.
Years League Active: 1939–
President: Ben J. Hayes.
President Emeritus: Robert F. Julian. **Treasurer:** Jon Dandes (Jamestown).

Ben Hayes

Directors: Tim Bawmann (Lowell), Steve Cohen (Brooklyn), Jon Dandes (Jamestown), Jeff Eiseman (Aberdeen), Tom Ganey (Auburn), Bill Gladstone (Tri-City), Jeff Goldklang (Hudson Valley), Chuck Greenberg (State College), CJ Knudsen (Vermont), Michael Savit (Mahoning Valley), E. Miles Prentice (Oneonta), Naomi Silver (Batavia), Art Matin (Staten Island), Paul Velte (Williamsport).

League Historian: Charles Wride.

Division Structure: McNamara—Aberdeen, Brooklyn, Hudson Valley, Staten Island. **Pinckney**—Auburn, Batavia, Jamestown, Mahoning Valley, State College, Williamsport. **Stedler**—Lowell, Oneonta, Tri-City, Vermont.

Regular Season: 76 games. **2009 Opening Date:** June 19. **Closing Date:** Sept. 6. **All-Star Game:** Aug. 18 at State College. **Hall of Fame Game:** Tri-City vs. Oneonta, July 25 in Cooperstown.

Playoff Format: Division winners and wild-card team meet in best-of-three semifinals. Winners meet in best-of-three series for league championship.

Roster Limit: 30 active, but only 25 may be in uniform and eligible to play in any given game. **Player Eligibility Rule:** No more than four players 23 or older; no more than three players on active list may have four or more years of prior service. **Brand of Baseball:** Rawlings. **Umpires:** Unavailable.

STADIUM INFORMATION

			Dimensions				
Club	Stadium	Opened	LF	CF	RF	Capacity	2007 Att.
Aberdeen	Ripken Stadium	2002	310	400	310	6,000	247,836
Auburn	Falcon Park	1995	330	400	330	2,800	64,052
Batavia	Dwyer Stadium	1996	325	400	325	2,600	43,167
Brooklyn	KeySpan Park	2001	315	412	325	7,500	265,220
Hudson Valley	Dutchess Stadium	1994	325	400	325	4,494	150,525
Jamestown	Russell E. Diethrick Jr. Park	1941	335	410	353	3,324	48,070
Lowell	Edward LeLacheur Park	1998	337	400	302	5,000	194,167
Mahoning Valley	Eastwood Field	1999	335	405	335	6,000	123,364
Oneonta	Damaschke Field	1906	350	406	350	4,200	39,609
State College	Medlar Field at Lubrano Park	2006	328	403	322	5,412	153,350
Staten Island	Richmond County Bank Ballpark	2001	325	400	325	6,500	189,876
Tri-City	Joseph L. Bruno Stadium	2002	325	400	325	5,000	140,631
Vermont	Centennial Field	1922	330	405	323	4,400	91,351
Williamsport	Bowman Field	1923	345	405	350	4,200	64,227

ABERDEEN IRONBIRDS

Office Address: 873 Long Drive, Aberdeen, MD 21001.
Telephone: (410) 297-9292. **Fax:** (410) 297-6653.
E-Mail Address: info@ironbirdsbaseball.com. **Website:** www.ironbirdsbaseball.com.
Affiliation (eighth year): Baltimore Orioles (2002). **Years in League:** 2002-

OWNERSHIP, MANAGEMENT

Operated By: Ripken Professional Baseball LLC.
Principal Owner: Cal Ripken Jr. **Co-Owner/Executive Vice President:** Bill Ripken. **VP:** Jeff Eiseman.
General Manager: Aaron Moszer. **Director, Sales:** Lev Shellenberger. **Director, Ticket Operations:** Brad Cox. **Director, Retail Merchandising:** Don Eney. **Manager, Facilities:** Dino Profili. **Head Groundskeeper:** Chris Walsh.

FIELD STAFF

Manager: Gary Kendall. **Coach:** Cesar Devarez. **Pitching Coach:** Scott McGregor. **Trainer:** Unavailable.

GAME INFORMATION

Radio Announcer: Unavailable. **No. of Games Broadcast:** Home-38, Away-38. **Flagship Station:** Unavailable.
PA Announcer: Jay Szech. **Official Scorer:** Joe Stetka.
Stadium Name: Ripken Stadium. **Location:** I-95 to exit 85 (Route 22), west on 22 West, right onto Long Drive. **Ticket**

Price Range: $6-15.
Visiting Club Hotel: Marriott Courtyard Aberdeen at Ripken Stadium. **Telephone:** 410-272-0440.

AUBURN DOUBLEDAYS

Office Address: 130 N. Division St., Auburn, NY 13021.
Telephone: (315) 255-2489. **Fax:** (315) 255-2675.
E-Mail Address: ddays@auburndoubledays.com. **Website:** www.auburndoubledays.com.
Affiliation (first year): Toronto Blue Jays (2001). **Years in League:** 1958-80, 1982-

OWNERSHIP, MANAGEMENT

Operated by: Auburn Community Non-Profit Baseball Association Inc.
CEO: Tom Ganey.
General Manager: Carl Gutelius. **Assistant GM:** Chris Reed. **Head Groundskeeper:** Rich Wild. **Director, Media/ Public Relations:** Unavailable.

FIELD STAFF

Manager: Dennis Holmberg. **Coach:** Charles Poe. **Pitching Coach:** Vince Horsman. **Trainer:** Daniel McIntosh.

GAME INFORMATION

Radio Announcer: Unavailable. **No of Games Broadcast:** Home-38 Away-38. **Flagship Station:** WAUB 1590-AM.
PA Announcer: Unavailable. **Official Scorer:** Unavailable.
Stadium Name: Falcon Park. **Location:** I-90 to exit 40, right on Route 34 for 8 miles to York Street, right on York, left on North Division Street. **Standard Game Times:** 7 p.m.; Sat.-Sun. 6. **Ticket Price Range:** $4-7.
Visiting Club Hotel: Days Inn, 37 Williams St., **Auburn, NY 13021. Telephone:** (315) 252-7567.

BATAVIA MUCKDOGS

Office Address: Dwyer Stadium, 299 Bank St, Batavia, NY 14020.
Telephone: (585) 343-5454. **Fax:** (585) 343-5620.
E-Mail Address: info@muckdogs.com. **Website:** www.muckdogs.com.
Affiliation (first year): St. Louis Cardinals (2007). **Years in League:** 1939-53, 1957-59, 1961-

OWNERSHIP, MANAGEMENT

Operated By: Red Wings Management, LLC.
General Manager, Baseball Operations: Travis Sick. **General Manager, Stadium Operations:** Casey Freeman. **Clubhouse Operations:** Tony Pecora.

FIELD STAFF

Manager: Mark DeJohn. **Hitting Coach:** Ramon Ortiz. **Pitching Coach:** Tim Leveque. **Trainer:** Manabu Kuwazuru.

GAME INFORMATION

Radio Announcer: Pat Melacaro. **No. of Games Broadcast:** Home-38 Away-12.
Flagship Station: WBTA 1490-AM. **PA Announcer:** Wayne Fuller. **Official Scorer:** Wayne Fuller. **Stadium Name:** Dwyer Stadium.
Location: I-90 to exit 48, left on Route 98 South, left on Richmond Avenue, left on Bank Street.
Standard Game Times: 7:05 p.m.; Sun. 5:05. **Ticket Price Range:** $5-7.
Visiting Club Hotel: Days Inn of Batavia, 200 Oak St., Batavia, NY 14020. **Telephone:** (585) 343-1440.

BROOKLYN CYCLONES

Office Address: 1904 Surf Ave, Brooklyn, NY 11224.
Telephone: (718) 449-8497. **Fax:** (718) 449-6368.
E-Mail Address: info@brooklyncyclones.com. **Website:** www.brooklyncyclones.com.
Affiliation (first year): New York Mets (2001). **Years in League:** 2001-

OWNERSHIP, MANAGEMENT

Chairman, CEO: Fred Wilpon.
President: Saul Katz. **COO:** Jeff Wilpon.
General Manager: Steve Cohen. **Assistant GM:** Kevin Mahoney. **Director, Communications:** Dave Campanaro. **Director, New Business Development:** Gary Perone. **Community Relations:** Sharon Lundy-Ross. **Group Sales Manager:** Joyce Huang. **Community Relations Manager:** Elizabeth Lombardi. **Operations Manager:** Vladimir Lipsman. **Video Production Manager:** Brendan McKeon. **Graphics Manager:** Kevin Jimenez. **Senior Accountant:** Sharif Soliman. **Staff Accountant:** Tatiana Isdith. **Accounts Payable Assistant:** Olena Gets. **Administrative Assistant, Ticket Manager:** Chris Nervegna. **Head Groundskeeper:** Kevin Ponte. **Account Executives:** Brandy Bercier, Katie Grenda, John Haley, Pat Toy, Ricky Viola.

FIELD STAFF

Manager: Pedro Lopez. **Hitting Coach:** Jack Voigt. **Pitching Coach:** Rick Tomlin.

GAME INFORMATION

Radio Announcer: Warner Fusselle. **No. of Games Broadcast:** Home-38, Away-38. **Flagship Station:** WKRB 90.3-FM.

PA Announcer: Dave Freeman. **Official Scorer:** Rose DeInnocentis.

Stadium Name: KeySpan Park. **Location:** Belt Parkway to Cropsey Ave. South, continue on Cropsey until it becomes West 17th St.; continue to Surf Ave., stadium on south side of Surf Ave. By subway, west/south to Stillwell Ave./Coney Island station. **Ticket Price Range:** $6-16.

Visiting Club Hotel: Staten Island Hotel, 1415 Richmond Ave, Staten Island, NY 10314. **Telephone:** (718) 698-5000.

HUDSON VALLEY RENEGADES

Office Address: Dutchess Stadium, Route 9D, Wappingers Falls, NY 12590.
Mailing Address: P.O. Box 661, Fishkill, NY 12524.
Telephone: (845) 838-0094. **Fax:** (845) 838-0014.
E-Mail Address: gadesinfo@hvrenegades.com. **Website:** www.hvrenegades.com.
Affiliation (first year): Tampa Bay Rays (1996). **Years in League:** 1994-.

OWNERSHIP, MANAGEMENT

Operated by: Keystone Professional Baseball Club Inc.

Principal Owner: Marv Goldklang. **President:** Jeff Goldklang.

General Manager: Eben Yager. **Assistant GM:** Corey Whitted. **Director, Food Services/Sales Manager:** Joe Ausanio. **Director, Media Relations:** Rick Kubitschek. **Director, Sales/Marketing:** Jack Weatherman. **Director, Ticket Sales:** Annie Rapalje. **Director, Customer Service:** Kristen Huss. **Sales Account Executive:** Kaitlin Lambert. **Community Relations Specialist:** Bob Outer. **Director, Mascot Entertainment:** Lisa Fulton. **Director, Business Operations:** Vicky DeFreese. **Director, Special Events/Renegades Charitable Foundation:** Rick Zolzer. **Entertainment Director/Assistant Director, PFK:** Eddie Cunningham. **Director, Promotions:** Andy Wilmert. **Director, Stadium Operations:** Tom Hubmaster. **Head Groundskeeper:** Evan Bardua. **Clubhouse Manager:** Anthony Dunnagan.

FIELD STAFF

Manager: Brady Williams. **Coaches:** Manny Castillo/Michael Johns. **Pitching Coach:** Rafael Montalvo. **Trainer:** Scott Thurston.

GAME INFORMATION

Radio Announcer: Unavailable. **No. of Games Broadcast:** Home-38, Away-38. **Flagship Stations:** WBNR 1260-AM/WLNA 1420-AM.

PA Announcer: Rick Zolzer. **Official Scorers:** Unavailable.

Stadium Name: Dutchess Stadium. **Location:** I-84 to exit 11 (Route 9D North), north one mile to stadium. **Standard Game Times:** 7:05 p.m.; Sun. 5:05.

Visiting Club Hotel: Ramada Inn, 20 Schuyler Blvd. and Route 9, Fishkill, NY 12524. **Telephone:** (845) 896-4995.

JAMESTOWN JAMMERS

Office Address: 485 Falconer St, Jamestown, NY 14701.
Mailing Address: P.O. Box 638, Jamestown, NY 14702.
Telephone: (716) 664-0915. **Fax:** (716) 664-4175.
E-Mail Address: email@jamestownjammers.com. **Website:** www.jamestownjammers.com.
Affiliation (first year): Florida Marlins (2002). **Years in League:** 1939-57, 1961-73, 1977-.

OWNERSHIP, MANAGEMENT

Operated By: Rich Baseball Operations.

President: Robert Rich Jr. **Chief Operating Officer:** Jonathon Dandes.

General Manager: Matthew Drayer. **Assistant GM:** George Sisson. **Director, Head Groundskeeper:** Jamie Bloomquist.

FIELD STAFF

Manager: Andy Haines. **Coach:** Frank Moore. **Pitching Coach:** Steve Watson. **Trainer:** Patrick Amorelli.

GAME INFORMATION

Radio: Unavailable.

PA Announcer: Unavailable. **Official Scorer:** Rim Riggs.

Stadium Name: Russell E. Diethrick Jr Park. **Location:** From I-90, south on Route 60, left on Buffalo Street, left on Falconer Street. **Standard Game Times:** 7:05 p.m.; Sun. 6:05. **Ticket Price Range:** $4.50-7.

Visiting Club Hotel: Red Roof Inn, 1980 Main St., Falconer, NY 14733. **Telephone:** (716) 665-3670.

LOWELL SPINNERS

Office Address: 450 Aiken St, Lowell, MA 01854.
Telephone: (978) 459-2255. **Fax:** (978) 459-1674.
E-Mail Address: generalinfo@lowellspinners.com. **Website:** www.lowellspinners.com.
Affiliation (first year): Boston Red Sox (1996). **Years in League:** 1996-

OWNERSHIP, MANAGEMENT

Operated By: Diamond Action Inc.
Owner/CEO: Drew Weber.
Vice President/General Manager: Tim Bawmann. **VP, Business Operations:** Brian Lindsay. **VP, Corporate Communications:** Jon Goode. **Controller:** Priscilla Harbour. **Director, Stadium Operations:** Dan Beaulieu. **Director, Facility Management:** Gareth Markey. **Media Relations Manager:** Jon Boswell. **Director, Merchandising:** Jeff Cohen. **Director, Ticket Group Sales:** Jon Healy. **Director, Ticket Operations:** Justin Williams. **Head Groundskeeper:** Jeff Paolino. **Clubhouse Manager:** Del Christman.

FIELD STAFF

Manager: Gary DiSarcina. **Hitting Coach:** Luis Lopez. **Pitching Coach:** Kevin Walker. **Trainer:** David Herrera

GAME INFORMATION

Radio Announcer: Ken Cail. **No. of Games Broadcast:** Home-38 Away-38. **Flagship Station:** WCAP 980-AM.
PA Announcer: George Brown. **Official Scorers:** David Rourke.
Stadium Name: Edward A. LeLacheur Park. **Location:** From Route 495 and 3, take exit 35C (Lowell Connector), follow connector to exit 5B (Thorndike Street) onto Dutton Street, left onto Father Morrissette Boulevard, right on Aiken Street. **Standard Game Times:** 7:05 p.m.; Sat.-Sun. 5:05. **Ticket Price Range:** $4-8.
Visiting Club Hotel: Doubletree Inn, 50 Warren St, Lowell, MA 01852. **Telephone:** (978) 452-1200.

MAHONING VALLEY SCRAPPERS

Office Address: 111 Eastwood Mall Blvd, Niles, OH 44446.
Mailing Address: 111 Eastwood Mall Blvd, Niles, OH 44446.
Telephone: (330) 505-0000. **Fax:** (303) 505-9696.
E-Mail Address: info@mvscrappers.com. **Website:** www.mvscrappers.com.
Affiliation (first year): Cleveland Indians (1999). **Years in League:** 1999-

OWNERSHIP, MANAGEMENT

Operated By: HWS Baseball Group.
Managing General Partner: Michael Savit.
General Manager: Dave Smith. **Assistant GM:** Jordan Taylor. **Director, Finance:** Debbie Primmer. **Director, Stadium Operations:** Dan Stricko. **Director, Concessions:** Brad Hooser. **Director, Promotions:** Billy Richards. **Director, Group Sales:** Matt Thompson. **Box Office Manager:** Stephanie Fife. **Creative Services Manager:** Jeff Holtke. **Ticket Sales Representatives:** Brad Ludwig, Marc Means. **Administrative Assistant:** Trish Trill.

FIELD STAFF

Manager: Travis Fryman. **Pitching Coach:** Ken Rowe. **Coach:** Phil Clark. **Trainer:** Issei Kamada.

GAME INFORMATION

Radio Announcer: Marc Means. **No. of Games Broadcast:** Home-38, Away-38. **Flagship Station:** WNIO 1390-AM.
PA Announcer: Unavailable. **Official Scorer:** Craig Antush.
Stadium Name: Eastwood Field. **Location:** I-80 to 11 North to 82 West to 46 South; stadium located behind Eastwood Mall. **Ticket Price Range:** $7-9.
Visiting Club Hotel: Days Inn & Suites, 1615 Liberty St., Girard, OH 44429. **Telephone:** (330) 759-9820

ONEONTA TIGERS

Office Address: 15 James Georgeson Ave., Oneonta, NY 13820.
Mailing Address: PO Box 1070, Oneonta, NY 13820
Telephone: (607) 432-6326. **Fax:** (607) 432-1965.
E-Mail Address: info@oneontatigers.com. **Website:** www.oneontatigers.com.
Affiliation (first year): Detroit Tigers (1999). **Years in League:** 1966-

OWNERSHIP, MANAGEMENT

Operated By: Oneonta Athletic Corp.

President: Miles Prenctice. **Executive Vice President:** John Gleason. **Executive Vice President:** Stephen Long. **Executive Vice President:** Bill Larkin. **General Manager:** Andrew Weber.

FIELD STAFF

Manager: Howard Bushong. **Hitting Coach:** Luis Quinones. **Pitching Coach:** Jorge Cordova. **Trainer:** Unavailable.

GAME INFORMATION

Radio: None.

PA Announcer: John Horne. **Official Scorer:** Tom Heitz.

Stadium Name: Damaschke Field. **Location:** Exit 15 off I-88. **Standard Game Times:** 7 p.m.; Sun. 6 p.m. **Ticket Price Range:** $5-10.

Visiting Club Hotel: Super 8 Motel, 4973 St Hwy 23, Oneonta, NY 13820. **Telephone:** (607) 432-9505.

STATE COLLEGE SPIKES

Office Address: Medlar Field, Lubrano Park, University Park, PA 16802.
Telephone: (814) 272-1711. **Fax:** (814) 272-1718.
Website: www.statecollegespikes.com
Affiliation (first year): Pittsburgh Pirates (2007). **Years in League:** 2006-.

OWNERSHIP, MANAGEMENT

Operated By: State College Professional Baseball LP.

Chairman/Managing Partner: Chuck Greenberg. **President:** Todd Parnell. **Executive Vice President:** Rick Janac.

General Manager: Jason Dambach. **Assistant General Manager:** Chris Phillips. **Director, Promotions/Community Relations:** Jen Orlando. **Director, Food/Beverage:** Unavailable. **Director, Stadium Operations:** Dan Petrazzolo. **Box Office Manager:** Ethan Stewart-Smith. **Administrative Assistant/Office Manager:** Rani Poague. **Ticket Sales Associates:** Brian Murphy, Scott Walker.

FIELD STAFF

Manager: Gary Robinson. **Hitting Coach:** Brandon Moore. **Pitching Coach:** Mike Steele. **Trainer:** Mike Zalno.

GAME INFORMATION

Radio Announcers: Steve Jones. **No of Games Broadcast:** Home-38 Road-38. **Flagship Station:** WZWW 95.3-FM.

PA Announcer: Dean Devore. **Official Scorer:** Dave Baker.

Stadium Name: Medlar Field at Lubrano Park. **Location:** From west, U.S. 322 to Mount Nittany Expressway, I-80 to exit 158 (old exit 23/Milesburg), follow Route 150 South to Route 26 South. From east, I-80 to exit 161(old exit 24/Bellefonte) to Route 26 South or U.S. 220/I-99 South. **Standard Game Times:** 7:05 p.m., Sun. 6:05. **Ticket Price Range:** $6-14.

Visiting Club Hotel: Ramada Conference Center State College, 1450 Atherton St., State College, PA 16801. **Telephone:** (814) 238-3001.

STATEN ISLAND YANKEES

Stadium Address: 75 Richmond Terrace, Staten Island, NY 10301.
Telephone: (718) 720-9265. **Fax:** (718) 273-5763.
Website: www.siyanks.com.
Affiliation (first year): New York Yankees (1999). **Years in League:** 1999-.

OWNERSHIP, MANAGEMENT

Operated by: Mandalay Baseball Properties.

Principal Owners: Staten Island Minor League Holdings LLC.

President: Joseph Ricciutti.

Executive Vice President/General Manager: Jane Rogers. **VP, Ticket Sales:** Jason Cohen. **Finance Manager:** Wayne Seguin. **Ticket Manager:** Matt Gulino. **Director, Entertainment:** Mike d'Amboise. **Directors, Corporate Partnerships:** Bob Gearing. **Manager, Corporate Partnerships:** Peter Honig, Director, Sponsor Services: Heidi Silber. **Manager, Sponsor Services:** Tak Mihara, Josh Derman. **Marketing Coordinator:** John McCutchan. **Marketing/Sales Coordinator:** Samantha DiTata. **Senior Corporate Marketing Manager:** Domenick Loccisano. **Group Sales Coordinators:** Mike Cummings, Tom Kurtz, Joe Kronander, Skip Russell, Matt Schulman, Allison Stadtmueller, Thomas Sheridan. **Customer Account Managers:** Tom Conway, Nicole Carballeira. **Director, Stadium Operations:** Robert Brown. **Manager, Stadium Operations:** Pete Derwin. **Groundskeeper:** Aaron Madill.

FIELD STAFF

Manager: Josh Paul. **Hitting Coach:** Ty Hawkins. **Pitching Coach:** Pat Daneker. **Trainer:** Brian Duncan.

GAME INFORMATION

Radio Announcer: Unavailable. **No. of Games Broadcast:** Home-38, Away-38. **Flagship Station:** Unavailable.

PA Announcer: Unavailable. **Official Scorer:** Unavailable.

Stadium Name: Richmond County Bank Ballpark at St. George. **Location:** From I-95, take exit 13E (1-278 and Staten Island), cross Goethals Bridge, stay on I-278 East and take last exit before Verrazano Narrows Bridge, north on Father Cappodanno Boulevard, which turns into Bay Street, which goes to ferry terminal; ballpark next to Staten Island Ferry Terminal. **Standard Game Times:** 7:00 p.m.; Sun 2. **Ticket Price Range:** $9-11.

Visiting Club Hotel: The Navy Lodge, 408 North Path Rd., Staten Island, NY 10305. **Telephone:** (718) 442-0413.

TRI-CITY VALLEYCATS

Office Address: Joseph L. Bruno Stadium, 80 Vandenburg Ave, Troy, NY 12180.
Mailing Address: P.O. Box 694, Troy, NY 12181.
Telephone: (518) 629-2287. **Fax:** (518) 629-2299.
E-Mail Address: info@tcvalleycats.com. **Website:** www.tcvalleycats.com.
Affiliation (first year): Houston Astros (2001). **Years in League:** 2002-

OWNERSHIP, MANAGEMENT

Operated By: Tri-City ValleyCats Inc.

Principal Owners: Martin Barr, John Burton, William Gladstone, Rick Murphy, Alfred Roberts, Stephen Siegel.

President: William Gladstone.

Vice President, General Manager: Rick Murphy. **Assistant GM:** Vic Christopher. **Senior Advisors:** William Rowan, Buddy Caruso. **Ticket/Merchandise Manager:** Heather LaVine. **Stadium Operations Manager:** Keith Sweeney. **Community Relations Manager:** Chris Turner. **Media Relations Manager:** Matt Van Pelt. **Business Development Manager:** Matt Callahan. **Account Executives:** Ryan Burke, Chris Deck, Joey Menz. **Bookkeeper:** Gene Gleason.

FIELD STAFF

Manager: Jim Pankovits. **Coach:** Joel Chimelis. **Pitching Coach:** Gary Ruby. **Trainer:** Brian Baca.

GAME INFORMATION

Radio Announcer:. **No. of Games Broadcast:** Home-38, Away-38. **Flagship Station:**.

PA Announcer: Anthony Pettograsso. **Official Scorer:** William Rowan.

Stadium Name: Joseph L. Bruno Stadium. **Location:** From north, I-87 to exit 7 (Route 7), go east 1½ miles to I-787 South, to Route 378 East, go over bridge to Route 4, right to Route 4 South, one mile to Hudson Valley Community College campus on left. From south, I-87 to exit 23 (I-787), I-787 north six miles to exit for Route 378 east, over bridge to Route 4, right to Route 4 South, one mile to campus on left. From east, Massachusetts Turnpike to exit B-1 (I-90), nine miles to Exit 8 (Defreestville), left off ramp to Route 4 North, five miles to campus on right. From west, I-90 to exit 24 (I-90 East), I-90 East for six miles to I-787 North (Troy), 2.2 miles to exit for Route 378 East, over bridge to Route 4, right to Route 4 south for one mile to campus on left. **Standard Game Times:** 7 p.m.; Sun. 5. **Ticket Price Range:** $5-10.

Visiting Club Hotel: Days Inn, 16 Wolf Rd, Albany, NY 12205. **Telephone:** (518) 459-3600.

VERMONT LAKE MONSTERS

Office Address: 1 King Street Ferry Dock, Burlington, VT 05401.
Telephone: (802) 655-4200. **Fax:** (802) 655-5660.
E-Mail Address: info@vermontlakemonsters.com. **Website:** www.vermontlakemonsters.com.
Affiliation (first year): Washington Nationals (2005). **Years in League:** 1994-

OWNERSHIP, MANAGEMENT

Operated by: Vermont Expos Inc.

Principal Owner/President: Ray Pecor.

General Manager: C.J. Knudsen. **Assistant GM:** Nate Cloutier. **Director, Community Relations/Promotions:** Denny Madigan. **Director, Media Relations:** Paul Stanfield. **Director, Stadium Operations:** Jim O'Brien. **Director, Special Projects:** Onnie Matthews. **Clubhouse Operations:** Phil Schelzo.

FIELD STAFF

Manager: Jeff Garber. **Hitting Coach:** Unavailable. **Pitching Coach:** Franklyn Bravo.

GAME INFORMATION

Radio Announcers: Rob Ryan, George Commo. **No. of Games Broadcast:** Home-38, Away-38. **Flagship Station:** The Zone 960-AM (delete 96.7 FM).

PA Announcer: Rich Haskell. **Official Scorer:** Ev Smith.

Stadium Name: Centennial Field. **Location:** I-89 to exit 14W, right on East Avenue for one mile, right at Colchester Avenue. **Standard Game Times:** 7:05 p.m.; Sun. 5:05. **Ticket Price Range:** $5-8.

Visiting Club Hotel: Comfort Inn & Suites, 5 Dorset St., South Burlington, VT 05403. **Telephone:** (802) 863-5541.

WILLIAMSPORT CROSSCUTTERS

Office Address: Bowman Field, 1700 W. Fourth St, Williamsport, PA 17701.
Mailing Address: P.O. Box 3173, Williamsport, PA 17701.
Telephone: (570) 326-3389. **Fax:** (570) 326-3494.
E-Mail Address: mail@crosscutters.com. **Website:** www.crosscutters.com.
Affiliation (first year): Philadelphia Phillies (2007). **Years in League:** 1968-72, 1994-

OWNERSHIP, MANAGEMENT

Operated By: Geneva Cubs Baseball Inc.

Principal Owners: Paul Velte, John Schreyer. **President:** Paul Velte. **Vice President:** John Schreyer.

Vice President, General Manager: Doug Estes. **Vice President, Marketing/Public Relations:** Gabe Sinicropi. **Director, Concessions:** Bill Gehron. **Director, Ticket Operations/Community Relations:** Sarah Budd. **Director, Client Services:** Jenny Hoover. **Head Groundskeeper:** Unavailable.

FIELD STAFF

Manager: Chris Truby. **Coach:** Bobby Meacham. **Pitching Coach:** Tom Filer.

GAME INFORMATION

Radio Announcer: Todd Bartley. **No. of Games Broadcast:** Home-38, Away-38. **Flagship Station:** WLYC 1050-AM., 104.1-FM.

PA Announcer: Rob Thomas. **Official Scorer:** Ken Myers.

Stadium Name: Bowman Field. **Location:** From south, Route 15 to Maynard Street, right on Maynard, left on Fourth Street for one mile. From north, Route 15 to Fourth Street, left on Fourth. **Ticket Price Range:** $4.50-7.

Visiting Club Hotel: Best Western, 1840 E. Third St, Williamsport, PA 17701. **Telephone:** (570) 326-1981.

NORTHWEST LEAGUE

NORTHWEST LEAGUE OF PROFESSIONAL BASEBALL

SHORT-SEASON

Bob Richmond

Office Address: 620 W. Franklin St., Boise, ID 83702.

Mailing Address: P.O. Box 1645, Boise, ID 83701.

Telephone: (208) 429-1511. **Fax:** (208) 429-1525.

E-Mail Address: bobrichmond@qwestoffice.net. **Website:** www.northwestleague.com.

Years League Active: 1954-.

President, Treasurer: Bob Richmond.

Vice President: Brent Miles. **Corporate Secretary:** Jerry Walker (Salem-Keizer).

Directors: Bob Beban (Eugene), Bobby Brett (Spokane), Tom Volpe (Everett), Jake Kerr (Vancouver), Mike McMurray (Yakima), Brent Miles (Tri-City), Jerry Walker (Salem-Keizer), Neil Leibman (Boise). **Administrative Assistant:** Rob Richmond.

Division Structure: East—Boise, Spokane, Tri-City, Yakima. **West**—Eugene, Everett, Salem-Keizer, Vancouver.

Regular Season: 76 games. **2009 Opening Date:** June 20. **Closing Date:** Sept. 6.

Playoff Format: Division winners meet in best-of-five series for league championship.

All-Star Game: None.

Roster Limit: 30 active, 35 under control. **Player Eligibility Rule:** No more than three players on active list may have four or more years of prior service.

Brand of Baseball: Rawlings.

Umpires: Unavailable.

STADIUM INFORMATION

			Dimensions				
Club	**Stadium**	**Opened**	**LF**	**CF**	**RF**	**Capacity**	**2008 Att.**
Boise	Memorial Stadium	1989	335	405	335	4,500	109,082
Eugene	Civic Stadium	1938	335	400	328	6,800	130,069
Everett	Everett Memorial Stadium	1984	330	395	330	3,682	95,294
Salem-Keizer	Volcanoes Stadium	1997	325	400	325	4,100	112,425
Spokane	Avista Stadium	1958	335	398	335	7,162	188,982
Tri-City	Dust Devils Stadium	1995	335	400	335	3,730	82,021
Vancouver	Nat Bailey Stadium	1951	335	395	335	6,500	129,073
Yakima	Yakima County Stadium	1993	295	406	295	3,000	72,207

BOISE HAWKS

Office Address: 5600 N. Glenwood St., Boise, ID 83714.

Telephone: (208) 322-5000. **Fax:** (208) 322-6846.

Website: www.boisehawks.com.

Affiliation (first year): Chicago Cubs (2001). **Years in League:** 1975-76, 1978, 1987-

OWNERSHIP, MANAGEMENT

Operated by: Boise Baseball LLC.

CEO: Neil Leibman.

President/General Manager: Todd Rahr. **Assistant GM/Director, Business Operations:** Dina Duncan. **Director, Sales/Marketing:** Andy Simon. **Director, Stadium Operations:** Jeff Israel. **Sponsorship Sales Manager:** Pete Korstad. **Ticket Sales Manager:** Danny Dunbar. **Manager, Client Services/Merchandise:** Kelly Kerkvliet. **Marketing Manager:** Kristen Nimmo. **Group Sales Coordinator:** Bryan McMartin. **Creative Services Manager:** Ken Hyde.

FIELD STAFF

Manager: Casey Kopitske. **Hitting Coach:** Desi Wilson. **Pitching Coach:** David Rosario. **Trainer:** Dan Golden.

GAME INFORMATION

Radio Announcer: Mike Safford. **No. of Games Broadcast:** Home-38, Away-38. **Flagship Station:** KTIK 1350-AM.

PA Announcer: Unavailable. **Official Scorer:** Unavailable.

Stadium Name: Memorial Stadium. **Location:** I-84 to Cole Road, north to Western Idaho Fairgrounds at 5600 North Glenwood Street. **Standard Game Time:** 7:15 p.m. **Ticket Price Range:** $6-10.

Visiting Club Hotel: Owyhee Plaza Hotel, 1109 Main St., Boise, ID 83702. **Telephone:** (208) 343-4611.

EUGENE EMERALDS

Office Address: 2077 Willamette St, Eugene, OR 97405.
Mailing Address: P.O. Box 5566, Eugene, OR 97405.
Telephone: (541) 342-5367. **Fax:** (541) 342-6089.
E-Mail Address: ems@go-ems.com. **Website:** www.go-ems.com.
Affiliation (first year): San Diego Padres (2001). **Years in League:** 1955-68, 1974-

OWNERSHIP, MANAGEMENT

Operated By: Elmore Sports Group Ltd.

Principal Owner: David Elmore.

President/General Manager: Bob Beban. **Assistant GMs:** Bryan Beban, Nathan Skalsky. **Director, Business Operations:** Eileen Beban. **Director, Food Services:** Phil Bopp. **Directors, Tickets/Special Events:** Koo Yul Kim, Travis Anderson. **Director, Stadium Operations:** David Puente. **Director, Media Relations:** Bryan Beban. **Grounds Superintendent:** Brian Burroughs.

FIELD STAFF

Manager: Greg Riddoch. **Coach:** Eric Payton. **Pitching Coach:** Bronswell Patrick. **Trainer:** Nate Stewart.

GAME INFORMATION

Radio Announcer: Matt McCabe. **No. of Games Broadcast:** Home-38, Away-38. **Flagship Station:** KPNW 1120-AM.

PA Announcer: Grant McHill. **Official Scorer:** George McPherson.

Stadium Name: Civic Stadium. **Location:** From I-5, take I-105 to Exit 2, stay left and follow to downtown, cross over Ferry Street Bridge to Eighth Avenue, left on Pearl Street, south to 20th Avenue. **Ticket Price Range:** $5.50-9.

Visiting Club Hotel: Shilo Inn Eugene/Springfield, 3350 Gateway Street, Springfield, OR 97477. **Telephone:** (541) 747-0332.

EVERETT AQUASOX

Mailing Address: 3802 Broadway, Everett, WA 98201.
Telephone: (425) 258-3673. **Fax:** (425) 258-3675.
E-Mail Address: aquasox@aquasox.com. **Website:** www.aquasox.com.
Affiliation (first year): Seattle Mariners (1995). **Years in League:** 1984-

OWNERSHIP, MANAGEMENT

Operated by: 7th Inning Stretch, LLC

Directors: Tom Volpe, Pat Filippone

Executive Vice President: Tom Backemeyer. **General Manager:** Brian Sloan. **Director, Broadcasting/Corporate Sales:** Pat Dillon. **Director, Ballpark Operations:** Jason Jarett. **Director, Food/Beverage:** Todd Holterhoff. **Director, Accounting:** Teresa Sarsted. **Director, Tickets:** Rick Dooley. **Account Executive:** Troy Sherry.

FIELD STAFF

Manager: John Tamargo. **Coach:** R. Santo Domingo. **Pitching Coach:** Unavailable.

GAME INFORMATION

Radio Announcer: Pat Dillon. **No. of Games Broadcast:** Home-38, Away-38. **Flagship Station:** KRKO 1380-AM.

PA Announcer: Tom Lafferty. **Official Scorer:** Pat Castro.

Stadium Name: Everett Memorial Stadium. **Location:** I-5, exit 192. **Standard Game Times:** 7:05 p.m., Sun. 1:05. **Ticket Price Range:** $7-15.

Visiting Club Hotel: Holiday Inn, Downtown Everett, 3105 Pine St., Everett, WA 98201. **Telephone:** (425) 339-2000.

SALEM-KEIZER VOLCANOES

Street Address: 6700 Field of Dreams Way NE, Keizer, OR 97303.
Mailing Address: P.O. Box 20936, Keizer, OR 97307.
Telephone: (503) 390-2225. **Fax:** (503) 390-2227.
E-Mail Address: probasebal@aol.com. **Website:** www.volcanoesbaseball.com.
Affiliation (first year): San Francisco Giants (1997). **Years in League:** 1997-

OWNERSHIP, MANAGEMENT

Operated By: Sports Enterprises Inc.

Principal Owners: Jerry Walker, Bill Tucker.

President/General Manager: Jerry Walker. **Vice President, Operations:** Rick Nelson. **Corporate Sponsorships:** Jerry Howard. **Media Relations:** Rick Nelson. **Director, Community Relations:** Kelly Hurst. **Corporate Ticket Sales:** Greg Herbst. **Director, Merchandising/Ticket Office Operations:** Bea Howard.

FIELD STAFF

Manager: Tom Trebelhorn. **Coach:** Ricky Ward. **Pitching Coach:** Hensley Meulens. **Trainer:** TBA.

GAME INFORMATION

Radio Announcer: Mark Gilman. **No. of Games Broadcast:** Home-38, Away-38. **Flagship Station:** KBZY AM-1490.

PA Announcer: Bill Post. **Official Scorer:** Dawn Hills.

Stadium Name: Volcanoes Stadium. **Location:** I-5 to exit 260 (Chemawa Road), west one block to Stadium Way NE, north six blocks to stadium. **Standard Game Times:** 6:35 p.m.; Fri-Sat. 7:05; Sun. 5:05. **Ticket Price Range:** $7-11.

Visiting Club Hotel: Comfort Suites, 630 Hawthorne Ave. SE, Salem, OR 97301. **Telephone:** (503) 585-9705.

SPOKANE INDIANS

Office Address: Avista Stadium, 602 N. Havana, Spokane, WA 99202.

Mailing Address: P.O. Box 4758, Spokane, WA 99220.

Telephone: (509) 535-2922. **Fax:** (509) 534-5368.

E-Mail Address: mail@spokaneindiansbaseball.com. **Website:** www.spokaneindians-baseball.com.

Affiliation (first year): Texas Rangers (2003). **Years in League:** 1972, 1983-

OWNERSHIP, MANAGEMENT

Operated By: Longball Inc.

Principal Owners: Bobby Brett, J.B. Brett. **President:** Andrew Billig.

Vice President, General Manager: Chris Duff. **Senior VP:** Otto Klein. **VP, Tickets:** Josh Roys. **Assistant GM:** Lesley DeHart. **Assistant GM, Promotions:** Sarah Travis. **Director, Sponsorships/Operations:** Matt Almond. **Director, Ticket Sales:** Ryan Donckers. **Director, Stadium Operations:** Dimitri Perera. **Director, Group Sales:** Sheldon Weddle. **Group Sales Coordinator:** Briana K'Burg. **Director, Hospitality:** Kyle Ewert. **Coordinator, Promotions:** Seth Moir. **CFO:** Greg Sloan. **Accounting:** Dawnelle Shaw. **Director, Public Relations:** Keenan Bowen. **Head Groundskeeper:** Brennan Prestley. **Assistant Director, Stadium Operations:** Larry Blummer.

FIELD STAFF

Manager: Tim Hulett. **Coach:** Jason Hart. **Pitching Coach:** Jeff Andrews. **Trainer:** Unavailable.

GAME INFORMATION

Radio Announcer: Bob Robertson. **No. of Games Broadcast:** Home-38, Away-38. **Flagship Station:** 1510 KGA.

PA Announcer: Unavailable. **Official Scorer:** Unavailable.

Stadium Name: Avista Stadium at the Spokane Fair and Expo Center. **Location:** From west, I-90 to exit 283B (Thor/Freya), east on Third Avenue, left onto Havana. From east, I-90 to Broadway exit, right onto Broadway, left onto Havana. **Standard Game Time:** 6:30 p.m. **Ticket Price Range:** $4-9.

Visiting Club Hotel: Mirabeau Park Hotel & Convention Center, N. 1100 Sullivan Rd, Spokane, WA 99037. **Telephone:** (509) 924-9000.

TRI-CITY DUST DEVILS

Office Address: 6200 Burden Blvd., Pasco, WA 99301.

Telephone: (509) 544-8789. **Fax:** (509) 547-9570.

E-Mail Address: info@dustdevilsbaseball.com. **Website:** www.dustdevilsbaseball.com.

Affiliation (first year): Colorado Rockies (2001). **Years in League:** 1955-1974, 1983-1986, 2001-.

OWNERSHIP, MANAGEMENT

Operated by: Northwest Baseball Ventures.

Principal Owners: George Brett, Hoshino Dreams Corp., Brent Miles.

President: Brent Miles. **Vice President/General Manager:** Monica Ortega. **VP, Business Operations:** Tim Gittel. **Assistant GM, Operations:** Garrett Flowers. **Director, Season Tickets:** Matt Nash. **Director, Sponsorships:** Kelli Foos. **Director, Group Sales:** Jesse Robinson. **Account Executive:** Dennis da Silva. **Sponsorships Coordinator:** Ryan Millard. **Stadium Operations Coordinator:** Jeff Volaski. **Head Groundskeeper:** Michael Angel.

FIELD STAFF

Manager: Freddie Ocasio. **Coach:** Anthony Sanders. **Pitching Coach:** Darryl Scott. **Trainer:** Andy Stover.

GAME INFORMATION

Radio Announcer: Mike Boyle. **No. of Games Broadcast:** Home-38, Away-38. **Flagship Station:** Unavailable.

PA Announcer: Patrick Harvey. **Official Scorers:** Tony Wise, Scott Tylinski.

Stadium Name: Gesa Stadium. **Location:** I-182 to exit 9 (Road 68), north to Burden Blvd., right to stadium. **Standard Game Time:** 7:15 p.m. **Ticket Price Range:** $5-9.

Visiting Club Hotel: Red Lion Hotel-Columbia Center, 1101 N. Columbia Center Blvd., Kennewick, WA 99336. **Telephone:** (509) 783-0611.

VANCOUVER CANADIANS

Office Address: Nat Bailey Stadium, 4601 Ontario St., Vancouver, British Columbia V5V 3H4.

Telephone: (604) 872-5232. **Fax:** (604) 872-1714.

E-Mail Address: staff@canadiansbaseball.com. **Website:** www.canadiansbaseball.com.

Affiliation (first year): Oakland Athletics (2000). **Years in League:** 2000-

OWNERSHIP, MANAGEMENT

Operated by: Vancouver Canadians Professional Baseball LLP.

Principal Owners: Jake Kerr, Jeff Mooney. **President:** Andy Dunn.

General Manager: Andrew Seymour. **Controller:** Dolores Sebellin. **Senior Director, Sales/Marketing:** Graham Wall. **Coordinator, Sales/Marketing:** Cynthia Wildman. **Manager, Group Sales:** Spiro Khouri. **Outside Sales Representitive:** Stephen Hopkins. **Director, Media Relations/Broadcast:** Rob Fai. **Director, Ticket Operations:** Jason Takefman. **Manager, Ticket Operations:** Allan Bailey. **Ballpark Operations Manager:** JC Fraser. **Head Groundskeeper:** Tom Archibald. **Assistant Groundskeeper:** Trevor Sheffield.

FIELD STAFF

Manager: Rick Magnante. **Coach:** Casey Myers. **Pitching Coach:** Craig Lefferts. **Trainer:** Travis Tims.

GAME INFORMATION

Radio Announcer: Rob Fai. **No. of Games Broadcast:** Home-38, Away-38. **Flagship Station:** The Team 1040-AM.

PA Announcer: Don Andrews. **Official Scorer:** Pat Karl.

Stadium Name: Nat Bailey Stadium. **Location:** From downtown, take Cambie Street Bridge, left on East 25th Ave./King Edward Ave., right on Main Street, right on 33rd Ave., right on Ontario St. to stadium. From south, take Highway 99 to Oak Street, right on 41st Ave., left on Main Street to 33rd Ave., right on Ontario St. to stadium. **Standard Game Times:** 7:05 p.m., Sun. 1:05. **Ticket Price Range:** $9-20.

Visiting Club Hotel: Accent Inns, 10551 Edwards Dr., Richmond, B.C. V6X 3L8. **Telephone:** (604) 273-3311.

YAKIMA BEARS

Office Address: 17 N. 3rd Street, Suite 101, Yakima, WA 98901.

Mailing Address: P.O. Box 483, Yakima, WA 98907.

Telephone: (509) 457-5151. **Fax:** (509) 457-9909.

E-Mail Address: info@yakimabears.com. **Website:** www.yakimabears.com.

Affiliation (first year): Arizona Diamondbacks (2001). **Years in League:** 1955-66, 1990-

OWNERSHIP, MANAGEMENT

Operated by: Short Season LLC.

Managing Partners: Mike McMurray, Mike Ellis, Josh Weinman, Myron Levin, Mike Ormsby.

President: Mike McMurray.

General Manager: K.L. Wombacher. **Assistant GM, Sales:** Aaron Arndt. **Director, Ballpark Operations:** Jared Jacobs. **Director, Ticket Operations:** Ryan Coffey. **Director, Group Sales:** Ricky Torres. **Director, Merchandise:** Lauren Wombacher. **Office Assistant/Reception:** Andrea Russell. **Head Groundskeeper:** Bill Brown. **Director, Media Relations/Broadcasting:** Drew Bontadelli. **Administrative Assistants:** Megan Welsch, Colin Goodman.

FIELD STAFF

Manager: Bob Didier. **Hitting Coach:** Andy Abad. **Pitching Coach:** Dan Carlson. **Trainer:** Ben Fraser. **Clubhouse Manager:** Tyler Harris.

GAME INFORMATION

Radio Announcer: Drew Bontadelli. **No. of Games Broadcast:** Home-38, Away-38. **Flagship Station:** KUTI 1460-AM.

PA Announcer: Todd Lyons. **Official Scorer:** Unknown at this time.

Stadium Name: Yakima County Stadium. **Location:** 1301 S. Fair Avenue. I-82 to exit 34 (Nob Hill Boulevard), west to Fair Avenue, right on Fair, right on Pacific Avenue. **Standard Game Times:** 7:05 p.m., Sun. 5:35 p.m. **Ticket Price Range:** $4.50-$9.50.

Visiting Club Hotel: Best Western Ahtanum Inn, 2408 Rudkin Rd., Union Gap, WA 98903. **Telephone:** (509) 248-9700.

APPALACHIAN LEAGUE

APPALACHIAN LEAGUE
of professional baseball clubs

ROOKIE ADVANCED

Mailing Address: 283 Deerchase Circle, Statesville, NC 28625.
Telephone: (704) 873-5300. **Fax:** (704) 873-4333.
E-Mail Address: appylg@hughes.net. **Website:** www.appyleague.com.

Years League Active: 1921-25, 1937-55, 1957-.

President, Treasurer: Lee Landers. **Corporate Secretary:** Jim Holland (Princeton).

Directors: Ricky Bennett (Greeneville), Pedro Grifol (Pulaski), Mitch Lukevics (Princeton), Scott Sharp (Burlington), Buddy Bell (Bristol), Len Johnston (Bluefield), Jeff Luhnow (Johnson City), Kurt Kemp (Danville), Adam Wogan (Kingsport), Jim Rantz (Elizabethton).

Lee Landers

League Administrator: Bobbi Landers.

Division Structure: East—Bluefield, Burlington, Danville, Princeton, Pulaski. **West**—Bristol, Elizabethton, Greeneville, Johnson City, Kingsport.

Regular Season: 68 games. **2009 Opening Date:** June 23. **Closing Date:** Sept 1.

All-Star Game: None.

Playoff Format: Division winners meet in best-of-three series for league championship.

Roster Limit: 35 active. **Player Eligibility Rule:** No more than two years of prior minor league service.

Brand of Baseball: Rawlings.

Umpires: Unavailable

STADIUM INFORMATION

			Dimensions				
Club	**Stadium**	**Opened**	**LF**	**CF**	**RF**	**Capacity**	**2008 Att.**
Bluefield	Bowen Field	1939	335	400	335	2,250	29,867
Bristol	DeVault Memorial Stadium	1969	325	400	310	2,000	21,696
Burlington	Burlington Athletic Stadium	1960	335	410	335	3,000	28,196
Danville	Dan Daniel Memorial Park	1993	330	400	330	2,588	39,534
Elizabethton	Joe O'Brien Field	1974	335	414	326	1,500	28,131
Greeneville	Pioneer Park	2004	331	400	331	2,400	51,806
Johnson City	Howard Johnson Field	1956	320	410	320	2,500	21,327
Kingsport	Hunter Wright Stadium	1995	330	410	330	2,500	38,589
Princeton	Hunnicutt Field	1988	330	396	330	1,950	24,233
Pulaski	Calfee Park	1935	335	405	310	2,500	33,679

BLUEFIELD ORIOLES

Office Address: Stadium Drive, Bluefield, WV 24701.
Mailing Address: P.O. Box 356, Bluefield, WV 24701.
Telephone: (276) 326-1326. **Fax:** (276) 326-1318.
E-Mail Address: babybirds1@comcast.net. **Website:** www.bluefieldorioles.com.
Affiliation (first year): Baltimore Orioles (1958). **Years in League:** 1946-55, 1957-

OWNERSHIP, MANAGEMENT

Operated By: Adam Shaffer.

Director: Len Johnston (Baltimore Orioles).

Vice President: Cecil Smith. **Secretary:** M.K. Burton. **Counsel:** David Kersey.

President: George McGonagle. **General Manager:** Michael Showe. **Director, Creative Services:** Katherine Ward. **Director, Stadium Services:** Aaron Showe. **Director, Field Operations/Grounds:** Mike White. **Director, Concessions:** Gary Halsey.

FIELD STAFF

Manager: Einar Diaz. **Coach:** Jim Saul. **Pitching Coach:** Troy Mattes. **Trainer:** T.D. Swinford.

GAME INFORMATION

Radio Announcer: Buford Early. **No. of Games Broadcast:** Home-34 Road-34. **Flagship Station:** WHIS 1440-AM/ WTZE 1470-AM.

PA Announcer: Buford Early. **Official Scorer:** Unavailable.

Stadium Name: Bowen Field. **Location:** I-77 to Bluefield exit 1, Route 290 to Route 460 West, fourth light right onto Leatherwood Lane, left at first light, past Chevron station and turn right, stadium 1/4 mile on left. **Ticket Price Range:** $3.50.

Visiting Club Hotel: Holiday Inn Bluefield, 3350 Big Laurel Highway. U.S. 460, Bluefield, WV 24701. **Telephone:** (304) 325-6170.

BRISTOL WHITE SOX

Ballpark Location: 1501 Euclid Ave., Bristol, VA 24201.
Mailing Address: P.O. Box 1434, Bristol, VA 24203.
Telephone: (276) 206-9946. **Fax:** (276) 669-7686.
E-Mail Address: brisox@btes.tv. **Website:** www.bristolsox.com.
Affiliation (first year): Chicago White Sox (1995-). **Years in League:** 1921-25, 1940-55, 1969-

OWNERSHIP, MANAGEMENT

Owned by: Chicago White Sox.
Operated by: Bristol Baseball Inc.
Director: Buddy Bell (Chicago White Sox).
President: Mahlon Luttrell. **Vice Presidents:** Lynn Armstrong, Perry Hustad.
General Manager: Mahlon Luttrell. **Treasurer:** Dorothy Cox. **Secretary:** Bentley Hudgins.

FIELD STAFF

Manager: Ryan Newman. **Hitting Coach:** Jerry Hairston. **Pitching Coach:** Curt Hasler. **Trainer:** Cory Barton. **Conditioning Coach:** Ibrahim Rivera.

GAME INFORMATION

Radio: None. **PA Announcer:** Chuck Necessary. **Official Scorer:** Perry Hustad.

Stadium Name: DeVault Memorial Stadium. **Location:** I-81 to exit 3 onto Commonwealth Ave., right on Euclid Ave. for ½ mile. **Standard Game Time:** 7 p.m. **Ticket Price Range:** $3-5.

Visiting Club Hotel: Holiday Inn, 3005 Linden Drive Bristol VA 24202. **Telephone:** (276) 466-4100.

BURLINGTON ROYALS

Office Address: 1450 Graham St., Burlington, NC 27217.
Mailing Address: P.O. Box 1143, Burlington, NC 27216.
Telephone: (336) 222-0223. **Fax:** (336) 226-2498.
E-Mail Address: info@burlingtonroyals.com. **Website:** www.burlingtonroyals.com.
Affiliation (first year): Kansas City Royals (2007). **Years in League:** 1986-

OWNERSHIP, MANAGEMENT

Operated by: Burlington Baseball Club Inc.
Director: Scott Sharp (Kansas City Royals).
President: Miles Wolff. **Vice President:** Dan Moushon.
General Manager: Steve Brice. **Assistant GM:** Dan Hostetter. **Director, Stadium Operations:** Mike Thompson.

FIELD STAFF

Manager: Nelson Liriano. **Hitting Coach:** Omar Ramirez. **Pitching Coach:** Bobby St. Pierre. **Trainer:** Mark Stubblefield.

GAME INFORMATION

Radio Announcer: Unavailable. **No. of Games Broadcast:** Home-34, Away-34. **Flagship:** www.burlingtonroyals.com. **PA Announcer:** Bradford Hines. **Official Scorer:** Bob Lowe.

Stadium Name: Burlington Athletic Stadium. **Location:** I-40/85 to exit 145, north on Route 100 (Maple Avenue) for 1½ miles, right on Mebane Street for 1½ miles, right on Beaumont, left on Graham. **Standard Game Time:** 7 p.m. **Ticket Price Range:** $3-8.

DANVILLE BRAVES

Office Address: Dan Daniel Memorial Park, 302 River Park Dr., Danville, VA 24540.
Mailing Address: P.O. Box 378, Danville, VA 24543.
Telephone: (434) 797-3792. **Fax:** (434) 797-3799.
E-Mail Address: info@dbraves.com. **Website:** www.dbraves.com.
Affiliation (first year): Atlanta Braves (1993). **Years in League:** 1993-

OWNERSHIP, MANAGEMENT

Operated by: Atlanta National League Baseball Club Inc.
Director: Kurt Kemp (Atlanta Braves).
General Manager: David Cross. **Assistant GM:** Bob Kitzmiller. **Operations Manager:** Kyle Mikesell.
Head Groundskeeper: Jon Hall.

FIELD STAFF

Manager: Paul Runge. **Hitting Coach:** Carlos Mendez. **Pitching Coach:** Derrick Lewis. **Athletic Trainer:** Ty Cobbs.

GAME INFORMATION

Radio Announcer: Nick Pierce. **No. of Games Broadcast:** Home-34, Away-0. **Flagship Station:** WMNA 106.3-FM. **PA Announcer:** Jay Stephens. **Official Scorer:** Mark Bowman.

Stadium Name: American Legion Field Post 325 Field at Dan Daniel Memorial Park. **Location:** U.S. 29 Bypass to River Park Drive/Dan Daniel Memorial Park exit; follow signs to park. **Standard Game Times:** 7 p.m., Sun. 4. **Ticket Price Range:** $3.50-6.50.

Visiting Club Hotel: Innkeeper-West, 3020 Riverside Dr., Danville, VA 24541. **Telephone:** (434) 799-1202.

ELIZABETHTON TWINS

Office Address: 300 West Mill Street, Elizabethton, TN 37643
Stadium Address: 208 N. Holly Lane, Elizabethton, TN 37643.
Mailing Address: 136 S. Sycamore St., Elizabethton, TN 37643.
Telephone: (423) 547-6441. **Fax:** (423) 547-6442.
E-Mail Address: etwins@charterinternet.com. **Website:** www.elizabethtontwins.com.
Affiliation (first year): Minnesota Twins (1974). **Years in League:** 1937-42, 1945-51, 1974-

OWNERSHIP, MANAGEMENT

Operator: City of Elizabethton.
Director: Jim Rantz (Minnesota Twins).
President: Harold Mains.
General Manager: Mike Mains. **Clubhouse Operations/Head Groundskeeper:** David McQueen.

FIELD STAFF

Manager: Ray Smith. **Coach:** Jeff Reed. **Pitching Coach:** Jim Shellenback. **Trainer:** Ryan Headwall.

GAME INFORMATION

Radio Announcer: Unavailable. **No. of Games Broadcast:** Home-34, Away-6. **Flagship Station:** WBEJ 1240-AM. **PA Announcer:** Tom Banks. **Official Scorer:** Bill Crow.

Stadium Name: Joe O'Brien Field. **Location:** I-81 to Highway I-26, exit at Highway 321/67, left on Holly Lane. **Standard Game Time:** 7 p.m. **Ticket Price Range:** $3-5.

Visiting Club Hotel: Holiday Inn, 101 W. Springbrook Dr., Johnson City, TN 37601. **Telephone:** (423) 282-4611.

GREENEVILLE ASTROS

Office Address: 135 Shiloh Road., Greeneville, TN 37743.
Mailing Address: P.O. Box 5192, Greeneville, TN 37743.
Telephone: (423) 638-0411. **Fax:** (423) 638-9450.
E-Mail Address: info@greenevilleastros.com. **Website:** www.greenevilleastros.com.
Affiliation (first year): Houston Astros (2004). **Years in League:** 2004-

OWNERSHIP, MANAGEMENT

Operated by: Houston Astros Baseball Club.
Director: Ricky Bennett (Houston Astros).
General Manager: David Lane. **Assistant GM:** Hunter Reed. **Director, Marketing/Media Relations:** Hunter Reed. **Head Groundskeeper:** Izzy Hinojosa III. **Clubhouse Operations:** Unavailable.

FIELD STAFF

Manager: Rodney Linares. **Pitching Coach:** Travis Driskill. **Hitting Coach:** Stubby Clapp. **Trainer:** Grant Hufford.

GAME INFORMATION

Radio: None. **PA Announcer:** Unavailable. **Official Scorer:** Johnny Painter.

JOHNSON CITY CARDINALS

Office Address: 111 Legion St., Johnson City, TN 37601.
Mailing Address: P.O. Box 179, Johnson City, TN 37605.
Telephone: (423) 461-4866. **Fax:** (423) 461-4864.
E-Mail Address: info@jccardinals.com. **Website:** www.jccardinals.com.
Affiliation (first year): St. Louis Cardinals (1975). **Years in League:** 1911-13, 1921-24, 1937-55, 1957-61, 1964-

OWNERSHIP, MANAGEMENT

Operated by: Johnson City Sports Foundation Inc.
President: Mark Fox.
Director: John Vuch (St. Louis Cardinals).
General Manager: Chuck Arnold. **Assistant GM:** Andy Barnett. **Clubhouse Operations:** Unavailable. **Groundskeeper:** Unavailable.

FIELD STAFF

Manager: Mike Shildt. **Coach:** Johnny Rodriguez. **Pitching Coach:** Doug White. **Trainer:** Unavailable.

GAME INFORMATION

Radio: None. **PA Announcer:** Unavailable. **Official Scorer:** Unavailable.

Stadium Name: Howard Johnson Field at Cardinal Park. **Location:** I-26 to exit 23, left on East Main, through light onto Legion Street. **Standard Game Time:** 7 p.m. **Ticket Price Range:** $3-5.

Visiting Club Hotel: Holiday Inn, 101 W. Springbrook Dr., Johnson City, TN 37601. **Telephone:** (423) 282-4611.

KINGSPORT METS

Office Address: 800 Granby Rd, Kingsport, TN 37660.
Mailing Address: P.O. Box 1128, Kingsport, TN 37662.
Telephone: (423) 378-3744. **Fax:** (423) 392-8538.
E-Mail Address: info@kmets.com. **Website:** www.kmets.com.
Affiliation (first year): New York Mets (1980). **Years in League:** 1921-25, 1938-52, 1957, 1960-63, 1969-82, 1984-

OWNERSHIP, MANAGEMENT

Operated By: S&H Baseball LLC..
Director: Adam Wogan (New York Mets).
President: Rick Spivey. **Vice President:** Steve Harville. **VP/General Manager:** Roman Stout. **Director, Stadium Operations:** Adam Hall. **Accountant:** Bob Dingus. **Director, Concessions:** Teresa Haywood. **Head Groundskeeper:** Josh Warner. **Clubhouse Attendant:** Travis Baker.

FIELD STAFF

Manager: Nick Leyva. **Hitting Coach:** Ryan Ellis. **Pitching Coach:** Marc Valdes.

GAME INFORMATION

Radio: None.
PA Announcer: Don Spivey. **Official Scorer:** Eddie Durham.
Stadium Name: Hunter Wright Stadium. **Location:** I-81 to I-181 North, exit 1 (Stone Drive), left on West Stone Drive (U.S. 11W), right on Granby Road. **Ticket Price Range:** $3-5.
Visiting Club Hotel: The Jameson Inn, 3004 Bays Mountain Plaza, Kingsport, TN 37660. **Telephone:** (423) 282-4611.

PRINCETON RAYS

Office Address: Hunnicutt Field, Old Bluefield Rd, Princeton, WV 24740.
Mailing Address: P.O. Box 5646, Princeton, WV 24740.
Telephone: (304) 487-2000. **Fax:** (304) 487-8762.
E-Mail Address: raysball@sunlitsurf.com. **Website:** www.princetonrays.net.
Affiliation (first year): Tampa Bay Rays (1997). **Years in League:** 1988-

OWNERSHIP, MANAGEMENT

Operated By: Princeton Baseball Association Inc.
Director: Mitch Lukevics (Tampa Bay Rays).
President: Mori Williams.
General Manager: Jim Holland. **Director, Stadium Operations:** Mick Bayle.

FIELD STAFF

Manager: Jared Sandberg. **Hitting Coach:** Rafael Deleon. **Pitching Coach:** Marty DeMerritt. **Coach:** Dan DeMent. **Trainer:** Andrew Hauser.

GAME INFORMATION

Radio Announcer: Unavailable. **No. of Games Broadcast:** Home-34, Away-34. **Flagship Station:** WAEY 1490-AM. **PA Announcer:** Jordan Pruett. **Official Scorer:** Bob Redd.

Stadium Name: Hunnicutt Field. **Location:** Exit 9 off I-77, U.S. 460 West to downtown exit, left on Stafford Drive, stadium located behind Mercer County Technical Education Center. **Standard Game Times:** 7 p.m., Sun 4. **Ticket Price Range:** $3-5.

Visiting Club Hotel: Days Inn, I-77 and Ambrose Lane, Princeton, WV 24740. **Telephone:** (304) 425-8100.

PULASKI MARINERS

Mailing Address: P.O. Box 676, Pulaski, VA 24301.
Telephone: (540) 980-1070. **Fax:** (540) 980-1850.
E-Mail Address: info@pulaskimariners.net
Affiliation (first year): Seattle Mariners (2008). **Years in League:** 1946-50, 1952-55, 1957-58, 1969-77, 1982-92, 1997-2006, 2008-

OWNERSHIP, MANAGEMENT

Operated By: Pulaski Baseball Inc.
Director: Pedro Grifol (Seattle Mariners).
President: Tom Compton
General Manager: Tom Compton. **Assistant GM:** Marty Gordon.

FIELD STAFF

Manager: Rob Mummau. **Hitting Coach:** Rafael Santo Domingo. **Pitching Coach:** Nasusel Cabrera. **Trainer:** Colby Harris.

GAME INFORMATION

Radio: None.
PA Announcer: Taylor Snow. **Official Scorer:** Charles Altizer.
Stadium Name: Calfee Park. **Location:** Interstate 81 to Exit 89-B (Route 11), north to Pulaski, right on Pierce Avenue. **Standard Game Times:** 7 p.m.
Ticket Price Range: $4-6.
Visiting Club Hotel: Comfort Inn, 4424 Cleburne Blvd, Dublin, Virginia. **Telephone:** (540) 674-1100.

PIONEER LEAGUE

ROOKIE LEAGUE

Office Address: 157 S. Lincoln Ave., Spokane, WA 99201.
Mailing Address: P.O. Box 2564, Spokane, WA 99220.
Telephone: (509) 456-7615. **Fax:** (509) 456-0136.
E-Mail Address: fanmail@pioneerleague.com. **Website:** www.pioneerleague.com.
Years League Active: 1939-42, 1946-.
President/Secretary-Treasurer: Jim McCurdy.

Jim McCurdy

Vice President: Mike Ellis (Missoula).
Directors: Dave Baggott (Ogden), Mike Ellis (Missoula), D.G. Elmore (Helena), Kevin Greene (Idaho Falls), Kevin Haughian (Casper), Jeff Katofsky (Orem), Vinny Purpura (Great Falls), Jim Iverson (Billings).
Administrative Assistant: Teryl MacDonald.
Division Structure: North—Billings, Great Falls, Helena, Missoula. **South**—Casper, Idaho Falls, Ogden, Orem.
Regular Season: 76 games (split schedule). **2009 Opening Date:** June 23. **Closing Date:** Sept. 11.
Playoff Format: First-half division winners meet second-half division winners in best-of-three series. Winners meet in best-of-three series for league championship.
All-Star Game: None.
Roster Limit: 35 active, 30 dressed for each game. **Player Eligibility Rule:** No more than 17 players 21 and older, provided that no more than two are 23 or older. No player on active list may have three or more years of prior minor league service.
Brand of Baseball: Rawlings.
Umpires: Unavailable.

STADIUM INFORMATION

			Dimensions				
Club	Stadium	Opened	LF	CF	RF	Capacity	2008 Att.
Billings	Dehler Park	2008	329	410	350	3,071	113,166
Casper	Mike Lansing Field	2002	355	400	345	2,500	50,580
Great Falls	Centene Stadium at Legion Park	1956	335	414	335	3,800	106,831
Helena	Kindrick Field	1939	335	400	325	1,700	35,066
Idaho Falls	Melaleuca Field	1976	340	400	350	3,400	95,470
Missoula	Ogren Park at Allegiance Field	2004	309	398	287	3,500	81,001
Ogden	Lindquist Field	1997	335	396	334	5,000	138,555
Orem	Home of the Owlz	2005	305	408	312	4,500	108,283

BILLINGS MUSTANGS

Office Address: Dehler Park, 2611 Ninth Avenue North, Billings, MT 59101.
Mailing Address: P.O. Box 1553, Billings, MT 59103-1553.
Telephone: (406) 252-1241. **Fax:** (406) 252-2968.
E-Mail Address: mustangs@billingsmustangs.com. **Website:** www.billingsmustangs.com .
Affiliation (first year): Cincinnati Reds (1974). **Years in League:** 1948-63, 1969-

OWNERSHIP, MANAGEMENT

Operated By: Billings Pioneer Baseball Club Inc.
President: Woody Hahn.
General Manager: Gary Roller. **Assistant GM:** Matt Bender. **Director, Stadium Operations:** Chris Marshall. **Director, Field Maintenance:** John Barta. **Director, Clubhouse Operations:** Zachary Haden.

FIELD STAFF

Manager: Julio Garcia. **Coach:** Tony Jaramillo. **Pitching Coach:** Tom Browning.

GAME INFORMATION

Radio Announcer: Unavailable. **No. of Games Broadcast:** Home-38, Away-38. **Flagship Station:** KBUL 970-AM.
PA Announcer: Kyle Riley. **Official Scorer:** Phil Sites.
Stadium Name: Dehler Park. **Location:** I-90 to North 27th Street exit, north to Ninth Avenue North. **Standard Game Times:** 7:05 p.m.; Sun. 4:05. **Ticket Price Range:** $3-9.
Visiting Club Hotel: Rimrock Inn, 1203 North 27th Street, Billings, MT 59101. **Telephone:** (406) 252-7107.

CASPER GHOSTS

Office Address: 330 Kati Lane, Casper, WY 82601.
Mailing Address: P.O. Box 1293, Casper, WY 82602.
Telephone: (307) 232-1111. **Fax:** (307) 265-7867.
E-Mail Address: homerun@ghostsbaseball.com. **Website:** www.ghostsbaseball.com.
Affiliation (first year): Colorado Rockies (2001). **Years in League:** 2001-

OWNERSHIP, MANAGEMENT

Operated by: Casper Professional Baseball Club LLC.
Principal Owner, CEO: Kevin Haughian.
General Manager: Mike Sandler.

FIELD STAFF

Manager: Tony Diaz. **Hitting Coach:** Kevin Riggs. **Pitching Coach:** Craig Bjornson. **Trainer:** Josh Guterman.

GAME INFORMATION

Radio Announcer: Tim Ray. **No. of Games Broadcast:** Home-38, Away-38. **Flagship Station:** Unavailable.
PA Announcer: Unavailable. **Official Scorer:** Unavailable.
Stadium Name: Mike Lansing Field. **Location:** I-25 to Poplar Street exit, north on Poplar Street, right into Crossroads Park. **Standard Game Times:** 7:05 p.m., Sun. 4:05. **Ticket Price Range:** $7.50-9.
Visiting Club Hotel: Parkway Plaza, 123 West E St., Casper, WY 82601. **Telephone:** (307) 235-1777.

GREAT FALLS VOYAGERS

Office Address: 1015 25th St. N, Great Falls, MT 59401.
Mailing Address: P.O. Box 1621, Great Falls, MT 59403.
Telephone: (406) 452-5311. **Fax:** (406) 454-0811.
E-Mail Address: voyagers@gfvoyagers.com. **Website:** www.gfvoyagers.com .
Affiliation (first year): Chicago White Sox (2003). **Years in League:** 1948-1963, 1969-

OWNERSHIP, MANAGEMENT

Operated By: Great Falls Baseball Club, Inc.
President: Vinney Purpura. **General Manager:** Jim Keough. **Head Groundskeeper:** Billy Chafin. **Office Manager:** Karen Skolrud. **Director, Marketing/Community Affairs:** Lorie Harris.

FIELD STAFF

Manager: Chris Cron. **Hitting Coach:** Olmedo Saenz. **Pitching Coach:** Brian Drahman. **Trainer:** Unavailable. **Conditioning:** Jeremie Imbus.

GAME INFORMATION

Radio Announcer: Unavailable. **No. of Games Broadcast:** Home-38, Away-38. **Flagship Station:** KMON 560-AM.
PA Announcer: Tim Paul. **Official Scorer:** Mike Lewis.
Stadium Name: Centene Stadium located at Legion Park. **Location:** From I-15 to exit 281 (10th Ave. S), left on 26th, left on Eighth Ave. North, right on 25th, ballpark on right, past railroad tracks. **Ticket Price Range:** $5-8.
Visiting Club Hotel: Mid Town Motel, 526 Second Ave. N, Great Falls, MT 59401. **Telephone:** (406) 453-2411.

HELENA BREWERS

Office Address: 1300 N. Ewing, Helena, MT 59601.
Mailing Address: P.O. Box 6756, Helena, MT 59604.
Telephone: (406) 495-0500. **Fax:** (406) 495-0900.
E-Mail Address: info@helenabrewers.net. **Website:** www.helenabrewers.net.
Affiliation (first year): Milwaukee Brewers (2003). **Years in League:** 1978-2000, 2003-

OWNERSHIP, MANAGEMENT

Operated by: Helena Baseball Club LLC.
Principal Owner: D.G. Elmore.
General Manager: Paul Fetz. **Assistant GM:** Nick Bowsher. **Director, Tickets:** Nick Joyner. **Director, Broadcasting/Media Relations:** Unavailable.

FIELD STAFF

Manager: Rene Gonzales. **Batting Coach:** Ned Yost IV. **Pitching Coach:** Unavailable. **Trainer:** Jimmy Gentry.

GAME INFORMATION

Radio Announcer: Unavailable. **No. of Games Broadcast:** Home-38, Away-38. **Flagship Station:** KCAP 1340-AM.
PA Announcer: Randy Bowsher. **Official Scorers:** Kevin Higgens, Craig Struble, Jim Shope.

Stadium Name: Kindrick Field. **Location:** Cedar Street exit off I-15, west to Last Chance Gulch, left at Memorial Park. **Standard Game Time:** 7:05 p.m. **Sun. 4:**05. **Ticket Price Range:** $6-9.

Visiting Club Hotel: Colonial Red Lion Hotel. **Telephone:** 406-443-2100.

IDAHO FALLS CHUKARS

Office Address: 568 W. Elva, Idaho Falls, ID 83402.

Mailing Address: P.O. 2183, Idaho, ID 83403.

Telephone: (208) 522-8363. **Fax:** (208) 522-9858.

E-Mail Address: chukars@ifchukars.com. **Website:** www.ifchukars.com.

Affiliation (first year): Kansas City Royals (2004). **Years in League:** 1940-42, 1946-

OWNERSHIP, MANAGEMENT

Operated By: The Elmore Group. **Principal Owner:** David Elmore.

President/General Manager: Kevin Greene. **Assistant GM, Merchandise:** Andrew Daugherty. **Director, Concessions:** Paul Henderson. **Head Groundskeeper:** Jon Clark.

FIELD STAFF

Manager: Darryl Kennedy. **Hitting Coach:** Jon Williams. **Pitching Coach:** Carlos Martinez. **Trainer:** Unavailable.

GAME INFORMATION

Radio Announcers: John Balginy, Jim Garshow. **No. of Games Broadcast:** Home-38 Road-38. **Flagship Station:** KUPI 980-AM.

Official Scorer: John Balginy.

Stadium Name: Melaleuca Field. **Location:** I-15 to West Broadway exit, left onto Memorial Drive, right on Mound Avenue, ¼ mile to stadium. **Standard Game Times:** 7:15 p.m., **Sun. 4. Ticket Price Range:** $6-9.

Visiting Club Hotel: Guesthouse Inn & Suites, 850 Lindsay Blvd, Idaho Falls, ID 83402. **Telephone:** (208) 522-6260.

MISSOULA OSPREY

Office Address: 412 W. Alder St, Missoula, MT 59802.

Telephone: (406) 543-3300. **Fax:** (406) 543-9463.

E-Mail Address: info@missoulaosprey.com. **Website:** www.missoulaosprey.com.

Affiliation (first year): Arizona Diamondbacks (1999). **Years in League:** 1956-60, 1999-

OWNERSHIP, MANAGEMENT

Operated By: Mountain Baseball LLC.

President: Mike Ellis. **Vice President:** Judy Ellis.

Executive Vice President: Matt Ellis. **VP, Finance/Merchandising:** Shelly Ellis. **General Manager/Operations:** Jared Amoss. **General Manager/Sales, Marketing:** Jeff Griffin. **Director, Stadium Operations:** Byron Dike. **Office Administrator:** Nola Hunter. **Stadium Operations Intern:** Unavailable. **Promotions/PR Intern:** Unavailable. **Hospitality Intern:** Unavailable.

FIELD STAFF

Manager: Audo Vincente. **Hitting Coach:** Jason Hardtke. **Pitching Coach:** Steve Merriman. **Trainer:** Joseph Metz. **Strength/Conditioning:** Jason Mitchell.

GAME INFORMATION

Radio Announcer: Ben Catley. **No. of Games Broadcast:** Home-38, Away-38. **Flagship Station:** KMPT 930-AM.

PA Announcer: Unavailable. **Official Scorer:** David Kinsey.

Stadium Name: Ogren Park at Allegiance Field. **Location:** 700 Cregg Lane. **Directions:** Take Orange Street to Cregg Lane, west on Cregg Lane, stadium west of McCormick Park. **Standard Game Times:** 7:05 p.m.; Sun 5:05 p.m. **Ticket Price Range:** $5-10.

Visiting Club Hotel: Mountain Valley Inn, 420 W. Broadway, Missoula, Mt. 59802. **Telephone:** (406) 728-4500

OGDEN RAPTORS

Office Address: 2330 Lincoln Ave, Ogden, UT 84401.

Telephone: (801) 393-2400. **Fax:** (801) 393-2473.

E-Mail Address: homerun@ogden-raptors.com. **Website:** www.ogden-raptors.com.

Affiliation (first year): Los Angeles Dodgers (2003). **Years in League:** 1939-42, 1946-55, 1966-74, 1994-

OWNERSHIP, MANAGEMENT

Operated By: Ogden Professional Baseball, Inc.

Principal Owners: Dave Baggott, John Lindquist. **Chairman, President:** Dave Baggott.

General Manager: Joey Stein. **VP/Director, Marketing:** John Stein. **Controller:** Carol Spickler. **Head Groundskeeper:**

Ken Kopinski. **Director, Merchandising:** Geri Kopinski.

FIELD STAFF

Manager: Damon Berryhill. **Hitting Coach:** Henry Cruz. **Pitching Coach:** Chuck Crim. **Trainer:** Peter Hite.

GAME INFORMATION

Radio Announcer: Eric Knighton. **No. of Games Broadcast:** Home-38, Away-38. **Flagship Station:** 1490 AM KOGN.

PA Announcer: Pete Diamond. **Official Scorer:** Dennis Kunimura.

Stadium Name: Lindquist Field. **Location:** I-15 North to 21th Street exit, east to Lincoln Avenue, south three blocks to park. **Standard Game Times:** 7 p.m ., Sun. 1. **Ticket Price Range:** $6-9.

Visiting Club Hotel: Hotel Ben Lomond, 2510 Washington Blvd., Ogden, UT 84401. **Telephone:** (801) 627-1900.

OREM OWLZ

Office Address: 970 W. University Parkway, Orem, UT 84058.

Telephone: (801) 377-2255. **Fax:** (801) 377-2345.

E-Mail Address: fan@oremowlz.com. **Website:** www.oremowlz.com.

Affiliation (first year): Los Angeles Angels (2001). **Years in League:** 2001-

OWNERSHIP, MANAGEMENT

Operated By: Bery Bery Gud To Me LLC.

Principal Owner: Jeff Katofsky.

General Manager: Aaron Wells. **Assistant GM/Sales:** Blake Buswell. **Director, Baseball Operations/Clubhouse Manager:** Brett Crane. **Director, Ticketing:** Andrew Scott.

FIELD STAFF

Manager: Tom Kotchman. **Coach:** Mike Eylward. **Pitching Coach:** Zeke Zimmerman. **Trainer:** Mike Dart.

GAME INFORMATION

Radio Announcer: Matt Gittins. **No. of Games Broadcast:** Home-38, Away-38. **Flagship Station:** Unavailable.

PA Announcer: Lincoln Fillmore. **Official Scorer:** Unavailable.

Stadium Name: Home of the Owlz. **Location:** Exit 269 (University Parkway) off I-15 at Utah Valley University campus. **Ticket Price Range:** $4-9.

Visiting Club Hotel: Provo Days Inn, 1675 N. 200 West, Provo, UT 84604. **Telephone:** (801) 375-8600.

ARIZONA LEAGUE

ROOKIE

Office Address: 620 W. Franklin St., Boise, ID 83702.
Mailing Address: P.O. Box 1645, Boise, ID 83701.
Telephone: (208) 429-1511. **Fax:** (208) 429-1525. **E-Mail Address:** bobrichmond@qwestoffice.net
Years League Active: 1988-.
President/Treasurer: Bob Richmond.
Vice President: Oneri Fleita (Cubs). **Corporate Secretary:** Ted Polakowski (Athletics).
Administrative Assistant: Rob Richmond.
Division Structure: East/West divisions.
Regular Season: 56 games (split schedule). **2009 Opening Date:** June 21. **Closing Date:** Aug. 29.
Standard Game Times: 7 p.m.
Playoff Format: First-half divisional winners meet second-half winners in one-game divisional championships on August 30. East vs. West championship game on Aug. 31.
All-Star Game: None.
Roster Limit: 35 active. **Player Eligibility Rule:** No player may have three or more years of prior Minor League Service.
Brand of Baseball: Rawlings.

Clubs	Playing Site	Manager	Coach	Pitching Coach(es)
Angels	Angels complex, Tempe	Ty Boykin	Dick Schofield	Trevor Wilson
Athletics	Papago Park Baseball Complex, Phoenix	Marcus Jensen	Juan Dilone	A. Prieto/C. Lessner
Brewers	Maryvale Baseball Complex, Phoenix	Tony Diggs	Kenny Dominguez	S. Cline/J. Nunez
Cubs	Fitch Park, Mesa	Juan Cabreja	Ricardo Medina	Rick Tronerud
Dodgers	Camelback Ranch, Glendale	Jeff Carter	Leo Garcia	Casey Deskins
Giants	Giants complex, Scottsdale	Mike Goff	Victor Torres	Mike Caldwell
Indians	Indians complex, Goodyear	Ted Kubiak	D. Malave/A. Medrano	Jeff Harris
Mariners	Peoria Sports Complex	Jose Moreno	Andy Bottin	Gary Wheelock
Padres	Peoria Sports Complex	Jose Flores	Jimmy Jones	Bob Skube
Rangers	Surprise Recreation Campus	Bill Richardson	Josue Perez	J. Burgos/C. Pulido
Royals	Surprise Recreation Campus	Julio Bruno	Kenny Munoz	C. Reyes/M. Davis

GULF COAST LEAGUE

ROOKIE

Office Address: 1503 Clower Creek Dr., Suite H-262, Sarasota, FL 34231.
Telephone: (941) 966-6407. **Fax:** (941) 966-6872.
Years League Active: 1964-.
President/Secretary-Treasurer: Tom Saffell.
First Vice President: Steve Noworyta (Phillies). **Second Vice President:** Jim Rantz (Twins).
Administrative Assistant: Bill Ventolo.
Division Structure: East—Astros, Cardinals, Marlins, Mets, Nationals. **North**—Blue Jays, Braves, Phillies, Pirates, Tigers, Yankees. **South**—Orioles, Rays, Reds, Red Sox, Twins.
Regular Season: North: 60 games; East/South: 56 games. **2009 Opening Date:** June 23. **Closing Date:** Aug. **31.**
Playoff Format: Division winner with best regular season winning percentage meets wild card team in one-game playoff. Remaining two division winners meet in one-game playoff. Playoff winners advance to best-of-three championship series.
Roster Limit: 35 active, but only 30 eligible for each game. **Player Eligibility Rule:** No age restriction limits. No player who has three or more years of prior minor league and/or major league service time can participate.
Brand of Baseball: Rawlings.

Clubs	Playing Site	Manager	Coach(es)	Pitching Coach
Astros	Astros complex, Kissimmee	Omar Lopez	D.J. Boston	Rick Aponte
Blue Jays	Mattick Training Center, Dunedin	John Schneider	D. Pano/D. Solano	Pete Walker
Braves	Disney's Wide World of Sports, Orlando	Luis Ortiz	Sixto Lezcano	Gabe Luckert
Cardinals	Cardinals complex, Jupiter	Steve Turco	Javier Meza	Dernier Orozco
Marlins	Roger Dean complex, Jupiter	Andy Haines	Frank Moore	Doc Watson
Mets	St. Lucie Sports Complex, St. Lucie	Julio Franco	L. Rojas/T. McGraw	Jonathan Hurst
Nationals	Carl Barger Baseball Complex, Melbourne	Bobby Henley	Paul Sanagorski	Joel Sanchez
Orioles	Twin Lakes Park, Sarasota	Ramon Sambo	TBA	Calvin Maduro
Phillies	Carpenter Complex, Clearwater	Roly DeArmas	Luis Melendez	Aris Tirado
Pirates	Pirate City Complex, Bradenton	Tom Prince	R. Pena/W. Huyke	Miguel Bonilla
Rays	Charlotte County Complex, Port Charlotte	Joe Alvarez	B. Oglivie/R. Ruiz	Darwin Peguero
Reds	Ed Smith Complex, Sarasota	Pat Kelly	Tony Fossas	Ramon Ortiz
Red Sox	Red Sox complex	Dave Tomlin	U.L. Washington	G. Gregson/W. Miranda
Tigers	Tigertown, Lakeland	Basilio Cabrera	Garrett Guest	Greg Sabat
Twins	Lee County Complex, Fort Myers	Jake Mauer	Milt Cuyler	R. Hernandez/I. Arteaga
Yankees	Yankee complex, Tampa	Tom Slater	Derek Shumpert	Carlos Chantres

INDEPENDENT LEAGUES

AMERICAN ASSOCIATION

Office Address: 1415 Hwy. 54 West, Suite 210, Durham, NC 27707.
Telephone: (919) 401-8150. **FAX:** (919) 401-8152. **Website:** www.americanassociationbaseball.com.
Year Founded: 2006.
Commissioner: Miles Wolff. **President:** Dan Moushon.
Administrative Assistant: Jason Deans. **Director of Umpires:** Kevin Winn.
Division Structure: North—Lincoln, St. Paul, Sioux City, Sioux Falls, Wichita. South—El Paso, Fort Worth, Grand Prairie, Pensacola, Shreveport-Bossier.
Regular Season: 96 games (split schedule).
2009 Opening Date: May 14. **Closing Date:** August 30.
All-Star Game: July 21 at Grand Prairie (North Division vs. South Division).
Playoff Format: First-half division winners and second-half division winners in best-of-five series. Winners meet in best-of-five series for league championship.
Roster Limit: 22. **Player Eligibility Rule:** Minimum of five first-year players, maximum of four veterans with at least four years of professional experience.
Brand of Baseball: Rawlings.
Statistician: PA SportsTicker, 55 Realty Drive, Cheshire, CT 06410.

STADIUM INFORMATION

			Dimensions				
Club	**Stadium**	**Opened**	**LF**	**CF**	**RF**	**Capacity**	**2008 Att.**
El Paso	Cohen Stadium	1990	340	410	340	9,725	182,380
Fort Worth	LaGrave Field	2002	325	400	335	5,100	185,175
Grand Prairie	QuikTrip Park at Grand Prairie	2008	330	400	330	5,445	143,627
Lincoln	Haymarket Park	2001	335	395	325	4,500	182,852
Pensacola	Pelican Park	1991	320	390	320	2,500	82,999
St. Paul	Midway Stadium	1982	320	400	320	6,069	286,796
Shreveport-Bossier	Fair Grounds Field	1986	330	400	330	4,500	57,975
Sioux City	Lewis and Clark Park	1993	330	400	330	3,630	87,616
Sioux Falls	Sioux Falls Stadium	1964	312	410	312	4,029	150,837
Wichita	Lawrence-Dumont Stadium	1934	344	401	312	6,055	146,408

EL PASO DIABLOS

Office Address: 9700 Gateway North Blvd., El Paso, TX 79924.
Telephone: (915) 755-2000. **Fax:** (915) 757-0681.
E-mail Address: info@diablos.com. **Website:** www.diablos.com.
Managing Partner: Mark Schuster, Ventura Sports Group.
General Manager: Matt LaBranche. **Director, Sponsorships:** Bernie Ricono. **Director, Media/Community Relations:** Adriana Ruiz. **Director, Marketing/Promotions:** Holly McWatters. **Director of Group Sales:** Jeff Hoover. **Box Office Manager:** Steve Martinez. **Account Executives:** Donna Blair, Rachel Ross. **Business Manager:** Pat Hofman.
Manager: Butch Henry. **Coach:** Ryan Medrano.

GAME INFORMATION

Radio Announcer: Jon Barr. **Games Broadcast:** 96. **Flagship Station:** ESPN Radio 1380-AM. **Webcast Address:** www.diablos.com.
Stadium Name: Cohen Stadium. **Location:** I-10 to U.S. 54 (Patriot Freeway), east to Diana exit to Gateway North Boulevard.
Standard Game Times: 7:05 PM, Sunday, 6:05 PM.
Visiting Club Hotel: Holiday Inn Airport, 6655 Gateway West, El Paso, TX 79925. **Telephone:** (915) 342-5330.

FORT WORTH CATS

Office Address: 301 NE Sixth St., Fort Worth, TX 76164.
Telephone: (817) 226-2287. **Fax:** (817) 534-4620.
E-Mail Address: info@fwcats.com. **Website:** www.fwcats.com.
Principal Owner/CEO: Carl Bell.
President/COO: John Dittrich.
Executive Vice President/General Manager: John Bilbow. **VP:** Dick Smith. **VP, Special Projects:** Maury Wills. **VP, Communications:** David Hatchett. **Assistant VP, Communications:** Emil Moffatt. **Business Manager:** Lois Dittrich. **Stadium Operations:** Raleigh Smith. **Assistant GM:** Cody Crume. **Community Relations / Merchandise Manager:** Andrea Dailey. **Director, Manager of Ticket Operations:** Jeff Gogerty. **Ticket Sales:** Corey Troxell. **Account Executives:** Dave Moharter, Reg Robbins.

Director, Player Personnel/Manager: Chad Tredaway. **Coaches:** Heath Autrey, James Frisbie, Wayne Terwilliger. **Head Athletic Trainer:** Chuck McCandless.

GAME INFORMATION

Radio Announcers: Emil Moffatt, David Hatchett. **No. of Games Broadcast:** 96. **Flagship Station:** 1460-AM. **Webcast Address:** www.fwcats.com.

Stadium Name: LaGrave Field. **Location:** From 1-30, take 1-35 North to North Side Drive exit, left (west) off exit to Main Street, left (south) on Main, left (east) onto NE Sixth Street.

Standard Game Times: 7:05 p.m, Sunday, 6:05 p.m.

Visiting Club Hotel: Unavailable.

GRAND PRAIRIE AIRHOGS

Office Address: 1600 Lone Star Parkway, Grand Prairie, TX 75050

Telephone: (972) 504-9383. **Fax:** (972) 504-2288.

Website: www.airhogsbaseball.com.

VP/General Manager: Dave Burke. **VP, Sales:** Brian Rose. **Assistant General Managers:** Matt Barry, Tim Savona. **Ticket Sales Manager:** J Willms. **Group Sales Executives:** Tiffany Dilworth, Chris Shuffield. **Account Executive:** Ketra Dawson. **Box Office Manager:** Sam Ward. **Director, Food/Beverage:** Jay Vending Company. **CFO:** Greg Engeldinger

Manager: Pete Incaviglia. **Trainer:** Paul Gillilan

GAME INFORMATION

No. of Games Broadcast: 96. **Webcast Address:** www.allinbroadcasting.com.

Stadium Name: QuikTrip Park @ Grand Prairie. **Location:** From I-30, take Beltline Road exit going north. Once on Beltline Road (½ mile), take Lone Star Park entrance (gate #2) toward the stadium.

Standard Game Times: 7:05 pm, Sunday, 6:05 p.m.

Visiting Club Hotel: Hyatt Place, 1542 N. Highway 360, Grand Prairie, TX 75050. **Telephone:** (972) 988-6800.

LINCOLN SALTDOGS

Office Address: 403 Line Drive Circle, Suite A, Lincoln, NE 68508.

Telephone: (402) 474-2255. **Fax:** (402) 474-2254.

E-Mail Address: info@saltdogs.com. **Website:** www.saltdogs.com.

Owner: Jim Abel. **President:** Charlie Meyer.

Vice President/General Manager: Tim Utrup. **Assistant GM/Director, Sales/Marketing:** Bret Beer. **Director, Broadcasting/Communications:** Jason Van Arkel. **Director, Merchandising/Promotions:** Anne Duchek. **Director, Season Tickets/Ticket Packages:** Toby Antonson. **Director, Group Sales:** Scott Mauser. **Director, Stadium Operations:** Dave Aschwege. **Assistant Director, Stadium Operations:** Brett Myers. **Office Manager:** Alicia Oakeson. **Athletic Turf Manager:** Josh Klute. **Assistant Turf Managers:** J.J. Borecky, Jen Roeber.

Manager: Marty Scott.

GAME INFORMATION

Radio Announcer: Jason Van Arkel. **No. of Games Broadcast:** 96. **Flagship Station:** KFOR 1240-AM. **Webcast Address:** www.kfor1240.com.

Stadium Name: Haymarket Park. **Location:** I-80 to Cornhusker Highway West, left on First Street, right on Sun Valley Boulevard, left on Line Drive.

Standard Game Times: 7:05 p.m.; Sunday, 6:05 p.m.

Visiting Club Hotel: Holiday Inn Downtown, 141 N. Ninth St., Lincoln, NE 68508. **Telephone:** (402) 475-4011.

PENSACOLA PELICANS

Office Address: 41 North Jefferson Street, Suite 300 Pensacola, FL 32502.

Telephone: (850) 934-8444. **Fax:** (850) 791-6256.

E-Mail Address: info@pensacolapelicans.com. **Website:** www.pensacolapelicans.com.

Owners: Quint Studer, Rishy Studer. **President:** Rishy Studer. **Chief Executive Officer:** Quint Studer.

General Manager: Talmadge Nunnari. **Assistant GM:** Jason Libbert. **Vice President, Sales:** Gary Colon. **Chief Financial Officer:** Bess Abernathy. **Ticketing Director:** Shelley Welch. **Community Relations Director:** Carrie Smith. **Sales Executive:** Paul Chestnutt. **Promotions Coordinator:** Tim Mulroy.

Manager: Talmadge Nunnari. **Infield Coordinator:** Lou Henry. **Player Procurement:** James Gamble.

GAME INFORMATION

No. of Games Broadcast: 96. **Flagship Station:** WNRP 1620-AM. **Webcast Address:** www.pensacolapelicans.com.

Stadium Name: Jim Spooner Field at Pelican Park. **Location:** On the campus of University of West Florida. From I-10 West, north on Davis Highway (SR 291) to exit 13, left on University Parkway, right on Campus Drive, stadium 1/2 mile on right.

Standard Game Times: 6:35 p.m.; Saturday-Sunday, 6:05 p.m.
Visiting Club Hotel: Unavailable.

ST. PAUL SAINTS

Office Address: 1771 Energy Park Dr., St. Paul, MN 55108.
Telephone: (651) 644-3517. **Fax:** (651) 644-1627.
E-Mail Address: funsgood@saintsbaseball.com. **Website:** www.saintsbaseball.com.

Principal Owners: Marv Goldklang, Mike Veeck, Bill Murray. **Chairman:** Marv Goldklang.

President: Mike Veeck. **Executive Vice President/General Manager:** Derek Sharrer. **Executive Vice President:** Tom Whaley. **Assistant GM:** Dan Lehv. **Vice President, Customer Service/Community Partnerships:** Annie Huidekoper. **Director, Corporate Sales:** Scott Bush. **Director, Promotions/Merchandise:** Scott Riley. **Director, Ticket Sales:** Matt Teske. **Director, Special Events:** Amy Heimer. **Group/Season Ticket Sales Manager:** Mike Nachreiner. **Technology Manager/Group Ticket Sales:** Jeremy Loosbrock. **Ticket Sales Representative:** Erin Luehti. **Ticket Sales Representative:** Marc Elliot. **Director, Food/Beverage:** Curtis Nachtsheim. **Business Manager:** Leesa Anderson. **Director, Stadium Operations:** Bob Klepperich. **Groundskeeper:** Connie Rudolph.

Manager: George Tsamis. **Coaches:** Lamarr Rogers, TJ Wiesner.

GAME INFORMATION

Radio Announcer: Sean Aronson. **No. of Games Broadcast:** 96. **Flagship Station:** Relevant Radio 1330-AM. **Webcast Address:** www.saintsbaseball.com.

Stadium Name: Midway Stadium. **Location:** From I-94, take Snelling Avenue North exit, west onto Energy Park Drive.

Standard Game Times: 7:05 p.m., Sunday, 1:05 p.m.
Visiting Club Hotel: Unavailable.

SHREVEPORT-BOSSIER CAPTAINS

Office Address: 2901 Pershing Blvd, Shreveport, LA 71109.
Telephone: (318) 636-5555. **Fax:** (318) 636-5670.
Website: www.sbcaptains.com.
Chairman: Gary Elliston. **President:** Scott Berry.

Vice President/General Manager: Craig Brasfield. **Assistant General Manager:** Chet Carey. **Director of Stadium Operations, Merchandising:** Bobby Entrekin. **Director of Ticket Operations:** Jon Marshall. **Director of Group Sales & Food/Beverage:** Rob Gusick. **Director of Broadcasting & Media Relations:** Josh Hirsch. **Business Manager:** Carrie Brasfield. **Head Groundskeeper:** Pat Holmes. **Intern:** Desiree Mitchell.

Manager: Ricky VanAsselberg. **Coach:** Vince Moore.

GAME INFORMATION

Radio Announcer: Josh Hirsch. **No. of Games Broadcast:** 96. **Webcast Address:** www.sbcaptains.com.
Stadium Name: Fair Grounds Field. **Location:** Hearne Avenue (U.S. 171) exit off I-20 at Louisiana State Fairgrounds.
Standard Game Times: Monday-Saturday - 7:05 p.m., Sunday - 6:05 p.m..
Visiting Club Hotel: Boomtown Hotel and Casino, 300 Riverside Drive, Bossier City, LA 71111. **Telephone:** (318)746-0711.

SIOUX CITY EXPLORERS

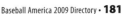

Office Address: 3400 Line Drive, Sioux City, IA 51106.
Telephone: (712) 277-9467. **Fax:** (712) 277-9406.
E-Mail Address: promotions@xsbaseball.com. **Website:** www.xsbaseball.com.
President: John Roost.

General Manager: Shane M. **Tritz. Assistant GM:** Ashley Schroenrock. **Office Manager:** Julie Stringer.

Field Manager/Player Procurement Director: Les Lancaster. **Coaches:** Darwin Marrero, Rafael Melchione, Billy Williams.

GAME INFORMATION

No. of Games Broadcast: 96. **Flagship Station:** KSCJ 1360-AM. **Webcast Address:** www.xsbaseball.com.
Stadium Name: Lewis and Clark Park. **Location:** I-29 to Singing Hills Blvd. North, right on Line Drive.
Standard Game Times: 7:05 p.m., Sunday, 6:05 p.m.
Visiting Club Hotel: Unavailable.

SIOUX FALLS CANARIES

Office Address: 1001 N. West Ave., Sioux Falls, SD 57104.
Telephone: (605) 333-0179. **Fax:** (605) 333-0139.
E-Mail Address: info@canariesbaseball.com. **Website:** www.canariesbaseball.com.
President: John Kuhn.

General Manager: Matt Hansen. **Assistant GM/Groundskeeper:** Larry McKenney. **Vice President, Assistant GM/Ticket Sales:** Chris Schwab. **Director, Media/Public Relations:** Matt Meola. **Director, Food/Beverage:** Bill Sedelmeier. **Group Sales Director:** Rustin Buysse. **Office Manager:** Peggy Ashdown. **Group Sales Executive:** Tyler Long. **Group Sales Executive:** Erin Kohles.

Manager: Steve Shirley. **Coaches:** John Harris, Mike Meyer.

GAME INFORMATION

Radio Announcer: Matt Meola. **No. of Games Broadcast:** 96. **Flagship Station:** KWSN 1230-AM. **Webcast Address:** www.kwsn.com.

Stadium Name: Sioux Falls Stadium. **Location:** I-29 to Russell Street, east one mile, right on West Avenue.
Standard Game Times: 7:05 p.m., Sunday, 2:05 p.m.
Visiting Club Hotel: Unavailable.

WICHITA WINGNUTS

Office Address: 300 South Sycamore, Wichita, KS 67213.
Telephone: (316) 264-4625. **Fax:** (316) 264-3037.
Website: www.wichitawingnuts.com.
Owners: Horn Chen, Steve Ruud, Dan Waller, Gary Austerman, Nick Easter, Nate Robertson, Josh Robertson.
President: Jeff Lund.

General Manager: Josh Robertson. **Assistant General Manager:** Matt Brokaw. **Assistant General Manager:** Joe Greene. **Director, Corporate Sales:** Bob Flanagan. **Director, Ticket Sales/Merchandise:** Sally Knofflock. **Director, Community Relations:** Amy Wilds. **Director, Broadcast:** Steve Schuster. **Director, Finance:** Kay Brown. **Director, Baseball Operations:** Ben Keiter. **Corporate Sales Associates:** Jeremy Mock, Chris Freshour. **Staff Assistants:** Scott Elbert, Mark Eckelberry, Jason Harrell. **Director, Stadium Operations:** Jeff Kline. **Assistant, Stadium Operations:** D.J. Giumento. **Director, Operations, NBC World Series:** Jerry Taylor. **Clubhouse Manager:** Brad Brungardt. **Assistant Clubhouse Manager:** Bill "Sarge" Cook.

Manager: Kevin Hooper. **Coaches:** Chris Mileham, Luke Robertson.

GAME INFORMATION

Radio Announcer: Steve Schuster. **Games Broadcast:** KGSO 1410-AM. **Webcast Address:** www.wichitawingnuts.com or www.kgso.com.

Stadium Name: Lawrence-Dumont Stadium. **Location:** 135 North to Kellogg (54) West. Take Seneca Street exit North to Maple. Go East on Maple to Sycamore. Stadium is located on corner of Maple and Sycamore.
Standard Game Times: 7:05 p.m.; Sunday, 5:05 p.m.
Visiting Club Hotel: Wichita Suites, 5211 E. Kellogg, Wichita, KS 67218. **Telephone:** (316) 685-2233.

ATLANTIC LEAGUE

Mailing Address: 401 N. Delaware Ave. Camden, NJ 08102.
Telephone: (856) 541-9400. **FAX:** (856) 541-9410.
E-Mail Address: info@atlanticleague.com. **Website:** www.atlanticleague.com.
Year Founded: 1998.
Chief Executive Officer/Founder: Frank Boulton. **Vice Presidents:** Peter Kirk, Steven Kalafer.
Executive Director: Joe Klein.
Directors: Marc Berson (Newark), Frank Boulton (Long Island), Mary Jane Foster (Bridgeport), Steve Kalafer (Somerset), Peter Kirk (Lancaster, Camden, York, Southern Maryland).
League Operations Latin Coordinator: Ellie Rodriguez. **Director, Baseball Administration:** Patty MacLuckie.
Division Structure: Liberty Division—Bridgeport Bluefish, Camden Riversharks, Long Island Ducks, Southern Maryland Bluecrabs. **Freedom Division**—Lancaster Barnstormers, Newark Bears, Somerset Patriots, York Revolution.
Regular Season: 140 games (split-schedule).
2009 Opening Date: April 25. **Closing Date:** Sept. 21.
All-Star Game: July 16 at Somerset.
Playoff Format: First-half division winners meet second-half winners in best-of-three series. Winners meet in best-of-five final for league championship.
Roster Limit: 25. **Eligibility Rule:** No restrictions.
Brand of Baseball: Rawlings.
Statistician: SportsTicker, ESPN Plaza, Building B, Bristol, CT 06010.

STADIUM INFORMATION

			Dimensions				
Club	**Stadium**	**Opened**	**LF**	**CF**	**RF**	**Capacity**	**2008 Att.**
Bridgeport	The Ballpark at Harbor Yard	1998	325	405	325	5,300	156,429
Camden	Campbell's Field	2001	325	405	325	6,425	236,526
Lancaster	Clipper Magazine Stadium	2005	372	400	300	6,000	343,720
Long Island	Citibank Park	2000	325	400	325	6,002	416,752
Newark	Bears & Eagles Riverfront Stadium	1999	302	394	323	6,201	181,240
Somerset	Commerce Bank Ballpark	1999	317	402	315	6,100	347,735
So. Maryland	Regency Stadium	2008	305	400	320	6,000	226,086
York	Sovereign Bank Stadium	2007	300	400	325	5,000	300,246

BRIDGEPORT BLUEFISH

Office Address: 500 Main St., Bridgeport, CT 06604.
Telephone: (203) 345-4800. **FAX:** (203) 345-4830.
Website: www.bridgeportbluefish.com.
Operated by: Past Time Partners, LLC.
Principal Owner/CEO, Past Time Partners: Frank Boulton. **Senior VP, Past Time Partners:** Mike Pfaff. **Partners, Past Time Partners:** Tony Rosenthal, Fred Heyman, Jeff Serkes.
General Manager: Todd Marlin. **Assistant General Manager:** Joe Izzo. **Ticket Sales Manager:** Rob Finn. **Groundskeeper:** Brian McLaughlin. **Facilities Coordinator:** Tom Healy. **Media Relations Coordinator:** Paul Herrmann. **Merchandise and Client Services Coordinator:** Kate Billings. **Group Sales Coordinator:** Karen Luciano. **Account Executive:** Marilyn Guarino, Matt Onderko.
Manager: Tommy John. **Coach:** Unavailable. **Pitching Coach:** Unavailable. **Trainer:** Unavailable.

GAME INFORMATION

Radio Announcer: Unavailable. **No. of Games Broadcast:** Unavailable. **Flagship Station:** Unavailable. **PA Announcer:** Bill Jensen. **Official Scorer:** Rick Cohen.
Stadium Name: The Ballpark at Harbor Yard. **Location:** I-95 to exit 27, Route 8/25 to exit 1. **Standard Game Times:** 7:05 p.m.; Saturday, 6:05 p.m.; Sunday, 2:05 p.m.
Visiting Club Hotel: Holiday Inn Bridgeport, 1070 Main St., Bridgeport, CT 06604. **Telephone:** (203) 334-1234.

CAMDEN RIVERSHARKS

Office Address: 401 N. Delaware Ave., Camden, NJ 08102.
Telephone: (856) 963-2600. **FAX:** (856) 963-8534.
E-Mail Address: riversharks@riversharks.com. **Website:** www.riversharks.com.
Operated by: Camden Baseball, LLC
Principal Owners: Frank Boulton, Peter Kirk. **President:** Jon Danos. **Senior Vice President:** Brad Sims. **Controller:** Emily Merrill **General Manager:** Adam Lorber. **Assistant General Manager:** Kristen Simon. **Director, Corporate Partnerships:** Joel Seiden. **Director, Business Development:** Stu Cohen. **Director, Group Events:** Bob Nehring. **Director, Finance:** Bryan Humphreys. **Director, Marketing:** Natalie Filomeno. **Facilities Manager:**

Barry Huver. **Group Account Manager:** Nikki Varoutsos. **Group Account Manager:** Jeremy VanEtten. **Corporate Partnerships Manager:** Elizabeth Stevenson. **Corporate Partnerships Manager:** Bill DeGeorge. **Community Relations Assistant:** Dolores Rozier. **Groundskeeper:** Kevin Moses. **Office Manager:** Cheryl Parker.

Director, Baseball Operations: David Keller. **Manager:** Joe Ferguson. **Pitching Coach:** Dick Such. **Hitting Coach:** Unavailable. **Trainer:** Unavailable.

GAME INFORMATION

Radio: Rowan Radio, WGLS-FM. **PA Announcer:** Kevin Casey. **Official Scorer:** Dick Shute.

Stadium Name: Campbell's Field. **Location:** From Philadelphia, right on Sixth Street, right after Ben Franklin Bridge toll booth, right on Cooper Street until it ends at Delaware Ave. From Camden, I-676 to exit 5B, follow signs to field. **Standard Game Times: Weekdays**—7:05 p.m., Saturdays- 5:05 p.m., Sundays- 1:05 p.m. Gates open one hour prior to game time.

Visiting Club Hotel: Holiday Inn, Route 70 and Sayer Avenue, Cherry Hill, NJ 08002. **Telephone:** (856) 663-5300.

LANCASTER BARNSTORMERS

Office Address: 650 North Prince St., Lancaster, PA 17603.

Telephone: (717) 509-4487. **FAX:** (717) 509-4486.

E-Mail Address: info@lancasterbarnstormers.com. **Website:** www.lancasterbarnstormers.com.

Operated by: Lancaster Baseball Club, LLC. **Principal Owners:** Opening Day Partners.

President: Jon Danos. **Senior Vice President:** Brad Sims. **Controller:** Emily Merrill. **General Manager:** Kevin Cummings. **Assistant GM:** Vince Bulik. **Director, Marketing/Public Relations:** Adam Aurand. **Director, Stadium Operations:** Don Pryer. **Director, Finance:** Barbara Wert. **Director, Premium Account Services:** Kaye Willis. **Creative Services Manager:** Brad Jagielski. **Community Relations Manager:** Kevin Manno. **Ticket Operations Manager:** Maureen Wheeler. **Assistant Director, Stadium Operations:** Jeffrey Daws. **Marketing/Public Relations Assistant:** Pamela Denlinger. **Corporate Partnerships Associates:** Robert Ford, Kristin Lovelace, Richard Molina, Brian Radle. **Group Events Coordinators:** Sean Dougherty, Michael Minney, Lindsay Minnich, Jonathan Naff, Benjamin Peifer. **Customer Service Specialists:** Dana Mundey, Emily Reinbold. **Administrative Assistant:** Susan Shue. **Centerplate General Manager (Concessions/Merchandise):** Josh Leatherman. **Centerplate Merchandise Manager (Merchandise):** John Farrell.

Senior Vice President, Baseball Operations: Keith Lupton. **Manager:** Von Hayes. **Pitching Coach:** Rick Wise. **Coach:** Sam Snider. **Trainer:** Unavailable.

GAME INFORMATION

Radio Announcer: Dave Collins. **No. of Games Broadcast:** Home-70, Away-70. **Flagship Station:** WLPA 1490-AM. **PA Announcer:** John Witwer. **Official Scorer:** Joel Schreiner.

Stadium Name: Clipper Magazine Stadium. **Location:** From Route 30, take Fruitville Pike or Harrisburg Pike toward downtown Lancaster, stadium at intersection of Prince Street and Harrisburg Pike. **Standard Game Times:** 7:05 p.m., Sun. 1:35 p.m.

Visiting Club Hotel: Sleep Inn, 314 Primose Lane, Mountville, Pa., 17554. **Telephone:** (717) 285-2500.

LONG ISLAND DUCKS

Mailing Address: 3 Court House Dr., Central Islip, NY 11722.

Telephone: (631) 940-3825. **FAX:** (631) 940-3800.

E-Mail Address: info@liducks.com. **Website:** www.liducks.com.

Operated by: Long Island Ducks Professional Baseball, LLC.

Principal Owner/CEO: Frank Boulton. **Owner/Senior Vice President, Baseball Operations:** Bud Harrelson.

General Manager: Michael Pfaff. **Assistant GMs:** Doug Cohen, Alex Scannella. **Director, Group Sales:** Bill Harney. **Director, Administration:** Gerry Anderson. **Director, Operations:** Russ Blatt. **Manager, Box Office:** Ben Harper. **Manager, Promotions:** Morgan Tranquist. **Manager, Media Relations:** Mike Solano. **Manager, Merchandise:** Anthony Barberio. **Manager, Facilities:** Chris Gee. **Manager, Ticket Sales:** Brad Kallman. **Manager, Community Relations:** Katie Capria. **Coordinator, Administration:** Stephanie Valentinetti. **Account Executive, Group Sales:** John Wolff. **Head Groundskeeper:** Brad Keith. **Clubhouse Manager:** Rich Jensen.

Manager: Dave LaPoint. **Coaches:** Bud Harrelson, Kevin Baez. **Trainers:** Tony Amin, Adam Lewis, Dorothy Pitchford.

GAME INFORMATION

Radio Announcers: Chris King, Mike Solano, David Weiss. **No. of Games Broadcast:** 140 on www.liducks.com. **Flagship Station:** Unavailable. **PA Announcer:** Bob Ottone. **Official Scorers:** Joe Donnelly, Red Foley.

Stadium Name: Citibank Park. **Location:** Southern State Parkway east to Carleton Avenue North (exit 43 A), right onto Courthouse Drive, stadium behind federal courthouse complex. **Standard Game Times:** 7:05 p.m.; 6:35 p.m. Sunday, 1:35/5:05.

Visiting Club Hotel: Radisson Hotel MacArthur Airport. 1730 North Ocean Avenue, Holtsville NY 11742. **Telephone:** (631) 758-2900 Fax: (631) 758-2612.

NEWARK BEARS

Office Address: 450 Broad St., Newark, NJ 07102.
Telephone: (973) 848-1000. **FAX:** (973) 621-0095.
Website: www.newarkbears.com.
Operated by: Bases Loaded Group, LLC. **Owner:** Tom Cetnar.
General Manager: Mark Skeels. **Chief Financial Officer:** Irene Weber. **Chief Strategic Officer:** Spencer Geissinger. **Director, Events/Marketing:** Sarah LaBier. **Director, Sales:** Lucia DeSimone. **Director, Ballpark Operations:** Robert Cuomo.
Manager: Tim Raines. **Pitching Coach:** Mike Torrez. **Hitting Coach:** Ron Karkovice. **Bench Coach:** Tony Ferrara

GAME INFORMATION

Radio Announcer: Unavailable. **No. of Games Broadcast:** Home-70, Away-70. **Flagship Station:** WSOU-89.5 FM. **Official Scorer:** Unavailable.
Stadium Name: Bears & Eagles Riverfront Stadium. **Location:** Garden State Parkway North/South to exit 145 (280 East), to exit 15; New Jersey Turnpike North/South to 280 West, to exit 15A. **Standard Game Times:** Monday - Friday 6:05 p.m., Saturday and Sunday 4:05 p.m.
Visiting Club Hotel: Unavailable.

SOMERSET PATRIOTS

Office Address: One Patriots Park, Bridgewater, NJ 08807. **Telephone:** (908) 252-0700. **FAX:** (908) 252-0776. **Website:** www.somersetpatriots.com.
Operated by: Somerset Patriots Baseball Club, LLC. **Principal Owners:** Steve Kalafer, Jack Cust, Byron Brisby, Don Miller. **Chairman:** Steve Kalafer.
President, General Manager: Patrick McVerry. **Senior Vice President, Marketing:** Dave Marek. **VP, Assistant GM:** Rob Lukachyk. **VP, Public Relations:** Marc Russinoff. **VP, Ticketing:** Bryan Iwicki. **Head Groundskeeper:** Ray Cipperly. **Director, Group Sales:** Matt Kopas. **Director, Sales:** Kevin Forrester. **Director, Operations:** Tim Ur. **Corporate Marketing Manager:** Mike Desmond. **Group Sales:** Adam Cobb, Robert Crossman, Ian Haggerty. **Account Executive:** Mark Burgoon, Don Walters. **Ticket Sales Manager:** Adam Lifson. **Executive Assistant to GM:** Michele DaCosta. **Controller:** Ron Schultz. **Accountants:** Stephanie Diez, Tom Unchester. **Receptionist:** Lorraine Ott. **GM, Centerplate:** Mike McDermott. **Groundskeeper:** Dan Purner.
Manager: Sparky Lyle. **Director, Player Procurement/Pitching Coach:** Brett Jodie. **Hitting Coach:** Kevin Dattola. **Trainer:** Ryan McMahon.

GAME INFORMATION

Radio Announcer: Brian Bender. **No. of Games Broadcast:** Home-70, Away-70. **Flagship Station:** WCTC 1450-AM. **PA Announcer:** Paul Spychala. **Official Scorer:** John Nolan.
Stadium Name: Commerce Bank Ballpark. **Location:** Route 287 North to exit 13B/Route 287 South to exit 13 (Somerville Route 28 West); follow signs to ballpark. **Standard Game Times:** 7:05 p.m.; Sunday, 1:35 p.m.
Visiting Club Hotel: Somerset Ramada, 60 Cottontail Lane, Somerset, NJ 08873. **Telephone:** (732) 560-9880.

SOUTHERN MARYLAND BLUE CRABS

Office Address: 11765 St. Linus Dr., Waldorf, MD 20602
Telephone: (301) 638-9788. **Fax:** (301) 638-9877.
E-Mail Address: info@somdbluecrabs.com. **Website:** www.somdbluecrabs.com
Principal Owners: Opening Day Partners LLC, Brooks Robinson.
Chairman: Peter Kirk. **President:** Jon Danos.
Controller: Emily Merrill.
General Manager: Chris Allen. **Assistant GM:** Omar Roque. **Marketing Manager:** Courtney Freeland. **Corporate Sales Executives:** Bill Snitcher; Candace Wyant. **Director Groups and Ticket Sales:** Kris Rutledge. **Group Sales Manager:** Kyle Knichel. **Group Sales Executives:** Adam Henry; John Watson.
Box Office Manager: Carrine Cole. **Centerplate General Manager-Concessions:** Darren Hubbard.
Manager: Butch Hobson. **Pitching Coach:** Andre Rabouin. **Bench Coach:** Andy Etchebarren.

GAME INFORMATION

Radio: Unavailable. **Stadium:** Regency Furniture Stadium. **Standard Game Times:** 7:05 p.m., Saturday: 6:35 p.m. Sun: 2:05 p.m.

YORK REVOLUTION

Office Address: 5 Brooks Robinson Way York, PA 17401.
Telephone: (717) 801-4487. **FAX:** (717) 801-4499.
E-Mail Address: info@yorkrevolution.com. **Website:** www.yorkrevolution.com
Operated by: York Professional Baseball Club, LLC.
Principal Owners: Opening Day Partners. **President:** Jon Danos. **Controller:** Emily Merrill.
General Manager: Matt O'Brien. **Assistant GM:** Neil Fortier. **Finance Manager:** Lori Brunson. **Sales Director:** Joe Charles. **Marketing/Promotions Director:** Greg Vojtanek. **Community Marketing Manager:** Tim Beckwith. **Corporate Sales Managers:** John Gibson, Mary Beth Hare. **Client Services Associate:** Scott Youcheff. **Facility Operations Manager:** Josh Brown. **Group Events Manager:** Michelle Gemmill. **Group Events Coordinators:** Dan App, Lisa Howell. **Box Office Manager:** Cindy Burkholder. **Head Groundskeeper:** Brandon Putman. **Centerplate General Manager (Concessions/Merchandise):** Travis Johnson.
Baseball Operations Director: Adam Gladstone. **Manager:** Chris Hoiles. **Pitching Coach:** Tippy Martinez.

GAME INFORMATION

Radio Announcer: Darrell Henry. **No. of Games Broadcast:** 140. **Flagship Station:** WSBA 910-AM. **PA Announcer:** Al Rose. **Official Scorer:** Brian Wisler.
Stadium Name: Sovereign Bank Stadium. **Location:** Take Route 30 West to North George Street. Turn left onto North George Street. Follow that straight for four lights, Sovereign Bank Stadium is on left. **Standard Game Times:** 7 p.m.; Sunday, 1 p.m. or 5 p.m.
Visiting Club Hotel: The Yorktowne Hotel, 48 E Market St. York, PA 17401. **Telephone:** 717-848-1111.

CAN-AM LEAGUE

Office Address: 1415 Hwy. 54 West, Suite 210, Durham, NC 27707.
Telephone: (919) 401-8150. **Fax:** (919) 401-8152.
Website: www.canamleague.com.
Year Founded: 2005.
Commissioner: Miles Wolff. **President:** Dan Moushon.
Administrative Assistant: Jason Deans. **Director of Umpires:** Kevin Winn.
Regular Season: 94 games (split-schedule).
2009 Opening Date: May 28. **Closing Date:** Sept. 7.
Playoff Format: First- and second-half winners meet two teams with best overall records in best-of-five series. Winners meet in best-of-five series for league championship.
Roster Limit: 22. **Eligibility Rule:** Minimum of five first-year players; maximum of four veterans with at least four years of professional experience.
Brand of Baseball: Rawlings.
Statistician: PA SportsTicker, 55 Realty Drive Cheshire, CT 06410.

STADIUM INFORMATION

			Dimensions				
Club	**Stadium**	**Opened**	**LF**	**CF**	**RF**	**Capacity**	**2008 Att.**
New Hampshire	Nokona Park at Holman Stadium	1937	307	401	315	4,375	69,995
Atlantic City	Bernie Robbins Stadium	1998	313	410	312	5,500	124,430
Brockton	Campanelli Stadium	2002	340	404	320	4,750	132,785
New Jersey	Yogi Berra Stadium	1998	308	398	308	3,784	103,817
Ottawa	Ottawa Stadium	1993	325	404	325	10,332	101,073
Quebec	Stade Municipal de Quebec	1938	315	385	315	4,800	140,933
Sussex	Skylands Park	1994	330	392	330	4,300	80,500
Worcester	Hanover Insurance Park-Fitton Field	1905	361	417	307	3,000	90,127

ATLANTIC CITY SURF

Office Address: 545 North Albany Avenue, Atlantic City, NJ 08401.
Telephone: (609) 344-8873. **Fax:** (609) 344-7873.
E-Mail: info@acsurf.com. **Website:** www.acsurf.com.
Owner: Mark Schuster.
President: Chris Carminucci. **Vice President:** Ryan Conley. **Director, Operations:** Hoffman Wolff. **Director, Sales:** Kerry Pritchard. **Director, Food/Beverage:** Sander Stotland. **Manager, Community Relations:** Barry Kraus.
Manager: Cecil Fielder. **Coaches:** J.C. Huguet, Brian Rodaway.

GAME INFORMATION

Announcer (Webcast): Matt Martucci. **No. of Games Broadcast:** 94. **Webcast Address:** www.acsurf.com.
Stadium Name: Bernie Robbins Stadium. **Location:** From Points South (Ocean City, Cape May): Take the Garden State Parkway North to Exit 38 (Atlantic City Expressway East), AC Expressway to Exit 2 (Rt. 40/322). Take Rt. 40/322 East for 1 1/2 miles to the ballpark. **From the West:** Take AC Expressway East to Exit 2 and follow directions from the south above. **From the North:** Take the Garden State Parkway South to Exit 38 (Atlantic City Expressway East). Follow directions from the South above (AC Expressway Exit 38).
Standard Game Times: 7:05 p.m.; May 26, 6:30 p.m.; May 28, June 11, July 16, July 30: 11:00 a.m.
Visiting Club Hotel: Comfort Inn Victorian, 6817 Black Horse Pike, West Atlantic City, NJ 08234. **Telephone:** (609) 646-8880.

BROCKTON ROX

Office Address: One Feinberg Way, Brockton, MA 02301
Telephone: (508)559-7000. **Fax:** (508)587-2802.
E-Mail: roxrock@brocktonrox.com. **Website:** www.brocktonrox.com
Principal Owner: Van Schley. **President:** Jack Yunits. **Executive Vice President:** Michael Canina.
General Manager: Brian Voelkel. **Director, Food/Beverage:** Steve Bowker. **Client Services Manager:** Allison Gemelli. **Director, Promotions/Merchandise:** Bailey Frye. **Director, Media Relations/Broadcasting:** Matt Futrell. **Group Sales Representative:** Chris Corbett, Loretta Sullivan. **Community Relations/Sales:** Terri Kuskoski. **Receptionist:** Me'Shay Hurt. **Bookkeeper:** Mary Scarlett. **Groundskeeper:** Tom Hassett.
Manager: Chris Miyake. **Coaches:** Ryan Kane, John Kelly. **Trainer:** Lauren Eck.

GAME INFORMATION

Radio Announcer: Matt Futrell. **No. of Games Broadcast:** 94. **Flagship Station:** WXBR 1460-AM. **Webcast Address:** www.brocktonrox.com.

Stadium Name: Campanelli Stadium. **Location:** Route 24 North/South to Route 123 east, stadium is two miles on right.

Standard Game Times: Monday/Saturday: 6:05 p.m.; Tuesday-Friday 7:05 p.m.; Sunday (May/June), 1:05 p.m. (July/August), 5:05 p.m.

Visiting Club Hotel: Holiday Inn Brockton, 195 Westgate Drive, Brockton, MA 02301. **Telephone:** (508) 588-6300.

NASHUA PRIDE

Office Address: 67 Amherst St., Nashua, NH 03064.
Telephone: (603) 883-2255. **Fax:** (603) 883-0880.
E-Mail Address: info@nashuapride.com. **Website:** www.nashuapride.com.
Operated by: Nashua Pride Baseball, LLC.
Principal Owner: John Stabile. **COO:** Jim Stabile

General Manager/Vice President, Baseball Operations: Chris Hall. **Assistant GM:** Courtney Hollis. **Director, Sales:** Cliff Jacques. **Director, Baseball Administration:** Beverly Taylor. **Manager, Media/Community Relations:** Nick Travalini. **Group Sales Manager:** Shaela Walsh.

Manager: Rick Miller. **Coach:** Richie Hebner.

GAME INFORMATION

Stadium Name: Historic Holman Stadium. **Location:** Route 3 to exit 7E (Amherst Street), stadium one mile on left.
Standard Game Times: 7:05 p.m.; Sunday, 5:05 p.m.
Visiting Club Hotel: Radisson-Nashua Hotel, 11 Tara Boulevard, Nashua, NH 03062.
Telephone: (603) 888-9970.

NEW JERSEY JACKALS

Office Address: One Hall Dr., Little Falls, NJ 07424.
Telephone: (973) 746-7434. **Fax:** (973) 655-8006.
E-Mail Address: info@jackals.com. **Website:** www.jackals.com.
Operated by: Floyd Hall Enterprises LLC.
Chairman: Floyd Hall. **President:** Greg Lockard.

General Manager: Larry Hall. **Business Manager:** Jennifer Fertig. **Director, Ticket Operations:** Pierson Van Raalte. **Director, Group Sales:** Sue Beck. **Facilities Manager:** Aldo Licitra. **Concessions Manager:** Michele Guarino. **Clubhouse Manager:** Wally Brackett.

Manager: Joe Calfapietra. **Coaches:** Bryan Gaal, Ed Ott, Ani Ramos.

GAME INFORMATION

Announcer (Webcast): Joe Ameruoso. **No. of Games Broadcast:** 94. **Webcast Address:** www.jackals.com.

Stadium Name: Yogi Berra Stadium. **Location:** Route 80 or Garden State Parkway to Route 46, take Valley Road exit to Montclair State University.

Standard Game Times: 7:05 p.m.; Sunday, 5:05 p.m.
Visiting Club Hotel: Ramada Inn, 130 Rte. 10 West, East Hanover, NJ 07936. **Telephone:** (973) 386-5622.

OTTAWA RAPIDS

Office Address: 300 Coventry Rd., Ottawa, Ontario K1K4P5.
Telephone: (613) 747-5969. **Fax:** (613) 747-0003
Email: info@baseballottawa.com. **Website:** www.baseballottawa.com.
Operated by: Ottawa Pro Baseball, Inc.

General Manager: Don Charrette. **Director, Sales:** Francois Marchand. **Office Administrator:** Lorraine Charrette. **Account Executive:** Richard Poulin. **Director, Marketing:** Angela Thompson. **Head Groundskeeper:** Josh Teuscher.

Manager: Ed Nottle. **Coach:** Mike Kusiewicz.

GAME INFORMATION

Stadium: Ottawa Stadium. **Location:** Hwy. 417 to Vanier Parkway exit. Vanier Parkway north, 1/2 mile to Coventry Rd. Turn right to stadium.

Standard Game Times: 7:05 p.m; Sunday, 1:05 p.m.
Visiting Club Hotel: Chimo Hotel. 119 Joseph Cyr Rd., Ottawa, Ontario K1K 3P5. **Telephone:** (613)744-1060.

QUEBEC CAPITALES

Office Address: 100 Rue du Cardinal Maurice-Roy, Quebec City, Quebec G1K8Z1.
Telephone: (418) 521-2255. **Fax:** (418) 521-2266.
E-Mail Address: baseball@capitalesdequebec.com. **Website:** www.capitalesdequebec.com.
Owner/President: Miles Wolff

General Manager: Alex Harvey. **Vice Presidents:** Michel Laplante, Stephane Dionne. **Sales Director:** Maxime Lamarche. **Promotions Director:** Guillaume Lamb. **Media Relations Director:** Pier-Luc Nappert. **Sales Representatives:** Jean-Philippe Auger, Jean Marois.

Manager: Michel Laplante. **Coaches:** Stephane Dionne, Patrick Scalabrini.

GAME INFORMATION

Radio Announcers: Jacques Doucet, Francois Paquet. **No. of Games Broadcast:** 94. **Flagship Station:** Info 800-AM. **Webcast Address:** www.info800.ca.

Stadium Name: Stade Municipal de Quebec. **Location:** Highway 40 to Highway 173 (Centre-Ville) exit 2 to Parc Victoria.

Standard Game Times: 7:05 p.m.; Sunday, 1:05 p.m.

Visiting Club Hotel: Hotel du Nord, 640 St. Vallier Ouest, Quebec City, QC G1N1C5. **Telephone:** (418) 522-1554.

SUSSEX SKYHAWKS

Office Address: 94 Championship Place Suite 11, Augusta, NJ 07822.
Telephone: (973) 300-1000. **Fax:** (973) 300-9000.
E-Mail Address: info@sussexskyhawks.com. **Website:** www.sussexskyhawks.com.
Operated By: Sussex Professional Baseball LLC.
President: Larry Hall.

General Manager: Ben Wittkowski. **Director, Corporate Sales:** Herm Sorcher. **Director, Corporate Partnerships:** Matt Millet. **Director, Ticket Sales/Operations:** Seth Bettan. **Group Sales Representatives:** Corinne Oravits, Amy Rude. **Concessions Manager:** Matt Myers. **Facility Manager:** Aldo Licitra.

Manager: Hal Lanier. **Coaches:** Brooks Carey, Dave Cash.

GAME INFORMATION

Television: Channel 10 Sussex County. **No. of Broadcasts:** 10 Games.

Stadium Name: Skylands Park. **Location:** From New Jersey, I-80 to exit 34B (Rt. 15 N) to Route 565; From Pennsylvania, I-84 to Route 6 to Route 206 North to Route 565 East. **Standard Game Times:** 7:05 p.m.; Saturday, 5:05 p.m.; Sunday, 2:05 p.m.

Visiting Club Hotel: Ramada Inn, 130 Rte. 10 West, East Hanover, NJ 07936.
Telephone: (973) 386-5622.

WORCESTER TORNADOES

Office Address: 303 Main St., Worcester, MA 01613.
Telephone: (508) 792-2288. **Fax:** (506) 926-3662.
E-Mail Address: info@worcestertornadoes.com. **Website:** www.worcestertornadoes.com.

Chairman: Theodore Tye. **Board of Directors:** Thomas Alperin, Mary DeFeudis, David Forsberg, Bruce Ginsberg, Tom Maher, Peter Merrigan, Bradly Michals, Bob Richards, Alan Stone.

Executive Vice President/General Manager: Jorg Bassiacos. **VP/Director, Sales:** Dave Peterson. **Account Executive/Tykes Program Coordinator:** Sara Farley. **Director, Group Sales:** Miriam Hyder. **Ticket Manager:** Alise Wales. **Ballpark Operations Manager:** Chris Leach. **Director of Interactive Media:** Mike Tetler.

Manager: Rich Gedman. **Coaches:** Roger LaFrancois, Ed Gallagher. **Director of Player Personnel:** Bradly Michals.

GAME INFORMATION

Radio Announcer: Jeremy Lechan. **No. of Games Broadcast:** 94. **Flagship Station:** WTAG 580-AM. **Webcast Address:** www.worcestertornadoes.com.

Stadium Name: Hanover Insurance Park at Fitton Field. **Location:** I-290 to exit 11 College Square, right on College Street, left on Fitton Avenue.

Standard Game Times: 6:05pm Mon-Sat (May-June) 7:05 p.m. Mon-Sat (July-August); 1:05 p.m. Sunday

Visiting Club Hotel: Hampton Inn, 110 Summer St., Worcester, MA 01609. **Telephone:** (508)754-0400.

FRONTIER LEAGUE

Office Address: 2041 Goose Lake Rd. Suite 2A, Sauget, Il. 62206
Telephone: (618) 215-4134. **FAX:** (618) 332-2115.
E-Mail Address: office@frontierleague.com. **Website:** www.frontierleague.com.
Year Founded: 1993.
Chairman: Dr. Chris Hanners
President: Rich Sauget (Gateway). **Vice Presidents:** Steve Malliet (River City) Leslye Wuerfel (Traverse City). **Corporate Secretary/Treasurer:** Bob Wolfe.
Commissioner: Bill Lee. **Legal Counsel/Deputy Commissioner:** Kevin Rouch.
Directors: Dan Brennan (Windy City), Clint Brown (Florence), Bill Bussing (Evansville), Kurt Carlson (Rockford), Steven Edelson (Lake Erie), Erik Haag (Southern Illinois), Rob Hilliard (Midwest), Steve Malliet (River City), Joe Rosenhagen (Kalamazoo), Rich Sauget (Gateway), John Swiatek (Washington), Leslye Wuerfel (Traverse City).
Division Structure: East—Florence, Kalamazoo, Lake Erie, Midwest, Traverse City, Washington. **West**—Evansville, Gateway, River City, Rockford, Southern Illinois, Windy City.
Regular Season: 96 games.
2009 Opening Date: May 20. **Closing Date:** Sept. 6.
All-Star Game: July 15 at Rockford.
Playoff Format: Division winners and two remaining teams with the best overall regular season records meet in best-of-five semifinal series. Winners meet in best-of-five series for league championship.
Roster Limit: 24. **Eligibility Rule:** Minimum of 10 first-year players; maximum of seven players with one year of professional experience, maximum of two players with two years of experience and maximum of three players with three or more years of experience. No player may be 27 prior to Jan. 1 of current season.
Brand of Baseball: Wilson.
Statistician: SportsTicker, 55 Reality Drive, Suite 200, Cheshire, CT 06410.

STADIUM INFORMATION

			Dimensions				
Club	Stadium	Opened	LF	CF	RF	Capacity	2008 Att.
Evansville	Bosse Field	1915	315	415	315	5,181	119,645
Florence	Champion Window Field	2004	325	395	325	4,200	106,707
Gateway	GCS Ballpark	2002	318	395	325	5,500	190,892
Kalamazoo	Homer Stryker Field	1995	306	400	330	4,806	83,157
Lake Erie	TBA	2009	325	400	325	5,000	N/A
Midwest	Oestrike Stadium	1971	340	390	325	1,300	N/A
River City	T.R. Hughes Ballpark	1999	320	382	299	4,989	106,114
Rockford	Road Ranger Stadium	2006	315	380	312	4,056	138,234
So. Illinois	Rent One Park	2007	325	400	330	4,500	218,191
Traverse City	Wuerfel Park	2006	320	400	320	4,600	193,724
Washington	Consol Energy Park	2002	325	400	325	3,200	154,444
Windy City	Standard Bank Stadium	1999	335	390	335	4,000	90,616

EVANSVILLE OTTERS

Mailing Address: 1701 N. Main St., Evansville, IN 47711.
Telephone: (812) 435-8686.
Operated by: Evansville Baseball, LLC.
President: Bill Bussing.
Senior Vice President: Pat Rayburn. **General Manager:** Liam Miller. **Assistant GM:** Casie Williams. **Operations Manager/Account Executive:** Brandon McClish. **Account Executives:** Kenton Hargis, Elizabeth Lewis. **Interns:** Greg Moore, Jake Weinzapfel, Nick Shanahan, Katie, Jaworski.
Manager/Director, Baseball Operations: Wayne Krenchicki. **Coaches:** Steve Foucault, Ryan Jones.

GAME INFORMATION

Radio Announcer: Unavailable. **No. of Games Broadcast:** Home-48, Away-48. **Flagship Station:** WUEV 91.5-FM. **PA Announcer:** Unavailable. **Official Scorer:** Unavailable.
Stadium Name: Bosse Field. **Location:** U.S. 41 to Lloyd Expressway West (IN-62), Main St. Exit, Right on Main St., ahead 1 mile to Bosse Field. **Standard Game Times:** 7:05 p.m.; Sunday, 6:05 p.m.
Visiting Club Hotel: Unavailable.

FLORENCE FREEDOM

Office Address: 7950 Freedom Way, Florence, KY 41042.
Telephone: (859) 594-4487. **FAX:** (859) 594-3194.
E-Mail Address: info@florencefreedom.com. **Website:** www.florencefreedom.com.

Operated by: Canterbury Baseball, LLC.

President: Clint Brown. **General Manager:** Kari Rumfield. **Director, Community Relations:** Kim Brown. **Box Office Manager:** Sarah Straughn. **Stadium Operations Manager:** Stephen Mace. **Director, Corporate Sales:** Elizabeth Quatman. **Promotions Manager:** Shawn Cox. **Sales Manager:** Johnathan Simon.

Baseball Operations/Manager: Toby Rumfield. **Coach:** Greg Stone. **Pitching Coach:** Bill Browett. **Trainer:** Dominic Favia.

GAME INFORMATION

Radio: 106.7 WNKR. **Radio Broadcaster:** Josh Anderson. **PA Announcer:** Kevin Schwab. **Official Scorer:** Unavailable.

Stadium: Champion Window Field. **Location:** I-71/75 South to exit 180, left onto US 42, right on Freedom Way; I-71/75 North to exit 180. **Standard Game Times:** 7:05 p.m.; Saturday 6:05 p.m. Sunday 2:05 p.m./6:05 p.m.

Visiting Club Hotel: Wildwood Inn.

GATEWAY GRIZZLIES

Mailing Address: 2301 Grizzlie Bear Blvd., Sauget, IL 62206.
Telephone: (618) 337-3000. **FAX:** (618) 332-3625.
E-Mail Address: grizzlies@accessus.net. **Website:** www.gatewaygrizzlies.com.
Operated by: Gateway Baseball, LLC.
Managing Officer: Richard Sauget.

General Manager: Steven Gomric. **Director, Group Sales:** Jason Murphy. **Stadium Operations:** Brent Pownall. **Media Relations Director/Events Coordinator:** Jeff O'Neill. **Director, Sales:** C.J. Hendrickson. **Director, Head Groundskeeper/Corporate Sales Associate:** Craig Kuhl. **Ticket Sales:** Will Myers. **Director, Guest Relations:** Evan Bolesta. **Director, Promotions:** Courtney Purcell. **Office Operations:** Chris Andrews. **Ticket Sales Associate:** Wes Hilliard. **Ticket Sales Associate:** Steven Gonzalez.

Manager: Phil Warren. **Pitching Coach:** Randy Martz. **Bench Coach:** Darin Kinsolving. **Trainer:** Geof Manzo. **Clubhouse Manager:** Mike Sartore

GAME INFORMATION

Radio Announcer: Joe Pott. **No of Games Broadcast:** Home-48, Away-48. **Flagship Station:** 88.7 FM WSIE. **PA Announcer:** Tom Calhoun. **Official Scorer:** Matthew Frey.

Stadium Name: GCS Ballpark. **Location:** I-255 at exit 15 (Mousette Lane). **Standard Game Times:** 7:05 p.m.; Sunday, 6:05 p.m./3:05 p.m.

Visiting Club Hotel: Ramada Inn, 6900 N. **Illinois St., Fairview Heights, IL 62208. Telephone:** (618) 632-4747.

LAKE ERIE CRUSHERS

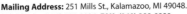

Mailing Address: 36711 American Way, Suite 4, Avon, OH, 44011.
Telephone: (440) 934-3636. **FAX:** (440) 934-2458.
E-Mail Address: info@lakeeriecrushers.com. **Website:** www.lakeeriecrushers.com.
Operated by: Avon Pro Baseball LLC.
Managing Officer: Steven Edelson.

General Manager: Ryan Gates. **Assistant GM, Operation:** Paul Siegwarth. **Business Manager:** Jen Doan. **Box Office Manager:** Kelly Dolan. **Account Executive:** Zack Krantz. **Director, Media/Community Relations:** Nicolle Meyer. **Corporate Sales Executive:** Brooke Novak. **Account Executive:** Derek Stapinski. **Director, Client Services/Merchandise:** Jason Vaughan.

Manager: John Massarelli. **Pitching Coach:** Chris Steinborn. **Hitting Coach:** Dave Schaub.

GAME INFORMATION

Stadium Name: Unavailable. **Location:** Intersection of I-90 and Colorado Ave. in Avon, OH. **Standard Game Times:** 7:05 p.m.; Sunday, 5:05 p.m.

KALAMAZOO KINGS

Mailing Address: 251 Mills St., Kalamazoo, MI 49048.
Telephone: (269) 388-8326. **FAX:** (269) 388-8333.
Website: www.kalamazookings.com.

Operated by: Team Kalamazoo, LLC. **Owners:** Bill Wright, Mike Seelye, Pat Seelye, Joe Rosenhagen, Ed Bernard, Scott Hocevar. **General Manager/Managing Partner:** Joe Rosenhagen. **Community Relations:** Chris Peake.

Director, Baseball Operations/Field Manager: Fran Riordan. **Pitching Coach:** John Sexton.

GAME INFORMATION

Radio Announcers: Unavailable. **No. of Games Broadcast:** Home-48, Away-48. **Flagship Station:** The Fan 1660-AM. **PA Announcer:** Jim Lefler. **Official Scorer:** Jason Zerban. **Stadium Name:** Homer Stryker Field. **Location:** I-94 to Sprinkle Road (exit 80), north on Sprinkle Road, left on Business Loop I-94, left on Kings Highway, right on Mills Street.

Standard Game Times: 7:05 p.m.; Sunday, 2:05 p.m.

Visiting Club Hotel: Red Roof Inn, 5425 W. Michigan Ave., Kalamazoo, MI 49009. **Telephone:** (269)375-7400.

MIDWEST SLIDERS

Mailing Address: P.O. Box 981408, Ypsilanti MI 48198

E-mail Address: info@cruisersbaseball.com. **Web Site:** www.midwestsliders.com

Operated By: Baseball Heroes of Oakland County, LP

President/Director, Team Personnel: Rob Hilliard

Manager/Director, Player Development: Eric Coleman. **Coaches:** Cory Domel, Gera Alvarez.

RIVER CITY RASCALS

Office Address: 900 T.R. Hughes Blvd., O'Fallon, MO 63366.

Telephone: (636) 240-2287. **FAX:** (636) 240-7313.

E-Mail Address: info@rivercityrascals.com. **Website:** www.rivercityrascals.com.

Operated by: PS and J Professional Baseball Club LLC. **Owners:** Tim Hoeksema, Jan Hoeksema, Fred Stratton, Anne Stratton, Pam Malliet, Steve Malliet, Michael Veeck.

Vice President/General Manager: Chris Franklin. **Business Manager:** Tammie Hopkins. **Senior Director, Ticket Sales:** Zach Ziler. **Groundskeeper:** Chris Young. **GM, Aramark Sports/Entertainment Services:** Mark Duffy.

Team Manager: Chad Parker. **Pitching Coach:** Bryce Florie. **Bench Coach:** Steve Brook.

GAME INFORMATION

Radio Announcer: Unavailable. **No. of Games Broadcast:** Home-48, Away-48. **Flagship Station:** 590 The FAN KFNS. **PA Announcer:** Unavailable. **Official Scorer:** Unavailable.

Stadium Name: T.R. Hughes Ballpark. **Location:** I-70 to exit 219, north on T.R. Hughes Road, follow signs to ballpark. **Standard Game Times:** 7:05 p.m.; Sunday, 6:05 p.m.

Visiting Club Hotel: Hilton Garden Inn, 2310 Technology Drive, O'Fallon, MO 63368, (636) 625-2700

ROCKFORD RIVERHAWKS

Office Address: 4503 Interstate Blvd., Loves Park, IL 61111.

Telephone: (815) 885-2255. **FAX:** (815) 964-2462.

Website: www.rockfordriverhawks.com.

Owners: Dennis Arouca, Kurt Carlson, Dave Ciarrachi, Brian McClure. **Managing Partner:** Dave Ciarrachi.

General Manager: Josh Olerud. **Assistant GM/Baseball Operations:** Todd Fulk. **Assistant GM/Marketing, Promotions:** Marshall Mackinder. **Director, Broadcasting/Media Relations:** Bill Czaja. **Director, Tickets/Finance:** Brad Sholes. **Director, Operations:** Chris Daleo. **Director, Group Sales:** Meredith Carlson. **Head Groundskeeper:** Travis Stephen.

Manager: Bob Koopmann. **Coaches:** J.D. Arndt, Sam Knaack, Spiro Lempesis. **Trainer:** Jim Halpin.

GAME INFORMATION

Radio Announcer: Bill Czaja. **No. of Games Broadcast:** Home-48, Away-48. **Flagship Station:** ESPN 1380 (WTJK, 1380-AM). **PA Announcers:** Scott Bentley, Brett Myhers, Bob Ace. **Official Scorer:** Unavailable.

Stadium Name: Road Ranger Stadium. **Location:** I-90 (Jane Addams Tollway) to Riverside Boulevard exit (automatic toll booth), east to Interstate Drive, left on Interstate Drive. **Standard Game Times:** Monday-Friday, 7:05 p.m.; Saturday, 6:05 p.m.; Sunday, 4:05 p.m.

Visiting Club Hotel: Days Inn, 220 S. Lyford Rd., Rockford, IL 61108. **Telephone:** (815) 332-4915.

SOUTHERN ILLINOIS MINERS

Office Address: Rent One Park, 1000 Miners Drive, Marion, IL 62959

Telephone: (618) 998-8499. **Fax:** (618) 969-8550

E-Mail Address: info@southernillinoisminers.com. **Website:** www.southernillinoisminers.com.

Operated by: Southern Illinois Baseball Group.

Vice President: Erik Haag. **General Manager:** Tim Arseneau. **Assistant GM:** Brad Grenoble. **Director, Ticket Operations:** Kyle Bass. **Manager, Client Services:** Sarah Chamness. **Director, Media Relations/Broadcasting:** Scott Gierman. **Director, Production:** Chris Hagstrom. **Executive Chef:** Dylan Lipe. **Team Merchandise:** Justin Moore. **Director, Finance:** Cathy Perry. **Director, Stadium Operations:** Billy Peterman. **Operations/Clubhouse Manager:** Jeff Pink. **Account Executive:** Jennifer Wade

Manager: Mike Pinto. **Pitching Coach:** Brendan Sagara. **Coaches:** Bart Zeller, Ralph Santana, Ron Biga.

GAME INFORMATION

Radio Announcer: Scott Gierman. **No. of Games Broadcast:** 96. **Flagship Station:** 97.7 WQUL-FM.

Stadium Name: Rent One Park. **Location:** US 57 to Route 13 East, right at Halfway Road to Fairmont Dr. **Standard Game Times:** 7:05 p.m.; Sunday, 5:05 p.m.

Visiting Club Hotel: Econo Lodge, 1806 Bittle Place, Marion, IL 62959

TRAVERSE CITY BEACH BUMS

Office Address: 333 Stadium Dr., Traverse City, MI 49684.
Telephone: (231) 943-0100.
FAX: (231) 943-0900.
E-Mail Address: info@tcbeachbums.com. **Website:** www.traversecitybeachbums.com.
Operated by: Traverse City Beach Bums, LLC.
Managing Partners: John Wuerfel, Leslye Wuerfel, Jason Wuerfel.

President/CEO: John Wuerfel. **General Manager:** Leslye Wuerfel. **Vice President:** Jason Wuerfel. **Director, Sales/Marketing:** Jeremy Crum. **Director, Promotions/Community Relations:** Michele LeMieux. **Director, Concessions:** Andy Benningfield. **Director, Merchandise:** Scott McDowell. **Director, Ticketing:** Nick Jacqmain. **Director, Media Relations:** Nate Jorgensen. **Director, Broadcasting:** Tim Calderwood.

Manager: Gregg Langbehn. **Hitting Coach:** Unavailable. **Pitching Coach:** Roger Mason. **Clubhouse Manager:** Denny Dame. **Trainer:** Unavailable.

GAME INFORMATION

Radio Announcer: Tim Calderwood. **No. of Games Broadcast:** Home-48, Away-48. **Flagship Stations:** WFCX 94.3-FM; WFDX 92.5-FM. **PA. Announcer:** Tim Moeggenberg. **Official Scorer:** Greg Rosinski.

Stadium Name: Wuerfel Park. **Location:** 3 miles south of the Grand Traverse Mall just off US-31 and M-37 in Chums Village. Stadium is visible from the highway (Or north of US 31 and M-37 Chums Corner intersection). Turn-west on Chums Village Drive, north on Village Park Drive, right on Stadium Drive. **Standard Game Times:** 7:05 p.m.; Sunday, 5:35 p.m.

Visiting Club Hotel: Days Inn & Suites of Traverse City.

WASHINGTON WILD THINGS

Office Address: One Washington Federal Way, Washington, PA 15301.
Telephone: (724) 250-9555. **FAX:** (724) 250-2333.
E-Mail Address: info@washingtonwildthings.com . **Website:** www.washingtonwildthings.com.
Owned by: Sports Facility, LLC. **Operated by:** Washington Frontier League Baseball, LLC.
Managing Partner: John Swiatek.
President/Chief Executive Officer: John Swiatek.

General Manager: Ross Vecchio. **Director, Marketing:** Christine Blaine. **Director. Stadium Operations:** Steve Zavacky. **Sponsorship Account Executive:** Greg Thompson. **Box Office Manager:** Joe Traynor. **Merchandise Manager:** Dee Lober. **Concessions Manager:** Joe Pagano. **Ticket Account Executives:** David Shrader, Dan Wolkiewicz, Ashlee Nichol, Phil Dillon, Peter Barakat

Manager: Greg Jelks. **Coach:** Bob Bozzuto. **Pitching Coach:** Unavailable. **Trainer:** Bobby Smith.

GAME INFORMATION

Radio Announcer: Bob Gregg. **No. of Games Broadcast:** Home-50, Away-45. **Flagship Station:** WJPA 95.3-FM . **PA Announcer:** Bill DiFabio. **Official Scorer:** Scott McGuinness.

Stadium Name: Location: I-70 to exit 15 (Chestnut Street), right on Chestnut Street to Washington Crown Center Mall, right at mall entrance, right on to Mall Drive to stadium. **Standard Game Times:** 7:05 p.m.; Sunday, 6:35 p.m.

Visiting Club Hotel: Unavailable.

WINDY CITY THUNDERBOLTS

Office Address: 14011 South Kenton Ave., Crestwood, IL 60445-2252.
Telephone: (708) 489-2255. **FAX:** (708) 489-2999.
E-Mail Address: info@wcthunderbolts.com. **Website:** www.wcthunderbolts.com.
Owned by: Crestwood Professional Baseball, LLC.

General Manager: Steve Tahsler. **Assistant GM:** Mike Lucas. **Director, Sales:** Pete Kelly. **Director, Group Sales:** Jim Rice. **Director, Community Relations:** Tom Linehan. **Director, Fundraising/Head Groundskeeper:** Mike VerSchave. **Director, Ticketing:** Adam Gorniak.

Field Manager: Tommy Thompson. **Pitching Coach:** Unavailable. **Hitting Coach:** Unavailable. **Bench Coach:** Mike Kashirsky. **Trainer:** Audric Warren.

GAME INFORMATION

Radio Announcers: Chad Cooper, Terry Bonadonna. **No. of Games Broadcast:** 96. **Flagship Station:** WXAV, 88.3 FM. **PA Announcer:** Unavailable. **Official Scorer:** Jason Collins.

Stadium Name: Standard Bank Stadium. **Location:** I-294 to S. Cicero Ave., exit (Route 50), south for 1 1/2 miles, left at Midlothian Turnpike, right on Kenton Ave.; I-57 to 147th Street, west on 147th to Cicero, north on Cicero, right on Midlothian Turnpike, right on Kenton. **Standard Game Times:** 7:05 p.m.; Sunday, 6:05 p.m.

Visiting Club Hotel: Georgio's Comfort Inn, 8800 W. 159th St., Orland Park, IL 60462. **Telephone:** (708) 403-1100. **Fax:** (708) 403-1105.

GOLDEN LEAGUE

Office Address: 7080 Donlon Way, Suite 109, Dublin, CA 94568.
Telephone: (925) 226-2889. **FAX:** (925) 226-2891.
E-mail Address: info@goldenbaseball.com. **Website:** www.goldenbaseball.com.
Founded: 2005.
CEO/President: David Kaval.
Commissioner/COO: Kevin Outcalt. **Vice President/Operations:** Curt Jacey. **Director, Administration:** Stephen Bedford. **League Historian/Secretary:** Bill Weiss. **Supervisor, Officials:** Ron Barnes.
Division Structure: North—Edmonton, Calgary, Chico, Victoria, Long Beach. **South**—Tucson, Tijuana, Orange County, St. George, Yuma.
Regular Season: 88 games.
2009 Opening Date: May 21. **Closing Date:** Aug. 31.
Playoff Format: First- and second-half division winners meet in best-of-five semifinals; winners meet in championship series.
Roster Limit: 22. **Eligibility Rules:** No minimum number of rookies, age limit of 28 as of Jan. 1 unless player has major league, Triple-A, Double-A, top foreign or former GBL experience.
Brand of Baseball: Rawlings
Statistician: SportsTicker, ESPN Plaza, Building B, Bristol, CT 06010.

STADIUM INFORMATION

			Dimensions				
Club	**Stadium**	**Opened**	**LF**	**CF**	**RF**	**Capacity**	**Attendance**
Calgary	Foothills Stadium	1966	345	400	325	8,000	45,686
Chico	Nettleton Stadium	1997	330	405	330	4,400	89,164
Edmonton	TELUS Field	1995	340	420	420	9,200	46,695
Long Beach	Blair Field	1958	348	400	348	3,500	67,255
Orange County	Goodwin Field	1992	330	400	330	3,500	26,604
*Tijuana	Calimax Stadium	1976	340	395	340	14,000	N/A
*Tucson	Hi Corbett Field	1937	366	392	348	9,500	N/A
St.George	Bruce Hurst Field	1994	340	390	335	3,000	23,870
*Victoria	Royal Athletic Park	1967	320	415	335	9,247	N/A
Yuma	Desert Sun Stadium	1969	335	410	335	7,100	66,899

*New franchises for 2009.

CALGARY VIPERS

Address: 2255 Crowchild Trail NW, Calgary, Alberta, Canada T2M4S7.
Telephone: (403) 277-2255
E-Mail Address: py@calgaryvipers.com. **Website:** www.calgaryvipers.com.
President/Chief Operating Officer: John Conrad. **Director, Baseball Operations:** Peter Young. **Facilities Director:** Rick Penner. **Senior Accountant:** John Kirkbride. **Director, Absolute Baseball Academy:** Neil Gidney. **Media Relations:** Patrich Haas. **Administrative Assistance:** Jaylene Church
Manager: Morgan Burkhart. **Coach:** Unavailable. **Pitching Coach:** Evan Greusel.

GAME INFORMATION

Radio Announcer: Patrick Haas. **No. of Games Broadcast:** Home-44 Away-44. **Flagship Station:** AM 770 CHQR. **PA Announcer:** Kramer. **Official Scorer:** Darcy Leitz/Gord Siminon.
Stadium Name: Foothills Athletic Park. **Standard Game Times:** 7:05 p.m., Sat. 5:05 Sun. 1:35.
Visiting Club Hotel: Unavailable.

CHICO OUTLAWS

Office Address: 308 Salem Street, Chico, CA 95928.
Telephone: (530) 345-3210.
E-Mail Address: cjacey@goldenbaseball.com. **Website:** www.chicooutlawsbaseball.com.
General Manager: Curt Jacey.
Manager: Greg Cadaret.

GAME INFORMATION

Radio Announcer: Unavailable. **No. of Games Broadcast:** Home-44, Away-44. **Flagship Station:** KPAY 1290-AM.
PA Announcer: Unavailable. **Official Scorer:** Unavailable.
Stadium Name: Nettleton Stadium. **Location:** California 99 North to California 32 West/East Eighth Street, right on Main Street, left on West First Street; stadium at 400 West First Street. **Standard Game Times:** 7:05 p.m., Sun. 1:05.
Visiting Club Hotel: Unavailable

EDMONTON CRACKER CATS

Address: 10233-96 Avenue, Edmonton, Alberta, Canada T5K0A5
Telephone: (780) 423-2255
E-Mail Address: teaminfo@crackercats.ca. **Website:** www.crackercats.ca
Owner: Unavailable.
Manager: Brent Bowers. **Coach:** Unavailable. **Pitching Coach:** Unavailable.

GAME INFORMATION

Radio Announcer: Al Coates. **No. of Games Broadcast:** Home-44 Away-44. **Flagship Station:** Unavailable.
PA Announcer: Unavailable. **Official Scorer:** Al Coates.
Stadium Name: Telus Field. **From North:** 101st Street to 96th Ave. Left on 96th, 1 block East. **From South:** Take Calgary Trail North to Queen Elizabeth Hill, make a right across Walterdale Bridge, and then a right on 96th Avenue. **Standard Game Times:** 7:05 p.m., Sun. 1:35.
Visiting Club Hotel: Sutton Place Hotel. 10235-101st Street, Edmonton, Alberta, Canada T5J3E9 (780) 428-7111.

LONG BEACH ARMADA

Office Address: 2900 Orange Avenue, Suite 203, Signal Hill, CA 90755
Telephone: (562) 427-4487
E-Mail Address: tsoares@goldenbaseball.com. **Website:** www.longbeacharmada.com .
President/General Manager: Tony Soares. **Office Manager:** Doug Cowgill.
Manager: Garry Templeton. **Coach:** Unavailable. **Pitching Coach:** Unavailable.

GAME INFORMATION

Radio Announcer: Unavailable. **Webcast Address:** www.longbeacharmada.com. **PA Announcer:** Unavailable Official Scorer: Unavailable.
Stadium Name: Blair Field. **Location:** From Orange County, take 405 North to Seventh Street/22 West, right at Park Avenue. From Los Angeles, take 405 South to Lakewood Boulevard South, go to traffic circle and get on Pacific Coast Highway South, right on Ximeno, left on 10th Street; park at intersection of 10th Street and Park Avenue. **Standard Game Times:** 7:05 p.m.; Sunday, 1:05 p.m.
Visiting Club Hotel: Unavailable.

ORANGE COUNTY FLYERS

Office Address: 2461 E. Orangethorpe, Suite 102, Fullerton, CA 92831.
Telephone: (714) 526-8326.
E-Mail Address: amintz@orangecountyflyers.com. **Website:** www.orangecountyflyers.com
President: Alan Mintz. **General Manager:** Unavailable.
Manager: Phil Nevin. **Coach:** Unavailable. **Pitching Coach:** Unavailable.

GAME INFORMATION

Radio: FM 90.1 KBPK; www.SportsNetUSA.net. **PA Announcer:** Unavailable. **Official Scorer:** Unavailable
Stadium Name: Goodwin Field. **Location:** From Orange Freeway, take Yorba Linda Blvd. Exit, west on Yorba Linda, left on Associated Road to parking lot G. **Standard Game Times:** 7:05 p.m.; Sunday, 1:05 p.m.
Visiting Club Hotel: Holiday Inn Express - Placentia, 118 E Orangethorpe Ave, Placentia, CA 92870 714-528-7778.

TUCSON TOROS

Office Address: 2919 E. Broadway, Suite 200, Tucson, AZ 85716.
Telephone: (520) 322-6989.
E-Mail Address: jay@tucsontoros.com . **Website:** www.tucsontoros.com
Owner: Jay Zucker.
General Manager: Sean Smock.
Manager: Tim Johnson. **Coach:** Unavailable. **Pitching Coach:** Unavailable.

GAME INFORMATION

Radio: Unavailable. **PA Announcer:** Unavailable. **Official Scorer:** Unavailable.
Stadium Name: Hi Corbett Field. **Standard Game Times:** 7:05 p.m.; Sunday, 1:05 p.m.
Visiting Club Hotel: Unavailable

ST. GEORGE ROAD RUNNERS

Office Address: 216 W. St. George Blvd, Suite A, St. George, Utah 84770.
Telephone: (435) 673-5333.
E-Mail Address: rberry@goldenbaseball.com. **Website:** www.stgeorgeroadrunners.com.
General Manager: Rick Berry. **Sales Executive:** Gary Webster.
Manager: Cory Snyder. **Pitching Coach:** Unavailable. **Hitting Coach:** Unavailable

GAME INFORMATION

Radio Announcer: John Potter. **No. of Games Broadcast:** Home-44, Away-44. **Flagship Station:** 1210 AM ESPN. **PA Announcer:** Ed Rogers. **Official Scorer:** Jeff Clough.
Stadium Name: Bruce Hurst Field. **Location:** 225 South 700 East Saint George, UT Standard Game Times: 7:05 p.m.
Visiting Club Hotels: Budget Inn & Suites, Comfort Suites, Holiday Inn, Ramada Inn, and Hilton Garden Inn all in St. George, Utah.

TIJUANA POTROS

Address: Unavailable.
Telephone: (323)423-0713
E-Mail Address: rockybeisbol@rocketmail.com. **Website:** Unavailable.
Owner/General Manager: Jose Pena Jr.
Manager: Mario Mendoza. **Coach:** Unavailable. **Pitching Coach:** Jose Pena Sr.

GAME INFORMATION

Radio Announcer: Unavailable. **No. of Games Broadcast:** Away-44. **Flagship Station:** Unavailable. **PA Announcer:** Unavailable. **Official Scorer:** Unavailable.
Stadium Name: Calimax Stadium. **Location:** Standard Game Times: 7:05 p.m., Sun. 1:05.
Visiting Club Hotel: Unavailable

VICTORIA SEALS

Address: 1014 Caledonia Avenue, Victoria, BC, CAN V8T1G1.
Telephone: (250)480-4487.
E-Mail Address: darren@victoriaseals.ca. **Website:** www.victoriaseals.ca.
Owner: Darren Parker, Russ Parker.
General Manager: Jay Longpre.
Manager: Darrell Evans. **Coach:** Unavailable. **Pitching Coach:** Unavailable.

GAME INFORMATION

Radio Announcer: Unavailable. **No. of Games Broadcast:** Away-44. **Flagship Station:** Unavailable. **PA Announcer:** Unavailable. **Official Scorer:** Unavailable.
Stadium Name: Royal Athletic Park. **Standard Game Times:** 7:05 p.m., **Sun. 1:**05.
Visiting Club Hotel: Unavailable.

YUMA SCORPIONS

Address: 1280 W. Desert Sun Dr., Yuma, AZ 85366.
Telephone: (928) 257-4700.
E-Mail Address: mmarshall@goldenbaseball.com. **Website:** www.yumascorpions.com.
General Manager: Mike Marshall. **Director, Sales/Marketing:** Glenn Dobson. **Director, Media Relations:** Cole St. Clair. **Office Manager:** Mary Marshall.
Manager: Mike Marshall. **Coach:** Kash Beauchamp. **Pitching Coach:** Unavailable.

GAME INFORMATION

Radio Announcer: Unavailable. **No. of Games Broadcast:** Away-44. **Flagship Station:** KBLU 560-AM. **PA Announcer:** Virgil Tudor. **Official Scorer:** Greg Abbott.
Stadium Name: Desert Sun Stadium. **Location:** From I-8, take Fourth Avenue or 16th Street exit to Avenue A. **Standard Game Times:** 7:05 p.m., Sun. 1:05.
Visiting Club Hotel: Best Western Inn Suites 1450 Castle Dome Ave. Yuma, AZ. (928) 783-4776.

NORTHERN LEAGUE

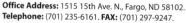

Office Addresses: 80 South Eighth Street, Suite 4920, Minneapolis, MN 55402 (Commissioner); One Mayor Art Schultz Dr, Joliet, IL 60432 (Treasurer); PO Box 1588, Soquel, CA 95073 (Director, Baseball Operations).

Telephone: (612) 338-9097. **Fax:** (612) 338-9098.

Email: commissioner@northernleague.com, baseballoperations@northernleague.com. **Website:** www.northern-league.com

Founded: 1993

Commissioner: Clark Griffith. **Director, Baseball Operations:** Harry Stavrenos.

Directors: John Ehlert (Kansas City), Rich Ehrenreich (Schaumburg), John Costello (Joliet), Sam Katz (Winnipeg), Pat Salvi (Gary), Bruce Thom (Fargo).

Regular Season: 96 games.

2009 Opening Date: May 15. **Closing Date:** August 31.

All-Star Game: July 7 at Silver Cross Field, Joliet, IL.

Playoff Format: Top four teams meet in best-of-five semifinal series. Winners meet in best-of-five championship.

Brand of Baseball: Rawlings

Statistician: PA SportsTicker, Cheshire, CT 06410

STADIUM INFORMATION

			Dimensions				
Club	**Stadium**	**Opened**	**LF**	**CF**	**RF**	**Capacity**	**Attendance**
Gary	Newman Outfoor Field	1996	318	400	318	4,513	159,586
Fargo-Moorhead	U.S. Steel Yard	2003	320	400	335	6,139	177,900
Joliet	Silver Cross Field	2002	330	400	327	4,616	184,638
Kansas City	Community America Ballpark	2003	300	396	328	4,365	280,795
Schaumburg	Alexian Field	1999	355	400	353	7,048	206,749
Winnipeg	CanWest Global Park	1999	325	400	325	7,481	300,938

FARGO-MOORHEAD REDHAWKS

Office Address: 1515 15th Ave. N., Fargo, ND 58102.

Telephone: (701) 235-6161. **FAX:** (701) 297-9247.

E-Mail Address: redhawks@fmredhawks.com. **Website:** www.fmredhawks.com.

Operated by: Fargo Baseball LLC.

President: Bruce Thom. **Executive Vice President:** Brad Thom.

General Manager: Josh Buchholz. **Assistant GM:** Megan Salic. **Senior Accountant:** Sue Wild. **Director, Stadium Operations:** Eric Jorgenson. **Director, Ticket Sales:** Michael Larson. **Director, Group Sales:** Karl Hoium. **Director, Food/Beverage:** Sean Kiernan. **Head Sports Turf Manager:** Matt Wallace.

Manager/Director, Player Procurement: Doug Simunic. **Assistant Director, Player Procurement/Consultant:** Jeff Bittiger. **Pitching Coach:** Steve Montgomery. **Coaches:** Bucky Burgau, Robbie Lopez. **Trainer:** Mike Bogenreif. **Clubhouse Operations:** Unavailable.

GAME INFORMATION

Radio Announcer: Scott Miller. **No. of Games Broadcast:** Home-48, Away-48. **Flagship Station:** WDAY 970-AM. **PA Announcer:** Erick Johnson. **Official Scorer:** Rob Olson.

Stadium Name: Newman Outdoor Field. **Location:** I-29 North to exit 67, right on 19th Ave. North, right on Albrecht Boulevard. **Standard Game Times:** 7:02 p.m.; Saturday 6 p.m.; Sunday, 1 p.m.

Visiting Club Hotel: Comfort Inn West, 3825 9th Ave. SW, Fargo, ND 58103. **Telephone:** (701) 282-9596.

GARY SOUTHSHORE RAILCATS

Office Address: One Stadium Plaza, Gary, IN 46402.

Telephone: (219) 882-2255. **FAX:** (219) 882-2259.

E-Mail Address: info@railcatsbaseball.com. **Website:** www.railcatsbaseball.com.

Operated by: SouthShore Baseball, LLC.

Owner/CEO: Pat Salvi. **Owner:** Lindy Salvi.

President/General Manager: Roger Wexelberg. **Sales/Marketing:** Mike Smith. **Assistant General Manager/CFO:** Becky Kremer. **Director, Merchandise:** Cydni Johnson. **Director, Media Relations/Broadcasting:** Andy Viano. **Manager, Stadium Operations:** Tony Wiedman. **Manager, Corporate Sales:** Patty Kostro. **Manager, Advertising/Promotions:** Dave Salvi. **Manager, Community Relations:** Laura Blakeley. **Manager, Stadium Maintenance:** Jim Kerr. **Account Executives:** Adam Harris, Radley Robinson, Danielle Turcovsky, Patrick Galvin. **Executive Assistant:** Arcella Moxley. **Stadium Maintenance:** Stephanie Tavorn. **General Counsel:** Patrick Salvi II.

Manager: Greg Tagert. **Coaches:** Jamie Bennett, Kenny Graham and Joe Gates.

GAME INFORMATION

Radio Announcer: Andy Viano. **No. of Games Broadcast:** Home-48, Away-48. **Flagship Station:** WLPR 89.1-FM.

Stadium Name: U.S. Steel Yard. **Location:** I-80/94 to Broadway Exit (Exit 10). North on Broadway to Fifth Avenue. East one block to stadium. **Standard Game Times:** 7 p.m.; Saturday, 6 p.m.; Sunday, 2 p.m.

Visiting Club Hotel: Radisson Hotel at Star Plaza, 800 E 81st Ave., Merrillville, IN 46410. **Telephone:** (219) 769-6311.

JOLIET JACKHAMMERS

Office Address: 1 Mayor Art Schultz Dr., Joliet, IL 60432.

Telephone: (815) 726-2255. **Fax:** (815) 726-9223.

E-Mail Address: info@jackhammersbaseball.com. **Website:** www.jackhammerbaseball.com.

Operated by: Joliet Professional Baseball Club, LLC.

Chairman: Peter Ferro. **Vice Chairman:** Charles Hammersmith. **CEO/General Counsel:** Michael Hansen. **Chief Financial Officer/President:** John Costello.

Executive Vice President/General Manager: Kelly Sufka. **Assistant GM:** Kyle Kreger. **Director, Corporate Partnerships:** Vince Maietta. **Box Office Manager:** Jeremy Timm. **Ticket Sales Manager:** Joe Verschueren. **Ticket Sales Representatives:** Mike Evans, Brett Piet. **Radio Broadcaster/Media Relations:** Unavailable. **Head Groundskeeper:** Nick Hill. **Director, Accounting/Human Resources:** Tammy Harvey. **Administrative Assistant/Team Travel Coordinator:** Kelly Drechsel.

Manager: Wally Backman. **Coach:** Unavailable.

GAME INFORMATION

Radio Announcers: Jon Versteeg, Bryan Dolgin. **No. of Games Broadcast:** Home-48, Away-48. **Flagship Station:** WJOL, 1340-AM.

Stadium Name: Silver Cross Field. **Location:** I-80 to Chicago Street/Route 53 North exit, go 1/2 mile on Chicago Street, right on Washington Street to Jefferson Street/U.S. 52, right on Jefferson, ballpark on left. **Standard Game Times:** 7:05 p.m. Tues: 6:05 p.m. Sunday: 2:05/5:05 p.m.

KANSAS CITY T-BONES

Office Address: 1800 Village West Parkway Kansas City, KS 66111.

Telephone: (913) 328-2255. **Fax:** (913) 328-5652.

E-mail Address: batterup@tbonesbaseball.com. **Website:** www.tbonesbaseball.com.

Operated By: T-Bones Baseball Club, LLC; Ehlert Development.

Owner, President: John Ehlert. **Vice President:** Adam Ehlert.

Vice President/General Manager: Chris Browne. **VP/Corporate Partnerships:** Scott Steckly. **Assistant GM/Group Sales:** Eric Marshall. **Director, Merchandise:** Laura Hayes. **Media Relations/Press Box:** Stan Duitsman. **Director, Promotions:** Colin Aldrich. **Director, Ticket Operations/Box Office Manager:** Kurt Sieker. **Head Groundskeeper:** Joey Fitzgerald. **Bookkeeper:** Theresa Bird. **Account Executive:** Michaela McCann.

Manager: Andy McCauley. **Coach:** Tim Doherty. **Pitching Coach:** Rick DeHart. **Trainer:** Josh Adams.

GAME INFORMATION

Radio Announcer: Unavailable. **No. of Games Broadcast:** Home-48, Away-48. **Flagship Station:** WDAF 1660am. **Official Scorer:** Louis Spry. **PA Announcer:** Dan Roberts.

Stadium Name: CommunityAmerica Ballpark. **Location:** State Avenue West off I-435 and State Avenue. **Standard Game Times:** Monday-Saturday 7:05pm; Sunday 5:05pm

Visiting Club Hotel: Hyatt Regency Crown Center.

SCHAUMBURG FLYERS

Office Address: 1999 S. Springinsguth Rd., Schaumburg, IL 60193.

Telephone: (847) 891-2255. **FAX:** (847) 891-6441.

E-Mail Address: info@flyersbaseball.com. **Website:** www.flyersbaseball.com.

Principal Owners: Richard Ehrenreich, John Hughes, Mike Conley. **Managing Partner:** Richard Ehrenreich.

General Manager: Ben Burke. **Assistant GM/Director, Tickets:** Scott Boor. **Assistant GM/Director, Operations:** Aaron Studebaker. **Director, Corporate Partnerships:** Robert Heck. **Director, Business Development:** Belinda Wiggins. **Director, Public Relations:** Sarah Eichenberger. **Ticket Manager:** Brian Gioia. **Promotions/Merchandise Manager:** Liz Hamilton. **Graphics Manager:** Rachel Irving. **Group Sales Associate:** Ray Gross. **Medical Director:** Tony Garofalo.

Manager: Michael Busch. **Coaches:** Jim Miksis, Brian Nelson.

GAME INFORMATION

Radio Announcer: Unavailable. **No. of Games Broadcast:** Home-48, Away-48. **Flagship Station:** WRMN 1410AM. **PA Announcer:** Unavailable. **Official Scorer:** Mark Madorin.

Stadium Name: Alexian Field. **Location:** From north, I-290 to Elgin-O'Hare Expressway (Thorndale), west on expressway to Irving Park Road exit, left on Springinsguth under expressway, stadium on left; From south, U.S. 20 West (Lake Street) to Elgin-O'Hare Expressway (Thorndale), east on expressway, south on Springinsguth Road. **Standard Game Times:** 7:05 p.m.; Friday 6:45 p.m.; Saturday, 6:05 p.m.; Sunday, 1:20 p.m.

Visiting Club Hotel: Country Inn and Suites/Hotel Indigo.

WINNIPEG GOLDEYES

Office Address: One Portage Ave. E., Winnipeg, Manitoba R3B 3N3.
Telephone: (204) 982-2273. **Fax:** (204) 982-2274.
E-Mail Address: goldeyes@goldeyes.com. **Website:** www.goldeyes.com.
Operated by: Winnipeg Goldeyes Baseball Club Inc.
Principal Owner, President: Sam Katz.

General Manager: Andrew Collier. **Assistant GM:** Regan Katz. **Director, Sales/Marketing:** Dan Chase. **Director, Communications:** Jonathan Green. **Promotions Coordinator:** Sarah Kyrylchuk. **Account Representatives:** Paul Duque, Paul Edmonds, Dennis McLean, Scott Taylor. **Retail Manager:** Shane Tucker. **Controller:** Judy Jones. **Chief Financial Officer:** Jason McRae-King. **Facility Manager:** Scott Horn. **Sales/Marketing Coordinator:** Angela Sanche. **Administrative Assistant:** Bonnie Benson. **Head Groundskeeper:** Don Ferguson.

Manager/Director, Player Procurement: Rick Forney. **Coaches:** Rudy Arias, Tom Vaeth. **Trainer:** Andrew Wautier.

GAME INFORMATION

Radio Announcer: Paul Edmonds. **No. of Games Broadcast:** Home-48, Road-48. **Flagship Station:** CFRW 1290-AM. **PA Announcer:** Ron Arnst. **Official Scorer:** Steve Eitzen.

Stadium Name: Canwest Park. **Location:** North on Pembina Highway to Broadway. East on Broadway to Main Street. North on Main Street to Water Avenue. East on Water Avenue to Westbrook Street. North on Westbrook Street to Lombard Avenue. East on Lombard Avenue to Mill Street. South on Mill Street to ballpark. **Standard Game Times:** 7 p.m.; Sunday, 1:30 p.m.

Visiting Club Hotel: The Marlborough, 331 Smith St., Winnipeg, Manitoba R3B 2G9. **Telephone:** (204) 942-6411.

CONTINENTAL LEAGUE

Office Address: 16633 Dallas Parkway, Suite 600, Addison, TX .
Telephone: (214) 234-0018. **Fax:** (972) 588-3363.
Website: www.cblproball.com

Chief Executive Officer/President: Ron Baron. **Director League Operations/Communications:** Bob Ibach. **Director, Marketing:** Laura Keith. **Director, Team Relations:** Jay Johnstone.

Year Founded: 2007.
Regular Season: 60 games.
2009 Opening Date: May 14. **Closing Date:** Aug. 23.
Member Clubs: Unavailable.
All-Star Game: July 7 in Alexandria, La.
Playoff Format: Unavailable.
Roster Limit: 25.
Official Baseball: Unavailable. **Statistician:** Unavailable.

INTERNATIONAL

AMERICAS

MEXICO

MEXICAN LEAGUE

Member, National Association

NOTE: The Mexican League is a member of the National Association of Professional Baseball Leagues and has a Triple-A classification. However, its member clubs operate largely independent of the 30 major league teams, and for that reason the league is listed in the international section.

Mailing Address: Angel Pola No. 16, Col. Periodista, CP 11220, Mexico, D.F. **Telephone:** (52) 555-557-1007. **Fax:** (52) 555-395-2454. **E-Mail Address:** oficina@lmb.com.mx. **Website:** www.lmb.com.mx.

Years League Active: 1955-.

President: Plinio Escalante Bolio. **Operations Manager:** Nestor Alba Brito.

Division Structure: North—Aquascalientes, Laguna, Monclova, Monterrey, Puebla, San Luis, Saltillo, Tijuana. South—Angelopolis, Campeche, Mexico City, Minatitlan, Oaxaca, Tabasco, Veracruz, Yucatan.

Regular Season: 110 games (split-schedule). **2009 Opening Date:** March 24. **Closing Date:** July 30.

All-Star Game: June 7, site unavailable.

Playoff Format: Top six teams in each division qualify; first- and second-place teams in each division receive first-round byes. First, second and semifinal rounds are best-of-seven series; division champions meet in best-of-seven series for league championship.

Roster Limit: 28. **Roster Limit, Imports:** 6.

PIRATAS DE CAMPECHE

Office Address: Unidad Deportiva 20 de Noviembre, Local 4, CP 24000, Campeche, Campeche. **Telephone:** (52) 981-816-2116. **Fax:** (52) 981-816-3807. **E-Mail Address:** Unavailable. **Website:** www.piratasdecampeche.com.mx.

President: Gabriel Escalante Castillo. **General Manager:** Maria del Socorro Morales.

Manager: Manual Cazarin.

DORADOS DE CHIHUAHUA

Office Address: Blvd. Juan Pablo II No. 4506, Col. Aeropuerto CP 31380. **Telephone:** (52) 614-459-0317. **Fax:** (52) 614-459-0336. **E-Mail Address:** Unavailable. **Website:** www.tunerosdeslp.com.

President: Marcelo de los Santos. **General Manager:** Leonardo Clayton Rodriguez.

Manager: Dan Firova.

VAQUEROS LAGUNA

Office Address: Juan Gutenberg s/n, Col. Centro, CP 27000, Torreon, Coahuila. **Telephone:** (52) 871-718-5515. **Fax:** (52) 871-717-4335. **E-Mail Address:** unionlag@prodigy.net.mx. **Website:** www.clubvaqueroslaguna.com.

President: Carlos Gomez del Campo. **General Manager:** Carlos de la Garza.

Manager: Fernando Elizardo.

DIABLOS ROJOS DEL MEXICO

Office Address: Av. Cuauhtemoc #451-101, Col. Narvarte, CP 03020, Mexico DF. **Telephone:** (52) 555-639-8722. **Fax:** (52) 555-639-9722. **E-Mail Address:** diablos@sportsya.com. **Website:** www.diablos.com.mx.

President: Roberto Mansur Galán. **General Manager:** Eduardo de la Cerda.

Manager: Marco Antonio Vazquez.

ACEREROS DE MONCLOVA

Office Address: Cuauhtemoc #299, Col. Ciudad Deportiva, CP 25750, Monclova, Coahuila. **Telephone:** (52) 866-636-2334. **Fax:** (52) 866-636-2688. **E-Mail Address:** acererosdelnorte@prodigy.net.mx. **Website:** www.aceros.com.mx.

President: Donaciano Garza Gutierrez. **General Manager:** Victor Favela Lopez.

Manager: Unavailable.

SULTANES DE MONTERREY

Office Address: Av. Manuel Barragan s/n, Estadio Monterrey, Apartado Postal 870, Monterrey, Nuevo Leon, CP 66460. **Telephone:** (52) 818-351-0209. **Fax:** (52) 818-351-8022. **E-Mail Address:** sultanes@sultanes.com.mx. **Website:** www.sultanes.com.mx.

President: José Maiz García. **General Manager:** Roberto Magdaleno Ramírez.

Manager: Bernardo Tatis.

TECOLATES DE NUEVO LAREDO

Office Address: Calle Manuel Madrigal y Juan de la Barrera, Colonia Heroes, Aguascalientes, Aguascalientes, CP 20250. **Telephone:** (52) 449-970-4585. **E-Mail Address:** rieleros@lmb.com.mx. **Website:** www.rielerosdeaguascalientes.com.

President: Jean Paul Mansur Beltran. **General Manager:** Carlos Hernandez.

Manager: Alex Taveras.

GUERREROS DE OAXACA

Office Address: Privada del Chopo #105, Fraccionamiento El Chopo, CP 68050, Oaxaca, Oaxaca. **Telephone:** (52) 951-515-5522. **Fax:** (52) 951-515-4966. **E-Mail Address:** guerreros@infosel.net.mx. **Website:** www.guerrerosdeoaxaca.com.

President: Vicente Pérez Avellá Villa. **General Manager:** Jose Diaz del la Vega.

Manager: Homer Rojas Villarreal.

PETROLEROS DE MINATITLAN

Club Information Unavailable.

Manager: Edgar Castro.

PERICOS DE PUEBLA

Office Address: Calle Paseo de las Fuentes, #13 Col Arboledas de Guadelupe, CP 72210, Puebla, Puebla. **Telephone:** (52) 222-236-3313. **Fax:** (52) 222-236-2906. **E-Mail Address:** oficina@pericosdepuebla.com.mx. **Website:** www.pericosdepuebla.com.mx.

President: Hassan Taja Abraham. **General Manager:** Francisco Minjarez Garcia.

Manager: Unavailable.

TIGRES DE QUINTANA ROO

Office Address: Calle Paseo de las Fuentes, #13 Col. Arbodedas de Guadelupe, CP 72210, Puebla, Puebla. **Telephone:** (52) 222-236-4909. **Fax:** (52) 222-234-0192. **E-Mail Address:** tigres@tigrescapitalinos.com.mx. **Website:** www.tigresdemexico.com.mx.

President: Cuauhtémoc Rodriguez. **General Manager:** Iram Campos Lara.

Manager: Unavailable.

SARAPEROS DE SALTILLO

Office Address: Blvd. Nazario Ortiz Esquina con Blvd. Jesus Sanchez, CP 25280, Saltillo, Coahuila. **Telephone:** (52) 844-416-9455. **Fax:** (52) 844-439-1330. **E-Mail Address:** aley@grupoley.com. **Website:** www.saraperos.com.mx.

President: Juan Manuel Ley. **General Manager:** Eduardo Valenzuela Guajardo.

Manager: Derek Bryant.

OLMECAS DE TABASCO

Office Address: Explanada de la Ciudad Deportiva, Parque de Beisbol Centenario del 27 de Febrero, Col. Atasta de Serra, CP 86100, Villahermosa, Tabasco. **Telephone:** (52) 993-352-2787. **Fax:** (52) 993-352-2788. **E-Mail Address:** olmecastab@prodigy.net.mx. **Website:** www.olmecasdetabasco.com.mx.

President: Raul Gonzalez Rodriguez. **General Manager:** Luis Guzman Ramos.

Manager: Mario Mendoza Aizpuro.

POTROS DE TIJUANA

Office Address: Blvd. Insurgentes 17017-21, Colonia Los Alamos, Tijuana, Baja California, Mexico 22320. **Telephone:**(52) 664-621-3787. **Fax:** (52) 664-621-3883. **E-Mail Address:** potros@potrosdetijuana.com. **Website:** www.potrosdetijuana.com.

President: Belisario Cabrera. **General Manager:** Raul Cano.

Manager: Domingo Rivera.

ROJOS DEL AGUILA DE VERACRUZ

Office Address: Av. Jacarandas s/n, Esquina España, Fraccionamiento Virginia, CP 94294, Boca del Rio, Veracruz. **Telephone:** (52) 229-935-5004. **Fax:** (229) 935-5008. **E-Mail Address:** rojosdelaguila@terra.com.mx. **Website:** www.aguiladeveracruz.com.

President: Jose Antonio Mansur Beltran. **General Manager:** Carlos Nahun Hernandez.

Manager: Juan Jose Pacho Burgos.

LEONES DE YUCATAN

Office Address: Calle 50 #406-B, Entre 35 y 37, Col. Jesus Carranza, CP 97109, Merida, Yucatán. **Telephone:** (52) 999-926-3022. **Fax:** (52) 999-926-3631. **E-Mail Addresses:** leonesy@sureste.com. **Website:** www.leonesdeyucatan.com.mx.

President: Gustavo Ricalde Durán. **General Manager:** Jose Rivero.

Manager: Lino Rivera.

MEXICAN ACADEMY

Rookie Classification

Mailing Address: Angel Pola No. 16, Col. Periodista, CP 11220, Mexico, D.F. **Telephone:** (52) 555-557-1007. **Fax:** (52) 555-395-2454. **E-Mail Address:** mbl@prodigy.net.mx. **Website:** www.lmb.com.mx.

Member Clubs: Celaya, Guanajuato, Queretaro, Salamanca.

Regular Season: 50 games. **2008 Opening Date:** Oct. 9. **Closing Date:** Dec. 21.

DOMINICAN REPUBLIC

DOMINICAN SUMMER LEAGUE

Member, National Association

Rookie Classification

Mailing Address: Calle Segunda No. 64, Reparto Antilla, Santo Domingo, Dominican Republic. **Telephone/Fax:** (809) 532-3619. **Website:** www.dominicansummerleague.com. **E-Mail Address:** ligadeverano@codetel.net.do.

Years League Active: 1985-.

President: Freddy Jana. **Administrative Assistant:** Orlando Diaz.

2008 Member Clubs/Participating Organizations: Angels, Astros, Athletics I, Athletics II, Blue Jays, Braves I, Braves II, Cardinals, Cubs, Diamondbacks, Dodgers I, Dodgers II, Giants, Indians I, Indians II, Mariners, Marlins, Mets, Nationals, Orioles, Padres, Phillies, Pirates, Rangers, Reds, Red Sox, Rockies, Royals, Tigers, Twins, White Sox, Yankees I, Yankees II.

Regular Season: 70-72 games, depending on divisions. **2008 Opening Date:** June 4. **Closing Date:** Aug. 24.

Playoff Format: Six divisions; two division champions with best winning percentages receive first-round byes. Four teams meet in best-of-three quarterfinals; winners and division champions with first-round byes meet in best-of-three semifinals; winners meet in best-of-five series for league championship.

Roster Limit: 35; 30 active. **Player Eligibility Rule:** No more than eight players 20 or older and no more than two players 21 or older. At least 10 players must be pitchers. No more than four years of prior service, excluding Rookie leagues outside the U.S. and Canada.

VENEZUELA

VENEZUELAN SUMMER LEAGUE

Member, National Association

Rookie Classification

Mailing Address: C.C. Caribbean Plaza Modulo 8, P.A. Local 173-174, Valencia, Carabobo, Venezuela. **Telephone:** (58) 241-824-0321, (011) 58-241-824-0980. **Fax:** (58) 241-824-0705. **Website:** www.vsl.com.ve.

Years League Active: 1997-.

Administrator: Saul Gonzalez Acevedo. **Coordinator:** Ramon Feriera.

2008 Member Clubs: Aguirre, Cagua, Ciudad Alienza, San Joaquin, Troconero 1, Tronconero 2, Universidad, Venoco 1, Venoco 2. **Participating Organizations:** Astros, Blue Jays, Mariners, Marlins, Mets, Orioles, Phillies, Pirates, Reds, Red Sox, Rockies, Twins.

Regular Season: 60 games. **2008 Opening Date:** May 16. **Closing Date:** Aug. 28.

Playoffs: Best-of-three series between top two teams in regular season.

Roster Limit: 35; 30 active. **Player Eligibility Rule:** No player on active list may have more than three years of minor league service. Open to players from all Latin American Spanish-speaking countries except the Dominican Republic and Puerto Rico.

INTERNATIONAL LEAGUES

ASIA

CHINA

CHINA BASEBALL ASSOCIATION

Mailing Address: 5, Tiyuguan Road, Beijing 100763, Peoples Republic of China. **Telephone:** (011-86) 10-85826002. **Fax:** (011-86) 10-85825994. **E-Mail Address:** chinabaseball2008@yahoo.com.cn.

Years League Active: 2002-.

Chairman: Hu Jian Guo. **Vice Chairmen:** Tom McCarthy, Shen Wei. **Executive Director:** Yang Jie. **General Manager, Marketing/Promotion:** Lin Xiao Wu.

Member Clubs: Beijing Tigers, China Hopestars, Guangdong Leopards, Shanghai Eagles, Sichuan Dragons, Tianjin Lions.

Regular Season: 30 games.

Playoff Format: Top two teams meet in best-of-five series for league championship.

JAPAN

NIPPON PROFESSIONAL BASEBALL

Mailing Address: Imperial Tower, 14F, 1-1-1 Uchisaiwai-cho, Chiyoda-ku, Tokyo 100-0011. **Telephone:** 03-3502-0022. **Fax:** 03-3502-0140. **Website:** www.npb.or.jp

Commissioner: Ryozo Kato.

Executive Secretary: Kazuo Hasegawa. **Director, Administration:** Kunio Shimoda. **Director, Baseball Operations:** Nobby Ito. **Director, Public Relations:** Minoru Hirata.

Director, Central League Operations: Hideo Okoshi. **Director, Pacific League Operations:** Shiromitsu Hanai.

Japan Series: Best-of-seven series between Central and Pacific League champions, begins Oct. 31 at home of Pacific League club.

All-Star Series: July 24 at Sapporo Dome; July 25 at Mazda Stadium, Hiroshima.

Roster Limit: 70 per organization (one major league club, one minor league club). Major league club is permitted to register 28 players at a time, though just 25 may be available for each game.

Roster Limit, Imports: Four in majors (no more than three position players or pitchers); unlimited in minors.

CENTRAL LEAGUE

Regular Season: 144 games.

2009 Opening Date: April 3. **Closing Date:** Sept. 30.

Playoff Format: Second-place team meets third-place team in best-of-three series. Winner meets first-place team in best-of-five series to determine representative in Japan Series (first-place team has one-game advantage to begin series).

CHUNICHI DRAGONS

Mailing Address: Chunichi Bldg. 6F, 4-1-1 Sakae, Naka-ku, Nagoya 460-0008. **Telephone:** 052-261-8811. **Fax:** 052-263-7696.

Chairman: Bungo Shirai. **President:** Junnosuke Nishikawa. **General Manager:** Kazumasa Ito. **Field Manager:** Hiromitsu Ochiai.

2009 Foreign Players: Tony Blanco, Tomas de la Rosa, Lee Byung Kyu, Maximo Nelson, Nelson Payano, Chen Wei Yin.

HANSHIN TIGERS

Mailing Address: 2-33 Koshien-cho, Nishinomiya-shi, Hyogo-ken 663-8152. **Telephone:** 0798-46-1515. **Fax:** 0798-46-3555.

Chairman: Shinya Sakai. **President:** Nobuo Minami. **Field Manager:** Akinobu Mayumi.

2009 Foreign Players: Scott Atchison, Aarom Baldiris, Kevin Mench, Chris Resop, Jeff Williams.

HIROSHIMA TOYO CARP

Mailing Address: 2-3-1 Minami Kaniya, Minami-ku, Hiroshima 732-8501. **Telephone:** 082-554-1000. **Fax:** 082-568-1190.

President: Hajime Matsuda. **General Manager:** Kiyoaki Suzuki. **Field Manager:** Marty Brown.

2009 Foreign Players: Scott Dohmann, Ben Kozlowski, Colby Lewis, Scott Seabol, Mike Schultz. **Coach:** Jeff Livesey.

TOKYO YAKULT SWALLOWS

Mailing Address: Shimbashi MCV Bldg. 5F, 5-13-5 Shimbashi, Minato-ku, Tokyo 105-0004. **Telephone:** 03-5470-8915. **Fax:** 03-5470-8916.

Chairman: Sumiya Hori. **President:** Tadashi Suzuki. **General Manager:** Kesanori Kurashima. **Field Manager:** Shigeru Takada.

2009 Foreign Players: Ricky Barrett, Jamie D'Antona, Aaron Guiel, Lee Hye Chun, Lim Chang Yong.

YOKOHAMA BAYSTARS

Mailing Address: Kannai Arai Bldg, 7F, 1-8 Onoe-cho, Naka-ku, Yokohama 231-0015. **Telephone:** 045-681-0811. **Fax:** 045-661-2500.

Chairman: Kiyoshi Wakabayashi. **President:** Kuniaki Sasaki. **Field Manager:** Akihiko Oya.

2009 Foreign Players: Ryan Glynn, Dan Johnson, Tom Mastny, Les Walrond. **Coach:** John Turney.

YOMIURI GIANTS

Mailing Address: Otemachi Nomura Bldg., 7F, 2-1-1 Otemachi, Chiyoda-ku, Tokyo 100-8151. **Telephone:** 03-3246-7733. **Fax:** 03-3246-2726.

Chairman: Takuo Takihana. **President:** Tsunekazu Momoi. **General Manager:** Hidetoshi Kiyotake. **Field Manager:** Tatsunori Hara.

2009 Foreign Players: Adrian Burnside, Dicky Gonzalez, Seth Greisinger, Marc Kroon, Wirfin Obispo, Alex Ramirez, Lee Seung Yeop.

PACIFIC LEAGUE

Regular Season: 144 games.

2009 Opening Date: April 3. **Closing Date:** Sept. 30.

Playoff Format: Second-place team meets third-place team in best-of-three series. Winner meets first-place team in best-of-five series to determine league's representative in Japan Series (first-place team has one-game advantage to begin series).

CHIBA LOTTE MARINES

Mailing Address: 1 Mihama, Mihama-ku, Chiba-shi, Chiba-ken 261-8587. **Telephone:** 043-296-1450. **Fax:** 043-296-7496.

Chairman: Takeo Shigemitsu. **President:** Ryuzo Setoyama. **Field Manager:** Bobby Valentine.

2009 Foreign Players: Benny Agbayani, Gary Burnham Jr., Chase Lambin, Brian Sikorski. **Coach:** Frank Ramppen. **Minor League Manager:** Lenn Sakata.

FUKUOKA SOFTBANK HAWKS

Mailing Address: Fukuoka Yahoo! Japan Dome, Hawks Town, Chuo-ku, Fukuoka 810-0065. **Telephone:** 092-844-1189. **Fax:** 092-844-4600.

Owner: Masayoshi Son. **Chairman:** Sadaharu Oh. **President:** Kazuhiko Kasai. **Field Manager:** Koji Akiyama.

2009 Foreign Players: Chris Aguila, Brian Falkenborg, Justin Germano, D.J. Houlton, Kameron Loe, Yang Yao-hsun.

HOKKAIDO NIPPON HAM FIGHTERS

Mailing Address: 1 Hitsujigaoka, Toyohira-ku, Sapporo 062-8655. **Telephone:** 011-857-7786. **Fax:** 011-857-3900.

Chairman: Hiroji Okoso. **President:** Junichi Fujii. **General Manager:** Masao Yamada. **Field Manager:** Masataka Nashida.

2009 Foreign Players: Jason Botts, Terrmel Sledge, Brian Sweeney, Ryan Wing.

ORIX BUFFALOES

Mailing Address: 3-Kita-2-30 Chiyozaki, Nishi-ku, Osaka 530-0023. **Telephone:** 06-6586-0221. **Fax:** 06-6586-0240.

Chairman: Yoshihiko Miyauchi. **President:** Yoshinori Matsuoka. **General Manager:** Katsuhiro Nakamura. **Field Manager:** Daijiro Oishi.

2009 Foreign Players: Alex Cabrera, Jose Fernandez, Greg LaRocca, Jon Leicester, Tuffy Rhodes, Ryan Vogelsong.

SAITAMA SEIBU LIONS

Mailing Address: 2135 Kami-Yamaguchi, Tokorozawa-shi, Saitama-ken 359-1189. **Telephone:** 04-2924-1155. **Fax:** 04-2928-1919.

President: Shinji Kobayashi. **Field Manager:** Hisanobu Watanabe.

2009 Foreign Players: Hiram Bocachica, Alex Graman, Hsu Ming-chieh, John Wasdin.

TOHOKU RAKUTEN GOLDEN EAGLES

Mailing Address: 2-11-6 Miyagino, Miyagino-ku, Sendai-shi, Miyagi-ken 983-0045. **Telephone:** 022-298-5300. **Fax:** 022-298-5360.

Chairman: Hiroshi Mikitani. **President:** Toru Shimada. **Field Manager:** Katsuya Nomura.

2009 Foreign Players: Matt Childers, Marc Gwyn, Lin En-yu, Darrell Rasner, Fernando Seguignol, Rick Short.

KOREA

KOREA BASEBALL ORGANIZATION

Mailing Address: 946-16 Dokokdong, Kangnam-gu, Seoul, Korea. **Telephone:** (02) 3460-4632. **Fax:** (02) 3460-4639.

Years League Active: 1982-.

Website: www.koreabaseball.com.

Commissioner: Shin Sang-woo. **Secretary General:** Ha Il-sung. **Deputy Secretary General:** Lee Sang-il.

Division Structure: None.

Regular Season: 133 games. **2009 Opening Date:** April 4.

Playoffs: Third- and fourth-place teams meet in best-of-three series; winner advances to meet second-place team in best-of-five series; winner meets first-place team in best-of-seven Korean Series for league championship.

Roster Limit: 26 active through Sept. 1, when rosters expand to 31. **Imports:** Two active.

DOOSAN BEARS

Mailing Address: Chamsil Baseball Stadium, 10 Chamsil-1 dong, Songpa-ku, Seoul, Korea 138-221. **Telephone:** (02) 2240-1777. **Fax:** (02) 2240-1788. **Website:** www.doosanbears.com. **President:** Kim Jin. **General Manager:** Kim Seung-young. **Manager:** Kim Kyung-Moon.

HANHWA EAGLES

Mailing Address: 22-1 Youngjeon-dong, Dong-ku, Daejeon, Korea 300-200. **Telephone:** (042) 637-6001. **Fax:** (042) 632-2929. **Website:** www.hanwhaeagles.co.kr. **President:** Lee Kyung-jae. **General Manager:** Song Kyu-Soo. **Manager:** Kim In-sik.

KIA TIGERS

Mailing Address: 266 Naebang-dong, Seo-ku, Gwangju, Korea 502-807. **Telephone:** (062) 370-1895. **Fax:** (062) 525-5350. **Website:** www.kiatigers.co.kr. **President:** Cho Nam-hong. **General Manager:** Jeong Jae-kong. **Manager:** Seo Jung-hwan.

LG TWINS

Mailing Address: Chamshil Baseball Stadium, 10 Chamshil 1-dong, Songpa-ku, Seoul, Korea 138-221. **Telephone:** (02) 2005-5760-5. **Fax:** (02) 2005-5801. **Website:** www.lgtwins.com. **President:** Kim Young-soo. **General Manager:** Kim Yeong-joong. **Manager:** Kim Jae-park.

LOTTE GIANTS

Mailing Address: 930 Sajik-dong Dongrae-Ku, Pusan, Korea, 607-120. **Telephone:** (051) 505-7422. **Fax:** 51-506-0090. **Website:** www.lotte-giants.co.kr. **President:** Ha Young-chul. **General Manager:** Lee Sang-koo. **Manager:** Jerry Royster.

SAMSUNG LIONS

Mailing Address: 184-3, Sunhwari-jinrliangyun, Kyungsan, Kyungsan, Kyungsangbuk-do, Korea 712-830. **Telephone:** (053) 859-3114. **Fax:** (053) 859-3117. **Website:** www.samsunglions.com. **President:** Kim Eung-yong. **General Manager:** Kim Jae-ha. **Manager:** Sun Dong-yeol.

SK WYVERNS

Mailing Address: 8 San, Moonhak-dong, Nam-ku, Inchon, Korea 402-070. **Telephone:** (032) 422-7949. **Fax:** (032) 429-4565. **Website:** www.skwyvers.com. **President:** Shin Young-chul. **General Manager:** Myung Young-chul. **Manager:** Kim Sung-keun.

SEOUL HEROES

Mailing Address: 914 Yangcheon Thu 1-dong, Seoul, Korea 158-050. **Telephone:** (02) 3660-1000. **Fax:** (02) 3660-1099. **Website:** www.woori-heroes.co.kr. **President:** Lee Changsuk. **General Manager:** Kim Si-jin. **Manager:** Park Rojun.

TAIWAN

CHINESE PROFESSIONAL BASEBALL LEAGUE

Mailing Address: 2F, No. 32, Pateh Road, Sec. 3, Taipei, Taiwan 10559. **Telephone:** 886-2-2577-6992. **Fax:** 886-2-2577-2606. **Website:** www.cpbl.com.tw.

Years League Active: 1990-.

Commissioner: Shou-Po Chao. **Secretary General:** Wayne Lee. **International Affairs:** Richard Wang. **E-Mail Address:** richard.wang@cpbl.com.tw.

Member Clubs: Brother Elephants (Taipei), Uni-President 7-Eleven Lions (Tainan), Sinon Bulls (Taichung), La New Bears (Kaohsiung).

Regular Season: 100 games. **2009 Opening Date:** March 28.

Playoffs: Second- and third-place teams meet in best-of-five series; winner advances to meet first-place team in best-of-seven championship series.

Import Rule: Only three import players may be active, and only two may be on the field at the same time.

EUROPE

HOLLAND

DUTCH MAJOR LEAGUE

Mailing Address: Koninklijke Nederlandse Baseball en Softball Bond (Royal Dutch Baseball and Softball Association), Postbus 2650, 3430 GB Nieuwegein, Holland. **Telephone:** 31-(0) 30-751-3650. **FAX:** 31-30-751-3651. **Website:** www.knbsb.nl.

President: Hans Meijer.

ADO

Mailing Address: Dr. G. Knuttlepark 93, 2552 LK Den Haag. **Telephone:** +31 (0) 64-583-7439. **Website:** www.svado.nl.

ALMERE '90

Mailing Address: B.S.C. Almere '90, Postbus 1076, 1300 BB Almere. **Telephone:** +31 (0) 36-549-9540. **Website:** www.almere90.nl.

AMSTERDAM PIRATES

Mailing Address: Postbus 8862, 1006 JB Amsterdam. **Telephone:** +31 (0) 20-612-6969. **Website:** www.amsterdampirates.nl.

HCAW

Mailing Address: Mr. Cocker HCAW, Postbus 1321, 1400 BH Bussum. **Telephone:** +31 (0) 35-693-1430. **Website:** www.hcaw.nl.

HOOFDDORP PIONIERS

Mailing Address: Postbus 475, 2130 AL Hoofddorp. **Telephone:** +31 (0) 23-561-3557. **Website:** www.hoofddorp-pioniers.nl.

KINHEIM

Mailing Address: Gemeentelijk Sportpark, Badmintonpad, 2023 BT Haarlem. **Telephone:** +31 (0) 23-526-0021. **Website:** www.kinheim.net.

NEPTUNUS

Mailing Address: Familiestadion Sportclub Neptunus, Abraham van Stolkweg 31, 3041 JA Rotterdam. **Telephone:** +31 (0) 10-462-5859. **Website:** www.neptunussport.com.

RCH PINGUINS

Mailing Address: Mediamonks RCH, Kantine "De Kuil", Ringvaartlaan 2, 2103 XW Heemstede. **Telephone:** +31 (0) 23-528-4388. **Website:** www.rch-pinguins.nl.

SPARTA/FEYENOORD

Mailing Address: Postbus 9211, 3007 AE Rotterdam. **Telephone:** +31 (0) 10-479-0483. **Website:** www.sparta-feyenoord.nl.

ITALY

SERIE A

Mailing Address: Federazione Italiana Baseball Softball, Viale Tiziano 74, 00196 Roma, Italy. **Telephone:** 39-06-36858376. **FAX:** 39-06-36858201. **Website:** www.fibs.it.

President: Riccardo Fraccari.

AVIGLIANA

Mailing Address: Via San Pietro 3, 10051 Avigliana. **Telephone:** 39-011-932-7774. **Website:** www.aviglianabaseball.com.

President: Antonio Carbone. **Manager:** Gian Mario Costa.

BOLOGNA

Mailing Address: Piazzale Atleti Azzurri d'Italia, 40122 Bologna. **Telephone:** 39-051-479618. **FAX:** 39-051-554000. **E-Mail Address:** fortitudobaseball@tin.it. **Website:** www.fortitudobaseball.com.

President: Marco Macchiavelli. **Manager:** Marco Nanni.

GODO

Mailing Address: Viale Baracca 17 48010 Godo di Russi (Ravenna). **Telephone:** 39-0544-414352. **E-Mail Address:** baseball-godo@libero.it. **Website:** www.baseball-godo.com.

President: Claudio Banchi. **Manager:** Mauro Mazzotti.

GROSSETO

Mailing Address: Via Papa Giovanni XXIII, 58100 Grosseto. **Telephone:** 39-0564-494149. **E-Mail Address:** info@bbcgrosseto.it. **Website:** www.bbcgrosseto.it.

President: Claudio Banchi. **Manager:** Mauro Mazzotti.

NETTUNO

Mailing Address: Via Borghese Scipione, 00048 Nettuno (Roma). **Telephone:** 39-06-9854966. **E-Mail Address:** web@nettunobaseball.net. **Website:** www.nettunobaseball.net.

President: Augusto Spigoni. **Manager:** Ruggero Bagialemani.

PARMA

Mailing Address: Via Donatore 4, Collecchio, 43044 Parma. **Telephone:** 39-0521-774-301. **E-Mail Address:** info@parmabaseball.it. **Website:** www.parmabaseball.it.

President: Rossano Rinaldi. **Manager:** Gilberto Gerali.

RIMINI

Mailing Address: Via Monaco 2, 47900 Rimini. **Telephone:** 39-0541-741761. **E-Mail Address:** info@baseballrimini.com. **Website:** www.baseballrimini.com.

President: Cesare Zangheri. **Manager:** Michele Romano.

SAN MARINO

Mailing Address: Via Piana 37, 47031 Republic of San Marino. **Telephone:** 39-0549-901412. **FAX:** 39-0549-901757. **E-Mail Address:** info@sanmarinobaseball.com. **Website:** www.sanmarinobaseball.com.

President: Paolo Achilli. **Manager:** Doriano Bindi.

WINTER BASEBALL

CARIBBEAN BASEBALL CONFEDERATION

Mailing Address: Frank Feliz Miranda No. 1 Naco, Santo Domingo, Dominican Republic. **Telephone:** (809) 381-2643. **Fax:** (809) 565-4654.

Commissioner: Juan Francisco Puello. **Secretary:** Benny Agosto.

Member Countries: Dominican Republic, Mexico, Puerto Rico, Venezuela.

2010 Caribbean Series: Venezuela, February.

DOMINICAN LEAGUE

Office Address: Estadio Quisqueya, 2da. Planta, Ens. La Fe, Santo Domingo, D.N., Dominican Republic. **Mailing Address:** Apartado Postal 1246, Santo Domingo, D.N., Dominican Republic. **Telephone:** (809) 563-5085. **Fax:** (809) 567-5720. **E-Mail Address:** info@besiboldominicano.com. **Website:** www.lidom.com.

Years League Active: 1951-.

Commisioner: Porfirio Veras Mercedes. **Administrator:** Marcos Rodríguez. **Public Relations Director:** Jorge Torres.

Regular Season: 50 games. **2009 Opening Date:** Oct. 16.

Playoff Format: Top four teams meet in 18-game round-robin. Top two teams advance to best-of-nine series for league championship. Winner advances to Caribbean Series.

Roster Limit: 30. **Imports:** 7.

AGUILAS CIBAENAS

Office Address: Estadio Cibao, Apartado 111, Santiago, Dom. Rep. **Mailing Address:** Calle 3, No. 16, Reparto Oquet, Santiago, Dom. Rep.. **Telephone:** (809) 575-8250. **Fax:** (809) 575-0865. **E-Mail Address:** info@lasaguilas.com. **Website:** www.lasaguilas.com.

President: Winston Llenas. **General Manager:** Reynaldo Bisono. **Manager:** Felix Fermin.

AZUCAREROS DEL ESTE

Mailing Address: Estadio Francisco Micheli, La Romana, Dom. Rep. **Telephone:** (809) 556-6189. **Fax:** (809) 550-1550. **E-Mail Address:** azucareros@verizon.net.do. **Website:** www.lostorosdeleste.com.

President: Francisco Micheli. **General Manager:** Jean Giraldi. **Manager:** Carlos Tosca.

ESTRELLAS DE ORIENTE

Office Address: Estadio Tetelo Vargas, San Pedro de Macoris, Dom. Rep. **Telephone:** (809) 246-4077. **Fax:** (809) 529-3618. **E-Mail Address:** info@estrellasdeoriente.com. **Website:** www.estrellasdeoriente.com.

President: Miguel Feris Iglesias. **General Manager:** Jose Mallen. **Manager:** Arturo DeFreites.

LEONES DEL ESCOGIDO

Office Address: Estadio Quisqueya, Ens. la Fe, Apartado Postal 1287, Santo Domingo, Dom. Rep. **Telephone:** (809) 562-6715. **Fax:** (809) 567-7643. **E-Mail Address:** info@escogido.com. **Website:** www.escogido.com.

President: Julio Hazim Risk. **General Manager:** Mario Soto. **Manager:** Donny Scott.

GIGANTES DEL CIBAO

Office Address: Estadio Julian Javier, San Francisco de Macoris, Dom. **Rep. Telephone:** (809) 566-1730. **Fax:** (809) 472-3504. **Website:** www.gigantesdelcibao.com.

President: Alberto Genao. **General Manager:** Patrick Guerrero. **Manager:** Mike Rojas.

TIGRES DE LICEY

Office Address: Estadio Quisqueya, Apartado Postal 1321, Santo Domingo, Dom. Rep. **Telephone:** (809) 567-3090. **Fax:** (809) 542-7714. **E-Mail Address:** fernando.ravelo@codetel.net.do. **Website:** www.licey.com.

President: Jose Manuel Busto. **General Manager:** Fernando Ravelo. **Manager:** Tim Tolman.

MEXICAN PACIFIC LEAGUE

Mailing Address: Av. Insurgentes No. 847 Sur, Interior 402, Edificio San Carlos, Col. Centro, CP 80120, Culiacan, Sinaloa. **Telephone:** (52) 667-761-2570. **Fax:** (52) 667-761-2571. **E-Mail Address:** ligadelpacifico@ligadelpacifico.com.mx. **Website:** www.ligadelpacifico.com.mx.

Years League Active: 1958-.

President: Renato Vega Alvarado. **General Manager:** Oviel Dennis Gonzalez.

Regular Season: 68 games. **2009 Opening Date:** Oct. 16.

Playoff Format: Six teams advance to best-of-seven quarterfinals. Three winners and losing team with best record advance to best-of-seven semifinals. Winners meet in best-of-seven series for league championship. Winner advances to Caribbean Series.

Roster Limit: 30. **Imports:** 5.

AGUILAS DE MEXICALI

Mailing Address: Estadio De Beisbol De La Cd. Deportiva, Calz. Cuautemoc s/n, Las Fuentes Mexicali, Baja, CA, Mexico. **Telephone:** (52) 686-567-0040. **Fax:** (52) 686-567-0095. **E-Mail Address:** aguilas2@telnor.net. **Website:** www.aguilasdemexicali.com.mx.

President: Dio Alberto Murillo. **General Manager:** Antonio Castro. **Manager:** Bobby Magallanes.

ALGODONEROS DE GUASAVE

Mailing Address: Obregon No. 43, CP 81000, Guasave, Sinaloa, Mexico. **Telephone:** (52) 687-872-2998. **Fax:** (52) 687-872-1431. **E-Mail Address:** algodon@prodigy.net.mx. **Website:** www.clubalgodoneros.com.mx.

President: Fausto Perez. **General Manager:** Luis Carlos Joffroy. **Manager:** Tim Johnson.

CANEROS DE LOS MOCHIS

Mailing Address: Francisco I. Madero No. 116 Oriente, CP 81200, Los Mochis, Sinaloa, Mexico. **Telephone:** (52) 668-815-0005. **Fax:** (52) 668-812-6740. **E-Mail Address:** verdes@prodigy.net.mx. **Website:** www.verdes.com.mx.

President: Mario Lopez Valdez. **General Manager:** Carlos Soto Castro. **Manager:** Marco Antonio Vazquez.

MAYOS DE NAVOJOA

Mailing Address: Antonio Rosales No. 102, E/Pesqueira Y no Reeleccion, CP 85830, Navojoa, Sonora, Mexico. **Telephone:** (52) 642-422-1433. **Fax:** (52) 642-422-8997. **E-Mail Address:** mayosbeisbol@mayosbeisbol.com. **Website:** www.mayosbeisbol.com.

President: Victor Cuevas Garibay. **General Manager:** Victor Cuevas. **Manager:** Mauricio Zazueta.

NARANJEROS DE HERMOSILLO

Mailing Address: Blvd. Solidaridad s/n, Estadio Hector Espino, E/Jose S. Healey Y Blvd., Luis Encinas, CP 83188, Hermosillo, Sonora, Mexico. **Telephone:** (52) 662-260-

6932. **Fax:** (52) 662-260-6931. **E-Mail Address:** webmaster@naranjeros.com.mx. **Website:** www.naranjeros.com.

President: Enrique Mazon Rubio. **General Manager:** Arturo Leon Lerma. **Manager:** Lorenzo Bundy.

TOMATEROS DE CULIACAN

Street Address: Av. Alvaro Obregon 348 Sur, CP 8000, Culiacan, Sinaloa, Mexico. **Telephone:** (52) 667-712-2446. **Fax:** (52) 667-715-6828. **E-Mail Address:** tomateros@infosel.com.mx. **Website:** www.tomateros.com.mx.

President: Juan Manuel Ley Lopez. **General Managers:** Jaime Blancarte. **Manager:** Marco Antonio Guzman.

VENADOS DE MAZATLAN

Mailing Address: Gutierrez Najera No. 821, CP 82000, Mazatlan, Sinaloa, Mexico. **Telephone:** (52) 669-981-1710. **Fax:** (52) 669-981-1711. **E-Mail Address:** club@venadosdemazatlan.com.mx. **Website:** www.venadosdemazatlan.com.mx.

President: José Luis Martínez Moreno. **General Manager:** Jesus Valdez. **Manager:** Juan Jose Pacho.

YAQUIS DE OBREGON

Mailing Address: Guerrero y Michoacan, Estadio de Beisbol Tomas Oroz Gaytan, CP 85130, Ciudad Obregon, Sonora, Mexico. **Telephone:** (52) 644-413-7766. **Fax:** (52) 644-414-1156. **E-Mail Address:** clubyaquisdeobregon@yaquisdeobregon.com.mx. **Website:** www.yaquisdeobregon.com.mx.

President: Luis Alfonso Lugo Platt. **General Manager:** Rene Arturo Rodriguez. **Manager:** Homar Rojas.

PUERTO RICAN LEAGUE

Office Address: Avenida Munoz Rivera 1056, Edificio First Federal, Suite 501, Rio Piedras, PR 00925. **Mailing Address:** P.O. Box 191852, San Juan, PR 00019. **Telephone:** (787) 765-6285, 765-7285. **Fax:** (787) 767-3028. **Website:** www.hitboricua.com.

Years League Active: 1938-2007; 2008-

President: Joaquin Monserrate Matienzo. **Executive Director:** Benny Agosto.

Regular Season: 42 games. **2009 Opening Date:** Nov. 11.

Playoff Format: Top four teams meet in best-of-seven semifinal series. Winners meet in best-of-nine series for league championship. Winner advances to Caribbean Series.

Roster Limit: 30. **Imports:** 5.

ATENIENSES DE MANTAI

Mailing Address: Direccion Postal Box 1155, Manati, PR 00674. **Telephone:** (787) 854-5757. **Fax:** (787) 854-6767.

President: Tony Valentin.

CRIOLLOS DE CAGUAS

Mailing Address: P.O. Box 1415, Caguas, PR 00726. **Telephone:** (787) 258-2222. **Fax:** (787) 743-0545.

President/General Manager: Frankie Thon.

GIGANTES DE CAROLINA

Mailing Address: Roberto Clemente Stadium, P.O. Box 366246, San Juan, PR 00936. **Telephone:** (787) 765-1152. **Fax:** (787) 765-2965.

President: Benjamin Rivera. **General Manager:** Angel Roman.

INDIOS DE MAYAGUEZ

Mailing Address: 3089 Marina Station, Mayaguez, PR 00681. **Telephone:** (787) 834-5211. **Fax:** (787) 834-7480.

President/General Manager: Ruben Escalera.

LEONES DE PONCE

Mailing Address: P.O. Box 363148, San Juan, PR 00936. **Telephone:** (787) 848-0150. **Fax:** (787) 848-8884.

President/General Manager: Ramon Conde.

LOBOS DE ARECIBO

Mailing Address: Unavailable. **Telephone:** (787) 315-1003. **Fax:** (787) 816-0456.

President/General Manager: Candy Maldonado.

VENEZUELAN LEAGUE

Mailing Address: Avenida Casanova, Centro Comercial "El Recreo," Torre Sur, Piso 3, Oficinas 6 y 7, Sabana Grande, Caracas, Venezuela. **Telephone:** (58) 212-761-6408. **Fax:** (58) 212-761-7661. **Website:** www.lvbp.com.

Years League Active: 1946-.

President: Ramon Guillermo Aveledo. **General Manager:** Jose Domingo Alvarez.

Division Structure: East—Caracas, La Guaira, Magallanes, Oriente; West—Aragua, Lara, Pastora, Zulia.

Regular Season: 62 games. **2009 Opening Date:** Oct. 18.

Playoff Format: Top two teams in each division, plus a wild-card team, meet in 16-game round-robin series. Top two finishers meet in best-of-seven series for league championship. Winner advances to Caribbean Series.

Roster Limit: 26. **Imports:** 7.

AGUILAS DEL ZULIA

Mailing Address: Avenida 8 con Calle 81, Urb. Santa Rita, Edificio Las Carolinas, Mezzanine Local M-3, Maracaibo, Zulia, Venezuela. **Telephone:** (58) 261-798-0541. **Fax:** (58) 261-798-0579. **Website:** www.aguilas.com.

President: Lucas Rincon Colmenares. **General Manager:** Luis Rodolfo Machado. **Manager:** Stan Cliburn.

BRAVOS DE MARGARITA

Mailing Address: Unavailable. **Telephone:** (58) 295-263-6316. **Fax:** (58) 295-263-4418.

President: Tobias Carrero. **General Manager:** Ruben Mijares. **Manager:** Phil Regan.

CARDENALES DE LARA

Mailing Address: Av. Rotaria, Estadio Antonio Herrera Gutiérrez, Barquisimeto, Lara, Venezuela. **Telephone:** (58) 251-442- 8321. **Fax:** (58) 251-442-1921. **E-Mail Address:** administrator@cardenalesdelara.com. **Website:** www.cardenalesdelara.com.

President: Adolfo Alvarez. **General Manager:** Humberto Oropeza. **Manager:** Luis Sojo.

CARIBES DE ORIENTE

Mailing Address: Avenida Estadio Alfonso Carrasquel, Oficina Caribes de Oriente, Centro Comercial Novocentro, Piso 2, Local 2-4, Puerto la Cruz, Anzoategui, Venezuela. **Telephone:** (58) 281-266-2536. **Fax:** (58) 281-267-2972. **E-Mail Address:** caribes@telcel.net.ve. **Website:** www.caribesbbc.com.

President: Aurelio Fernandez Concheso. **Vice President:** Pablo Ruggeri. **Manager:** Marco Davilillo.

LEONES DE CARACAS

Mailing Address: Av. Francisco de Miranda, Centro Seguros la Paz, Piso 4, ofc. 42-C, La California Norte. **Telephone:** (58) 212-761-3211. **Fax:** (58) 212-761-3211. **E-Mail Address:** contacto@leones.com. **Website:** www.leones.com.

President: Ariel Pratt Pinedo. **General Manager:** Oscar Prieto. **Manager:** Carlos Hernandez.

NAVEGANTES DEL MAGALLANES

Mailing Address: Centro Comercial Caribbean Plaza, Modulo 8, Local 173, Valencia, Carabobo, Venezuela. **Telephone:** (58) 241-824-0980. **Fax:** (58) 241-824-0705. **E-Mail Address:** magallanes@magallanesbbc.com.ve. **Website:** www.magallanesbbc.com.ve.

President: Jorge Latouche. **General Manager:** Juan Castillo. **Manager:** Al Pedrique.

TIBURONES DE LA GUAIRA

Mailing Address: 4ta., Avienda Urb. Los Palos Grandes, Torre Seguros Altamira, 1er. Piso, Officinas C, D y E, Caracas, Venezuela. **Telephone:** (58) 212-284-4456. **Fax:** (58) 212-286-8373. **E-Mail Addres:** prensa@tiburonesdelaguiara.com.ve. **Website:** www.tiburonesdelaguaira.com.ve.

President: Francisco Arocha. **Vice President, General Manager:** Alejandro Herrera. **Manager:** Julio Vina.

TIGRES DE ARAGUA

Mailing Address: Estadio Jose Perez Colmenares, Calle Campo Elias, Barrio Democratico, Maracay, Aragua, Venezuela. **Telephone:** (58) 243-554-4134. **Fax:** (58) 243-553-8655. **E-Mail Address:** tigres@telcel.net.ve. **Website:** www.tigresdearagua.net.

President, General Manager: Rafael Rodriguez Rendon. **Manager:** Buddy Bailey.

COLOMBIAN LEAGUE

Office/Mailing Address: Unavailable. **Telephone:** Unavailable.

Website: www.teamrenteria.com.

Regular season: 65 games. **2008 Opening Date:** Oct. 28. **Closing Date:** Jan. 12.

Active Teams: Barranquilla, Cartagena, Monteria, Sincelejo.

Playoff Format: Top two teams meet in best-of-seven finals for league championship.

NICARAGUAN LEAGUE

Office Address/Mailing Address: Managua de Canal 2, Casa 1013 en Bolonia, Managua, Nicaragua. **Telephone:** (011) 505-266-1009. **Website:** www.lnbp.net.

President: Enrique Gasteazoro. **Vice President:** Eduardo Ureuyo.

Regular Season: 40 games. **2008 Opening Date:** Dec. 1. **Closing Date:** Jan. 16.

Active Teams: Boer, Leon, Chinandega, San Fernando.

Playoff Format: Top two teams meet in best-of-seven finals for league championship.

DOMESTIC WINTER LEAGUES

ARIZONA FALL LEAGUE

Mailing Address: 2415 E. Camelback Road, Suite 850, Phoenix, AZ 85016. **Telephone:** (602) 281-7250. **Fax:** (602) 281-7313. **E-Mail Address:** afl@mlb.com. **Website:** www.mlb.com.

Years League Active: 1992-.

Operated by: Major League Baseball.

Executive Director: Steve Cobb. **Seasonal Assistant:** Joan McGrath.

Teams: Mesa Solar Sox, Peoria Javelinas, Peoria Saguaros, Phoenix Desert Dogs, Scottsdale Scorpions, Surprise Rafters.

2009 Opening Date: Unavailable. Play usually opens in early October.

Playoff Format: Division champions meet in one-game championship.

Roster Limit: 30. Players with less than one year of major league service are eligible, with one foreign player and one player below the Double-A level allowed per team.

FLORIDA WINTER BASEBALL LEAGUE

(Scheduled to debut, October 2009)

Office Address: 1172 South Dixie Highway, Suite 551, Coral Gables, FL 33146.

Telephone: (877) 999-3925. **Website:** www.fwbl.com. **E-Mail Address:** info@fwbl.com.

President: Mickey Filippucci. **Commissioner:** James Gamble. **Director, Operations:** Kevin Davidson.

League Structure: Four teams, sites unavailable.

Roster Limit: 22. **Eligibility Rules:** None.

Regular Season: 60 games. **2009 Opening Date:** Unavailable; scheduled to run October-January.

Playoffs: Top two teams play in best-of-three championship series.

Statistician: SportsTicker.

MINOR LEAGUE SCHEDULES

TRIPLE-A

INTERNATIONAL LEAGUE

BUFFALO

APRIL
9-12 . . . . .Pawtucket
13-16 . . . . . . Scranton/WB
17-20 . . . . at Syracuse
21-22 . . . . at Scranton/WB
24-27 . . . . Syracuse
28-29 . . . . . . at Rochester
30 . . . . Louisville

MAY
1-3. . . . . Louisville
4-7. . . . . . at Lehigh Valley
8-11 . . . . .Norfolk
12-15 . . . . Gwinnett
16-19 . . . . . . at Pawtucket
21-24 . . . . Columbus
25-28 . . . . . . Lehigh Valley
29-31 . . . . .at Durham

JUNE
2-5. . . . . at Norfolk
6-9. . . . . .Indianapolis
11-14 . . . . Durham
15-16 . . . . at Syracuse
17-18 . . . . .Syracuse
19-22 . . . . . . .at Charlotte
23-26 . . . . . . .at Gwinnett
27-30 . . . . Charlotte

JULY
2-3. . . . . Rochester
4-6. . . . . at Rochester
7-8. . . . . Scranton/WB
9-10 . . . . at Pawtucket
11-12 . . . . at Scranton/WB
16-19 . . . . Toledo
20-23 . . . . at Louisville
24-27 . . . . . at Indianapolis
28-31 . . . . .Pawtucket

AUGUST
1-4. . . . . .at Toledo
6-9. . . . . at Columbus
10-13 . . . . Rochester
14-17 . . . . . . Lehigh Valley
18-19 . . . . at Syracuse
20-21 . . . . Syracuse
22-25 . . . . at Scranton/WB
26-27 . . . . at Pawtucket
28-30 . . . . at Rochester
31 . . . . Rochester

SEPTEMBER
1 . . . . Rochester
2-3. . . . . Scranton/WB
4-7. . . . . . . at Lehigh Valley

CHARLOTTE

APRIL
9-12. . . . . Gwinnett
13-16 . . . . .Norfolk
17-19 . . . . Durham
20-23 . . . . at Norfolk
23-26 . . . . .at Gwinnett
28-29 . . . . .at Durham
30 . . . . Syracuse

MAY
1-3. . . . . Syracuse
4-5. . . . . at Durham
6-7. . . . . Durham
8-11 . . . . at Rochester
12-15 . . . . . at Scranton/WB
16-19 . . . . Toledo
21-24 . . . . .Indianapolis
25-28 . . . . at Columbus
29-31 . . . . at Toledo

JUNE
1 . . . . .at Toledo
2-5. . . . . .Columbus
6-9. . . . . Scranton/WB
11-14 . . . . . at Lehigh Valley
15-18 . . . . at Pawtucket
19-22 . . . . Buffalo
23-26 . . . . Louisville
27-30 . . . . at Buffalo

JULY
2-3. . . . . at Durham
4-6. . . . . Durham
7-9. . . . . .Norfolk
10-12 . . . . Gwinnett
16-19 . . . . at Norfolk
20-23 . . . . Lehigh Valley
24-27 . . . . Rochester
28-31 . . . . at Syracuse

AUGUST
1-4. . . . . at Louisville
6-9. . . . . at Indianapolis
10-13 . . . . .Pawtucket
14-17 . . . . .Norfolk
18-21 . . . . .at Durham
22-24 . . . . .at Gwinnett
26-28 . . . . Gwinnett
29-31 . . . . at Norfolk

SEPTEMBER
1 . . . . at Norfolk
2-4. . . . . Durham
5-7. . . . . .at Gwinnett

COLUMBUS

APRIL
9-12 . . . . at Louisville
13-15 . . . . . at Indianapolis
16-17 . . . . .at Toledo
18-19 . . . . Toledo
20-22 . . . . Louisville
23-26 . . . . .Indianapolis
27-28 . . . . .at Toledo
30 . . . . .at Durham

MAY
1-3. . . . . .at Durham
4-7. . . . . at Norfolk
8-11 . . . . .Pawtucket
12-15 . . . . . . Lehigh Valley
16-19 . . . . at Scranton/WB
21-24 . . . . at Buffalo
25-28 . . . . Charlotte
29-31 . . . . .Norfolk

JUNE
1 . . . . .Norfolk
2-5. . . . . at Charlotte
6-9. . . . . at Gwinnett
11-14 . . . . Louisville
15-18 . . . . Rochester
19-22 . . . . at Syracuse
23-26 . . . . . . at Rochester
27-30 . . . . Durham

JULY
1-2. . . . . Toledo
3-5. . . . . .at Toledo
7-9. . . . . .Indianapolis
10-12 . . . . at Louisville
16-19 . . . . Syracuse
20-23 . . . . . . Scranton/WB
24-27 . . . . . . at Pawtucket
28-31 . . . . at Lehigh Valley

AUGUST
1-4. . . . . Gwinnett
6-9. . . . . Buffalo
10-12 . . . . . at Indianapolis
13-16 . . . . . . .Indianapolis
17-18 . . . . .at Toledo
19-22 . . . . Toledo
23-26 . . . . . at Indianapolis
27-30 . . . . at Louisville
31 . . . . Louisville

SEPTEMBER
1-2. . . . . Louisville
3-4. . . . . .at Toledo
5-7. . . . . Toledo

DURHAM

APRIL
9-12. . . . . .Norfolk
13-16 . . . . Gwinnett
17-19 . . . . . . .at Charlotte
20-22 . . . . . . .at Gwinnett
23-26 . . . . at Norfolk
28-29 . . . . Charlotte
30 . . . . Columbus

MAY
1-3. . . . . Columbus
4-5. . . . . Charlotte
6-7. . . . . .at Charlotte
8-11 . . . . at Gwinnett
12-15 . . . . Louisville
16-19 . . . . Rochester
21-24 . . . . at Lehigh Valley
25-28 . . . . . . at Rochester
29-31 . . . . Buffalo

JUNE
1 . . . . Buffalo
2-5. . . . . Toledo
6-9. . . . . at Pawtucket
11-14 . . . . at Buffalo
15-18 . . . . . . Lehigh Valley
19-22 . . . . .Pawtucket
23-25 . . . . .at Toledo
29-30 . . . . . . at Columbus

JULY
2-3. . . . . Charlotte
5-6. . . . . .at Charlotte
7-9. . . . . Gwinnett
10-12 . . . . at Norfolk
16-19 . . . . at Louisville
20-23 . . . . . at Indianapolis
24-27 . . . . Norfolk
28-31 . . . . at Scranton/WB

AUGUST
1-4. . . . . .Indianapolis
6-9. . . . . Syracuse
10-13 . . . . at Gwinnett
14-17 . . . . . . Scranton/WB
18-21 . . . . Charlotte
22-25 . . . . at Syracuse
26-28 . . . . at Norfolk
29-31 . . . . Gwinnett

SEPTEMBER
1 . . . . Gwinett County
2-4. . . . . .at Charlotte
5-7. . . . . .Norfolk

GWINNETT

APRIL
9-12 . . . . .at Charlotte
13-16 . . . . .at Durham
17-19 . . . . .Norfolk
20-22 . . . . Durham
23-26 . . . . Charlotte
28-29 . . . . at Norfolk
30 . . . . at Pawtucket

MAY
1-3. . . . . at Pawtucket
4-7. . . . . Syracuse
8-11 . . . . Durham
12-15 . . . . at Buffalo
16-19 . . . . at Lehigh Valley
21-24 . . . . Toledo
25-28 . . . . .Indianapolis
29-31 . . . . at Syracuse

JUNE
1 . . . . at Syracuse
2-5. . . . . at Rochester
6-9. . . . . Columbus
11-14 . . . . . . Scranton/WB
15-18 . . . . . at Indianapolis
19-22 . . . . at Louisville
23-26 . . . . Buffalo
27-30 . . . . Louisville

JULY
2-3. . . . . at Norfolk
4-6. . . . . .Norfolk
7-9. . . . . .at Durham
10-12 . . . . at Charlotte
16-19 . . . . at Scranton/WB
20-23 . . . . .Norfolk
24-27 . . . . . . Lehigh Valley
28-31 . . . . Rochester

AUGUST
1-4. . . . . at Columbus
6-9. . . . . .at Toledo
10-13 . . . . Durham
14-17 . . . . .Pawtucket

- 18-21 . . . at Norfolk
- 22-24 . . . Charlotte
- 26-28 . . . at Charlotte
- 29-31 . . . at Durham

SEPTEMBER
- 1 . . . at Durham
- 2-4 . . . at Norfolk
- 5-7 . . . Charlotte

INDIANAPOLIS

APRIL
- 9-12 . . . Toledo
- 13-15 . . . Columbus
- 16-17 . . . Louisville
- 18-19 . . . at Louisville
- 21-22 . . . at Toledo
- 23-26 . . . at Columbus
- 27-28 . . . at Louisville
- 30 . . . Rochester

MAY
- 1-3 . . . Rochester
- 4-7 . . . Scranton/WB
- 8-11 . . . at Syracuse
- 12-15 . . . at Rochester
- 16-19 . . . Syracuse
- 21-24 . . . at Charlotte
- 25-28 . . . at Gwinnett
- 29-31 . . . Pawtucket

JUNE
- 1 . . . Pawtucket
- 2-5 . . . Lehigh Valley
- 6-9 . . . at Buffalo
- 11-14 . . . Norfolk
- 15-18 . . . Gwinnett
- 19-22 . . . at Scranton/WB
- 23-26 . . . at Lehigh Valley
- 27-30 . . . Toledo

JULY
- 2-3 . . . at Louisville
- 4-6 . . . Louisville
- 7-9 . . . at Columbus
- 10-12 . . . at Toledo
- 16-19 . . . at Pawtucket
- 20-23 . . . Durham
- 24-27 . . . Buffalo
- 28-31 . . . at Norfolk

AUGUST
- 1-4 . . . at Durham
- 6-9 . . . Charlotte
- 10-12 . . . Columbus
- 13-16 . . . at Columbus
- 17-19 . . . at Louisville
- 20-22 . . . Louisville
- 23-26 . . . Columbus
- 27-30 . . . at Toledo
- 31 . . . Toledo

SEPTEMBER
- 1-2 . . . Toledo
- 3-5 . . . Louisville
- 6-7 . . . at Louisville

LEHIGH VALLEY

APRIL
- 9-12 . . . Scarnton/WB
- 13-16 . . . Syracuse
- 17-20 . . . at Pawtucket
- 21-22 . . . at Syracuse
- 24-27 . . . Pawtucket
- 28-29 . . . at Scranton/WB
- 30 . . . Toledo

MAY
- 1-3 . . . Toledo
- 4-7 . . . Buffalo
- 8-11 . . . at Toledo
- 12-15 . . . at Columbus
- 16-19 . . . Gwinnett
- 21-24 . . . Durham
- 25-28 . . . at Buffalo
- 29-31 . . . Rochester

JUNE
- 1 . . . Rochester
- 2-5 . . . at Indianapolis
- 6-9 . . . at Louisville
- 11-14 . . . Charlotte
- 15-18 . . . at Durham
- 19-22 . . . at Norfolk
- 23-26 . . . Indianapolis
- 27-30 . . . Norfolk

JULY
- 2-3 . . . Syracuse
- 4-6 . . . at Syracuse
- 7-8 . . . Pawtucket
- 9-10 . . . at Scranton/WB
- 11-12 . . . at Rochester
- 16-19 . . . Rochester
- 20-23 . . . at Charlotte
- 24-27 . . . at Gwinnett
- 28-31 . . . Columbus

AUGUST
- 1-4 . . . at Rochester
- 6-7 . . . at Scranton/WB
- 8-9 . . . Scranton/WB
- 10-13 . . . Louisville
- 14-17 . . . at Buffalo
- 18-19 . . . at Scranton/WB
- 20-21 . . . Scranton/WB
- 22-25 . . . at Pawtucket
- 26-27 . . . at Rochester
- 28-30 . . . at Syracuse
- 31 . . . Pawtucket

SEPTEMBER
- 1 . . . Pawtucket
- 2-3 . . . Syracuse
- 4-7 . . . Buffalo

LOUISVILLE

APRIL
- 9-12 . . . Columbus
- 13-15 . . . Toledo
- 16-17 . . . at Indianapolis
- 18-19 . . . Indianapolis
- 20-22 . . . at Columbus
- 23-26 . . . at Toledo
- 27-28 . . . Indianapolis
- 30 . . . at Buffalo

MAY
- 1-3 . . . at Buffalo
- 4-7 . . . Rochester
- 8-11 . . . Scranton/WB
- 12-15 . . . at Durham
- 16-19 . . . at Norfolk
- 21-24 . . . Syracuse
- 25-28 . . . Pawtucket
- 29-31 . . . at Scranton/WB

JUNE
- 1 . . . at Scranton/WB
- 2-5 . . . at Pawtucket
- 6-9 . . . Lehigh Valley
- 11-14 . . . at Columbus
- 15-18 . . . Norfolk
- 19-22 . . . Gwinnett
- 23-26 . . . at Charlotte
- 27-30 . . . at Gwinnett

JULY
- 2-3 . . . Indianapolis
- 4-6 . . . at Indianapolis
- 7-9 . . . at Toledo
- 10-12 . . . Columbus
- 16-19 . . . Durham
- 20-23 . . . Buffalo
- 24-27 . . . at Syracuse
- 28-31 . . . Toledo

AUGUST
- 1-4 . . . Charlotte
- 6-9 . . . at Rochester
- 10-13 . . . at Lehigh Valley
- 14-16 . . . Toledo
- 17-19 . . . Indianapolis
- 20-22 . . . at Indianapolis
- 23-26 . . . at Toledo
- 27-30 . . . Columbus
- 31 . . . at Columbus

SEPTEMBER
- 1-2 . . . at Columbus
- 3-5 . . . at Indianapolis
- 6-7 . . . Indianapolis

NORFOLK

APRIL
- 9-12 . . . at Durham
- 13-16 . . . at Charlotte
- 17-19 . . . at Gwinnett
- 20-22 . . . Charlotte
- 23-26 . . . Durham
- 28-29 . . . Gwinnett
- 30 . . . Gwinnett

MAY
- 1-3 . . . at Scranton/WB
- 4-7 . . . Columbus
- 8-11 . . . at Buffalo
- 12-15 . . . at Syracuse
- 16-19 . . . Louisville
- 21-14 . . . Rochester
- 25-28 . . . at Toledo
- 29-31 . . . at Columbus

JUNE
- 1 . . . at Columbus
- 2-5 . . . Buffalo
- 6-9 . . . Toledo
- 11-14 . . . at Indianapolis
- 15-18 . . . at Louisville
- 19-22 . . . Lehigh Valley
- 23-26 . . . Pawtucket
- 27-30 . . . at Lehigh Valley

JULY
- 2-3 . . . Gwinnett
- 4-6 . . . at Gwinnett
- 7-9 . . . at Charlotte
- 10-12 . . . Durham
- 16-19 . . . Charlotte
- 20-23 . . . at Gwinnett
- 24-27 . . . at Durham
- 28-31 . . . Indianapolis

AUGUST
- 1-4 . . . Syracuse
- 5-8 . . . at Pawtucket
- 10-13 . . . Scranton/WB
- 14-17 . . . at Charlotte
- 18-21 . . . Gwinnett
- 22-25 . . . at Rochester
- 26-28 . . . Durham
- 29-31 . . . Charlotte

SEPTEMBER
- 1 . . . Charlotte
- 2-4 . . . Gwinnett
- 5-7 . . . at Durham

PAWTUCKET

APRIL
- 9-12 . . . at Buffalo
- 13-16 . . . at Rochester
- 17-20 . . . Lehigh Valley
- 21-22 . . . Rochester
- 24-27 . . . at Lehigh Valley
- 28-29 . . . at Syracuse
- 30 . . . Gwinnett

MAY
- 1-3 . . . Gwinnett
- 4-7 . . . Toledo
- 8-11 . . . at Columbus
- 12-15 . . . at Toledo
- 16-19 . . . Buffalo
- 21-24 . . . Scranton/WB
- 25-28 . . . at Louisville
- 29-31 . . . at Indianapolis

JUNE
- 1 . . . at Indianapolis
- 2-5 . . . Louisville
- 6-9 . . . Durham
- 11-14 . . . at Syracuse
- 15-18 . . . Charlotte
- 19-22 . . . at Durham
- 23-26 . . . at Norfolk
- 27-30 . . . Syracuse

JULY
- 2-3 . . . Scranton/WB
- 4-6 . . . at Scranton/WB
- 7-8 . . . at Lehigh Valley
- 9-10 . . . Buffalo
- 11-12 . . . Syracuse
- 16-19 . . . Indianapolis
- 20-23 . . . at Rochester
- 24-27 . . . Columbus
- 28-31 . . . at Buffalo

AUGUST
- 1-2 . . . at Scranton/WB
- 3-4 . . . Scranton/WB
- 5-8 . . . Norfolk
- 10-13 . . . at Charlotte
- 14-17 . . . at Gwinnett
- 18-21 . . . Rochester
- 22-25 . . . Lehigh Valley
- 26-27 . . . Buffalo
- 28-30 . . . at Scranton/WB
- 31 . . . at Lehigh Valley

SEPTEMBER
1 . . . . at Lehigh Valley
2-3 . . . . Rochester
4-5 . . . . Syracuse
6-7 . . . . at Syracuse

ROCHESTER

APRIL
9-10 . . . . at Syracuse
11-12 . . . . Syracuse
13-16 . . . . Pawtucket
17-20 . . . . at Scranton/WB
21-22 . . . . . . at Pawtucket
24-27 . . . . . Scranton/WB
28-29 . . . . Buffalo
30 . . . . at Indianapolis

MAY
1-3 . . . . at Indianapolis
4-7 . . . . at Louisville
8-11 . . . . Charlotte
12-15 . . . . Indianapolis
16-19 . . . . at Durham
21-24 . . . . at Norfolk
25-28 . . . . Durham
29-31 . . . . at Lehigh Valley

JUNE
1 . . . . at Lehigh Valley
2-5 . . . . Gwinnett
6-9 . . . . Syracuse
11-14 . . . . at Toledo
15-18 . . . . . . at Columbus
19-22 . . . . Toledo
23-26 . . . . Columbus
27-28 . . . . . . Scranton/WB
29-30 . . . . at Scranton/WB

JULY
2-3 . . . . at Buffalo
4-6 . . . . Buffalo
7-10 . . . . at Syracuse
11-12 . . . . . . Lehigh Valley
16-19 . . . . at Lehigh Valley
20-23 . . . . Pawtucket
24-27 . . . . at Charlotte
28-31 . . . . at Gwinnett

AUGUST
1-4 . . . . Lehigh Valley
6-9 . . . . Louisville
10-13 . . . . at Buffalo
14-15 . . . . at Syracuse
16-17 . . . . Syracuse
18-21 . . . . . . at Pawtucket
22-25 . . . . Norfolk
26-27 . . . . . . Lehigh Valley
28-30 . . . . Buffalo
31 . . . . at Buffalo

SEPTEMBER
1 . . . . at Buffalo
2-3 . . . . at Pawtucket
4-5 . . . . Scranton/WB
6-7 . . . . . . at Scranton/WB

SCRANTON/WILKES-BARRE

APRIL
9-12 . . . . . at Lehigh Valley
13-16 . . . . at Buffalo
17-20 . . . . Rochester
21-22 . . . . Buffalo
24-27 . . . . . . at Rochester
28-29 . . . . . . Lehigh Valley
30 . . . . Norfolk

MAY
1-3 . . . . Norfolk
4-7 . . . . at Indianapolis
8-11 . . . . at Louisville
12-15 . . . . Charlotte
16-19 . . . . Columbus
21-24 . . . . . . at Pawtucket
25-28 . . . . at Syracuse
29-31 . . . . Louisville

JUNE
1 . . . . Louisville
2-5 . . . . Syracuse
6-9 . . . . at Charlotte
11-14 . . . . at Gwinnett
15-18 . . . . Toledo
19-22 . . . . Indianapolis
23-24 . . . . Syracuse
25-26 . . . . at Syracuse
27-28 . . . . . . at Rochester
29-30 . . . . Rochester

JULY
2-3 . . . . at Pawtucket
4-6 . . . . Pawtucket
7-8 . . . . at Buffalo
9-10 . . . . Lehigh Valley
11-12 . . . . Buffalo
16-19 . . . . Gwinnett
20-23 . . . . at Columbus
24-27 . . . . at Toledo
28-31 . . . . Durham

AUGUST
1-2 . . . . Pawtucket
3-4 . . . . at Pawtucket
6-7 . . . . Lehigh Valley
8-9 . . . . . . at Lehigh Valley
10-13 . . . . at Norfolk
14-17 . . . . at Durham
18-19 . . . . . . Lehigh Valley
20-21 . . . . at Lehigh Valley
22-25 . . . . Buffalo
26-27 . . . . Syracuse
28-30 . . . . Pawtucket
31 . . . . at Syracuse

SEPTEMBER
1 . . . . at Syracuse
2-3 . . . . at Buffalo
4-5 . . . . at Rochester
6-7 . . . . Rochester

SYRACUSE

APRIL
9-10 . . . . Rochester
11-12 . . . . at Rochester
13-16 . . . . at Lehigh Valley
17-20 . . . . Buffalo
21-22 . . . . . . Lehigh Valley
24-27 . . . . at Buffalo
28-29 . . . . Pawtucket
30 . . . . at Charlotte

MAY
1-3 . . . . at Charlotte
4-7 . . . . at Gwinnett
8-11 . . . . Indianapolis
12-15 . . . . Norfolk
16-19 . . . . . at Indianapolis
21-24 . . . . at Louisville
25-28 . . . . . . Scranton/WB
29-31 . . . . Gwinnett

JUNE
1 . . . . Gwinnett
2-5 . . . . . . at Scranton/WB
6-9 . . . . at Rochester
11-14 . . . . Pawtucket
15-16 . . . . Buffalo
17-18 . . . . at Buffalo
19-22 . . . . Columbus
23-24 . . . . at Scranton/WB
25-26 . . . . . . Scranton/WB
27-30 . . . . . . at Pawtucket

JULY
2-3 . . . . . . at Lehigh Valley
4-6 . . . . Lehigh Valley
7-10 . . . . Rochester
11-12 . . . . . . at Pawtucket
16-19 . . . . . . at Columbus
20-23 . . . . at Toledo
24-27 . . . . Louisville
28-31 . . . . Charlotte

AUGUST
1-4 . . . . at Norfolk
6-9 . . . . at Durham
11-13 . . . . Toledo
14-15 . . . . Rochester
16-17 . . . . . . at Rochester
18-19 . . . . Buffalo
20-21 . . . . at Buffalo
22-25 . . . . Durham
26-27 . . . . at Scranton/WB
28-30 . . . . . . Lehigh Valley
31 . . . . Scranton/WB

SEPTEMBER
1 . . . . Scranton/WB
2-3 . . . . . . at Lehigh Valley
4-5 . . . . at Pawtucket
6-7 . . . . Pawtucket

TOLEDO

APRIL
9-12 . . . . . . at Indianapolis
13-15 . . . . at Louisville
16-17 . . . . Columbus
18-19 . . . . . . at Columbus
21-22 . . . . Indianapolis
23-26 . . . . Louisville
27-28 . . . . Columbus
30 . . . . . . at Lehigh Valley

MAY
1-3 . . . . . . at Lehigh Valley
4-7 . . . . at Pawtucket
8-11 . . . . Lehigh Valley
12-15 . . . . Pawtucket
16-19 . . . . at Charlotte
21-24 . . . . at Gwinnett
25-28 . . . . Norfolk
29-31 . . . . Charlotte

JUNE
1 . . . . Charlotte
2-5 . . . . at Durham
6-9 . . . . at Norfolk
11-14 . . . . Rochester
15-18 . . . . at Scranton/WB
19-22 . . . . . . at Rochester
23-26 . . . . Durham
27-30 . . . . . at Indianapolis

JULY
1-2 . . . . at Columbus
3-5 . . . . Columbus
7-9 . . . . Louisville
10-12 . . . . Indianapolis
16-19 . . . . at Buffalo
20-23 . . . . Syracuse
24-27 . . . . . . Scranton/WB
28-31 . . . . at Louisville

AUGUST
1-4 . . . . Buffalo
6-9 . . . . Gwinnett
11-13 . . . . at Syracuse
14-16 . . . . at Louisville
17-18 . . . . Columbus
19-22 . . . . at Columbus
23-26 . . . . Louisville
27-30 . . . . Indianapolis
31 . . . . at Indianapolis

SEPTEMBER
1-2 . . . . at Indianapolis
3-4 . . . . Columbus
5-7 . . . . at Columbus

PACIFIC COAST LEAGUE

ALBUQUERQUE

APRIL
9-12 . . . . Omaha
13-16 . . . . Iowa
17-20 . . . . at Omaha
21-24 . . . . at Iowa
25-28 . . . . . at New Orleans
30 . . . . Round Rock

MAY
1-3 . . . . Round Rock
4-7 . . . . . at Oklahoma City
8-11 . . . . New Orleans
12-15 . . . . . . at Sacramento
16-19 . . . . at Fresno
21-24 . . . . Salt Lake
25-28 . . . Colorado Springs
29-31 . . . at Oklahoma City

JUNE
1 . . . . . . at Oklahoma City
2-5 . . . . at New Orleans
6-9 . . . . Oklahoma City
11-14 . . . . . . at Round Rock
15-17 . . . . at Memphis
18-21 . . . . Omaha
22-23 . . . . Nashville
27-30 . . . . at Omaha

JULY
1-3 . . . . Memphis
4-7 . . . . at Nashville

8-12 . . . at Memphis
16-19 . . . New Orleans
20-23 . . . at Round Rock
24-27 . . . Iowa
28-31 . . . Oklahoma City

AUGUST

1-4 . . . at Nashville
5-8 . . . Portland
9-12 . . . Tacoma
14-17 . . . at Las Vegas
18-21 . . . at Reno
22-25 . . . Nashville
26-30 . . . Memphis
31 . . . Round Rock

SEPTEMBER

1-3 . . . Round Rock
4-7 . . . at Iowa

COLORADO SPRINGS

APRIL

9-12 . . . Las Vegas
13-16 . . . Reno
17-20 . . . at Las Vegas
21-24 . . . at Reno
25-28 . . . Tacoma
30 . . . Sacramento

MAY

1-3 . . . Sacramento
4-7 . . . at Portland
8-11 . . . at Tacoma
12-15 . . . Iowa
16-19 . . . Omaha
21-24 . . . at Round Rock
25-28 . . . at Albuquerque
29-31 . . . Tacoma

JUNE

1 . . . Tacoma
2-5 . . . Fresno
6-9 . . . at Sacramento
11-14 . . . Las Vegas
15-17 . . . at Salt Lake
18-21 . . . at Fresno
23-26 . . . at Sacramento
27-30 . . . Portland

JULY

1-3 . . . Salt Lake
4-7 . . . at Portland
8-12 . . . at Salt Lake
16-19 . . . Fresno
20-23 . . . at Las Vegas
24-27 . . . Sacramento
28-31 . . . at Fresno

AUGUST

1-4 . . . at Reno
5-8 . . . Nashville
9-12 . . . Memphis
14-17 . . . at New Orleans
18-21 . . . at Oklahoma City
22-25 . . . Reno
26-30 . . . Salt Lake
31 . . . Portland

SEPTEMBER

1-3 . . . Portland
4-7 . . . at Tacoma

FRESNO

APRIL

9-12 . . . Portland
13-16 . . . Tacoma
17-20 . . . at Portland
21-24 . . . at Las Vegas
25-28 . . . Reno
30 . . . at Tacoma

MAY

1-3 . . . at Tacoma
4-7 . . . Las Vegas
8-11 . . . at Reno
12-15 . . . Round Rock
16-19 . . . Albuquerque
21-24 . . . at Iowa
25-28 . . . at Omaha
29-31 . . . Portland

JUNE

1 . . . Portland
2-5 . . . at Colorado Springs
6-9 . . . Salt Lake
11-14 . . . at Portland
15-17 . . . Sacramento
18-21 . . . Colorado Springs
23-26 . . . at Salt Lake
27-30 . . . Salt Lake

JULY

1-3 . . . at Sacramento
4-7 . . . Las Vegas
8-12 . . . Sacramento
16-19 . . . at Colorado Springs
20-23 . . . at Salt Lake
24-27 . . . Reno
28-31 . . . Colorado Springs

AUGUST

1-4 . . . at Tacoma
5-8 . . . New Orleans
9-12 . . . Oklahoma City
14-17 . . . at Nashville
18-21 . . . at Memphis
22-25 . . . Tacoma
26-30 . . . at Sacramento
31 . . . at Las Vegas

SEPTEMBER

1-3 . . . at Las Vegas
4-7 . . . at Reno

IOWA

APRIL

9-12 . . . at Round Rock
13-16 . . . at Albuquerque
17-20 . . . Round Rock
21-24 . . . Albuquerque
25-28 . . . at Nashville
30 . . . at Memphis

MAY

1-3 . . . at Memphis
4-7 . . . Nashville
8-11 . . . Memphis
12-15 . . . at Colorado Springs
16-19 . . . at Salt Lake
21-24 . . . Fresno
25-28 . . . Sacramento
29-31 . . . at Memphis

JUNE

1 . . . at Memphis
2-5 . . . at Nashville
6-9 . . . Round Rock
11-14 . . . Omaha
15-17 . . . at Oklahoma City
18-21 . . . Memphis
23-26 . . . New Orleans
27-30 . . . at Round Rock

JULY

1-3 . . . Oklahoma City
4-7 . . . at New Orleans
9-12 . . . at Oklahoma City
16-19 . . . Nashville
20-23 . . . Omaha
24-27 . . . at Albuquerque
28-31 . . . at Omaha

AUGUST

1-4 . . . at New Orleans
5-8 . . . Reno
9-12 . . . Las Vegas
14-17 . . . at Tacoma
18-21 . . . at Portland
22-25 . . . New Orleans
26-30 . . . Oklahoma City
31 . . . at Omaha

SEPTEMBER

1-3 . . . at Omaha
4-7 . . . Albuquerque

LAS VEGAS

APRIL

9-12 . . . at Colorado Springs
13-16 . . . at Salt Lake
17-20 . . . Colorado Springs
21-24 . . . Fresno
25-28 . . . at Sacramento
30 . . . Salt Lake

MAY

1-3 . . . Salt Lake
4-7 . . . at Fresno
8-11 . . . Sacramento
12-15 . . . at Memphis
16-19 . . . at Nashville
21-24 . . . Oklahoma City
25-28 . . . New Orleans
29-31 . . . at Sacramento

JUNE

1 . . . at Sacramento
2-5 . . . Portland
6-9 . . . Tacoma
11-14 . . . at Colorado Springs
15-17 . . . at Reno
18-21 . . . Portland
23-26 . . . at Tacoma
27-30 . . . Sacramento

JULY

1-3 . . . Reno
4-7 . . . at Fresno
8-12 . . . at Reno
16-19 . . . Tacoma
20-23 . . . Colorado Springs
24-27 . . . at Tacoma
28-31 . . . at Portland

AUGUST

1-3 . . . Salt Lake
5-8 . . . at Omaha
9-12 . . . at Iowa
14-17 . . . Albuquerque
18-21 . . . Round Rock
22-25 . . . at Salt Lake
26-30 . . . Reno
31 . . . Fresno

SEPTEMBER

1-3 . . . Fresno
4-7 . . . at Portland

MEMPHIS

APRIL

9-12 . . . Oklahoma City
13-16 . . . New Orleans
17-20 . . . Oklahoma City
21-24 . . . Nashville
25-28 . . . at Round Rock
30 . . . Iowa

MAY

1-3 . . . Iowa
4-7 . . . at Omaha
8-11 . . . at Iowa
12-15 . . . Las Vegas
16-19 . . . Reno
21-24 . . . at Tacoma
25-28 . . . at Portland
29-31 . . . Iowa

JUNE

1 . . . Iowa
2-5 . . . at Oklahoma City
6-9 . . . New Orleans
11-14 . . . at Nashville
15-17 . . . Albuquerque
18-21 . . . at Iowa
22-26 . . . Omaha
27-30 . . . at New Orleans

JULY

1-3 . . . at Albuquerque
4-7 . . . Round Rock
8-12 . . . Albuquerque
16-19 . . . at Omaha
20-23 . . . Nashville
24-27 . . . at New Orleans
28-31 . . . Round Rock

AUGUST

1-4 . . . Omaha
5-8 . . . at Salt Lake
9-12 . . . at Colorado Springs
14-17 . . . Sacramento
18-21 . . . Fresno
22-25 . . . at Round Rock
26-30 . . . at Albuquerque
31 . . . at Nashville

SEPTEMBER

1-3 . . . at Nashville
4-7 . . . Oklahoma City

NASHVILLE

APRIL
9-12 . . . . New Orleans
13-16 . . . . .Oklahoma City
17-20 . . . . .at New Orleans
21-24 . . . . . . .at Memphis
25-28 . . . . Iowa
30 . . . . .Omaha

MAY
1-3. . . . . .Omaha
4-7. . . . . .at Iowa
8-11 . . . . at Omaha
12-15 . . . . Reno
16-19 . . . . Las Vegas
21-24 . . . . at Portland
25-28 . . . . at Tacoma
29-31 . . . . .Omaha

JUNE
2-5. . . . . Iowa
6-8. . . . . at Omaha
11-14 . . . . Memphis
15-17 . . . . . . .Round Rock
18-21 . . . at Oklahoma City
23-26 . . . . at Albuquerque
27-30 . . . . .Oklahoma City

JULY
1-3. . . . . . . at Round Rock
4-7. . . . . Albuquerque
8-11 . . . . .Round Rock
16-19 . . . . at Iowa
20-23 . . . . at Memphis
24-27 . . . at Oklahoma City
28-31 . . . . . . New Orleans

AUGUST
1-4. . . . . Albuquerque
5-8. . . .at Colorado Springs
9-12 . . . . at Salt Lake
14-17 . . . . Fresno
18-21 . . . . . . .Sacramento
22-25 . . . . at Albuquerque
26-30 . . . . . at Round Rock
31 . . . . Memphis

SEPTEMBER
1-3. . . . . Memphis
4-7. . . . . . .at New Orleans

NEW ORLEANS

APRIL
9-12 . . . . at Nashville
13-16 . . . . at Memphis
17-20 . . . . .Nashville
21-24 . . . . . at Round Rock
25-28 . . . . . . Albuquerque
30 . . . . . at Oklahoma City

MAY
1-3. . . . . at Oklahoma City
4-7. . . . . .Round Rock
8-11 . . . . . at Albuquerque
12-15 . . . . .Tacoma
16-19 . . . . Portland
21-24 . . . . .at Reno
25-28 . . . . at Las Vegas
29-31 . . . . . . .Round Rock

JUNE
1 . . . . .Round Rock
2-5. . . . . Albuquerque
6-9. . . . . .at Memphis
11-14 . . . . .Oklahoma City
15-17 . . . . .Omaha
18-21 . . . . . at Round Rock
23-26 . . . . at Iowa
27-30 . . . . Memphis

JULY
1-3. . . . . at Omaha
4-7. . . . . Iowa
8-12 . . . . .Omaha
16-19 . . . . at Albuquerque
20-23 . . . . .Oklahoma City
24-27 . . . . Memphis
28-31 . . . . at Nashville

AUGUST
1-4. . . . . Iowa
5-8. . . . . .at Fresno
9-12 . . . . . . at Sacramento
14-17 . . . Colorado Springs
18-21 . . . . .Salt Lake
22-25 . . . . at Iowa
26-30 . . . . at Omaha
31 . . . . . at Oklahoma City

SEPTEMBER
1-3. . . . . at Oklahoma City
4-7. . . . . .Nashville

OKLAHOMA CITY

APRIL
9-12 . . . . .at Memphis
13-16 . . . . at Nashville
17-20 . . . . Memphis
21-24 . . . . .Omaha
25-28 . . . . at Omaha
30 . . . . New Orleans

MAY
1-3. . . . . New Orleans
4-7. . . . . Albuquerque
8-11 . . . . . . at Round Rock
12-15 . . . . Portland
16-18 . . . . .Tacoma
21-24 . . . . at Las Vegas
25-28 . . . . at Reno
29-31 . . . . . . Albuquerque

JUNE
1 . . . . Albuquerque
2-5. . . . . Memphis
6-9. . . . . . at Albuquerque
11-14 . . . . .at New Orleans
15-17 . . . . Iowa
18-21 . . . . .Nashville
23-26 . . . . .Round Rock
27-30 . . . . at Nashville

JULY
1-3. . . . . at Iowa
4-7. . . . . .Omaha
9-12 . . . . Iowa
16-19 . . . . . at Round Rock
20-23 . . . . .at New Orleans
24-27 . . . . .Nashville
28-31 . . . . at Albuquerque

AUGUST
1-4. . . . . .Round Rock
5-8. . . . . . . at Sacramento
9-12 . . . . .at Fresno
14-17 . . . . .Salt Lake
18-21 . . . Colorado Springs
22-25 . . . . at Omaha
26-30 . . . . at Iowa
31 . . . . New Orleans

SEPTEMBER
1-3. . . . . New Orleans
4-7. . . . . at Memphis

OMAHA

APRIL
9-12 . . . . . at Albuquerque
13-16 . . . . . at Round Rock
17-20 . . . . . . Albuquerque
21-24 . . . at Oklahoma City
25-28 . . . . .Oklahoma City
30 . . . . at Nashville

MAY
1-3. . . . . at Nashville
4-7. . . . . Memphis
8-11 . . . . .Nashville
12-15 . . . . at Salt Lake
16-19 . .at Colorado Springs
21-24 . . . . . . .Sacramento
25-28 . . . . Fresno
29-31 . . . . .Nashville

JUNE
2-5. . . . . .Round Rock
6-8. . . . . .Nashville
11-14 . . . . at Iowa
15-17 . . . . .at New Orleans
18-21 . . . . at Albuquerque
23-26 . . . . at Memphis
27-30 . . . . . . Albuquerque

JULY
1-3. . . . . New Orleans
4-7. . . . . at Oklahoma City
8-12 . . . . . .at New Orleans
16-19 . . . . Memphis
20-23 . . . . at Iowa
24-27 . . . . . . .Round Rock
28-31 . . . . Iowa

AUGUST
1-4. . . . . .at Memphis
5-8. . . . . Las Vegas
9-12 . . . . Reno
14-17 . . . . at Portland
18-21 . . . . at Tacoma
22-25 . . . . .Oklahoma City
26-30 . . . . . . New Orleans
31 . . . . Iowa

SEPTEMBER
1-3. . . . . Iowa
4-7. . . . . . . at Round Rock

RENO

APRIL
9-12 . . . . at Salt Lake
13-16 . .at Colorado Springs
17-20 . . . . .Salt Lake
21-24 . . . Colorado Springs
25-28 . . . . at Fresno
30 . . . . Portland

MAY
1-3. . . . . Portland
4-7. . . . . . . at Sacramento
8-11 . . . . Fresno
12-15 . . . . at Nashville
16-19 . . . . at Memphis
21-24 . . . . . . New Orleans
25-28 . . . . .Oklahoma City
29-31 . . . . at Salt Lake

JUNE
1 . . . . at Salt Lake
2-5. . . . . at Tacoma
6-9. . . . . at Portland
11-14 . . . . .Salt Lake
15-17 . . . . Las Vegas
18-21 . . . . at Tacoma
23-26 . . . . at Portland
27-30 . . . . .Tacoma

JULY
1-3. . . . . .at Las Vegas
4-7. . . . . .Sacramento
8-12 . . . . Las Vegas
16-19 . . . . . at Sacramento
20-23 . . . . Portland
24-27 . . . . .at Fresno
28-31 . . . . .Tacoma

AUGUST
1-4. . . . . Colorado Springs
5-8. . . . . at Iowa
9-12 . . . . at Omaha
14-17 . . . . . . .Round Rock
18-21 . . . . . . Albuquerque
22-25 . .at Colorado Springs
26-30 . . . . . . .at Las Vegas
31 . . . . .Sacramento

SEPTEMBER
1-3. . . . . .Sacramento
4-7. . . . . Fresno

PORTLAND

APRIL
9-12 . . . . .at Fresno
13-16 . . . . . at Sacramento
17-20 . . . . Fresno
21-24 . . . . . . .Sacramento
25-28 . . . . at Salt Lake
30 . . . . .at Reno

MAY
1-3. . . . . .at Reno
4-7. . . . . Colorado Springs
8-11 . . . . .Salt Lake
12-15 . . . at Oklahoma City
16-19 . . . . .at New Orleans
21-24 . . . . .Nashville
25-28 . . . . Memphis
29-31 . . . . .at Fresno

JUNE
1 . . . . .at Fresno
2-5. . . . . .at Las Vegas
6-9. . . . . Reno
11-14 . . . . Fresno
15-17 . . . . .Tacoma
18-21 . . . . . . .at Las Vegas
23-26 . . . . Reno
27-30 . .at Colorado Springs

JULY
1-3. . . . . at Tacoma
4-7. . . . . Colorado Springs

8-12 . . . . at Tacoma
16-19 . . . . Salt Lake
20-23 . . . . .at Reno
24-27 . . . . at Salt Lake
28-31 . . . . Las Vegas
14-17 . . . . Omaha
18-21 . . . . Iowa
22-25 . . . . . at Sacramento
26-30 . . . . Tacoma
31 . . . .at Colorado Springs

AUGUST

1-4. . . . . Sacramento
5-8. . . . . . at Albuquerque
9-12 . . . . . . at Round rock

SEPTEMBER

1-3. . . .at Colorado Springs
4-7. . . . . Las Vegas

ROUND ROCK

APRIL

9-12 . . . . Iowa
13-16 . . . . Omaha
17-20 . . . . at Iowa
21-24 . . . . . . New Orleans
25-28 . . . . Memphis
30 . . . . . . at Albuquerque

MAY

1-3. . . . . . at Albuquerque
4-7. . . . . . at New Orleans
8-11 . . . . . . Oklahoma City
12-15 . . . . at Fresno
16-19 . . . . . at Sacramento
21-24 . . . Colorado Springs
25-28 . . . . Salt Lake
29-31 . . . . at New Orleans

JUNE

1 . . . . at New Orleans
2-5. . . . . at Omaha
6-9. . . . . at Iowa
11-14 . . . . . . Albuquerque
15-17 . . . . at Nashville
18-21 . . . . . . New Orleans
23-26 . . . at Oklahoma City
27-30 . . . . Iowa

JULY

1-3. . . . . Nashville
4-7. . . . . at Memphis
8-11 . . . . at Nashville
16-19 . . . . . Oklahoma City
20-23 . . . . . . Albuquerque
24-27 . . . . at Omaha
28-31 . . . . at Memphis

AUGUST

1-4. . . . . at Oklahoma City
5-8. . . . . Tacoma
9-12 . . . . Portland
14-17 . . . . at Reno
18-21 . . . . at Las Vegas
22-25 . . . . Memphis
26-30 . . . . Nashville
31 . . . . . . at Albuquerque

SEPTEMBER

1-3. . . . . . at Albuquerque
4-7. . . . . Omaha

SACRAMENTO

APRIL

9-12 . . . . Tacoma
13-16 . . . . Portland
17-20 . . . . at Tacoma
21-24 . . . . at Portland
25-28 . . . . Las Vegas
30 . . . .at Colorado Springs

MAY

1-3. . . .at Colorado Springs
4-7. . . . . Reno
8-11 . . . . at Las Vegas
12-15 . . . . . . Albuquerque
16-19 . . . . Round Rock
21-24 . . . . at Omaha
25-28 . . . . at Iowa
29-31 . . . . Las Vegas

JUNE

1 . . . . Las Vegas
2-5. . . . . at Salt Lake
6-9. . . . . Colorado Springs
11-14 . . . . Tacoma
15-17 . . . . at Fresno
18-21 . . . . Salt Lake
23-26 . . . Colorado Springs
27-30 . . . . at Las Vegas

JULY

1-3. . . . . Fresno
4-7. . . . . at Reno
8-12 . . . . at Fresno
16-19 . . . . Reno
20-23 . . . . at Tacoma
24-27 . .at Colorado Springs
28-31 . . . . Salt Lake

AUGUST

1-4. . . . . at Portland
5-8. . . . . . . Oklahoma City
9-12 . . . . New Orleans
14-17 . . . . at Memphis
18-21 . . . . at Nashville
22-25 . . . . Portland
27-30 . . . . Fresno
31 . . . . .at Reno

SEPTEMBER

1-3. . . . . .at Reno
4-7. . . . . at Salt Lake

SALT LAKE

APRIL

9-12 . . . . Reno
13-16 . . . . Las Vegas
17-20 . . . . at Reno
21-24 . . . . at Tacoma
25-28 . . . . Portland
30 . . . . at Las Vegas

MAY

1-3. . . . . at Las Vegas
4-7. . . . . Tacoma
8-11 . . . . at Portland
12-15 . . . . Omaha
16-19 . . . . Iowa
21-24 . . . . at Albuquerque
25-28 . . . . . at Round Rock
29-31 . . . . Reno

JUNE

1 . . . . Reno
2-5. . . . . Sacramento
6-9. . . . . at Fresno
11-14 . . . . at Reno
15-17 . . . Colorado Springs
18-21 . . . . . at Sacramento
23-26 . . . . Fresno
27-30 . . . . at Fresno

JULY

1-3. . . .at Colorado Springs
4-7. . . . . Tacoma
8-12 . . . . Colorado Springs
16-19 . . . . at Portland
20-23 . . . . Fresno
24-27 . . . . Portland
28-31 . . . . . at Sacramento

AUGUST

1-3. . . . . at Las Vegas
5-8. . . . . Memphis
9-12 . . . . Nashville
14-17 . . . at Oklahoma City
18-21 . . . . .at New Orleans
22-25 . . . . Las Vegas
26-30 . .at Colorado Springs
31 . . . . at Tacoma

SEPTEMBER

1-3. . . . . at Tacoma
5-7. . . . . Sacramento

TACOMA

APRIL

9-12 . . . . . . at Sacramento
13-16 . . . . at Fresno
17-20 . . . . Sacramento
21-24 . . . . Salt Lake
25-28 . .at Colorado Springs
30 . . . . Fresno

MAY

1-3. . . . . Fresno
4-7. . . . . at Salt Lake
8-11 . . . . Colorado Springs
12-15 . . . . .at New Orleans
16-18 . . . at Oklahoma City
21-24 . . . . Memphis
25-28 . . . . Nashville
29-31 . .at Colorado Springs

JUNE

1 . . . . .at Colorado Springs
2-5. . . . . Reno
6-9. . . . . at Las Vegas
11-14 . . . . . at Sacramento
15-17 . . . . at Portland
18-21 . . . . Reno
23-26 . . . . Las Vegas
27-30 . . . . at Reno

JULY

1-3. . . . . Portland
4-7. . . . . at Salt Lake
8-12 . . . . Portland
16-19 . . . . at Las Vegas
20-23 . . . . Sacramento
24-27 . . . . Las Vegas
28-31 . . . . at Reno

AUGUST

1-4. . . . . Fresno
5-8. . . . . . . at Round Rock
9-12 . . . . . at Albuquerque
14-17 . . . . Iowa
18-21 . . . . Omaha
22-25 . . . . at Fresno
26-30 . . . . at Portland
31 . . . . Salt Lake

SEPTEMBER

1-3. . . . . Salt Lake
4-7. . . . . Colorado Springs

DOUBLE-A

EASTERN LEAGUE

AKRON

APRIL
8-11 . . . . Bowie
13-15 . . . . Altoona
16-19 . . . . at Bowie
20-22 . . . . at Harrisburg
23-26 . . . . Altoona
28-30 . . . . Harrisburg

MAY
1-3 . . . . at Bowie
4-7 . . . . at Altoona
8-10 . . . . Harrisburg
11-13 . . . . Bowie
14-17 . . . . at Altoona
19-21 . . . . at Trenton
22-25 . . . . Erie
26-28 . . . . Reading
29-31 . . . . at Erie

JUNE
1-4 . . . . at Reading
5-7 . . . . at Altoona
9-11 . . . . New Hampshire
13-15 . . . . Portland
16-18 . . . . at New Hampshire
19-21 . . . . at Portland
23-25 . . . . Trenton
26-29 . . . . Binghamton
30 . . . . at Bowie

JULY
1-3 . . . . at Bowie
4-6 . . . . at Harrisburg
7-9 . . . . Reading
10-13 . . . . at Erie
16-19 . . . . Bowie
20-23 . . . . at Erie
24-26 . . . . Altoona
27-30 . . . . Erie
31 . . . . at Binghamton

AUGUST
1-2 . . . . at Binghamton
4-6 . . . . Connecticut
7-9 . . . . New Britain
11-13 . . . . at Connecticut
14-16 . . . . at New Britain
18-20 . . . . Bowie
21-24 . . . . at Erie
25-27 . . . . at Bowie
28-31 . . . . Binghamton

SEPTEMBER
1-3 . . . . at Altoona
4-7 . . . . Erie

ALTOONA

APRIL
8-11 . . . . at Erie
13-15 . . . . at Akron
16-19 . . . . Erie
20-22 . . . . Reading
23-26 . . . . at Akron
28-30 . . . . at Reading

MAY
1-3 . . . . Erie
4-7 . . . . Akron
8-10 . . . . at Reading
11-13 . . . . at Harrisburg
14-17 . . . . Akron
19-21 . . . . at Bowie
22-25 . . . . Reading
26-28 . . . . Bowie
29-31 . . . . at Trenton

JUNE
1-4 . . . . at Erie
5-7 . . . . Akron
9-11 . . . . at New Britain
12-14 . . . . at Connecticut
16-18 . . . . New Britain
19-21 . . . . Connecticut
23-25 . . . . at Erie
26-29 . . . . Bowie
30 . . . . at Reading

JULY
1-3 . . . . at Reading
4-6 . . . . Bowie
7-9 . . . . Erie
10-13 . . . . at Bowie
16-19 . . . . Harrisburg
20-23 . . . . Reading
24-26 . . . . at Akron
27-30 . . . . Binghamton
31 . . . . Trenton

AUGUST
1-2 . . . . Trenton
4-6 . . . . at Portland
7-9 . . . . at New Hampshire
11-13 . . . . Portland
14-16 . . . . New Hampshire
18-20 . . . . at Harrisburg
21-24 . . . . at Bowie
25-27 . . . . Trenton
28-31 . . . . at Erie

SEPTEMBER
1-3 . . . . Akron
4-7 . . . . at Binghamton

BINGHAMTON

APRIL
8-11 . . . . at Trenton
13-15 . . . . at Reading
16-19 . . . . Portland
20-22 . . . . Trenton
23-26 . . . . at New Hampshire
28-30 . . . . at Portland

MAY
1-3 . . . . New Hampshire
4-7 . . . . Portland
8-10 . . . . at Trenton
11-13 . . . . at New Hampshire
14-17 . . . . Trenton
19-21 . . . . at Connecticut
22-25 . . . . New Britain
26-28 . . . . Connecticut
29-31 . . . . at New Britain

JUNE
1-4 . . . . at Portland
5-7 . . . . Connecticut
9-11 . . . . Harrisburg
12-14 . . . . at Trenton
16-18 . . . . at Harrisburg
19-21 . . . . Trenton
23-25 . . . . Bowie
26-29 . . . . at Akron
30 . . . . New Hampshire

JULY
1-3 . . . . New Hampshire
4-6 . . . . Erie
7-9 . . . . at Portland
10-13 . . . . at New Britain
16-19 . . . . Erie
20-23 . . . . Connecticut
24-26 . . . . at Erie
27-30 . . . . at Altoona
31 . . . . Akron

AUGUST
1-2 . . . . Akron
4-6 . . . . at Harrisburg
7-9 . . . . Reading
11-13 . . . . Harrisburg
14-16 . . . . at Reading
18-20 . . . . New Britain
21-24 . . . . at Connecticut
25-27 . . . . Portland
28-31 . . . . at Akron

SEPTEMBER
1-3 . . . . at Bowie
4-7 . . . . Altoona

BOWIE

APRIL
8-11 . . . . at Akron
13-15 . . . . at Erie
16-19 . . . . Akron
20-22 . . . . Erie
23-26 . . . . at Reading
27-29 . . . . at Erie

MAY
1-3 . . . . Akron
4-7 . . . . Trenton
8-10 . . . . at Erie
11-13 . . . . at Akron
14-17 . . . . Erie
19-21 . . . . Altoona
22-25 . . . . at Harrisburg
26-28 . . . . at Altoona
29-31 . . . . Harrisburg

JUNE
1-4 . . . . at Trenton
5-7 . . . . Erie
9-11 . . . . at Connecticut
12-14 . . . . at New Britain
16-18 . . . . Reading
19-21 . . . . New Britain
23-25 . . . . at Binghamton
26-29 . . . . at Altoona
30 . . . . Akron

JULY
1-3 . . . . Akron
4-6 . . . . at Altoona
7-9 . . . . Harrisburg
10-13 . . . . Altoona
16-19 . . . . at Akron
20-23 . . . . at Harrisburg
24-26 . . . . Reading
27-30 . . . . Connecticut
31 . . . . at New Britain

AUGUST
1-2 . . . . at New Britain
4-6 . . . . at New Hampshire
7-9 . . . . at Portland
11-13 . . . . New Hampshire
14-16 . . . . Portland
18-20 . . . . at Akron
21-24 . . . . Altoona
25-27 . . . . Akron
28-31 . . . . at Reading

SEPTEMBER
1-3 . . . . Binghamton
4-7 . . . . Harrisburg

CONNECTICUT

APRIL
9-12 . . . . at Portland
13-15 . . . . at New Hampshire
16-19 . . . . Trenton
20-22 . . . . New Hampshire
23-26 . . . . at Portland
28-30 . . . . at Trenton

MAY
1-3 . . . . Portland
4-7 . . . . Reading
8-10 . . . . at New Hampshire
11-13 . . . . at New Britain
14-17 . . . . New Hampshire
19-21 . . . . Binghamton
22-25 . . . . at Portland
26-28 . . . . at Binghamton
29-31 . . . . Portland

JUNE
1-4 . . . . New Britain
5-7 . . . . at Binghamton
9-11 . . . . Bowie
12-14 . . . . Altoona
16-18 . . . . at Trenton
19-21 . . . . at Altoona
23-25 . . . . Portland
26-29 . . . . at New Britain
30 . . . . Harrisburg

JULY
1-3 . . . . Harrisburg
4-6 . . . . at Reading
7-9 . . . . at New Britain
10-13 . . . . Trenton
16-19 . . . . at New Hampshire
20-23 . . . . at Binghamton
24-26 . . . . New Britain
27-30 . . . . at Bowie
31 . . . . New Hampshire

AUGUST
1-2 . . . . New Hampshire
4-6 . . . . at Akron
7-9 . . . . at Erie
11-13 . . . . Akron

14-16 . . . . Erie
18-20 . . at New Hampshire
21-24 . . . . . . Binghamton
25-27 . . . . New Britain
28-31 . . . . . . at Harrisburg

SEPTEMBER

1-3. . . . . . New Hampshire
4-7. . . . . Reading

ERIE

APRIL

8-11 . . . . Altoona
13-15 . . . . .Bowie
16-19 . . . . .at Altoona
20-22 . . . . at Bowie
23-26 . . . . .Harrisburg
27-29 . . . . .Bowie

MAY

1-3. . . . . .at Altoona
4-7. . . . . at Harrisburg
8-10. . . . . .Bowie
11-13 . . . . Reading
14-17 . . . . at Bowie
18-20 . . . . .Harrisburg
22-25 . . . . at Akron
26-28 . . . . . . at Harrisburg
29-31 . . . . .Akron

JUNE

1-4. . . . . Altoona
5-7. . . . . at Bowie
9-11 . . . . Portland
12-14 . . . . New Hampshire
16-18 . . . . at Portland
19-21 . . at New Hampshire
23-25 . . . . Altoona
26-29 . . . . . . at Harrisburg
30 . . . . Trenton

JULY

1-3. . . . . Trenton
4-6. . . . . . . at Binghamton
7-9. . . . . at Altoona
10-13 . . . . .Akron
16-19 . . . . . at Binghamton
20-23 . . . . .Akron
24-26 . . . . . . Binghamton
27-30 . . . . at Akron
31 . . . . Reading

AUGUST

1-2. . . . . Reading
4-6. . . . . New Britain
7-9. . . . . .Connecticut
11-13 . . . . . at New Britain
14-16 . . . . . at Connecticut
18-20 . . . . at Trenton
21-24 . . . . .Akron
25-27 . . . . .at Reading
28-31 . . . . Altoona

SEPTEMBER

1-3. . . . . at Harrisburg
4-7. . . . . at Akron

HARRISBURG

APRIL

9-11 . . . . .at Reading
13-15 . . . . .at Trenton
16-19 . . . . Reading
20-22 . . . . .Akron
23-26 . . . . at Erie
28-30 . . . . at Akron

MAY

1-3. . . . . Reading
4-7. . . . . Erie
8-10. . . . . at Akron
11-13 . . . . Altoona
14-17 . . . . .at Reading
18-20 . . . . at Erie
22-25 . . . . .Bowie
26-28 . . . . Erie
29-31 . . . . at Bowie

JUNE

1-4. . . . . . New Hampshire
5-7. . . . . New Britain
9-11 . . . . . .at Binghamton
12-15 . . . . at Reading
16-18 . . . . . . Binghamton
19-21 . . . . .at Reading
23-25 . . . . . at New Britain
26-29 . . . . Erie
30 . . . . at Connecticut

JULY

1-3. . . . . . . at Connecticut
4-6. . . . . .Akron
7-9. . . . . at Bowie
10-13 . . . . Reading
16-19 . . . . .at Altoona
20-23 . . . . .Bowie
24-26 . . . . Trenton
27-30 . . . . at Trenton
31 . . . . Portland

AUGUST

1-2. . . . . Portland
4-6. . . . . Binghamton
7-9. . . . . at Trenton
11-13 . . . . . at Binghamton
14-16 . . . . Trenton
18-20 . . . . Altoona
21-24 . . . . at Portland
25-27 . . at New Hampshire
28-31 . . . . . . .Connecticut

SEPTEMBER

1-3. . . . . Erie
4-7. . . . . at Bowie

NEW BRITAIN

APRIL

8-11 . . . at New Hampshire
13-15 . . . . at Portland
16-19 . . . . New Hampshire
20-22 . . . . Portland
23-26 . . . . at Trenton
28-30 . . at New Hampshire

MAY

1-3. . . . . Trenton
4-7. . . . . . New Hampshire
8-10. . . . . at Portland
11-13 . . . . . . .Connecticut
14-17 . . . . Portland
19-21 . . . . .at Reading
22-25 . . . . . at Binghamton
26-28 . . . . Trenton
29-31 . . . . . . Binghamton

JUNE

1-4. . . . . at Connecticut
5-7. . . . . at Harrisburg
9-11 . . . . Altoona
12-14 . . . . .Bowie
16-18 . . . . .at Altoona
19-21 . . . . at Bowie
23-25 . . . . .Harrisburg
26-29 . . . . .Connecticut
30 . . . . at Portland

JULY

1-3. . . . . at Portland
4-6. . . . . at Trenton
7-9. . . . . .Connecticut
10-13 . . . . . . Binghamton
16-19 . . . . .at Reading
20-23 . . . . Portland
24-26 . . . . . at Connecticut
27-30 . . at New Hampshire
31 . . . . .Bowie

AUGUST

1-2. . . . . .Bowie
4-6. . . . . at Erie
7-9. . . . . at Akron
11-13 . . . . Erie
14-16 . . . . .Akron
18-20 . . . . . at Binghamton
21-24 . . . . Reading
25-27 . . . . . at Connecticut
28-31 . . . . at Trenton

SEPTEMBER

1-3. . . . . Reading
4-7. . . . . Trenton

NEW HAMPSHIRE

APRIL

8-11 . . . . New Britain
13-15 . . . . .Connecticut
16-19 . . . . . at New Britain
20-22 . . . . . at Connecticut
23-26 . . . . . . Binghamton
28-30 . . . . New Britain

MAY

1-3. . . . . . .at Binghamton
4-7. . . . . . . at New Britain
8-10. . . . . . . .Connecticut
11-13 . . . . . . Binghamton
14-17 . . . . . at Connecticut
19-21 . . . . at Portland
22-25 . . . . Trenton
26-28 . . . . Portland
29-31 . . . . at Reading

JUNE

1-4. . . . . at Harrisburg
5-7. . . . . Reading
9-11 . . . . at Akron
12-14 . . . . at Erie
16-18 . . . . Akron
19-21 . . . . Erie
23-25 . . . . .at Reading
26-29 . . . . Portland
30 . . . . at Binghamton

JULY

1-3. . . . . . .at Binghamton
4-6. . . . . Portland
7-9. . . . . at Trenton
10-13 . . . . at Portland
16-19 . . . . . . .Connecticut
20-23 . . . . Trenton
24-26 . . . . at Portland
27-30 . . . . New Britain
31 . . . . at Connecticut

AUGUST

1-2. . . . . . . at Connecticut
4-6. . . . . .Bowie
7-9. . . . . Altoona
11-13 . . . . at Bowie
14-16 . . . . .at Altoona
18-20 . . . . . . .Connecticut
21-24 . . . . at Trenton
25-27 . . . . .Harrisburg
28-31 . . . . Portland

SEPTEMBER

1-3. . . . . . . at Connecticut
4-7. . . . . at Portland

PORTLAND

APRIL

9-12 . . . . .Connecticut
13-15 . . . . New Britain
16-19 . . . . .at Binghamton
20-22 . . . . . at New Britain
23-26 . . . . . . .Connecticut
28-30 . . . . . . Binghamton

MAY

1-3. . . . . . . at Connecticut
4-7. . . . . . .at Binghamton
8-10. . . . . New Britain
11-13 . . . . .at Trenton
14-17 . . . . . at New Britain
19-21 . . . . New Hampshire
22-25 . . . . . . .Connecticut
26-28 . . at New Hampshire
29-31 . . . . . at Connecticut

JUNE

1-4. . . . . Binghamton
5-7. . . . . Trenton
9-11 . . . . at Erie
12-14 . . . . at Akron
16-18 . . . . Erie
19-21 . . . . .Akron
23-25 . . . . . at Connecticut
26-29 . . at New Hampshire
30 . . . . New Britain

JULY

1-3. . . . . New Britain
4-6. . . . at New Hampshire
7-9. . . . . Binghamton
10-13 . . . . . New Hampshire
16-19 . . . . at Trenton
20-23 . . . . . at New Britain
24-26 . . . . New Hampshire
27-30 . . . . .at Reading
31 . . . . at Harrisburg

AUGUST

1-2. . . . . at Harrisburg
4-6. . . . . Altoona
7-9. . . . . .Bowie
11-13 . . . . .at Altoona
14-16 . . . . at Bowie
18-20 . . . . Reading
21-24 . . . . .Harrisburg
25-27 . . . . .at Binghamton
28-31 . . at New Hampshire

SEPTEMBER

1-3. . . . . Trenton
4-7. . . . . . New Hampshire

READING

APRIL
9-11 Harrisburg
13-15 Binghamton
16-19 at Harrisburg
20-22 at Altoona
23-26 Bowie
28-30 Altoona

MAY
1-3 at Harrisburg
4-7 at Connecticut
8-10 Altoona
11-13 at Erie
14-17 Harrisburg
19-21 New Britain
22-25 at Altoona
26-28 at Akron
29-31 New Hampshire

JUNE
1-4 Akron
5-7 at New Hampshire
9-11 Trenton
12-15 Harrisburg
16-18 at Bowie
19-21 Harrisburg
23-25 New Hampshire
26-29 at Trenton
30 Altoona

JULY
1-3 Altoona
4-6 Connecticut
7-9 at Akron
10-13 at Harrisburg
16-19 New Britain
20-23 at Altoona
24-26 at Bowie
27-30 Portland
31 at Erie

AUGUST
1-2 at Erie
4-6 Trenton
7-9 at Binghamton
11-13 at Trenton
14-16 Binghamton
18-20 at Portland
21-24 at New Britain
25-27 Erie
28-31 Bowie

SEPTEMBER
1-3 at New Britain
4-7 at Connecticut

TRENTON

APRIL
8-11 Binghamton
13-15 Harrisburg
16-19 at Connecticut
20-22 at Binghamton
23-26 New Britain
28-30 Connecticut

MAY
1-3 at New Britain
4-7 at Bowie
8-10 Binghamton
11-13 Portland
14-17 at Binghamton
19-21 Akron
22-25 at New Hampshire
26-28 at New Britain
29-31 Altoona

JUNE
1-4 Bowie
5-7 at Portland
9-11 at Reading
12-14 Binghamton
16-18 Connecticut
19-21 at Binghamton
23-25 at Akron
26-29 Reading
30 at Erie

JULY
1-3 at Erie
4-6 New Britain
7-9 New Hampshire
10-13 at Connecticut
16-19 Portland
20-23 at New Hampshire
24-26 at Harrisburg
27-30 Harrisburg
31 at Altoona

AUGUST
1-2 at Altoona
4-6 at Reading
7-9 Harrisburg
11-13 Reading
14-16 at Harrisburg
18-20 Erie
21-24 New Hampshire
25-27 at Altoona
28-31 New Britain

SEPTEMBER
1-3 at Portland
4-7 at New Britain

SOUTHERN LEAGUE

BIRMINGHAM

APRIL
9-13 Chattanooga
15-19 at Tennessee
20-24 Jacksonville
25-29 at Mobile
30 West Tenn

MAY
1-4 West Tenn
5-9 at Montgomery
11-15 Carolina
16-20 at West Tenn
21-25 at Tennessee
26-30 Mississippi
31 at Huntsville

JUNE
1-4 at Huntsville
5-9 Montgomery
11-15 at Mississippi
17-21 Huntsville
22-27 at Mississippi
28-30 Mobile

JULY
1-3 Mobile
4-7 at Montgomery
8-11 Mississippi
15-19 at Mobile
21-25 Montgomery
27-31 at Jacksonville

AUGUST
1-5 Mobile
6-10 Tennessee
12-16 at Carolina
17-21 Montgomery
22-26 at West Tenn
28-31 Huntsville

SEPTEMBER
1 Huntsville
3-7 at Chattanooga

CAROLINA

APRIL
9-13 at Mississippi
14-18 at Mobile
20-24 Huntsville
25-29 at Tennessee
30 Chattanooga

MAY
1-4 Chattanooga
5-9 Mobile
11-15 at Birmingham
16-20 Jacksonville
21-25 at Chattanooga
26-30 Montgomery
31 Tennessee

JUNE
1-4 Tennessee
5-9 at Jacksonville
11-15 West Tenn
17-21 at Tennessee
22-27 Jacksonville
28-30 at Chattanooga

JULY
1-3 at Chattanooga
4-7 Tennessee
9-11 at Jacksonville
15-19 Chattanooga
21-25 at Huntsville
27-31 Chattanooga

AUGUST
1-5 at Tennessee
6-10 at West Tenn
12-16 Birmingham
17-21 at Jacksonville
22-26 Tennessee
28-31 at Montgomery

SEPTEMBER
1 at Montgomery
3-7 Mississippi

CHATTANOOGA

APRIL
9-13 at Birmingham
14-18 Montgomery
20-24 at Mississippi
25-29 Huntsville
30 at Carolina

MAY
1-4 at Carolina
5-9 Jacksonville
11-15 at Huntsville
16-20 Tennessee
21-25 Carolina
26-30 at West Tenn
31 Mobile

JUNE
1-4 Mobile
5-9 at Tennessee
11-15 at Montgomery
17-21 Mississippi
22-27 at Huntsville
28-30 Carolina

JULY
1-3 Carolina
4-7 at Mobile
8-11 Huntsville
15-19 at Carolina
21-25 Mobile
27-31 at Carolina

AUGUST
1-5 West Tenn
6-10 Jacksonville
12-15 at West Tenn
17-21 at Tennessee
22-26 Mississippi
28-31 at Jacksonville

SEPTEMBER
1 at Jacksonville
3-7 Birmingham

HUNTSVILLE

APRIL
9-13 Mobile
14-18 Mississippi
20-24 at Carolina
25-29 at Chattanooga
30 Tennessee

MAY
1-4 Tennessee
5-9 at West Tenn
11-15 Chattanooga
16-20 at Mobile
21-25 West Tenn
26-30 at Tennessee
31 Birmingham

JUNE
1-4 Birmingham
5-9 at West Tenn
11-15 Jacksonville
17-21 at Birmingham
22-27 Chattanooga
28-30 at Tennessee

JULY
1-3 . . . at Tennessee
4-7 . . . West Tenn
8-11 . . . at Chattanooga
15-19 . . . at Mississippi
21-25 . . . Carolina
27-31 . . . at Montgomery

AUGUST
1-5 . . . at Jacksonville
7-11 . . . Mississippi
12-16 . . . at Mobile
17-21 . . . West Tenn
22-26 . . . Montgomery
28-31 . . . at Birmingham

SEPTEMBER
1 . . . at Birmingham
3-7 . . . Jacksonville

JACKSONVILLE

APRIL
9-13 . . . Tennessee
14-18 . . . West Tenn
20-24 . . . at Birmingham
25-29 . . . at Montgomery
30 . . . Mobile

MAY
1-4 . . . Mobile
5-9 . . . at Chattanooga
11-15 . . . Mississippi
16-20 . . . at Carolina
21-25 . . . Montgomery
26-30 . . . at Mobile
31 . . . at Montgomery

JUNE
1-4 . . . at Montgomery
5-9 . . . Carolina
11-15 . . . at Huntsville
17-21 . . . Mobile
22-27 . . . at Carolina
28-30 . . . Montgomery

JULY
1-3 . . . Montgomery
4-7 . . . at Mississippi
9-11 . . . Carolina
15-19 . . . Tennessee
21-25 . . . at West Tenn
27-31 . . . Birmingham

AUGUST
1-5 . . . Huntsville
6-10 . . . at Chattanooga
11-15 . . . at Tennessee
17-21 . . . Carolina
22-26 . . . at Mobile
28-31 . . . Chattanooga

SEPTEMBER
1 . . . Chattanooga
3-7 . . . at Huntsville

MISSISSIPPI

APRIL
9-13 . . . Carolina
14-18 . . . at Huntsville
20-24 . . . Chattanooga
25-29 . . . at West Tenn
30 . . . Montgomery

MAY
1-4 . . . Montgomery
5-9 . . . Tennessee
11-15 . . . at Jacksonville
16-20 . . . at Montgomery
21-25 . . . Mobile
26-30 . . . at Birmingham
31 . . . West Tenn

JUNE
1-4 . . . West Tenn
5-9 . . . at Mobile
11-15 . . . Birmingham
17-21 . . . at Chattanooga
22-27 . . . Birmingham
28-30 . . . at West Tenn

JULY
1-3 . . . at West Tenn
4-7 . . . Jacksonville
8-11 . . . at Birmingham
15-19 . . . Huntsville
21-25 . . . at Tennessee
27-31 . . . West Tenn

AUGUST
1-5 . . . Montgomery
7-11 . . . at Huntsville
12-16 . . . at Montgomery
17-21 . . . Mobile
22-26 . . . at Chattanooga
28-31 . . . West Tenn

SEPTEMBER
1 . . . West Tenn
3-7 . . . at Carolina

MOBILE

APRIL
9-13 . . . at Huntsville
14-18 . . . Carolina
20-24 . . . at Montgomery
25-29 . . . Birmingham
30 . . . at Jacksonville

MAY
1-4 . . . at Jacksonville
5-9 . . . at Carolina
11-15 . . . Montgomery
16-20 . . . Huntsville
21-25 . . . at Mississippi
26-30 . . . Jacksonville
31 . . . at Chattanooga

JUNE
1-4 . . . at Chattanooga
5-9 . . . Mississippi
11-15 . . . Tennessee
17-21 . . . at Jacksonville
22-27 . . . West Tenn
28-30 . . . at Birmingham

JULY
1-3 . . . at Birmingham
4-7 . . . Chattanooga
8-11 . . . at West Tenn
15-19 . . . Birmingham
21-25 . . . at Chattanooga
27-31 . . . Tennessee

AUGUST
1-5 . . . at Birmingham
6-10 . . . at Montgomery
12-16 . . . Huntsville
17-21 . . . at Mississippi
22-26 . . . Jacksonville
28-31 . . . at Tennessee

SEPTEMBER
1 . . . at Tennessee
3-7 . . . Montgomery

MONTGOMERY

APRIL
9-13 . . . West Tenn
14-18 . . . at Chattanooga
20-24 . . . Mobile
25-29 . . . Jacksonville
30 . . . at Mississippi

MAY
1-4 . . . at Mississippi
5-9 . . . Birmingham
11-15 . . . at Mobile
16-20 . . . Mississippi
21-25 . . . at Jacksonville
26-30 . . . at Carolina
31 . . . Jacksonville

JUNE
1-4 . . . Jacksonville
5-9 . . . at Birmingham
11-15 . . . Chattanooga
17-20 . . . at West Tenn
22-27 . . . Tennessee
28-30 . . . at Jacksonville

JULY
1-3 . . . at Jacksonville
4-7 . . . Birmingham
8-11 . . . at Tennessee
15-19 . . . West Tenn
21-25 . . . at Birmingham
27-31 . . . Huntsville

AUGUST
1-5 . . . at Mississippi
6-10 . . . Mobile
12-16 . . . Mississippi
17-21 . . . at Birmingham
22-26 . . . at Huntsville
28-31 . . . Carolina

SEPTEMBER
1 . . . Carolina
3-7 . . . at Mobile

TENNESSEE

APRIL
9-13 . . . at Jacksonville
15-19 . . . Birmingham
20-24 . . . at West Tenn
25-29 . . . Carolina
30 . . . at Huntsville

MAY
1-4 . . . at Huntsville
5-9 . . . at Mississippi
11-15 . . . West Tenn
16-20 . . . at Chattanooga
21-25 . . . Birmingham
26-30 . . . Huntsville
31 . . . at Carolina

JUNE
1-4 . . . at Carolina
5-9 . . . Chattanooga
11-15 . . . at Mobile
17-21 . . . Carolina
22-27 . . . at Montgomery
28-30 . . . Huntsville

JULY
1-3 . . . Huntsville
4-7 . . . at Carolina
8-11 . . . Montgomery
15-19 . . . at Jacksonville
21-25 . . . Mississippi
27-31 . . . at Mobile

AUGUST
1-5 . . . Carolina
6-10 . . . at Birmingham
11-15 . . . Jacksonville
17-21 . . . Chattanooga
22-26 . . . at Carolina
28-31 . . . Mobile

SEPTEMBER
1 . . . Mobile
3-7 . . . at West Tenn

WEST TENN

APRIL
9-13 . . . at Montgomery
14-18 . . . at Jacksonville
20-24 . . . Tennessee
25-29 . . . Mississippi
30 . . . at Birmingham

MAY
1-4 . . . at Birmingham
5-9 . . . Huntsville
11-15 . . . at Tennessee
16-20 . . . Birmingham
21-25 . . . at Huntsville
26-30 . . . Chattanooga
31 . . . at Mississippi

JUNE
1-4 . . . at Mississippi
5-9 . . . Huntsville
11-15 . . . at Carolina
17-20 . . . Montgomery
22-27 . . . at Mobile
28-30 . . . Mississippi

JULY
1-3 . . . Mississippi
4-7 . . . at Huntsville
8-11 . . . Mobile
15-19 . . . at Montgomery
21-25 . . . Jacksonville
27-31 . . . at Mississippi

AUGUST
1-5 . . . at Chattanooga
6-10 . . . Carolina
12-15 . . . Chattanooga
17-21 . . . at Huntsville
22-26 . . . Birmingham
28-31 . . . at Mississippi

SEPTEMBER
1 . . . at Mississippi
3-7 . . . Tennessee

TEXAS LEAGUE

ARKANSAS

APRIL
9-11 . . . . Midland
12-14 . . . . .Frisco
16-18 . . . . at Midland
19-21 . . . . at Frisco
23-26 . . . . . . NW Arkansas
27-30 . . . . .at Tulsa

MAY
1-4. . . . . . at NW Arkansas
5-8. . . . . Tulsa
9-12. . . . . Springfield
13-16 . . . . .at Tulsa
18-21 . . . . . .at Springfield
22-25 . . . . . . NW Arkansas
27-29 . . . .at Corpus Christi
30-31 . . . . .at San Antonio

JUNE
1 . . . . .at San Antonio
3-5. . . . . . . Corpus Christi
6-8. . . . . San Antonio
10-13 . . . . at NW Arkansas
14-17 . . . . Springfield
18-21 . . . . Tulsa
22-25 . . . . . .at Springfield
26-29 . . . . at NW Arkansas

JULY
2-4. . . . . Midland
5-7. . . . . .Frisco
9-11 . . . . at Midland
12-14 . . . . at Frisco
16-19 . . . . Tulsa
20-23 . . . . at NW Arkansas
24-27 . . . . Tulsa
28-30 . . . . Springfield
31 . . . . .at Tulsa

AUGUST
1-3. . . . . .at Tulsa
4-6. . . . . . . .at Springfield
7-10 . . . . .NW Arkansas
12-14 . . . .at Corpus Christi
15-17 . . . . .at San Antonio
19-21 . . . . . Corpus Christi
22-24 . . . . . . San Antonio
25-28 . . . . .at Tulsa
29-31 . . . . Springfield

SEPTEMBER
1-4. . . . . NW Arkansas
5-7. . . . . . . .at Springfield

CORPUS CHRISTI

APRIL
9-11 . . . . Tulsa
12-14 . . . . . . NW Arkansas
16-18 . . . . .at Tulsa
19-21 . . . . at NW Arkansas
23-26 . . . . .Frisco
27-30 . . . . at Midland

MAY
1-4. . . . . at Frisco
5-8. . . . . Midland
9-10 . . . . . .at San Antonio
11-12 . . . . . . San Antonio
13-16 . . . . .Frisco
17-18 . . . . . . San Antonio
20-21 . . . . .at San Antonio
22-25 . . . . at Midland
27-29 . . . . .Arkansas
30-31 . . . . Springfield

JUNE
1 . . . . Springfield
3-5. . . . . at Arkansas
6-8. . . . . . . .at Springfield
10-13 . . . . Midland
14-17 . . . . .at San Antonio
18-21 . . . . at Frisco
22-25 . . . . . . San Antonio
26-29 . . . . at Frisco

JULY
2-4. . . . . Tulsa
5-7. . . . . NW Arkansas
9-11 . . . . .at Tulsa
12-14 . . . . at NW Arkansas
16-19 . . . . .Frisco
20-23 . . . . at Midland
24-27 . . . . .Frisco
28-30 . . . . . . San Antonio
31 . . . . at Midland

AUGUST
1-3. . . . . at Midland
4-6. . . . . . .at San Antonio
7-10 . . . . Midland
12-14 . . . . .Arkansas
15-17 . . . . Springfield
19-21 . . . . at Arkansas
22-24 . . . . . .at Springfield
25-28 . . . . Midland
29-31 . . . . .at San Antonio

SEPTEMBER
1-4. . . . . at Frisco
5-7. . . . . San Antonio

FRISCO

APRIL
9-11 . . . . . . .at Springfield
12-14 . . . . at Arkansas
16-18 . . . . Springfield
19-21 . . . . .Arkansas
23-26 . . . .at Corpus Christi
27-30 . . . . .at San Antonio

MAY
1-4. . . . . . . Corpus Christi
5-8. . . . . San Antonio
9-12. . . . . at Midland
13-16 . . . .at Corpus Christi
18-21 . . . . Midland
22-25 . . . . . . San Antonio
27-29 . . . . .at Tulsa
30-31 . . . . at NW Arkansas

JUNE
1 . . . . at NW Arkansas
3-5. . . . . Tulsa
6-8. . . . . .NW Arkansas
10-13 . . . . .at San Antonio
14-17 . . . . at Midland
18-21 . . . . . Corpus Christi
22-25 . . . . Midland
26-29 . . . . . Corpus Christi

JULY
2-4. . . . . . . .at Springfield
5-7. . . . . at Arkansas
9-11 . . . . Springfield
12-14 . . . . .Arkansas
16-19 . . . .at Corpus Christi
20-23 . . . . . . San Antonio
24-27 . . . .at Corpus Christi
28-30 . . . . Midland
31 . . . . . . .at San Antonio

AUGUST
1-3. . . . . . .at San Antonio
4-6. . . . . at Midland
7-10 . . . . San Antonio
12-14 . . . . .at Tulsa
15-17 . . . . at NW Arkansas
19-21 . . . . Tulsa
22-24 . . . . . . NW Arkansas
25-28 . . . . .at San Antonio
29-31 . . . . Midland

SEPTEMBER
1-4. . . . . . . Corpus Christi
5-7. . . . . at Midland

MIDLAND

APRIL
9-11 . . . . at Arkansas
12-14 . . . . . .at Springfield
16-18 . . . . .Arkansas
19-21 . . . . Springfield
23-26 . . . . .at San Antonio
27-30 . . . . . Corpus Christi
26-29 . . . . . . San Antonio

MAY
1-4. . . . . San Antonio
5-8. . . . . .at Corpus Christi
9-12. . . . . .Frisco
13-16 . . . . .at San Antonio
18-21 . . . . at Frisco
22-25 . . . . . Corpus Christi
27-29 . . . . at NW Arkansas
30-31 . . . . .at Tulsa

JUNE
1 . . . . .at Tulsa
3-5. . . . . NW Arkansas
6-8. . . . . Tulsa
10-13 . . . .at Corpus Christi
14-17 . . . . .Frisco
18-21 . . . . . . San Antonio
22-25 . . . . at Frisco

JULY
2-4. . . . . at Arkansas
5-7. . . . . . . .at Springfield
9-11 . . . . .Arkansas
12-14 . . . . Springfield
16-19 . . . . .at San Antonio
20-23 . . . . . Corpus Christi
24-27 . . . . .at San Antonio
28-30 . . . . at Frisco
31 . . . . Corpus Christi

AUGUST
1-3. . . . . . . Corpus Christi
4-6. . . . . .Frisco
7-10 . . . . .at Corpus Christi
12-14 . . . . at NW Arkansas
15-17 . . . . .at Tulsa
19-21 . . . . . . NW Arkansas
22-24 . . . . Tulsa
25-28 . . . .at Corpus Christi
29-31 . . . . at Frisco

SEPTEMBER
1-4. . . . . San Antonio
5-7. . . . . .Frisco

NORTHWEST ARKANSAS

APRIL
9-11 . . . . . .at San Antonio
12-14 . . . .at Corpus Christi
16-18 . . . . . . San Antonio
19-21 . . . . . Corpus Christi
23-26 . . . . at Arkansas
27-30 . . . . Springfield

MAY
1-4. . . . . .Arkansas
5-8. . . . . . . .at Springfield
9-12. . . . . .at Tulsa
13-16 . . . . Springfield
18-21 . . . . Tulsa
22-25 . . . . at Arkansas
27-29 . . . . Midland
30-31 . . . . .Frisco

JUNE
1 . . . . .Frisco

3-5 at Midland
6-8 at Frisco
10-13 Arkansas
14-17 Tulsa
18-21 at Springfield
22-25 at Tulsa
26-29 Arkansas

JULY

2-4 at San Antonio
5-7 at Corpus Christi
9-11 San Antonio
12-14 Corpus Christi
16-19 at Springfield
20-23 Arkansas
24-27 at Springfield
28-30 at Tulsa
31 Springfield

AUGUST

1-3 Springfield
4-6 Tulsa
7-10 at Arkansas
12-14 Midland
15-17 Frisco
19-21 at Midland
22-24 at Frisco
25-28 Springfield
29-31 Tulsa

SEPTEMBER

1-4 at Arkansas
5-7 at Tulsa

SAN ANTONIO

APRIL

9-11 NW Arkansas
12-14 Tulsa
16-18 at NW Arkansas
19-21 at Tulsa
23-26 Midland
27-30 Frisco

MAY

1-4 at Midland
5-8 at Frisco
9-10 Corpus Christi
11-12 at Corpus Christi
13-16 Midland
17-18 at Corpus Christi
20-21 Corpus Christi
22-25 at Frisco
27-29 Springfield
30-31 Arkansas

JUNE

1 Arkansas
3-5 at Springfield
6-8 at Arkansas
10-13 Frisco
14-17 Corpus Christi
18-21 at Midland
22-25 at Corpus Christi
26-29 at Midland

JULY

2-4 NW Arkansas
5-7 Tulsa
9-11 at NW Arkansas
12-14 at Tulsa
16-19 Midland
20-23 at Frisco
24-27 Midland
28-30 at Corpus Christi
31 Frisco

AUGUST

1-3 Frisco
4-6 Corpus Christi
7-10 at Frisco
12-14 Springfield
15-17 Arkansas
19-21 at Springfield
22-24 at Arkansas
25-28 Frisco
29-31 Corpus Christi

SEPTEMBER

1-4 at Midland
5-7 at Corpus Christi

SPRINGFIELD

APRIL

9-11 Frisco
12-14 Midland
16-18 at Frisco
19-21 at Midland
23-26 Tulsa
27-30 at NW Arkansas

MAY

1-4 at Tulsa
5-8 NW Arkansas
9-12 at Arkansas
13-16 at NW Arkansas
18-21 Arkansas
22-25 Tulsa
27-29 at San Antonio
30-31 at Corpus Christi

JUNE

1 at Corpus Christi
3-5 San Antonio
6-8 Corpus Chrisit
10-13 at Tulsa
14-17 at Arkansas
18-21 NW Arkansas
22-25 Arkansas
26-29 at Tulsa

JULY

2-4 Frisco
5-7 Midland
9-11 at Frisco
12-14 at Midland
16-19 NW Arkansas
20-23 at Tulsa
24-27 NW Arkansas
28-30 at Arkansas
31 at NW Arkansas

AUGUST

1-3 at NW Arkansas
4-6 Arkansas
7-10 Tulsa
12-14 at San Antonio
15-17 at Corpus Christi
19-21 San Antonio
22-24 Corpus Christi
25-28 at NW Arkansas
29-31 at Arkansas

SEPTEMBER

1-4 Tulsa
5-7 Arkansas

TULSA

APRIL

9-11 at Corpus Christi
12-14 at San Antonio
16-18 Corpus Christi
19-21 San Antonio
23-26 at Springfield
27-30 Arkansas

MAY

1-4 Springfield
5-8 at Arkansas
9-12 NW Arkansas
13-16 Arkansas
18-21 at NW Arkansas
22-25 at Springfield
27-29 Frisco
30-31 Midland

JUNE

1 Midland
3-5 at Frisco
6-8 at Midland
10-13 Springfield
14-17 at NW Arkansas
18-21 at Arkansas
22-25 NW Arkansas
26-29 Springfield

JULY

2-4 at Corpus Christi
5-7 at San Antonio
9-11 Corpus Christi
12-14 San Antonio
16-19 at Arkansas
20-23 Springfield
24-27 at Arkansas
28-30 NW Arkansas
31 Arkansas

AUGUST

1-3 Arkansas
4-6 at NW Arkansas
7-10 at Springfield
12-14 Frisco
15-17 Midland
19-21 at Frisco
22-24 at Midland
25-28 Arkansas
29-31 at NW Arkansas

SEPTEMBER

1-4 at Springfield
5-7 NW Arkansas

HIGH CLASS A

CALIFORNIA LEAGUE

BAKERSFIELD

APRIL

9-12 at Modesto
13-15 at San Jose
16-19 Lake Elsinore
20-22 at Visalia
23-26 Stockton
28-30 Modesto

MAY

1-4 at Stockton
5-7 San Jose
8-10 Visalia
12-14 Modesto
15-18 at Visalia
19-21 at Stockton
22-25 Inland Empire
27-30 Stockton
31 at Visalia

JUNE

1-3 at Visalia
4-7 at San Jose
9-11 San Jose
12-14at Rancho Cucamonga
15-17 at Lake Elsinore
18-21 Visalia
25-27 at High Desert
28-30 Visalia

JULY

1-3 at Modesto
4-6 Stockton
7-9 Modesto
10-13 at Stockton
15-18 Visalia
19-21 at San Jose
22-24 High Desert
25-27 at Modesto
28-30 Visalia
31 at Visalia

AUGUST

1-2 at Visalia
4-6 at Modesto
7-9 Lancaster
11-13 San Jose
14-16 at Lancaster
18-20 at Inland Empire
21-23 Modesto
24-26 Stockton
27-30 at Modesto

SEPTEMBER

1-3 at Stockton
4-7 Rancho Cucamonga

HIGH DESERT

APRIL

9-12 Lancaster
13-15 at Lake Elsinore
16-19 at Lancaster
20-22 Rancho Cucamonga
23-26 San Jose

28-30 at Inland Empire

MAY
1-4 at Rancho Cucamonga
5-7 Inland Empire
8-10 at Lake Elsinore
12-14 at Rancho Cucamonga
15-18 Stockton
19-21 Rancho Cucamonga
22-25 at Lancaster
27-30 Lake Elsinore
31 Inland Empire

JUNE
1-3 Inland Empire
4-7 at Stockton
8-10 at Visalia
12-14 Lancaster
15-17 Rancho Cucamonga
18-21 at Inland Empire
25-27 Bakersfield
28-30 Lake Elsinore

JULY
1-3 at Rancho Cucamonga
4-6 Visalia
7-9 at San Jose
10-13 at Modesto
15-18 Lancaster
19-21 at Rancho Cucamonga
22-24 at Bakersfield
25-27 Lancaster
28-30 at Lancaster
31 Lake Elsinore

AUGUST
1-2 Lake Elsinore
4-6 at Lancaster
7-9 at Lake Elsinoe
11-13 at Rancho Cucamonga
14-16 at Inland Empire
18-20 Rancho Cucamonga
21-23 Inland Empire
24-26 Lancaster
27-30 at Inland Empire

SEPTEMBER
1-3 Lancaster
4-7 Modesto

INLAND EMPIRE

APRIL
9-12 Rancho Cucamonga
13-15 at Lancaster
16-19 at Rancho Cucamonga
20-22 Lancaster
23-26 at Lake Elsinore
28-30 High Desert

MAY
1-4 Lake Elsinore
5-7 at High Desert
8-10 at Lancaster
12-14 Stockton
15-18 Lake Elsinore
19-21 at San Jose
22-25 at Bakersfield
27-30 Modesto
31 at High Desert

JUNE
1-3 at High Desert
5-8 at Lake Elsinore
9-11 Lancaster
12-14 Lake Elsinore
15-17 at Lancaster
18-21 High Desert
25-27 at Lake Elsinore
28-30 Rancho Cucamonga

JULY
1-3 at Visalia
4-6 Lancaster
7-9 at Lake Elsinore
10-13 at Lancaster
15-18 Rancho Cucamonga
19-21 Lake Elsinore
22-24 at Rancho Cucamonga
25-27 Visalia
28-30 at Lake Elsinore
31 Lancaster

AUGUST
1-2 Lancaster
4-6 Rancho Cucamonga
7-9 at Stockton
10-12 at Modesto
14-16 High Desert
18-20 Bakersfield
21-23 at High Desert
24-26 at Rancho Cucamonga
27-30 High Desert

SEPTEMBER
1-3 San Jose
4-7 at Lancaster

LAKE ELSINORE

APRIL
9-12 Visalia
13-15 High Desert
16-19 at Bakersfield
20-22 at San Jose
23-26 Inland Empire
28-30 at Rancho Cucamonga

MAY
1-4 at Inland Empire
5-7 Lancaster
8-10 High Desert
12-14 at Lancaster
15-18 at Inland Empire
19-21 Lancaster
22-25 Rancho Cucamonga
27-30 at High Desert
31 Rancho Cucamonga

JUNE
1-2 Rancho Cucamonga
3 at Rancho Cucamonga
5-8 Inland Empire
9 at Rancho Cucamonga
10 Rancho Cucamonga
11 at Rancho Cucamonga
12-14 at Inland Empire
15-17 Bakersfield
18-21 at Rancho Cucamonga
25-27 Inland Empire
28-30 at High Desert

JULY
1-3 at Lancaster
4-6 Rancho Cucamonga
7-9 Inland Empire
10-13 at Rancho Cuacmonga
15-18 Stockton
19-21 at Inland Empire
22-24 at Lancaster
25-27 Rancho Cucamonga
28-30 Inland Empire
31 at High Desert

AUGUST
1-2 at High Desert
4-6 at Stockton
7-9 High Desert
11-13 at Lancaster
14-16 at Rancho Cucamonga
18-20 Lancaster
21-23 Rancho Cucamonga
24-26 at Modesto
27-30 at Visalia

SEPTEMBER
1-3 Modesto
4-7 San Jose

LANCASTER

APRIL
9-12 at High Desert
13-15 Inland Empire
16-19 High Desert
20-22 at Inland Empire
23-26 Rancho Cucamonga
27-29 San Jose

MAY
1-4 at Visalia
5-7 at Lake Elsinore
8-10 Inland Empire
12-14 Lake Elsinore
15-18 at Rancho Cucamonga
19-21 at Lake Elsinore
22-25 High Desert
27-30 at Rancho Cucamonga
31 Modesto

JUNE
1-3 Modesto
4-7 Rancho Cucamonga
9-11 at Inland Empire
12-14 at High Desert
15-17 Inland Empire
18-21 at Modesto
25-27 Rancho Cucamonga
28-30 at Stockton

JULY
1-3 Lake Elsinore
4-6 at Inland Empire
7-9 at Rancho Cucamonga
10-13 Inland Empire
15-18 at High Desert
19-21 Stockton
22-24 Lake Elsinore
25-27 at High Desert
28-30 High Desert
31 at Inland Empire

AUGUST
1-2 at Inland Empire
4-6 High Desert
7-9 at Bakersfield
11-13 Lake Elsinore
14-16 Bakersfield
18-20 at Lake Elsinore
21-23 Visalia
24-26 at High Desert
27-30 at San Jose

SEPTEMBER
1-3 at High Desert
4-7 Inland Empire

MODESTO

APRIL
9-12 Bakersfield
13-15 Stockton
16-19 at Visalia
20-22 at Stockton
23-26 Visalia
28-30 at Bakersfield

MAY
1-4 at San Jose
5-7 Rancho Cucamonga
8-10 San Jose
12-14 at Bakersfield
15-18 San Jose
19-21 Visalia
22-25 at San Jose
27-30 at Inland Empire
31 at Lancaster

JUNE
1-3 at Lancaster
4-7 Visalia
9-11 Stockton
12-14 at San Jose
15-17 at Stockton
18-21 Lancaster
25-27 at Visalia
28-30 San Jose

JULY
1-3 Bakersfield
4-6 at San Jose
7-9 at Bakersfield
10-13 High Desert
15-18 at San Jose
19-21 Visalia
22-24 at Stockton
25-27 Bakersfield
28-30 at Rancho Cucamonga
31 Stockton

AUGUST
1-2 Stockton
4-6 Bakersfield
7-9 at Visalia
10-12 Inland Empire
14-16 Visalia
18-20 at Stockton
21-23 at Bakersfield
24-26 Lake Elsinore
27-30 Bakersfield

SEPTEMBER
1-3 at Lake Elsinore
4-7 at High Desert

RANCHO CUCAMONGA

APRIL
9-12 at Inland Empire
13-15 Visalia
16-19 Inland Empire
20-22 at High Desert
23-26 at Lancaster
28-30 Lake Elsinore

MAY
1-4 High Desert
5-7 at Modesto
8-10 at Stockton
12-14 High Desert
15-18 Lancaster
19-21 at High Desert
22-25 at Lake Elsinore
27-30 Lancaster
31 at Lake Elsinore

JUNE
1-2 at Lake Elsinore
3 Lake Elsinore

4-7 . . . at Lancaster
9 . . . Lake Elsinore
10 . . . at Lake Elsinore
11 . . . Lake Elsinore
12-14 . . . Bakersfield
15-17 . . . at High Desert
18-21 . . . Lake Elsinore
25-27 . . . at Lancaster
28-30 . . . at Inland Empire

JULY

1-3 . . . High Desert
4-6 . . . at Lake Elsinore
7-9 . . . Lancaster
10-13 . . . Lake Elsinore
15-18 . . . at Inland Empire
19-22 . . . High Desert
23-24 . . . Inland Empire
25-27 . . . at Lake Elsinore
28-30 . . . Modesto
31 . . . at San Jose

AUGUST

1-2 . . . at San Jose
4-6 . . . at Inland Empire
7-9 . . . San Jose
11-13 . . . High Desert
14-16 . . . Lake Elsinore
18-20 . . . at High Desert
21-23 . . . at Lake Elsinore
24-26 . . . Inland Empire
27-30 . . . Stockton

SEPTEMBER

1 . . . at Stockton
2-3 . . . at Visalia
4-7 . . . at Bakersfield

SAN JOSE

APRIL

9-12 . . . Stockton
13-15 . . . Bakersfield
16-19 . . . at Stockton
20-22 . . . Lake Elsinore
23-26 . . . at High Desert
27-29 . . . at Lancaster

MAY

1-4 . . . Modesto
5-7 . . . at Bakersfield
8-10 . . . at Modesto
12-14 . . . at Visalia
15-18 . . . at Modesto
19-21 . . . Inland Empire
22-25 . . . Modesto
27-30 . . . at Visalia
31 . . . Stockton

JUNE

1-3 . . . Stockton
4-7 . . . Bakersfield
9-11 . . . at Bakersfield
12-14 . . . Modesto
15-17 . . . Visalia
18-21 . . . at Stockton
25-27 . . . Stockton
28-30 . . . at Modesto

JULY

1-3 . . . at Stockton
4-6 . . . Modesto
7-9 . . . High Desert
0-13 . . . at Visalia
15-18 . . . Modesto
19-21 . . . Bakersfield
22-24 . . . at Visalia
25-27 . . . Stockton
28-30 . . . at Stockton
31 . . . Rancho Cucamonga

AUGUST

1-2 . . . Rancho Cucamonga
4-6 . . . Visalia
7-9 . . . at Rancho Cucamonga
11-13 . . . at Bakersfield
14-16 . . . Stockton
18-20 . . . at Visalia
21-23 . . . at Stockton
24-26 . . . Visalia
27-30 . . . Lancaster

SEPTEMBER

1-3 . . . at Inland Empire
4-7 . . . at Lake Elsinore

STOCKTON

APRIL

9-12 . . . at San Jose
13-15 . . . at Modesto
16-19 . . . San Jose
20-22 . . . Modesto
23-26 . . . at Bakersfield
28-30 . . . Visalia

MAY

1-4 . . . Bakersfield
5-7 . . . at Visalia
8-10 . . Rancho Cucamonga
12-14 . . . at Inland Empire
15-18 . . . at High Desert
19-21 . . . Bakersfield
22-25 . . . Visalia
27-30 . . . at Bakersfield
31 . . . at San Jose

JUNE

1-3 . . . at San Jose
4-7 . . . High Desert
9-11 . . . at Modesto
12-14 . . . at Visalia
15-17 . . . Modesto
18-21 . . . San Jose
25-27 . . . at San Jose
28-30 . . . Lancaster

JULY

1-3 . . . San Jose
4-6 . . . at Bakersfield
7-9 . . . at Visalia
10-13 . . . Bakersfield
15-18 . . . at Lake Elsinore
19-21 . . . at Lancaster
22-24 . . . Modesto
25-27 . . . at San Jose
28-30 . . . San Jose
31 . . . at Modesto

AUGUST

1-2 . . . at Modesto
4-6 . . . Lake Elsinore
7-9 . . . Inland Empire
11-13 . . . at Visalia
14-16 . . . at San Jose
18-20 . . . Modesto
21-23 . . . San Jose
24-26 . . . at Bakersfield
27-30at Rancho Cucamonga

SEPTEMBER

1-3 . . . Bakersfield
4-7 . . . Visalia

VISALIA

APRIL

9-12 . . . at Lake Elsinore
13-15at Rancho Cucamonga
16-19 . . . Modesto
20-22 . . . Bakersfield
23-26 . . . at Modesto
28-30 . . . at Stockton

MAY

1-4 . . . Lancaster
5-7 . . . Stockton
8-10 . . . at Bakersfield
12-14 . . . San Jose
15-18 . . . Bakersfield
19-21 . . . at Modesto
22-25 . . . at Stockton
27-30 . . . San Jose
31 . . . Bakersfield

JUNE

1-3 . . . Bakersfield
4-7 . . . at Modesto
8-10 . . . High Desert
12-14 . . . Stockton
15-17 . . . at San Jose
18-21 . . . at Bakersfield
25-27 . . . Modesto
28-30 . . . at Bakersfield

JULY

1-3 . . . Inland Empire
4-6 . . . at High Desert
7-9 . . . Stockton
11-13 . . . San Jose
15-18 . . . at Bakersfield
19-21 . . . at Modesto
22-24 . . . San Jose
25-27 . . . at Inland Empire
28-30 . . . at Bakersfield
31 . . . Bakersfield

AUGUST

1-2 . . . Bakersfield
4-6 . . . at San Jose
7-9 . . . Modesto
11-13 . . . Stockton
14-16 . . . at Modesto
18-20 . . . San Jose
21-23 . . . at Lancaster
24-26 . . . at San Jose
27-30 . . . Lake Elsinore

SEPTEMBER

1-3 . . . Rancho Cucamonga
4-7 . . . at Stockton

CAROLINA LEAGUE

FREDERICK

APRIL

9-12 . . . at Salem
13-16 . . . at Myrtle Beach
17-19 . . . Salem
20-22 . . . at Lynchburg
23-26 . . . Potomac
28-30 . . . at Winston-Salem

MAY

1-3 . . . at Potomac
4-7 . . . Winston-Salem
8-10 . . . Wilmington
11-14 . . . Myrtle Beach
15-17 . . . at Kinston
18-21 . . . Lynchburg
22-24 . . . Kinston
26-28 . . . at Wilmington
29-31 . . . at Salem

JUNE

1-3 . . . Lynchburg
4-7 . . . Salem
9-11 . . . at Lynchburg
12-14 . . . Potomac
15-17 . . . at Winston-Salem
19-21 . . . at Myrtle Beach
25-27 . . . Winston-Salem
28-30 . . . Wilmington

JULY

1 . . . Wilmington
2-5 . . . at Potomac
7-9 . . . at Kinston
10-12 . . . Myrtle Beach
13-16 . . . Kinston
17-19 . . . at Wilmington
21-23 . . . at Salem
24-26 . . . Lynchburg
27-29 . . . Salem
30-31 . . . at Lynchburg

AUGUST

1-2 . . . at Lynchburg
3-5 . . . Potomac
6-9 . . . at Winston-Salem
10-13 . . . at Potomac
14-16 . . . Winston-Salem
18-20 . . . Wilmington
22 . . . at Myrtle Beach
24-27 . . . at Kinston
28-30 . . . Myrtle Beach

SEPTEMBER

1-3 . . . Kinston
4-7 . . . at Wilmington

KINSTON

APRIL

9-12 . . . Winston-Salem
13-16 . . . Wilmington
17-19 . . . Winston-Salem
20-22 . . . at Myrtle Beach
23-26 . . . Lynchburg
28-30 . . . Salem

MAY

1-3 . . . at Lynchburg

4-7 . . . at Salem
8-10 . . . Myrtle Beach
12-14 . . . at Wilmington
15-17 . . . Frederick
18-21 . . . Potomac
22-24 . . . at Frederick
25-27 . . . at Potomac
29-31 . . . at Winston-Salem

JUNE

1-3 . . . Wilmington
4-7 . . . at Winston-Salem
9-11 . . . at Myrtle Beach
12-14 . . . Lynchburg
15-17 . . . at Salem
18-21 . . . at Lynchburg
25-27 . . . Salem
28-30 . . . Myrtle Beach

JULY

1 . . . Myrtle Beach
2-5 . . . at Wilmington
7-9 . . . Frederick
10-12 . . . Potomac
13-16 . . . at Frederick
17-19 . . . at Potomac
21-23 . . . Winston-Salem
24-26 . . . Wilmington
27-29 . . . at Winston-Salem
30-31 . . . at Myrtle Beach

AUGUST

1-2 . . . at Myrtle Beach
3-5 . . . Lynchburg
6-9 . . . Salem
11-13 . . . at Lynchburg
14-16 . . . at Salem
18-20 . . . Myrtle Beach
21-23 . . . at Wilmington
24-27 . . . Frederick
28-30 . . . Potomac

SEPTEMBER

1-3 . . . at Frederick
4-7 . . . at Potomac

LYNCHBURG

APRIL

9-12 . . . Potomac
13-16 . . . Winston-Salem
17-19 . . . at Wilmington
20-22 . . . Frederick
23-26 . . . at Kinston
27-29 . . . at Myrtle Beach

MAY

1-3 . . . Kinston
4-7 . . . Myrtle Beach
8-10 . . . at Salem
12-14 . . . at Winston-Salem
15-17 . . . Wilmington
18-21 . . . at Frederick
22-24 . . . at Potomac
26-28 . . . Salem
29-31 . . . Potomac

JUNE

1-3 . . . at Frederick
4-7 . . . at Wilmington
9-11 . . . Frederick
12-14 . . . at Kinston
15-17 . . . at Myrtle Beach
18-21 . . . Kinston
25-27 . . . Myrtle Beach
28-29 . . . at Salem
30 . . . Salem

JULY

1 . . . Salem
2 . . . at Winston-Salem
3-5 . . . Winston-Salem
7-9 . . . Wilmington
10-12 . . . at Winston-Salem
13-16 . . . at Potomac
17-19 . . . Salem
21-23 . . . Potomac
24-26 . . . at Frederick
27-29 . . . at Wilmington
30-31 . . . Frederick

AUGUST

1-2 . . . Frederick
3-5 . . . at Kinston
6-9 . . . at Myrtle Beach
11-13 . . . Kinston
14-16 . . . Myrtle Beach
18-20 . . . at Salem
21-23 . . . Winston-Salem
24-27 . . . Wilmington
28-30 . . . at Winston-Salem

SEPTEMBER

1-3 . . . at Potomac
4-5 . . . at Salem
6-7 . . . Salem

MYRTLE BEACH

APRIL

9-12 . . . Wilmington
13-16 . . . Frederick
17-19 . . . at Potomac
20-22 . . . Kinston
23-26 . . . at Salem
27-29 . . . Lynchburg

MAY

1-3 . . . Salem
4-7 . . . at Lynchburg
8-10 . . . at Kinston
11-14 . . . at Frederick
15-17 . . . Potomac
18-21 . . . at Winston-Salem
22-24 . . . Wilmington
26-28 . . . Winston-Salem
29-31 . . . at Wilmington

JUNE

1-3 . . . at Winston-Salem
4-7 . . . at Potomac
9-11 . . . Kinston
12-14 . . . at Salem
15-17 . . . Lynchburg
19-21 . . . Frederick
25-27 . . . at Lynchburg
28-30 . . . at Kinston

JULY

1 . . . at Kinston
2-5 . . . Salem
7-9 . . . Potomac
10-12 . . . at Frederick
13-16 . . . at Wilmington
18-20 . . . Winston-Salem
21-23 . . . Wilmington
24-26 . . . at Winston-Salem
27-29 . . . at Potomac
30-31 . . . Kinston

AUGUST

1-2 . . . Kinston
3-5 . . . at Salem
6-9 . . . Lynchburg
11-13 . . . Salem
14-16 . . . at Lynchburg
18-20 . . . at Kinston
21-23 . . . Frederick
24-27 . . . Potomac
28-30 . . . at Frederick
31 . . . at Wilmington

SEPTEMBER

1-2 . . . at Wilmington
4-7 . . . Winston-Salem

POTOMAC

APRIL

9-12 . . . at Lynchburg
13-16 . . . at Salem
17-19 . . . Myrtle Beach
20-22 . . . Winston-Salem
23-26 . . . at Frederick
28-30 . . . Wilmington

MAY

1-3 . . . Frederick
4-7 . . . at Wilmington
8-10 . . . at Winston-Salem
12-14 . . . Salem
15-17 . . . at Myrtle Beach
18-21 . . . at Kinston
22-24 . . . Lynchburg
25-27 . . . Kinston
29-31 . . . at Lynchburg

JUNE

1-3 . . . at Salem
4-7 . . . Myrtle Beach
9-11 . . . Winston-Salem
12-14 . . . at Frederick
15-17 . . . Wilmington
18-21 . . . Salem
25-27 . . . at Wilmington
28-30 . . . at Winston-Salem

JULY

1 . . . at Winston-Salem
2-5 . . . Frederick
7-9 . . . at Myrtle Beach
10-12 . . . at Kinston
13-16 . . . Lynchburg
17-19 . . . Kinston
21-23 . . . at Lynchburg
24-26 . . . at Salem
27-29 . . . Myrtle Beach
30-31 . . . Winston-Salem

AUGUST

1-2 . . . Winston-Salem
3-5 . . . at Frederick
6-9 . . . Wilmington
11-13 . . . Frederick
14-16 . . . at Wilmington
18-20 . . . at Winston-Salem
21-23 . . . Salem
24-27 . . . at Myrtle Beach
28-30 . . . at Kinston

SEPTEMBER

1-3 . . . Lynchburg
4-7 . . . Kinston

SALEM

APRIL

9-12 . . . Frederick
13-16 . . . Potomac
17-19 . . . at Frederick
20-22 . . . at Wilmington
23-26 . . . Myrtle Beach
28-30 . . . at Kinston

MAY

1-3 . . . at Myrtle Beach
4-7 . . . Kinston
8-10 . . . Lynchburg
12-14 . . . at Potomac
15-17 . . . Winston-Salem
18-21 . . . Wilmington
22-24 . . . at Winston-Salem
26-28 . . . at Lynchburg
29-31 . . . Frederick

JUNE

1-3 . . . Potomac
4-7 . . . at Frederick
8-10 . . . at Wilmington
12-14 . . . Myrtle Beach
15-17 . . . Kinston
18-21 . . . at Potomac
25-27 . . . at Kinston
28-29 . . . Lynchburg
30 . . . at Lynchburg

JULY

1 . . . at Lynchburg
2-5 . . . at Myrtle Beach
6-9 . . . at Winston-Salem
10-12 . . . Wilmington
14-16 . . . Winston-Salem
17-19 . . . at Lynchburg
21-23 . . . Frederick
24-26 . . . Potomac
27-29 . . . at Frederick
30-31 . . . at Wilmington

AUGUST

1-2 . . . at Wilmington
3-5 . . . Myrtle Beach
6-9 . . . at Kinston
11-13 . . . at Myrtle Beach
14-16 . . . Kinston
18-20 . . . Lynchburg
21-23 . . . at Potomac
24-27 . . . Winston-Salem
28-30 . . . Wilmington

SEPTEMBER

1-3 . . . at Winston-Salem
4-5 . . . Lynchburg
6-7 . . . at Lynchburg

WILMINGTON

APRIL

9-12 . . . at Myrtle Beach
13-16 . . . at Kinston
17-19 . . . Lynchburg
20-22 . . . Salem
23-26 . . . at Winston-Salem
28-30 . . . at Potomac

MAY

1-3 . . . Winston-Salem
4-7 . . . Potomac
8-10 . . . at Frederick
12-14 . . . Kinston
15-17 . . . at Lynchburg
18-21 . . . at Salem
22-24 . . . at Myrtle Beach
26-28 . . . Frederick
29-31 . . . Myrtle Beach

JUNE

1-3 . . . at Kinston
4-7 . . . Lynchburg

8-10 . . . Salem
12-14 . . . at Winston-Salem
15-17 . . . at Potomac
18-21 . . . Winston-Salem
25-27 . . . Potomac
28-30 . . . at Frederick

JULY

1 . . . Frederick
2-5 . . . Kinston
7-9 . . . at Lynchburg
10-12 . . . at Salem
13-16 . . . Myrtle Beach
17-19 . . . Frederick
21-23 . . . at Myrtle Beach
24-26 . . . at Kinston
27-29 . . . Lynchburg
30-31 . . . Salem

AUGUST

1-2 . . . Salem
3-5 . . . at Winston-Salem
6-9 . . . at Potomac
11-13 . . . Winston-Salem
14-16 . . . Potomac
18-20 . . . at Frederick
21-23 . . . Kinston
24-27 . . . at Lynchburg
28-30 . . . at Salem
31 . . . Myrtle Beach

SEPTEMBER

1-2 . . . Myrtle Beach
4-7 . . . Frederick

WINSTON-SALEM

APRIL

9-12 . . . at Kinston
13-16 . . . at Lynchburg
17-19 . . . at Kinston
20-22 . . . at Potomac
23-26 . . . Wilmington
28-30 . . . Frederick

MAY

1-3 . . . at Wilmington
4-7 . . . at Frederick
8-10 . . . Potomac
12-14 . . . Lynchburg
15-17 . . . at Salem
18-21 . . . Myrtle Beach
22-24 . . . Salem
26-28 . . . at Myrtle Beach
29-31 . . . Kinston

JUNE

1-3 . . . Myrtle Beach
4-7 . . . Kinston
9-11 . . . at Potomac
12-14 . . . Wilmington
15-17 . . . Frederick
18-21 . . . at Wilmington
25-27 . . . at Frederick
28-30 . . . Potomac

JULY

1 . . . Potomac
2 . . . Lynchburg
3-5 . . . at Lynchburg
6-9 . . . Salem
10-12 . . . Lynchburg
14-16 . . . at Salem
18-20 . . . at Myrtle Beach
21-23 . . . at Kinston
24-26 . . . Myrtle Beach
27-29 . . . Kinston
30-31 . . . at Potomac

AUGUST

1-2 . . . at Potomac
3-5 . . . Wilmington
6-9 . . . Frederick
11-13 . . . at Wilmington
14-16 . . . at Frederick
18-20 . . . Potomac
21-23 . . . at Lynchburg
24-27 . . . at Salem
28-30 . . . Lynchburg

SEPTEMBER

1-3 . . . Salem
4-7 . . . at Myrtle Beach

FLORIDA STATE LEAGUE

BREVARD COUNTY

APRIL

9 . . . Daytona
10-12 . . . at Daytona
14-16 . . . Tampa
17-19 . . . Dunedin
21-23 . . . at Tampa
24 . . . at Dunedin
27 . . . Daytona
28 . . . at Daytona
29 . . . Daytona
30 . . . at Daytona

MAY

1-3 . . . Lakeland
4-6 . . . at Clearwater
7-9 . . . at Lakeland
10-12 . . . Clearwater
14-16 . . . at Lakeland
17-19 . . . Tampa
20 . . . Daytona
21-24 . . . at Dunedin
26-27 . . . St. Lucie
28-29 . . . at St. Lucie
30-31 . . . Fort Myers

JUNE

1-2 . . . Fort Myers
3-6 . . . at Sarasota
7-10 . . . Charlotte
11-14 . . . at Palm Beach
15-18 . . . at Jupiter
22-24 . . . Dunedin
25-28 . . . Palm Beach
29-30 . . . at Charlotte

JULY

1-2 . . . at Charlotte
3-4 . . . Daytona
5-7 . . . at Tampa
8-10 . . . Clearwater
11-13 . . . Lakeland
15-17 . . . at Clearwater
18-21 . . . Jupiter
22-23 . . . St. Lucie
24-25 . . . at St. Lucie
26-29 . . . at Fort Myers
30-31 . . . Sarasota

AUGUST

1-2 . . . Sarasota
3-6 . . . at Daytona
7 . . . Daytona
8-10 . . . Lakeland
11-13 . . . Dunedin
14-16 . . . at Lakeland
17-20 . . . at Dunedin
21-23 . . . Daytona
25-27 . . . Clearwater
28-30 . . . at Tampa

SEPTEMBER

1-3 . . . at Clearwater
4-6 . . . Tampa

CHARLOTTE

APRIL

9 . . . Fort Myers
10 . . . at Fort Myers
11 . . . Fort Myers
12 . . . at Fort Myers
14-16 . . . at St. Lucie
17-19 . . . at Palm Beach
21-23 . . . Sarasota
24-26 . . . St. Lucie
27-29 . . . at Sarasota
30 . . . at Fort Myers

MAY

1-2 . . . Fort Myers
3 . . . at Fort Myers
4-6 . . . at Jupiter
7-9 . . . Palm Beach
11-13 . . . Jupiter
14-16 . . . at Palm Beach
17-19 . . . St. Lucie
20-22 . . . Palm Beach
23 . . . at Fort Myers
24 . . . Fort Myers
26-29 . . . at Clearwater
30-31 . . . at Tampa

JUNE

1-2 . . . at Tampa
3-6 . . . Daytona
7-10 . . . at Brevard County
11-14 . . . Dunedin
15-18 . . . Lakeland
22-24 . . . at St. Lucie
25-28 . . . at Dunedin
29-30 . . . Brevard County

JULY

1-2 . . . Brevard County
3 . . . at Fort Myers
4 . . . Fort Myers
5-7 . . . Sarasota
8-10 . . . at Jupiter
11-13 . . . at Sarasota
15-17 . . . Jupiter
18-21 . . . at Lakeland
22-25 . . . Clearwater
26-29 . . . Tampa
30-31 . . . at Daytona

AUGUST

1-2 . . . at Daytona
4 . . . at Fort Myers
5 . . . Fort Myers
6-7 . . . at Fort Myers
8-10 . . . Palm Beach
11-13 . . . St. Lucie
14-16 . . . at Palm Beach
17-19 . . . at St. Lucie
20 . . . at Fort Myers
21-23 . . . Fort Myers
25-27 . . . Jupiter
28-30 . . . at Sarasota

SEPTEMBER

1-3 . . . at Jupiter
4-6 . . . Sarasota

CLEARWATER

APRIL

9 . . . Dunedin
10 . . . at Dunedin
11 . . . Dunedin
13 . . . at Dunedin
14-16 . . . Lakeland
17-19 . . . Tampa
21-23 . . . at Lakeland
24-26 . . . at Tampa
27 . . . Dunedin
28 . . . at Dunedin
29 . . . Dunedin
30 . . . at Dunedin

MAY

1-3 . . . Daytona
4-6 . . . Brevard County
7-9 . . . at Daytona
10-12 . . . at Brevard County
14-16 . . . Daytona
17-19 . . . at Lakeland
20-21 . . . at Dunedin
22-24 . . . at Tampa
26-29 . . . Charlotte
30-31 . . . at St. Lucie

JUNE

1-2 . . . at St. Lucie
3-5 . . . at Fort Myers
7-10 . . . Palm Beach
11-14 . . . Jupiter
15-18 . . . at Sarasota
22 . . . Tampa
23-24 . . . at Tampa
25-28 . . . at Jupiter
29-30 . . . at Palm Beach

JULY

1-2 . . . at Palm Beach
3 . . . Dunedin
4 . . . at Dunedin
5-7 . . . Lakeland
8-10 . . . at Brevard County
11-13 . . . at Daytona
15-17 . . . Brevard County
18-21 . . . Sarasota
22-25 . . . at Charlotte
26-29 . . . St. Lucie
30-31 . . . Fort Myers

AUGUST

1-2 . . . Fort Myers
4-5 . . . at Dunedin
6 . . . Dunedin
7 . . . at Dunedin
8 . . . at Tampa
9-10 . . . Tampa
11 . . . at Lakeland
12-13 . . . Lakeland
14-16 . . . Tampa
17 . . . at Lakeland
18 . . . Lakeland
19 . . . Lakeland
20-24 . . . Dunedin

- 25-27 at Brevard County
- 28-30 at Daytona

SEPTEMBER

- 1-3 Brevard County
- 4-6 Daytona

DAYTONA

APRIL

- 9 at Brevard County
- 10-13 Brevard County
- 14-16 Dunedin
- 17-19 at Lakeland
- 20-22 at Dunedin
- 24-26 Lakeland
- 27 at Brevard County
- 28 Brevard County
- 29 at Brevard County
- 30 Brevard County

MAY

- 1-3 at Clearwater
- 4-6 at Tampa
- 7-9 Clearwater
- 11-13 Tampa
- 14-16 at Clearwater
- 17-19 at Dunedin
- 20 at Brevard County
- 21 Brevard County
- 22-24 Lakeland
- 26-29 at Palm Beach
- 30-31 Sarasota

JUNE

- 1-2 Sarasota
- 3-6 at Charlotte
- 7-10 at Jupiter
- 11-14 Fort Myers
- 15-18 St. Lucie
- 22-24 at Lakeland
- 25-28 at Fort Myers
- 29-30 Jupiter

JULY

- 1-2 Jupiter
- 3-4 at Brevard County
- 5-7 Dunedin
- 8-10 at Tampa
- 11-13 Clearwater
- 15-17 Tampa
- 18-21 at St. Lucie
- 22-25 Palm Beach
- 26-29 at Sarasota
- 30-31 Charlotte

AUGUST

- 1-2 Charlotte
- 3-6 Brevard County
- 7 at Brevard County
- 8-10 at Dunedin
- 11-13 Tampa
- 14-16 Dunedin
- 17-19 at Tampa
- 20 Brevard County
- 21-23 at Brevard County
- 25-27 Lakeland
- 28-30 Clearwater

SEPTEMBER

- 1-3 at Lakeland
- 4-6 at Clearwater

DUNEDIN

APRIL

- 9 at Clearwater
- 10 Clearwater
- 11 at Clearwater
- 13 Clearwater
- 14-16 at Daytona
- 17-19 at Brevard County
- 20-22 Daytona
- 24-26 Brevard County
- 27 at Clearwater
- 28 Clearwater
- 29 at Clearwater
- 30 Clearwater

MAY

- 1-3 at Tampa
- 4-6 at Lakeland
- 7-9 Tampa
- 11-13 Lakeland
- 14-16 at Tampa
- 17-19 Daytona
- 20-21 Clearwater
- 22-24 Brevard County
- 26-29 at Sarasota
- 30-31 Jupiter

JUNE

- 1-2 Jupiter
- 3-6 Palm Beach
- 7-10 at St. Lucie
- 11-14 at Charlotte
- 15-18 Fort Myers
- 22-24 at Brevard County
- 25-28 Charlotte
- 29-30 St. Lucie

JULY

- 1-2 St. Lucie
- 3 at Clearwater
- 4 Clearwater
- 5-7 at Daytona
- 8-10 Lakeland
- 11-13 Tampa
- 15-17 at Lakeland
- 18-21 at Fort Myers
- 22-25 Sarasota
- 26-29 at Jupiter
- 30-31 at Palm Beach

AUGUST

- 1-2 at Palm Beach
- 4-5 Clearwater
- 6 at Clearwater
- 7 Clearwater
- 8-10 Daytona
- 11-13 at Brevard County
- 14-16 at Daytona
- 17-19 Brevard County
- 20-24 at Clearwater
- 25-27 Tampa
- 28-30 Lakeland

SEPTEMBER

- 1-3 at Tampa
- 4-6 at Lakeland

FORT MYERS

APRIL

- 9 at Charlotte
- 10 Charlotte
- 11 at Charlotte
- 13 Charlotte
- 14-16 Jupiter
- 17-19 at St. Lucie
- 21-23 Palm Beach
- 24-26 at Jupiter
- 27-29 at Palm Beach
- 30 Charlotte

MAY

- 1-2 at Charlotte
- 3 Charlotte
- 4-6 at Sarasota
- 7-9 St. Lucie
- 11-13 Sarasota
- 14-16 at St. Lucie
- 17-19 at Jupiter
- 20-22 St. Lucie
- 23 Charlotte
- 24 at Charlotte
- 26 at Tampa
- 27-29 Tampa
- 30-31 at Brevard County

JUNE

- 1-2 at Brevard County
- 3-6 at Clearwater
- 7-10 Lakeland
- 11-14 at Daytona
- 15-18 at Dunedin
- 22-24 Jupiter
- 25-28 Daytona
- 29-30 at Lakeland

JULY

- 1-2 at Lakeland
- 3 Charlotte
- 4 at Charlotte
- 5-7 at Palm Beach
- 8-10 Sarasota
- 11-13 Palm Beach
- 15-17 at Sarasota
- 18-21 Dunedin
- 22-24 at Tampa
- 25 Tampa
- 26-29 at Brevard County
- 30-31 at Clearwater

AUGUST

- 1-2 at Clearwater
- 4 Charlotte
- 5 at Charlotte
- 6-7 Charlotte
- 8 Sarasota
- 9-10 at Sarasota
- 11-13 Palm Beach
- 14-15 Sarasota
- 16 at Sarasota
- 17-19 at Palm Beach
- 20 Charlotte
- 21-23 at Charlotte
- 24-26 St. Lucie
- 28-30 Jupiter

SEPTEMBER

- 1-3 at St. Lucie
- 4-6 at Jupiter

JUPITER

APRIL

- 9-10 at Palm Beach
- 11-13 Palm Beach
- 14-16 at Fort Myers
- 17-19 at Sarasota
- 21-23 St. Lucie
- 24-26 Fort Myers
- 27-29 at St. Lucie
- 30 Palm Beach

MAY

- 1 Palm Beach
- 2-3 at Palm Beach
- 4-6 Charlotte
- 7-9 Sarasota
- 11-13 at Charlotte
- 14-16 at Sarasota
- 17-19 Fort Myers
- 20-22 Sarasota
- 23 at Palm Beach
- 24 Palm Beach
- 26-29 at Lakeland
- 30-31 at Dunedin

JUNE

- 1-2 at Dunedin
- 3-6 Tampa
- 7-10 Daytona
- 11-14 at Clearwater
- 15-18 Brevard County
- 22-24 at Fort Myers
- 25-28 Clearwater
- 29-30 at Daytona

JULY

- 1-2 at Daytona
- 3 Palm Beach
- 4 at Palm Beach
- 5-7 at St. Lucie
- 8-10 Charlotte
- 11-13 St. Lucie
- 15-17 at Charlotte
- 18-21 at Brevard County
- 22-25 Lakeland
- 26-29 Dunedin
- 30-31 at Tampa

AUGUST

- 1-2 at Tampa
- 4 Palm Beach
- 5-7 at Palm Beach
- 8-10 St. Lucie
- 11-13 Sarasota
- 14-16 at St. Lucie
- 17-19 at Sarasota
- 20 at Palm Beach
- 21-23 Palm Beach
- 25-27 at Charlotte
- 28-30 at Fort Myers

SEPTEMBER

- 1-3 Charlotte
- 4-6 Fort Myers

LAKELAND

APRIL

- 9 Tampa
- 10 at Tampa
- 11 Tampa
- 13 at Tampa
- 14-16 at Clearwater
- 17-19 Daytona
- 21-23 Clearwater
- 24-26 at Daytona
- 27-29 Tampa
- 30 at Tampa

MAY

- 1-3 at Brevard County
- 4-6 Dunedin
- 7-9 Brevard County
- 11-13 at Dunedin
- 14-16 Brevard County
- 17-19 Clearwater
- 20-21 at Tampa
- 22-24 at Daytona
- 26-29 Jupiter
- 30-31 at Palm Beach

JUNE

- 1-2 at Palm Beach
- 3-6 at St. Lucie
- 7-10 at Fort Myers

11-14 . . . Sarasota
15-18 . . . at Charlotte
22-24 . . . Daytona
25-28 . . . at Sarasota
29-30 . . . Fort Myers

JULY

1-2 . . . Fort Myers
3 . . . at Tampa
4 . . . Tampa
5-7 . . . at Clearwater
8-10 . . . at Dunedin
11-13 . . . at Brevard County
15-17 . . . Dunedin
18-21 . . . Charlotte
22-25 . . . at Jupiter
26-29 . . . Palm Beach
30-31 . . . at St. Lucie

AUGUST

1-2 . . . at St. Lucie
4-5 . . . at Tampa
6-7 . . . Tampa
8-10 . . . at Brevard County
11 . . . Clearwater
12-13 . . . at Clearwater
14-16 . . . Brevard County
17 . . . Clearwater
18 . . . at Clearwater
19 . . . Clearwater
20 . . . at Tampa
21 . . . Tampa
22 . . . at Tampa
23 . . . Tampa
25-27 . . . at Daytona
28-30 . . . at Dunedin

SEPTEMBER

1-3 . . . Daytona
4-6 . . . Dunedin

PALM BEACH

APRIL

9-10 . . . Jupiter
11-13 . . . at Jupiter
14-16 . . . Sarasota
17-19 . . . Charlotte
21-23 . . . at Fort Myers
24-26 . . . at Sarasota
27-29 . . . Fort Myers
30 . . . at Jupiter

MAY

1 . . . at Jupiter
2-3 . . . Jupiter
4-6 . . . at St. Lucie
7-9 . . . at Charlotte
11-13 . . . St. Lucie
14-16 . . . Charlotte
17-19 . . . at Sarasota
20-22 . . . at Charlotte
23 . . . Jupiter
24 . . . at Jupiter
26-29 . . . Daytona
30-31 . . . Lakeland

JUNE

1-2 . . . Lakeland
3-6 . . . at Dunedin
7-10 . . . at Clearwater
11-14 . . . Brevard County
15-18 . . . at Tampa
22-24 . . . Sarasota
25-28 . . . at Brevard County
29-30 . . . Clearwater

JULY

1-2 . . . Clearwater
3 . . . at Jupiter
4 . . . Jupiter
5-7 . . . Fort Myers
8-10 . . . at St. Lucie
11-13 . . . at Fort Myers
15-17 . . . St. Lucie
18-21 . . . Tampa
22-25 . . . at Daytona
26-29 . . . at Lakeland
30-31 . . . Dunedin

AUGUST

1-2 . . . Dunedin
4 . . . at Jupiter
5-7 . . . Jupiter
8-10 . . . at Charlotte
11-13 . . . at Fort Myers
14-16 . . . Charlotte
17-19 . . . Fort Myers
20 . . . Jupiter
21-23 . . . at Jupiter
25-27 . . . Sarasota
28-30 . . . St. Lucie

SEPTEMBER

1-3 . . . at Sarasota
4-6 . . . at St. Lucie

ST. LUCIE

APRIL

9-12 . . . Sarasota
14-16 . . . Charlotte
17-19 . . . Fort Myers
21-23 . . . at Jupiter
24-26 . . . at Charlotte
27-29 . . . Jupiter
30 . . . Sarasota

MAY

1 . . . Sarasota
2-3 . . . at Sarasota
4-6 . . . Palm Beach
7-9 . . . at Fort Myers
11-13 . . . at Palm Beach
14-16 . . . Fort Myers
17-19 . . . at Charlotte
20-22 . . . at Fort Myers
23-24 . . . at Sarasota
26-27 . . . at Brevard County
28-29 . . . Brevard County
30-31 . . . Clearwater

JUNE

1-2 . . . Clearwater
3-6 . . . at Lakeland
7-10 . . . Dunedin
11-14 . . . Tampa
15-18 . . . at Daytona
22-24 . . . Charlotte
25-28 . . . at Tampa
29-30 . . . at Dunedin

JULY

1-2 . . . at Dunedin
3-4 . . . Sarasota
5-7 . . . Jupiter
8-10 . . . Palm Beach
11-13 . . . at Jupiter
15-17 . . . at Palm Beach
18-21 . . . Daytona
22-23 . . . at Brevard County
24-25 . . . Brevard County
26-29 . . . at Clearwater
30-31 . . . Lakeland

AUGUST

1-2 . . . Lakeland
4-5 . . . Sarasota
6-7 . . . at Sarasota
8-10 . . . at Jupiter
11-13 . . . at Charlotte
14-16 . . . Jupiter
17-19 . . . Charlotte
20-23 . . . at Sarasota
24-26 . . . at Fort Myers
28-30 . . . at Palm Beach

SEPTEMBER

1-3 . . . Fort Myers
4-6 . . . Palm Beach

SARASOTA

APRIL

9-12 . . . at St. Lucie
14-16 . . . at Palm Beach
17-19 . . . Jupiter
21-23 . . . at Charlotte
24-26 . . . Palm Beach
27-29 . . . Charlotte
30 . . . at St. Lucie

MAY

1 . . . at St. Lucie
2-3 . . . St. Lucie
4-6 . . . Fort Myers
7-9 . . . at Jupiter
11-13 . . . at Fort Myers
14-16 . . . Jupiter
17-19 . . . Palm Beach
20-22 . . . at Jupiter
23-24 . . . St. Lucie
26-29 . . . Dunedin
30-31 . . . at Daytona

JUNE

1-2 . . . at Daytona
3-6 . . . Brevard County
7-10 . . . at Tampa
11-14 . . . at Lakeland
15-18 . . . Clearwater
22-24 . . . at Palm Beach
25-28 . . . Lakeland
29-30 . . . Tampa

JULY

1-2 . . . Tampa
3-4 . . . at St. Lucie
5-7 . . . at Charlotte
8-10 . . . at Fort Myers
11-13 . . . Charlotte
15-17 . . . Fort Myers
18-21 . . . at Clearwater
22-25 . . . at Dunedin
26-29 . . . Daytona
30-31 . . . at Brevard County

AUGUST

1-2 . . . at Brevard County
4-5 . . . at St. Lucie
6-7 . . . St. Lucie
8 . . . at Fort Myers
9-10 . . . Fort Myers
11-13 . . . at Jupiter
14-15 . . . at Fort Myers
16 . . . Fort Myers
17-19 . . . Jupiter
20-23 . . . St. Lucie
25-27 . . . at Palm Beach
28-30 . . . Charlotte

SEPTEMBER

1-3 . . . Palm Beach
4-6 . . . at Charlotte

TAMPA

APRIL

9 . . . at Lakeland
10 . . . Lakeland
11 . . . at Lakeland
13 . . . Lakeland
14-16 . . . at Brevard County
17-19 . . . Clearwater
21-23 . . . Brevard County
24-26 . . . Clearwater
27-29 . . . at Lakeland
30 . . . Lakeland

MAY

1-3 . . . Dunedin
4-6 . . . Daytona
7-9 . . . at Dunedin
11-13 . . . at Daytona
14-16 . . . Dunedin
17-19 . . . at Brevard County
20-21 . . . Lakeland
22-24 . . . Clearwater
26 . . . Fort Myers
27-29 . . . at Fort Myers
30-31 . . . Charlotte

JUNE

1-2 . . . Charlotte
3-6 . . . at Jupiter
7-10 . . . Sarasota
11-14 . . . at St. Lucie
15-18 . . . Palm Beach
22 . . . at Clearwater
23-24 . . . Clearwater
25-28 . . . St. Lucie
29-30 . . . at Sarasota

JULY

1-2 . . . at Sarasota
3 . . . Lakeland
4 . . . at Lakeland
5-7 . . . Brevard County
8-10 . . . Daytona
11-13 . . . at Dunedin
15-17 . . . at Daytona
18-21 . . . at Palm Beach
22-24 . . . Fort Myers
25 . . . at Fort Myers
26-29 . . . at Charlotte
30-31 . . . Jupiter

AUGUST

1-2 . . . Jupiter
4-5 . . . Lakeland
6-7 . . . at Lakeland
9-10 . . . at Clearwater
11-13 . . . at Daytona
14-16 . . . at Clearwater
17-19 . . . Daytona
20 . . . Lakeland
21 . . . at Lakeland
22 . . . Lakeland
23 . . . at Lakeland
25-27 . . . at Dunedin
28-30 . . . Brevard County

SEPTEMBER

1-3 . . . Dunedin
4-6 . . . at Brevard County

LOW CLASS A

MIDWEST LEAGUE

BELOIT

APRIL
- 9-11 at Cedar Rapids
- 13-15 at Quad Cities
- 16-19 Burlington
- 21-24 Quad Cities
- 25-28 at Kane County
- 29-30 Dayton

MAY
- 1 Dayton
- 2-4 Great Lakes
- 5-7 at West Michigan
- 8-10 at Lansing
- 12-15 at Clinton
- 16-19 Peoria
- 20-22 Fort Wayne
- 23-25 Wisconsin
- 26-28 at South Bend
- 29-31 Kane County

JUNE
- 2-5 at Peoria
- 6-9 at Wisconsin
- 10-13 at Burlington
- 14-17 Clinton
- 18-21 Quad Cities
- 25-28 at Clinton
- 30 Cedar Rapids

JULY
- 1-3 Cedar Rapids
- 4-7 at Peoria
- 8-10 South Bend
- 11-13 West Michigan
- 15-17 at Burlington
- 18-20 at Dayton
- 22-24 Cedar Rapids
- 25-27 Lansing
- 28-30 at Great Lakes
- 31 at Fort Wayne

AUGUST
- 1-2 at Fort Wayne
- 3-6 Peoria
- 7-10 at Cedar Rapids
- 11-14 Clinton
- 15-18 at Wisconsin
- 20-23 Kane County
- 24-27 at Kane County
- 28-31 Burlington

SEPTEMBER
- 2-4 at Quad Cities
- 5-7 Wisconsin

BURLINGTON

APRIL
- 9-11 Clinton
- 13-15 at Kane County
- 16-19 at Beloit
- 21-24 Kane County
- 25-28 at Clinton
- 29-30 Peoria

MAY
- 1 Peoria
- 2-4 West Michigan
- 5-7 at Wisconsin
- 8-10 at Great Lakes
- 12-15 at Kane County
- 16-19 Cedar Rapids
- 20-22 South Bend
- 23-25 Dayton
- 26-28 at Lansing
- 29-31 at Fort Wayne

JUNE
- 1-5 Quad Cities
- 6-9 at Cedar Rapids
- 10-13 Beloit
- 14-17 Wisconsin
- 18-21 at Peoria
- 25-28 Cedar Rapids
- 30 at Quad Cities

JULY
- 1-3 at Quad Cities
- 4-7 Wisconsin
- 8-10 at Kane County
- 11-13 Lansing
- 15-17 Beloit
- 18-20 at South Bend
- 22-24 Great Lakes
- 25-27 Fort Wayne
- 28-30 at West Michigan
- 31 at Dayton

AUGUST
- 1-2 at Dayton
- 3-6 at Clinton
- 7-10 Quad Cities
- 11-14 at Peoria
- 15-18 Kane County
- 20-23 at Quad Cities
- 24-27 Wisconsin
- 28-31 at Beloit

SEPTEMBER
- 2-4 Clinton
- 5-7 at Cedar Rapids

CEDAR RAPIDS

APRIL
- 9-11 Beloit
- 13-15 at Clinton
- 16-19 at Kane County
- 21-24 Clinton
- 25-28 at Peoria
- 29-30 West Michigan

MAY
- 1 West Michigan
- 2-4 Peoria
- 5-7 at South Bend
- 8-10 at Quad Cities
- 12-15 Wisconsin
- 16-19 at Burlington
- 20-22 Great Lakes
- 23-25 Lansing
- 26-28 at Fort Wayne
- 29-31 at Dayton

JUNE
- 2-5 at Wisconsin
- 6-9 Burlington
- 10-13 at Quad Cities
- 14-17 Kane County
- 18-21 Clinton
- 25-28 at Burlington
- 30 at Beloit

JULY
- 1-3 at Beloit
- 4-7 Quad Cities
- 8-10 Fort Wayne
- 11-13 Dayton
- 15-17 at Lansing
- 18-20 at Great Lakes
- 22-24 at Beloit
- 25-27 South Bend
- 28-30 Kane County
- 31 at West Michigan

AUGUST
- 1-2 at West Michigan
- 3-6 at Quad Cities
- 7-10 Beloit
- 11-14 Wisconsin
- 15-18 at Clinton
- 20-23 at Wisconsin
- 24-27 Clinton
- 28-31 Peoria

SEPTEMBER
- 2-4 at Wisconsin
- 5-7 Burlington

CLINTON

APRIL
- 9-11 at Burlington
- 13-15 Cedar Rapids
- 16-19 Wisconsin
- 21-24 at Cedar Rapids
- 25-28 Burlington
- 29-30 Fort Wayne

MAY
- 1 Fort Wayne
- 2-4 Quad Cities
- 5-7 at Dayton
- 8-10 at West Michigan
- 12-15 Beloit
- 16-19 at Wisconsin
- 20-22 Lansing
- 23-25 Great Lakes
- 26-28 at Peoria 6:30
- 29-31 at South Bend

JUNE
- 2-5 Kane County
- 6-9 at Quad Cities
- 10-13 Peoria
- 14-17 at Beloit
- 18-21 at Cedar Rapids
- 25-28 Beloit
- 30 at Wisconsin

JULY
- 1-3 at Wisconsin
- 4-7 Kane County
- 8-10 Dayton
- 11-13 at Quad Cities
- 15-17 at Fort Wayne
- 18-20 Peoria
- 22-24 South Bend
- 25-27 West Michigan
- 28-30 at Lansing
- 31 at Great Lakes

AUGUST
- 1-2 at Great Lakes
- 3-6 Burlington
- 7-10 at Kane County
- 11-14 at Beloit
- 15-18 Cedar Rapids
- 20-23 at Peoria
- 24-27 at Cedar Rapids
- 28-31 Quad Cities

SEPTEMBER
- 2-4 at Burlington
- 5-7 Peoria

DAYTON

APRIL
- 9-11 Great Lakes
- 13-15 at Peoria
- 16-19 at Fort Wayne
- 21-24 Great Lakes
- 25-28 at South Bend
- 29-30 at Beloit

MAY
- 1 at Beloit
- 2-4 at Fort Wayne
- 5-7 Clinton
- 8-10 Kane County
- 12-15 West Michigan
- 16-19 at Lansing
- 20-22 at Quad Cities
- 23-25 at Burlington
- 26-28 Wisconsin
- 29-31 Cedar Rapids

JUNE
- 2-5 South Bend
- 6-9 at Great Lakes
- 10-13 at Fort Wayne
- 14-17 Lansing
- 18-21 West Michigan
- 25-28 at Lansing
- 30 Fort Wayne

JULY
- 1-3 Fort Wayne
- 4-7 at West Michigan
- 8-10 at Clinton
- 11-13 at Cedar Rapids
- 15-17 Quad Cities
- 18-20 Beloit
- 22-24 at Wisconsin
- 25-27 at Kane County
- 28-30 Peoria
- 31 Burlington

AUGUST
- 1-2 Burlington
- 3-6 Great Lakes
- 7-10 at Lansing
- 11-14 West Michigan
- 15-18 at Fort Wayne
- 20-23 West Michigan
- 24-27 at South Bend
- 28-31 Lansing

SEPTEMBER
- 2-4 South Bend
- 5-7 at Great Lakes

FORT WAYNE

APRIL
9-11 at Lansing
13-15 at Wisconsin
16-19 Dayton
21-24 West Michigan
25-28 at Great Lakes
29-30 at Clinton

MAY
1 at Clinton
2-4 Dayton
5-7 Kane County
8-10 Peoria
12-15 at Great Lakes
16-17 South Bend
18-19 at South Bend
20-22 at Beloit
23-25 at Quad Cities
26-28 Cedar Rapids
29-31 Burlington

JUNE
2-5 Lansing
6-7 South Bend
8-9 at South Bend
10-13 Dayton
14-17 at West Michigan
18-21 at South Bend
25-28 South Bend
30 at Dayton

JULY
1-3 at Dayton
4-7 Great Lakes
8-10 at Cedar Rapids
11-13 at Peoria
15-17 Clinton
18-20 Quad Cities
22-24 at Kane County
25-27 at Burlington
28-30 Wisconsin
31 Beloit

AUGUST
1-2 Beloit
3-6 Lansing
7-10 at South Bend
11-14 at Great Lakes
15-18 Dayton
20-23 Lansing
24-27 at Great Lakes
28-31 at West Michigan

SEPTEMBER
2-4 Great Lakes
5-7 at West Michigan

GREAT LAKES

APRIL
9-11 at Dayton
13-15 West Michigan
16-19 South Bend
21-24 at Dayton
25-28 Fort Wayne
29-30 at Wisconsin

MAY
1 at Wisconsin
2-4 at Beloit
5-7 Quad Cities
8-10 Burlington
12-15 Fort Wayne
16-19 at West Michigan
20-22 at Cedar Rapids
23-25 at Clinton
26-28 Kane County
29-31 Peoria

JUNE
2-5 at West Michigan
6-9 Dayton
10-13 at Lansing
14-17 at South Bend
18-21 Lansing
25-28 at West Michigan
30 Lansing

JULY
1-3 Lansing
4-7 at Fort Wayne
8-10 at Peoria
11-13 at Kane County
15-17 Wisconsin
18-20 Cedar Rapids
22-24 at Burlington
25-27 at Quad Cities
28-30 Beloit
31 Clinton

AUGUST
1-2 Clinton
3-6 at Dayton
7-10 West Michigan
11-14 Fort Wayne
15-18 at Lansing
20-23 at South Bend
24-27 Fort Wayne
28-31 South Bend

SEPTEMBER
2-4 at Fort Wayne
5-7 Dayton

KANE COUNTY

APRIL
9-11 at Peoria
13-15 Burlington
16-19 Cedar Rapids
21-24 at Burlington
25-28 Beloit
29-30 Lansing

MAY
1 Lansing
2-4 South Bend
5-7 at Fort Wayne
8-10 at Dayton
12-15 Burlington
16-19 at Quad Cities
20-22 Wisconsin
23-25 West Michigan
26-28 at Great Lakes
29-31 at Beloit

JUNE
2-5 at Clinton
6-9 Peoria
10-13 at Wisconsin
14-17 at Cedar Rapids
18-21 Wisconsin
25-28 at Quad Cities
30 Peoria

JULY
1-3 Peoria
4-7 at Clinton
8-10 Burlington
11-13 Great Lakes
15-17 at South Bend
18-20 at West Michigan
22-24 Fort Wayne
25-27 Dayton
28-30 at Cedar Rapids
31 at Lansing

AUGUST
1-2 at Lansing
3-6 at Wisconsin
7-10 Clinton
11-14 Quad Cities
15-18 at Burlington
20-23 at Beloit
24-27 Beloit
28-31 Wisconsin

SEPTEMBER
2-4 at Peoria
5-7 Quad Cities

LANSING

APRIL
9-11 Fort Wayne
13-15 at South Bend
17-20 West Michigan
21-24 South Bend
25-28 at West Michigan
29-30 at Kane County

MAY
1 at Kane County
2-4 at Wisconsin
5-7 Peoria
8-10 Beloit
12-15 at South Bend
16-19 Dayton
20-22 at Clinton
23-25 at Cedar Rapids
26-28 Burlington
29-31 Quad Cities

JUNE
2-5 at Fort Wayne
6-9 West Michigan
10-13 Great Lakes
14-17 at Dayton
18-21 at Great Lakes
25-28 Dayton
30 at Great Lakes

JULY
1-3 at Great Lakes
4-7 South Bend
8-10 at Quad Cities
11-13 at Burlington
15-17 Cedar Rapids
18-20 Wisconsin
22-24 at Peoria
25-27 at Beloit
28-30 Clinton
31 Kane County

AUGUST
1-2 Kane County
3-6 at Fort Wayne
7-10 Dayton
11-14 at South Bend
15-18 Great Lakes
20-23 at Fort Wayne
24-27 West Michigan
28-31 at Dayton

SEPTEMBER
1 at South Bend
2-4 West Michigan
6-7 at South Bend

PEORIA

APRIL
9-11 Kane County
13-15 Dayton
16-19 at Quad Cities
21-24 at Wisconsin
25-28 Cedar Rapids
29-30 at Burlington

MAY
1 at Burlington
2-4 at Cedar Rapids
5-7 at Lansing
8-10 at Fort Wayne
12-15 Quad Cities
16-19 at Beloit
20-22 West Michigan
23-25 South Bend
26-28 Clinton
29-31 at Great Lakes

JUNE
2-5 Beloit
6-9 at Kane County
10-13 at Clinton
14-17 Quad Cities
18-21 Burlington
25-28 at Wisconsin
30 at Kane County

JULY
1-3 at Kane County
4-7 Beloit
8-10 Great Lakes
11-13 Fort Wayne
15-17 at West Michigan
18-20 at Clinton
22-24 Lansing
25-27 Wisconsin
28-30 at Dayton
31 at South Bend

AUGUST
1-2 at South Bend
3-6 at Beloit
7-10 Wisconsin
11-14 Burlington
15-18 at Quad Cities
20-23 Clinton
24-27 Quad Cities
28-31 at Cedar Rapids

SEPTEMBER
2-4 Kane County
5-7 at Clinton

QUAD CITIES

APRIL
9-11 at Wisconsin
13-15 Beloit
16-19 Peoria
21-24 at Beloit
25-28 Wisconsin
29-30 South Bend

MAY
1 South Bend
2-4 at Clinton
5-7 at Great Lakes
8-10 Cedar Rapids
12-15 at Peoria
16-19 Kane County

20-22 . . . . Dayton
23-25 . . . . . . Fort Wayne
26-28 . . . at West Michigan
29-31 . . . . at Lansing

JUNE

1-2 . . . . at Burlington
4-5 . . . . at Burlington
6-9 . . . . Clinton
10-13 . . . . . Cedar Rapids
14-17 . . . . at Peoria
18-21 . . . . at Beloit
25-28 . . . . . Kane County
30 . . . . Burlington

JULY

1-3 . . . . Burlington
4-7 . . . . . at Cedar Rapids
8-10 . . . . Lansing
11-13 . . . . Clinton
15-17 . . . . at Dayton
18-20 . . . . . . at Fort Wayne
22-24 . . . . West Michigan
25-27 . . . . . . Great Lakes
28-30 . . . . . at South Bend
31 . . . . at Wisconsin

AUGUST

1-2 . . . . at Wisconsin
3-6 . . . . Cedar Rapids
7-10 . . . . at Burlington
11-14 . . . . at Kane County
15-18 . . . . Peoria
20-23 . . . . Burlington
24-27 . . . . at Peoria
28-31 . . . . at Clinton

SEPTEMBER

2-4 . . . . Beloit
5-7 . . . . . at Kane County

SOUTH BEND

APRIL

9-11 . . . . at West Michigan
13-15 . . . . Lansing
16-19 . . . . . at Great Lakes
21-24 . . . . at Lansing
25-28 . . . . Dayton
29-30 . . . . . at Quad Cities

MAY

1 . . . . at Quad Cities
2-4 . . . . . at Kane County
5-7 . . . . Cedar Rapids
8-10 . . . . Wisconsin
12-15 . . . . Lansing
16-17 . . . . . . at Fort Wayne
18-19 . . . . . . Fort Wayne
20-22 . . . . . . at Burlington
23-25 . . . . at Peoria
26-28 . . . . Beloit
29-31 . . . . Clinton

JUNE

2-5 . . . . at Dayton
6-7 . . . . at Fort Wayne
8-9 . . . . Fort Wayne
10-13 . . . at West Michigan
14-17 . . . . . . Great Lakes
18-21 . . . . . . Fort Wayne
25-28 . . . . . at Fort Wayne
30 . . . . . . West Michigan

JULY

1-3 . . . . . . West Michigan
4-7 . . . . at Lansing
8-10 . . . . at Beloit
11-13 . . . . . . at Wisconsin
15-17 . . . . . Kane County
18-20 . . . . Burlington
22-24 . . . . at Clinton
25-27 . . . . at Cedar Rapids
28-30 . . . . . . Quad Cities
31 . . . . Peoria

AUGUST

1-2 . . . . Peoria
3-6 . . . . at West Michigan
7-10 . . . . Fort Wayne
11-14 . . . . Lansing
15-18 . . . at West Michigan
20-23 . . . . . . Great Lakes
24-27 . . . . Dayton
28-31 . . . . . at Great Lakes

SEPTEMBER

1 . . . . Lansing
2-4 . . . . at Dayton
6-7 . . . . Lansing

WEST MICHIGAN

APRIL

9-11 . . . . South Bend
13-15 . . . . . at Great Lakes
17-20 . . . . at Lansing
21-24 . . . . . . at Fort Wayne
25-28 . . . . Lansing
29-30 . . . . at Cedar Rapids

MAY

1 . . . . at Cedar Rapids
2-4 . . . . at Burlington
5-7 . . . . Beloit
8-10 . . . . Clinton
12-15 . . . . at Dayton
16-19 . . . . . . Great Lakes
20-22 . . . . at Peoria
23-25 . . . . at Kane County
26-28 . . . . . . Quad Cities
29-31 . . . . Wisconsin

JUNE

2-5 . . . . Great Lakes
6-9 . . . . at Lansing
10-13 . . . . . . South Bend
14-17 . . . . . . Fort Wayne
18-21 . . . . at Dayton
25-28 . . . . . . Great Lakes
30 . . . . at South Bend

JULY

1-3 . . . . . . at South Bend
4-7 . . . . Dayton
8-10 . . . . at Wisconsin
11-13 . . . . at Beloit
15-17 . . . . Peoria
18-20 . . . . . Kane County
22-24 . . . . . at Quad Cities
25-27 . . . . at Clinton
28-30 . . . . Burlington
31 . . . . Cedar Rapids

AUGUST

1-2 . . . . Cedar Rapids
3-6 . . . . South Bend
7-10 . . . . . . at Great Lakes
11-14 . . . . at Dayton
15-18 . . . . . . South Bend
20-23 . . . . at Dayton
24-27 . . . . at Lansing
28-31 . . . . . . Fort Wayne

SEPTEMBER

2-4 . . . . at Lansing
5-7 . . . . Fort Wayne

WISCONSIN

APRIL

9-11 . . . . Quad Cities
13-15 . . . . . . Fort Wayne
16-19 . . . . at Clinton
21-24 . . . . Peoria
25-28 . . . . . at Quad Cities
29-30 . . . . . . Great Lakes

MAY

1 . . . . Great Lakes
2-4 . . . . Lansing
5-7 . . . . Burlington
8-10 . . . . . . at South Bend
12-15 . . . . at Cedar Rapids
16-19 . . . . Clinton
20-22 . . . . at Kane County
23-25 . . . . at Beloit
26-28 . . . . at Dayton
29-31 . . . at West Michigan

JUNE

2-5 . . . . Cedar Rapids
6-9 . . . . Beloit
10-13 . . . . . Kane County
14-17 . . . . . . at Burlington
18-21 . . . . at Kane County
25-28 . . . . Peoria
30 . . . . Clinton

JULY

1-3 . . . . Clinton
4-7 . . . . at Burlington
8-10 . . . . . West Michigan
11-13 . . . . . . South Bend
15-17 . . . . . at Great Lakes
18-20 . . . . at Lansing
22-24 . . . . Dayton
25-27 . . . . at Peoria
28-30 . . . . . . at Fort Wayne
31 . . . . Quad Cities

AUGUST

1-2 . . . . Quad Cities
3-6 . . . . Kane County
7-10 . . . . at Peoria
11-14 . . . . at Cedar Rapids
15-18 . . . . Beloit
20-23 . . . . . Cedar Rapids
24-27 . . . . . . at Burlington
28-31 . . . . at Kane County

SEPTEMBER

2-4 . . . . Cedar Rapids
5-7 . . . . at Beloit

SOUTH ATLANTIC LEAGUE

ASHEVILLE

APRIL

9-12 . . . . at Kannapolis
13-16 . . . . Greensboro
17-20 . . . . Hickory
21-24 . . . . . at Greensboro
25-26 . . . . Greenville
28-30 . . . . Charleston

MAY

1 . . . . Charleston
2-5 . . . . at Savannah
6-9 . . . . at Charleston
11-14 . . . . Rome
15-18 . . . . Augusta
20-23 . . . . at Rome
24-27 . . . . at Augusta
28-31 . . . . Savannah

JUNE

2-4 . . . . at Greenville
5-7 . . . . . . Bowling Green
8-10 . . . . at Lexington
11-12 . . . . . . at Greenville
13-15 . . . . Lexington
16-18 . . . . Greenville
19-21 . . . at Bowling Green
25-28 . . . . Greenville
30 . . . . at Savannah

JULY

1-3 . . . . at Savannah
4-7 . . . . Charleston
8-11 . . . . Augusta
13-16 . . . . . at Lake County
17-20 . . . . . at Hagerstown
22-25 . . . . Lakewood
26-29 . . . . Delmarva
30-31 . . . . at Rome

AUGUST

1-2 . . . . at Rome
4-7 . . . . Bowling Green
8-11 . . . . at Lexington
13-16 . . . . Kannapolis
17-20 . . . . at West Virginia
21-24 . . . . at Hickory
25-28 . . . . Greensboro
29-31 . . . at Bowling Green

SEPTEMBER

1-3 . . . . Lexington
4-7 . . . . at Greenville

AUGUSTA

APRIL

9-12 . . . . at Savannah
14-15 . . . . . . at Charleston
16-19 . . . . Savannah
20-21 . . . . Rome
22-24 . . . . Charleston
25-27 . . . . at Rome
28-30 . . . at Bowling Green

MAY

1 . . . . . . at Bowling Green
2-5 . . . . Lexington

6-9 Bowling Green
11-14 at Greenville
15-18 at Asheville
20-23 Greenville
24-27 Asheville
29-31 at Lexington

JUNE

1 at Lexington
2-5 at Rome
6-8 Savannah
9-11 at Charleston
12-14 at Savannah
15-17 Charleston
18-26 Rome
27-29 at Rome
30 Lexington

JULY

1-3 Lexington
4-7 at Bowling Green
8-11 at Asheville
13-16 West Virginia
17-20 Greensboro
22-25 at Kannapolis
26-29 at Hickory
30-31 Greenville

AUGUST

1-2 Greenville
4-8 Charleston
10-13 at Lake County
14-17 at Hagerstown
19-21 Savannah
22-24 Charleston
25-27 at Savannah
28-30 at Charleston
31 Savannah

SEPTEMBER

1-2 Savannah
3-4 at Rome
5-7 Rome

BOWLING GREEN

APRIL

9-12 at Hickory
13-16 at West Virginia
17-20 Kannapolis
21-24 West Virginia
25-26 at Lexington
28-30 Augusta

MAY

1 Augusta
2-5 at Rome
6-9 at Augusta
11-14 Savannah
15-18 Charleston
20-23 at Savannah
24-27 at Charleston
29-31 Rome

JUNE

1 Rome
2-4 Lexington
5-7 at Asheville
8-10 Greenville
11-12 Lexington
13-15 at Greenville
16-18 at Lexington
19-21 Asheville
25-28 at Lexington
30 at Rome

JULY

1-3 at Rome
4-7 Augusta
8-11 Charleston
13-16 at Lakewood
17-20 at Delmarva
22-25 Hagerstown
26-29 Lake County
31 at Savannah

AUGUST

1-3 at Savannah
4-7 at Asheville
8-11 Greenville
13-16 Hickory
17-20 at Greensboro
21-24 at Kannapolis
25-28 West Virginia
29-31 Asheville

SEPTEMBER

1-3 at Greenville
4-7 Lexington

CHARLESTON

APRIL

9-12 Rome
14-15 Augusta
16-19 at Rome
20-21 at Savannah
22-24 at Augusta
25-27 Savannah
28-30 at Asheville

MAY

1 at Asheville
2-5 Greenville
6-9 Asheville
11-14 at Lexington
15-18 at Bowling Green
20-23 Lexington
24-27 Bowling Green
28-31 at Greenville

JUNE

2-5 at Savannah
6-8 Rome
9-11 Augusta
12-14 at Rome
15-17 at Augusta
18-21 Savannah
25-29 at Savannah
30 Greenville

JULY

1-3 Greenville
4-7 at Asheville
8-11 at Bowling Green
13-16 Hickory
17-20 Kannapolis
22-25 at Greensboro
26-29 at West Virginia
31 Lexington

AUGUST

1-3 Lexington
4-8 at Augusta
10-13 Delmarva
14-17 Lakewood
19-21 at Rome
22-24 at Augusta
25-27 Rome
28-30 Augusta
31 at Rome

SEPTEMBER

1-2 at Rome
3-7 Savannah

DELMARVA

APRIL

9-12 at Lakewood
13-15 at Hagerstown
16-19 Lake County
20-22 Hagerstown
23-25 at Lake County
27-29 Lakewood
30 at Greensboro

MAY

1-3 at Greensboro
5-8 West Virginia
9-12 Greensboro
14-17 at West Virginia
18-21 at Hickory
22-25 Kannapolis
26-29 Hickory
30-31 at Kannapolis

JUNE

1-2 at Kannapolis
3-6 Lakewood
8-11 at Lake County
12-14 at Hagerstown
15-16 at Lakewood
17-18 Lake County
19-21 Hagerstown
25-29 at Lakewood
30 Hickory

JULY

1-3 Hickory
4-7 at Kannapolis
8-11 at West Virginia
13-16 Lexington
17-20 Bowling Green
22-25 at Greenville
26-29 at Asheville
31 Greensboro

AUGUST

1-3 Greensboro
4-8 Hagerstown
10-13 at Charleston
14-17 at Savannah
19-21 Lake County
22-24 Hagerstown
25-27 at Lake County
28-30 at Hagerstown
31 Lake County

SEPTEMBER

1-2 Lake County
3-7 Lakewood

GREENSBORO

APRIL

9-12 Greenville
13-16 at Asheville
17-20 at Greenville
21-24 Asheville
25-26 at West Virginia
28-29 West Virginia
30 Delmarva

MAY

1-3 Delmarva
5-8 at Hagerstown
9-12 at Delmarva
14-17 Hagerstown
18-21 Lake County
22-25 at Lakewood
26-29 at Lake County
30-31 Lakewood

JUNE

1-2 Lakewood
4-5 Hickory
6-8 at Hickory
9-10 at West Virginia
11-12 Kannapolis
13-14 at Kannapolis
15-17 Hickory
18-19 at Kannapolis
20-21 Kannapolis
25-28 West Virginia
30 at Lakewood

JULY

1-3 at Lakewood
4-7 Lake County
8-11 Hagerstown
13-16 at Rome
17-20 at Augusta
22-25 Charleston
26-29 Savannah
31 at Delmarva

AUGUST

1-3 at Delmarva
4-7 Hickory
8-11 at Kannapolis
13-16 at Greenville
17-20 Bowling Green
21-24 Lexington
25-28 at Asheville
29-31 Kannapolis

SEPTEMBER

1-3 at Hickory
4-7 at West Virginia

GREENVILLE

APRIL

9-12 at Greensboro
13-16 Hickory
17-20 Greensboro
21-24 at Kannapolis
25-26 at Asheville
28-30 Savannah

MAY

1 Savannah
2-5 at Charleston
6-9 at Savannah
11-14 Augusta
15-18 Rome
20-23 at Augusta
24-27 at Rome
28-31 Charleston

JUNE

2-4 Asheville
5-7 at Lexington
8-10 at Bowling Green
11-12 Asheville
13-15 Bowling Green
16-18 at Asheville
19-21 Lexington
25-28 at Asheville
30 at Charleston

JULY

1-3 at Charleston
4-7 Savannah
8-11 Rome
13-16 at Hagerstown
17-20 at Lake County
22-25 Delmarva

26-29 .... Lakewood
30-31 .... at Augusta

AUGUST

1-2 .... at Augusta
4-7 .... Lexington
8-11 .... at Bowling Green
13-16 ...... Greensboro
17-20 .... at Hickory
21-24 .... at West Virginia
25-28 ...... Kannapolis
29-31 ...... at Lexington

SEPTEMBER

1-3 ...... Bowling Green
4-7 .... Asheville

HAGERSTOWN

APRIL

9-12 ...... at Lake County
13-15 .... Delmarva
16-19 .... Lakewood
20-22 .... at Delmarva
23-25 ...... at Lakewood
27-29 ..... Lake County
30 ...... at West Virginia

MAY

1-3 ..... at West Virginia
5-8 .... Greensboro
9-12 ...... West Virginia
14-17 ..... at Greensboro
18-21 ...... at Kannapolis
22-25 .... Hickory
26-29 ...... Kannapolis
30-31 .... at Hickory

JUNE

1-2 .... at Hickory
3-6 .... Lake County
8-11 .... at Lakewood
12-14 .... Delmarva
15-16 .... at Lake County
17-18 .... Lakewood
19-21 .... at Delmarva
25-29 .... at Lake County
30 .... Kannapolis

JULY

1-3 .... Kannapolis
4-7 .... at Hickory
8-11 ...... at Greensboro
13-16 .... Greenville
17-20 .... Asheville
22-25 ... at Bowling Green
26-29 ...... at Lexington
30-31 ..... West Virginia

AUGUST

1-2 .... West Virginia
4-8 .... at Delmarva
10-13 .... Rome
14-17 .... Augusta
19-21 ...... at Lakewood
22-24 .... at Delmarva
25-27 .... Lakewood
28-30 .... Delmarva
31 .... at Lakewood

SEPTEMBER

1-2 .... at Lakewood
3-7 .... Lake County

HICKORY

APRIL

9-12 ..... Bowling Green
13-16 ...... at Greenville
17-20 .... at Asheville
21-24 .... Lexington
25-26 ...... Kannapolis
28-29 ...... at Kannapolis
30 .... Lakewood

MAY

1-3 .... Lakewood
5-8 ...... at Lake County
9-12 .... at Lakewood
14-17 ..... Lake County
18-21 .... Delmarva
22-25 ..... at Hagerstown
26-29 .... at Delmarva
30-31 ...... Hagerstown

JUNE

1-2 .... Hagerstown
4-5 ...... at Greensboro
6-8 .... Greensboro
9-10 .... Kannapolis
11-14 .... at West Virginia
15-17 ..... at Greensboro
18-21 ..... West Virginia
25-28 ...... Kannapolis
30 .... at Delmarva

JULY

1-3 .... at Delmarva
4-7 .... Hagerstown
8-11 ...... Lake County
13-16 ...... at Charleston
17-20 .... at Savannah
22-25 .... Rome
26-29 .... Augusta
31 .... at Lakewood

AUGUST

1-3 .... at Lakewood
4-7 ...... at Greensboro
8-11 ...... West Virginia
13-16 ... at Bowling Green
17-20 .... Greenville
21-24 .... Asheville
25-28 ...... at Lexington
29-31 .... at West Virginia

SEPTEMBER

1-3 .... Greensboro
4-7 .... at Kannapolis

KANNAPOLIS

APRIL

9-12 .... Asheville
13-16 ...... at Lexington
17-20 ... at Bowling Green
21-24 .... Greenville
25-26 .... at Hickory
28-29 .... Hickory
30 .... Lake County

MAY

1-3 .... Lake County
5-8 .... at Lakewood
9-12 ...... at Lake County
14-17 .... Lakewood
18-21 ...... Hagerstown
22-25 .... at Delmarva
26-29 ..... at Hagerstown
30-31 .... Delmarva

JUNE

1-2 .... Delmarva
3-7 .... West Virginia
9-10 .... at Hickory
11-12 ..... at Greensboro
13-14 ...... Greensboro
15-17 .... at West Virginia
18-19 ..... Greensboro
20-21 ..... at Greensboro
25-28 .... at Hickory
30 .... at Hagerstown

JULY

1-3 ...... at Hagerstown
4-7 .... Delmarva
8-11 .... Lakewood
13-16 .... at Savannah
17-20 ...... at Charleston
22-25 .... Augusta
26-29 .... Rome
31 .... at Lake County

AUGUST

1-3 ...... at Lake County
4-7 ..... at West Virginia
8-11 .... Greensboro
13-16 .... at Asheville
17-20 .... Lexington
21-24 .... Bowling Green
25-28 ...... at Greenville
29-31 ..... at Greensboro

SEPTEMBER

1-3 .... West Virginia
4-7 .... Hickory

LAKE COUNTY

APRIL

9-12 .... Hagerstown
13-15 .... Lakewood
16-19 .... at Delmarva
20-22 ...... at Lakewood
23-25 .... Delmarva
27-29 ..... at Hagerstown
30 .... at Kannapolis

MAY

1-3 .... at Kannapolis
5-8 .... Hickory
9-12 .... Kannapolis
14-17 .... at Hickory
18-21 ..... at Greensboro
22-25 ..... West Virginia
26-29 ..... Greensboro
30-31 .... at West Virginia

JUNE

1-2 ..... at West Virginia
3-6 ...... at Hagerstown
8-11 .... Delmarva
12-14 .... Lakewood
15-16 ..... Hagerstown
17-18 ...... at Delmarva
19-21 ...... at Lakewood
25-29 ..... Hagerstown
30 .... West Virginia

JULY

1-3 .... West Virginia
4-7 ...... at Greensboro
8-11 .... at Hickory
13-16 .... Asheville
17-20 .... Greenville
22-25 ...... at Lexington
26-29 ... at Bowling Green
31 .... Kannapolis

AUGUST

1-3 .... Kannapolis
4-8 .... at Lakewood
10-13 .... Augusta
14-17 .... Rome
19-21 ...... at Delmarva
22-24 ...... at Lakewood
25-27 .... Delmarva
28-30 .... Lakewood
31 .... at Delmarva

SEPTEMBER

1-2 .... at Delmarva
3-7 ...... at Hagerstown

LAKEWOOD

APRIL

9-12 .... Delmarva
13-15 ..... at Lake County
16-19 ..... at Hagerstown
20-22 ..... Lake County
23-25 ..... Hagerstown
27-29 ...... at Delmarva
30 .... at Hickory

MAY

1-3 .... at Hickory
5-8 .... Kannapolis
9-12 .... Hickory
14-17 ..... at Kannapolis
18-21 .... at West Virginia
22-25 ...... Greensboro
26-29 ..... West Virginia
30-31 ..... at Greensboro

JUNE

1-2 ...... at Greensboro
3-6 .... at Delmarva
8-11 .... Hagerstown
12-14 ..... at Lake County
15-16 .... Delmarva
17-18 ..... at Hagerstown
19-21 ..... Lake County
25-29 .... Delmarva
30 .... Greensboro

JULY

1-3 .... Greensboro
4-7 ..... at West Virginia
8-11 .... at Kannapolis
13-16 .... Bowling Green
17-20 .... Lexington
22-25 .... at Asheville
26-29 ...... at Greenville
31 .... Hickory

AUGUST

1-3 .... Hickory
4-8 .... Lake County
10-13 .... at Savannah
14-17 ...... at Charleston
19-21 ..... Hagerstown
22-24 ..... Lake County
25-27 ..... at Hagerstown
28-30 ..... at Lake County
31 .... Hagerstown

SEPTEMBER

1-2 .... Hagerstown
3-7 .... at Delmarva

LEXINGTON

APRIL
9-12 . . . . . at West Virginia
13-16 . . . . . . Kannapolis
17-20 . . . . . West Virginia
21-24 . . . . at Hickory
25-26 . . . . Bowling Green
28-30 . . . . Rome

MAY
1 . . . . Rome
2-5 . . . . at Augusta
6-9 . . . . at Rome
11-14 . . . . Charleston
15-18 . . . . Savannah
20-23 . . . . . . at Charleston
24-27 . . . . at Savannah
29-31 . . . . Augusta

JUNE
1 . . . . Augusta
2-4 . . . . at Bowling Green
5-7 . . . . Greenville
8-10 . . . . Asheville
11-12 . . . at Bowling Green
13-15 . . . . at Asheville
16-18 . . . . Bowling Green
19-21 . . . . at Greenville
25-28 . . . . Bowling Green
30 . . . . at Augusta

JULY
1-3 . . . . at Augusta
4-7 . . . . Rome
8-11 . . . . Savannah
13-16 . . . . at Delmarva
17-20 . . . . at Lakewood
22-25 . . . . . . Lake County
26-29 . . . . . . Hagerstown
31 . . . . at Charleston

AUGUST
1-3 . . . . at Charleston
4-7 . . . . at Greenville
8-11 . . . . Asheville
12-15 . . . . . West Virginia
17-20 . . . . . . at Kannapolis
21-24 . . . . . at Greensboro
25-28 . . . . Hickory
29-31 . . . . Greenville

SEPTEMBER
1-3 . . . . at Asheville
4-7 . . . . at Bowling Green

SAVANNAH

APRIL
9-12 . . . . Augusta
14-15 . . . . at Rome
16-19 . . . . at Augusta
20-21 . . . . Charleston
22-24 . . . . Rome
25-27 . . . . . . at Charleston
28-30 . . . . . . at Greenville

MAY
1 . . . . at Greenville
2-5 . . . . Asheville
6-9 . . . . Greenville
11-14 . . . at Bowling Green
15-18 . . . . . . at Lexington
20-23 . . . . . Bowling Green
24-27 . . . . Lexington
28-31 . . . . at Asheville

JUNE
2-5 . . . . Charleston
6-8 . . . . at Augusta
9-11 . . . . Rome
12-14 . . . . Augusta
15-17 . . . . at Rome
18-21 . . . . at Charleston
25-29 . . . . Charleston
30 . . . . Asheville

JULY
1-3 . . . . Asheville
4-7 . . . . at Greenville
8-11 . . . . at Lexington
13-16 . . . . Kannapolis
17-20 . . . . Hickory
22-25 . . . . at West Virginia
26-29 . . . . . at Greensboro
31 . . . . Bowling Green

AUGUST
1-3 . . . . . . Bowling Green
4-8 . . . . at Rome
10-13 . . . . Lakewood
14-17 . . . . Delmarva
19-21 . . . . at Augusta
22-24 . . . . at Rome
25-27 . . . . Augusta
28-30 . . . . Rome
31 at . . . . Augusta

SEPTEMBER
1-2 at . . . . Augusta
3-7 at . . . . Charleston

ROME

APRIL
9-12 . . . . at Charleston
14-15 . . . . Savannah
16-19 . . . . Charleston
20-21 . . . . at Augusta
22-24 . . . . at Savannah
25-27 . . . . Augusta
28-30 . . . . . . at Lexington

MAY
1 at . . . . Lexington
2-5 . . . . . . Bowling Green
6-9 . . . . Lexington
11-14 . . . . at Asheville
15-18 . . . . . . at Greenville
20-23 . . . . Asheville
24-27 . . . . Greenville
29-31 . . . at Bowling Green

JUNE
1 . . . . . . at Bowling Green
2-5 . . . . Augusta
6-8 . . . . at Charleston
9-11 . . . . at Savannah
12-14 . . . . Charleston
15-17 . . . . Savannah
18-26 . . . . at Augusta
27-29 . . . . Augusta
30 . . . . . . Bowling Green

JULY
1-3 . . . . . . Bowling Green
4-7 . . . . at Lexington
8-11 . . . . at Greenville
13-16 . . . . Greensboro
17-20 . . . . West Virginia
22-25 . . . . at Hickory
26-29 . . . . . . at Kannapolis
30-31 . . . . Asheville

AUGUST
1-2 . . . . Asheville
4-8 . . . . Savannah
10-13 . . . . . . at Hagerstown
14-17 . . . . . at Lake County
19-21 . . . . Charleston
22-24 . . . . Savannah
25-27 . . . . at Charleston
28-30 . . . . at Savannah
31 . . . . Charleston

SEPTEMBER
1-2 . . . . Charleston
3-4 . . . . Augusta
5-7 . . . . at Augusta

WEST VIRGINIA

APRIL
9-11 . . . . Lexington
13-16 . . . . . Bowling Green
17-20 . . . . at Lexington
21-24 . . . at Bowling Green
25-26 . . . . Greensboro
28-29 . . . . . . at Greensboro
30 . . . . Hagerstown

MAY
1-3 . . . . Hagerstown
5-8 . . . . at Delmarva
9-12 . . . . . . at Hagerstown
14-17 . . . . Delmarva
18-21 . . . . Lakewood
22-25 . . . . . at Lake County
26-29 . . . . at Lakewood
30-31 . . . . Lake County

JUNE
1-2 . . . . Lake County
3-7 . . . . at Kannapolis
9-10 . . . . Greensboro
11-14 . . . . Hickory
15-17 . . . . Kannapolis
18-21 . . . . at Hickory
25-28 . . . . . at Greensboro
30 . . . . at Lake County

JULY
1-3 . . . . . . at Lake County
4-7 . . . . Lakewood
8-11 . . . . Delmarva
13-16 . . . . at Augusta
17-20 . . . . at Rome
22-25 . . . . Savannah
26-29 . . . . Charleston
30-31 . . . . . . at Hagerstown

AUGUST
1-2 . . . . . . at Hagerstown
4-7 . . . . Kannapolis
8-11 . . . . at Hickory
12-15 . . . . . . at Lexington
17-20 . . . . Asheville
21-24 . . . . Greenville
25-28 . . . at Bowling Green
29-31 . . . . Hickory

SEPTEMBER
1-3 . . . . at Kannapolis
4-7 . . . . Greensboro

SHORT SEASON

NEW YORK-PENN LEAGUE

ABERDEEN

JUNE
19-21 . . . . at Hudson Valley
22-24 . . . . . . Staten Island
25-27 . . . . Brooklyn
28-30 . . . . at Staten Island

JULY
1-3. . . . . Oneonta
4-6. . . . . at Oneonta
7-9. . . . . at Brooklyn
10 . . . . . . at Hudson Valley
11-12 . . . . . Hudson Valley
14-16 . . . . at Lowell
17-19 . . . . Vermont
20-22 . . . Mahoning Valley
23 . . . . Hudson Valley
24-26 . . . at Hudson Valley
27-28 . . . . at Brooklyn
29-31 . . . . . Hudson Valley

AUGUST
1 . . . . Hudson Valley
2-3. . . . . Staten Island
4-6. . . . . . at State College
7-9. . . . . at Auburn
11-13 . . . . . . Williamsport
14-16 . . . . . . at Jamestown
19-21 . . . . Batavia
22-23 . . . . Brooklyn
24-26 . . . . Lowell
27-29 . . . . at Vermont
30-31 . . . . at Tri-City

SEPTEMBER
1 . . . . at Tri-City
2-3. . . . . . at Staten Island
4-6. . . . . Tri-City

AUBURN

JUNE
19	at Batavia
20	Batavia
21	at Batavia
22-24	at Jamestown
25-27	State College
28-30	Jamestown

JULY
1-3	at State College
4	at Batavia
5-6	Batavia
7-9	at Mahoning Valley
10-12	at Williamsport
14-16	Oneonta
17-19	at Brooklyn
20-22	at Tri-City
23-24	Williamsport
25-26	at Jamestown
27-28	State College
29-30	Mahoning Valley
31	at State College

AUGUST
1	at State College
2-3	at Mahoning Valley
4-6	Vermont
7-9	Aberdeen
11-13	at Staten Island
14-16	Hudson Valley
19-21	at Lowell
22-24	Mahoning Valley
25-27	Williamsport
28	at Batavia
29	Batavia
30	at Batavia
31	Jamestown

SEPTEMBER
1	Jamestown
2	Batavia
3	at Batavia
4	Batavia
5-6	at Williamsport

BATAVIA

JUNE
19	Auburn
20	at Auburn
21	Auburn
22-24	Williamsport
25	at Jamestown
26	Jamestown
27	at Jamestown
28-30	at Williamsport

JULY
1	Jamestown
2	at Jamestown
3	Jamestown
4	Auburn
5-6	at Auburn
7-9	at State College
10-12	Mahoning Valley
14-16	at Hudson Valley
17-19	Tri-City
20-22	at Oneonta
23	at Jamestown
24	Jamestown
25-26	at State College
27-28	Mahoning Valley
29-30	at Williamsport
31	at Mahoning Valley

AUGUST
1	at Mahoning Valley
2-3	Williamsport
4-6	Brooklyn
7-9	at Lowell
11-13	Vermont
14-16	Staten Island
19-21	at Aberdeen
22-24	State College
25-27	at Mahoning Valley
28	Auburn
29	at Auburn
30	Auburn
31	State College

SEPTEMBER
1	State College
2	at Auburn
3	Auburn
4	at Auburn
5	Jamestown
6	at Jamestown

BROOKLYN

JUNE
19	Staten Island
20	at Staten Island
21	Staten Island\
22	at Hudson Valley
23	Hudson Valley
24	at Hudson Valley
25-27	at Aberdeen
28	Hudson Valley
29	at Hudson Valley
30	Hudson Valley

JULY
1-3	Tri-City
4-6	at Tri-City
7-9	Aberdeen
10	at Staten Island
11	Staten Island
12	at Staten Island
14-16	Williamsport
17-19	Auburn
20-22	at Vermont
23	Staten Island
24	at Staten Island
25	Staten Island
26	at Staten Island
27-28	Aberdeen
29-30	Staten Island
31	at Staten Island

AUGUST
1	at Staten Island
2	at Hudson Valley
3	Hudson Valley
4-6	at Batavia
7-9	Jamestown
11-13	at Mahoning Valley
14-16	Oneonta
19-21	at State College
22-23	at Aberdeen
24-26	Vermont
27-29	at Oneonta
30-31	at Lowell

SEPTEMBER
1	at Lowell
2	Hudson Valley
3	at Hudson Valley
4-6	Lowell

HUDSON VALLEY

JUNE
19-21	Aberdeen
22	Brooklyn
23	at Brooklyn
24	Brooklyn
25-27	at Staten Island
28	at Brooklyn
29	Brooklyn
30	at Brooklyn

JULY
1-3	Vermont
4-6	at Vermont
7-8	Staten Island
9	at Staten Island
10	Aberdeen
11-12	at Aberdeen
14-16	Batavia
17-19	at Jamestown
20-22	at Williamsport
23	at Aberdeen
24-26	Aberdeen
27	Staten Island
28	at Staten Island
29-31	at Aberdeen

AUGUST
1	at Aberdeen
2	Brooklyn
3	at Brooklyn
4-6	Lowell
7-9	State College
11-13	at Tri-City
14-16	at Auburn
19-21	Mahoning Valley
22-23	Staten Island
24-26	Tri-City
27-29	at Lowell
30-31	at Oneonta

SEPTEMBER
1	at Oneonta
2	at Brooklyn
3	Brooklyn
4-6	Oneonta

JAMESTOWN

JUNE
19-21	at Mahoning Valley
22-24	Auburn
25	Batavia
26	at Batavia
27	Batavia
28-30	at Auburn

JULY
1	at Batavia
2	Batavia
3	at Batavia
4-6	Mahoning Valley
7-9	Williamsport
10-12	at State College
14-16	Vermont
17-19	Hudson Valley
20-22	at Staten Island
23	Batavia
24	at Batavia
25-26	Auburn
27-28	at Williamsport
29-30	State College
31	Williamsport

AUGUST
1	Williamsport
2-3	at State College
4-6	at Oneonta
7-9	at Brooklyn
11-13	Lowell
14-16	Aberdeen
19-21	at Vermont
22-24	at Williamsport
25-27	State College
28-30	Mahoning Valley
31	at Auburn

SEPTEMBER
1	at Auburn
2-4	Mahoning Valley
5	at Batavia
6	Batavia

LOWELL

JUNE
19-21	Vermont
22-24	Oneonta
25-27	at Tri-City
28-30	at Oneonta

JULY
1-3	Staten Island
4-6	at Staten Island
7-9	Tri-City
10-12	at Vermont
14-16	Aberdeen
17-19	Williamsport
20-22	at State College
23-24	Vermont
25-26	at Vermont
27-28	at Tri-City
29-30	Tri-City
31	at Vermont

AUGUST
1	at Vermont
2-3	Vermont
4-6	at Hudson Valley
7-9	Batavia
11-13	at Jamestown
14-16	at Mahoning Valley
19-21	Auburn
22-23	Oneonta
24-26	at Aberdeen
27-29	Hudson Valley
30-31	Brooklyn

SEPTEMBER
1	Brooklyn
2-3	at Oneonta
4-6	at Brooklyn

MAHONING VALLEY

JUNE
19-21	Jamestown
22-24	State College
25-27	at Williamsport
28-30	at State College

JULY
1-3	Williamsport
4-6	at Jamestown
7-9	Auburn
10-12	at Batavia

- 14-16 Staten Island
- 17-19 Oneonta
- 20-22 at Aberdeen
- 23-24 at State College
- 25-26 Williamsport
- 27-28 at Batavia
- 29-30 at Auburn
- 31 Batavia

AUGUST

- 1 Batavia
- 2-3 Auburn
- 4-6 at Tri-City
- 7-9 at Vermont
- 11-13 Brooklyn
- 14-16 Lowell
- 19-21 at Hudson Valley
- 22-24 at Auburn
- 25-27 Batavia
- 28-30 at Jamestown
- 31 at Williamsport

SEPTEMBER

- 1 at Williamsport
- 2-4 Jamestown
- 5-6 State College

ONEONTA

JUNE

- 19 Tri-City
- 20 at Tri-City
- 21 Tri-City
- 22-24 at Lowell
- 25-27 at Vermont
- 28-30 Lowell

JULY

- 1-3 at Aberdeen
- 4-6 Aberdeen
- 7-9 Vermont
- 10 at Tri-City
- 11 Tri-City
- 12 at Tri-City
- 14-16 at Auburn
- 17-19 at Mahoning Valley
- 20-22 Batavia
- 23-24 at Tri-City
- 25-26 Tri-City
- 27-28 Vermont
- 29-30 at Vermont
- 31 Tri-City

AUGUST

- 1 at Tri-City
- 2 Tri-City
- 3 at Tri-City
- 4-6 Jamestown
- 7-9 Staten Island
- 11-13 at State College
- 14-16 at Brooklyn
- 19-21 Williamsport
- 22-23 at Lowell
- 24-26 at Staten Island
- 27-29 Brooklyn
- 30-31 Hudson Valley

SEPTEMBER

- 1 Hudson Valley
- 2-3 Lowell
- 4-6 at Hudson Valley

STATE COLLEGE

JUNE

- 19 Williamsport
- 20 at Williamsport
- 21 Williamsport
- 22-24 at Mahoning Valley
- 25-27 at Auburn
- 28-30 Mahoning Valley

JULY

- 1-3 Auburn
- 4 Williamsport
- 5-6 at Williamsport
- 7-9 Batavia
- 10-12 Jamestown
- 14-16 at Tri-City
- 17-19 at Staten Island
- 20-22 Lowell
- 23-24 Mahoning Valley
- 25-26 Batavia
- 27-28 at Auburn
- 29-30 at Jamestown
- 31 Auburn

AUGUST

- 1 Auburn
- 2-3 Jamestown
- 4-6 Aberdeen
- 7-9 at Hudson Valley
- 11-13 Oneonta
- 14-16 at Vermont
- 19-21 Brooklyn
- 22-24 at Batavia
- 25-27 at Jamestown
- 28-30 Williamsport
- 31 at Batavia

SEPTEMBER

- 1 at Batavia
- 2-4 at Williamsport
- 5-6 at Mahoning Valley

STATEN ISLAND

JUNE

- 19 at Brooklyn
- 20 Brooklyn
- 21 at Brooklyn
- 22-24 at Aberdeen
- 25-27 Hudson Valley
- 28-30 Aberdeen

JULY

- 1-3 at Lowell
- 4-6 Lowell
- 7-8 at Hudson Valley
- 9 Hudson Valley
- 10 Brooklyn
- 11 at Brooklyn
- 12 Brooklyn
- 14-16 at Mahoning Valley
- 17-19 State College
- 20-22 Jamestown
- 23 at Brooklyn
- 24 Brooklyn
- 25 at Brooklyn
- 26 Brooklyn
- 27 at Hudson Valley
- 28 Hudson Valley
- 29-30 at Brooklyn
- 31 Brooklyn

AUGUST

- 1 Brooklyn
- 2-3 at Aberdeen
- 4-6 at Williamsport
- 7-9 at Oneonta
- 11-13 Auburn
- 14-16 at Batavia
- 19-20 Tri-City
- 21 at Tri-City
- 22-23 at Hudson Valley
- 24-26 Oneonta
- 27 Tri-City
- 28-29 at Tri-City
- 30-31 at Vermont

SEPTEMBER

- 1 at Vermont
- 2-3 Aberdeen
- 4-6 Vermont

TRI-CITY

JUNE

- 19 at Oneonta
- 20 Oneonta
- 21 at Oneonta
- 22-24 at Vermont
- 25-27 Lowell
- 28-30 Vermont

JULY

- 1-3 at Brooklyn
- 4-6 Brooklyn
- 7-9 at Lowell
- 10 Oneonta
- 11 at Oneonta
- 12 Oneonta
- 14-16 State College
- 17-19 at Batavia
- 20-22 Auburn
- 23-24 Oneonta
- 25-26 at Oneonta
- 27-28 Lowell
- 29-30 at Lowell
- 31 at Oneonta

AUGUST

- 1 Oneonta
- 2 at Oneonta
- 3 Oneonta
- 4-6 Mahoning Valley
- 7-9 at Williamsport
- 11-13 Hudson Valley
- 14-16 at Williamsport
- 19-20 at Staten Island
- 21 Staten Island
- 22-23 Vermont
- 24-26 at Hudson Valley
- 27 at Staten Island
- 28-29 Staten Island
- 30-31 Aberdeen

SEPTEMBER

- 1 Aberdeen
- 2-3 at Vermont
- 4-6 at Aberdeen

VERMONT

JUNE

- 19-21 at Lowell
- 22-24 Tri-City
- 25-27 Oneonta
- 28-30 at Tri-City

JULY

- 1-3 at Hudson Valley
- 4-6 Hudson Valley
- 7-9 at Oneonta
- 10-12 Lowell
- 14-16 at Jamestown
- 17-19 at Aberdeen
- 20-22 Brooklyn
- 23-24 at Lowell
- 25-26 Lowell
- 27-28 at Oneonta
- 29-30 Oneonta
- 31 Lowell

AUGUST

- 1 Lowell
- 2-3 at Lowell
- 4-6 at Auburn
- 7-9 Mahoning Valley
- 11-13 at Batavia
- 14-16 State College
- 19-21 Jamestown
- 22-23 at Tri-City
- 24-26 at Brooklyn
- 27-29 Aberdeen
- 30-31 Staten Island

SEPTEMBER

- 1 Staten Island
- 2-3 Tri-City
- 4-6 at Staten Island

WILLIAMSPORT

JUNE

- 19 at State College
- 20 State College
- 21 at State College
- 22-24 at Batavia
- 25-27 Mahoning Valley
- 28-30 Batavia

JULY

- 1-3 at Mahoning Valley
- 4 at State College
- 5-6 State College
- 7-9 at Jamestown
- 10-12 Auburn
- 14-16 at Brooklyn
- 17-19 at Lowell
- 20-22 Hudson Valley
- 23-24 at Auburn
- 25-26 at Mahoning Valley
- 27-28 Jamestown
- 29-30 Batavia
- 31 at Jamestown

AUGUST

- 1 at Jamestown
- 2-3 at Batavia
- 4-6 Staten Island
- 7-9 Tri-City
- 11-13 at Aberdeen
- 14-16 Tri-City
- 19-21 at Oneonta
- 22-24 Jamestown
- 25-27 at Auburn
- 28-30 at State College
- 31 Mahoning Valley

SEPTEMBER

- 1 Mahoning Valley
- 2-4 State College
- 5-6 Auburn

NORTHWEST LEAGUE

BOISE

JUNE
- 20-22 Tri-City
- 23-27 at Salem-Keizer
- 28-30 Yakima

JULY
- 1-3 at Tri-City
- 4-8 Eugene
- 10-14 at Vancouver
- 15-17 Yakima
- 18-22 Salem-Keizer
- 23-27 at Eugene
- 29-31 Vancouver

AUGUST
- 1-2 Vancouver
- 3-7 at Everett
- 8-10 at Yakima
- 11-15 Everett
- 17-19 Spokane
- 20-22 at Yakima
- 23-28 at Spokane
- 29-31 at Tri-City

SEPTEMBER
- 1-3 Spokane
- 4-6 Tri-City

EUGENE

JUNE
- 20-22 Salem-Keizer
- 23-27 at Yakima
- 28-30 Everett

JULY
- 1-3 Everett
- 4-8 at Boise
- 9-13 Spokane
- 15-17 at Salem-Keizer
- 18-22 at Tri-City
- 23-27 Boise
- 28-31 at Spokane

AUGUST
- 1 at Spokane
- 3-7 Tri-City
- 8-10 at Everett
- 11-13 at Vancouver
- 14-18 Yakima
- 20-22 Vancouver
- 23-25 at Everett
- 26-28 Vancouver
- 29-31 at Vancouver

SEPTEMBER
- 1-3 Salem-Keizer
- 4-6 at Salem-Keizer

EVERETT

JUNE
- 20-22 at Vancouver
- 23-27 Spokane
- 28-30 at Eugene

JULY
- 1-3 at Eugene
- 4-8 Yakima
- 9-13 at Tri-City
- 15-17 Vancouver
- 18-22 at Spokane
- 23-27 Tri-City
- 28-31 at Yakima

AUGUST
- 1 at Yakima
- 3-7 Boise
- 8-10 Eugene
- 11-15 at Boise
- 16-18 at Salem-Keizer
- 20-22 Salem Keizer
- 23-25 Eugene
- 26-28 at Salem-Keizer
- 29-31 Salem-Keizer

SEPTEMBER
- 1-3 Vancouver
- 4-6 at Vancouver

SALEM-KEIZER

JUNE
- 20-22 at Eugene
- 23-27 Boise
- 28-30 at Vancouver

JULY
- 1-3 at Vancouver
- 4-8 Tri-City
- 9-13 at Yakima
- 15-17 Eugene
- 18-22 at Boise
- 23-27 Yakima
- 28-31 at Tri-City

AUGUST
- 1 at Tri-City
- 3-7 Spokane
- 8-10 Vancouver
- 11-15 at Spokane
- 16-18 Everett
- 20-22 at Everett
- 23-25 Vancouver
- 26-28 Everett
- 29-31 at Everett

SEPTEMBER
- 1-3 at Eugene
- 4-6 Eugene

SPOKANE

JUNE
- 20-22 Yakima
- 23-27 at Everett
- 28-30 Tri-City

JULY
- 1-3 at Yakima
- 4-8 Vancouver
- 9-13 at Eugene
- 15-17 Tri-City
- 18-22 Everett
- 23-27 at Vancouver
- 28-31 Eugene

AUGUST
- 1 Eugene
- 3-7 at Salem-Keizer
- 8-10 at Tri-City
- 11-15 Salem-Keizer
- 17-19 at Boise
- 20-22 at Tri-City
- 23-28 Boise
- 29-31 at Yakima

SEPTEMBER
- 1-3 at Boise
- 4-6 Yakima

TRI-CITY

JUNE
- 20-22 at Boise
- 23-27 Vancouver
- 28-30 at Spokane

JULY
- 1-3 Boise
- 4-8 at Salem-Keizer
- 9-13 Everett
- 15-17 at Spokane
- 18-22 Eugene
- 23-27 at Everett
- 28-31 Salem-Keizer

AUGUST
- 1 Salem Keizer
- 3-7 at Eugene
- 8-10 Spokane
- 11-13 at Yakima
- 14-18 at Vancouver
- 20-22 Spokane
- 23-25 Yakima
- 26-28 at Yakima
- 29-31 Boise

SEPTEMBER
- 1-3 Yakima
- 4-6 at Boise

VANCOUVER

JUNE
- 20-22 Everett
- 23-27 at Tri-City
- 28-30 Salem-Keizer

JULY
- 1-3 Salem-Keizer
- 4-8 at Spokane
- 10-14 Boise
- 15-17 at Everett
- 18-22 at Yakima
- 23-27 Spokane
- 29-31 at Boise

AUGUST
- 1-2 at Boise
- 3-7 Yakima
- 8-10 at Salem-Keizer
- 11-13 Eugene
- 14-18 Tri-City
- 20-22 at Eugene
- 23-25 at Salem-Keizer
- 26-28 at Eugene
- 29-31 Eugene

SEPTEMBER
- 1-3 at Everett
- 4-6 Everett

YAKIMA

JUNE
- 20-22 at Spokane
- 23-27 Eugene
- 28-30 at Boise

JULY
- 1-3 Spokane
- 4-8 at Everett
- 9-13 Salem-Keizer
- 15-17 at Boise
- 18-22 Vancouver
- 23-27 at Salem-Keizer
- 28-31 Everett

AUGUST
- 1 Everett
- 3-7 at Vancouver
- 8-10 Boise
- 11-13 Tri-City
- 14-18 at Eugene
- 20-22 Boise
- 23-25 at Tri-City
- 26-28 Tri-City
- 29-31 Spokane

SEPTEMBER
- 1-3 at Tri-City
- 4-6 at Spokane

ROOKIE

APPALACHIAN LEAGUE

BLUEFIELD

JUNE
23-25 Elizabethton
26-28 at Kingsport
29-30 at Burlington

JULY
1 at Burlington
2 at Pulaski
3 Pulaski
4 at Pulaski
5-7 Burlington
8 Danville
9-10 at Danville
11-13 Princeton
15-17 at Bristol
18-20 Johnson City
21-23 Greeneville
24 Danville
25-26 at Danville
27-29 Princeton
30 at Princeton
31 at Johnson City

AUGUST
1-2 at Johnson City
4-6 at Greeneville
7-9 at Elizabethton
10-11 Pulaski
12 at Pulaski
13-15 at Princeton
16-18 Bristol
20-22 Kingsport
23-25 at Pulaski
26 Princeton
27-28 at Danville
29 Danville
30-31 Burlington

SEPTEMBER
1 Burlington

BRISTOL

JUNE
23-25 Greeneville
26-27 Princeton
29-30 at Elizabethton

JULY
1 at Elizabethton
2-4 Johnson City
5-7 at Johnson City
8-10 Burlington
11-13 at Kingsport
15-17 Bluefield
18-20 at Danville
21-23 at Burlington
24-27 at Pulaski
28-30 Greeneville
31 Danville

AUGUST
1-2 Danville
4-6 Kingsport
7-9 at Greeneville
10-12 at Johnson City
13-15 Elizabethton
16-18 at Bluefield
20-22 at Princeton
23-25 Kingsport
26-29 Pulaski
30-31 at Elizabethton

SEPTEMBER
1 at Elizabethton

BURLINGTON

JUNE
23-25 at Princeton
26-28 at Johnson City
29-30 Bluefield

JULY
1 Bluefield
2-4 Kingsport
5-7 at Bluefield
8-10 at Bristol
11-13 Danville
15-17 at Pulaski
18-20 Elizabethton
21-23 Bristol
24-26 at Greeneville
27 at Danville
28-30 Danville
31 at Elizabethton

AUGUST
1-2 at Elizabethton
4-6 Pulaski
7-9 Princeton
10-12 at Kingsport
13-15 at Danville
16-18 Pulaski
20-22 Johnson City
23-25 at Princeton
26 Danville
27-29 Greeneville
30-31 at Bluefield

SEPTEMBER
1 at Bluefield

DANVILLE

JUNE
23-25 at Pulaski
26-28 at Greeneville
29-30 Kingsport

JULY
1 Kingsport
2-4 Princeton
5-7 at Pulaski
8 at Bluefield
9-10 Bluefield
11-13 at Burlington
15-17 Elizabethton
18-20 Bristol
21-23 at Johnson City
24 at Bluefield
25-26 Bluefield
27 Burlington
28-30 at Burlington
31 at Bristol

AUGUST
1-2 at Bristol
4-6 Princeton
7-9 Pulaski
10-12 at Princeton
13-15 Burlington
16-18 at Elizabethton
20-22 Greeneville
23-25 Johnson City
26 at Burlington
27-28 Bluefield
29 at Bluefield
30-31 at Kingsport

SEPTEMBER
1 at Kingsport

ELIZABETHTON

JUNE
23-25 at Bluefield
26-28 Pulaski
29-30 Bristol

JULY
1 Bristol
2-4 at Greeneville
5-7 at Princeton
8-10 at Kingsport
11-13 Johnson City
15-17 at Danville
18-20 at Burlington
21-23 Princeton
24-26 at Kingsport
27-30 Johnson City
31 Burlington

AUGUST
1-2 Burlington
4-6 at Johnson City
7-9 Bluefield
10-12 Greeneville
13-15 at Bristol
16-18 Danville
20-22 at Pulaski
23-25 at Greeneville
26 at Johnson City
27-29 Kingsport
30-31 Bristol

SEPTEMBER
1 Bristol

GREENEVILLE

JUNE
23-25 at Bristol
26-28 Danville
29-30 at Princeton

JULY
1 at Princeton
2-4 Elizabethton
5-7 at Kingsport
8-10 at Johnson City
11-13 Pulaski
15-17 at Johnson City
18-20 Kingsport
21-23 at Bluefield
24-26 Burlington
27 at Kingsport
28-30 at Bristol
31 Kingsport

AUGUST
1-2 Kingsport
4-6 Bluefield
7-9 Bristol
10-12 at Elizabethton
13-15 at Pulaski
16-18 Johnson City
20-22 at Danville
23-25 Elizabethton
26 Kingsport
27-29 at Burlington
30-31 Princeton

SEPTEMBER
1 Princeton

JOHNSON CITY

JUNE
23-25 at Kingsport
26-28 Burlington
29-30 at Pulaski

JULY
1 at Pulaski
2-4 at Bristol
5-7 Bristol
8-10 Greeneville
11-13 at Elizabethton
15-17 Greeneville
18-20 at Bluefield
21-23 Danville
24-26 at Princeton
27-30 at Elizabethton
31 Bluefield

AUGUST
1-2 Bluefield
4-6 Elizabethton
7-9 at Kingsport
10-12 Bristol
13-15 Kingsport
16-18 at Greeneville
20-22 at Burlington
23-25 at Danville
26 Elizabethton
27-29 Princeton
30-31 Pulaski

SEPTEMBER
1 Pulaski

KINGSPORT

JUNE
23-25 Johnson City
26-28 Bluefield
29-30 at Danville

JULY
1 at Danville
2-4 at Burlington
5-7 Greeneville
8-10 Elizabethton

11-13 . . . . Bristol
15-17 . . . . . . .at Princeton
18-20 . . . . . .at Greeneville
21-23 . . . . at Pulaski
24-26 . . . . . . Elizabethton
27 . . . . Greeneville
28-30 . . . . Pulaski
31 . . . . .at Greeneville

AUGUST

1-2. . . . . . . .at Greeneville
4-6. . . . . .at Bristol
7-9. . . . . Johnson City
10-12 . . . . .Burlington
13-15 . . . . at Johnson City
16-18 . . . . Princeton
20-22 . . . . at Bluefield
23-25 . . . . at Bristol
26 . . . . .at Greeneville
27-29 . . . . .at Elizabethton
30-31 . . . . Danville

SEPTEMBER

1 . . . . Danville

PRINCETON

JUNE

23-25 . . . . .Burlington
26-28 . . . . at Bristol
29-30 . . . . Greeneville

JULY

1 . . . . Greeneville
2-4. . . . . .at Danville
5-7. . . . . Elizabethton
8-9. . . . . Pulaski
10 . . . . at Pulaski
11-13 . . . . at Bluefield
15-17 . . . . Kingsport
18-20 . . . . Pulaski
21-23 . . . . .at Elizabethton
24-26 . . . . . . Johnson City
27-29 . . . . at Bluefield
30 . . . . Bluefield
31 . . . . Pulaski

AUGUST

1-2. . . . . at Pulaski
4-6. . . . . .at Danville
7-9. . . . . at Burlington
10-12 . . . . Danville
13-15 . . . . .Bluefield
16-18 . . . . at Kingsport
20-22 . . . . Bristol
23-25 . . . . .Burlington
26 . . . . at Bluefield
27-29 . . . . at Johnson City
30-31 . . . . . .at Greeneville

SEPTEMBER

1 . . . . .at Greeneville

PULASKI

JUNE

23-25 . . . . Danville
26-28 . . . . .at Elizabethton
29-30 . . . . . . Johnson City

JULY

1 . . . . Johnson City
2 . . . . .Bluefield
3 . . . . at Bluefield
4 . . . . .Bluefield
5-7. . . . . Danville
8-9. . . . . .at Princeton
10 . . . . Princeton
11-13 . . . . . .at Greeneville
15-17 . . . . .Burlington
18-20 . . . . .at Princeton
21-23 . . . . Kingsport
24-27 . . . . Bristol
28-30 . . . . at Kingsport
31 . . . . .at Princeton

AUGUST

1-2. . . . . Princeton
4-6. . . . . at Burlington
7-9. . . . . .at Danville
10-11 . . . . at Bluefield
12 . . . . .Bluefield
13-15 . . . . Greeneville
16-18 . . . . . . at Burlington
20-22 . . . . Elizabethton
23-25 . . . . .Bluefield
26-29 . . . . .at Bristol
30-31 . . . . at Johnson City

SEPTEMBER

1 . . . . at Johnson City

PIONEER LEAGUE

BILLINGS

JUNE

23-25 . . . . Great Falls
26-28 . . . . . . at Great Falls
29-30 . . . . at Helena

JULY

1-3. . . . . Helena
4-5. . . . . .Missoula
7-10 . . . . at Orem
11-13 . . . . at Ogden
15-17 . . . . Orem
18-21 . . . . Ogden
23-26 . . . . at Missoula
27-28 . . . . Great Falls
29-30 . . . . .Missoula
31 . . . . at Helena

AUGUST

1-2. . . . . at Helena
3-5. . . . . .Great Falls
6-8. . . . . Helena
10-13 . . . . . . at Idaho Falls
14-16 . . . . at Casper
17-19 . . . . Idaho Falls
20-23 . . . . Casper
25-27 . . . . at Helena
28-31 . . . . .Missoula

SEPTEMBER

1-3. . . . . at Great Falls
4-5. . . . . Helena
6-9. . . . . at Missoula
10-11 . . . . . . at Great Falls

CASPER

JUNE

23-26 . . . . . . at Idaho Falls
27-29 . . . . at Ogden
30 . . . . .Idaho Falls

JULY

1-3. . . . . Idaho Falls
4-5. . . . . Ogden
7-10 . . . . at Missoula
11-13 . . . . at Helena
15-17 . . . . .Missoula
18-21 . . . . Helena
23-24 . . . . at Ogden
25-27 . . . . at Orem
28-30 . . . . Ogden
31 . . . . Orem

AUGUST

1-2. . . . . Orem
3-5. . . . . at Ogden
6-8. . . . . at Orem
10-13 . . . . Great Falls
14-16 . . . . Billings
17-19 . . . . . . at Great Falls
20-23 . . . . at Billings
25-27 . . . . Orem
28-30 . . . . Ogden
31 . . . . at Orem

SEPTEMBER

1 . . . . at Orem
2-5. . . . . at Idaho Falls
6-7. . . . . Orem
8-11 . . . . .Idaho Falls

GREAT FALLS

JUNE

23-25 . . . . at Billings
26-28 . . . . Billings
29-30 . . . . .Missoula

JULY

1-3. . . . . at Missoula
4-5. . . . . Helena
7-10 . . . . at Ogden
11-13 . . . . at Orem
15-17 . . . . Ogden
18-21 . . . . Orem
23-24 . . . . at Helena
25-26 . . . . Helena
27-28 . . . . at Billings
29-30 . . . . at Helena
31 . . . . .Missoula

AUGUST

1-2. . . . . .Missoula
3-5. . . . . at Billings
6-8. . . . . .Missoula
10-13 . . . . at Casper
14-16 . . . . . . at Idaho Falls
17-19 . . . . Casper
20-23 . . . . .Idaho Falls
25-27 . . . . at Missoula
28-29 . . . . at Helena
30-31 . . . . Helena

SEPTEMBER

1-3. . . . . Billings
4-5. . . . . at Missoula
6-7. . . . . at Helena
8-9. . . . . Helena
10-11 . . . . Billings

HELENA

JUNE

23-25 . . . . .Missoula
26-28 . . . . at Missoula
29-30 . . . . Billings

JULY

1-3. . . . . at Billings
4-5. . . . . at Great Falls
7-10 . . . . .Idaho Falls
11-13 . . . . Casper
15-17 . . . . . . at Idaho Falls
18-21 . . . . at Casper
23-24 . . . . Great Falls
25-26 . . . . at Great Falls
27-28 . . . . at Missoula
29-30 . . . . Great Falls
31 . . . . Billings

AUGUST

1-2. . . . . .Billings
3-5. . . . . at Missoula
6-8. . . . . at Billings
10-13 . . . . Ogden
15-16 . . . . Orem
17-19 . . . . at Ogden
20-23 . . . . at Orem
25-27 . . . . Billings
28-29 . . . . Great Falls
30-31 . . . . at Great Falls

SEPTEMBER

1-3. . . . . Missoula
4-5. . . . . at Billings
6-7. . . . . Great Falls
8-9. . . . . at Great Falls
10-11 . . . . .Missoula

IDAHO FALLS

JUNE

23-26 . . . . Casper
27-29 . . . . at Orem
30 . . . . at Casper

JULY

1-3. . . . . at Casper
4-5. . . . . Orem
7-10 . . . . at Helena
11-13 . . . . at Missoula
15-17 . . . . Helena
18-21 . . . . .Missoula
23-24 . . . . at Orem
25-27 . . . . at Ogden
28-30 . . . . Orem
31 . . . . Ogden

AUGUST

1-2. . . . . Ogden
3-5. . . . . at Orem
6-8. . . . . at Ogden
10-13 . . . . Billings
14-16 . . . . Great Falls
17-19 . . . . at Billings
20-23 . . . . at Great Falls
25-27 . . . . Ogden
28-30 . . . . Orem
31 . . . . at Ogden

SEPTEMBER

1 at Ogden
2-5 Casper
6-7 Ogden
8-11 at Casper

MISSOULA

JUNE

23-25 at Helena
26-28 Helena
29-30 at Great Falls

JULY

1-3 Great Falls
4-5 at Billings
7-10 Casper
11-13 Idaho Falls
15-17 at Casper
18-21 at Idaho Falls
23-26 Billings
27-28 Helena
29-30 at Billings
31 at Great Falls

AUGUST

1-2 at Great Falls
3-5 Helena
6-8 at Great Falls
10-13 Orem
14-16 Ogden
17-19 at Orem
20-23 at Ogden
25-27 Great Falls
28-31 at Billings

SEPTEMBER

1-3 at Helena
4-5 Great Falls
6-9 Billings
10-11 at Helena

OGDEN

JUNE

23-24 Orem
25-26 at Orem
27-29 Casper
30 Orem

JULY

. . . . Orem
2-3 at Orem
4-5 at Casper
7-10 Great Falls
11-13 Billings
15-17 at Great Falls
18-21 at Billings
23-24 Casper
25-27 Idaho Falls
28-30 at Casper
31 at Idaho Falls

AUGUST

1-2 at Idaho Falls
3-5 Casper
6-8 Idaho Falls
10-13 at Helena
14-16 at Missoula
17-19 Helena
20-23 Missoula
25-27 at Idaho Falls
28-30 at Casper
31 Idaho Falls

SEPTEMBER

1 Idaho Falls
2-3 at Orem
4-5 Orem
6-7 at Idaho Falls
8-9 at Orem
10-11 Orem

OREM

JUNE

23-24 at Ogden
25-26 Ogden
27-29 Idaho Falls
30 at Ogden

JULY

1 at Ogden
2-3 Ogden
4-5 at Idaho Falls
7-10 Billings
11-13 Great Falls
15-17 at Billings
18-21 at Great Falls
23-24 Idaho Falls
25-27 Casper
28-30 at Idaho Falls
31 at Casper

AUGUST

1-2 at Casper
3-5 Idaho Falls
6-8 Casper
10-13 at Missoula
14-16 at Helena
17-19 Missoula
20-23 Helena
25-27 at Casper
28-30 at Idaho Falls
31 Casper

SEPTEMBER

1 Casper
2-3 Ogden
4-5 at Ogden
6-7 at Casper
8-9 Ogden
10-11 at Ogden

ARIZONA LEAGUE

HOME GAMES ONLY

ROYALS

JUNE

22 Dodgers
23 Indians
26 Mariners
28 Padres

JULY

1/9/22 Rangers
3 Angels
7/29 Mariners
11 Dodgers
13/23 Indians
16 Brewers
19 Athletics
26 Padres
31 Giants

AUGUST

3 Giants
6/23 Rangers
8 Indians
11 Mariners
12/26 Dodgers
15 Angels
17 Cubs
20/27 Padres

RANGERS

JUNE

21 Indians
24 Royals
27 Padres
30 Dodgers

JULY

2 Brewers
4/31 Cubs
6 Padres
10/21/25 Mariners
12 Royals
14/29 Indians
17 Athletics
20 Giants
26 Dodgers

AUGUST

4 Angels
8 Mariners
9/24 Padres
10/28 Royals
13 Indians
15 Giants
18 Athletics
20/25 Dodgers

PADRES

JUNE

21 Royals
23 Dodgers
26 Rangers
30 Mariners

JULY

1 Giants
3 Athletics
7/12/21 Indians
8/28 Royals
11 Mariners
13/23 Dodgers
15/30 Rangers
17 Cubs
18 Angels

AUGUST

4 Brewers
6 Brewers
7 Dodgers
11 Indians
14 Rangers
17 Giants
19 Athletics
21 Indians
22 Dodgers
25 Royals
26 Mariners
29 at Mariners

MARINERS

JUNE

21 at Dodgers
22 Rangers
24 at Indians
25 Padres
26 at Royals
27 Indians
29 Royals
30 at Padres

JULY

2 Cubs
5 Giants
6/12/30 Dodgers
9 Indians
14/24 Royals
16 Rangers
20 Brewers
22/27 Padres

AUGUST

1 Angels
3 Athletics
5 Cubs
9 Dodgers
10/15 Padres
13 Royals
18 Brewers
23/28 Indians
29 Rangers

DODGERS

JUNE

21 Mariners
25 Rangers
27 Royals
28 Indians

JULY

1 Angels
5 Athletics
7/27 Rangers
10/13/25 Padres
15/30 Mariners
17/28 Indians
18 Giants
21 Royals

AUGUST

1/19 Brewers
2/15 Cubs
5/21 Royals
6 Angels
11 Rangers
14/24 Mariners
27 Indians
29 Padres

INDIANS

JUNE
- 22 . . . . . Padres
- 24 . . . . . Mariners
- 26 . . . . . Dodgers
- 29 . . . . . Rangers

JULY
- 2/6/27 . . . . . Royals
- 4 . . . . . Brewers
- 8/22 . . . . . Dodgers
- 11/24 . . . . . Rangers
- 12 . . . . . Padres
- 16 . . . . . Angels
- 19 . . . . . Cubs
- 26 . . . . . Mariners

AUGUST
- 1/12 . . . . . Padres
- 2/6 . . . . . Athletics
- 7 . . . . . Giants
- 10/16 . . . . . Dodgers
- 17 . . . . . Angels
- 20/25 . . . . . Mariners
- 22 . . . . . Royals
- 26 . . . . . Rangers

BREWERS

JUNE
- 21 . . . . . Giants
- 25 . . . . . Athletics
- 27 . . . . . Angels
- 29 . . . . . Cubs

JULY
- 1 . . . . . Mariners
- 5 . . . . . Padres
- 6/27 . . . . . Angels
- 9/21 . . . . . Giants
- 12/29 . . . . . Cubs
- 15/25 . . . . . Athletics
- 17 . . . . . Royals
- 19 . . . . . Rangers

AUGUST
- 3 . . . . . Rangers
- 5/15 . . . . . Indians
- 8/24 . . . . . Athletics
- 10/26 . . . . . Angels
- 14/20 . . . . . Giants
- 16 . . . . . Royals
- 28 . . . . . Cubs

ATHLETICS

JUNE
- 22 . . . . . Cubs
- 24 . . . . . Giants
- 28 . . . . . Angels
- 30 . . . . . Brewers

JULY
- 2 . . . . . Dodgers
- 4 . . . . . Mariners
- 8/24 . . . . . Giants
- 10/30 . . . . . Brewers
- 12/28 . . . . . Angels
- 14/22 . . . . . Cubs
- 18 . . . . . Indians
- 20 . . . . . Padres

AUGUST
- 1/7 . . . . . Royals
- 4 . . . . . Mariners
- 9/23 . . . . . Giants
- 11/29 . . . . . Brewers
- 12/21 . . . . . Cubs
- 16 . . . . . Rangers
- 17 . . . . . Dodgers
- 27 . . . . . Angels

ANGELS

JUNE
- 22 . . . . . Brewers
- 23 . . . . . Athletics
- 26 . . . . . Cubs
- 30 . . . . . Giants

JULY
- 2 . . . . . Padres
- 5 . . . . . Rangers
- 7/23 . . . . . Athletics
- 8/26 . . . . . Cubs
- 11/22 . . . . . Brewers
- 15/30 . . . . . Giants
- 17 . . . . . Mariners
- 20 . . . . . Dodgers
- 31 . . . . . Indians

AUGUST
- 2 . . . . . Royals
- 5 . . . . . Padres
- 9/21 . . . . . Brewers
- 11/25 . . . . . Cubs
- 14/22 . . . . . Athletics
- 16 . . . . . Mariners
- 19 . . . . . Rangers
- 29 . . . . . Giants

GIANTS

JUNE
- 23 . . . . . Cubs
- 25 . . . . . Angels
- 26 . . . . . Brewers
- 29 . . . . . Athletics

JULY
- 3 . . . . . Indians
- 4 . . . . . Royals
- 6/23 . . . . . Cubs
- 10/25 . . . . . Angels
- 13/29 . . . . . Athletics
- 14/26 . . . . . Brewers
- 16 . . . . . Dodgers
- 19 . . . . . Mariners

AUGUST
- 2 . . . . . Padres
- 4 . . . . . Dodgers
- 5 . . . . . Rangers
- 8/22 . . . . . Cubs
- 12/24 . . . . . Angels
- 13/28 . . . . . Athletics
- 18 . . . . . Indians
- 19 . . . . . Mariners
- 25 . . . . . Brewers

CUBS

JUNE
- 21 . . . . . Angels
- 24 . . . . . Brewers
- 27 . . . . . Athletics
- 28 . . . . . Giants

JULY
- 1 . . . . . Indians
- 3 . . . . . Dodgers
- 7/24 . . . . . Brewers
- 9/27 . . . . . Athletics
- 11/28 . . . . . Giants
- 13/21 . . . . . Angels
- 16 . . . . . Padres
- 18 . . . . . Royals

AUGUST
- 1 . . . . . Rangers
- 3 . . . . . Indians
- 6 . . . . . Mariners
- 7/20 . . . . . Angels
- 10/27 . . . . . Giants
- 13/23 . . . . . Brewers
- 16 . . . . . Padres
- 18 . . . . . Royals
- 26 . . . . . Athletics

GULF COAST LEAGUE

ASTROS

JUNE
- 23 . . . . . at Mets
- 25 . . . . . Nationals
- 26 . . . . . Marlins
- 27 . . . . . Cardinals
- 28 . . . . . Mets
- 30 . . . . . at Nationals

JULY
- 1/6/16/26 . . . . . at Marlins
- 2/22/27 . . . . . Cardinals
- 3/13/23 . . . . . at Mets
- 5/15/25 . . . . . Nationals
- 7/12/17 . . . . . at Cardinals
- 8/18/28 . . . . . Mets
- 10/20/30 . . . . . at Nationals
- 11/21/31 . . . . . Marlins

AUGUST
- 1/6/21/26 . . . . . at Cardinals
- 2/12/22 . . . . . at Mets
- 4/14/24 . . . . . Nationals
- 5/15/25 . . . . . at Marlins
- 7/17/27 . . . . . Mets
- 9/16/19/29 . . . . . at Nationals
- 10/20/30 . . . . . Marlins
- 11/31 . . . . . Cardinals

BLUE JAYS

JUNE
- 23 . . . . . at Phillies
- 24 . . . . . Phillies
- 25 . . . . . at Braves
- 26 . . . . . Braves
- 27 . . . . . at Tigers
- 29 . . . . . Tigers
- 30 . . . . . at Yankees

JULY
- 1/11/24/28 . . . . . Yankees
- 2/15/27 . . . . . at Pirates
- 3/14/25 . . . . . Pirates
- 4/17 . . . . . Phillies
- 6/16/29 . . . . . at Phillies
- 7/20/30 . . . . . Braves
- 8/18/31 . . . . . at Braves
- 9/22 . . . . . Tigers
- 10/21 . . . . . at Tigers
- 13/23 . . . . . at Yankees

AUGUST
- 1/14/25 . . . . . Tigers
- 3/13/26 . . . . . at Tigers
- 4/17/27 . . . . . Yankees
- 5/15/28 . . . . . at Yankees
- 6/18/31 . . . . . at Pirates
- 7/19/29 . . . . . Pirates
- 8/21 . . . . . at Phillies
- 10/20 . . . . . Phillies
- 11/24 . . . . . at Braves
- 12/22 . . . . . Braves

BRAVES

JUNE
- 23 . . . . . Tigers
- 24/30 . . . . . at Tigers
- 25 . . . . . Blue Jays
- 26 . . . . . at Blue Jays
- 27 . . . . . Pirates
- 29 . . . . . at Pirates

JULY
- 1/11/24 . . . . . at Phillies
- 2/15/25 . . . . . Yankees
- 3/14/27 . . . . . at Yankees
- 4/17/28 . . . . . at Tigers
- 6/16 . . . . . Tigers
- 7/20/30 . . . . . at Blue Jays
- 8/18/31 . . . . . Blue Jays
- 9/22 . . . . . at Pirates
- 10/21 . . . . . Pirates
- 13/23 . . . . . Phillies

AUGUST
- 1/14/25 . . . . . at Pirates
- 3/13/26 . . . . . Pirates
- 4/17/27 . . . . . at Phillies
- 5/15/28 . . . . . Phillies
- 6/19/29 . . . . . at Yankees
- 7/18/31 . . . . . Yankees
- 8/21 . . . . . Tigers
- 10/20 . . . . . at Tigers
- 11/24 . . . . . Blue Jays
- 12/22 . . . . . at Blue Jays

CARDINALS

JUNE

23 . . . Marlins
24 . . . at Nationals
25 . . . Mets
27 . . . at Astros
28 . . . at Marlins
29 . . . Nationals
30 . . . at Mets

JULY

2/22/27 . . . at Astros
3/13/23 . . . Marlins
4/14/24 . . . at Nationals
5/15/25 . . . Mets
7/12/17 . . . Astros
8/18/28 . . . at Marlins
9/19/29 . . . Nationals
10/20/30 . . . at Mets

AUGUST

1/6/26/21 . . . Astros
2/12/22 . . . Marlins
3/9//13/23 . . . at Nationals
4/14/29 . . . Mets
7/17/27 . . . at Marlins
8/18/28 . . . Nationals
11/16/31 . . . at Astros
19/21 . . . at Mets

MARLINS

JUNE

23 . . . at Cardinals
24 . . . Mets
26 . . . at Astros
27 . . . Nationals
28 . . . Cardinals
29 . . . at Mets

JULY

1/6/16/26 . . . Astros
2/22/27 . . . Nationals
3/13/23 . . . at Cardinals
4/14/24 . . . Mets
7/12/17 . . . at Nationals
8/18/28 . . . Cardinals
9/19/29 . . . at Mets
11/21/31 . . . at Astros

AUGUST

1/6/16/26 . . . at Nationals
2/12/22 . . . at Cardinals
3/8/13/23 . . . Mets
5/15/25 . . . Astros
7/17/27 . . . Cardinals
10/20/30 . . . at Astros
11/21/31 . . . Nationals
18/28 . . . at Mets

METS

JUNE

23 . . . Astros
24 . . . at Marlins
25 . . . at Cardinals
26 . . . Nationals
28 . . . at Astros
29 . . . Marlins
30 . . . Cardinals

JULY

1/11/21 . . . at Nationals
3/13/23 . . . Astros
4/14/24 . . . at Marlins
5/15/25 . . . at Cardinals
6/16/26 . . . Nationals
8/18/28 . . . at Astros
9/19/29 . . . Marlins
10/30 . . . Cardinals

AUGUST

2/12/22 . . . Astros
3/13/23 . . . at Marlins
4/14/29 . . . at Cardinals
5/15/25 . . . Nationals
7/17/27 . . . at Astros
8/18/28 . . . Marlins
9/19/24 . . . Cardinals
10/20/30 . . . at Nationals

NATIONALS

JUNE

24 . . . Cardinals
25 . . . at Astros
26 . . . at Mets
27 . . . at Marlins
29 . . . at Cardinals
30 . . . Astros

JULY

1/11/21/31 . . . Mets
2/22/27 . . . at Marlins
4/14/24 . . . Cardinals
5/15/25 . . . at Astros
6/16/26 . . . at Mets
7/12/17 . . . Marlins
9/19/29 . . . at Cardinals
10/20/30 . . . Astros

AUGUST

1/6/16/26 . . . Marlins
3/13/23 . . . Cardinals
4/14/24 . . . at Astros
5/15/25 . . . at Mets
8/18/28 . . . at Cardinals
9/19/29 . . . Astros
10/20/30 . . . Mets
11/21/31 . . . at Marlins

PHILLIES

JUNE

23 . . . Blue Jays
24 . . . at Blue Jays
25 . . . Pirates
26 . . . at Pirates
27 . . . Yankees
29 . . . at Yankees
30 . . . at Braves

JULY

1/11/24 . . . Braves
2/15/25 . . . Tigers
3/14/27 . . . at Tigers
4/17/28 . . . at Blue Jays
6/16/29 . . . Blue Jays
7/20/30 . . . at Pirates
8/18/31 . . . Pirates
9/22 . . . at Yankees
10/21 . . . Yankees
13/23 . . . at Braves

AUGUST

1/14/25 . . . at Yankees
3/13/26 . . . Yankees
4/17/27 . . . Braves
5/15/28 . . . at Braves
6/19/29 . . . at Tigers
7/18/31 . . . Tigers
8/21 . . . Blue Jays
10/20/22 . . . at Blue Jays
11/24 . . . Pirates
12 . . . at Pirates

PIRATES

JUNE

23 . . . at Yankees
24 . . . Yankees
25 . . . at Phillies
26 . . . Phillies
27 . . . at Braves
29 . . . Braves
30 . . . at Tigers

JULY

1/11/24 . . . Tigers
2/15/27 . . . Blue Jays
3/14/25 . . . at Blue Jays
4/17/28 . . . Yankees
6/16/29 . . . at Yankees
7/20/30 . . . Phillies
8/18/31 . . . at Phillies
9/22 . . . Braves
10/21 . . . at Braves
13/23 . . . at Tigers

AUGUST

1/14/25 . . . Braves
3/8/13/26 . . . at Braves
4/1727 . . . Tigers
5/15/28 . . . at Tigers
6/18/31 . . . Blue Jays
7/19/29 . . . at Blue Jays
10/20 . . . Yankees
11/24 . . . at Phillies
12/22 . . . Phillies
21 . . . at Yankees

TIGERS

JUNE

23 . . . at Braves
24 . . . Braves
25 . . . at Yankees
26 . . . Yankees
27 . . . Blue Jays
29 . . . at Blue Jays
30 . . . Pirates

JULY

1/11/24 . . . at Pirates
2/16/25 . . . at Phillies
3/14/27 . . . Phillies
4/7/20/30 . . . Yankees
6/29 . . . at Braves
8/18/31 . . . at Yankees
9/22 . . . at Blue Jays
10/21 . . . Blue Jays
13/23 . . . Pirates
17/28 . . . Braves

AUGUST

1/14/25 . . . at Blue Jays
3/13/26 . . . Blue Jays
4/17/27 . . . at Pirates
5/15/28 . . . Pirates
6/19/29 . . . Phillies
7/18/31 . . . at Phillies
8/21 . . . at Braves
1/200 . . . Braves
11/24 . . . at Yankees
12/22 . . . Yankees

ORIOLES

JUNE

23 . . . at Reds
24 . . . Twins
26 . . . Rays
27 . . . at Red Sox
28 . . . Reds

JULY

1/11/21/31 . . . at Rays
2/12/22 . . . Red Sox
3/13/23 . . . at Reds
4/14/24 . . . Twins
6/16/26 . . . Rays
7/17/27 . . . at Red Sox
8/28/28 . . . Reds
9/19/29 . . . at Twins

AUGUST

1/11/21/31 . . . Red Sox
2/7/22 . . . at Reds
3/8/23 . . . Twins
5/15/25 . . . Rays
6/16/26 . . . at Red Sox
10/20/30 . . . at Rays
13/18/28 . . . at Twins
17/27 . . . Reds

RAYS

JUNE

23 . . . at Twins
25 . . . Red Sox
26 . . . at Orioles
27 . . . Reds
28 . . . Twins
30 . . . at Red Sox

JULY

1/11/21/31 . . . Orioles
2/27 . . . at Reds
3/13/23/28 . . . at Twins
5/15/25/30 . . . Red Sox
6/16/26 . . . at Orioles
7/12/17/22 . . . Reds
8/18 . . . Twins
10/20 . . . at Red Sox

AUGUST

1/11/21/31 . . . at Reds
2/12/17/27 . . . Twins
4/24 . . . Red Sox

5/15/25 . . . at Orioles
6/16/26 . . . Reds
7/22 . . . at Twins
9/14/19/29 . . . at Red Sox
10/20/30 . . . Orioles

REDS

JUNE
23 . . . Orioles
24/30 . . . at Red Sox
25 . . . Twins
27 . . . at Rays
28 . . . at Orioles
29 . . . Red Sox

JULY
2/27 . . . Rays
3/13 . . . Orioles
4/14/19/29 . . . at Red Sox
5/15/25 . . . Twins
7/12/17/22 . . . at Rays
8/18/28 . . . at Orioles
9/24 . . . Red Sox
10/20/30 . . . at Twins

AUGUST
1/11/21/26/31 . . . Rays
2/4/14/24 . . . Twins
3/8/18/28 . . . Red Sox
6/16 . . . at Rays
7/12/22/27 . . . Orioles
9/19/29 . . . at Twins
13/23 . . . at Red Sox

RED SOX

JUNE
24 . . . Reds
25 . . . at Rays
26 . . . at Twins
27 . . . Orioles
29 . . . at Reds
30 . . . Rays

JULY
1/11/21/31 . . . Twins
2/12/22 . . . at Orioles
4/14/19/29 . . . Reds
5/15/25/31 . . . at Rays
6/16/26 . . . at Twins
7/17/27 . . . Orioles
9/24 . . . at Reds
10/20 . . . Rays

AUGUST
1/11/21/31 . . . at Orioles
3/13/23 . . . Reds
4/14/24 . . . at Rays
5/15/25 . . . at Twins
6/16/26 . . . Orioles
8/18/28 . . . at Reds
9/19/29 . . . Rays
10/20/30 . . . Twins

TWINS

JUNE
23 . . . Rays
24 . . . at Orioles
25 . . . at Reds
26 . . . Red Sox
28 . . . at Rays
29 . . . Orioles
30 . . . Reds

JULY
1/11/21 . . . at Red Sox
3/13/23/28 . . . Rays
4/14/24 . . . at Orioles
5/15/25 . . . at Reds
7/17/27 . . . Red Sox
8/18 . . . at Rays
9/19/29 . . . Orioles
10/20/30 . . . Reds
19/29 . . . Orioles

AUGUST
2/12/22 . . . at Rays
3/8/23 . . . at Orioles
4/14/24 . . . at Reds
5/15/25 . . . Red Sox
7/17/27 . . . Rays
9/19/29 . . . Reds
10/20/30 . . . at Red Sox
13/18/28 . . . Orioles

YANKEES

JUNE
23 . . . Pirates
24 . . . at Pirates
25 . . . Tigers
26 . . . at Tigers
27 . . . at Phillies
29 . . . Phillies
30 . . . Blue Jays

JULY
1/11/24 . . . at Blue Jays
2/15/25 . . . at Braves
3/14/27 . . . Braves
4/17/28 . . . at Pirates
6/16/29 . . . Pirates
7/20/30 . . . at Tigers
8/28/31 . . . Tigers
9/22 . . . Phillies
10/21 . . . at Phillies
13/23 . . . Blue Jays

AUGUST
1/14/25 . . . Phillies
3/13/26 . . . at Phillies
4/17/27 . . . at Blue Jays
5/15/28 . . . Blue Jays
6/19/29 . . . Braves
7/18/31 . . . at Braves
8/21 . . . Pirates
10/20 . . . at Pirates
11/24 . . . Tigers
12/22 . . . at Tigers

INDEPENDENT

AMERICAN ASSOCIATION

HOME GAMES ONLY

EL PASO

MAY
14-17 . . . Sioux City
19-21 . . . Pensacola
29-31 . . Shreveport-Bossier

JUNE
1-3 . . . Wichita
8-10 . . . Grand Prairie
19-21 . . . Fort Worth
30 . . . Grand Prairie

JULY
1-2 . . . Grand Prairie
3-5 . . . Shreveport-Bossier
14-16 . . . Grand Prairie
23-25 . . . Grand Prairie
26-29 . . Shreveport-Bossier

AUGUST
3-5 . . . Lincoln
14-16 . . . Pensacola
17-19 . . . Fort Worth
27-30 . . . Fort Worth

FORT WORTH

MAY
14-17 . . . Grand Prairie
18-20 . . . Sioux City
29-31 . . . Wichita

JUNE
4-7 . . . El Paso
12-14 . . . El Paso
16-18 . . . Lincoln
23-25 . . Shreveport-Bossier

JULY
3-5 . . . Pensacola
14-16 . . . St. Paul
17-19 . . . El Paso
26-29 . . . Grand Prairie

AUGUST
4-6 . . . Shreveport-Bossier
14-16 . . . Wichita
21-23 . . Shreveport-Bossier
24-26 . . . Pensacola

GRAND PRAIRIE

MAY
22-24 . . . Pensacola
26-28 . . Shreveport-Bossier

JUNE
1-3 . . . Fort Worth
4-6 . . . Pensacola
12-14 . . . Pensacola
15-18 . . . El Paso
26-28 . . . Fort Worth

JULY
3-5 . . . Sioux Falls
6-8 . . . Shreveport-Bossier
11-13 . . . Fort Worth
17-19 . . Shreveport-Bossier
30-31 . . . El Paso

AUGUST
1-2 . . . El Paso
3-6 . . . Pensacola
14-16 . . Shreveport-Bossier
24-26 . . . St. Paul

LINCOLN

MAY
22-24 . . . Fort Worth
25-27 . . . Sioux City

JUNE
1-4 . . . St. Paul
8-10 . . . Sioux City
12-14 . . . Sioux Falls
23-25 . . . El Paso
26-28 . . . Sioux City

JULY
3-5 . . . Wichita
10-12 . . . Sioux Falls
17-19 . . . Wichita
27-30 . . . Sioux City

AUGUST
7-9 . . . Sioux Falls
10-13 . . . Wichita
18-20 . . . Grand Prairie
21-23 . . . St. Paul

PENSACOLA

MAY
14-17 . Shreveport-Bossier
25-27 . . . El Paso
29-31 . . . Grand Prairie

JUNE
8-10 . . . Fort Worth
19-21 . . . Lincoln
22-25 . . . Grand Prairie
30 . . . Sioux Falls

JULY
1-2 . . . Sioux Falls
7-12 . . . El Paso
17-19 . . . St. Paul
31 . . . Fort Worth

AUGUST
1-2 . . . Fort Worth
7-9 . . . Fort Worth
10-12 . . . Grand Prairie
21-23 . . . El Paso
27-30 . . Shreveport-Bossier

SHREVEPORT-BOSSIER

MAY
19-21 . . . . . . Grand Prairie
22-24 . . . . El Paso

JUNE
1-3 . . . . Pensacola
15-18 . . . . Pensacola
19-21 . . . . . . Grand Prairie
26-28 . . . . Pensacola
29-30 . . . . Fort Worth

JULY
1-2 . . . . Fort Worth
10-12 . . . . Wichita
14-16 . . . . Pensacola
22-25 . . . . Fort Worth
July 31 . . . . Lincoln

AUGUST
1-2 . . . . Lincoln
7-9 . . . . Grand Prairie
10-12 . . . . Fort Worth
17-19 . . . . Pensacola
24-26 . . . . El Paso

SIOUX CITY

MAY
22-24 . . . . Wichita
29-31 . . . . St. Paul

JUNE
1-4 . . . . Sioux Falls
11-13 . . Shreveport-Bossier
15-17 . . . . St. Paul
22-25 . . . . Wichita

JULY
3-5 . . . . St. Paul
7-9 . . . . Lincoln
14-16 . . . . Lincoln
23-26 . . . . Pensacola
31 . . . . St. Paul

AUGUST
1-2 . . . . St. Paul
7-9 . . . . Wichita
10-12 . . . . El Paso
21-23 . . . . . . Grand Prairie
24-26 . . . . Sioux Falls

SIOUX FALLS

MAY
14-17 . . . . St. Paul
25-27 . . . . Fort Worth
29-31 . . . . Lincoln
5-7 . . . Shreveport-Bossier
8-11 . . . . Wichita
19-21 . . . . Sioux City
26-28 . . . . El Paso

JULY
7-9 . . . . Fort Worth
17-19 . . . . Sioux City
31 . . . . Wichita

AUGUST
1-2 . . . . Wichita
4-6 . . . . Sioux City
11-13 . . . . St. Paul
14-16 . . . . Sioux City
21-23 . . . . Wichita
27-30 . . . . Lincoln

ST. PAUL

MAY
19-21 . . . . Lincoln
22-24 . . . . Sioux Falls

JUNE
5-7 . . . . Sioux City
8-10 . . . Shreveport-Bossier
19-21 . . . . Wichita
23-25 . . . . Sioux Falls
29-30 . . . . Lincoln

JULY
1-2 . . . . Lincoln
10-12 . . . . Sioux City
23-25 . . . . Lincoln
27-30 . . . . Sioux Falls

AUGUST
4-6 . . . . Wichita
7-9 . . . . El Paso
14-16 . . . . Lincoln
18-20 . . . . Sioux Falls
27-30 . . . . Sioux City

WICHITA

MAY
14-17 . . . . Lincoln
19-21 . . . . Sioux Falls
26-28 . . . . St. Paul

JUNE
5-7 . . . . Lincoln
12-14 . . . . St. Paul
15-17 . . . . Sioux Falls
26-28 . . . . St. Paul
30 . . . . Sioux City

JULY
1-2 . . . . Sioux City
6-9 . . . . St. Paul
13-16 . . . . Sioux Falls
24-26 . . . . Sioux Falls
27-29 . . . . Pensacola

AUGUST
18-20 . . . . Sioux City
24-26 . . . . Lincoln
28-30 . . . . . . Grand Prairie

ATLANTIC LEAGUE

HOME GAMES ONLY

BRIDGEPORT

APRIL
23-26 . . . . York
28-30 . . . . Camden

MAY
8-10 . . . . Long Island
15-17 . . . . Newark
26-28 . . . . Somerset

JUNE
1-3 . . . . Long Island
9-11 . . . . Lancaster
12-14 . . Southern Maryland
19-21 . . . . York
29-30 . . . . Camden

JULY
1 . . . . Camden
6-8 . . . . Somerset
17-19 . . . . Newark
20-23 . . . . Camden
28-30 . . . . York

AUGUST
3-6 . . . . Southern Maryland
7-9 . . . . Lancaster
14-16 . . Southern Maryland
20-23 . . . . Somerset
31 . . . . Lancaster

SEPTEMBER
1-3 . . . . Lancaster
10-13 . . . . Long Island
17-20 . . . . Newark

CAMDEN

MAY
1-3 . . . . Southern Maryland
4-7 . . . . Bridgeport
12-14 . . . . Somerset
18-20 . . . . York
22-24 . . Southern Maryland
29-31 . . . . Lancaster

JUNE
1-3 . . . . Newark
12-14 . . . . Somerset
19-21 . . . . Newark
25-28 . . . . Long Island

JULY
2-5 . . . . Newark
10-13 . . . . Somerset
14-16 . . . . Bridgeport
24-26 . . . . Lancaster
31 . . . . Long Island

AUGUST
1-2 . . . . Long Island
11-13 . . . . York
20-23 . . . . Lancaster
24-26 . . . . Long Island
31 . . . . Southern Maryland

SEPTEMBER
1-3 . . . . Southern Maryland
7-9 . . . . York
14-16 . . . . Bridgeport

LANCASTER

APRIL
23-26 . . . . Newark
28-30 . . . . Long Island

MAY
8-10 . . . . Camden
15-17 . . Southern Maryland
22-24 . . . . Bridgeport
25-27 . . . . Newark

JUNE
4-7 . . . . Camden
15-18 . . . . Bridgeport
29-30 . . . . Somerset

JULY
1 . . . . Somerset
2-5 . . . . York
17-19 . . . . York
20-23 . . . . Long Island
28-30 . . . . Newark

AUGUST
3-6 . . . . Somerset
14-16 . . . . Camden
17-19 . . . . Somerset
24-26 . . . . Bridgeport
28-30 . . . . York

SEPTEMBER
4-6 . . . . Long Island
7-9 . . . . Southern Maryland
17-20 . . Southern Maryland

LONG ISLAND

MAY
1-3 . . . . Somerset
4-7 . . . . Lancaster
15-17 . . . . Camden
18-21 . . . . Newark
26-28 . . Southern Maryland
29-31 . . . . York

JUNE
9-11 . . . . Camden
12-14 . . . . Newark
19-21 . . . . Lancaster
29-30 . . . . York

JULY
1 . . . . York
2-5 . . . . Bridgeport
10-13 . . Southern Maryland
14-16 . . . . Lancaster
24-26 . . . . Bridgeport
28-30 . . Southern Maryland

AUGUST
7-9 . . . . Somerset
17-19 . . . . Bridgeport
20-23 . . . . York
31 . . . . Somerset

SEPTEMBER
1-3 . . . . Somerset
7-9 . . . . Newark
17-20 . . . . Camden

NEWARK

MAY
1-3 . . . Bridgeport
4-7 . . . Somerset
12-14 . . . Lancaster
22-24 . . . York
29-31 . . . Somerset

JUNE
4-7 . . . Southern Maryland
9-11 . . . York
25-28 . . . Bridgeport
29-30 . . Southern Maryland

JULY
1 . . . Southern Maryland
6-8 . . . Long Island
10-13 . . . Lancaster
14-16 . . . Somerset
24-26 . . Southern Maryland
31 . . . Bridgeport

AUGUST
1-2 . . . Bridgeport
3-6 . . . Long Island
11-13 . . . Lancaster
17-19 . . . Camden
28-30 . . . Long Island
31 . . . York

SEPTEMBER
1-3 . . . York
4-6 . . . Camden
10-13 . . . Camden

SOMERSET

APRIL
23-26 . . . Camden
28-30 . . . Newark

MAY
8-10 . . . York
18-21 . . . Lancaster
22-24 . . . Long Island

JUNE
1-3 . . . Lancaster
4-7 . . . Bridgeport
15-18 . . . Long Island
19-21 . . Southern Maryland

JULY
2-5 . . . Southern Maryland
17-19 . . . Long Island
20-23 . . . Newark
28-30 . . . Camden
31 . . . York

AUGUST
1-2 . . . York
11-13 . . . Bridgeport
14-16 . . . Newark
24-26 . . Southern Maryland
28-30 . . . Camden

SEPTEMBER
7-9 . . . Bridgeport
14-16 . . . Lancaster
17-20 . . . York

SOUTHERN MARYLAND

APRIL
23-26 . . . Long Island
28-30 . . . York

MAY
8-10 . . . Newark
12-14 . . . Long Island
18-21 . . . Bridgeport
29-31 . . . Bridgeport

JUNE
1-3 . . . York
9-11 . . . Somerset
15-18 . . . Camden
25-28 . . . Lancaster

JULY
6-8 . . . Lancaster
17-19 . . . Camden
20-23 . . . York
31 . . . Lancaster

AUGUST
1-2 . . . Lancaster
7-9 . . . Camden
11-13 . . . Long Island
20-23 . . . Newark
28-30 . . . Bridgeport

SEPTEMBER
4-6 . . . Somerset
10-13 . . . Somerset
14-16 . . . Newark

YORK

MAY
1-3 . . . Lancaster
4-7 . . . Southern Maryland
12-14 . . . Bridgeport
15-17 . . . Somerset
25-27 . . . Camden

JUNE
4-7 . . . Long Island
12-14 . . . Lancaster
15-18 . . . Newark
25-28 . . . Somerset

JULY
6-8 . . . Camden
10-13 . . . Bridgeport
14-16 . . Southern Maryland
24-26 . . . Somerset

AUGUST
3-6 . . . Camden
7-9 . . . Newark
14-16 . . . Long Island
17-19 . . Southern Maryland
24-26 . . . Newark

SEPTEMBER
4-6 . . . Bridgeport
11-13 . . . Lancaster
14-16 . . . Long Island

CAN-AM LEAGUE

HOME GAMES ONLY

ATLANTIC CITY

JUNE
4-7 . . . Quebec
8-10 . . . Ottawa
19-21 . . . New Hampshire
22-24 . . . New Jersey
29-30 . . . Worcester

JULY
1 . . . Worcester
3-5 . . . Sussex
13 . . . New Jersey
15-18 . . . Brockton
27-29 . . . Quebec
31 . . . Ottawa

AUGUST
1-2 . . . Ottawa
10-13 . . . New Hampshire
14-16 . . . Brockton
21-23 . . . Worcester
24-27 . . . Sussex

SEPTEMBER
5-7 . . . New Jersey

BROCKTON

MAY
28-31 . . . Sussex

JUNE
2-3 . . . New Hampshire
9 . . . New Hampshire
12-14 . . . New Jersey
16-18 . . . Quebec
25-28 . . . Atlantic City

JULY
6-8 . . . Ottawa
10-12 . . . Worcester
19-21 . . . Sussex
23-26 . . . New Hampshire

AUGUST
3-6 . . . New Jersey
7-9 . . . Quebec
18-20 . . . Worcester
28-30 . . . Ottawa
31 . . . Atlantic City

SEPTEMBER
1-2 . . . Atlantic City
5 . . . Worcester

NEW JERSEY

MAY
28-31 . . . Worcester

JUNE
1-3 . . . Quebec
4-7 . . . Ottawa
16-18 . . . New Hampshire
19-21 . . . Brockton
25-28 . . . Worcester

JULY
7-9 . . . Sussex
10-12 . . . Atlantic City
23-26 . . . Quebec
28-30 . . . Ottawa

AUGUST
7-9 . . . New Hampshire
10-13 . . . Brockton
18-20 . . . Atlantic City
28-30 . . . Sussex

SEPTEMBER
1-3 . . . Worcester
4 . . . Atlantic City

OTTAWA

MAY
28-31 . . . New Jersey

JUNE
1-3 . . . Atlantic City
12-14 . . . Sussex
15-17 . . . Worcester
25-28 . . . New Hampshire
30 . . . Brockton

JULY
1-2 . . . Brockton
10-13 . . . Quebec
19-21 . . . New Jersey
23-26 . . . Atlantic City

AUGUST
3-6 . . . Sussex
7-9 . . . Worcester
18-19 . . . Quebec
21-23 . . . Brockton
31 . . . New Hampshire

SEPTEMBER
1-2 . . . New Hampshire

QUEBEC

MAY
28-31 . . . Atlantic City

JUNE
9-11 . . . Sussex
12-14 . . . Worcester
22-24 . . . Ottawa

JULY
3-5 . . . Brockton
7-9 . . . New Hampshire
15-18 . . . New Jersey
20-22 . . . Atlantic City
31 . . . Sussex

AUGUST
1-2 . . . Sussex
3-6 . . . Worcester
14-16 . . . New Jersey
20 . . . Ottawa
24-27 . . . Brockton
28-31 . . . New Hampshire

SEPTEMBER
4-5 . . . Ottawa
7 . . . Ottawa

SUSSEX

JUNE
1-3 . . . Worcester
4-7 . . . Brockton
15-17 . . . Atlantic City
19-21 . . . Ottawa
25-28 . . . Quebec
30 . . . New Jersey

JULY
1-2 . . . New Jersey
10-13 . . . New Hampshire
23-26 . . . Worcester
28-30 . . . Brockton

AUGUST
7-9 . . . Atlantic City
10-13 . . . Ottawa
18-20 . . . New Hampshire
21-23 . . . New Jersey
31 . . . Quebec

SEPTEMBER
1-2 . . . Quebec

WORCESTER

JUNE
4-7 . . . New Hampshire
9-11 . . . New Jersey
19-21 . . . Quebec
22-24 . . . Brockton

JULY
3-5 . . . Ottawa
7-9 . . . Atlantic City
14 . . . Brockton
15-18 . . . Sussex
28-30 . . . New Hampshire
31 . . . New Jersey

AUGUST
1-2 . . . New Jersey
10-13 . . . Quebec
14-16 . . . Sussex
24-27 . . . Ottawa
28-30 . . . Atlantic City

SEPTEMBER
4 . . . Brockton
6-7 . . . Brockton

FRONTIER LEAGUE

HOME GAMES ONLY

EVANSVILLE

MAY
22-24 . . . Southern Illinois

JUNE
2-4 . . . Kalamazoo
5-7 . . . Traverse City
15-17 . . . Rockford
18-20 . . . River City
24-26 . . . Windy City

JULY
1-2 . . . River City
7-9 . . . Florence
17-19 . . . Washington
23-25 . . . Gateway
29-31 . . . Rockford

AUGUST
1-3 . . . Windy City
14-16 . . . Lake Erie
18-20 . . . Midwest
25-27 . . . Southern Illinois

SEPTEMBER
4-6 . . . Gateway

FLORENCE

MAY
20-23 . . . Midwest
29-31 . . . Gateway

JUNE
2-4 . . . River City
12-14 . . . Kalamazoo
15-17 . . . Washington
24-26 . . . Lake City
27-28 . . . Midwest

JULY
10-12 . . . Southern Illinois
20-22 . . . Evansville
26-28 . . . Traverse City
29-31 . . . Washington

AUGUST
4-6 . . . Kalamazoo
7-9 . . . Traverse City
18-20 . . . Windy City
21-23 . . . Rockford

SEPTEMBER
1-3 . . . Lake Erie

GATEWAY

MAY
22-24 . . . River City
26-28 . . . Washington

JUNE
5-7 . . . Florence
15-17 . . . Southern Illinois
18-20 . . . Rockford
25-26 . . . River City
27-29 . . . Evansville

JULY
3-5 . . . Windy City
17-9 . . . Lake Erie
20-22 . . . Midwest
26-28 . . . Southern Illinois
29-31 . . . Windy City

AUGUST
7-9 . . . Evansville
18-20 . . . Traverse City
21-23 . . . Kalamazoo
29 . . . River City

SEPTEMBER
1-3 . . . Rockford

KALAMAZOO

MAY
22-24 . . . Traverse City
26-28 . . . Evansville

JUNE
5-7 . . . Southern Illinois
9-11 . . . Lake Erie
15-17 . . . Midwest
18-20 . . . Florence
21-23 . . . Lake Erie
27-29 . . . Washington

JULY
3-5 . . . Washington
10-12 . . . Rockford
20-22 . . . Windy City
29-31 . . . Midwest

AUGUST
11-13 . . . River City
14-16 . . . Gateway
25-27 . . . Traverse City
28-30 . . . Florence

LAKE ERIE

JUNE
2-4 . . . Windy City
5-7 . . . Rockford
12-14 . . . Washington
15-17 . . . Traverse City
18-20 . . . Midwest
27-29 . . . Traverse City

JULY
3-5 . . . Florence
7-9 . . . Gateway
10-12 . . . River City
23-25 . . . Florence
26-28 . . . Kalamazoo

AUGUST
1-3 . . . Kalamazoo
7-9 . . . Midwest
11-13 . . . Southern Illinois
21-23 . . . Evansville
25-27 . . . Washington

SEPTEMBER
4-6 . . . Midwest

MIDWEST

MAY
29-31 . . . Windy City

JUNE
2-4 . . . Rockford
9-11 . . . Florence
24-26 . . . Kalamazoo
30 . . . Lake Erie

JULY
1 . . . Lake Erie
7-9 . . . River City
10-12 . . . Gateway
23-25 . . . Kalamazoo

AUGUST
1-3 . . . Washington
4-6 . . . Traverse City
11-13 . . . Evansville
14-16 . . . Southern Illinois
25-27 . . . Florence
28-30 . . . Washington
31 . . . Traverse City

SEPTEMBER
1-2 . . . Traverse City

RIVER CITY

MAY
23 . . . Gateway
26-28 . . . Florence

JUNE
10-11 . . . Gateway
13-14 . . . Evansville
21-23 . . . Windy City
27-29 . . . Southern Illinois

JULY
3-5 . . . Rockford
17-19 . . . Midwest
20-22 . . . Lake Erie
26-28 . . . Rockford

AUGUST
4-6 . . . Southern Illinois
7-9 . . . Windy City
18-20 . . . Kalamazoo
21-23 . . . Traverse City
28-30 . . . Gateway

SEPTEMBER
1-3 . . . Evansville

ROCKFORD

MAY
26-28 . . . Midwest
29-31 . . . Lake Erie

JUNE
9-11 . . . Windy City
12-14 . . . Gateway
21-23 . . . Evansville
30 . . . Gateway

JULY
1-2 . . . Gateway
7-9 . . . Traverse City
17-19 . . . Kalamazoo
23-25 . . . Southern Illinois

AUGUST
1-3 . . . River City
4-6 . . . Evansville
11-13 . . . Washington
14-16 . . . Florence
25-27 . . . River City
28-30 . . . Southern Illinois

SEPTEMBER
4-6 . . . Windy City

SOUTHERN ILLINOIS

MAY
29-31 . . . . Kalamazoo

JUNE
2-4. . . . . Traverse City
9-11 . . . . Evansville
12-14 . . . . Windy City
21-23 . . . . Gateway
24-26 . . . . Rockford

JULY
3-5. . . . . Evansville
17-19 . . . . Florence
20-22 . . . . Washington
29-31 . . . . River City

AUGUST
1-3. . . . . Gateway
7-9. . . . . Rockford
18-20 . . . . Lake Erie
21-23 . . . . Midwest

SEPTEMBER
1-3. . . . . Windy City
4-6. . . . . River City

TRAVERSE CITY

MAY
26-28 . . . . Southern Illinois
29-31 . . . . Evansville

JUNE
9-11 . . . . Washington
12-14 . . . . Midwest
21-23 . . . . Florence
24-26 . . . . Washington
30 . . . . Kalamazoo

JULY
1-2. . . . . Kalamazoo
3-5. . . . . Midwest
17-19 . . . . Windy City
20-22 . . . . Rockford
29-31 . . . . Lake Erie

AUGUST
1-3. . . . . Florence
11-13 . . . . Gateway
14-16 . . . . River City
28-30 . . . . Lake Erie

SEPTEMBER
4-6. . . . . Kalamazoo

WASHINGTON

MAY
22-24 . . . . Lake Erie

JUNE
2-4. . . . . Gateway
5-7. . . . . River City
18-20 . . . . . . Traverse City
21-23 . . . . Midwest
30 . . . . Florence

JULY
1-2. . . . . Florence
7-9. . . . . . Southern Illinois
10-12 . . . . Evansville
23-25 . . . . . . Traverse City
26-28 . . . . Midwest

AUGUST
4-6. . . . . Lake Erie
7-9. . . . . Kalamazoo
18-20 . . . . Rockford
21-23 . . . . Windy City

SEPTEMBER
1-3. . . . . Kalamazoo
4-6. . . . . Florence

WINDY CITY

MAY
21-24 . . . . Rockford
26-28 . . . . Lake Erie

JUNE
5-7. . . . . Midwest
15-17 . . . . River City
18-20 . . . . Southern Illinois
27-29 . . . . Rockford
30 . . . . . . Southern Illinois

JULY
1-2. . . . . . Southern Illinois
7-9. . . . . Kalamazoo
10-12 . . . . . . Traverse City
23-25 . . . . River City
26-28 . . . . Evansville

AUGUST
4-6. . . . . Gateway
11-13 . . . . Florence
14-16 . . . . Washington
25-27 . . . . Gateway
28-30 . . . . Evansville

GOLDEN LEAGUE

HOME GAMES ONLY

CALGARY VIPERS

MAY
21-24 . . . . Long Beach
25-27 . . . . Victoria

JUNE
5-7. . . . . . Orange County
8-10 . . . . Saint George
15-17 . . . . Victoria
23-25 . . . . Victoria
26-28 . . . . Tucson

JULY
10-12 . . . . Yuma
16-19 . . . . Chico
24-26 . . . . Edmonton

AUGUST
4-6. . . . . Tucson
7-9. . . . . Tijuana
14-16 . . . . Victoria
25-27 . . . . Edmonton

CHICO OUTLAWS

MAY
25-27 . . . . . Orange County
29-31 . . . . Calgary

JUNE
5-7. . . . . Victoria
16-18 . . . . Tucson
19-21 . . . . Long Beach
22-24 . . . . . Orange County
30 . . . . Edmonton

JULY
1-3. . . . . Edmonton
10-12 . . . . Tijuana
24-26 . . . . Yuma
28-30 . . . . . . Saint George
31 . . . . Long Beach

AUGUST
1-2. . . . . Long Beach
14-16 . . . . Tucson
25-27 . . . . Edmonton
28-31 . . . . . Orange County

EDMONTON CRACKER-CATS

MAY
21-24 . . . . Victoria
25-27 . . . . Long Beach

JUNE
5-7. . . . . Saint George
8-10 . . . . Yuma
23-25 . . . . Long Beach
26-28 . . . . Victoria

JULY
7-9. . . . . Saint George
10-12 . . . . Victoria
21-23 . . . . Calgary
31 . . . . Tucson

AUGUST
1-2. . . . . Tucson
4-5. . . . . Chico
17-19 . . . . Calgary
21-23 . . . . Tijuana
28-31 . . . . Calgary

LONG BEACH ARMADA

JUNE
9-11 . . . . Tijuana
12-14 . . . . Yuma
15-17 . . . . Edmonton
26-28 . . . . . Orange County
30 . . . . Tijuana

JULY
1-3. . . . . Tijuana
7-9. . . . . Chico
10-12 . . . . Tucson
21-23 . . . . . . Saint George
24-26 . . . . . Orange County
28-30 . . . . Yuma

AUGUST
11-13 . . . . Tijuana
14-16 . . . . Yuma
18-20 . . . . . . Saint George
28-31 . . . . Victoria

ORANGE COUNTY FLYERS

JUNE
9-11 . . . . Victoria
12-13 . . . . Edmonton
19-20 . . . . . . Saint George
30 . . . . Yuma

JULY
1-3. . . . . Yuma
4-5. . . . . Saint George
6-8. . . . . Calgary
16-18 . . . . Yuma
21-23 . . . . Chico
28-30 . . . . Tijuana
31 . . . . Saint George

AUGUST
1 . . . . Saint George
4-6. . . . . Long Beach
11-13 . . . . Chico
14-15 . . . . . . Saint George
25-27 . . . . Long Beach

ST. GEORGE ROADRUNNERS

MAY
26-28 . . . . Yuma
29-30 . . . . Edmonton

JUNE
1-3. . . . . Chico
12-13 . . . . Tucson
15-18 . . . . . Orange County
23-25 . . . . Yuma
30 . . . . Calgary

JULY
1-3. . . . . Calgary
10-12 . . . . . Orange County
16-20 . . . . Tucson
24-27 . . . . Tijuana

AUGUST
3-5. . . . . Victoria
7-10 . . . . Long Beach
21-24 . . . . Long Beach
25-27 . . . . Tucson

TIJUANA POTROS

MAY
21-24 . . . . Orange County
26-28 . . . . Tucson

JUNE
2-3. . . . . Long Beach
5-7. . . . . Tucson
12-14 . . . . Chico
19-21 . . . . Calgary
26-28 . . . . . . Saint George

JULY
4-6. . . . . Chico
16-19 . . . . Long Beach
21-23 . . . . Victoria
31 . . . . Calgary

AUGUST
1-2. . . . . Calgary
3-5. . . . . Yuma
14-15 . . . . Edmonton
18-20 . . . . Chico

TUCSON TOROS

MAY
21-24 . . . . Chico
29-31 . . . . Orange County

JUNE
1-3. . . . . Edmonton
9-11 . . . . Chico
19-21 . . . . Yuma
23-25 . . . . Tijuana

JULY
4-6. . . . . Long Beach
7-9. . . . . Tijuana
24-26 . . . . Victoria
28-30 . . . . Calgary

AUGUST
7-9. . . . . Edmonton
11-13 . . . . . . Saint George
21-23 . . . . Orange County
28-31 . . . . . . Saint George

VICTORIA SEALS

MAY
29-31 . . . . Long Beach

JUNE
2-4. . . . . . . Orange County
12-14 . . . . Calgary
19-21 . . . . Edmonton
30 . . . . Tucson

JULY
1-3. . . . . Tucson
4-6. . . . . Edmonton
7-9. . . . . Yuma
16-19 . . . . Edmonton
28-30 . . . . Edmonton

AUGUST
7-9. . . . . Chico
11-13 . . . . Calgary
18-20 . . . . . Orange County
21-23 . . . . Calgary
25-27 . . . . Tijuana

YUMA SCORPIONS

MAY
22-25 . . . . . . Saint George
29-31 . . . . Tijuana

JUNE
1-3. . . . . Calgary
4-6. . . . . Long Beach
16-18 . . . . Tijuana
26-28 . . . . Chico

JULY
4-5. . . . . Calgary
21-23 . . . . Tucson
31 . . . . Victoria

AUGUST
1-2. . . . . Victoria
7-9. . . . . . . Orange County
11-13 . . . . Edmonton
18-20 . . . . Tucson
21-23 . . . . Chico
28-31 . . . . Tijuana

NORTHERN LEAGUE

HOME GAMES ONLY

FARGO-MOORHEAD

MAY
15-17 . . . . Gary
19-21 . . . . Winnipeg
29-31 . . . . Gary

JUNE
1-4. . . . . Schaumburg
12-14 . . . . Kansas City
16-18 . . . . Winnipeg
23-25 . . . . Gary

JULY
3-5. . . . . Joliet
17-19 . . . . Winnipeg
21-23 . . . . Joliet
24-26 . . . . . . Schaumburg

AUGUST
3-6. . . . . Kansas City
7-9. . . . . Joliet
21-23 . . . . Gary
24-27 . . . . Kansas City

GARY

MAY
18-19 . . . . Joliet
22-24 . . . Fargo-Moorhead

JUNE
2 . . . . Joliet
5-7. . . . . Joliet
12-14 . . . . . . Schaumburg
15-18 . . . . Kansas City
26-28 . . . . Joliet
30 . . . . . Fargo-Moorhead

JULY
1-2. . . . . Fargo-Moorhead
3-5. . . . . Winnipeg
13-16 . . . . Kansas City
17-19 . . . . . . Schaumburg
30 . . . . Joliet

AUGUST
3-6. . . . . Schaumburg
13-16 . . . . Winnipeg
25-27 . . . . . . Schaumburg
28-31 . . . Fargo-Moorhead

JOLIET

MAY
15-17 . . . . . . Schaumburg
20-21 . . . . Gary
29-31 . . . . Winnipeg

JUNE
3-4. . . . . Gary
14-15 . . . . Winnipeg
16-18 . . . . . . Schaumburg
29-30 . . . . Kansas City

JULY
1-2. . . . . Kansas City
9-12 . . . . Schaumburg
14-16 . . . Fargo-Moorhead
24-26 . . . . Kansas City
28-29 . . . . Gary
31 . . . . . Fargo-Moorhead

AUGUST
1-2. . . . . Fargo-Moorhead
10-12 . . . . Winnipeg
14-16 . . . Fargo-Moorhead
17-19 . . . . Gary
28-31 . . . . Kansas City

KANSAS CITY

MAY
15-17 . . . . Winnipeg
18-20 . . . . . . Schaumburg
26-28 . . . . Joliet
29-31 . . . . . . Schaumburg

JUNE
1-3. . . . . Winnipeg
9-11 . . . . Fargo-Moorhead
19-21 . . . . Fargo Moorhead
23-25 . . . . Winnipeg

JULY
9-12 . . . . Fargo-Moorhead
17-19 . . . . Joliet
28-30 . . . . Winnipeg
31 . . . . Gary

AUGUST
1-2. . . . . Gary
7-11 . . . . Gary
18-19 . . . . . . Schaumburg
20-23 . . . . Joliet

SCHAUMBURG

MAY
22-24 . . . . Joliet
25-27 . . . Fargo-Moorhead

JUNE
5-7. . . . . Kansas City
9-11 . . . . Joliet
19-21 . . . . Gary
23-25 . . . . Joliet
26-28 . . . . Kansas City

JULY
3-5. . . . . Kansas City
13-16 . . . . Winnipeg
20-22 . . . . Gary
28-30 . . . Fargo-Moorhead
31 . . . . Winnipeg

AUGUST
1-2. . . . . Winnipeg
10-13 . . . Fargo-Moorhead
14-16 . . . . Kansas City
20-23 . . . . Winnipeg

WINNIPEG

MAY
22-24 . . . . Kansas City
25-27 . . . . Gary

JUNE
5-7. . . . . Fargo-Moorhead
8-11 . . . . Gary
19-22 . . . . Joliet
26-28 . . . Fargo-Moorhead
29-30 . . . . . . Schaumburg

JULY
1 . . . . Schaumburg
10-12 . . . . Gary
21-23 . . . . Kansas City
24-26 . . . . Gary

AUGUST
4-6. . . . . Joliet
7-9. . . . . Schaumburg
17-19 . . . Fargo-Moorhead
24-26 . . . . Joliet
28-31 . . . . . . Schaumburg

COLLEGE

COLLEGE ORGANIZATIONS

NATIONAL COLLEGIATE ATHLETIC ASSOCIATION

Mailing Address: PO Box 6222, Indianapolis, IN 46206. **Telephone:** (317) 917-6222. **Fax:** (317) 917-6826 (championships), 917-6710 (baseball). **E-Mail Addresses:** dpoppe@ncaa.org (Dennis Poppe), rbuhr@ncaa.org (Randy Buhr), dleech@ncaa.org (Damani Leech), jhamilton@ncaa.org (J.D. Hamilton), ryurk@ncaa.org (Russ Yurk), phairston@ncaa.org (Patrick Hairston). **Websites:** www.ncaa.org, www.ncaa.com.

President: Myles Brand. **Vice President for Division I Baseball and Football:** Dennis Poppe. **Director, Baseball:** Damani Leech. **Associate Director, Championships:** Randy Buhr. **Division II Assistant Director, Championships:** Russ Yurk. **Division III Associate Director, Championships:** Patrick Hairston. **Media Contact, Division I College World Series:** J.D. Hamilton. **Contact, Statistics:** Sean Straziscar, Jeff Williams.

Chairman, Division I Baseball Committee: Tim Weiser (Deputy Commissioner, Big 12 Conference). **Division I Baseball Committee:** John Anderson (head coach, Minnesota), Pat Murphy (head coach, Arizona State), Brian Quinn (athletic director, Cal State Fullerton), Bobby Staub (athletic director, Louisiana-Monroe).

Assistant Athletics Director: Gary Overton (East Carolina University). **Athletics Director, Director of Athletics:** John P. Hardt (Bucknell), Lynn W. Thompson (Bethune-Cookman), Chris Monasch (St. John's). **Commissioner:** Kyle Kallander (Big South Conference).

Chairman, Division II Baseball Committee: Joseph Clinton (Dominican College). **Chairman, Division III Baseball Committee:** Malcolm Driggers Jr. (baseball coach, McMurry).

2009 National Convention: Jan. 14-17 at Washington, D.C.

2009 CHAMPIONSHIP TOURNAMENTS

NCAA Division I

62nd College World Series . . . . Omaha, June 13-23/24
Super Regionals (8) . . . . Campus sites, June 5-8
Regionals (16) . . . . Campus sites, May 29-June 1

NCAA Division II

42nd World Series . . USA Baseball National Training Complex, May 23-30.
Regionals (8) . . . . Campus sites, May 14-17.

NCAA Division III

32nd World Series . . . . Appleton, Wis., May 22-26
Regionals (8) . . . . Campus sites, May 13-17

NATIONAL ASSOCIATION OF INTERCOLLEGIATE ATHLETICS

Mailing Address: 1200 Grand Blvd., Kansas City, MO 64106. **Telephone:** (816) 595-8000. **Fax:** (816) 595-8200. **Website:** www.naia.org.

President/CEO: Jim Carr. **VP for Championships:** Lori Thomas. **Manager, Championship Sports:** Scott McClure. **Director, Sports Information:** Chad Waller. **President, Coaches Association:** Denney Crabaugh.

2009 CHAMPIONSHIP TOURNAMENT

Opening rounds: May 12-15, campus locations.

53rd Annual Avista-NAIA World Series: Lewiston, Idaho, May 22-29.

NATIONAL JUNIOR COLLEGE ATHLETIC ASSOCIATION

Mailing Address: 1755 Telstar Dr., Suite 103, Colorado Springs, CO 80920. **Telephone:** (719) 590-9788. **Fax:** (719) 590-7324. **Website:** www.njcaa.org.

Executive Director (acting): Mary Ellen Leight. **Director, Division I Baseball Tournament:** Jamie Hamilton. **Director, Division II Baseball Tournament:** Billy Mayberry. **Director, Division III Baseball Tournament:** Tim Drain. **Director, Media Relations:** Mark Krug.

2009 CHAMPIONSHIP TOURNAMENTS

Division I

World Series . . . . Grand Junction, Colo., May 23-30

Division II

World Series . . . . Enid, Okla., May 23-29

Division III

World Series . . . . Tyler, Texas, May 16-22

CALIFORNIA COMMUNITY COLLEGE COMMISSION ON ATHLETICS

Mailing Address: 2017 O St., Sacramento, CA 95814. **Telephone:** (916) 444-1600. **Fax:** (916) 444-2616. **E-Mail Address:** ccarter@coasports.org. **Website:** www.coasports.org.

Executive Director: Carlyle Carter. **Director, Member Services:** Debra Wheeler.

2009 CHAMPIONSHIP TOURNAMENT

State Championship . . . . Fresno, Calif., May 23-25

NORTHWEST ATHLETIC ASSOCIATION OF COMMUNITY COLLEGES

Mailing Address: Clark College PLS-033, 1933 Fort Vancouver Way, Vancouver, WA 98663-3598. **Telephone:** (360) 992-2833. **Fax:** (360) 696-6210. **Website:** www.nwaacc.org. **E-Mail Address:** nwaacc@clark.edu.

Executive Director: Dick McClain. **Executive Assistant:** Carol Hardin. **Director, Marketing:** Charlie Warner. **Sports Information Director:** Tracy Swisher.

2009 CHAMPIONSHIP TOURNAMENT

NWAACC Championship . . . . . Longview, Wash., May 21-25

AMERICAN BASEBALL COACHES ASSOCIATION

Office Address: 108 S. University Ave., Suite 3, Mount Pleasant, MI 48858-2327. **Telephone:** (989) 775-3300. **Fax:** (989) 775-3600. **E-Mail Address:** abca@abca.org. **Website:** www.abca.org.

Executive Director: Dave Keilitz. **Assistant to Executive Director:** Betty Rulong. **Membership/Convention Coordinator:** Nick Phillips. **Assistant Coordinator:** Juahn Clark.

Chairman: Glen Tuckett (Brigham Young). **President:** Pat McMahon.

2010 National Convention: Jan. 7-10 at Dallas Anatole.

NCAA DIVISION I CONFERENCES

AMERICA EAST CONFERENCE

Mailing Address: 215 First Street, Suite 140, Cambridge, MA 02142. **Telephone:** (617) 695-6369. **Fax:** (617) 695-6385. **E-Mail Address:** hanna@americaeast.com. **Website:** www.americaeast.com.

Baseball Members (First Year): Albany (2002), Binghamton (2002), Hartford (1990), Maine (1990), Maryland-Baltimore County (2004), Stony Brook (2002), Vermont (1990).

Director, Communications: Sean Tainsh.

2009 Tournament: Four teams, double-elimination. May 21-23 at highest-seeded team with lights.

ATLANTIC COAST CONFERENCE

Office Address: 4512 Weybridge Lane, Greensboro, NC 27407. **Mailing Address:** PO Drawer ACC, Greensboro, NC 27417. **Telephone:** (336) 851-6062. **Fax:** (336) 854-8797. **E-Mail Address:** sphillips@theacc.org. **Website:** www.theacc.com.

Baseball Members (First Year): Boston College (2006), Clemson (1954), Duke (1954), Florida State (1992), Georgia Tech (1980), Maryland (1954), Miami (2005), North Carolina (1954), North Carolina State (1954), Virginia (1955), Virginia Tech (2005), Wake Forest (1954).

Assistant Director, Media Relations: Steve Phillips.

2009 Tournament: Eight teams, group play. May 20-24 at Durham, N.C.

ATLANTIC SUN CONFERENCE

Mailing Address: 3370 Vineville Ave., **Suite 108-B, Macon, GA 31204. Telephone:** (478) 474-3394. **Fax:** (478) 474-4272. **E-Mail Address:** emoyer@atlanticsun.org. **Website:** www.atlanticsun.org.

Baseball Members (First Year): Belmont (2002), Campbell (1995), East Tennessee State (2006), Florida Gulf Coast (2008), Jacksonville (1999), Kennesaw State (2006), Lipscomb (2004), Mercer (1979), North Florida (2006), South Carolina Upstate (2008), Stetson (1986).

Assistant Commissioner, Championships/Communications: Eric Moyer.

2009 Tournament: Six teams, double-elimination. **May 20-23 at DeLand, Fla. (Stetson).**

ATLANTIC 10 CONFERENCE

Mailing Address: 230 S. Broad St., Suite 1700, Philadelphia, PA 19102. **Telephone:** (215) 545-6678. **Fax:** (215) 545-3342. **E-Mail Address:** shaug@atlantic10.org. **Website:** www.atlantic10.org.

Baseball Members (First Year): Charlotte (2006), Dayton (1996), Duquesne (1977), Fordham (1996), George Washington (1977), LaSalle (1996), Massachusetts (1977), Rhode Island (1981), Richmond (2002), St. Bonaventure (1980), Saint Joseph's (1983), Saint Louis (2006), Temple (1983), Xavier (1996).

Director, Baseball Communications: Stephen Haug.

2009 Tournament: Six teams, double elimination. May 20-23 at Fifth Third Field, Dayton, OH.

BIG EAST CONFERENCE

Mailing Address: 222 Richmond St., Suite 110, Providence, RI 02903. **Telephone:** (401) 453-0660. **Fax:** (401) 751-8540. **E-Mail Address:** jgust@bigeast.org. **Website:** www.bigeast.org.

Baseball Members (First Year): Cincinnati (2006), Connecticut (1985), Georgetown (1985), Louisville (2006), Notre Dame (1996), Pittsburgh (1985), Rutgers (1996), St. John's (1985), Seton Hall (1985), South Florida (2006), Villanova (1985), West Virginia (1996).

Director, Communications: Chuck Sullivan.

2009 Championship: Eight teams, double-elimination. May 19-23 at Clearwater, Fla.

BIG SOUTH CONFERENCE

Mailing Address: 7233 Pineville-Matthews Rd., Suite 100, Charlotte, NC 28226. **Telephone:** (704) 341-7990. **Fax:** (704) 341-7991. **E-Mail Address:** marks@bigsouth.org. **Website:** www.bigsouthsports.com.

Baseball Members (First Year): Charleston Southern (1983), Coastal Carolina (1983), Gardner-Webb (2009), High Point (1999), Liberty (1991), UNC Asheville (1985), Presbyterian (2009), Radford (1983), Virginia Military Institute (2004), Winthrop (1983).

Assistant Commissioner, Public Relations: Mark Simpson.

2009 Tournament: Eight teams, single-elimination in first round followed by six-team double-elimination. May 19-23 at Asheville, N.C.

BIG 10 CONFERENCE

Mailing Address: 1500 W. Higgins Rd., Park Ridge, IL 60068. **Telephone:** (847) 696-1010. **Fax:** (847) 696-1110. **E-Mail Addresses:** schipman@bigten.org; vtodryk@bigten.org. **Website:** www.bigten.org.

Baseball Members (First Year): Illinois (1896), Indiana (1906), Iowa (1906), Michigan (1896), Michigan State (1950), Minnesota (1906), Northwestern (1898), Ohio State (1913), Penn State (1992), Purdue (1906).

Assistant Commissioner, Communications: Scott Chipman. **Assistant Director, Communications:** Valerie Todryk.

2009 Tournament: Six teams, double-elimination. May 20-23 at Huntington Park in Columbus, Ohio.

BIG 12 CONFERENCE

Mailing Address: 400 E. John Carpenter Freeway, Irving, TX 75062. **Telephone:** (469) 524-1000. **E-Mail Address:** carmen@big12sports.com. **Website:** www.big12sports.com.

Baseball Members (First Year): Baylor (1997), Kansas (1997), Kansas State (1997), Missouri (1997), Nebraska (1997), Oklahoma (1997), Oklahoma State (1997), Texas (1997), Texas A&M (1997), Texas Tech (1997).

Assistant Director of Communications: Carmen Branch.

2009 Tournament: Two divisions, pool play format. May 20-24 at AT&T Bricktown Ballpark, Oklahoma City.

BIG WEST CONFERENCE

Mailing Address: 2 Corporate Park, Suite 206, Irvine, CA 92606. **Telephone:** (949) 261-2525. **Fax:** (949) 261-2528. **E-Mail Address:** jstcyr@bigwest.org. **Website:** www.bigwest.org.

Baseball Members (First Year): Cal Poly (1997), UC Davis (2008), UC Irvine (2002), UC Riverside (2002), UC Santa Barbara (1970), Cal State Fullerton (1975), Cal State Northridge (2001), Long Beach State (1970), Pacific (1972).

Associate Information Director: Julie St. Cyr.

2009 Tournament: None.

COLONIAL ATHLETIC ASSOCIATION

Mailing Address: 8625 Patterson Ave., Richmond, VA 23229. **Telephone:** (804) 754-1616. **Fax:** (804) 754-1830. **E-Mail Address:** rwashburn@caasports.com. **Website:** www.caasports.com.

Baseball Members (First Year): Delaware (2002), George Mason (1986), Georgia State (2006), Hofstra

(2002), James Madison (1986), UNC Wilmington (1986), Northeastern (2006), Old Dominion (1992), Towson (2002), Virginia Commonwealth (1996), William & Mary (1986).

Sports Information Director: Rob Washburn.

2009 Tournament: Six teams, double-elimination. May 20-23 at Wilmington, N.C. (UNC Wilmington).

CONFERENCE USA

Mailing Address: 5201 N. O'Connor Blvd., Suite 300, Irving, TX 75039. **Telephone:** (214) 774-1300. **Fax:** (214) 496-0055. **E-Mail Address:** rdanderson@c-usa.org. **Website:** www.c-usasports.com.

Baseball Members (First Year): Alabama-Birmingham (1996), Central Florida (2006), East Carolina (2002), Houston (1997), Marshall (2006), Memphis (1996), Rice (2006), Southern Mississippi (1996), Tulane (1996).

Assistant Commissioner, Media Relations: Russell Anderson.

2009 Tournament: Eight teams, double-elimination. May 20-24 at Hattiesburg, Miss. (Southern Mississippi).

HORIZON LEAGUE

Mailing Address: 201 S. Capitol Ave., Suite 500, Indianapolis, IN 46225. **Telephone:** (317) 237-5621. **Fax:** (317) 237-5620. **E-Mail Address:** msegal@horizonleague.org. **Website:** www.horizonleague.org.

Baseball Members (First Year): Butler (1979), Cleveland State (1994), Illinois-Chicago (1994), Wisconsin-Milwaukee (1994), Valparaiso (2008), Wright State (1994), Youngstown State (2002).

Director, Communications: Matt Segal.

2009 Tournament: Seven teams, double-elimination. May 19-23 at Pipe Yard Stadium in Lorain, Ohio (Cleveland State).

IVY LEAGUE

Mailing Address: 228 Alexander Rd., Second Floor, Princeton, NJ 08544. **Telephone:** (609) 258-6426. **Fax:** (609) 258-1690. **E-Mail Address:** info@ivyleaguesports.com. **Website:** www.ivyleaguesports.com.

Baseball Members (First Year): Rolfe—Brown (1948), Dartmouth (1930), Harvard (1948), Yale (1930). Gehrig—Columbia (1930), Cornell (1930), Pennsylvania (1930), Princeton (1930).

Assistant Director, Communications: Alex Searle.

2009 Tournament: Best-of-three series between division champions. May 2-3 at team with best overall record.

METRO ATLANTIC ATHLETIC CONFERENCE

Mailing Address: 712 Amboy Ave., Edison, NJ 08837. Telephone: (732) 738-5455. **Fax:** (732) 738-8366. **E-Mail Address:** jill.skotarczak@maac.org. **Website:** www.maacsports.com.

Baseball Members (First Year): Canisius (1990), Fairfield (1982), Iona (1982), Manhattan (1982), Marist (1998), Niagara (1990), Rider (1998), St. Peter's (1982), Siena (1990).

Assistant Commissioner, Media Relations: Jill Skotarczak.

2009 Tournament: Four teams, double-elimination. May 20-22 at Trenton, NJ (Rider).

MID-AMERICAN CONFERENCE

Mailing Address: 24 Public Square, 15th Floor, Cleveland, OH 44113. **Telephone:** (216) 566-4622. **Fax:** (216) 858-9622. **E-Mail Address:** jguy@mac-sports.com. **Website:** www.mac-sports.com.

Baseball Members (First Year): Akron (1992), Ball State (1973), Bowling Green State (1952), Buffalo (2001), Central Michigan (1971), Eastern Michigan (1971), Kent State (1951), Miami (1947), Northern Illinois (1997), Ohio (1946). Toledo (1950), Western Michigan (1947).

Associate Director, Media Relations: Jeremy Guy.

2009 Tournament: Eight teams (two division winners, six wild-card teams with next-best conference winning percentage), double-elimination. May 20-23 at VA Memorial Stadium (Chillicothe, Ohio).

MID-EASTERN ATHLETIC CONFERENCE

Mailing Address: 222 Central Park Ave., Suite 1150, Virginia Beach, VA 23462. **Telephone:** (757) 416-7100. **Fax:** (757) 416-7109. **E-Mail Address:** jinksm@themeac.com; allemanm@themeac.com. **Website:** www.meacsports.com.

Baseball Members (First Year): Bethune-Cookman (1979), Coppin State (1985), Delaware State (1970), Florida A&M (1979), Maryland-Eastern Shore (1970), Norfolk State (1998), North Carolina A&T (1970).

Assistant Director, Media Relations/Baseball Contact: Sahar Abdur-Rashid.

2009 Tournament: Six teams, double-elimination. May 14-17 at Ormond Beach, Fla. (Bethune-Cookman).

MISSOURI VALLEY CONFERENCE

Mailing Address: 1818 Chouteau Ave., St. Louis, MO 63103. **Telephone:** (314) 421-0339. **Fax:** (314) 421-3505. **E-Mail Address:** kbriscoe@mvc.org. **Website:** www.mvc.org.

Baseball Members (First Year): Bradley (1955), Creighton (1976), Evansville (1994), Illinois State (1980), Indiana State (1976), Missouri State (1990), Northern Iowa (1991), Southern Illinois (1974), Wichita State (1945).

Assistant Director, Communications: Kelli Briscoe.

2009 Tournament: A six-team tournament with two three-team pods and the winner of each pod meeting in a single championship game. May 20-23 at Wichita, Kan.

MOUNTAIN WEST CONFERENCE

Mailing Address: 15455 Gleneagle Dr., Suite 200B, Colorado Springs, CO 80921. **Telephone:** (719) 488-4052. **Fax:** (719) 487-7241. **E-Mail Address:** medge@themwc.com. **Website:** www.themwc.com.

Baseball Members (First Year): Air Force (2000), BYU (2000), UNLV (2000), New Mexico (2000), San Diego State (2000), TCU (2006), Utah (2000).

Assistant Director, Communications: Marlon Edge.

2009 Tournament: Six teams, double-elimination. May 19-23 at Fort Worth, Texas (Texas Christian).

NORTHEAST CONFERENCE

Mailing Address: 399 Campus Drive, Somerset, NJ 08873. **Telephone:** (732) 469-0440. **Fax:** (732) 469-0744. **E-Mail Address:** rratner@northeastconference.org. **Website:** www.northeastconference.org.

Baseball Members (First Year): Central Connecticut State (1999), Fairleigh Dickinson (1981), Long Island (1981), Monmouth (1985), Mount St. Mary's (1989), Quinnipiac (1999), Sacred Heart (2000), Wagner (1981).

Associate Commissioner: Ron Ratner.

2009 Tournament: Four teams, double-elimination. May 21-23. Site TBA.

OHIO VALLEY CONFERENCE

Mailing Address: 215 Centerview Dr., Suite 115, Brentwood, TN 37027. **Telephone:** (615) 371-1698. **Fax:** (615) 371-1788. **E-Mail Address:** kschwartz@ovc.org. **Website:** www.ovcsports.com.

Baseball Members (First Year): Austin Peay State (1962), Eastern Illinois (1996), Eastern Kentucky (1948), Jacksonville State (2003), Morehead State (1948), Murray

State (1948), Southeast Missouri State (1991), Tennessee-Martin (1992), Tennessee Tech (1949).

Assistant Commissioner: Kyle Schwartz.

2009 Tournament: Six teams, double-elimination. May 20-24 at Paducah, Ky.

PACIFIC-10 CONFERENCE

Mailing Address: 1350 Treat Blvd., Suite 500. **Telephone:** (925) 932-4411. **Fax:** (925) 932-4601. **Website:** www.pac-10.org.

Baseball Members (First Year): Arizona (1979), Arizona State (1979), California (1916), UCLA (1928), Oregon (1916-1981, 2009) Oregon State (1916), Southern California (1923), Stanford (1918), Washington (1916), Washington State (1919).

Public Relations Intern: Regina Verlengiere.

2009 Tournament: None.

PATRIOT LEAGUE

Mailing Address: 3773 Corporate Pkwy., Suite 190, Center Valley, PA 18034. **Telephone:** (610) 289-1963. **Fax:** (610) 289-1952. **E-Mail Address:** mdougherty@patriotleague.com. **Website:** www.patriotleague.com.

Baseball Members (First Year): Army (1993), Bucknell (1991), Holy Cross (1991), Lafayette (1991), Lehigh (1991), Navy (1993).

Assistant Director, Media Relations: Matt Dougherty.

2009 Tournament: Four teams, May 9-10 and May 16-17 at site of higher seeds.

SOUTHEASTERN CONFERENCE

Mailing Address: 2201 Richard Arrington Blvd. N., Birmingham, AL 35203. **Telephone:** (205) 458-3000. **Fax:** (205) 458-3030. **E-Mail Address:** cdunlap@sec.org. **Website:** www.secsports.com.

Baseball Members (First Year): East—Florida (1933), Georgia (1933), Kentucky (1933), South Carolina (1992), Tennessee (1933), Vanderbilt (1933). West—Alabama (1933), Arkansas (1992), Auburn (1933), Louisiana State (1933), Mississippi (1933), Mississippi State (1933).

Associate Director, Media Relations: Chuck Dunlap.

2009 Tournament: Eight teams, modified double-elimination. May 20-24 at Hoover, Ala.

SOUTHERN CONFERENCE

Mailing Address: 702 N. Pine St., Spartanburg, SC 29303. **Telephone:** (864) 591-5100. **Fax:** (864) 591-4282. **E-Mail Address:** jcaskey@socon.org. **Website:** www.soconsports.com.

Baseball Members (First Year): Appalachian State (1971), Charleston (1998), The Citadel (1936), Davidson (1991), Elon (2004), Furman (1936), Georgia Southern (1991), UNC Greensboro (1997), Samford (2009, Western Carolina (1976), Wofford (1997).

Media Relations: Jonathan Caskey.

2009 Tournament: Ten teams, double-elimination. May 20-24 at Fluor Field in Greenville, S.C.

SOUTHLAND CONFERENCE

Mailing Address: 2600 Network Blvd., Suite 150, Frisco, Texas 75034. **Telephone:** (972) 422-9500. **Fax:** (972) 422-9225. **E-Mail Address:** tlamb@southland.org. **Website:** www.southland.org.

Baseball Members (First Year): Central Arkansas (2007), Lamar (1999), Louisiana-Monroe (1983), McNeese State (1973), Nicholls State (1992), Northwestern State (1988), Sam Houston State (1988), Southeastern Louisiana (1998), Stephen F. Austin (2006), Texas State (1988), Texas-Arlington (1964), Texas-San Antonio (1992), Texas A&M-Corpus Christi (2007).

Baseball Contact/Assistant Commissioner: Todd Lamb.

2009 Tournament: Two four-team brackets, double-elimination. May 20-23 at Whataburger Field, Corpus Christi, Texas.

SOUTHWESTERN ATHLETIC CONFERENCE

Mailing Address: A.G. Gaston Building, 1527 Fifth Ave. N., Birmingham, AL 35203. **Telephone:** (205) 252-7573, ext. 111. **Fax:** (205) 252-9997. **E-Mail Address:** d.lewis@swac.org. **Website:** www.swac.org.

Baseball Members (First Year): East—Alabama A&M (2000), Alabama State (1982), Alcorn State (1962), Jackson State (1958), Mississippi Valley State (1968). West—Arkansas-Pine Bluff (1999), Grambling State (1958), Prairie View A&M (1920), Southern (1934), Texas Southern (1954).

Assistant Commissioner, Media Relations: Duane Lewis.

2009 Tournament: Eight teams, double-elimination. May 20-24 at Baton Rouge, La.

SUMMIT LEAGUE

Mailing Address: 340 W. Butterfield Rd., Suite 3-D, Elmhurst, IL 60126. **Telephone:** (630) 516-0661. **Fax:** (630) 516-0673. **E-Mail Addresses:** brauer@thesummitleague.org, mette@thesummitleague.org. **Website:** www.thesummitleague.org.

Baseball Members (First Year): Centenary (2004), IPFW (2008), North Dakota State (2008), Oakland (2000), Oral Roberts (1998), South Dakota State (2008), Southern Utah (2000), Western Illinois (1984).

Director, Media Relations: David Brauer. **Assistant Director (baseball contact):** Greg Mette.

2009 Tournament: Four teams, double-elimination. May 21-23 at Tulsa, Okla. (Oral Roberts).

SUN BELT CONFERENCE

Mailing Address: 601 Poydras St., Suite 2355, New Orleans, LA 70130. **Telephone:** (504) 299-9066. **Fax:** (504) 299-9068. **E-Mail Address:** kristofak@sunbeltsports.org. **Website:** www.sunbeltsports.org.

Baseball Members (First Year): Arkansas-Little Rock (1991), Arkansas State (1991), Florida Atlantic (2007), Florida International (1999), Louisiana-Lafayette (1991), Louisiana-Monroe (2007), Middle Tennessee (2001), New Orleans (1976/1991), South Alabama (1976), Troy (2006), Western Kentucky (1982).

Director, Media Relations: Melissa Kristofak.

2009 Tournament: Eight teams, double-elimination. May 20-23 at Troy, Ala.

WEST COAST CONFERENCE

Mailing Address: 1250 Bayhill Dr., Suite 101, San Bruno, CA 94066. **Telephone:** (650) 873-8622. **Fax:** (650) 873-7846. **E-Mail Addresses:** jwilson@westcoast.org; apatel@westcoast.org. **Website:** www.wccsports.com.

Baseball Members (First Year): Gonzaga (1996), Loyola Marymount (1968), Pepperdine (1968), Portland (1996), Saint Mary's (1968), San Diego (1979), San Francisco (1968), Santa Clara (1968).

Director, Communications: Jae Wilson. **Associate Director, Communications:** Anish Patel.

2009 Tournament: Top two teams meet in best-of-three series at home of regular-season winner, May 22-24.

WESTERN ATHLETIC CONFERENCE

Mailing Address: 9250 East Costilla Ave., Suite 300,

Englewood, CO 80112. **Telephone:** (303) 799-9221. **Fax:** (303) 799-3888. **E-Mail Address:** jerickson@wac.org. **Website:** www.wacsports.com.

Baseball Members (First Year): Fresno State (1993), Hawaii (1980), Louisiana Tech (2002), Nevada (2001), New Mexico State (2006), Sacramento State (2006), San Jose State (1997).

Commissioner: Karl Benson. **Senior Associate Commissioner:** Jeff Hurd. **Director, Sports Information:** Jason Erickson.

2009 Tournament: Six teams, double elimination. May 21-24 at Honolulu (University of Hawaii).

NCAA DIVISION I TEAMS

AIR FORCE FALCONS

Conference: Mountain West.

Mailing Address: 2169 Field House Drive, USAF Academy, CO 80840. **Website:** goairforcefalcons.com.

Head Coach: Mike Hutcheon. **Assistant Coaches:** Shane Davis, *Scott Marchand, Chandler Rose. **Telephone:** (719) 333-0835. **Baseball SID:** Nick Arseniak. **Telephone:** (719) 333-9251. **Fax:** (719) 333-3798.

Home Field: Falcon Field. **Seating Capacity:** 1,000. **Outfield Dimensions:** LF—349, CF—400, RF—316. **Press Box Telephone:** (719) 333-3472.

AKRON ZIPS

Conference: Mid-American (East).

Mailing Address: University of Akron, Rhodes Arena, Akron, OH 44325. **Website:** www.GoZips.com.

Head Coach: Pat Bangtson. **Assistant Coaches:** *Brian Donohew, Trent Luyster, Ernest Simpson. **Telephone:** (330) 972-7290. **Baseball SID:** Rita Chinyere. **Telephone:** (330) 972-7171. **Fax:** (330) 374-8844.

Home Field: Lee Jackson Field. **Seating Capacity:** 1,500. **Outfield Dimensions:** LF—330, CF—400, RF—330. **Press Box Telephone:** (330) 972-8896.

ALABAMA CRIMSON TIDE

Conference: Southeastern (East).

Mailing Address: Box 870393, Tuscaloosa, AL 35487. **Website:** www.rolltide.com.

Head Coach: Jim Wells. **Assistant Coaches:** *Mitch Gaspard, B.J. Green, Dax Norris. **Telephone:** (205) 348-6171. **Baseball SID:** Barry Allen. **Telephone:** (205) 348-8836. **Fax:** (205) 348-8841.

Home Field: Sewell-Thomas Stadium. **Seating Capacity:** 6,800. **Outfield Dimensions:** LF—320, CF—400, RF—320.

ALABAMA A&M BULLDOGS

Conference: Southwestern Athletic.

Mailing Address: PO Box 1597, Normal, AL 35762. **Website:** www.aamusports.com.

Head Coach: Jay Martin. **Assistant Coaches:** Jason Harrison, Demetrius Mitchell. **Telephone:** (256) 372-4004. **Baseball SID:** Thomas Galbraith. **Telephone:** (256) 372-4005. **Fax:** (256) 851-5919.

ALABAMA STATE HORNETS

Conference: Southwestern Athletic.

Mailing Address: 915 S. Jackson St, Montgomery, AL 36101. **Website:** www.bamastatesports.com.

Head Coach: Larry Watkins. **Assistant Coaches:** Anthony Hall, Tony Macon. **Telephone:** (334) 229-4228. **Baseball SID:** La Tonia Thirston. **Telephone:** (334) 229-4511. **Fax:** (334) 262-2971.

ALABAMA-BIRMINGHAM BLAZERS

Conference: Conference USA.

Mailing Address: U 236, 1530 3rd Ave S., Birmingham, AL 35294. **Website:** www.uabsports.com.

Head Coach: Brian Shoop. **Assistant Coaches:** Doug Kovash, Ron Polk, *Perry Roth. **Telephone:** (205) 934-5181. **Baseball SID:** Tyson Mathews. **Telephone:** (205) 996-2576. **Fax:** (205) 934-7505.

Home Field: Young Memorial Field. **Seating Capacity:** 1,000. **Outfield Dimensions:** LF—330, CF—400, RF—330. **Press Box Telephone:** (205) 934-0200.

ALBANY GREAT DANES

Conference: America East.

Mailing Address: 1400 Washington Ave, PE Bldg 123, Albany, NY 12222. **Website:** www.ualbanysports.com.

Head Coach: Jon Mueller. **Assistant Coaches:** Garett Baron, *Drew Pearce. **Telephone:** (518) 442-3014. **Baseball SID:** Brianna LaBrecque. **Telephone:** (518) 442-5733. **Fax:** (518) 442-3139.

Home Field: Varsity Field. **Seating Capacity:** 1,000. **Outfield Dimensions:** LF—345, CF—375, RF—325.

ALCORN STATE BRAVES

Conference: Southwestern Athletic.

Mailing Address: 1000 ASU Drive, Alcorn State, MS 39096. **Website:** www.alcornsports.com.

Head Coach: Willie McGowan, Sr. **Assistant Coaches:** *Marqus Johnson, LaBarry Jones. **Telephone:** (601) 877-6279. **Baseball SID:** LaToya Shields. **Telephone:** (601) 877-6466. **Fax:** (601) 877-3821.

APPALACHIAN STATE MOUNTAINEERS

Conference: Southern.

Mailing Address: Appalachian State University, Owens Field House, Boone, NC 28607. **Website:** www.goasu.com.

Head Coach: Chris Pollard. **Assistant Coaches:** *Matt Boykin, Josh Jordan, Craig Scheffler. **Telephone:** (828) 262-6097. **Baseball SID:** Mike Flynn. **Telephone:** (828) 262-2845. **Fax:** (828) 262-6106.

Home Field: Jim and Bettie Smith Stadium. **Seating Capacity:** 2,000. **Outfield Dimensions:** LF—330, CF—400, RF—330.

ARIZONA WILDCATS

Conference: Pacific-10.

Mailing Address: McKale Center, 1 National Championship Drive, Tucson, AZ 85721-0096. **Website:** www.arizonaathletics.com.

Head Coach: Andy Lopez. **Assistant Coaches:** Keith Franics, Jeff Pickler, *Mark Wasikowski. **Telephone:** (520) 621-4102. **Baseball SID:** Blair Willis. **Telephone:** (520) 621-0914. **Fax:** (520) 621-2681.

Home Field: Jerry Kindall Field at Frank Sancet Stadium. **Seating Capacity:** 6,500. **Outfield Dimensions:** LF—360, CF—400, RF—360. **Press Box Telephone:** (520) 621-4440.

ARIZONA STATE SUN DEVILS

Conference: Pacific-10.

Mailing Address: 500 East Veteran's Way, Tempe, AZ 85287. **Website:** www.TheSunDevils.com.

Head Coach: Pat Murphy. **Assistant Coaches:** Tim Esmay, *Josh Holliday, Andy Stankiewicz. **Telephone:** (480) 965-1904. **Baseball SID:** Randy Policar. **Telephone:** (480) 965-6594. **Fax:** (480) 965-5408.

Home Field: Winkles Field-Packard Stadium at Brock Ballpark. **Seating Capacity:** 3,879. **Outfield Dimensions:**

LF—338, CF—395, RF—338. **Press Box Telephone:** (480) 727-7253.

ARKANSAS RAZORBACKS

Conference: Southeastern (West).

Mailing Address: 1255 South Razorback Rd, Fayetteville, AR 72702. **Website:** www.hogwired.com.

Head Coach: Dave Van Horn. **Assistant Coaches:** *Todd Butler, Dave Jorn. **Telephone:** (479) 575-3655. **Baseball SID:** Phil Pierce. **Telephone:** (479) 575-7430. **Fax:** (479) 575-7481.

Home Field: Baum Stadium. **Seating Capacity:** 10,737. **Outfield Dimensions:** LF—320, CF—400, RF—320. **Press Box Telephone:** (479) 575-4141.

ARKANSAS STATE RED WOLVES

Conference: Sun Belt.

Mailing Address: PO Box 1000, State University, AR 72467. **Website:** www.asuindians.com.

Head Coach: Tommy Raffo. **Assistant Coaches:** Chris Cook, Anthony Everman, *Justin Meccage. **Telephone:** (870) 680-4337. **Baseball SID:** Anthony Reynolds. **Telephone:** (870) 972-3547. **Fax:** (870) 972-3367.

Home Field: Tomlinson Stadium Kell Field. **Seating Capacity:** 1,500. **Outfield Dimensions:** LF—335, CF—400, RF—335. **Press Box Telephone:** (870) 972-3383.

ARKANSAS-LITTLE ROCK TROJANS

Conference: Sun Belt.

Mailing Address: 2801 S. University Ave, Little Rock, AR 72204. **Website:** www.ualrtrojans.com.

Head Coach: Scott Norwood. **Assistant Coaches:** Jeremy Haworth, *Dirk Kinney, J.J. Yant. **Telephone:** (501) 663-8095. **Baseball SID:** Joe Angolia. **Telephone:** (501) 569-3449. **Fax:** (501) 683-7002.

Home Field: Gary Hogan Field. **Seating Capacity:** 1,000. **Outfield Dimensions:** LF—330, CF—400, RF—325. **Press Box Telephone:** (501) 351-1060.

ARKANSAS-PINE BLUFF GOLDEN LIONS

Conference: Southwestern Athletic.

Mailing Address: 1200 N. University Drive, Mail Slot 4805, Pine Bluff AR 71601. **Website:** www.uapblionsroar.com.

Head Coach: Michael Bumpers. **Assistant Coaches:** Michael Birmingham, Willie Smith, *Michael Wilson. **Telephone:** (870) 575-8089. **Baseball SID:** Tim Munn. **Telephone:** (870) 575-7174. **Fax:** (870) 575-7880.

ARMY BLACK KNIGHTS

Conference: Patriot.

Mailing Address: 639 Howard Road, West Point, NY 10996. **Website:** www.goarmysports.com.

Head Coach: Joe Sottolano. **Assistant Coaches:** Matt Reid, Chris Tracz. **Telephone:** (845) 938-3712. **Baseball SID:** Bob Beretta. **Telephone:** (845) 938-6416. **Fax:** (845) 446-2556.

AUBURN TIGERS

Conference: Southeastern (West).

Mailing Address: PO Box 351, Auburn, AL 36830. **Website:** www.auburntigers.com.

Head Coach: John Pawlowski. **Assistant Coaches:** Jeff Duncan, *Scott Foxhall, Matt Heath. **Telephone:** (334) 844-4975. **Baseball SID:** Dan Froehlich. **Telephone:** (334) 844-9803. **Fax:** (334) 844-9807.

Home Field: Plainsman Park. **Seating Capacity:** 4,096. **Outfield Dimensions:** LF—315, CF—385, RF—331. **Press Box Telephone:** (334) 844-4138.

AUSTIN PEAY STATE GOVERNORS

Conference: Ohio Valley.

Mailing Address: Box 4515, Clarksville, TN 37044. **Website:** www.letsgopeay.com.

Head Coach: Gary McClure. **Assistant Coaches:** Dan Burton, *Seth Kenny, Jake Peterson. **Telephone:** (931) 221-6266. **Baseball SID:** Cody Bush. **Telephone:** (931) 221-7561. **Fax:** (931) 221-7830.

Home Field: Raymond C. **Hand Park. Seating Capacity:** 2,000. **Outfield Dimensions:** LF—321, CF—392, RF—327. **Press Box Telephone:** (931) 221-7406.

BALL STATE CARDINALS

Conference: Mid-American (West).

Mailing Address: HP 245, Muncie, IN 47306. **Website:** www.ballstatesports.com.

Head Coach: Greg Beals. **Assistant Coaches:** Michael Dalton, Alex Marconi, *Mike Stafford. **Telephone:** (765) 285-8226. **Baseball SID:** Matt McCollester. **Telephone:** (765) 285-8242. **Fax:** (765) 285-8929.

Home Field: Ball Diamond. **Seating Capacity:** 1,500. **Outfield Dimensions:** LF—330, CF—400, RF—330. **Press Box Telephone:** (765) 285-8932.

BAYLOR BEARS

Conference: Big 12 (South).

Mailing Address: Simpson Building Room 161, 1500 South University Parks Drive, Waco, TX 76706. **Website:** www.baylorbears.com.

Head Coach: Steve Smith. **Assistant Coaches:** Steve Johnigan, Trevor Mote, *Mitch Thompson. **Telephone:** (254) 710-3029. **Baseball SID:** Larry Little. **Telephone:** (254) 710-4389. **Fax:** (254) 710-1369.

Home Field: Baylor Ballpark. **Seating Capacity:** 5,000. **Outfield Dimensions:** LF—330, CF—400, RF—330. **Press Box Telephone:** (254) 754-5546.

BELMONT BRUINS

Conference: Atlantic Sun.

Mailing Address: 1900 Belmont Blvd, Nashville, TN 37212. **Website:** belmontbruins.cstv.com.

Head Coach: Dave Jarvis. **Assistant Coaches:** *Matt Barnett, Scott Hall. **Telephone:** (615) 460-6166. **Baseball SID:** Marcel Pourtout. **Telephone:** (615) 460-6165. **Fax:** (615) 460-5584.

Home Field: Greer Stadium. **Seating Capacity:** 10,000. **Outfield Dimensions:** LF—330, CF—400, RF—327. **Press Box Telephone:** (615) 400-7504.

BETHUNE-COOKMAN WILDCATS

Conference: Mid-Eastern Athletic.

Mailing Address: 640 Dr. Mary McLeod Bethune Blvd, Daytona Beach, FL 32114**. Website:** www.bccathletics.com.

Head Coach: Mervyl Melendez. **Assistant Coaches:** Jason Arnold, Phil Enright, Jose Vasquez. **Telephone:** (386) 481-2224. **Baseball SID:** Mark Johnson. **Telephone:** (386) 481-2206. **Fax:** (386) 481-2238.

BINGHAMTON BEARCATS

Conference: America East.

Mailing Address: Binghamton University, Events Center Office #110, Binghamton, NY, 13902. **Website:** bubearcats.com.

Head Coach: Tim Sinicki. **Assistant Coaches:** Ed Folli, Ryan Hurba, Andy Hutchings. **Telephone:** (607) 777-2525. **Baseball SID:** John Hartrick. **Telephone:** (607) 777-6800. **Fax:** (607) 777-4597.

Home Field: Varsity Field. **Seating Capacity:** 1,000.

Outfield Dimensions: LF—315, CF—390, RF—315.

BOSTON COLLEGE EAGLES

Conference: Atlantic Coast (Atlantic).

Mailing Address: 140 Commonwealth Ave, Chestnut Hill, MA 02467.

Head Coach: Mikio Aoki. **Assistant Coaches:** Steve Englert, *Joe Hastings, Jesse Woods. **Telephone:** (617) 552-2674. **Baseball SID:** Matt Lynch. **Telephone:** (617) 552-2193. **Fax:** (617) 552-4903.

Home Field: Shea Field. **Seating Capacity:** 1,000. **Outfield Dimensions:** LF—330, CF—410, RF—318.

BOWLING GREEN STATE FALCONS

Conference: Mid-American (East).

Mailing Address: 201 Doyt Perry Stadium East, Bowling Green, OH 43403. **Website:** www.bgsufalcons.com.

Head Coach: Danny Schmitz. **Assistant Coaches:** *Rick Blanc, Luke Harrigan, Spencer Schmitz. **Telephone:** (419) 372-7065. **Baseball SID:** Steve Barr. **Telephone:** (419) 372-7105. **Fax:** (419) 372-6015.

Home Field: Warren E. Steller Field. **Seating Capacity:** 1,100. **Outfield Dimensions:** LF—340, CF—400, RF—340. **Press Box Telephone:** (419) 372-1234.

BRADLEY BRAVES

Conference: Missouri Valley.

Mailing Address: 1501 West Bradley Ave, Peoria, IL 61625. **Website:** www.bubraves.com.

Head Coach: Elvis Dominguez. **Assistant Coaches:** *John Corbin, Jonathan Hadra. **Telephone:** (309) 677-2671. **Baseball SID:** Bobby Parker. **Telephone:** (309) 677-2624. **Fax:** (309) 677-2626.

Home Field: O'Brien Field. **Seating Capacity:** 7,500. **Outfield Dimensions:** LF—310, CF—400, RF—310. **Press Box Telephone:** (309) 680-4045.

BRIGHAM YOUNG COUGARS

Conference: Mountain West.

Mailing Address: 30 SFH, BYU, Provo, UT 84602. **Website:** www.byucougars.com.

Head Coach: Vance Law. **Assistant Coaches:** Bobby Applegate, *Ryan Roberts. **Telephone:** (801) 422-5049. **Baseball SID:** Ralph Zobell. **Telephone:** (801) 422-9769. **Fax:** (801) 422-0633.

Home Field: Larry H. Miller Field. **Seating Capacity:** 2,204. **Outfield Dimensions:** LF—345, CF—400, RF—345. **Press Box Telephone:** (801) 422-4041.

BROWN BEARS

Conference: Ivy League (Rolfe).

Mailing Address: 235 Hope St, Box 1932, Providence, RI 02912. **Website:** www.BrownBears.com.

Head Coach: Marek Drabinski. **Assistant Coaches:** *Bill Cilento, Dave Cunningham, Jason Lefkowitz. **Telephone:** (401) 863-3090. **Baseball SID:** Isaac Goodling. **Telephone:** (401) 863-6069. **Fax:** (401) 863-1436.

Home Field: Murray Stadium. **Seating Capacity:** 1,000. **Outfield Dimensions:** LF—340, CF—405, RF—330. **Press Box Telephone:** (401) 863-9427.

BRYANT BULLDOGS

Conference: Independent.

Mailing Address: 1150 Douglas Pike, Smithfield, RI 02917. **Website:** www.bryantbulldogs.com.

Head Coach: Jamie Pinzino. **Assistant Coaches:** Jay Iannoni, *Brian Murphy, Matt Ponte. **Telephone:** (401) 232-6397. **Baseball SID:** Allie Weinberger. **Telephone:** (401) 232-6558. **Fax:** (910) 893-1330.

BUCKNELL BISON

Conference: Patriot.

Mailing Address: Bucknell University, Moore Ave, Lewisburg, PA 17837. **Website:** www.bucknellbison.com.

Head Coach: Gene Depew. **Assistant Coaches:** Jim Gulden, *Scott Heather, Ben Krentzman. **Telephone:** (570) 577-3593. **Baseball SID:** Todd Merriett. **Telephone:** (570) 577-3488. **Fax:** (570) 577-1660.

Home Field: Depew Field. **Seating Capacity:** 500. **Outfield Dimensions:** LF—330, CF—400, RF—330. **Press Box Telephone:** (570) 428-5393.

BUFFALO BULLS

Conference: Mid-American (East).

Mailing Address: University at Buffalo, Division of Athletics, 175 Alumni Arena, Buffalo, NY 14260. **Website:** www.buffalobulls.com.

Head Coach: Ron Torgalski. **Assistant Coaches:** Tony Fuller, *Jim Koerner, Devin McIntosh. **Telephone:** (716) 645-6834. **Baseball SID:** Will Nowadly. **Telephone:** (716) 645-5523. **Fax:** (716) 645-6840.

Home Field: Amherst Audubon Field. **Seating Capacity:** 500. **Outfield Dimensions:** LF—330, CF—400, RF—330. **Press Box Telephone:** (716) 867-1908.

BUTLER BULLDOGS

Conference: Horizon.

Mailing Address: 510 W. 49th Street, Indianapolis, IN 46208. **Website:** butlersports.com.

Head Coach: Steve Farley. **Assistant Coaches:** Jeff Brown, Craig Lacy, *Matt Tyner. **Telephone:** (317) 940-9721. **Baseball SID:** Chris Urban. **Telephone:** (317) 940-9994. **Fax:** (317) 940-9808.

Home Field: Bulldog Park. **Seating Capacity:** 500. **Outfield Dimensions:** LF—330, CF—400, RF—330. **Press Box Telephone:** (317) 945-8943.

CALIFORNIA GOLDEN BEARS

Conference: Pacific-10.

Mailing Address: 66 Haas Pavilion, Berkeley, CA 94720. **Website:** www.calbears.com.

Head Coach: David Esquer. **Assistant Coaches:** Tony Arnerich, *Dan Hubbs, Jon Zuber. **Telephone:** (510) 643-6006. **Baseball SID:** Scott Ball. **Telephone:** (510) 643-1741. **Fax:** (510) 643-7778.

Home Field: Evans Diamond. **Seating Capacity:** 2,500. **Outfield Dimensions:** LF—320, CF—400, RF—320. **Press Box Telephone:** (510) 642-3098.

UC DAVIS AGGIES

Conference: Big West.

Mailing Address: Hickey Gym 264, One Shields Ave, Davis, CA 95616. **Website:** ucdavisaggies.com.

Head Coach: Rex Peters. **Assistant Coaches:** *Anthony Schifano, Adam Sorgi, Matt Vaughn. **Telephone:** (530) 752-7513. **Baseball SID:** Wes Collins. **Telephone:** (530) 752-3505. **Fax:** (530) 754-5674.

Home Field: Dobbins Stadium. **Seating Capacity:** 3,500. **Outfield Dimensions:** LF—310, CF—410, RF—310. **Press Box Telephone:** (530) 752-3673.

UC IRVINE ANTEATERS

Conference: Big West.

Mailing Address: UC Irvine, Crawford Hall, 903 W. Peltason Dr, Irvine, CA 92697-4500. **Website:** www.ucirvinesports.com.

Head Coach: Mike Gillespie. **Assistant Coaches:** Bob Macaluso, *Pat Shine, Ted Silva. **Telephone:** (949) 824-4292. **Baseball SID:** Fumi Kimura. **Telephone:** (949) 824-

9474. **Fax:** (949) 824-5260.

Home Field: Anteater Ballpark. **Seating Capacity:** 3,200. **Outfield Dimensions:** LF—335, CF—405, RF—335. **Press Box Telephone:** (949) 824-9905.

UCLA BRUINS

Conference: Pacific-10.

Mailing Address: J.D. Morgan Center, 325 Westwood Plaza, Los Angeles, CA 90095. **Website:** www.uclabruins.com.

Head Coach: John Savage. **Assistant Coaches:** Steve Pearse, P.C. Shaw, *Rick Vanderhook. **Telephone:** (310) 794-2470. **Baseball SID:** Alex Timiraos. **Telephone:** (310) 206-4008. **Fax:** (310) 825-8664.

Home Field: Jackie Robinson Stadium. **Seating Capacity:** 1,250. **Outfield Dimensions:** LF—330, CF—395, RF—330. **Press Box Telephone:** (310) 794-8213.

UC RIVERSIDE HIGHLANDERS

Conference: Big West.

Mailing Address: Dept. of Athletics, UC Riverside, 900 University Ave, Riverside, CA 92521. **Website:** www.athletics.ucr.edu.

Head Coach: Doug Smith. **Assistant Coaches:** Randy Betten, *Nathan Choate, Rusty McNamara. **Telephone:** (951) 827-5441. **Baseball SID:** Unavailable. **Telephone:** (951) 827-5438.

Home Field: UCR Sports Complex. **Seating Capacity:** 2,800. **Outfield Dimensions:** LF—330, CF—400, RF—330.

UC SANTA BARBARA GAUCHOS

Conference: Big West.

Mailing Address: ICA Building, UC Santa Barbara, CA 93106-5200. **Website:** www.ucsbgauchos.com.

Head Coach: Bob Brontsema. **Assistant Coaches:** John Kirkgard, *Tom Myers. **Telephone:** (805) 893-3690. **Baseball SID:** Matt Hurst. **Telephone:** (805) 893-8603. **Fax:** (805) 893-4537.

Home Field: Caesar Uyesaka Stadium. **Seating Capacity:** 1,000. **Outfield Dimensions:** LF—335, CF—400, RF—335. **Press Box Telephone:** (805) 893-4671.

CAL POLY MUSTANGS

Conference: Big West.

Mailing Address: 1 Grand Ave, San Luis Obispo, CA 93407-0388. **Website:** www.GoPoly.com.

Head Coach: Larry Lee. **Assistant Coaches:** Dustin Kelly, Jason Kelly, *Jesse Zepeda. **Telephone:** (805) 756-6367. **Baseball SID:** Eric Burdick. **Telephone:** (805) 756-6550. **Fax:** (805) 756-2650.

Home Field: Baggett Stadium. **Seating Capacity:** 1,734. **Outfield Dimensions:** LF—335, CF—405, RF—335. **Press Box Telephone:** (805) 756-7456.

CAL STATE BAKERSFIELD ROADRUNNERS

Conference: Independent.

Mailing Address: 9001 Stockdale Hwy-8GYM, Bakersfield, CA 93311-1022. **Website:** www.gorunners.com.

Head Coach: Bill Kernen. **Assistant Coaches:** Bill Gentry, *Dennis Machado, Jody Robinson. **Telephone:** (661) 654-2628. **Baseball SID:** Sarah Finney. **Telephone:** (661) 654-3071. **Fax:** (661) 654-6978.

Home Field: Roadrunner Baseball Complex. **Seating Capacity:** Unavailable. **Outfield Dimensions:** LF—325, CF—390, RF—325.

CAL STATE FULLERTON TITANS

Conference: Big West.

Mailing Address: 800 N. State College Blvd, Fullerton, CA 92831. **Website:** fullertontitans.com.

Head Coach: Dave Serrano. **Assistant Coaches:** Greg Bergeron, *Sergio Brown, Brett Lindgren. **Telephone:** (714) 278-3780. **Baseball SID:** Michael Greenlee. **Telephone:** (714) 278-3081. **Fax:** (714) 278-3141.

Home Field: Goodwin Field. **Seating Capacity:** 3,500. **Outfield Dimensions:** LF—330, CF—400, RF—330. **Press Box Telephone:** (714) 278-5327.

CAL STATE NORTHRIDGE MATADORS

Conference: Big West.

Mailing Address: 18111 Nordhoff Street, Northridge, CA 91330. **Website:** gomatadors.cstv.com.

Head Coach: Stephen Rousey. **Assistant Coaches:** *Mark Kertenian, Rob McKinley, Phil Van Horn. **Telephone:** (818) 677-7055. **Baseball SID:** Eric Bankston. **Telephone:** (818) 677-3860. **Fax:** (818) 677-4950.

Home Field: Matador Field. **Seating Capacity:** 1,000. **Outfield Dimensions:** LF—325, CF—395, RF—325. **Press Box Telephone:** (818) 677 4292.

CAMPBELL FIGHTING CAMELS

Conference: Atlantic Sun.

Mailing Address: 78 McKoy Dr, Buies Creek, NC 27506. **Website:** www.gocamels.com.

Head Coach: Greg Goff. **Assistant Coaches:** Aubrey Blackwell, John Caddell, *Justin Haire. **Telephone:** (910) 893-1354. **Baseball SID:** Stan Cole. **Telephone:** (910) 893-1331. **Fax:** (910) 893-1330.

Home Field: Taylor Field. **Seating Capacity:** 1,000. **Outfield Dimensions:** LF—337, CF—395, RF—328. **Press Box Telephone:** (910) 814-4781.

CANISIUS GOLDEN GRIFFINS

Conference: Metro Atlantic.

Mailing Address: 2001 Main St, Buffalo, NY 14208. **Website:** www.gogriffs.com.

Head Coach: Mike McRae. **Assistant Coaches:** Matt Mazurek, *Mike Medici, Jerry Shank. **Telephone:** (716) 888-3207. **Baseball SID:** Matt Lozar. **Telephone:** (716) 888-3756. **Fax:** (716) 888-8444.

Home Field: Demske Sports Complex. **Seating Capacity:** 1,000. **Outfield Dimensions:** LF—310, CF—400, RF—310. **Press Box Telephone:** (716) 477-3777.

CENTENARY GENTS

Conference: Summit.

Mailing Address: 2911 Centenary Blvd, Shreveport, LA 71134. **Website:** www.gocentenary.com.

Head Coach: Ed McCann. **Assistant Coaches:** Mike Diaz, Pat Holmes. **Telephone:** (318) 869-5298. **Baseball SID:** David Pratt. **Telephone:** (318) 869-5092. **Fax:** (318) 869-5128.

CENTRAL ARKANSAS BEARS

Conference: Southland.

Mailing Address: 2401 College Ave, Conway, AR 72034. **Website:** www.ucasports.com.

Head Coach: Doug Clark. **Assistant Coaches:** *Ronnie Goodwin, Ryan Johnson. **Telephone:** (501) 450-3407. **Baseball SID:** Steve East. **Telephone:** (501) 450-5743. **Fax:** (501) 450-5740.

Home Field: Bear Field. **Seating Capacity:** 1,500. **Outfield Dimensions:** LF—320, CF—400, RF—320. **Press Box Telephone:** (501) 450-5972.

CENTRAL CONNECTICUT STATE BLUE DEVILS

Conference: Northeast.

Mailing Address: 16151 Stanley St, New Britain, CT

06050. **Website:** ccsubluedevils.com.

Head Coach: Charlie Hickey. **Assistant Coaches:** *Paul LaBella, Jim Ziogas. **Telephone:** (860) 832-3074. **Baseball SID:** Tom Pincince. **Telephone:** (860) 832-3089. **Fax:** (860) 832-3754.

CENTRAL FLORIDA KNIGHTS

Conference: Conference USA.

Mailing Address: PO Box 163555, Orlando, FL 32816. **Website:** ucfathletics.com.

Head Coach: Terry Rooney. **Assistant Coaches:** *Cliff Godwin, Jeff Palumbo, Aaron Smith. **Telephone:** (407) 823-0140. **Baseball SID:** Brian Ormiston. **Telephone:** (407) 823-2409. **Fax:** (407) 823-5293.

Home Field: Jay Bergman Field. **Seating Capacity:** 2,230. **Outfield Dimensions:** LF—320, CF—390, RF—320. **Press Box Telephone:** (407) 823-4487.

CENTRAL MICHIGAN CHIPPEWAS

Conference: Mid-American (West).

Mailing Address: Rose Center 120, Mt. Pleasant, MI 48859. **Website:** www.cmuchippewas.com.

Head Coach: Steve Jaksa. **Assistant Coaches:** Jeff Opalewski, *Mike Villano. **Telephone:** (989) 774-4392. **Baseball SID:** Mike Boseak. **Telephone:** (989) 774-3277. **Fax:** (989) 774-7324.

Home Field: Theunissen Stadium. **Seating Capacity:** 2,046. **Outfield Dimensions:** LF—330, CF—400, RF—330.

CHARLESTON COUGARS

Conference: Southern.

Mailing Address: 66 George St, Charleston, SC 29424. **Website:** www.cofcsports.com.

Head Coach: Monte Lee. **Assistant Coaches:** Chris Morris, *Dan Roszel. **Telephone:** (843) 953-5916. **Baseball SID:** Tony Ciuffo. **Telephone:** (843) 953-6720. **Fax:** (843) 953-6534.

Home Field: Patriots Point Field. **Seating Capacity:** 2,500. **Outfield Dimensions:** LF—310, CF—400, RF—320.

CHARLESTON SOUTHERN BUCCANEERS

Conference: Big South.

Mailing Address: PO Box 118087, Charleston, SC 29423-8087. **Website:** csusports.com.

Head Coach: Stuart Lake. **Assistant Coaches:** *Charles Assey, Anthony Hayes, Stan Kowalski. **Telephone:** (843) 863-7591. **Baseball SID:** Niki Turner. **Telephone:** (843) 863-7037. **Fax:** (843) 863-7676.

Home Field: Buccaneer Field. **Seating Capacity:** 500. **Outfield Dimensions:** LF—330, CF—400, RF—330. **Press Box Telephone:** (843) 863-7764.

CHARLOTTE 49ERS

Conference: Atlantic 10.

Mailing Address: Wachovia Fieldhouse, 9201 University City Blvd, Charlotte, N.C. 28223. **Website:** www.charlotte49ers.com.

Head Coach: Loren Hibbs. **Assistant Coaches:** Bo Durkac, *Brandon Hall, Brett Hall. **Telephone:** (704) 687-3935. **Baseball SID:** Ryan Rose. **Telephone:** (704) 687-6312. **Fax:** (704) 687-4918.

Home Field: Robert and Mariam Hayes Stadium. **Seating Capacity:** 3,000. **Outfield Dimensions:** LF—335, CF—390, RF—335. **Press Box Telephone:** (704) 687-5959.

CHICAGO STATE COUGARS

Conference: Independent.

Mailing Address: 9501 S. King Drive, JCC 1532, Chicago, IL 60628. **Website:** www.csu.edu/athletics.

Head Coach: Michael Caston. **Assistant Coaches:** Juan Alonso, *Neal Frendling. **Telephone:** (773) 995-3659. **Baseball SID:** Corey Miggins. **Telephone:** (773) 995-2217. **Fax:** (773) 821-4961.

Home Field: Gwendolyn Brooks Field. **Seating Capacity:** 800. **Outfield Dimensions:** LF—320, CF—400, RF—320.

CINCINNATI BEARCATS

Conference: Big East.

Mailing Address: 2751 O'Varsity Way, Suite 764, Cincinnati, OH 45221. **Website:** gobearcats.com.

Head Coach: Brian Cleary. **Assistant Coaches:** *Brad Meador, Chris Reilly, A.J. Upton. **Telephone:** (513) 556-0566. **Baseball SID:** John Berry. **Telephone:** (513) 556-0618. **Fax:** (513) 556-0619.

Home Field: Marge Schott Stadium. **Seating Capacity:** 3,085. **Outfield Dimensions:** LF—325, CF—400, RF—325. **Press Box Telephone:** (513) 556-9645.

CITADEL BULLDOGS

Conference: Big South.

Mailing Address: 171 Moultrie St, Charleston, SC 29409. **Website:** www.citadelsports.com.

Head Coach: Fred Jordan. **Assistant Coaches:** Jon Aughey, *David Beckley, Randy Carlson. **Telephone:** (843) 953-5901. **Baseball SID:** Patrick Walsh. **Telephone:** (843) 953-7590. **Fax:** (843) 953-6727.

Home Field: Joseph P. Riley Jr. Park. **Seating Capacity:** 6,000. **Outfield Dimensions:** LF—305, CF—398, RF—337. **Press Box Telephone:** (843) 965-4151.

CLEMSON TIGERS

Conference: Atlantic Coast (Atlantic).

Mailing Address: PO Box 31, Clemson, SC 29633. **Website:** clemsontigers.com.

Head Coach: Jack Leggett. **Assistant Coaches:** Kyle Bunn, Michael Johnson, *Tom Riginos. **Telephone:** (864) 656-1947. **Baseball SID:** Brian Hennessy. **Telephone:** (864)656-1921. **Fax:** (864) 656-0299.

Home Field: Doug Kingsmore Stadium. **Seating Capacity:** 6,217. **Outfield Dimensions:** LF—320, CF—400, RF—330. **Press Box Telephone:** (864) 656-7731.

CLEVELAND STATE VIKINGS

Conference: Horizon.

Mailing Address: 2451 Euclid Ave, Cleveland, OH 44115. **Website:** www.csuvikings.com.

Head Coach: Kevin Kocks. **Assistant Coaches:** Cliff Cook, *Rob Henry, Craig Moro. **Telephone:** (216) 687-4822. **Baseball SID:** Greg Murphy. **Telephone:** (216) 687-5288. **Home Field:** Pipe Yard Stadium. **Seating Capacity:** 2,000. **Outfield Dimensions:** LF—330, CF—400, RF—330.

COASTAL CAROLINA CHANTICLEERS

Conference: Big South.

Mailing Address: 132 Chanticleer Drive West, Conway, SC 29526. **Website:** www.GoCCUSports.com.

Head Coach: Gary Gilmore. **Assistant Coaches:** Brendan Dougherty, *Kevin Schnall, Drew Thomas. **Telephone:** (843) 349-2816. **Baseball SID:** Kent Reichert. **Telephone:** (843) 349-2840. **Fax:** (843) 349-2819.

Home Field: Charles Watson Stadium/Vrooman Field. **Seating Capacity:** 2,000. **Outfield Dimensions:** LF—320, CF—390, RF—325. **Press Box Telephone:** (843) 421-8244.

COLUMBIA LIONS

Conference: Ivy League (Gehrig).

Mailing Address: 3030 Broadway, Mail Code 1901, New York, NY 10027. **Website:** www.gocolumbialions.com.

Head Coach: Brett Boretti. **Assistant Coaches:** *Pete Maki, Jay Quinn, Jim Walsh. **Telephone:** (212) 854-8448. **Baseball SID:** Pete McHugh. **Telephone:** (212) 854-7064. **Fax:** (212) 854-8168.

Home Field: Robertson Field. **Seating Capacity:** 300. **Outfield Dimensions:** LF—330, CF—350, RF—325. **Press Box Telephone:** (917) 678-3621.

CONNECTICUT HUSKIES

Conference: Big East.

Mailing Address: 2095 Hillside Rd, Unit 1173, Storrs, CT 06269. **Website:** www.UConnHuskies.com.

Head Coach: James Penders. **Assistant Coaches:** *Justin Blood, Steve Malinowski, Chris Podeszwa. **Telephone:** (860) 486-4089. **Baseball SID:** Kristen Altieri. **Telephone:** (860) 486-3531. **Fax:** (860) 486-5085.

Home Field: J.O. Christian Field**. Seating Capacity:** Unavailable. **Outfield Dimensions:** LF—337, CF—400, RF—325.

COPPIN STATE EAGLES

Conference: Mid-Eastern Athletic.

Mailing Address: 2500 W. North Ave, Baltimore, MD 21216. **Website:** www.coppinstatesports.com.

Head Coach: Mike Scolinos. **Telephone:** (410) 951-3723. **Baseball SID:** Roger McAfee. **Telephone:** (410) 951-3729. **Fax:** (410) 951-3718.

CORNELL BIG RED

Conference: Ivy League (Rolfe).

Mailing Address: Cornell Baseball, Teagle Hall, Campus Rd, Ithaca, NY 14853. **Website:** cornellbigred.com.

Head Coach: Bill Walkenbach. **Assistant Coaches:** Tom Ford, *Scott Marsh. **Telephone:** (607) 255-3812. **Baseball SID:** Kevin Zeise. **Telephone:** (607) 255-5627. **Fax:** (607) 255-9791.

Home Field: Hoy Field. **Seating Capacity:** 500. **Outfield Dimensions:** LF—315, CF—400, RF—325. **Press Box Telephone:** (603) 748-1268.

CREIGHTON BLUEJAYS

Conference: Missouri Valley.

Mailing Address: 2500 California Ave, Omaha, NE 68178. **Website:** www.gocreighton.com.

Head Coach: Ed Servais. **Assistant Coaches:** Brent Alwine, *Rob Smith, Johnny Sweeney. **Telephone:** (402) 280-2483. **Baseball SID:** Rob Beuerlein. **Telephone:** (402) 280-5801. **Fax:** (402) 280-2459.

Home Field: Creighton Sports Complex. **Seating Capacity:** 1,000. **Outfield Dimensions:** LF—330, CF—400, RF—330. **Press Box Telephone:** (402) 280-1676.

DALLAS BAPTIST PATRIOTS

Conference: Independent.

Mailing Address: 3000 Mt. Creek Parkway, Dallas, TX 75211. **Website:** www.dbu.edu/athletics.

Head Coach: Dan Heefner. **Assistant Coaches:** *Nate Frieling, Brad Welker, Travis Wyckoff. **Telephone:** (214) 333-5327. **Baseball SID:** Tyler Knox. **Telephone:** (214) 333-5349. **Fax:** (214) 333-5306.

Home Field: Patriot Field. **Seating Capacity:** 1,500. **Outfield Dimensions:** LF—330, CF—400, RF—330. **Press Box Telephone:** (214) 333-5542.

DARTMOUTH BIG GREEN

Conference: Ivy League (Rolfe).

Mailing Address: 6083 Alumni Gym, Hanover, NH 03755. **Website:** dartmouthsports.com.

Head Coach: Bob Whalen. **Assistant Coaches:** Nicholas Enriquez, George Roig. **Telephone:** (603) 646-2477. **Baseball SID:** Rick Bender. **Telephone:** (603) 646-1030. **Fax:** (603) 646-1286.

DAVIDSON WILDCATS

Conference: Southern.

Mailing Address: Box 7158, Davidson, N.C. 28035. **Website:** www.davidsonwildcats.com.

Head Coach: Dick Cooke. **Assistant Coaches:** Toby Bicknell, Sean Lennox, *Mike Zandler. **Telephone:** (704) 894-2368. **Baseball SID:** Lauren Biggers. **Telephone:** (704) 894-2815. **Fax:** (704) 894-2636.

Home Field: Wilson Field. **Seating Capacity:** 700. **Outfield Dimensions:** LF—320, CF—385, RF—325. **Press Box Telephone:** (704) 894-2740.

DAYTON FLYERS

Conference: Atlantic 10.

Mailing Address: 300 College Park, Dayton, OH 45469. **Website:** daytonflyers.com.

Head Coach: Tony Vittorio. **Assistant Coaches:** Terry Bell, Brian Harrison, *Todd Linklater. **Telephone:** (937) 229-4456. **Baseball SID:** Seth Iiames. **Telephone:** (937) 229-4419. **Fax:** (937) 229-4461.

Home Field: Time Warner Cable Stadium. **Seating Capacity:** 2,000. **Outfield Dimension:** LF—330, CF—400, RF—335.

DELAWARE FIGHTIN' BLUE HENS

Conference: Colonial Athletic.

Mailing Address: 629 South College Ave, Newark, DE 19716. **Website:** www.bluehens.com.

Head Coach: Jim Sherman. **Assistant Coaches:** *Dan Hammer, Steve Harden, Brian Walker. **Telephone:** (302) 831-8596. **Baseball SID:** Kenny Kline. **Telephone:** (302) 831-2186. **Fax:** (302) 831-8653.

Home Field: Bob Hannah Stadium. **Seating Capacity:** 1,300. **Outfield Dimensions:** LF—330, CF—400, RF—330. **Press Box Telephone:** (302) 831-4122.

DELAWARE STATE HORNETS

Conference: Mid-Eastern Athletic.

Mailing Address: 1200 N. Dupont Hwy, Dover, DE 19901. **Website:** www.dsuhornets.com.

Head Coach: J.P. Blandin. **Assistant Coach:** Michael August, Russ Steinhorn, Nick Wenger. **Telephone:** (302) 857-6035. **Baseball SID:** Dennis Jones. **Telephone:** (302) 857-6068. **Fax:** (302) 857-6069.

DUKE BLUE DEVILS

Conference: Atlantic Coast (Coastal).

Mailing Address: 118 Cameron Indoor Stadium, Durham, NC 27708. **Website:** www.goduke.com.

Head Coach: Sean McNally. **Assistant Coaches:** Jonathan Anderson, *Matthew Boggs, Sean Snedeker. **Telephone:** (919) 668-0255. **Baseball SID:** Chris Cook. **Telephone:** (919) 684-8708. **Fax:** (919) 684-2489.

Home Field: Jack Coombs Field. **Seating Capacity:** 1,500. **Outfield Dimensions:** LF—330, CF—400, RF—330.

DUQUESNE DUKES

Conference: Atlantic 10.

Mailing Address: 600 Forbes Ave, Pittsburgh, PA

15282. **Website:** www.goduquesne.com.

Head Coach: Mike Wilson. **Assistant Coaches:** Buck Bollinger, Jeff Minick. **Telephone:** (412) 396-5245. **Baseball SID:** George Nieman. **Telephone:** (412) 396-5376. **Fax:** (412) 396-6210.

Home Field: Duquesne Field. **Seating Capacity:** 1,500. **Outfield Dimensions:** LF—330, CF—390, RF—330.

EAST CAROLINA PIRATES

Conference: Conference USA.

Mailing Address: 102 Clark-LeClair Stadium, Greenville, NC 27858. **Website:** www.ecupirates.com.

Head Coach: Billy Godwin. **Assistant Coaches:** Tommy Atkinson, Bill Jarman, *Link Jarrett. **Telephone:** (252) 737-1985. **Baseball SID:** Malcolm Gray. **Telephone:** (252) 737-4523. **Fax:** (252) 737-4528.

Home Field: Clark-LeClair Stadium. **Seating Capacity:** 5,000. **Outfield Dimensions:** LF—320, CF—400, RF—320. **Press Box Telephone:** (252) 328-0068.

EAST TENNESSEE STATE BUCCANEERS

Conference: Atlantic Sun.

Mailing Address: PO Box 70707, Johnson City, TN 37604. **Website:** www.etsubucs.com.

Head Coach: Tony Skole. **Assistant Coaches:** Reid Casey, *Clay Greene. **Telephone:** (423) 439-4496. **Baseball SID:** Jeff Schneider. **Telephone:** (423) 439-5612. **Fax:** (423) 439-6138.

Home Field: Cardinal Park. **Seating Capacity:** 2,000. **Outfield Dimensions:** LF—325, CF—430, RF—320. **Press Box Telephone:** (423) 741-5297.

EASTERN ILLINOIS PANTHERS

Conference: Ohio Valley.

Mailing Address: 600 Lincoln Avenue, Charleston, IL 61920. **Website:** www.EIUpanthers.com.

Head Coach: Jim Schmitz. **Assistant Coaches:** *Sean Lyons, Skylar Meade, Gil Metzger. **Telephone:** (217) 581-2522. **Baseball SID:** Ben Turner. **Telephone:** (217) 581-7020. **Fax:** (217) 581-6434.

Home Field: Coaches Stadium. **Seating Capacity:** 550. **Outfield Dimensions:** LF—340, CF—380, RF—340. **Press Box Telephone:** (217) 581-8464.

EASTERN KENTUCKY COLONELS

Conference: Ohio Valley.

Mailing Address: 521 Lancaster Ave, Richmond, KY 40475. **Website:** www.ekusports.com.

Head Coach: Jason Stein. **Assistant Coaches:** *Jerry Edwards, Shawn Thompson, Cory Whitby. **Telephone:** (859) 622-2128. **Baseball SID:** Steve Fohl. **Telephone:** (859) 622-1253. **Fax:** (859) 622-5108.

Home Field: Turkey Hughes Field. **Seating Capacity:** 1,000. **Outfield Dimensions:** LF—340, CF—415, RF—330.

EASTERN MICHIGAN EAGLES

Conference: Mid-American (West).

Mailing Address: 799 N. Hewitt Rd, Room 307, Ypsilanti, MI 48197. **Website:** www.emueagles.com.

Head Coach: Jay Alexander. **Assistant Coaches:** Aaron Hepner, *Andrew Maki, Dan O'Brien. **Telephone:** (734) 487-0315. **Baseball SID:** Dan Wyar. **Telephone:** (734) 487-0317. **Fax:** (734) 485-3840.

Home Field: Oestrike Stadium. **Seating Capacity:** 1,200. **Outfield Dimensions:** LF—330, CF—390, RF—330. **Press Box Telephone:** (734) 481-9328.

ELON PHOENIX

Conference: Southern.

Mailing Address: 2500 Campus Box, Elon, NC 27244. **Website:** www.elonphoenix.com.

Head Coach: Mike Kennedy. **Assistant Coaches:** Robbie Huffstetler, *Greg Starbuck. **Telephone:** (336) 278-6741. **Baseball SID:** Chris Rash. **Telephone:** (336) 278-6712. **Fax:** (336) 278-6768.

Home Field: Latham Park. **Seating Capacity:** 2,000. **Outfield Dimensions:** LF—317, CF—385, RF—327. **Press Box Telephone:** (336) 278-6788.

EVANSVILLE PURPLE ACES

Conference: Missouri Valley.

Mailing Address: 1800 Lincoln Ave, Evansville, IN 47722. **Website:** www.gopurpleaces.com.

Head Coach: Wes Carroll. **Assistant Coaches:** Mike Gilner, Josh Reynolds, *Marc Wagner. **Telephone:** (812) 488-2059. **Baseball SID:** Tom Benson. **Telephone:** (812) 488-1152. **Fax:** (812) 488-2090.

Home Field: Charles H. Braun Stadium. **Seating Capacity:** 1,200. **Outfield Dimensions:** LF—330, CF—400, RF—330. **Press Box Telephone:** (812) 479-2587.

FAIRFIELD STAGS

Conference: Metro Atlantic.

Mailing Address: 1073 North Benson Rd, Fairfield, CT 06824. **Website:** www.fairfieldstags.com.

Head Coach: *John Slosar. **Assistant Coaches:** Sean Fesh, Dennis Whalen. **Telephone:** (203) 254-4000, ext 2605. **Baseball SID:** Kelly McCarthy. **Telephone:** (203) 254-4000, ext 2877. **Fax:** (203) 254-4117.

Home Field: Alumni Baseball Diamond. **Seating Capacity:** Unavailable. **Outfield Dimensions:** LF—330, CF—400, RF—330.

FAIRLEIGH DICKINSON KNIGHTS

Conference: Northeast.

Mailing Address: 1000 River Rd, Teaneck, NJ 07666. **Website:** fduknights.com.

Head Coach: Jerry Defabbia. **Assistant Coaches:** *Todd Leathers, Paul Magrini. **Telephone:** (201) 692-2245. **Baseball SID:** Wes Heinel. **Telephone:** (201) 692-2208. **Fax:** (201) 692-9361.

FLORIDA GATORS

Conference: Southeastern.

Mailing Address: University Athletic Association, PO Box 14485; Gainesville, FL 32604. **Website:** www.GatorZone.com.

Head Coach: *Kevin O'Sullivan. **Assistant Coaches:** Craig Bell, Don Norris, Brad Weitzel. **Telephone:** (352) 375-4683. **Baseball SID:** John Hines. **Telephone:** (352) 375-4683. **Fax:** (352) 375-4809.

Home Field: Alfred A. McKethan Stadium at Perry Field. **Seating Capacity:** 5,500. **Outfield Dimensions:** LF—329, CF—400, RF—325. **Press Box Telephone:** (352) 375-4683.

FLORIDA A&M RATTLERS

Conference: Mid-Eastern Athletic.

Mailing Address: 1500 Wahnish Way, Tallahassee, FL 32307. **Website:** famurattlersports.com.

Head Coach: Robert Lucas. **Assistant Coaches:** Brett Richardson, Kentaus Carter. **Telephone:** (850) 599-3202. **Baseball SID:** Ronnie Johnson. **Telephone:** (850) 561-2701. **Fax:** (850) 599-3206.

FLORIDA ATLANTIC OWLS

Conference: Sun Belt.

Mailing Address: 777 Glades Rd, Boca Raton, FL 33431. **Website:** www.fausports.com.

Head Coach: John McCormack. **Assistant Coaches:** Brad Frick, *Jason Jackson, Ben Sanderson. **Telephone:** (561) 297-3477. **Baseball SID:** Nick Mirkovich. **Telephone:** (561) 297-3063. **Fax:** (561) 297-3963.

Home Field: FAU Stadium. **Seating Capacity:** 2,500. **Outfield Dimensions:** LF—330, CF—400, RF—330. **Press Box Telephone:** (561) 297-3455.

FLORIDA GULF COAST EAGLES

Conference: Atlantic Sun.

Mailing Address: 10501 FGCU Blvd, South Fort Myers, FL 33965. **Website:** www.fgcuathletics.com.

Head Coach: Dave Tollett. **Assistant Coaches:** *Rusty McKee, Nolan Neiman, Derek Tate. **Telephone:** (239) 590-7051. **Baseball SID:** Chris Perry. **Telephone:** (239) 590-7061. **Fax:** (239) 590-7014.

Home Field: Swanson Stadium. **Seating Capacity:** 1,800. **Outfield Dimensions:** LF—330, CF—400, RF—330. **Press Box Telephone:** (239) 590-7012.

FLORIDA INTERNATIONAL PANTHERS

Conference: Sun Belt.

Mailing Address: 11200 SW 8th St, Miami, FL 33199. **Website:** www.fiusports.com.

Head Coach: Turtle Thomas. **Assistant Coaches:** *Sean Allen, Frank Damas, Scott Humes. **Telephone:** (305) 348-3165. **Baseball SID:** Ivan Irizarry. **Telephone:** (305) 348-6666. **Fax:** (305) 348-2963.

Home Field: University Park. **Seating Capacity:** 2,000. **Outfield Dimensions:** LF—325, CF—400, RF—325. **Press Box Telephone:** 305-348-7403.

FLORIDA STATE SEMINOLES

Conference: Atlantic Coast (Atlantic).

Mailing Address: 403 Stadium Drive West, Room D0107, Tallahassee, FL 32306. **Website:** www.seminoles.com.

Head Coach: Mike Martin. **Assistant Coaches:** Brian Hoop, Mike Martin Jr., *Jamey Shouppe. **Telephone:** (850) 644-1073. **Baseball SID:** Jason Leturmy. **Telephone:** (850) 644-5656. **Fax:** (850) 644-3820.

Home Field: Dick Howser Stadium. **Seating Capacity:** 6,700. **Outfield Dimensions:** LF—340, CF—400, RF—320. **Press Box Telephone:** (850) 644-1553.

FORDHAM RAMS

Conference: Atlantic 10.

Mailing Address: 441 East Fordham Road, Bronx, NY 10458. **Website:** www.fordhamsports.com.

Head Coach: Nick Restaino. **Assistant Coaches:** Anthony DeCicco, Andrew Lang, Mark Stevens. **Telephone:** (718) 817-4292. **Baseball SID:** Scott Kwiatkowski. **Telephone:** (718) 817-4219. **Fax:** (718) 817-4244.

Home Field: Houlihan Park at Jack Coffey Field. **Seating Capacity:** 1,000. **Outfield Dimension:** LF—330, CF—400, RF—330. **Press Box Telephone:** (718) 817-0773.

FRESNO STATE BULLDOGS

Conference: Western Athletic.

Mailing Address: 1510 E. Shaw Ave, Suite 103, Fresno, CA 93710. **Website:** gobulldogs.com.

Head Coach: Mike Batesole. **Assistant Coaches:** *Matt Curtis, Pat Waer. **Telephone:** (559) 278-2178. **Baseball SID:** Theresa Kurtz. **Telephone:** (559) 244-5619. **Fax:** (559) 244-6032.

Home Field: Beiden Field. **Seating Capacity:** 3,575. **Outfield Dimensions:** LF—330, CF—400, RF—330. **Press Box Telephone:** (559) 278-7678.

FURMAN PALADINS

Conference: Southern.

Mailing Address: 3300 Poinsett Highway, Greenville, SC 29613. **Website:** furmanpaladins.com.

Head Coach: Ron Smith. **Assistant Coaches:** Britt Rheames, Jeff Whitfield. **Telephone:** (864) 294-2146. **Baseball SID:** Hunter Reid. **Telephone:** (864) 294-2061. **Fax:** (864) 294-3061.

GARDNER-WEBB RUNNING BULLDOGS

Conference: Atlantic Sun.

Mailing Address: PO Box 877, Boiling Springs, NC 28017. **Website:** www.gwusports.com.

Head Coach: Rusty Stroupe. **Assistant Coaches:** Jason Burke, *Kent Cox. **Telephone:** (704) 406-4421. **Baseball SID:** Marc Rabb. **Telephone:** (704) 406-4355. **Fax:** (704) 406-4739.

GEORGE MASON PATRIOTS

Conference: Colonial Athletic.

Mailing Address: 4400 University Dr, Fairfax, VA 22030. **Website:** gomason.com.

Head Coach: Bill Brown. **Assistant Coaches:** *Steve Hay, Robbie Jacobsen, Kyle Werman. **Telephone:** (703) 993-3282. **Baseball SID:** Richard Coco. **Telephone:** (703) 993-3264. **Fax:** (703) 993-3259.

Home Field: Hap Spuhler Field. **Seating Capacity:** 900. **Outfield Dimensions:** LF—320, CF—400, RF—320.

GEORGE WASHINGTON COLONIALS

Conference: Atlantic 10.

Mailing Address: 600 22nd Street NW, Washington, DC 20052. **Website:** gwsports.cstv.com.

Head Coach: Steve Mrowka. **Assistant Coaches:** *Pat O'Brien, Bob Smith. **Telephone:** (202) 994-7399. **Baseball SID:** Simon Ogus. **Telephone:** (202) 994-0339. **Fax:** (202) 994-2713.

GEORGETOWN HOYAS

Conference: Big East.

Mailing Address: McDonough Arena, 37th & O Streets, Washington DC 20057. **Website:** guhoyas.com.

Head Coach: Pete Wilk. **Assistant Coaches:** J.J. Brock, *Curtis Brown, Tom Shaffer. **Telephone:** (202) 687-2462. **Baseball SID:** Drew Wiseman. **Telephone:** (202) 687-6591. **Fax:** (202) 687-2491.

Home Field: Shirley Povich Field. **Seating Capacity:** 1,500. **Outfield Dimensions:** LF—330, CF—375, RF—330. **Press Box Telephone:** (267) 304-2440.

GEORGIA BULLDOGS

Conference: Southeastern (East).

Mailing Address: One Selig Circle, Athens, GA 30602. **Website:** www.georgiadogs.com.

Head Coach: David Perno. **Assistant Coaches:** *Jason Eller, Justin Holmes, Brady Wiederhold. **Telephone:** (706) 542-7971. **Baseball SID:** Ben Beaty. **Telephone:** (706) 542-9344. **Fax:** (706) 542-9339.

Home Field: Foley Field. **Seating Capacity:** 3,291. **Outfield Dimensions:** LF—350, CF—404, RF—314. **Press Box Telephone:** (706) 542-6161.

GEORGIA SOUTHERN EAGLES

Conference: Southern.

Mailing Address: PO Box 8095, Statesboro GA 30460. **Website:** www.georgiasoutherneagles.com.

Head Coach: Rodney Hennon. **Assistant Coaches:** Jason Beverlin, *Mike Tidick. **Telephone:** (912) 478-7360. **Baseball SID:** Pat Osterman. **Telephone:** (912) 478-5239.

Fax: (912) 478-0046.

Home Field: JI Clements Stadium. **Seating Capacity:** 3,000. **Outfield Dimensions:** LF—325, CF—385, RF—325. **Press Box Telephone:** (912) 478-5764.

GEORGIA STATE PANTHERS

Conference: Colonial Athletic.

Mailing Address: 125 Decatur St, Suite 201, Atlanta, GA 30329. **Website:** www.georgiastatesports.com.

Head Coach: Greg Frady. **Assistant Coaches:** Blaine McFerrin, *Brad Stromdahl, Peter Wermuth. **Telephone:** (404) 413-4077. **Baseball SID:** Mike Holmes. **Telephone:** (404) 413-4033. **Fax:** (404) 413-4035.

Home Field: The Field at Panthersville. **Seating Capacity:** 1,000. **Outfield Dimensions:** LF—334, CF—385, RF—338. **Press Box Telephone:** (404) 244-5801.

GEORGIA TECH YELLOW JACKETS

Conference: Atlantic Coast (Coastal).

Mailing Address: 150 Bobby Dodd Way, Atlanta, GA 30332. **Website:** www.ramblinwreck.com.

Head Coach: Danny Hall. **Assistant Coaches:** Tom Kinkelaar, *Bryan Prince, Matt White. **Telephone:** (404) 894-5471. **Baseball SID:** Cheryl Watts. **Telephone:** (404) 894-5445. **Fax:** (404) 894-1248.

Home Field: Russ Chandler Stadium. **Seating Capacity:** 4,157. **Outfield Dimensions:** LF—328, CF—400, RF—334. **Press Box Telephone:** (404) 894-3167.

GONZAGA BULLDOGS

Conference: West Coast.

Mailing Address: 502 E. Boone Ave, Spokane, WA 99258. **Website:** gozags.com.

Head Coach: Mark Machtolf. **Assistant Coaches:** Steve Bennent, Bobby Carlson, *Danny Evans. **Telephone:** (509) 313-4209. **Baseball SID:** Bobby Alworth. **Telephone:** (509) 313-4227. **Fax:** (509) 313-5730.

Home Field: Patterson Baseball Complex and Washington Trust Field. **Seating Capacity:** 1,500. **Outfield Dimensions:** LF—328, CF—398, RF—328. **Press Box Telephone:** (509) 279-1005.

GRAMBLING STATE TIGERS

Conference: Southwestern Athletic.

Mailing Address: PO Box 868, Grambling, LA 71245. **Website:** www.gsutigers.com.

Head Coach: Barret Rey. **Assistant Coach:** Olen Parker. **Telephone:** (318) 274-6566. **Baseball SID:** Ryan McGinty. **Telephone:** (318) 274-6562. **Fax:** (318) 274-2761.

HARTFORD HAWKS

Conference: America East.

Mailing Address: Sports Center, 200 Bloomfield Ave, West Hartford, CT 06117. **Website:** www.hartfordhawks.com.

Head Coach: Jeff Calcaterra. **Assistant Coaches:** Inaki Ormaechea, *Mike Susi, John Turner. **Telephone:** (860) 768-5760. **Baseball SID:** Dan Ruede. **Telephone:** (860) 768-4501. **Fax:** (860) 768-5047.

Home Field: Hartford Field. **Seating Capacity:** 1,500. **Outfield Dimensions:** LF—325, CF—400, RF—325.

HARVARD CRIMSON

Conference: Ivy League (Rolfe).

Mailing Address: 65 North Harvard St, Boston, MA 02163. **Website:** www.gocrimson.com.

Head Coach: Joe Walsh. **Assistant Coaches:** Aaron Landes, Tom Lo Ricco. **Telephone:** (617) 495-2629. **Baseball SID:** Kurt Svoboda. **Telephone:** (617) 495-2206. **Fax:** (617) 495-2130.

HAWAII RAINBOWS

Conference: Western Athletic.

Mailing Address: 1337 Lower Campus Road, Honolulu, HI 96822. **Website:** hawaiiathletics.com.

Head Coach: Mike Trapasso. **Assistant Coaches:** Keith Komeiji, *Chad Konishi. **Telephone:** (808) 956-6247. **Baseball SID:** Pakalani Bello. **Telephone:** (808) 956-7506. **Fax:** (808) 956-3543.

HIGH POINT PANTHERS

Conference: Big South.

Mailing Address: 833 Montlieu Ave, High Point, NC 27262. **Website:** highpointpanthers.com.

Head Coach: Craig Cozart. **Assistant Coaches:** Daniel Latham, *Bryan Peters, Rich Wallace. **Telephone:** (336) 841-9190. **Baseball SID:** Manny Nieves. **Telephone:** (336) 841-4640. **Fax:** (336) 841-9182.

Home Field: Coy O. Williard Baseball Stadium. **Seating Capacity:** 550. **Outfield Dimensions:** LF—350, CF—400, RF—330. **Press Box Telephone:** (336) 888-6334.

HOFSTRA PRIDE

Conference: Colonial Athletic.

Mailing Address: 228 PFC, 230 Hofstra University, Hempstead, NY 11549. **Website:** www.hofstra.edu/Athletics/index_Athletics.cfm.

Head Coach: Patrick Anderson. **Assistant Coaches:** Marshall Canosa, *John Russo. **Telephone:** (516) 463-5065. **Baseball SID:** Len Skoros. **Telephone:** (516) 463-4602. **Fax:** (516) 463-5033.

Home Field: University Field. **Seating Capacity:** 500. **Outfield Dimensions:** LF—331, CF—380, RF—340.

HOLY CROSS CRUSADERS

Conference: Patriot.

Mailing Address: One College St, Worcester, MA 01610. **Website:** goholycross.com.

Head Coach: Greg DiCenzo. **Assistant Coaches:** *Bruce Elliott, Keving Gately, Chris King. **Telephone:** (508) 793-2753. **Baseball SID:** Michelle Bradley. **Telephone:** (508) 793-2583. **Fax:** (508) 793-2309.

Home Field: Fitton Field. **Seating Capacity:** 3,000. **Outfield Dimensions:** LF—332, CF—385, RF—313.

HOUSTON COUGARS

Conference: Conference USA.

Mailing Address: 3100 Cullen Blvd, Houston, Texas 77204. **Website:** UHCougars.com.

Head Coach: Rayner Noble. **Assistant Coaches:** Jorge Garza, *Russell Stockton. **Telephone:** (713) 743-9396. **Baseball SID:** Jamie Zarda. **Telephone:** (713) 743-9406. **Fax:** (713) 743-9411.

Home Field: Cougar Field. **Seating Capacity:** 2,000. **Outfield Dimensions:** LF—330, CF—390, RF—330. **Press Box Telephone:** (713) 743-0840.

HOUSTON BAPTIST HUSKIES

Conference: Independent.

Mailing Address: 7502 Fondren Rd, Houston, TX 77074. **Website:** www.hbuhuskies.com.

Head Coach: Jared Moon. **Assistant Coaches:** Chris Hill, Steve Hughes. **Telephone:** (281) 649-3262. **Baseball SID:** Jeff Sutton. **Telephone:** (281) 649-3098. **Fax:** (281) 649-3496.

ILLINOIS FIGHTING ILLINI

Conference: Big 10.

Mailing Address: 1700 S. Fourth St, Champaign, IL 61820. **Website:** www.fightingillini.com.

Head Coach: Dan Hartleb. **Assistant Coaches:** *Eric Snider, Ken Westray. **Telephone:** (217) 244-8144. **Baseball SID:** Ben Taylor. **Telephone:** (217) 244-5045. **Fax:** (217) 333-5540.

Home Field: Illinois Field. **Seating Capacity:** 1,500. **Outfield Dimensions:** LF—330, CF—400, RF—330. **Press Box Telephone:** (217) 333-1227.

ILLINOIS STATE REDBIRDS

Conference: Missouri Valley.

Mailing Address: Illinois State Athletic Media Relations, 202 Horton Field House, Normal, IL 61671. **Website:** GoRedbirds.com.

Head Coach: Jim Brownlee. **Assistant Coaches:** Mike Current, Matt Fowles, *Mark Kingston. **Telephone:** (309) 438-5151. **Baseball SID:** Kevin McCarty. **Telephone:** (309) 438-3249. **Fax:** (309) 438-5634.

Home Field: Duffy Bass Field. **Seating Capacity:** 1,500. **Outfield Dimensions:** LF—330, CF—400, RF—330.

ILLINOIS-CHICAGO FLAMES

Conference: Horizon.

Mailing Address: 839 W. Roosevelt Rd, MC 195, Chicago, IL 60608. **Website:** uicflames.cstv.com.

Head Coach: Mike Dee. **Assistant Coaches:** John Flood, Sean McDermott, *Mike Nall. **Telephone:** (312) 996-8645. **Baseball SID:** John Jaramillo. **Telephone:** (312) 996-5880. **Fax:** (312) 996-8349.

Home Field: Les Miller Field. **Seating Capacity:** 1,000. **Outfield Dimensions:** LF—330, CF—400, RF—330. **Press Box Telephone:** (312) 355-1190.

INDIANA HOOSIERS

Conference: Big 10.

Mailing Address: 1001 E. 17th St, Bloomington IN 47408. **Website:** iuhoosiers.com.

Head Coach: Tracy Smith. **Assistant Coaches:** Ben Greenspan, *Ty Neal. **Telephone:** (812) 856-0215. **Baseball SID:** Matt Brady. **Telephone:** (812) 856-0215. **Fax:** (812) 855-9401.

Home Field: Sembower Field. **Seating Capacity:** 1,500. **Outfield Dimensions:** LF—330, CF—400, RF—330. **Press Box Telephone:** (812) 855-4787.

INDIANA STATE SYCAMORES

Conference: Missouri Valley.

Mailing Address: 401 N. 4th St, Terre Haute, IN 47809. **Website:** gosycamores.com.

Head Coach: Lindsay Meggs. **Assistant Coaches:** Ryan Heil, *Tyler Herbst, T.J. Merritt. **Telephone:** (812) 237-4051. **Baseball SID:** Mike Williams. **Telephone:** (812) 237-4161. **Fax:** (812) 237-4157.

Home Field: Sycamore Field. **Seating Capacity:** Unavailable. **Outfield Dimensions:** LF—330, CF—400, RF—330.

IPFW MASTODONS

Conference: Summit.

Mailing Address: 2101 East Coliseum Blvd, Fort Wayne, IN 46805. **Website:** gomastodons.com.

Head Coach: Bobby Pierce. **Assistant Coaches:** Grant Birely, *Josh Schultz. **Telephone:** (260) 481-5480. **Baseball SID:** Rudy Yovich. **Telephone:** (260) 481-6646. **Fax:** (260) 481-6002.

IONA GAELS

Conference: Metro Atlantic.

Mailing Address: 715 North Ave, New Rochelle, NY 10801. **Website:** icgaels.com.

Head Coach: *Pat Carey. **Assistant Coaches:** James LaSalla, Adam Taraska, Chuck Todd. **Telephone:** (914) 633-2419. **Baseball SID:** Brian Beyrer. **Telephone:** (914) 633-2334. **Fax:** (914) 633-2072.

IOWA HAWKEYES

Conference: Big 10.

Mailing Address: 232 Carver Hawkeye Arena, Iowa City, IA 52242.

Head Coach: Jack Dahm. **Assistant Coaches:** *Ryan Brownlee, Chris Maliszewksi, pitching coach Kris Welker, volunteer coach. **Telephone:** 319-335-9390. **Baseball SID:** Matt Weitzel. **Telephone:** 319-335-6590. **Fax:** 319-335-9417.

Home Field: Duane Banks Field. **Seating Capacity:** 3,000. **Outfield Dimensions:** LF—330, CF—400, RF—330. **Press Box Telephone:** 319-335-9520.

JACKSON STATE TIGERS

Conference: Southwestern Athletic.

Mailing Address: 1400 John R. Lynch Street, Jackson, MS 39217. **Website:** www.jsutigers.com.

Head Coach: Omar Johnson. **Assistant Coaches:** Frank Adams, Anton Shinhoster. **Telephone:** (601) 979-3930. **Baseball SID:** Wesley Peterson. **Telephone:** (601) 979-5899. **Fax:** (601) 979-2000.

JACKSONVILLE DOLPHINS

Conference: Atlantic Sun.

Mailing Address: 2800 University Blvd North, Jacksonville, FL 32211. **Website:** judolphins.com.

Head Coach: Terry Alexander. **Assistant Coaches:** Todd Claus, Ben Kerr, *Tim Montez. **Telephone:** (904) 256-7412. **Baseball SID:** Josh Ellis. **Telephone:** (904) 256-7402. **Fax:** (904) 256-7424.

JACKSONVILLE STATE GAMECOCKS

Conference: Ohio Valley.

Mailing Address: 700 Pelham Road North, Jacksonville, AL 36265. **Website:** www.jsugamecocksports.com.

Head Coach: Jim Case. **Assistant Coaches:** *Steve Gillispie, Travis Janssen. **Telephone:** (256) 782-5367. **Baseball SID:** Greg Seitz. **Telephone:** (256) 782-5279. **Fax:** (256) 782-5958.

Home Field: Rudy Abbott Field. **Seating Capacity:** 1,500. **Outfield Dimensions:** LF—330, CF—405, RF—330. **Press Box Telephone:** (256) 782-5533.

JAMES MADISON DUKES

Conference: Colonial Athletic.

Mailing Address: MSC 2301, Godwin Hall Room 304, Harrisonburg, VA 22807. **Website:** jmusports.com.

Head Coach: Spanky McFarland. **Assistant Coaches:** Jason Middleton, *Jay Sullenger, Ted White. **Telephone:** (540) 568-3932. **Baseball SID:** Kevin Warner. **Telephone:** (540) 568-6154. **Fax:** (540) 568-3703.

Home Field: Long Field/Mauck Stadium. **Seating Capacity:** 1,200. **Outfield Dimensions:** LF—340, CF—400, RF—320. **Press Box Telephone:** (540) 568-6545.

KANSAS JAYHAWKS

Conference: Big 12.

Mailing Address: Allen Fieldhouse, 1651 Naismith Dr, Lawrence, KS 66045. **Website:** www.kuathletics.com.

Head Coach: Ritch Price. **Assistant Coaches:** Kevin Frady, Ryan Graves, *John Szefc. **Telephone:** (785) 864-7907. **Baseball SID:** Mike Cummings. **Telephone:** (785) 864-3575. **Fax:** (785) 864-7944.

Home Field: Hoglund Ballpark. **Seating Capacity:** 2,500. **Outfield Dimensions:** LF—330, CF—392, RF—330. **Press Box Telephone:** (785) 864-4037.

KANSAS STATE WILDCATS

Conference: Big 12.

Mailing Address: 1800 College Ave, Manhattan, KS 66502. **Website:** www.kstatesports.com.

Head Coach: Brad Hill. **Assistant Coaches:** *Sean McCann, Craig Ringe, Andy Sawyers. **Telephone:** (785) 532-3926. **Baseball SID:** Ryan Lackey. **Telephone:** (785) 532-7708. **Fax:** (785) 532-6093.

Home Field: Tointon Family Stadium. **Seating Capacity:** 2,331. **Outfield Dimensions:** LF—340, CF—40, RF—325. **Press Box Telephone:** (785) 532-5801.

KENNESAW STATE OWLS

Conference: Atlantic Sun.

Mailing Address: 1000 Chastain Rd, Kennesaw, Georgia 30144. **Website:** ksuowls.com.

Head Coach: Mike Sansing. **Assistant Coaches:** *Ryan Coe, Kevin Erminio. **Telephone:** (770) 423-6264. **Baseball SID:** Jason Hanes. **Telephone:** (678) 797-2562. **Fax:** (770) 423-6555.

Home Field: Stillwell Stadium. **Seating Capacity:** 1,065. **Outfield Dimensions:** LF—331, CF—400, RF—330.

KENT STATE GOLDEN FLASHES

Conference: Mid-American (East).

Mailing Address: 234 MAC Center, Kent, OH 44242. **Website:** www.kentstatesports.com.

Head Coach: Scott Stricklin. **Assistant Coaches:** Mike Birkbeck, *Scott Daeley. **Telephone:** (330) 672-8432. **Baseball SID:** Matthew Lofton. **Telephone:** (330) 672-2254. **Fax:** (330) 672-2112.

Home Field: Schoonover Stadium. **Seating Capacity:** 1,148. **Outfield Dimensions:** LF—330, CF—415, RF—320. **Press Box Telephone:** (330) 672-3696.

KENTUCKY WILDCATS

Conference: Southeastern (East).

Mailing Address: Joe Craft Center, 338 Lexington Ave, Lexington, KY 40506. **Website:** www.ukathletics.com.

Head Coach: Gary Henderson. **Assistant Coaches:** *Brad Bohannon, Brian Green. **Telephone:** (859) 257-8052. **Baseball SID:** Brent Ingram. **Telephone:** (859) 257-3838. **Fax:** (859) 323-4310.

Home Field: Cliff Hagan Stadium. **Seating Capacity:** 3,000. **Outfield Dimensions:** LF—340, CF—390, RF—310. **Press Box Telephone:** 859.257.9011.

LA SALLE EXPLORERS

Conference: Atlantic 10.

Mailing Address: 1900 West Olney Ave, Box 805, Philadelphia, PA 19141. **Website:** www.goexplorers.com.

Head Coach: *Mike Lake. **Assistant Coaches:** Mike Dertouzos, Toby Fisher. **Telephone:** (215) 951-1995. **Baseball SID:** Marc Mullen. **Telephone:** (215) 951-1633. **Fax:** (215) 951-1694. **Fax:** (215) 951-1694.

Home Field: Hank DeVincent Field. **Seating Capacity:** 1,000. **Outfield Dimensions:** LF—305, CF—458, RF—321.

LAFAYETTE LEOPARDS

Conference: Patriot.

Mailing Address: Kirby Sports Center, Easton, PA 18042. **Website:** www.goleopards.com.

Head Coach: Joe Kinney. **Assistant Coaches:** *Rick Clagett, Gregg Durrah, Brandt Godshalk. **Telephone:** (610) 330-5476. **Baseball SID:** Katie Meier. **Telephone:** (610) 330-5518. **Fax:** (610) 330-5519.

Home Field: Kamine Stadium. **Seating Capacity:** 500. **Outfield Dimensions:** LF—332, CF—403, RF—335.

LAMAR CARDINALS

Conference: Southland.

Mailing Address: PO Box 10066, Beaumont, TX, 77710. **Website:** lamarcardinals.com.

Head Coach: Jim Gilligan. **Assistant Coaches:** Scott Hatten, *Jim Ricklefsen. **Telephone:** (409) 880-8351. **Baseball SID:** Brian Henry. **Telephone:** (409) 880-8329. **Fax:** (409) 880-2338.

Home Field: Vincent-Beck Stadium. **Seating Capacity:** 3,500. **Outfield Dimensions:** LF—325, CF—380, RF—325. **Press Box Telephone:** (409) 880-8327.

LE MOYNE DOLPHINS

Conference: Independent.

Mailing Address: 1419 Salt Springs Rd, Syracuse, NY 13214. **Website:** www.lemoynedolphins.com.

Head Coach: Steve Owens. **Assistant Coaches:** Pete Hoy, Scott Landers, Bob Nandin. **Telephone:** (315) 445-4415. **Baseball SID:** Craig Lane. **Telephone:** (315) 445-4412. **Fax:** (315) 445-4678.

Home Field: Dick Rockwell Field. **Seating Capacity:** 2,500. **Outfield Dimensions:** LF—314, CF—375, RF—337.

LEHIGH MOUNTAIN HAWKS

Conference: Patriot.

Mailing Address: 641 Taylor St, Bethlehem, PA 18015. **Website:** www.lehighsports.com.

Head Coach: Sean Leary. **Assistant Coaches:** John Bisco, Tim Fisher, *Brian Hirschberg. **Telephone:** (610) 758-4315. **Baseball SID:** Unavailable. **Telephone:** (610) 758-5101. **Fax:** (610) 758-4407.

LIBERTY FLAMES

Conference: Big South.

Mailing Address: 1971 University Blvd, Lynchburg, VA 24502. **Website:** www.libertyflames.com.

Head Coach: Jim Toman. **Assistant Coaches:** Garrett Quinn, Jeremiah Boles, *Nick Schnabel. **Telephone:** (434) 582-2103. **Baseball SID:** Ryan Bomberger. **Telephone:** (434) 582-2292. **Fax:** (434) 582-2076.

Home Field: Worthington Stadium. **Seating Capacity:** 1,000. **Outfield Dimensions:** LF—325, CF—390, RF—325. **Press Box Telephone:** (434) 582-2914.

LIPSCOMB BISONS

Conference: Atlantic Sun.

Mailing Address: 1 University Park Dr, Nashville, TN 37204. **Website:** lipscombsports.com.

Head Coach: Jeff Forehand. **Assistant Coaches:** *Chris Collins, Brian Ryman, Lantz Wheeler. **Telephone:** (615) 966-5716. **Baseball SID:** Mark McGee. **Telephone:** (615) 966-5862. **Fax:** (615) 966-1806.

Home Field: Dugan Field. **Seating Capacity:** 1,500. **Outfield Dimensions:** LF—330, CF—405, RF—330. **Press Box Telephone:** (615) 479-3794.

LONG BEACH STATE DIRTBAGS

Conference: Big West.

Mailing Address: 1250 Bellflower Blvd, Long Beach, CA 90840. **Website:** www.longbeachstate.com.

Head Coach: Mike Weathers. **Assistant Coaches:** T.J. Bruce, *Andy Rojo, Jon Strauss. **Telephone:** (562) 985-7548. **Baseball SID:** Roger Kirk. **Telephone:** (562) 985-8569. **Fax:** (562) 985-1549.

Home Field: Blair Field. **Seating Capacity:** 3,200. **Outfield Dimensions:** LF—348, CF—400, RF—348.

LONG ISLAND BLACKBIRDS

Conference: Northeast.

Mailing Address: 1 University Plaza, Brooklyn, NY 11201. **Website:** www.liuathletics.com.

Head Coach: Don Maines. **Assistant Coaches:** Joshua MacDonald, *Craig Noto, Chris Reyes. **Telephone:** (718) 488-1538. **Baseball SID:** Shawn Sweeney. **Telephone:** (718) 488-1307. **Fax:** (718) 488-3302.

Home Field: LIU Field. **Seating Capacity:** 500. **Outfield Dimensions:** LF—315, CF—416, RF—315.

LONGWOOD LANCERS

Conference: Independent.

Mailing Address: 201 High St, Farmville, VA 23909. **Website:** www.longwoodlancers.com.

Head Coach: Buddy Bolding. **Assistant Coaches:** *Shawn Abell, Erik Supplee. **Telephone:** (434) 395-2352. **Baseball SID:** Greg Prouty. **Telephone:** (434) 395-2097. **Fax:** (434) 395-2568.

Home Field: Lancer Stadium. **Seating Capacity:** 500. **Outfield Dimensions:** LF—335, CF—400, RF—335.

LOUISIANA STATE TIGERS

Conference: Southeastern (West).

Mailing Address: PO Box 25095, Baton Rouge, LA 70894. **Website:** www.LSUsports.net.

Head Coach: Paul Mainieri. **Assistant Coaches:** Will Davis, *David Grewe, Javi Sanchez. **Telephone:** (225) 578-4148. **Baseball SID:** Bill Franques. **Telephone:** (225) 578-2527. **Fax:** (225) 578-1861.

Home Field: Alex Box Stadium. **Seating Capacity:** 8,786. **Outfield Dimensions:** LF—330, CF—405, RF—330. **Press Box Telephone:** (225) 578-4149.

LOUISIANA TECH BULLDOGS

Conference: Western Athletic.

Mailing Address: PO Box 3166, Ruston, LA 71272. **Website:** www.latechsports.com.

Head Coach: Wade Simoneaux. **Assistant Coaches:** Fran Andermann, *Brian Rountree, Dr. David Szymanski. **Telephone:** (318) 257-5318. **Baseball SID:** Ryan Jones. **Telephone:** (318) 257-5314. **Fax:** (318) 257-3757.

Home Field: J.C. Love Field at Pat Patterson Park. **Seating Capacity:** 3,500. **Outfield Dimensions:** LF—315, CF—385, RF—325. **Press Box Telephone:** (318) 257-3144.

LOUISIANA-LAFAYETTE RAGIN' CAJUNS

Conference: Sun Belt.

Mailing Address: 201 Reinhardt Dr, Cox Communications Athletic Complex, Lafayette, LA 70506. **Website:** www.ragincajuns.com.

Head Coach: Tony Robichaux. **Assistant Coaches:** Anthony Babineaux, Chris Domingue, *Mike Trahan. **Telephone:** (337) 482-6189. **Baseball SID:** John Strawn. **Telephone:** (337) 482-6332. **Fax:** (337) 482-6529.

Home Field: M.L. "Tigue" Moore Field. **Seating Capacity:** 3,755. **Outfield Dimensions:** LF—330, CF—400, RF—330. **Press Box Telephone:** (337) 851-2255.

LOUISVILLE CARDINALS

Conference: Big East.

Mailing Address: 215 Central Ave, Louisville, KY 40292. **Website:** www.UofLSports.com.

Head Coach: Dan McDonnell. **Assistant Coaches:** Xan Barksdale, *Chris Lemonis, Roger Williams. **Telephone:** (502) 852-0103. **Baseball SID:** Garett Wall. **Telephone:** (502) 852-3088. **Fax:** (502) 852-7401.

Home Field: Jim Patterson Stadium. **Seating Capacity:** 2,500. **Outfield Dimensions:** LF—330, CF—402, RF—330. **Press Box Telephone:** (502) 852-3700.

LOYOLA MARYMOUNT LIONS

Conference: West Coast.

Mailing Address: 1 LMU Drive, Los Angeles, CA 90045. **Website:** lmulions.com.

Head Coach: Jason Gill. **Assistant Coaches:** *Drew Keehn, Jeff Walker, Scott Walter. **Telephone:** (310) 338-2949. **Baseball SID:** Tyler Geivett. **Telephone:** (310) 338-7638. **Fax:** (310) 338-2703.

Home Field: Page Stadium. **Seating Capacity:** 600. **Outfield Dimensions:** LF—326, CF—413, RF—330. **Press Box Telephone:** (310) 338-3046.

MAINE BLACK BEARS

Conference: America East.

Mailing Address: 5747 Memorial Gym, Orono, ME 04469. **Website:** www.goblackbears.com.

Head Coach: Steve Trimper. **Assistant Coaches:** *Jared Holowaty, Aaron Izaryk. **Telephone:** (207) 581-1090. **Baseball SID:** Laura Reed. **Telephone:** (207) 581-3646. **Fax:** (207) 581-3297.

Home Field: Mahaney Diamond. **Seating Capacity:** 4,400. **Outfield Dimensions:** LF—330, CF—300, RF—330. **Press Box Telephone:** (207) 581-1049.

MANHATTAN JASPERS

Conference: Metro Atlantic.

Mailing Address: 4513 Manhattan College Pkwy, Riverdale, NY 10471. **Website:** www.gojaspers.com.

Head Coach: Kevin Leighton. **Assistant Coaches:** *Ryan Darcy, Jason Spaulding. **Telephone:** (718) 862-7936. **Baseball SID:** Steve Dombroski. **Telephone:** (718) 862-7228. **Fax:** (718) 862-8020.

Home Field: Van Cortlandt Park. **Seating Capacity:** 500. **Outfield Dimensions:** LF—320, CF—398, RF—320.

MARIST RED FOXES

Conference: Metro Atlantic.

Mailing Address: 3399 North Road, Poughkeepsie, NY 12601. **Website:** goredfoxes.com.

Head Coach: Dennis Healy. **Assistant Coaches:** Joe Michalski, Tom Shanley. **Telephone:** (845) 575-3699, ext 2570. **Baseball SID:** Mike Haase. **Telephone:** (914) 575-3699, ext 6047. **Fax:** (914) 471-0466.

MARSHALL THUNDERING HERD

Conference: Conference USA.

Mailing Address: 2001 3rd Ave, Huntington,WV 25715. **Website:** herdzone.com.

Head Coach: Jeff Waggoner. **Assistant Coaches:** *Tim Adkins, George Brumfield, Tim Donnelly. **Telephone:** (304) 696-5277. **Baseball SID:** Chris Attwood. **Telephone:** (304) 696-4662. **Fax:** (304) 696-2325.

Home Field: Appalachian Power Park. **Seating Capacity:** 4,500. **Outfield Dimensions:** LF—330, CF—400, RF—320.

MARYLAND TERRAPINS

Conference: Atlantic Coast (Atlantic).

Mailing Address: Comcat Center, 1 Terrapin Trail, College Park, MD 20742. **Website:** umterps.com.

Head Coach: Terry Rupp. **Assistant Coaches:** Blaine Brown, *Jim Farr. **Telephone:** (301) 314-7122. **Baseball SID:** Joey Flyntz. **Telephone:** (301) 314-8093. **Fax:** (301) 314-5472.

Home Field: Shipley Field. **Seating Capacity:** 2,500. **Outfield Dimensions:** LF—320, CF—380, RF—325. **Press Box Telephone:** (301) 314-0379.

MARYLAND-BALTIMORE COUNTY RETRIEVERS

Conference: America East.

Mailing Address: 1000 Hilltop Circle, Baltimore, MD 21250. **Website:** www.umbcretrievers.com.

Head Coach: John Jancuska. **Assistant Coaches:** Kevin Daly, Bob Mumma, Tim O'Brien. **Telephone:** (410) 455-2239. **Baseball SID:** Tom Fenstermaker. **Telephone:** (410) 455-1530. **Fax:** (410) 455-3994.

MARYLAND-EASTERN SHORE HAWKS

Conference: Mid-Eastern.

Mailing Address: William P. Hytche Athletic Center, One Backbone Rd, Princess Anne, MD 21853. **Website:** umeshawks.com.

Head Coach: *Will Gardner. **Assistant Coaches:** Eric Armstrong. **Telephone:** (410) 651-8908. **Baseball SID:** G. Stan Bradley. **Telephone:** (410) 651-6499. **Fax:** (410) 651-7514.

MASSACHUSETTS MINUTEMEN

Conference: Atlantic 10.

Mailing Address: 131 Commonwealth Ave, Amherst, MA 01003. **Website:** umassathletics.com.

Head Coach: Mike Stone. **Assistant Coaches:** Justin Keadle, Ernie May, Mike Sweeney. **Telephone:** (413) 545-3120. **Baseball SID:** Jillian Jakuba. **Telephone:** (413) 577-0053. **Fax:** (413) 545-5439.

MCNEESE STATE COWBOYS

Conference: Southland.

Mailing Address: 615 Bienville Street, Lake Charles, LA 70607. **Website:** mcneesesports.com.

Head Coach: Terry Burrows. **Assistant Coaches:** *Bubbs Merrill, Clay Van Hook. **Telephone:** (337) 475-5484. **Baseball SID:** Louis Bonnette. **Telephone:** (337) 475-5207. **Fax:** (337) 475-5202.

Home Field: Cowboy Diamond. **Seating Capacity:** 2,000. **Outfield Dimensions:** LF—330, CF—400, RF—330. **Press Box Telephone:** (337) 475-8007.

MEMPHIS TIGERS

Conference: Conference USA.

Mailing Address: 570 Normal, Memphis, TN 38152. **Website:** www.gotigersgo.com.

Head Coach: Daron Schoenrock. **Assistant Coaches:** Derrick Dunbar, *Michael Federico, Jerry Zulli. **Telephone:** (901) 678-2452. **Baseball SID:** Jason C. Redd. **Telephone:** (901) 678-4640. **Fax:** (901) 678-4131.

Home Field: USA Stadium. **Seating Capacity:** 5,000. **Outfield Dimensions:** LF—334, CF—414, RF—334.

MERCER BEARS

Conference: Atlantic Sun.

Mailing Address: 1400 Coleman Ave, Macon, GA 31207. **Website:** www.mercerbears.com.

Head Coach: Craig Gibson. **Assistant Coaches:** Tim Boeth, *Brent Shade. **Telephone:** (478) 301-2396. **Baseball SID:** Bryan Geelan. **Telephone:** (478) 301-5209. **Fax:** (478) 301-5350.

Home Field: Claude Smith Field. **Seating Capacity:** 500. **Outfield Dimensions:** LF—330, CF—400, RF—320. **Press Box Telephone:** (478) 301-2339.

MIAMI HURRICANES

Conference: Atlantic Coast (Coastal).

Mailing Address: 5821 San Amaro Dr, Coral Gables, FL 33146. **Website:** www.hurricanesports.com.

Head Coach: Jim Morris. **Assistant Coaches:** *J.D. Arteaga, Rey Fuentes, Joe Mercadante. **Telephone:** (305) 284-4171. **Baseball SID:** Rob Dunning. **Telephone:** (305) 284-3230. **Fax:** (305) 284-2807.

Home Field: Alex Rodriguez Park at Mark Light Field. **Seating Capacity:** 3,000. **Outfield Dimensions:** LF—330, CF—400, RF—330.

MIAMI (OHIO) REDHAWKS

Conference: Mid-American (East).

Mailing Address: 120 Withrow Court, Oxford, OH 45056. **Website:** www.muredhawks.com.

Head Coach: Dan Simonds. **Assistant Coaches:** *Ben Bachmann, Jeremy Ison, Nick Otte. **Telephone:** (513) 529-6631. **Baseball SID:** Jeff Symonds. **Telephone:** (513) 529-1601. **Fax:** (513) 529-6739.

Home Field: McKie Field at Hayden Park. **Seating Capacity:** 1,000. **Outfield Dimensions:** LF—332, CF—400, RF—343. **Press Box Telephone:** (513) 529-4331.

MICHIGAN WOLVERINES

Conference: Big 10.

Mailing Address: 1000 South State St, Ann Arbor, MI 48109. **Website:** www.mgoblue.com.

Head Coach: Rich Maloney. **Assistant Coaches:** *Matt Husted, Bob Keller. **Telephone:** (734) 647-4555. **Baseball SID:** Matt Fancett. **Telephone:** (734) 647-1726. **Fax:** (734) 647-1188.

Home Field: Wilpon Complex/Ray Fisher Stadium. **Seating Capacity:** 4,500. **Outfield Dimensions:** LF—312, CF—395, RF—320. **Press Box Telephone:** (734) 647-1283.

MICHIGAN STATE SPARTANS

Conference: Big 10.

Mailing Address: 304 Jenison Field House, East Lansing, MI 48824. **Website:** msuspartans.com.

Head Coach: Jake Boss. **Assistant Coaches:** Jake Boss Sr., Billy Gernon, *Mark Van Ameyde. **Telephone:** (517) 355-4486. **Baseball SID:** Jeff Barnes. **Telephone:** (517) 355-2271. **Fax:** (517) 353-9636.

Home Field: McLane Stadium. **Seating Capacity:** 2,500. **Outfield Dimensions:** LF—305, CF—395, RF—305. **Press Box Telephone:** (517) 353-3009.

MIDDLE TENNESSEE STATE BLUE RAIDERS

Conference: Sun Belt.

Mailing Address: PO Box 90, Murfreesboro, TN 37132. **Website:** www.goblueraiders.com.

Head Coach: Steve Peterson. **Assistant Coaches:** *Jim McGuire, Michael McLaury. **Telephone:** (615) 898-2984. **Baseball SID:** Jessica Stauffacher. **Telephone:** (615) 904-8115. **Fax:** (615) 898-5626.

Home Field: Reese Smith Field. **Seating Capacity:** 2,100. **Outfield Dimensions:** LF—330, CF—390, RF—330. **Press Box Telephone:** (615) 898-2117.

MINNESOTA GOLDEN GOPHERS

Conference: Big 10.

Mailing Address: University of Minnesota, 516 15th Ave SE, Minneapolis, MN 55455. **Website:** www.gophersports.com.

Head Coach: John Anderson. **Assistant Coaches:** *Rob Fornasiere, Todd Oakes, Lee Swenson. **Telephone:** (612) 625-4057. **Baseball SID:** Steve Geller. **Telephone:** (612) 624-9396. **Fax:** (612) 625-0359.

Home Field: Siebert Field. **Seating Capacity:** 2,000. **Outfield Dimensions:** LF—330, CF—380, RF—330. **Press Box Telephone:** (612) 625-4031.

MISSISSIPPI REBELS

Conference: Southeastern (West).

Mailing Address: Ole Miss Baseball Office, University Place, University, MS 38677. **Website:** www.OleMissSports.com.

Head Coach: Mike Bianco. **Assistant Coaches:** Carl Lafferty, Matt Mossberg, *Rob Reinstetle. **Telephone:** (662) 915-6643. **Baseball SID:** Bill Bunting. **Telephone:** (662) 915-1083. **Fax:** (662) 915-7006.

Home Field: Oxford University Stadium/Swayze Field. **Seating Capacity:** 11,000. **Outfield Dimensions:** LF—330, CF—390, RF—330. **Press Box Telephone:** (662) 915-7858.

MISSISSIPPI STATE BULLDOGS

Conference: Southeastern (West).

Mailing Address: PO Box 5327, Mississippi State, MS 39762. **Website:** www.mstateathletics.com.

Head Coach: John Cohen. **Assistant Coaches:** Lane Burroughs, Nick Mingione, *Butch Thompson. **Telephone:** (662) 325-3597. **Baseball SID:** Joe Dier. **Telephone:** (662) 325-8040. **Fax:** (662) 325-3600.

Home Field: Dudy Noble Field/Polk-DeMent Stadium. **Seating Capacity:** 15,000. **Outfield Dimensions:** LF—330, CF—390, RF—326. **Press Box Telephone:** (662) 325-3776.

MISSISSIPPI VALLEY STATE DELTA DEVILS

Conference: Southwestern Athletic.

Mailing Address: 14000 Highway 82 West, No. 7246, Itta Bena, MS 38941. **Website:** www.mvsu.edu/athletics.

Head Coach: Doug Shanks. **Assistant Coach:** Aaron Stevens. **Telephone:** (662) 254-3834. **Baseball SID:** Roderick Mosely. **Telephone:** (662) 254-3011. **Fax:** (662) 254-3639.

MISSOURI TIGERS

Conference: Big 12.

Mailing Address: 100 Mizzou Athletic Training Complex, Columbia, MO 65211. **Website:** mutigers.com.

Head Coach: Tim Jamieson. **Assistant Coaches:** Luke Cassis, Evan Pratte*, Tony Vitello. **Telephone:** (573) 882-0721. **Baseball SID:** Josh Murray. **Telephone:** (573) 882-0711. **Fax:** (573) 882-4720.

Home Field: Taylor Stadium at Simmons Field. **Seating Capacity:** 3,000. **Outfield Dimensions:** LF—340, CF—400, RF—340.

MISSOURI STATE BEARS

Conference: Missouri Valley.

Mailing Address: 901 S. National Ave, Springfield, MO 65897. **Website:** www.missouristatebears.com.

Head Coach: Keith Guttin. **Assistant Coaches:** *Paul Evans, Brent Thomas. **Telephone:** (417) 836-4497. **Baseball SID:** Ben Adamson. **Telephone:** (417) 836-4584. **Fax:** (417) 836-4868.

Home Field: Hammons Field. **Seating Capacity:** 8,000. **Outfield Dimensions:** LF—315, CF—400, RF—330. **Press Box Telephone:** (417) 863-0395, ext 3070.

MONMOUTH HAWKS

Conference: Northeast.

Mailing Address: 400 Cedar Ave, West Long Branch, NJ, 07764. **Website:** www.gomuhawks.com.

Head Coach: Dean Ehehalt. **Assistant Coaches:** Jeff Barbalinardo, Ty Megahee, *Chuck Ristano. **Telephone:** (732) 263-5186. **Baseball SID:** Chris Tobin. **Telephone:** (732) 263-5180. **Fax:** (732) 571-3535.

Home Field: MU Baseball Field. **Seating Capacity:** 500. **Outfield Dimensions:** LF—320, CF—380, RF—320.

MOREHEAD STATE EAGLES

Conference: Ohio Valley.

Mailing Address: Allen Field, Morehead, KY 40351. **Website:** www.msueagles.com.

Head Coach: Jay Sorg. **Assistant Coaches:** Drew Hall, *Jason Neal, Ryan Wheat. **Telephone:** (606) 783-2881. **Baseball SID:** Randy Stacy. **Telephone:** (606) 783-2500. **Fax:** (606) 783-2550.

Home Field: Allen Field. **Seating Capacity:** 1,500. **Outfield Dimensions:** LF—320, CF—370, RF—310.

MOUNT ST. MARY'S MOUNTAINEERS

Conference: Northeast.

Mailing Address: 16300 Old Emmitsburg Rd, Emmitsburg, MD 21727. **Website:** www.mountathletics.com.

Head Coach: Scott Thomson. **Assistant Coaches:** Scott Biesecker, Eric Haines, Eric Smith. **Telephone:** (301) 447-3806. **Baseball SID:** Mark Vandergrift. **Telephone:** (301) 447-5384. **Fax:** (301) 447-5300.

MURRAY STATE THOROUGHBREDS

Conference: Ohio Valley.

Mailing Address: 217 Stewart Stadium, Murray, KY, 42071. **Website:** goracers.com.

Head Coach: Rob McDonald. **Assistant Coaches:** *Paul Wyczawski. **Telephone:** (270) 809-4892. **Baseball SID:** John Brush. **Telephone:** (270) 809-7044. **Fax:** (270) 809-3814.

Home Field: Reagan Field. **Seating Capacity:** 800. **Outfield Dimensions:** LF—330, CF—400, RF—330. **Press Box Telephone:** (270) 809-5650.

NAVY MIDSHIPMEN

Conference: Patriot.

Mailing Address: 566 Brownson Rd, Annapolis, MD 21402. **Website:** navysports.com.

Head Coach: Paul Kostacopoulos. **Assistant Coaches:** *Scott Friedholm, Matt Reynolds, Jason Ronai. **Telephone:** (410) 293-5571. **Baseball SID:** Jonathan Maggart. **Telephone:** (410) 293-8771. **Fax:** (410) 293-8954.

Home Field: Terwilliger Brothers Field at Max Bishop Stadium. **Seating Capacity:** 1,500. **Outfield Dimensions:** LF—323, CF—397, RF—304. **Press Box Telephone:** (410) 293-5430.

NEBRASKA CORNHUSKERS

Conference: Big 12.

Mailing Address: 403 Line Drive Circle, Suite B, Lincoln, NE 68588. **Website:** huskers.com.

Head Coach: Mike Anderson. **Assistant Coaches:** *Dave Bingham, Eric Newman, Nate Thompson. **Telephone:** (402) 472-2269. **Baseball SID:** Shamus McKnight. **Telephone:** (402) 472-7772. **Fax:** (402) 472-2005.

Home Field: Hawks Field at Haymarket Park. **Seating Capacity:** 8,486. **Outfield Dimensions:** LF—335, CF—395, RF—325. **Press Box Telephone:** (402) 434-6861.

NEVADA WOLF PACK

Conference: Western Athletic.

Mailing Address: 1664 N. Virginia St, Reno, NV 89557. **Website:** www.nevadawolfpack.com.

Head Coach: Gary Powers. **Assistant Coaches:** Gary McNamara, *Stan Stolte, Jay Uhlman. **Telephone:** (775) 682-6978. **Baseball SID:** Jack Kuestermeyer. **Telephone:** (775) 682-6984. **Fax:** (775) 784-4386.

Home Field: Peccole Park. **Seating Capacity:** 3,000. **Outfield Dimensions:** LF—340, CF—401, RF—340. **Press Box Telephone:** (775) 784-1585.

NEVADA-LAS VEGAS REBELS

Conference: Mountain West.

Mailing Address: 4505 S. Maryland Parkway, Las Vegas, NV 89154. **Website:** unlvrebels.com.

Head Coach: Buddy Gouldsmith. **Assistant Coaches:** Bob Fenn, *David Martinez, Jeff Prieto. **Telephone:** (702) 895-3499. **Baseball SID:** Bryan Haines. **Telephone:** (702) 895-3764. **Fax:** (702) 895-0989.

Home Field: Earl E. Wilson Stadium. **Seating Capacity:** 3,000. **Outfield Dimensions:** LF—335, CF—400, RF—335. **Press Box Telephone:** (702) 895-1595.

NEW JERSEY TECH HIGHLANDERS

Conference: Independent.

Mailing Address: University Heights, Newark, NJ 07102-1982. **Website:** www.njithighlanders.com.

Head Coach: Brian Callahan. **Assistant Coaches:** Chris Reardon, Ed Ward. **Telephone:** (973) 596-5827. **Baseball SID:** Tim Camp. **Telephone:** (973) 596-5827. **Fax:** Unavailable.

NEW MEXICO LOBOS

Conference: Mountain West.

Mailing Address: Collen J. Maloof Administration Building, 1 University of New Mexico, MSC04 2680, Albuquerque, NM 87131. **Website:** golobos.com.

Head Coach: Ray Birmingham. **Assistant Coaches:** *Ken Jacome, Chad Tidwell. **Telephone:** (505) 925-5720. **Baseball SID:** Judy Willson. **Telephone:** (505) 925-5851. **Fax:** (505) 925-5529.

Home Field: Isotopes Park. **Seating Capacity:** 11,124. **Outfield Dimensions:** LF—335, CF—400, RF—335. **Press Box Telephone:** (505) 688-2364.

NEW MEXICO STATE AGGIES

Conference: Western Athletic.

Mailing Address: Regents Row Athletics Complex, MSC 3145, 1 Regents Row, Las Cruces, NM 88001-8001. **Website:** nmstatesports.com.

Head Coach: Rocky Ward. **Assistant Coaches:** *Chase Tidwell, Gary Ward. **Telephone:** (575) 646-5813. **Baseball SID:** Eddie Morelos. **Telephone:** (575) 646-3269. **Fax:** (575) 646-5221.

Home Field: Presley-Askew Field. **Seating Capacity:** 1,000. **Outfield Dimensions:** LF—340, CF—400, RF—340.

NEW ORLEANS PRIVATEERS

Conference: Sun Belt.

Mailing Address: 2000 Lakeshore Dr, New Orleans, LA 70148. **Website:** www.unoprivateers.com.

Head Coach: Tom Walter. **Assistant Coaches:** Kirk Bullinger, *Bruce Peddie, Jason Walck. **Telephone:** (504) 280-7021. **Baseball SID:** Rob Broussard. **Telephone:** (504) 280-7027. **Fax:** (504) 280-3977.

Home Field: Maestri Field at Privateer Park. **Seating Capacity:** 4,200. **Outfield Dimensions:** LF—330, CF—405, RF—330. **Press Box Telephone:** (504) 280-3874.

NEW YORK TECH BEARS

Conference: Independent.

Mailing Address: PO Box 8000, Old Westbury, NY 11568. **Website:** www.nyit.edu/athletics.

Head Coach: Bob Hirschfield. **Assistant Coaches:** Mike Caulfield, Ron McKay. **Telephone:** (516) 686-7513. **Baseball SID:** Ben Arcuri. **Telephone:** (516) 686-7504. **Fax:** (516) 686-1219.

NIAGARA EAGLES

Conference: Metro Atlantic.

Mailing Address: PO Box 2009, Niagara University, NY 14109. **Website:** www.purpleeagles.com.

Head Coach: Chris Chernisky. **Assistant Coaches:** Rob McCoy. **Telephone:** (716) 286-8624. **Baseball SID:** Kevin Carver. **Telephone:** (716) 286-8588. **Fax:** (716) 286-8609.

NICHOLLS STATE COLONELS

Conference: Southland.

Mailing Address: PO Box 2032, Thibodaux, LA 70310. **Website:** geauxcolonels.com.

Head Coach: Chip Durham. **Assistant Coaches:** Ricky Newman, Chris Prothro, *Seth Thibodeaux. **Telephone:** (985) 448-4808. **Baseball SID:** Elizabeth Ballard. **Telephone:** (985) 448-4282. **Fax:** (985) 448-4814.

Home Field: Ray Didier Field. **Seating Capacity:** 3,000. **Outfield Dimensions:** LF—340, CF—400, RF—330.

NORFOLK STATE SPARTANS

Conference: Mid-Eastern Athletic.

Mailing Address: 700 Park Ave, Norfolk, VA 23504. **Website:** www.nsuspartans.com.

Head Coach: *Claudell Clark. **Assistant Coaches:** A.J. Corbin, Quentin Jones. **Telephone:** (757) 449-8948. **Baseball SID:** Matt Michalec. **Telephone:** (757) 823-2628. **Fax:** (757) 823-8218.

Home Field: Marty L. Miller Field. **Seating Capacity:** 1,500. **Outfield Dimensions:** LF—330, CF—404, RF—318. **Press Box Telephone:** (757) 823-8196.

NORTH CAROLINA TAR HEELS

Conference: Atlantic Coast (Coastal).

Mailing Address: PO Box 2126, Chapel Hill, NC 27515. **Website:** tarheelblue.com.

Head Coach: Mike Fox. **Assistant Coaches:** *Scott Jackson, Scott Forbes, Matt McCay. **Telephone:** (919) 962-4396. **Baseball SID:** John Martin. **Telephone:** (919) 962-0084. **Fax:** (919) 962-0612.

Home Field: Bryson Field at Boshamer Stadium. **Seating Capacity:** 4,100. **Outfield Dimensions:** LF—335, CF—400, RF—340.

NORTH CAROLINA A&T AGGIES

Conference: Mid-Eastern Athletic.

Mailing Address: 1601 E. Market St, Greensboro, NC 27411-0001. **Website:** www.ncataggies.com.

Head Coach: *Keith Shumate. **Assistant Coaches:** Austin Love, Tim Wilson. **Telephone:** (336) 334-7371. **Baseball SID:** Brian Holloway. **Telephone:** (336) 334-7141. **Fax:** (336) 334-7181.

Home Field: War Memorial Stadium. **Seating Capacity:** 2,500. **Outfield Dimensions:** LF—327, CF—400, RF—327.

NORTH CAROLINA CENTRAL EAGLES

Conference: Independent.

Mailing Address: 1801 Fayetteville St, Durham, NC 27707. **Website:** www.nccueaglepride.com.

Head Coach: Henry White. **Assistant Coaches:** Chris Smith, Michael Swann, Ken Valentine. **Telephone:** (919) 530-6723. **Baseball SID:** Oralia Washington. **Telephone:** (919) 530-6892. **Fax:** (919) 530-5426.

NORTH CAROLINA STATE WOLFPACK

Conference: Atlantic Coast (Atlantic).

Mailing Address: 1081 Varsity Drive, Campus Box 8505, Raleigh, NC 27695. **Website:** gopack.com.

Head Coach: Elliott Avent. **Assistant Coaches:** Chris

Hart, *Tom Holliday. **Telephone:** (919) 515-3613. **Baseball SID:** Bruce Winkworth. **Telephone:** (919) 515-2102. **Fax:** (919) 515-2898.

Home Field: Doak Field at Dail Park. **Seating Capacity:** 2,500. **Outfield Dimensions:** LF—320, CF—400, RF—330. **Press Box Telephone:** (919) 513-0653.

UNC ASHEVILLE BULLDOGS

Conference: Big South.

Mailing Address: One University Heights, Justice Gymnasium, Asheville, NC 28804. **Website:** www.uncabulldogs.com.

Head Coach: Willie Stewart. **Assistant Coaches:** Elliot Arrington, *Tim Perry, Tom Smith. **Telephone:** (828) 251-6920. **Baseball SID:** Everett Hutto. **Telephone:** (828) 251-6931. **Fax:** (828) 251-6386.

Home Field: McCormick Field. **Seating Capacity:** 4,000. **Outfield Dimensions:** LF—326, CF—370, RF—297. **Press Box Telephone:** (828) 254-5125.

UNC GREENSBORO SPARTANS

Conference: Southern.

Mailing Address: 1400 Spring Garden St, Greensboro, NC 27412. **Website:** www.uncgspartans.com.

Head Coach: Mike Gaski. **Assistant Coaches:** *Jamie Athas, Dustin Ijames. **Telephone:** (336) 334-3247. **Baseball SID:** David Percival. **Telephone:** (336) 334-5615. **Fax:** (336) 334-3182.

Home Field: UNCG Baseball Stadium. **Seating Capacity:** 3,500. **Outfield Dimensions:** LF—340, CF—405, RF—340. **Press Box Telephone:** (336) 334-3885.

UNC WILMINGTON SEAHAWKS

Conference: Colonial Athletic.

Mailing Address: 601 South College Rd, Wilmington, NC 28403. **Website:** www.uncwsports.com.

Head Coach: Mark Scalf. **Assistant Coaches:** *Randy Hood, Jason Howell, Josh Simmons. **Telephone:** (910) 962-3570. **Baseball SID:** Tom Riordan. **Telephone:** (910) 962-4099. **Fax:** (910) 962-3686.

Home Field: Brooks Field. **Seating Capacity:** 3,500. **Outfield Dimensions:** LF—340, CF—380, RF—330. **Press Box Telephone:** (910) 395-5141.

NORTH DAKOTA FIGHTING SIOUX

Conference: Independent.

Mailing Address: Hyslop Sports Center, Room 126, 2751 2nd Ave N., Stop 9013, Grand Forks, NC 58202-9013. **Website:** www.fightingsioux.com.

Head Coach: Jeff Dodson. **Assistant Coaches:** Brian DeVillers, J.C. Field, Eric Hoffman. **Telephone:** (701) 777-4038. **Baseball SID:** Ryan Powell. **Telephone:** (701) 777-2986. **Fax:** (701) 777-4352.

NORTH DAKOTA STATE BISON

Conference: Summit.

Mailing Address: NDSU Dept 1200, PO Box 6050, Fargo, ND 58108-6050. **Website:** www.gobison.com.

Head Coach: Tod Brown. **Assistant Coaches:** Steve Montgomery, *David Pearson, Tyrus Powe. **Telephone:** (701) 231-8853. **Baseball SID:** Ryan Perreault. **Telephone:** (701) 231-8331. **Fax:** (701) 231-8022.

Home Field: Newman Outdoor Field. **Seating Capacity:** 4,513. **Outfield Dimensions:** LF—318, CF—408, RF—314. **Press Box Telephone:** (701) 235-5204.

NORTH FLORIDA OSPREYS

Conference: Atlantic Sun.

Mailing Address: 1 UNF Drive, Jacksonville, FL 32224. **Website:** www.unfospreys.com.

Head Coach: Dusty Rhodes. **Assistant Coaches:** Greg Labbe, Trey Leonard, *Bob Shepherd, Telephone: (904) 620-1556. **Baseball SID:** Eric Scott. **Telephone:** (904) 620-4029. **Fax:** (904) 620-2836.

Home Field: Harmon Stadium. **Seating Capacity:** 1,000. **Outfield Dimensions:** LF—325, CF—400, RF—325. **Press Box Telephone:** (904) 620-1557

NORTHEASTERN HUSKIES

Conference: Colonial Athletic.

Mailing Address: 219 Cabot Center, 360 Huntington Ave, Boston, MA 02115. **Website:** www.gonu.com.

Head Coach: Neil McPhee. **Assistant Coaches:** Justin Gordon, Mike Glavine, Patrick Mason. **Telephone:** (617) 373-3657. **Baseball SID:** Jon Litchfield. **Telephone:** (617) 373-3643. **Fax:** (617) 373-3152.

NORTHERN COLORADO BEARS

Conference: Independent.

Mailing Address: 251 Butler-Hancock Hall, Box 117, Greeley, CO 80639. **Website:** uncbears.com.

Head Coach: Kevin Smallcomb. **Assistant Coach:** Ryan Strain. **Telephone:** (970) 351-1714. **Baseball SID:** Heather Kennedy. **Telephone:** (970) 351-1065. **Fax:** (970) 351-1995.

NORTHERN ILLINOIS HUSKIES

Conference: Mid-American (West).

Mailing Address: 209 Convocation Center, 1525 W. Lincoln Highway, DeKalb, IL 60115. **Website:** niuhuskies.com.

Head Coach: Ed Mathey. **Assistant Coaches:** *Steven Joslyn, Ray Napientek. **Telephone:** (815) 753-2225. **Baseball SID:** Zach Peters. **Telephone:** (815) 753-9572. **Fax:** (815) 753-9540.

Home Field: Ralph McKinzie Field. **Seating Capacity:** 2,000. **Outfield Dimensions:** LF—312, CF—395, RF—322. **Press Box Telephone:** (815) 753-8094.

NORTHERN IOWA PANTHERS

Conference: Missouri Valley.

Mailing Address: West Gym 206, Cedar Falls, Iowa 50614-0163. **Website:** unipanthers.com.

Head Coach: Rick Heller. **Assistant Coaches:** Scott Brickman, Brian Grunzke, *Marty Sutherland. **Telephone:** (319) 273-6323. **Baseball SID:** Kara Moran. **Telephone:** (319) 273-5455. **Fax:** (319) 273-3602.

Home Field: Riverfront Stadium. **Seating Capacity:** 4,500. **Outfield Dimensions:** LF—335, CF—375, RF—335. **Press Box Telephone:** (319) 232-5633.

NORTHWESTERN WILDCATS

Conference: Big 10.

Mailing Address: 1501 Central St, Evanston, IL 60208. **Website:** nusports.com.

Head Coach: Paul Stevens. **Assistant Coaches:** *Gabe Ribas, Tim Stoddard. **Telephone:** (847) 491-4652. **Baseball SID:** Nick Brilowski. **Telephone:** (847) 467-3831. **Fax:** (847) 491-8818.

Home Field: Rocky Miller Park. **Seating Capacity:** 1,000. **Outfield Dimensions:** LF—330, CF—400, RF—320. **Press Box Telephone:** (847) 491-4200.

NORTHWESTERN STATE DEMONS

Conference: Southland.

Mailing Address: Athletic Fieldhouse, Natchitoches, LA 71497. **Website:** www.nsudemons.com.

Head Coach: John Paul Davis. **Assistant Coaches:** Bobby Barbier, *Jeff McCannon. **Telephone:** (318) 354-4139. **Baseball SID:** Matt Bonnette. **Telephone:** (318)

357-6469. **Fax:** (318) 357-4515.

Home Field: Brown Stroud Field. **Seating Capacity:** 1,214. **Outfield Dimensions:** LF—320, CF—400, RF—330. **Press Box Telephone:** (318)357-4606.

NOTRE DAME FIGHTING IRISH

Conference: Big East.

Mailing Address: Frank Eck Stadium, Notre Dame, IN 46556. **Website:** und.com.

Head Coach: Dave Schrage. **Assistant Coaches:** Sherrard Clinkscales, *Scott Lawler, Graham Sikes. **Telephone:** (574) 631-6366. **Baseball SID:** Michael Bertsch. **Telephone:** (574) 631-8642. **Fax:** (574) 631-7941.

Home Field: Frank Eck Stadium. **Seating Capacity:** 2,500. **Outfield Dimensions:** LF—330, CF—400, RF—330. **Press Box Telephone:** (574) 631-9018.

OAKLAND GOLDEN GRIZZLIES

Conference: Summit.

Mailing Address: 2200 N. Squirrel Athletics Center, Rochester, MI 48309. **Website:** www.ougrizzlies.com.

Head Coach: John Musachio. **Assistant Coaches:** Mike Takashima, Del Young. **Telephone:** (248) 370-4059. **Baseball SID:** Paul Smith. **Telephone:** (248) 370-3123. **Fax:** (248) 370-4056.

OHIO BOBCATS

Conference: Mid-American (East).

Mailing Address: N117 Convocation Center, Athens, OH 45701. **Website:** www.ohiobobcats.com.

Head Coach: Joe Carbone. **Assistant Coaches:** Scott Malinowski, *Andrew See. **Telephone:** (740) 593-1180. **Baseball SID:** Michael Weisman. **Telephone:** (740) 597-1784. **Fax:** (740) 597-1838.

Home Field: Bob Wren Stadium. **Seating Capacity:** 4,000. **Outfield Dimensions:** LF—340, CF—405, RF—340. **Press Box Telephone:** (740) 593-0526.

OHIO STATE BUCKEYES

Conference: Big 10.

Mailing Address: 650 Borror Drive, Suite 250, Columbus, Ohio 43210. **Website:** www.ohiostatebuckeyes.com.

Head Coach: Bob Todd. **Assistant Coaches:** *Greg Cypret, Pete Jenkins, Eric Parker. **Telephone:** (614) 292-1075. **Baseball SID:** Jerry Emig. **Telephone:** (614) 688-0343. **Fax:** (614) 292-8547.

Home Field: Bill Davis Stadium. **Seating Capacity:** 4,450. **Outfield Dimensions:** LF—330, CF—400, RF—330. **Press Box Telephone:** (614) 292-0021.

OKLAHOMA SOONERS

Conference: Big 12.

Mailing Address: 401 W. Imhoff, Norman, OK 73019. **Website:** www.soonersports.com.

Head Coach: Sunny Golloway. **Assistant Coaches:** Mike Bell, *Tim Tadlock. **Telephone:** (405) 325-8354. **Baseball SID:** Craig Moran. **Telephone:** (405) 325-6449. **Fax:** (405) 325-7623.

Home Field: L. Dale Mitchell Park. **Seating Capacity:** 2,700. **Outfield Dimensions:** LF—335, CF—411, RF—335. **Press Box Telephone:** (405) 325-8363.

OKLAHOMA STATE COWBOYS

Conference: Big 12.

Mailing Address: 220 Athletics Center, Stillwater, OK 74078. **Website:** www.okstate.com.

Head Coach: Frank Anderson. **Assistant Coaches:** Greg Evans, *Billy Jones. **Telephone:** (405) 744-5849. **Baseball SID:** Wade McWhorter. **Telephone:** (405) 744-7853. **Fax:** (405) 744-7754.

Home Field: Allie P. Reynolds Stadium. **Seating Capacity:** 4,000. **Outfield Dimensions:** LF—330, CF—398, RF—330. **Press Box Telephone:** (405) 744-5757.

OLD DOMINION MONARCHS

Conference: Colonial Athletic.

Mailing Address: Athletic Admin. Bldg., Norfolk, VA 23529-0201. **Website:** www.odusports.com.

Head Coach: Jerry Meyers. **Assistant Coaches:** Nate Goulet, *Ryan Morris. **Telephone:** (757) 683-4230. **Baseball SID:** Carol Hudson, Jr. **Telephone:** (757) 683-3395. **Fax:** (757) 683-3119.

Home Field: Bud Metheny Complex. **Seating Capacity:** 2,500. **Outfield Dimensions:** LF—325, CF—395, RF—325. **Press Box Telephone:** (757) 683-5036.

ORAL ROBERTS GOLDEN EAGLES

Conference: Summit.

Mailing Address: 7777 S. Lewis Avenue, Tulsa, OK 74147. **Website:** www.orugoldeneagles.com.

Head Coach: Rob Walton. **Assistant Coaches:** Wes Davis, Ryan Folmar, Ryan Neill. **Telephone:** (918) 495-7205. **Baseball SID:** Kyle Seay. **Telephone:** (918) 495-7094. **Fax:** (918) 495-7142.

Home Field: J.L. Johnson Stadium. **Seating Capacity:** 2,418. **Outfield Dimensions:** LF—330, CF—400, RF—330. **Press Box Telephone:** (918) 495-7165.

OREGON DUCKS

Conference: Pacific-10.

Mailing Address: 2727 Leo Harris Parkway, Eugene, OR 97401. **Website:** www.goducks.com.

Head Coach: George Horton. **Assistant Coaches:** *Andrew Checketts, Mike Kirby, Bryson LeBlanc. **Telephone:** (541) 346-5776. **Baseball SID:** Andria Wenzel. **Telephone:** (541) 346-0962. **Fax:** (541) 346-5449.

Home Field: PK Park. **Seating Capacity:** 2,000. **Outfield Dimensions:** LF—335, CF—400, RF—325. **Press Box Telephone:** (916) 838-2346.

OREGON STATE BEAVERS

Conference: Pacific-10.

Mailing Address: 103 Gill Coliseum, Corvallis, OR 97331. **Website:** www.osubeavers.com.

Head Coach: Pat Casey. **Assistant Coaches:** Pat Bailey, *Marty Lees, Nate Yeskie. **Telephone:** (541) 737-2825. **Baseball SID:** Hank Hager. **Telephone:** (541) 737-7472. **Fax:** (541) 737-3072.

Home Field: Goss Stadium. **Seating Capacity:** 3,000. **Outfield Dimensions:** LF—330, CF—400, RF—330. **Press Box Telephone:** (541) 737-7475.

PACIFIC TIGERS

Conference: Big West.

Mailing Address: 3601 Pacific Ave, Stockton, CA 95211. **Website:** pacifictigers.com.

Head Coach: Ed Sprague. **Assistant Coaches:** *Don Barbara, Mike McCormick, Chris McCormack. **Telephone:** (209) 946-2709. **Baseball SID:** Monique Moyal. **Telephone:** (209) 946-2479. **Fax:** (209) 946-2757.

Home Field: Klein Family Field. **Seating Capacity:** 2,000. **Outfield Dimensions:** LF—314, CF—405, RF—325. **Press Box Telephone:** (209) 946-2722.

PENN STATE NITTANY LIONS

Conference: Big 10.

Mailing Address: 112 Bryce Jordan Center, University Park, PA 16802. **Website:** www.GoPSUsports.com.

Head Coach: Robbie Wine. **Assistant Coaches:** Jason

Bell, *Eric Folmar, Will Hoover. **Telephone:** (814) 863-0239. **Baseball SID:** Jay Monahan. **Telephone:** (814) 865-1757. **Fax:** (814) 863-3165.

Home Field: Medlar Field at Lubrano Park. **Seating Capacity:** 5,406. **Outfield Dimensions:** LF—325, CF—399, RF—320.

PENNSYLVANIA QUAKERS

Conference: Ivy League (Gehrig).

Mailing Address: James D. Dunning Coaches Center, 235 South 33rd Street, Philadelphia, PA 19104. **Website:** www.pennathletics.com.

Head Coach: John Cole. **Assistant Coaches:** Jon Cross, *John Yurkow. **Telephone:** (215) 898-6282. **Baseball SID:** Chas Dorman. **Telephone:** (215) 898-6128. **Fax:** (215) 898-1747.

Home Field: Meiklejohn Stadium. **Seating Capacity:** 900. **Outfield Dimensions:** LF—325, CF—380, RF—355.

PEPPERDINE WAVES

Conference: West Coast.

Mailing Address: 24255 Pacific Coast Hwy., Malibu, CA 90263. **Website:** www.PepperdineSports.com.

Head Coach: Steve Rodriguez. **Assistant Coaches:** Greg Garrison, Rick Hirtensteiner, *Sean Kenny. **Telephone:** (310) 506-4371. **Baseball SID:** Chris Macaluso. **Telephone:** (310) 506-4333. **Fax:** (310) 506-4322.

Home Field: Eddy D. Field Stadium. **Seating Capacity:** 1,800. **Outfield Dimensions:** LF—330, CF—400, RF—330. **Press Box Telephone:** (310) 456-4598.

PITTSBURGH PANTHERS

Conference: Big East.

Mailing Address: Petersen Events Center, 3719 Terrace Street, Pittsburgh, PA 15261. **Website:** pittsburghpanthers.com.

Head Coach: Joe Jordano. **Assistant Coaches:** Ryan Leahy, *Danny Lopaze, Brandon Rowan. **Telephone:** (412) 648-8208. **Baseball SID:** Paul Pancoe. **Telephone:** (412) 383-8650. **Fax:** (412) 648-8248.

Home Field: Trees Field. **Seating Capacity:** 500. **Outfield Dimensions:** LF—300, CF—405, RF—330. **Press Box Telephone:** (330) 559-1131.

PORTLAND PILOTS

Conference: West Coast.

Mailing Address: 5000 North Willamette Blvd, Portland, OR 97203. **Website:** www.portlandpilots.com.

Head Coach: Chris Sperry. **Assistant Coaches:** Tucker Brack, Larry Casian. **Telephone:** (503) 943-7707. **Baseball SID:** Adam Linnman. **Telephone:** (503) 943-7731. **Fax:** (503) 943-7242.

PRAIRIE VIEW A&M PANTHERS

Conference: Southwestern Athletic.

Mailing Address: PO Box 519 MS 1500, Prairie View, TX 77446. **Website:** www.pvamu.edu/pages/104.asp.

Head Coach: Waskyla Cullivan. **Assistant Coaches:** *Byron Carter, Matthew Chase, Oscar Goldman. **Telephone:** (936) 261 9121. **Baseball SID:** Reginald Rouzan. **Telephone:** (936) 261-9106. **Fax:** (936) 261-9159.

PRINCETON TIGERS

Conference: Ivy League (Gehrig).

Mailing Address: Jadwin Gymnasium, Princeton, NJ 08544. **Website:** www.GoPrincetonTigers.com.

Head Coach: Scott Bradley. **Assistant Coaches:** *Lloyd Brewer, Jeremy Meccage. **Telephone:** (609) 258-5059. **Baseball SID:** Yariv Amir. **Telephone:** (609) 258-5701. **Fax:** (609) 258-2399.

Home Field: Clarke Field. **Seating Capacity:** 500. **Outfield Dimensions:** LF—335, CF—400, RF—325. **Press Box Telephone:** (609) 462-0248.

PURDUE BOILERMAKERS

Conference: Big 10.

Mailing Address: 1225 Northwestern Ave, West Lafayette, IN 47907. **Website:** purduesports.com.

Head Coach: Doug Schreiber. **Assistant Coaches:** *Spencer Allen, Chadd Blasko, Ryan Sawyers. **Telephone:** (765) 494-3998. **Baseball SID:** Matt Rector. **Telephone:** (765) 494-3196. **Fax:** (765) 494-5447.

Home Field: Lambert Field. **Seating Capacity:** 1,100. **Outfield Dimensions:** LF—340, CF—408, RF—340. **Press Box Telephone:** (765) 494-1522.

QUINNIPIAC BOBCATS

Conference: Northeast.

Mailing Address: 275 Mount Carmel Ave, Hamden, CT 06518. **Website:** quinnipiacbobcats.com.

Head Coach: *Dan Gooley. **Assistant Coaches:** Dan Scarpa, Marc Stonaha, Joe Tonelli. **Telephone:** (203) 582-8966. **Baseball SID:** Ken Sweeten. **Telephone:** (203) 582-8625. **Fax:** (203) 582-5385.

RADFORD HIGHLANDERS

Conference: Big South.

Mailing Address: PO Box 6913, Radford, VA 24142. **Website:** www.ruhighlanders.com.

Head Coach: Joe Raccuia. **Assistant Coaches:** *Brian Anderson, Allen Rice. **Telephone:** (540) 831-5881. **Baseball SID:** Patrick Reed. **Telephone:** (540) 831-5211. **Fax:** (540) 831-5556.

Home Field: Radford University Baseball Field. **Seating Capacity:** 1,000. **Outfield Dimensions:** LF—330, CF—400, RF—330. **Press Box Telephone:** (540) 257-1159.

RHODE ISLAND RAMS

Conference: Atlantic 10.

Mailing Address: 3 Keaney Rd, Suite One, Kingston, RI 02881. **Website:** gorhody.com.

Head Coach: Jim Foster. **Assistant Coaches:** *Steve Breitbach, Eric Cirella, Idris Liasu. **Telephone:** (401) 874-4550. **Baseball SID:** Jodi Pontbriand. **Telephone:** (401) 874-5356. **Fax:** (401) 874-5354.

Home Field: Bill Beck Field. **Seating Capacity:** Unavailable. **Outfield Dimensions:** LF—330, CF—400, RF—330.

RICE OWLS

Conference: Conference USA.

Mailing Address: 6100 Main St, MS 547, Houston, TX 77251. **Website:** www.riceowls.com.

Head Coach: Wayne Graham. **Assistant Coaches:** Patrick Hallmark, *David Pierce, *Mike Taylor. **Telephone:** (713) 348-8864. **Baseball SID:** John Sullivan. **Telephone:** (713) 348-5636. **Fax:** (713) 348-6019.

Home Field: Reckling Park. **Seating Capacity:** 5,700. **Outfield Dimensions:** LF—330, CF—400, RF—330. **Press Box Telephone:** (713) 348-4931.

RICHMOND SPIDERS

Conference: Atlantic 10.

Mailing Address: The Robins Center, Richmond, VA 23173. **Website:** RichmondSpiders.com.

Head Coach: Mark McQueen. **Assistant Coaches:** Joe Frostick, Chad Oxendine, *Ryan Wheeler. **Telephone:** (804) 289-8391. **Baseball SID:** Mike DeGeorge. **Telephone:** (804) 287-6313. **Fax:** (804) 289-8820.

Home Field: Pitt Field. **Seating Capacity:** 600.

Outfield Dimensions: LF—320, CF—380, RF—320. **Press Box Telephone:** (804) 289-8714.

RIDER BRONCS

Conference: Metro Atlantic.

Mailing Address: 2083 Lawrenceville Road, Lawrenceville, NJ 08648. **Website:** www.gobroncs.com.

Head Coach: Barry Davis. **Assistant Coaches:** Jim Maher, Jaime Steward. **Telephone:** (609) 896-5055. **Baseball SID:** Bud Focht. **Telephone:** (609) 896-5138. **Fax:** (609) 896-0341.

RUTGERS SCARLET KNIGHTS

Conference: Big East.

Mailing Address: Louis Brown Athletic Center, 83 Rockafeller Rd, Piscataway, NJ 08854. **Website:** www.scarletknights.com.

Head Coach: Fred Hill. **Assistant Coaches:** Jay Blackwell, *Darren Fenster, Rick Freeman, Glen Gardner. **Telephone:** (732) 445-7834. **Baseball SID:** Doug Drabik. **Telephone:** (732) 445-7884. **Fax:** (732) 445-3063.

Home Field: Bainton Field. **Seating Capacity:** 1,500. **Outfield Dimensions:** LF—330, CF—410, RF—320. **Press Box Telephone:** (732) 921-1067.

SACRAMENTO STATE HORNETS

Conference: Western Athletic.

Mailing Address: 6000 J Street, Sacramento, CA 95819-6099. **Website:** www.hornetsports.com.

Head Coach: John Smith. **Assistant Coaches:** Jim Barr, John Callahan, *Reggie Christiansen. **Telephone:** (916) 278-7225. **Baseball SID:** J.D. Fox. **Telephone:** (916) 278-6896. **Fax:** (916) 278-5429.

Home Field: Hornet Field. **Seating Capacity:** 1,267. **Outfield Dimensions:** LF—333, CF—400, RF—333. **Press Box Telephone:** (209) 210-8858.

SACRED HEART PIONEERS

Conference: Northeast.

Mailing Address: 5151 Park Ave, Fairfield, CT 06825. **Website:** www.sacredheartpioneers.com.

Head Coach: Nick Giaguinto. **Assistant Coaches:** Earl Mathewson, Wayne Mazzoni. **Telephone:** (203) 365-7632. **Baseball SID:** Gene Gumbs. **Telephone:** (203) 396-8127. **Fax:** (203) 371-7889.

ST. BONAVENTURE BONNIES

Conference: Atlantic 10.

Mailing Address: PO Box G, Reilly Center, St. Bonaventure, NY 14778. **Website:** gobonnies.com.

Head Coach: Larry Sudbrook. **Assistant Coaches:** *, Kieran Malone, Nick LaBella. **Telephone:** (716) 375-2641. **Baseball SID:** Patrick Pierson. **Telephone:** (716) 375-2575. **Fax:** (716) 375-2280.

Home Field: Fred Handler Park. **Seating Capacity:** Unavailable. **Outfield Dimensions:** LF—330, CF—402, RF—330.

ST. JOHN'S RED STORM

Conference: Big East.

Mailing Address: 8000 Utopia Parkway, Queens, NY 11439. **Website:** www.redstormsports.com.

Head Coach: Ed Blankmeyer. **Assistant Coaches:** Scott Brown, *Mike Hampton, Julio Vega. **Telephone:** (718) 990-6148. **Baseball SID:** Tim Brown. **Telephone:** (718) 990-1521. **Fax:** (718) 969-8468.

Home Field: Kaiser Stadium. **Seating Capacity:** 3,500. **Outfield Dimensions:** LF—325, CF—400, RF—325. **Press Box Telephone:** (718) 990-2725.

SAINT JOSEPH'S HAWKS

Conference: Atlantic 10.

Mailing Address: 5600 City Ave, Philadelphia, PA 19131. **Website:** sjuhawks.com.

Head Coach: Fritz Hamburg. **Assistant Coaches:** *Jacob Gill, Greg Manco. **Telephone:** (610) 660-1718. **Baseball SID:** Joe Greenwich. **Telephone:** (610) 660-1738. **Fax:** (610) 660-1724.

Home Field: Latshaw-McCarthy Field. **Seating Capacity:** 1,000. **Outfield Dimensions:** LF—328, CF—393, RF—328.

SAINT LOUIS BILLIKENS

Conference: Atlantic 10.

Mailing Address: 3303 Laclede Ave, Saint Louis, MO 63103. **Website:** www.slubillikens.com.

Head Coach: Darin Hendrickson. **Assistant Coaches:** Will Bradley, Danny Jackson, *Kevin Moulder. **Telephone:** (314) 977-3172. **Baseball SID:** Brian Kunderman. **Telephone:** (314) 977-3346. **Fax:** (314) 977-3178.

Home Field: Billiken Sports Center. **Seating Capacity:** 500. **Outfield Dimensions:** LF—330, CF—403, RF—330. **Press Box Telephone:** (314) 808-4868.

SAINT MARY'S GAELS

Conference: West Coast.

Mailing Address: PO Box 5100, Moraga, CA 94575. **Website:** www.smcgaels.com.

Head Coach: Jedd Soto. **Assistant Coaches:** *Lloyd Acosta, Mike McCormick, Gabe Zappin. **Telephone:** (925) 631-4637. **Baseball SID:** Matt Fontenot. **Telephone:** (925) 631-4950. **Fax:** (925) 631-4405.

Home Field: Louis Guisto Field. **Seating Capacity:** 500. **Outfield Dimensions:** LF—340, CF—400, RF—340. **Press Box Telephone:** (925) 376-3906.

SAINT PETER'S PEACOCKS

Conference: Metro Atlantic.

Mailing Address: 2641 Kennedy Blvd, Jersey City, NJ 07306. **Website:** www.spc.edu/pages/408.asp.

Head Coach: Derek England. **Assistant Coaches:** Ben Cueto, Tim Nagurka, *Corky Thompson. **Telephone:** (201) 761-7318. **Baseball SID:** David Freeman. **Telephone:** (201) 761-7315. **Fax:** (201) 761-7317.

SAM HOUSTON STATE BEARKATS

Conference: Southland.

Mailing Address: PO Box 2268, Huntsville, TX 77341. **Website:** gobearkats.com.

Head Coach: Mark Johnson. **Assistant Coaches:** Jim Blair, Chris Berry, Phillip Miller. **Telephone:** (936) 294-1731. **Baseball SID:** Paul Ridings. **Telephone:** (936) 294-1764. **Fax:** (936) 294-3538.

SAMFORD BULLDOGS

Conference: Ohio Valley.

Mailing Address: Samford Athletics, 800 Lakeshore Dr, Birmingham, AL 35229. **Website:** samfordsports.com.

Head Coach: Casey Dunn. **Assistant Coaches:** *Tony David, Mick Fieldbinder, Rucker Taylor. **Telephone:** (205) 726-2134. **Baseball SID:** Joey Mullins. **Telephone:** (205) 726-2799. **Fax:** (205) 726-2545.

Home Field: Joe Lee Griffin Field. **Seating Capacity:** 1,000. **Outfield Dimensions:** LF—330, CF—390, RF—335. **Press Box Telephone:** (205) 726-4167.

SAN DIEGO TOREROS

Conference: West Coast.

Mailing Address: 5998 Alcala Park, San Diego, CA

92110. **Website:** www.usdtoreros.com.

Head Coach: Rich Hill. **Assistant Coaches:** Jay Johnson, *Eric Valenzuela, Mark Viramontes. **Telephone:** (619) 260-5953. **Baseball SID:** Chris Loucks. **Telephone:** (619) 260-7930. **Fax:** (619) 260-2990.

Home Field: Cunningham Stadium. **Seating Capacity:** 1,200. **Outfield Dimensions:** LF—309, CF—395, RF—329. **Press Box Telephone:** (619) 260-8829.

SAN DIEGO STATE AZTECS

Conference: Mountain West.

Mailing Address: 5500 Campanile Dr, San Diego, CA 92182. **Website:** www.goaztecs.com.

Head Coach: Tony Gwynn. **Assistant Coaches:** *Rusty Filter, Mark Martinez, Jody Stevens. **Telephone:** (619) 594-6889. **Baseball SID:** Dave Kuhn. **Telephone:** (619) 594-5242. **Fax:** (619) 582-6541.

Home Field: Tony Gwynn Stadium. **Seating Capacity:** 3,000. **Outfield Dimensions:** LF—340, CF—410, RF—340. **Press Box Telephone:** (619) 594-4103.

SAN FRANCISCO DONS

Conference: West Coast.

Mailing Address: 2130 Fulton Street, San Francisco, CA 94117-1080. **Website:** www.usfdons.com.

Head Coach: Nino Giarratano. **Assistant Coaches:** *Greg Moore, Troy Nakamura, John Norfolk. **Telephone:** (415) 422 2934. **Baseball SID:** Jordan Wilcox. **Telephone:** (415) 422 6161. **Fax:** (415) 422 2929.

Home Field: Benedetti Diamond. **Seating Capacity:** 2,000. **Outfield Dimensions:** LF—301, CF—400, RF—305. **Press Box Telephone:** (415) 422 2919.

SAN JOSE STATE SPARTANS

Conference: Western Athletic.

Mailing Address: 1393 S. 7th Street, San Jose, CA 95112. **Website:** www.sjsuspartans.com.

Head Coach: Sam Piraro. **Assistant Coaches:** Tom Kunis, *Jeff Pritchard, Brian Yocke. **Telephone:** (408) 924-1255. **Baseball SID:** Doga Gur. **Telephone:** (408) 924-1211. **Fax:** (408) 924-1291.

Home Field: Municipal Stadium. **Seating Capacity:** 5,200. **Outfield Dimensions:** LF—320, CF—390, RF—320. **Press Box Telephone:** (408) 924-7276.

SANTA CLARA BRONCOS

Conference: West Coast.

Mailing Address: 500 El Camino Real, Santa Clara, CA 95053. **Website:** www.santaclarabroncos.com.

Head Coach: Mark O'Brien. **Assistant Coaches:** Chad Baum, Shawn Epidendio, *Mike Zirelli. **Telephone:** (408) 554-4680. **Baseball SID:** Sabrina Polidoro. **Telephone:** (408) 554-4659. **Fax:** (408) 554-6942.

Home Field: Stephen Schott Stadium. **Seating Capacity:** 2,200. **Outfield Dimensions:** LF—340, CF—402, RF—335. **Press Box Telephone:** (408) 554-4752.

SAVANNAH STATE TIGERS

Conference: Independent.

Mailing Address: 3219 College Street, Savannah, GA 31404. **Website:** www.savstate.edu/Athletics.

Head Coach: Carlton Hardy. **Assistant Coaches:** Trey Mock, Emmanuel Wheeler. **Telephone:** (912) 356-2801. **Baseball SID:** Opio Mashariki. **Telephone:** (912) 356-2446. **Fax:** (912) 353-5287.

SETON HALL PIRATES

Conference: Big East.

Mailing Address: 400 South Orange Ave, South Orange, NJ 07079. **Website:** www.shupirates.com.

Head Coach: Rob Sheppard. **Assistant Coaches:** Phil Cundari, Jim Duffy, Zach Porcello. **Telephone:** (973) 761-9557. **Baseball SID:** Joe Montefusco. **Telephone:** (973) 761-9493. **Fax:** (973) 761-9061.

Home Field: Owen T. Carroll Field. **Seating Capacity:** 1,000. **Outfield Dimensions:** LF—315, CF—401, RF—330. **Press Box Telephone:** (973) 670-2752.

SIENA SAINTS

Conference: Metro Atlantic.

Mailing Address: 515 Loudon Rd, Loudonville, NY 12211. **Website:** www.sienasaints.com.

Head Coach: Tony Rossi. **Assistant Coaches:** Rob DiToma, Jimmy Jackson, *Joe Sinicola. **Telephone:** (518) 786-5044. **Baseball SID:** Jason Rich. **Telephone:** (518) 783-2441. **Fax:** (518) 783-2992.

Home Field: Siena Field. **Seating Capacity:** 500. **Outfield Dimensions:** LF—300, CF—400, RF—325.

SOUTH ALABAMA JAGUARS

Conference: Sun Belt.

Mailing Address: 1209 Mitchell Center, Mobile, AL 36688. **Website:** www.usajaguars.com.

Head Coach: Steve Kittrell. **Assistant Coaches:** *Scot Sealy, *Seth Von Behren. **Telephone:** (251) 461-1397. **Baseball SID:** David Kaye. **Telephone:** (251) 414-8034. **Fax:** (251) 460-7297.

Home Field: Stanky Field. **Seating Capacity:** 3,575. **Outfield Dimensions:** LF—330, CF—400, RF—330. **Press Box Telephone:** (251) 461-1842.

SOUTH CAROLINA GAMECOCKS

Conference: Southeastern (East).

Mailing Address: 1300 Rosewood Drive, Columbia, SC 29208. **Website:** www.gamecocksonline.com.

Head Coach: Ray Tanner. **Assistant Coaches:** Mark Calvi, Sammy Esposito, *Chad Holbrook. **Telephone:** (803) 777-0116. **Baseball SID:** Andrew Kitick. **Telephone:** (803) 777-5257. **Fax:** (803) 777-2967.

Home Field: Carolina Stadium. **Seating Capacity:** 9,000. **Outfield Dimensions:** LF—325, CF—400, RF—325. **Press Box Telephone:** (803) 777-6648.

SOUTH CAROLINA-UPSTATE SPARTANS

Conference: Atlantic Sun.

Mailing Address: 800 University Way, Spartanburg, SC 29303. **Website:** upstatespartans.cstv.com.

Head Coach: Matt Fincher. **Assistant Coaches:** Ryan Fecteau, Grant Rembert, *Russell Triplett. **Telephone:** (864) 503-5135. **Baseball SID:** Joe Guistina. **Telephone:** (864) 503-5152. **Fax:** (864) 503-5127.

Home Field: Harley Park. **Seating Capacity:** 500. **Outfield Dimensions:** LF—325, CF—402, RF—325. **Press Box Telephone:** (864) 503-5058.

SOUTH DAKOTA STATE JACKRABBITS

Conference: Summit.

Mailing Address: 1047 16th Ave, Brookings, SD 57007. **Website:** gojacks.com.

Head Coach: Ritchie Price. **Assistant Coaches:** *Jake Angier, Ryan Neale, Ryan Overland. **Telephone:** (605) 688-5027. **Baseball SID:** Jason Hove. **Telephone:** (605) 688-4623. **Fax:** (605) 688-5999.

Home Field: Erv Huether Field. **Seating Capacity:** 400. **Outfield Dimensions:** LF—330, CF—400, RF—330. **Press Box Telephone:** (605) 695-1827.

SOUTH FLORIDA BULLS

Conference: Big East.

Mailing Address: 4202 E. Fowler Ave, ATH 100, Tampa,

FL 33620. **Website:** www.GoUSFBulls.com.

Head Coach: Lelo Prado. **Assistant Coaches:** *Lazer Collazo, Bryant Ward. **Telephone:** (813) 974-2504. **Baseball SID:** Amy Woodruff. **Telephone:** (813) 974-4087. **Fax:** (813) 974-5328.

Home Field: Red McEwen Field. **Seating Capacity:** 1,500. **Outfield Dimensions:** LF—375, CF—400, RF—375. **Press Box Telephone:** (813) 410-1194.

SOUTHEAST MISSOURI STATE REDHAWKS

Conference: Ohio Valley.

Mailing Address: 1 University Plaza, MS 0200, Cape Girardeau, MO 63701. **Website:** gosoutheast.com.

Head Coach: Mark Hogan. **Assistant Coaches:** Chris Cafalone, *Rick McCarty, Lance Rhodes. **Telephone:** (573) 651-2645. **Baseball SID:** Tyler Koonce. **Telephone:** (573) 651-2294. **Fax:** (573) 651-2294.

Home Field: Capaha Field. **Seating Capacity:** 2,000. **Outfield Dimensions:** LF—335, CF—400, RF—335.

SOUTHEASTERN LOUISIANA LIONS

Conference: Southland.

Mailing Address: SLU 10309, Hammond, LA 70402. **Website:** www.lionsports.net.

Head Coach: Jay Artigues. **Assistant Coaches:** *Justin Hill, Matt Riser, Jordan Rogers. **Telephone:** (985) 549-3566. **Baseball SID:** Charlie Gillingham. **Telephone:** (985) 549-3774. **Fax:** (985) 549-3495.

Home Field: Pat Kennelly Diamond at Alumni Field. **Seating Capacity:** 5,000. **Outfield Dimensions:** LF—320, CF—365-400-365, RF—320.

SOUTHERN JAGUARS

Conference: Southwestern Athletic.

Mailing Address: Baseball Office, F.G.Clark Center, Harding Blvd, Baton Rouge, LA 70813. **Website:** gojagsports.com.

Head Coach: Roger Cador. **Assistant Coaches:** *Fernando Puebla. **Telephone:** (225) 771-2513. **Baseball SID:** Kevin Manns. **Telephone:** (225) 771-4142. **Fax:** (225) 771-4400.

Home Field: Lee-Hines Field. **Seating Capacity:** 1,500. **Outfield Dimensions:** LF—360, CF—395, RF—325.

SOUTHERN CALIFORNIA TROJANS

Conference: Pacific-10.

Mailing Address: Dedeaux Field, 1021 Childs Way, Los Angeles, CA 90089-0731. **Website:** usctrojans.com.

Head Coach: Chad Kreuter. **Assistant Coaches:** Frank Cruz, *Doyle Wilson, Tom House. **Telephone:** (213) 740-8446. **Baseball SID:** Jason Pommier. **Telephone:** (213) 740-3807. **Fax:** (213) 740-7584.

Home Field: Dedeaux Field. **Seating Capacity:** 2,500. **Outfield Dimensions:** LF—335, CF—395, RF—335. **Press Box Telephone:** (213) 748-3449.

SOUTHERN ILLINOIS SALUKIS

Conference: Missouri Valley.

Mailing Address: 130B Lingle Hall-SIU Arena, Carbondale, IL 62901-6620. **Website:** siusalukis.com.

Head Coach: Dan Callahan. **Assistant Coaches:** Tim Dixon, *Ken Henderson, Brian Neal. **Telephone:** (618) 453-2802. **Baseball SID:** Jeff Honza. **Telephone:** (618) 453-5470. **Fax:** (618) 453-2648.

Home Field: Abe Martin Field. **Seating Capacity:** 2,000. **Outfield Dimensions:** LF—340, CF—390, RF—340. **Press Box Telephone:** (618) 453-3794.

SOUTHERN ILLINOIS-EDWARDSVILLE COUGARS

Conference: Independent.

Mailing Address: Box 1129 SIUE, Edwardsville, IL 62026. **Website:** www.siuecougars.com.

Head Coach: Gary Collins. **Assistant Coach:** Tony Stoecklin. **Telephone:** (618) 650-2331. **Baseball SID:** Eric Hess. **Telephone:** (618) 650-3608. **Fax:** (618) 650-2296.

SOUTHERN MISSISSIPPI GOLDEN EAGLES

Conference: Conference USA.

Mailing Address: 118 College Dr, No. 5161, Hattiesburg, MS 39401. **Website:** www.southernmiss.com.

Head Coach: Corky Palmer. **Assistant Coaches:** Scott Berry, *Chad Cailliet. **Telephone:** (601) 266-5017. **Baseball SID:** Jason Kirksey. **Telephone:** (601) 266-5332. **Fax:** (601) 266-5332.

Home Field: Pete Taylor Park. **Seating Capacity:** 6,600. **Outfield Dimensions:** LF—340, CF—400, RF—340. **Press Box Telephone:** (601) 266-5684.

SOUTHERN UTAH THUNDERBIRDS

Conference: Summit.

Mailing Address: 351 West University Blvd, Cedar City, UT 84720. **Website:** www.suutbirds.com.

Head Coach: David Eldredge. **Assistant Coaches:** Chase Hudson, Loren Murillo, *Robert Stephens. **Telephone:** (435) 327-0452. **Baseball SID:** Kyle Cottam. **Telephone:** (435) 586-7752. **Fax:** (435) 586-5444.

Home Field: Thunderbird Park. **Seating Capacity:** 500. **Outfield Dimensions:** LF—345, CF—410, RF—330.

STANFORD CARDINAL

Conference: Pacific-10.

Mailing Address: 641 E. Campus Dr, Stanford, CA 94305. **Website:** gostanford.com.

Head Coach: Mark Marquess. **Assistant Coaches:** Jeff Austin, Dave Nakama, *Dean Stotz. **Telephone:** (650) 723-4528. **Baseball SID:** Matt Hodson. **Telephone:** (650) 725-2959. **Fax:** (650) 725-2957.

Home Field: Klein Field at Sunken Diamond. **Seating Capacity:** 4,000. **Outfield Dimensions:** LF—335, CF—400, RF—335. **Press Box Telephone:** (650) 723-4629.

STEPHEN F. AUSTIN STATE LUMBERJACKS

Conference: Southland.

Mailing Address: PO Box 13010, SFA Station, Nacogdoches, TX 75962. **Website:** www.sfajacks.com.

Head Coach: Johnny Cardenas. **Assistant Coaches:** *Chris Connally, Chad Massengale. **Telephone:** (936) 468-4599. **Baseball SID:** Ben Rikard. **Telephone:** (936) 468-5801. **Fax:** (936) 468-4593.

Home Field: Jaycees Field. **Seating Capacity:** 1,000. **Outfield Dimensions:** LF—330, CF—400, RF—300. **Press Box Telephone:** (936) 559-8344.

STETSON HATTERS

Conference: Atlantic Sun.

Mailing Address: 421 N. Woodland Blvd, DeLand, FL 32723. **Website:** www.gohatters.com.

Head Coach: Pete Dunn. **Assistant Coaches:** Clint Chrysler, Mitch Markham, Chris Roberts. **Telephone:** (386) 822-8106. **Baseball SID:** Dean Watson. **Telephone:** (386) 822-8130. **Fax:** (386) 822-8132.

Home Field: Melching Field. **Seating Capacity:** 2,500. **Outfield Dimensions:** LF—335, CF—403, RF—335. **Press Box Telephone:** (386) 736-7360.

STONY BROOK SEAWOLVES

Conference: America East.

Mailing Address: Indoor Sports Complex, Stony Brook, NY 11794-3500. **Website:** goseawolves.cstv.com.

Head Coach: Matt Senk. **Assistant Coaches:** *Joe

Pennucci, Chris Sipp, Anthony Stutz. **Telephone:** (631) 632-9226. **Baseball SID:** Jeremy Cohen. **Telephone:** (631) 632-6328. **Fax:** (631) 632-8841.

TEMPLE OWLS

Conference: Atlantic 10.

Mailing Address: 1700 North Broad St, Philadelphia, PA. **Website:** www.owlsports.com.

Head Coach: Rob Valli. **Assistant Coaches:** Brandon Anderson, *Justin Gordon, Greg Lemon. **Telephone:** (215) 204-8639. **Baseball SID:** Kevin Bonner. **Telephone:** (215) 204-9149. **Fax:** (215) 204-7499.

Home Field: Skip Wilson Field. **Seating Capacity:** 1,000. **Outfield Dimensions:** LF—330, CF—400, RF—330. **Press Box Telephone:** (484) 880-3382.

TENNESSEE VOLUNTEERS

Conference: Southeastern (East).

Mailing Address: 1720 Volunteer Blvd, Knoxville,TN 37996. **Website:** www.UTsports.com.

Head Coach: Todd Raleigh. **Assistant Coaches:** Fred Corral, Nate Headley, *Bradley LeCroy. **Telephone:** (865) 974-1223. **Baseball SID:** Melissa Anderson. **Telephone:** (865) 974-0884. **Fax:** (865) 974-1269.

Home Field: Lindsey Nelson Stadium. **Seating Capacity:** 3,800. **Outfield Dimensions:** LF—320, CF—387, RF—320. **Press Box Telephone:** (865) 974-3376.

TENNESSEE TECH GOLDEN EAGLES

Conference: Ohio Valley.

Mailing Address: Box 5057, Cookeville, TN 38505. **Website:** www.ttusports.com.

Head Coach: Matt Bragga. **Assistant Coaches:** Larry Bragga, Chris Cole, Justin Hogan. **Telephone:** (931) 372-3853. **Baseball SID:** Nick Heidelberger. **Telephone:** (931) 372-3293. **Fax:** (931) 372-6139.

Home Field: Howell Bush Stadium. **Seating Capacity:** 1,000. **Outfield Dimensions:** LF—331, CF—405, RF—329.

TENNESSEE-MARTIN SKYHAWKS

Conference: Ohio Valley.

Mailing Address: 1037 Elam Center, Martin, TN 38238. **Website:** www.utmsports.com.

Head Coach: Victor Cates. **Assistant Coaches:** Brad Goss, Joe Scarano, Jake Weghorst. **Telephone:** (731) 881-7337. **Baseball SID:** Joe Lofaro. **Telephone:** (731) 881-7632. **Fax:** (731) 881-7624.

Home Field: Skyhawk Field. **Seating Capacity:** 300. **Outfield Dimensions:** LF—330, CF—385, RF—330.

TEXAS LONGHORNS

Conference: Big 12.

Mailing Address: 2100 San Jacinto Boulevard, 327 Bellmont Hall, Austin, TX 78712. **Website:** www.TexasSports.com.

Head Coach: Augie Garrido. **Assistant Coaches:** *Tommy Harmon, Skip Johnson, Tommy Nicholson. **Telephone:** (512) 471-5732. **Baseball SID:** Thomas Dick. **Telephone:** (512) 471-6039. **Fax:** (512) 471-4060.

Home Field: UFCU Disch Falk Field. **Seating Capacity:** 6,876. **Outfield Dimensions:** LF—340, CF—400, RF—320.

TEXAS A&M AGGIES

Conference: Big 12.

Mailing Address: PO Box 30017, College Station, TX 77842-3017. **Website:** AggieAthletics.com.

Head Coach: Rob Childress. **Assistant Coaches:** Matt Deggs, *Jeremy Talbot. **Telephone:** (979) 845-4810. **Baseball SID:** Matt Simon. **Telephone:** (979) 845-3239. **Fax:** (979) 845-0564.

Home Field: Olsen Field. **Seating Capacity:** 7,053. **Outfield Dimensions:** LF—330, CF—400, RF—330. **Press Box Telephone:** (979) 458-3604.

TEXAS A&M-CORPUS CHRISTI ISLANDERS

Conference: Southland.

Mailing Address: 6300 Ocean Drive, Corpus Christi, TX 78412. **Website:** www.goislanders.com.

Head Coach: Scott Malone. **Assistant Coaches:** Josh Blakley, Rusty Miller, *Chris Ramirez. **Telephone:** (361) 825-3413. **Baseball SID:** Aaron Ames. **Telephone:** (361) 825-3410. **Fax:** (361) 825-3218.

Home Field: Whataburger Field. **Seating Capacity:** 8,000. **Outfield Dimensions:** LF—327, CF—400, RF—315. **Press Box Telephone:** (361) 561-4665.

TEXAS CHRISTIAN HORNED FROGS

Conference: Mountain West.

Mailing Address: 2900 Stadium Dr, Fort Worth, TX 76129. **Website:** www.gofrogs.com.

Head Coach: Jim Schlossnagle. **Assistant Coaches:** Randy Mazey, Ryan Shotzberger, *Todd Whitting. **Telephone:** (817) 257-5354. **Baseball SID:** Brandie Davidson. **Telephone:** (817) 257-7479. **Fax:** (817) 257-7964.

Home Field: Lupton Stadium. **Seating Capacity:** 3,500. **Outfield Dimensions:** LF—330, CF—400, RF—330. **Press Box Telephone:** (817) 257-7966.

TEXAS STATE BOBCATS

Conference: Southland.

Mailing Address: 601 University Drive, San Marcos, TX 78666. **Website:** txstatebobcats.com.

Head Coach: Ty Harrington. **Assistant Coaches:** Jeremy Fikac, Aaron Fuller, *Derek Matlock. **Telephone:** (512) 245-3383. **Baseball SID:** Amber Arterberry. **Telephone:** (512) 245-4692. **Fax:** (512) 245-2967.

Home Field: Bobcat Field. **Seating Capacity:** 2,000. **Outfield Dimensions:** LF—370, CF—395, RF—330.

TEXAS SOUTHERN TIGERS

Conference: Southwestern Athletic.

Mailing Address: 3100 Cleburne Street, Houston, TX 77004. **Website:** www.tsu.edu/athletics.

Head Coach: Michael Robertson. **Assistant Coaches:** Core Alexander, Candy Robinson, Brian White. **Telephone:** (713) 313-7993. **Baseball SID:** Rodney Bush. **Telephone:** (713) 313-6829. **Fax:** (713) 313-1045.

TEXAS TECH RED RAIDERS

Conference: Big 12.

Mailing Address: Box 43021, 6th and Boston Ave, Lubbock, TX 79409. **Website:** www.texastech.com.

Head Coach: Dan Spencer. **Assistant Coaches:** Ed Gustafson, Andy Jarvis, *Trent Petrie. **Telephone:** (806) 742-3355. **Baseball SID:** Blayne Beal. **Telephone:** (806) 742-2770. **Fax:** (806) 742-1970.

Home Field: Dan Law Field. **Seating Capacity:** 5,050. **Outfield Dimensions:** LF—330, CF—405, RF—305. **Press Box Telephone:** (806) 742-3688.

TEXAS-ARLINGTON MAVERICKS

Conference: Southland.

Mailing Address: 1309 West Mitchell Street, Arlington, TX 76019. **Website:** utamavs.com.

Head Coach: Darin Thomas. **Assistant Coaches:** Mark Flatten, K.J. Hendricks, *Jay Sirianni. **Telephone:** (817) 272-2542. **Baseball SID:** Scott Lacefield. **Telephone:** (817)

272-2239. **Fax:** (817) 272-2254.

Home Field: Clay Gould Ballpark. **Seating Capacity:** 1,600. **Outfield Dimensions:** LF—330, CF—400, RF—330. **Press Box Telephone:** (817) 462-4225.

TEXAS-PAN AMERICAN BRONCS

Conference: Independent.

Mailing Address: 1201 W. University Drive, Edinburg, TX 78539. **Website:** utpabroncs.com.

Head Coach: Manny Mantrana. **Assistant Coaches:** Norbert Lopez, *Stephen Piercefield. **Telephone:** (956) 381-2235. **Baseball SID:** Bernie Saenz. **Telephone:** (956) 381-2240. **Fax:** (956) 381-2398.

TEXAS-SAN ANTONIO ROADRUNNERS

Conference: Southland.

Mailing Address: One UTSA Circle, San Antonio, TX 78249-0691. **Website:** www.goutsa.com.

Head Coach: Sherman Corbett. **Assistant Coaches:** Mike Clement, Brett Lawler, *Jason Marshall. **Telephone:** (210) 458-4805. **Baseball SID:** Brian Hernandez. **Telephone:** (210) 458-4907. **Fax:** (210) 458-4569.

Home Field: Roadrunner Field. **Seating Capacity:** 800. **Outfield Dimensions:** LF—335, CF—405, RF—340. **Press Box Telephone:** (210) 458-4612.

TOLEDO ROCKETS

Conference: Mid-American (West).

Mailing Address: 2801 West Bancroft St, MS-408, Toledo, OH 43606. **Website:** utrockets.com.

Head Coach: Cory Mee. **Assistant Coaches:** *Josh Bradford, Nick McIntyre, Oliver Wolcott. **Telephone:** (419) 530-6263. **Baseball SID:** Brian DeBenedictis. **Telephone:** (419) 530-4919. **Fax:** (419) 530-4930.

Home Field: Scott Park. **Seating Capacity:** 1,000. **Outfield Dimensions:** LF—330, CF—400, RF—330. **Press Box Telephone:** (419) 530-3089.

TOWSON TIGERS

Conference: Colonial Athletic.

Mailing Address: 8000 York Road, Towson, MD 21252-0001. **Website:** www.towsontigers.com.

Head Coach: Mike Gottlieb. **Assistant Coaches:** Lance Mauck, *Scott Roane. **Telephone:** (410) 704-3775. **Baseball SID:** Dan O'Connell. **Telephone:** (410) 704-3102. **Fax:** (410) 704-3861.

Home Field: John B. Schuerholz Park. **Seating Capacity:** 1,200. **Outfield Dimensions:** LF—312, CF—424, RF—302. **Press Box Telephone:** (410) 704-5810.

TROY TROJANS

Conference: Sun Belt.

Mailing Address: 5000 Veterans Stadium Dr, Troy, AL 36082. **Website:** www.TroyTrojans.com.

Head Coach: Bobby Pierce. **Assistant Coaches:** Jeff Crane, Mike Murphree, *Mark Smartt. **Telephone:** (334) 670-3489. **Baseball SID:** Ricky Hazel. **Telephone:** (334) 670-3832. **Fax:** (334) 670-3278.

Home Field: Riddle-Pace Field. **Seating Capacity:** 2,000. **Outfield Dimensions:** LF—340, CF—400, RF—310. **Press Box Telephone:** (334) 670-5701.

TULANE GREEN WAVE

Conference: Conference USA.

Mailing Address: James Wilson Center, New Orleans, LA 70118-5698. **Website:** www.TulaneGreenWAvecom.

Head Coach: Rick Jones. **Assistant Coaches:** Jack Cressend, Billy Mohl, *Chad Sutter. **Telephone:** (504) 862-8216. **Baseball SID:** Colleen LeMasters. **Telephone:** (504) 314-7219. **Fax:** (504) 865-5379.

Home Field: Greer Field at Turchin Stadium. **Seating Capacity:** 5,000. **Outfield Dimensions:** LF—325, CF—400, RF—325. **Press Box Telephone:** (504) 862-8224.

UTAH UTES

Conference: Mountain West.

Mailing Address: 1825 E. South Campus Dr, Salt Lake City, UT 84112. **Website:** utahutes.com.

Head Coach: Bill Kinneberg. **Assistant Coaches:** *Mike Crawford, Pete Flores, Bryan Kinneberg. **Telephone:** (801) 581-3526. **Baseball SID:** Brooke Frederickson. **Telephone:** (801) 581-8302. **Fax:** (801) 581-4358.

Home Field: Franklin Covey Field. **Seating Capacity:** 15,000. **Outfield Dimensions:** LF—320, CF—410, RF—315.

UTAH VALLEY STATE WOLVERINES

Conference: Independent.

Mailing Address: 800 W. University Parkway, Orem, UT 84058. **Website:** www.WolverineGreen.com.

Head Coach: Eric Madsen. **Assistant Coaches:** *Dave Carter, Mike Martin. **Telephone:** (801) 863-6509. **Baseball SID:** Clint Burgi. **Telephone:** (801) 863-8644. **Fax:** (801) 863-8813.

Home Field: Brent Brown Ballpark. **Seating Capacity:** 5,000. **Outfield Dimensions:** LF—312, CF—408, RF—315. **Press Box Telephone:** (801) 362-1548.

VALPARAISO CRUSADERS

Conference: Horizon.

Mailing Address: 1009 Union St, Valparaiso, IN 46383. **Website:** www.valpoathletics.com.

Head Coach: Tracy Woodson. **Assistant Coaches:** Josh Dietz, *Brian Schmack, Eric Osborn. **Telephone:** (219) 464-5239. **Baseball SID:** Ryan Wronkowicz. **Telephone:** (219) 464-5232. **Fax:** (219) 464-5762.

Home Field: Emory G. Bauer Field. **Seating Capacity:** 500. **Outfield Dimensions:** LF—330, CF—400, RF—330. **Press Box Telephone:** (219) 464-6006.

VANDERBILT COMMODORES

Conference: Southeastern (East).

Mailing Address: 2601 Jess Neely Dr, Nashville, TN 37212. **Website:** www.vucommodores.com.

Head Coach: Tim Corbin. **Assistant Coaches:** *Erik Bakich, Larry Day, Derek Johnson. **Telephone:** (615) 322-7725. **Baseball SID:** Thomas Samuel. **Telephone:** (615) 343-0020. **Fax:** (615) 343-7064.

Home Field: Hawkins Field. **Seating Capacity:** 4,100. **Outfield Dimensions:** LF—315, CF—400, RF—335. **Press Box Telephone:** (615) 320-0436.

VERMONT CATAMOUNTS

Conference: America East.

Mailing Address: 97 Spear St, Burlington, VT 05405. **Website:** www.uvmathletics.com.

Head Coach: Bill Currier. **Assistant Coaches:** Keith Carter, *Mike Cole, Josh Santerre. **Telephone:** (802) 656-7701. **Baseball SID:** Bruce Bosley. **Telephone:** (802) 656-1109. **Fax:** (802) 656-8328.

Home Field: Centennial Field. **Seating Capacity:** 4,400. **Outfield Dimensions:** LF—324, CF—405, RF—320. **Press Box Telephone:** (802) 324-8334.

VILLANOVA WILDCATS

Conference: Big East.

Mailing Address: 800 Lancaster Ave, Villanova, PA 19085. **Website:** villanova.com.

Head Coach: Joe Godri. **Assistant Coaches:** *Jim Carone, Rod Johnson, Chris Madonna. **Telephone:** (610)

519-4529. **Baseball SID:** David Berman. **Telephone:** (610) 519-4122. **Fax:** (610) 519-7323.

Home Field: Villanova Ballpark at Plymouth. **Seating Capacity:** 750. **Outfield Dimensions:** LF—330, CF—405, RF—330. **Press Box Telephone:** (610) 490-6398.

VIRGINIA CAVALIERS

Conference: Atlantic Coast (Coastal).

Mailing Address: PO Box 400853, Charlottesville, VA 22904-4853. **Website:** www.virginiasports.com.

Head Coach: Brian O'Connor. **Assistant Coaches:** Karl Kuhn, *Kevin McMullan, Eddie Smith. **Telephone:** (434) 982-4932. **Baseball SID:** Andy Fledderjohann. **Telephone:** (434) 982-5131. **Fax:** (434) 982-5525.

Home Field: Davenport Field. **Seating Capacity:** 3,283. **Outfield Dimensions:** LF—335, CF—408, RF—335. **Press Box Telephone:** (434) 244-4071.

VIRGINIA COMMONWEALTH RAMS

Conference: Colonial Athletic.

Mailing Address: 1300 W. Broad Street, Richmond, VA 23284. **Website:** www.vcuathletics.com.

Head Coach: Paul Keyes. **Assistant Coaches:** Tim Haynes, *Shawn Stiffler. **Telephone:** (804) 828-4820. **Baseball SID:** Scott Day. **Telephone:** (804) 828-1727. **Fax:** (804) 828-9428.

Home Field: The Diamond. **Seating Capacity:** 12,134. **Outfield Dimensions:** LF—330, CF—402, RF—330. **Press Box Telephone:** (302) 593-0115.

VIRGINIA MILITARY INSTITUTE KEYDETS

Conference: Big South.

Mailing Address: Virginia Military Institute, Lexington, VA 24450. **Website:** www.VMIKeydets.com.

Head Coach: Marlin Ikenberry. **Assistant Coaches:** James Conrad, *Ryan Mau, Barry Shelton. **Telephone:** (540) 464-7609. **Baseball SID:** Christian Hoffman. **Telephone:** (540) 464-7514. **Fax:** (540) 464-7583.

Home Field: Gray-Minor Stadium. **Seating Capacity:** 1,400. **Outfield Dimensions:** LF—330, CF—395, RF—335. **Press Box Telephone:** (540) 460-6920.

VIRGINIA TECH HOKIES

Conference: Atlantic Coast (Coastal).

Mailing Address: 460 Jamerson Athletic Center, Blacksburg, VA 24061. **Website:** www.hokiesports.com.

Head Coach: Pete Hughes. **Assistant Coaches:** *Mike Gambino, Mike Kunigonis, Dave Turgeon. **Telephone:** (540) 231-3671. **Baseball SID:** Matt Kovatch. **Telephone:** (540) 231-1894. **Fax:** (540) 231-6984.

Home Field: English Field. **Seating Capacity:** 4,000. **Outfield Dimensions:** LF—330, CF—400, RF—330. **Press Box Telephone:** (540) 231-8974.

WAGNER SEAHAWKS

Conference: Northeast.

Mailing Address: Spiro Sports Center, One Campus Rd, Staten Island, NY 10301. **Website:** wagnerathletics.com.

Head Coach: *Joe Litterio. **Assistant Coaches:** Jason Jurgens, Billy Malloy. **Telephone:** (718) 390-3154. **Baseball SID:** Kevin Ross. **Telephone:** (718) 390-3215. **Fax:** (718) 420-4015.

Home Field: Richmond County Bank Ballpark. **Seating Capacity:** 6,900. **Outfield Dimensions:** LF—320, CF—390, RF—318. **Press Box Telephone:** (718) 969-6126.

WAKE FOREST DEMON DEACONS

Conference: Atlantic Coast (Atlantic).

Mailing Address: 211 Wingate Drive, 310 Miller Center, Winston-Salem, NC 27109. **Website:** wakeforestsports.com.

Head Coach: Rick Rembielak. **Assistant Coaches:** Greg Bauer, *Jon Palmieri. **Telephone:** (336) 758-5570. **Baseball SID:** Chad Crunk. **Telephone:** (336) 758-5842. **Fax:** (336) 758-5140.

Home Field: Ernie Shore Stadium. **Seating Capacity:** 6,000. **Outfield Dimensions:** LF—325, CF—400, RF—325.

WASHINGTON HUSKIES

Conference: Pacific-10.

Mailing Address: Box 354070, Seattle, WA 98195. **Website:** www.gohuskies.com.

Head Coach: Ken Knutson. **Assistant Coaches:** Tighe Dickinson, Kevin Miller, *Joe Ross. **Telephone:** (206) 616-4335. **Baseball SID:** Jeff Bechthold. **Telephone:** (206) 685-7910. **Fax:** (206) 543-5000.

Home Field: Husky Ballpark. **Seating Capacity:** 1,500. **Outfield Dimensions:** LF—327, CF—395, RF—317. **Press Box Telephone:** (206) 685-1994.

WASHINGTON STATE COUGARS

Conference: Pacific-10.

Mailing Address: PO Box 641602, Pullman, WA 99164. **Website:** wsucougars.cstv.com.

Head Coach: Donnie Marbut. **Assistant Coaches:** Gabe Boruff, *Travis Jewett, Gregg Swenson. **Telephone:** (509) 335-0332. **Baseball SID:** Craig Lawson. **Telephone:** (509) 335-0265. **Fax:** (509) 335-0328.

Home Field: Bailey-Brayton Field. **Seating Capacity:** 3,500. **Outfield Dimensions:** LF—340, CF—400, RF—315.

WEST VIRGINIA MOUNTAINEERS

Conference: Big East.

Mailing Address: PO Box 0877, Morgantown, WV 26507. **Website:** www.msnsportsnet.com.

Head Coach: Greg Van Zant. **Assistant Coaches:** Tad Reida, Patrick Sherald. **Telephone:** (304) 293-9881. **Baseball SID:** Steve Stone. **Telephone:** (304) 293-2821. **Fax:** (304) 293-4105.

Home Field: Hawley Field. **Seating Capacity:** 1,500. **Outfield Dimensions:** LF—325, CF—390, RF—325.

WESTERN CAROLINA CATAMOUNTS

Conference: Southern.

Mailing Address: Ramsey Center, Cullowhee, NC 28723. **Website:** catamountsports.com.

Head Coach: Bobby Moranda. **Assistant Coaches:** Grant Achilles, *Alan Beck, David Haverstick. **Telephone:** (828) 227-7338. **Baseball SID:** Daniel Hooker. **Telephone:** (828) 227-2339. **Fax:** (828) 227-7688.

Home Field: Childress Field/Hennon Stadium. **Seating Capacity:** 1,500. **Outfield Dimensions:** LF—325, CF—390, RF—325. **Press Box Telephone:** (828) 227-7020.

WESTERN ILLINOIS LEATHERNECKS

Conference: Summit.

Mailing Address: 204 Western Hall, 1 University Circle, Macomb, IL 61455. **Website:** www.wiuathletics.com.

Head Coach: Stan Hyman. **Assistant Coaches:** Brock Bainter, Steve Barry, *Tom Radz. **Telephone:** (309) 298-1521. **Baseball SID:** Brock Wissmiller. **Telephone:** (309) 298-1133. **Fax:** (309) 298-2060.

Home Field: Alfred D. Boyer Stadium. **Seating Capacity:** 500. **Outfield Dimensions:** LF—330, CF—400, RF—330. **Press Box Telephone:** (309) 298-1190.

WESTERN KENTUCKY HILLTOPPERS

Conference: Sun Belt.

Mailing Address: 1605 Avenue of Champions, Bowling Green, KY 42101. **Website:** www.wkusports.com.

Head Coach: Chris Finwood. **Assistant Coaches:** *Blake Allen, Casey Hamilton, Matt Myers. **Telephone:** (270) 745-2277. **Baseball SID:** Brad Fields. **Telephone:** (270) 745-5045. **Fax:** (270) 745-6187.

Home Field: Nick Denes Field. **Seating Capacity:** 2,500. **Outfield Dimensions:** LF—330, CF—400, RF—330.

WESTERN MICHIGAN BRONCOS

Conference: Mid-American (West).

Mailing Address: 1903 West Michigan Ave, Kalamazoo, MI 49008. **Website:** www.wmubroncos.com.

Head Coach: Randy Ford. **Assistant Coaches:** Scott Bates, *Scott Demetral. **Telephone:** (269) 276-3205. **Baseball SID:** Kristin Keirns. **Telephone:** (269) 387-4123. **Fax:** (269) 387-4139.

Home Field: Hyames Field. **Seating Capacity:** 2,500. **Outfield Dimensions:** LF—320, CF—390, RF—340.

WICHITA STATE SHOCKERS

Conference: Missouri Valley.

Mailing Address: 1845 Fairmount, Campus Box 18, Wichita, KS 67260-0018. **Website:** www.goshockers.com.

Head Coach: Gene Stephenson. **Assistant Coaches:** Jerod Goodale, *Brent Kemnitz, Jim Thomas. **Telephone:** (316) 978-3636. **Baseball SID:** Tami Cutler. **Telephone:** (316) 978-5559. **Fax:** (316) 978-3336.

Home Field: Eck Stadium. **Seating Capacity:** 7,851. **Outfield Dimensions:** LF—330, CF—390, RF—330. **Press Box Telephone:** (316) 978-3390.

WILLIAM & MARY TRIBE

Conference: Colonial Athletic.

Mailing Address: PO Box 399, Williamsburg, VA 23187. **Website:** www.tribeathletics.com.

Head Coach: Frank Leoni. **Assistant Coaches:** Kyle Padgett, Tim Park, *Jad Prachniak. **Telephone:** (757) 221-3399. **Baseball SID:** Jake Skipper. **Telephone:** (757) 221-3344. **Fax:** (757) 221-2989.

Home Field: Plumeri Park. **Seating Capacity:** 1,200. **Outfield Dimensions:** LF—330, CF—400, RF—330. **Press Box Telephone:** (757) 221-3562.

WINTHROP EAGLES

Conference: Big South.

Mailing Address: 1162 Eden Terrace Road, Rock Hill, SC 29733. **Website:** www.winthropeagles.com.

Head Coach: Joe Hudak. **Assistant Coaches:** Kyle DiEduardo, *Mike McGuire, Jason Murray. **Telephone:** (803) 323-2129, ext 6235. **Baseball SID:** Wesley Herring. **Telephone:** (803) 323-2129, ext 6067. **Fax:** (803) 323-2433.

Home Field: The Winthrop Ballpark. **Seating Capacity:** 1,700. **Outfield Dimensions:** LF—325, CF—390, RF—325. **Press Box Telephone:** (803) 323-2155.

WISCONSIN-MILWAUKEE PANTHERS

Conference: Horizon.

Mailing Address: 3409 N. Downer Ave, Milwaukee, WI 53201. **Website:** uwmpanthers.com.

Head Coach: Scott Doffek. **Assistant Coaches:** *Cory Bigler, Dean Haase, Steve Sanfilippo. **Telephone:** (414) 229-5670. **Baseball SID:** Chris Zills. **Telephone:** (414) 229-4593. **Fax:** (414) 229-6759.

Home Field: Henry Aaron Field. **Seating Capacity:** Unavailable. **Outfield Dimensions:** LF—320, CF—390, RF—320. **Press Box Telephone:** (414) 750-2090.

WOFFORD TERRIERS

Conference: Southern.

Mailing Address: 429 N. Church Street, Spartanburg, SC 29303. **Website:** athletics.woffoRdedu.

Head Coach: Todd Interdonato. **Assistant Coaches:** *Dusty Blake, Anthony Dillenger, Chris Wiley. **Telephone:** (864) 597-4497. **Baseball SID:** Brent Williamson. **Telephone:** (864) 597-4093. **Fax:** (864) 597-4129.

Home Field: Russell C. **King Field. Seating Capacity:** 2,500. **Outfield Dimensions:** LF—325, CF—395, RF—325. **Press Box Telephone:** (864) 597-4478.

WRIGHT STATE RAIDERS

Conference: Horizon.

Mailing Address: 3640 Colonel Glenn Hwy., Dayton, OH 45435. **Website:** wsuraiders.cstv.com.

Head Coach: Rob Cooper. **Assistant Coaches:** Kyle Geswein, *Greg Lovelady, Matt Smith. **Telephone:** (937) 775-2771. **Baseball SID:** Greg Campbell. **Telephone:** (937) 775-4687. **Fax:** (937) 775-2368.

Home Field: Nischwitz Stadium. **Seating Capacity:** 750. **Outfield Dimensions:** LF—330, CF—400, RF—370. **Press Box Telephone:** (937) 602-0326.

XAVIER MUSKETEERS

Conference: Atlantic 10.

Mailing Address: 3800 Victory Parkway, Cincinnati, OH 45207. **Website:** www.goxavier.com.

Head Coach: Scott Googins. **Assistant Coaches:** Jeff Fontaine, *J.D. Heilmann, Zach Schmidt. **Telephone:** (513) 745-2891. **Baseball SID:** Jenna Willhoit. **Telephone:** (513) 745-3961. **Fax:** (513) 745-2825.

Home Field: Hayden Field. **Seating Capacity:** 500. **Outfield Dimensions:** LF—310, CF—385, RF—310.

YALE BULLDOGS

Conference: Ivy League (Rolfe).

Mailing Address: PO Box 208216, New Haven, CT 06520. **Website:** yalebulldogs.com.

Head Coach: John Stuper. **Assistant Coaches:** John Dorman, Tucker Frawley. **Telephone:** (203) 432-1466. **Baseball SID:** Steve Conn. **Telephone:** (203) 432-1455. **Fax:** (203) 432-1454.

YOUNGSTOWN STATE PENGUINS

Conference: Horizon.

Mailing Address: One University Plaza, Youngstown, OH 44555. **Website:** www.ysusports.com.

Head Coach: Rich Pasquale. **Assistant Coaches:** Craig Antush, *Tom Lipari. **Telephone:** (330) 941-3485. **Baseball SID:** John Vogel. **Telephone:** (330) 941-1480. **Fax:** (330) 941-3191.

Home Field: Eastwood Field. **Seating Capacity:** 6,000. **Outfield Dimensions:** LF—335, CF—405, RF—335. **Press Box Telephone:** (330) 505-0000 ext 229.

AMATEUR & YOUTH

INTERNATIONAL ORGANIZATIONS

INTERNATIONAL OLYMPIC COMMITTEE

Mailing Address: Chateau de Vidy, 1007 Lausanne, Switzerland. **Telephone:** (41-21) 621-6111. **Fax:** (41-21) 621-6216. **Website:** www.olympic.org.

President: Jacques Rogge. **Director, Communications:** Giselle Davies.

Games of the XXIX Olympiad: Aug. 8-24, 2008, at Beijing, China.

U.S. OLYMPIC COMMITTEE

Mailing Address: One Olympic Plaza, Colorado Springs, CO 80909. **Telephone:** (719) 632-5551. **Fax:** (719) 866-4654. **Website:** www.usoc.org.

Chief Executive Officer: Jim Scherr. **Chief Communications Officer:** Darryl Seibel.

INTERNATIONAL BASEBALL FEDERATION

Headquarters: Avenue de Mon Repos 24, Case Postale 6099, 1002 Lausanne, Switzerland. **Telephone: (+41-21) 318-82-40. FAX: (41-21) 318-82-41.**

Website: www.ibaf.org. E-Mail: ibafmedia@yahoo.com.

Year Founded: 1938.

President: Dr. Harvey W. Schiller.

Assistant to President: Katharine Romaine. **Manager, Media Relations:** Jake Fehling. **Manager, Anti-Doping:** Jean-Pierre Moser.

Coordinator, Projects/Events: Carlota Bincaz. **Coordinator, Anti-Doping/Communications Support:** Olivia Bille Peña.

Coordinator, Media Relations: Bradley Young. **Coordinator, Information Services for the 2009 Baseball World Cup:** Ian Young.

Coordinator, Media Rights: David Schiller.

Executive Committee Members: Harvey W. Schiller (USA), Masatake Matsuda (JPN), Martin Miller (GER), Alonso Perez (MEX), John C. Ostermeyer (AUS), Rene Laforce (BEL), Alex W.J. Huang (TPE), Eric Pierre Dufour (FRA), David Molina (GUA), Ishola Williams (NGR), Eduardo De Bello (PAN), Nae-Heun Lee, Riccardo Fraccari (ITA), Robert Steffy (GUM), Shen Wei (CHN), Lei Jun (CHN), Dr. Ndi Okereke-Onyiuke (NGR), Sandra Monteiro (POR), Rodolfo Puente (CUB).

CONTINENTAL ASSOCIATIONS

CONFEDERATION PAN AMERICANA DE BEISBOL (COPABE)

Mailing Address: Calle 3, Francisco Filos, Vista Hermosa, Edificio 74, Planta Baja Local No. 1, Panama City, Panama. **Telephone:** (507) 229-8684. **Fax:** Unavailable. **E-Mail Address:** copabe@sinfo.net.

President: Eduardo De Bello (Panama). **Secretary General:** Hector Pereyra (Dominican Republic).

AFRICAN BASEBALL/SOFTBALL ASSOCIATION

Mailing Address: Paiko Road, Changaga, Minna, Niger State, PMB 150, Nigeria. **Telephone:** (234-66) 224-555. **Fax:** (234-66) 224-555. **E-Mail Address:** absasecretariat@yahoo.com.

President: Ishola Williams (Nigeria). **Executive Director:** Friday Ichide (Nigeria). **Secretary General:** Fridah Shiroya (Kenya).

BASEBALL FEDERATION OF ASIA

Mailing Address: No. 946-16 Dogok-Dong, Kangnam-Gu, Seoul, 135-270 Korea. **Telephone:** (82-2) 572-8413. **Fax:** (82-2) 572-8416.

President: Nae-Heun Lee (Korea). **Secretary General:** Kyung-Hoon Minn (Korea).

EUROPEAN BASEBALL CONFEDERATION

Mailing Address: Zatopkova 100/2, P.O. Box 40, 160 17 Prague 6 (Czech Republic). **Telephone/Fax:** (420-2) 33017459. **E-Mail Address:** info@baseballeurope.com. **Website:** baseballeurope.com.

President: Martin Miller (Germany). **Secretary General:** Petr Ditrich (Czech Republic).

BASEBALL CONFERERATION OF OCEANIA

Mailing Address: 48 Partridge Way, Mooroolbark, Victoria 3138, Australia. **Telephone:** (61-2) 6214-1236. **Fax:** (61-3) 6214-1926. **E-Mail Address:** bcosecgeneral@baseballoceania.com. **Website:** www.baseballoceania.com.

President: John Ostermeyer (Australia). **Secretary General:** Chet Gray (Australia).

ORGANIZATIONS

INTERNATIONAL GOODWILL SERIES, INC.

Mailing Address: P.O. Box 213, Santa Rosa, CA 95402. **Telephone:** (707) 975-7894. **Fax:** (707) 525-0214. **E-Mail Address:** rwilliams@goodwillseries.org. **Website:** www.goodwillseries.org.

President, Goodwill Series, Inc.: Bob Williams.

17th International Friendship Series (16 and Under): Aug. **8-18, China. Goodwill Series:** Australia, Dec. **14-31.**

INTERNATIONAL SPORTS GROUP

Mailing Address: 11430 Kestrel Rd., Klamath Falls, OR 97601. **Telephone:** (541) 882-4293. **E-Mail Address:** isg-baseball@yahoo.com. **Website:** www.isgbaseball.com.

President: Jim Jones. **Vice President:** Tom O'Connell. **Secretary/Treasurer:** Randy Town.

NATIONAL ORGANIZATIONS

USA BASEBALL

Mailing Address, Corporate Headquarters: P.O. Box 1131, Durham, NC 27702. **Office Address:** 403 Blackwell St., **Durham, NC 27701 Telephone:** (919) 474-8721. **Fax:** (919) 474-8822. **E-Mail Address:** info@usabaseball.com. **Website:** www.usabaseball.com.

President: Mike Gaski. **Secretary General:** Ernie Young. **Treasurer:** Jason Dobis.

Executive Director, Chief Executive Officer: Paul Seiler. **General Manager, Professional and National Teams:** Eric Campbell. **Chief Financial Officer:** Ray Darwin. **Director, Media & Public Relations:** Jake Fehling. **Coordinator, Special Projects:** Nate Logan. **Chief Operating Officer:** David Perkins. **Director, 18U National Team:** Rick Riccobono. **Director, 16U National Team:** Jeff Singer. **Director, Baseball Administration:** Matt Titus.

National Members: Amateur Athletic Union (AAU), American Amateur Baseball Congress (AABC), American Baseball Coaches Association (ABCA), American Legion Baseball, Babe Ruth Baseball, Dixie Baseball, Little League Baseball, National Amateur Baseball Federation (NABF), National Association of Intercollegiate Athletics (NAIA), National Baseball Congress (NBC), National Collegiate Athletic Association (NCAA), National Federation of State High School Athletic Associations, National High School Baseball Coaches Association (BCA), National Junior College Athletic Association (NJCAA), Police Athletic League (PAL), PONY Baseball, T-Ball USA, United States Specialty Sports Association (USSSA), YMCAs of the USA.

2009 Events

Team USA—Professional Level

World Baseball Classic . . . . March 5-23, various sites
World Cup Training Camp . . . . Sept. 1-5, Cary, NC
IBAF Baseball World Cup . . . . Sept. 9-27, Europe

USA Baseball National Team Collegiate

National Team Trials . . . . June 20-24, Cary, NC
National Team Tour . . . . June 25-July 7, various sites
USA/Japan Collegiate Series . . . . July 11-16, Japan
World Baseball Challenge . . . July 18-26, Prince Georgia, B.C.

USA Baseball 18U National Team

Tournament of Stars . . . . June 23-28, Cary, NC
COPABE Pan Am Championships . . . . Dates TBD, Venezuela
National Team ID Series (17U) . . . . Sept. 18-20, Cary, NC

USA Baseball 16U National Team

16U Championships—West . Peoria/Surprise, AZ, June 19-27
16U Championships—East . . . . Jupiter, FL, June 19-27
IBAF World Champ. . . . . Taichung, Taiwan, Aug. 15-23
National Team ID Series (15U) . . . . Sept. 18-20, Cary, NC

USA Baseball 14U National Team

COPABE Pan Am Champ.. . . . . Dates TBD, Ecuador
National Team ID Series (13U) . . . . Sept. 18-20, Cary, NC

USA Baseball Baseball Athlete Development Camps

Youth Development Camp . . . . June 15-16, Cary, NC
Athlete Prospect Camp. . . . . June 16-18, Peoria, Ariz.
Athlete Prospect Camp. . . . . June 17-19, Cary, NC

BASEBALL CANADA

Mailing Address: 2212 Gladwin Cres., Suite A7, Ottawa, Ontario K1B 5N1. **Telephone:** (613) 748-5606. **FAX:** (613) 748-5767. **E-Mail Address:** info@baseball.ca. **Website:** www.baseball.ca.

Director General: Jim Baba. **Head Coach/Director, National Teams:** Greg Hamilton. **Manager, Baseball Operations:** Andre Lachance. **Manager, Media/Public Relations:** Andre Cormier. **Administrative Coordinator:** Denise Thomas.

2009 Events

Baseball Canada Cup (17 & under) . . Kindersley, SK, Aug. 5-9

NATIONAL BASEBALL CONGRESS

Mailing Address: 300 S. Sycamore, Wichita, KS 67213. **Telephone:** (316) 264-4625. **Fax:** (316) 264-3037. **Website:** www.nbcbaseball.com.

Year Founded: 1931.

General Manager: Josh Robertson. **Tournament Director:** Jerry Taylor.

ATHLETES IN ACTION

Mailing Address: 651 Taylor Dr., Xenia, OH 45385. **Telephone:** (937) 352-1000. **Fax:** (937) 352-1245. **E-Mail Address:** baseball@aia.com. **Website:** www.aiabaseball.org.

Director, AIA Baseball: Jason Lester. **U.S. Teams Director:** Chris Beck. **International Teams Director:** John McLaughlin. **General Manager, Great Lakes:** John Henschen. **Athletic Trainer:** Natalie McLaughlin.

SUMMER COLLEGE LEAGUES

NATIONAL ALLIANCE OF COLLEGE SUMMER BASEBALL

Telephone: (508) 801-8741. **E-Mail Address:** pgalop@comcast.net.

Executive Director: Jeff Carter (Southern Collegiate Baseball League). **Assistant Executive Directors:** Kim Lance (Great Lakes Summer Collegiate League), David Biery (Valley Baseball League). **Secretary:** Sara Whiting (Florida Collegiate Summer League). **Treasurer:** Jim Phillips (Valley Baseball League).

Member Leagues: Atlantic Collegiate Baseball League, Cape Cod Baseball League, Central Illinois Collegiate League, Florida Collegiate Summer League, Great Lakes Summer Collegiate League, New York Collegiate Baseball League, Southern Collegiate Baseball League, Valley Baseball League.

SUMMER COLLEGIATE BASEBALL ASSOCIATION

Mailing Address: 4900 Waters Edge Dr, Suite 201, Raleigh, NC 27606. **Telephone:** (919) 852-1960. **Fax:** 919-852-1973 E-Mail Address: peteb@coastalplain.com. **Website:** www.summercollegiatebaseball.com.

President: Pete Bock (Coastal Plain League). **Vice President:** Dick Radatz, Jr. **(Northwoods League).**

Affiliated Leagues: Coastal Plain League, Northwoods League, West Coast Collegiate League.

ALASKA BASEBALL LEAGUE

Mailing Address: 651 Taylor Drive, Xenia, OH 45385. **Telephone:** (907) 283-6186.

Year Founded: 1974 (reunited, 1998).

President: Chris Beck (Athletes In Action). **First Vice President/Marketing:** Pete Christopher (Mat-Su Miners). **League Spokesperson:** Mike Baxter. **League Stats:** Dick

Lobdell.

Regular Season: 45 league games and approximately 5 non-league games. **2009 Opening Date:** June 10. **Closing Date:** August 3.

Playoff Format: League champion and second-place finisher qualify for National Baseball Congress World Series.

Roster Limit: 24 plus exemption for Alaska residents. **Player Eligibility Rule:** Players with college eligibility, except drafted seniors.

ANCHORAGE BUCS

Mailing Address: PO Box 240061, Anchorage, AK 99524. **Telephone:** (907) 561-2827. **Fax:** (907) 561-2920. **E-Mail Address:** admin@anchoragebucs.com. **Website:** www.anchoragebucs.com. **General Manager:** Dennis Mattingly. **Head Coach:** Thom Dreier (Arizona State).

ANCHORAGE GLACIER PILOTS

Mailing Address: 207 East Northern Lights Blvd, Anchorage, AK 99503. **Telephone:** (907) 274-3627. **Fax:** (907) 274-3628. **E-Mail Address:** gpilots@alaska.net. **Website:** www.glacierpilots.com. **General Manager:** Jon Dyson. **Head Coach:** Dennis Machado (Cal State Bakersfield).

ATHLETES IN ACTION

Mailing Address: 651 Taylor Dr, Xenia, OH 45385. **Telephone:** (937) 352-1237. **Fax:** (937) 352-1245. **E-Mail Address:** chris.beck@aia.com. **Website:** www.aiabaseball.org. **General Manager:** Chris Beck. **Head Coach:** Rob Ramseyer (Mid American Nazerene).

FAIRBANKS ALASKA GOLDPANNERS

Mailing Address: PO Box 71154, Fairbanks, AK 99707. **Telephone:** (907) 451-0095, (619) 561-4581. **Fax:** (907) 456-6429. **E-Mail Address:** addennis@cox.net. **Website:** www.goldpanners.com. **General Manager:** Don Dennis. **Head Coach:** Tim Gloyd (Yuba, Calif., CC).

MAT-SU MINERS

Mailing Address: PO Box 2690, Palmer, AK 99645. **Telephone:** (907) 746-4914. **Fax:** (907) 746-5068. **E-Mail Address:** generalmanager@matsuminers.org. **Website:** www.matsuminers.org. **General Manager:** Pete Christopher. **Head Coach:** Russell Raley (University of Oklahoma).

PENINSULA OILERS

Mailing Address: 601 S. Main St, Kenai, AK 99611. **Telephone:** (907) 283-7133. **Fax:** (907) 283-3390. **E-Mail Address:** shawn@oilersbaseball.com. **Website:** www.oilersbaseball.com. **General Manager:** Shawn Maltby. **Head Coach:** Jeff Walker (Loyola Marymount).

ATLANTIC COLLEGIATE LEAGUE

Mailing Address: 1760 Joanne Drive, Quakertown, PA 18951. **Telephone:** 215-536-5777. **Fax:** 215-536-5177. **E-Mail:** tbonekemper@comcast.net. **Website:** www.acbl-online.com.

Year Founded: 1967.

Commissioner: Ralph Addonizio. **President:** Tom Bonekemper. **Secretary:** Ed Kull. **Treasurer:** Bob Hoffman.

Division Structure: Wolff—Jersey, Kutztown, Lehigh Valley, Northern Jersey, Peekskill, Quakertown. Kaiser—Long Island, Mattituck, Riverhead, Sag Harbor, Southampton, Westhampton.

Regular Season: 40 games. **2009 Opening Date:** June 1. **Closing Date:** Aug. 15.

All-Star Game: July 13, St. John's University.

Playoff Format: Top four teams, winners play best-of-three division series and then one game championship at field of division winner of All-Star game.

Roster Limit: 25 (college-eligible players only).

HAMPTON WHALERS

Mailing Address: PO Box 835, Montauk, NY 11954. **Telephone:** (631) 668-3901. **General Manager:** Mike Caulfield. **Head Coach:** Julio Vega..

JERSEY PILOTS

Mailing Address: 401 Timber Dr, Berkeley Heights, NJ 07922. **Telephone:** (908) 464-8042. **E-Mail Address:** bensmookler@aol.com. **President/General Manager:** Ben Smookler. **Head Coach:** Evan Davis.

KUTZTOWN ROCKIES

Mailing Address: 429 Baldy Rd, Kutztown, PA 19530. **Telephone:** (610) 683-5273. **E-Mail Address:** kutztownrockies@aol.com. **President/General Manager:** Jon Yeakel. **Head Coach:** Jon Yeakel.

LEHIGH VALLEY CATZ

Mailing Address: 103 Logan Dr, Easton, PA 18045. **Telephone:** (610) 533-9349. **E-Mail Address:** valleycatz@hotmail.com. **Website:** www.lvcatz.com. **General Manager:** Pat O'Connell. **Head Coach:** Dennis Morgan.

LONG ISLAND MUSTANGS

Mailing Address: 825 East Gate Blvd, Suite 101, Garden City, NY 11530. **E-Mail Address:** phil.andriola@yahoo.com. **Website:** www.limustangsbaseball.com. **General Manager:** Phillip Andriola. **Head Coach:** Pete Murphy.

NORTH FORK OSPREYS

Operated by: Hamptons Collegiate Baseball. **Telephone:** (631) 680-7870. **Website:** www.hamptonsbaseball.org. **General Manager:** Joe Finora.

NORTHERN NEW JERSEY EAGLES

Mailing Address: 107 Pleasant Avenue, Upper Saddle River, NJ 07458. **General Manager:** Doug Cinnella. **Head Coach:** Jorge Hernandez.

PEEKSKILL ROBINS

Mailing Address: PO Box 113254, Stamford, CT 06911. **Telephone:** (203) 981-7516. **E-Mail Address:** michaelhalo3131@aol.com. **Website:** www.robinsbaseball.com. **General Manager:** Mike DeAngelo. **Head Coach:** Raphael Vellajo.

QUAKERTOWN BLAZERS

Mailing Address: 2345 Allentown Road, Quakertown, PA 18951. **Telephone:** (610) 844-5030. **General Manager:** Clyde Smoll. **Head Coach:** Clay Kuklick.

RIVERHEAD TOMCATS

Operated by: Hamptons Collegiate Baseball. **Website:** www.hamptonsbaseball.org. **Head Coach:** Ron Davies.

SAG HARBOR WHALERS

Operated by: Hamptons Collegiate Baseball. **Website:** www.hamptonsbaseball.org. **Head Coach:** Jason Lefkowitz.

SOUTHAMPTON BREAKERS

Operated by: Hamptons Collegiate Baseball. **Website:** www.hamptonsbaseball.org. **Head Coach:** Brad Howland.

WESTHAMPTON AVIATORS

Operated by: Hamptons Collegiate Baseball. **Telephone:** (631) 466-4393. **Website:** www.hamptons-baseball.org. **General Manager:** Henry Bramwell. **Head Coach:** Dan Gallagher.

CALIFORNIA COLLEGIATE LEAGUE

Mailing Address: 4299 Carpinteria Ave, Suite 201, Carpinteria, CA 93013. **Telephone:** (805) 684-0657. **Fax:** (805) 684-8596. **Website:** www.calsummerball.com.

Year Founded: 1993.

President: Pat Burns.

Member Clubs: Conejo Oaks, MLB Urban Youth Academy, Monterey Bay Sox, San Luis Obispo Rattlers, Santa Barbara Foresters.

Regular Season: 30 games. **2009 Opening Date:** June 5. **Closing Date:** July 30.

Playoff Format: League champion and runner-up advance to NBC World Series.

Roster Limit: 33.

CAL RIPKEN SR. COLLEGIATE LEAGUE

Address: PO Box 22471, Baltimore, MD 21203. **Telephone:** (410) 588-9900. **E-Mail:** athompson@crscbl.org. **Website:** www.ripkensrcollegebaseball.org.

Year Founded: 2005.

Commissioner: William Spencer. **Deputy Commissioner:** Robert Douglas. **Executive Director:** Alex Thompson.

Regular Season: 42 games. **2009 Opening Date:** June 4. **Closing Date:** July 26.

All-Star Game: Unavailable.

Playoff Format: Four-team double-elimination league championship series, July 29-August 2.

Roster Limit: 30 (college-eligible players 22 and under).

ALEXANDRIA ACES

Address: Potomac Station, 1908 Mount Vernon Ave, PO Box 2566, Alexandria, VA 22301. **Telephone:** (202) 465-4830. **E-Mail:** pat@alexandriaaces.org. **Website:** www.alexandriaaces.org. **General Manager:** Brian Midkiff. **Head Coach:** Eric Williams.

BETHESDA BIG TRAIN

Address: PO Box 30306, Bethesda, MD 20824. **Telephone:** (301) 983-1006. **Fax:** (301) 652-0691. **E-Mail:** david@bigtrain.org. **Website:** www.bigtrain.org. **General Manager:** Jordan Henry. **Head Coach:** Sal Colangelo.

COLLEGE PARK BOMBERS

Address: 5033 56th Ave, Hyattsville, MD 20781. **Telephone:** (301) 674-7362. **Fax:** (301) 927-6997. **E-Mail:** collegeparkbombers@gmail.com. **Website:** www.collegeparkbombers.org. **President/Head Coach:** Gene Bovello. **General Manager:** Scott Weaver.

HERNDON BRAVES

Address: PO Box 631, Haymarket, VA 20168. **Telephone:** (703) 754-6808. **Fax:** (703) 783-1319. **E-Mail:** herndon-braves@cox.net. **Website:** www.herndonbraves.com. **Administrator:** Lauren Taggart. **Head Coach:** Chris Smith.

MARYLAND REDBIRDS

Address: 10819 Sandringham Rd, Cockeysville, MD 21030. **Telephone:** (410) 823-3399, ext. 118. **Fax:** (410) 823-4144. **E-Mail:** redbird1@hotmail.com. **Website:** www.mdredbirds.com. **GM/Head Coach:** Mark Russo.

ROCKVILLE EXPRESS

Address: PO Box 10188, Rockville, MD 20849. **Telephone:** (301) 928-6608. **Fax:** (240) 567-7586. **E-Mail:** shaffer048@hotmail.com. **Website:** www.rockvilleexpress.org. **General Manager:** Jim Kazunas. **Head Coach:** Jim Pereira.

SILVER SPRING-TAKOMA THUNDERBOLTS

Address: 326 Lincoln Ave, Takoma Park, MD 20912. **Telephone:** (301) 270-0598. **E-Mail:** tboltsbaseball@gmail.com. **Website:** www.tbolts.org. **President/General Manager:** Richard O'Connor. **Head Coach:** Jason Walck.

YOUSE'S MARYLAND ORIOLES

Address: 6451 St. Phillips Rd, Linthicum, MD 21090. **Telephone:** (443) 690-6550. **E-Mail:** daalbany22@cablespeed.com. **General Manager:** Dean Albany. **Head Coach:** Tim Norris.

CAPE COD LEAGUE

Mailing Address: PO Box 266, Harwich Port, MA 02646. **Telephone:** (508) 432-6909. **E-Mail:** info@capecodbaseball.org. **Website:** www.capecodbaseball.org.

Year Founded: 1885.

Commissioner: Paul Galop. **President:** Judy Walden Scarafile. **Senior Vice President:** Jim Higgins. **Vice Presidents:** Phil Edwards, Peter Ford. **Deputy Commissioner:** Richard Sullivan. **Deputy Commissioner/Director, Officiating:** Sol Yas. **Treasurer/Website Manager:** Steven Wilson. **Director, Public Relations/Broadcast Media:** John Garner. **Director, Communications:** Jim McGonigle. **Director, Publications:** Lou Barnicle.

Division Structure: East—Brewster, Chatham, Harwich, Orleans, Yarmouth-Dennis. West—Bourne, Cotuit, Falmouth, Hyannis, Wareham.

Regular Season: 44 games. **2009 Opening Date:** June 11. **Closing Date:** Aug. 15.

All-Star Game: July 23.

Playoff Format: Top two teams in each division meet in best-of-three semifinals. Winners meet in best-of-three series for league championship.

Roster Limit: 25 (college-eligible players only).

BOURNE BRAVES

Mailing Address: PO Box 895, Monument Beach, MA 02553. **Telephone:** (508) 345-1013. **Fax:** (508) 759-4062. **E-Mail Address:** bournebravesgm@hotmail.com. **Website:** www.bournebraves.org. **President:** Thomas Fink. **General Manager:** Michael Carrier. **Head Coach:** Harvey Shapiro.

BREWSTER WHITE CAPS

Mailing Address: PO Box 2349, Brewster, MA 02631. **Telephone:** (508) 896-7442. **Fax:** (508) 896-9372. **E-Mail Address:** contact@brewsterwhitecaps.com, cgradone@hotmail.com. **Website:** www.brewsterwhitecaps.com. **President:** Claire Gradone. **General Manager:** Ned Monthie. **Head Coach:** Tom Myers (UC Santa Barbara).

CHATHAM ANGLERS

Mailing Address: PO Box 428, Chatham, MA 02633. **Telephone:** (508) 945-3841. **Fax:** (508) 945-4787. **E-Mail Address:** ruddock4@yahoo.com. **Website:** www.chathamas.com. **President:** Peter Troy. **General Manager:** Andy Ruddock. **Head Coach:** John Schiffner.

COTUIT KETTLEERS

Mailing Address: PO Box 411, Cotuit, MA 02635.

Telephone: (508) 428-3358. **Fax:** (508) 420-5584. **E-Mail Address:** info@kettleers.org. **Website:** www.kettleers.org. **President:** Paul Logan. **General Manager:** Bruce Murphy. **Head Coach:** Mike Roberts.

FALMOUTH COMMODORES

Mailing Address: PO Box 808 Falmouth, MA 02541. **Telephone:** (508) 472-7922. **Fax:** (508) 862-6011. **E-Mail Address:** jreilly@falcommodores.org. **Website:** www.falcommodores.org. **President:** Jerry Reilly. **General Manager:** Dan Dunn. **Head Coach:** Jeff Trundy.

HARWICH MARINERS

Mailing Address: PO Box 201, Harwich Port, MA 02646. **Telephone:** (508) 432-2000. **Fax:** (508) 432-5357. **E-Mail Address:** mehendy@comcast.net. **Website:** www.harwichmariners.org. **President:** Mary Henderson. **General Manager:** John Reid. **Head Coach:** Steve Englert (Boston College).

HYANNIS METS

Mailing Address: PO Box 852, Hyannis, MA 02601. **Telephone:** (508) 420-0962. **Fax:** (508) 428-8199. **E-Mail Address:** bbussiere@hyannismets.org. **Website:** www.hyannismets.org. **General Manager:** Bill Bussiere. **Head Coach:** Chad Gassman.

ORLEANS FIREBIRDS

Mailing Address: PO Box 504, Orleans, MA 02653. **Telephone:** (508) 255-0793. **Fax:** (508) 255-2237. **Website:** www.orleansfirebirds.com. **Acting President:** Bob Korn. **General Manager:** Sue Horton. **Head Coach:** Kelly Nicholson.

WAREHAM GATEMEN

Mailing Address: 71 Towhee Rd, Wareham, MA 02571. **Telephone:** (508) 748-0287. **Fax:** (508) 880-2602. **E-Mail Address:** tom@ggflaw.com. **Website:** www.gatemen.org. **President:** John Wylde. **General Manager:** Tom Gay. **Head Coach:** Cooper Farris (Mississippi Gulf Coast CC).

YARMOUTH-DENNIS RED SOX

Mailing Address: PO Box 814, South Yarmouth, MA 02664. **Telephone:** (508) 394-9387. **Fax:** (508) 398-2239. **E-Mail Address:** jimmartin321@yahoo.com. **Website:** www.ydredsox.org. **President:** Bob Mayo. **General Manager:** Jim Martin. **Head Coach:** Scott Pickler (Cypress, Calif., CC).

CLARK GRIFFITH COLLEGIATE LEAGUE

Mailing Address: 10915 Howland Dr, Reston, VA 20191. **Telephone:** (703) 860-0946. **Fax:** (703) 860-0143. **E-Mail Address:** info@clarkgriffithbaseball.com. **Website:** www.clarkgriffithbaseball.com.

Year Founded: 1945.

Commissioner: Tom Davis. **Executive Vice President:** Frank Fannan. **Treasurer:** Tom Dellinger. **Vice President/ Rules Enforcement:** Byron Zeigler.

Regular Season: 40 games. **2009 Opening Date:** June 1. **Closing Date:** July 28.

Playoff Format: Top four teams, double-elimination tournament.

Roster Limit: 25 (college-eligible players only).

ARLINGTON DIAMONDS

Mailing Address: Unavailable. **Telephone:** Unavailable. **E-Mail Address:** mojojojo@aol.com. **Website:** www.arlingtondiamonds.net. **President:** Dan Hodgson. **General Manager:** Unavailable. **Manager:** Unavailable.

BELTWAY BLUECAPS

Mailing Address: 6404 Ruffin Road, Chevy Chase, MD 20815. **Telephone:** (301) 461-0602. **E-Mail Address:** jonassinger@gmail.com. **Website:** www.bluecapsbaseball.com. **General Manager/Head Coach:** Jonas Singer.

CARNEY PIRATES

Mailing Address: 13309 Caswell Court, Clifton, VA 20124. **Telephone:** (571) 233-3994. **E-Mail Address:** bemerson@paulvi.net. **Website:** www.carneypirates.com. **General Manager/Head Coach:** Billy Emerson.

DC GRAYS

Mailing Address: 1406-B Leslie Avenue, Alexandria, VA 22301. **Telephone:** (202) 315-6945. **Fax:** (703) 684-9702. **E-Mail Address:** antonio@dcgrays.net. **Website:** www.dcgrays.net. **General Manager:** Antonio Scott. **Head Coach:** Doug Remer.

FAIRFAX NATIONALS

Mailing Address: 1844 Horseback Trail, Vienna, VA 22182. **Telephone:** (703) 201-3346. **E-Mail Address:** garyboss@fairfaxnationals.com. **Website:** www.fairfaxnationals.com. **President:** Jim Beck. **General Manager:** Gary Boss. **Head Coach:** Unavailable.

MCLEAN RAIDERS

Mailing Address: 10915 Howland Dr, Herndon, VA 20191. **Telephone:** (301) 447-3806. **E-Mail Address:** ericm_smith@email.msmary.edu. **Website:** www.mcelanraiders.com. **General Manager:** Frank Whitchy. **Head Coach:** Eric Smith.

VIENNA SENATORS

Mailing Address: 308 Hillwood Ave, Suite G2, Vienna, VA 22046. **Telephone:** (703) 534-5081. **Fax:** (703) 534-5085. **E-Mail Address:** cburr17@hotmail.com. **Website:** www.viennasenators.com. **President:** Bill McGillicuddy. **General Manager:** Bob Menefee. **Head Coach:** Chris Burr.

COASTAL PLAIN LEAGUE

Mailing Address: 4900 Waters Edge Dr, Suite 201, Raleigh, NC 27606. **Telephone:** (919) 852-1960. **Fax:** (919) 852-1973. **Website:** www.coastalplain.com.

Year Founded: 1997.

Chairman/CEO: Jerry Petitt. **President/Commissioner:** Pete Bock. **Assistant Commissioner:** Justin Sellers.

Division Structure: North—Edenton, Outer Banks, Peninsula, Petersburg. South—Columbia, Fayetteville, Florence, Wilmington, Wilson. West—Asheboro, Forest City, Gastonia, Martinsville, Thomasville.

Regular Season: 56 games (split schedule). **2009 Opening Date:** May 27. **Closing Date:** Aug. 4.

All-Star Game: July 21 at Wilmington, N.C.

Playoff Format: Eight-team tournament, August 6-14.

Roster Limit: 27 (college-eligible players only).

ASHEBORO COPPERHEADS

Mailing Address: PO Box 4006, Asheboro, NC 27204. **Telephone:** (336) 460-7018. **Fax:** (336) 629-2651. **E-Mail Address:** info@teamcopperhead.com. **Website:** www.teamcopperhead.com. **Owners:** Ronnie Pugh, Steve Pugh, Doug Pugh, Mike Pugh. **Co-General Managers:** Aaron Pugh, William Davis. **Head Coach:** Tim Murray.

COLUMBIA BLOWFISH

Mailing Address: PO Box 1328, Columbia, SC 29202.

Telephone: (803) 254-3474. **Fax:** (803) 254-4482. **E-Mail Address:** bill@blowfishbaseball.com. **Website:** www.blowfishbaseball.com. **Owner:** HWS Baseball V (Michael Savit, Bill Shanahan). **General Manager:** Skip Anderson. **Head Coach:** Tim Medlin.

EDENTON STEAMERS

Mailing Address: PO Box 86, Edenton, NC 27932. **Telephone:** (252) 482-4080. **Fax:** (252) 482-1717. **E-Mail Address:** edentonsteamers@hotmail.com. **Website:** www.edentonsteamers.com. **Owner:** Edenton-Chowan Community Foundation Inc. **President:** Katy Ebersole. **Head Coach:** Marty Smith (Angelo State).

FAYETTEVILLE SWAMPDOGS

Mailing Address: PO Box 64691, Fayetteville, NC 28306. **Telephone:** (910) 426-5900. **Fax:** (910) 426-3544. **E-Mail Address:** info@fayettevilleswampdogs.com. **Website:** www.goswampdogs.com. **Owner:** Lew Handelsman, Darrell Handelsman. **Head Coach/Director, Operations:** Darrell Handelsman.

FLORENCE REDWOLVES

Mailing Address: PO Box 809, Florence, SC 29503. **Telephone:** (843) 629-0700. **Fax:** (843) 629-0703. **E-Mail Address:** Jamie@florenceredwolves.com. **Website:** www.florenceredwolves.com. **President:** Kevin Barth. **General Manager:** Jamie Young. **Head Coach:** Wes Davis (Oral Roberts).

FOREST CITY OWLS

Mailing Address: PO Box 1062, Forest City, NC 28043. **Telephone:** (828) 245-0000. **Fax:** (828) 245-6666. **E-Mail Address:** jwolfe@forestcitybaseball.com. **Website:** www.forestcitybaseball.com. **President:** Ken Silver. **General Manager:** James Wolfe. **Head Coach:** Matt Hayes (Indiana).

GASTONIA GRIZZLIES

Mailing Address: PO Box 177, Gastonia, NC 28053. **Telephone:** (704) 866-8622. **Fax:** (704) 864-6122. **E-Mail Address:** jesse@gastoniagrizzlies.com. **Website:** www.gastoniagrizzlies.com. **President:** Ken Silver. **General Manager:** Jesse Cole. **Head Coach:** Eli Benefield.

MARTINSVILLE MUSTANGS

Mailing Address: PO Box 1112, Martinsville, VA 24114. **Telephone:** (276) 403-5250. **Fax:** (276) 403-5387. **E-Mail Address:** mustangsgm28@aol.com. **Website:** www.martinsvillemustangs.com. **General Manager:** Doug Gibson. **Head Coach:** Barry Powell.

OUTER BANKS DAREDEVILS

Mailing Address: PO Box 7596, Kill Devil Hills, NC 27948. **Telephone:** (252) 441-0600. **Fax:** (252) 441-0606. **E-Mail Address:** owen@obxdaredevils.com. **Website:** www.obxdaredevils.com. **Owner:** Marcus Felton. **General Manager:** Owen Hassell. **Head Coach:** Jeff Wicker (South Carolina—Salkehatchie).

PENINSULA PILOTS

Mailing Address: PO Box 7376, Hampton, VA 23666. **Telephone:** (757) 245-2222. **Fax:** (757) 245-8030. **E-Mail Address:** jeffscott@peninsulapilots.com. **Website:** www.peninsulapilots.com. **Owner:** Henry Morgan. **General Manager:** Jeffrey Scott. **Head Coach:** Hank Morgan.

PETERSBURG GENERALS

Mailing Address: 1981 Midway Ave, Petersburg, VA 23803. **Telephone:** (804) 722-0141. **Fax:** (804) 733-7370. **E-Mail Address:** pbgenerals@aol.com. **Website:** www.generals.petersburgsports.com. **President:** Larry Toombs. **General Manager, Baseball Operations:** Jeremy Toombs. **Head Coach:** Dave Carfley (California, Pa.).

THOMASVILLE HI-TOMS

Mailing Address: 7003 Ballpark Road, Thomaasville, NC 27360. **Telephone:** (336) 472-8667. **Fax:** (336) 472-7198. **E-Mail Address:** info@hitoms.com. **Website:** www.hitoms.com. **President:** Greg Suire. **General Manager:** Chris Marmo. **Head Coach:** Ray Greene (Pfeiffer).

WILMINGTON SHARKS

Mailing Address: PO Box 15233, Wilmington, NC 28412. **Telephone:** (910) 343-5621. **Fax:** (910) 343-8932. **E-Mail Address:** info@wilmingtonsharks.com. **Website:** www.wilmingtonsharks.com. **Owners:** Lew Handelsman, Darrell Handelsman, Conor Caloia. **General Manager:** Chris Reavis. **Head Coach:** Jake Tenhouse (Saint Joseph's College).

WILSON TOBS

Mailing Address: PO Box 633, Wilson, NC 27894. **Telephone:** (252) 291-8627. **Fax:** (252) 291-1224. **E-Mail Address:** wilsontobs@earthlink.net. **Website:** www.wilsontobs.com. **President:** Greg Turnage. **General Manager:** Ben Jones. **Head Coach:** Jeff Steele (Lubbock, Texas, Christian).

FLORIDA COLLEGIATE SUMMER LEAGUE

Mailing Address: 1778 N. Park Ave, Suite 201, Maitland, FL 32751. **Telephone:** (321) 206-9174. **Fax:** (407) 628-8535. **E-Mail Address:** info@floridaleague.com. **Website:** www.floridaleague.com.

Year Founded: 2004.

President: Sara Whiting. **Vice President:** Rob Sitz.

Division Structure: East—Orlando, Sanford, Winter Park. West—Belleview, Clermont, Leesburg.

Regular Season: 44 games. **2009 Opening Date:** June 4. **Closing Date:** July 29.

All-Star Game: July 20 at Sanford.

Playoff Format: Six-team, modified double-elimination tournament.

Roster Limit: 25 (college-eligible players only).

BELLEVIEW BULLDOGS

Operated through league office. **E-Mail Address:** belleviewbulldogs@floridaleague.com. **Head Coach:** Ricky Plante (Seminole, Fla., CC).

CLERMONT OUTLAWS

Operated through league office. **E-Mail Address:** clermontoutlaws@floridaleague.com. **President:** Tim Dye. **Head Coach:** Stephen Piercefield (Florida Southern).

LEESBURG LIGHTNING

Mailing Address: 318 South 2nd St, Leesburg, FL 34748 Telephone: (352) 728-9885. **E-Mail Address:** leesburglightning@floridaleague.com. **President:** Bruce Ericson. **Head Coach:** Frank Viola.

ORLANDO SUNS

Operated through league office. **E-Mail Address:** orlandosuns@floridaleague.com. **President:** Ken Gordon. **Head Coach:** Scott Benedict.

SANFORD RIVER RATS

Operated through league office. **E-Mail Address:** sanfordriverrats@floridaleague.com. **President:** Charles Davis. **Head Coach:** Kenne Brown.

WINTER PARK DIAMOND DAWGS

Operated through league office. **E-Mail Address:** winterparkdiamonddawgs@floridaleague.com. **President:** Joe Russell. **Head Coach:** Derek Wolfe (Central Florida).

GREAT LAKES LEAGUE

Mailing Address: 133 W. Winter St, Delaware, OH 43015. **Telephone:** (740) 368-3527. **Fax:** (740) 368-3999. **E-Mail Address:** kalance@greatlakesleague.org. **Website:** www.greatlakesleague.org.

Year Founded: 1986.

President, Commissioner: Kim Lance.

Regular Season: 36 games. **2009 Opening Date:** June 12.

Playoff Format: Top six teams meet in double-elimination tournament.

Roster Limit: 28 (college-eligible players only).

ANDERSON SERVANTS

Mailing Address: 8888 Fitness Lane, Fishers, IN, 46038. **Telephone:** (317) 842-2555. **Website:** www.servantsbaseball.com. **General Manager:** Greg Lymberopolous. **Head Coach:** Kyle Lymberopolous.

CINCINNATI STEAM

Mailing Address: 2745 Anderson Ferry Rd, Cincinnati, OH 45238. **Telephone:** (513) 922-4272. **Website:** www.cincinnatisteam.com. **General Manager:** Max McLeary. **Head Coach:** Dave Collins.

GRAND LAKE MARINERS

Mailing Address: 717 W. Walnut St, Coldwater, OH 45828. **Telephone:** (513) 207-5977. **Website:** www.grandlakemariners.com. **General Manager:** Wayne Miller. **Head Coach:** Unavailable.

HAMILTON JOES

Mailing Address: 6218 Greens Way, Hamilton, OH 45011. **E-mail address:** darrelgrisson@fuse.net. **General Manager:** Darrel Grisson. **Head Coach:** Darrel Grissom.

LAKE ERIE MONARCHS

Mailing Address: 26670 Cranden Drive, Perrysburg, OH 43551. **Telephone:** (734) 626-1166. **Website:** www.lakeeriemonarchs.com. **General Manager:** Jim DeSana. **Head Coach:** Jim DeSana.

LICKING COUNTY SETTLERS

Mailing Address: 958 Camden Drive, Newark, OH 43055. **Telephone:** (740) 344-1063. **Website:** www.settlersbaseball.com. **General Manager:** Dave Froelich. **Head Coach:** Kyle Sobecki.

LIMA LOCOS

Mailing Address: 3588 South Conant Rd, Spencerville, OH 45887. **Telephone:** (419) 647-5242. **Website:** www.limalocos.com. **General Manager:** Steve Meyer. **Head Coach:** Rob Livchak.

SOUTHERN OHIO COPPERHEADS

Mailing Address: PO Box 442, Athens, OH 45701. **Telephone:** (740) 541-9284. **Website:** www.copperheadsbaseball.com. **General Manager:** David Palmer. **Head Coach:** Mike Florak.

STARK COUNTY TERRIERS

Mailing Address: 1019 35th St Northwest, Canton, OH, 44709. **Telephone:** (330) 492-9220. **Website:** www.terriersbaseballclub.com. **General Manager:** Greg Trbovich. **Head Coach:** Eric Bunnell.

XENIA ATHLETES IN ACTION

Mailing Address: 651 Taylor Dr, Xenia, OH 45385. **Telephone:** (937) 352-1239. **E-Mail Address:** john.mclaughlin@aia.com. **Website:** www.aiabaseball.org. **General Manager:** John McLaughlin. **Head Coach:** Josh Hulin.

JAYHAWK LEAGUE

Mailing Address: 865 Fabrique, Wichita, KS 67218. **Telephone:** (316) 942-6333. **Fax:** (316) 942-2009. **Website:** www.jayhawkbaseballleague.org.

Year Founded: 1976.

Commissioner: Bob Considine. **President:** J.D. Schneider. **Vice President:** Frank Leo. **Public Relations/Statistician:** Gary Karr. **Secretary:** Christi Billups.

Regular Season: 32 games. **2009 Opening Date:** June 4.

Playoff Format: Top two teams qualify for National Baseball Congress World Series in Wichita, KS.

Roster Limit: 30 to begin season; 28 at midseason.

DERBY TWINS

Mailing Address: 1245 N. Pine Grove, Wichita, KS 67212. **Telephone:** (316) 992-3623. **Fax:** 316-667-2286. **E-mail:** derbytwins@earthlink.net. **Website:** www.derbytwins.com. **General Manager:** Jeff Wells. **Head Coach:** Unavailable.

DODGE CITY A'S

Mailing Address: 2914 Center, Dodge City, KS 67801. **Telephone:** 620-339-5231. **E-mail:** no1teammom@hotmail.com. **General Manager:** Doug Bell. **Head Coach:** Phil Stevenson.

EL DORADO BRONCOS

Mailing Address: 865 Fabrique, Wichita, KS 67218. **Telephone:** (316) 687-2309. **Fax:** (316) 942-2009. **Website:** www.eldoradobroncos.org. **General Manager:** J.D. Schneider. **Head Coach:** Steve Johnson.

HAYS LARKS

Mailing Address: 2715 Walnut., Hays, KS 67601. **Telephone:** (785) 259-1430. **Fax:** (630) 848-2236. **E-Mail Address:** cbieber@sbcglobal.net. **General Manager:** Frank Leo. **Head Coach:** Frank Leo.

LIBERAL BEEJAYS

Mailing Address: PO Box 793, Liberal, KS 67901. **Telephone:** (620) 624-1904. **Fax:** (620) 624-1906. **General Manager:** Bob Carlisle.

M.I.N.K. LEAGUE

(Missouri, Iowa, Nebraska, Kansas)

Mailing Address: 3350 Chatham Avenue, St. Joseph, MO, 64506. **Telephone:** (816) 232-7964, (816) 294-6677. **Fax:** (660) 646-2107. **Email Address:** jodo1986@aol.com. **Website:** www.minkleaguebaseball.com.

Year Founded: 1995.

Commissioner: Linden Black. **President:** Bob Steinkamp (Beatrice Bruins). **Vice President:** Liz Fechtig (Chillicothe Mudcats). **Secretary:** Jim Hamlin.

Regular Season: 30 games. **2009 Opening Date:** May 31. **Closing Date:** July 23.

Playoff Format: Top team qualifies for National Baseball Congress World Series in Wichita.

Roster Limit: None.

BEATRICE BRUINS

Mailing Address: PO Box 2, Beatrice, NE 68310. **Telephone:** (402) 223-3081. **E-Mail address:** ksteinkamp@alltel.net. **Website:** www.beatricebaseball.com. **General Manager/Head Coach:** Bob Steinkamp.

CHILLICOTHE MUDCATS

Mailing Address: PO Box 1155, Chillicothe, MO 64601. **Telephone:** (660) 646-2165. **Fax:** (660) 646-6933. **E-Mail Address:** hitit@chillicothemudcats.com. **Website:** www.chillicothemudcats.com. **General Manager:** Liz Fechtig. **Head Coach:** Jud Kindle.

CLARINDA A'S

Mailing Address: 225 East Lincoln, Clarinda, IA 61632. **Telephone:** (712) 542-4272. **E-Mail Address:** memrse@heartland.net. **Website:** www.clarindaiowa-as-baseball.org. **General Manager:** Merle Eberly. **Head Coach:** Ryan Eberly.

FELLOWSHIP OF CHRISTIAN ATHLETES GRAYS

Mailing Address: FCA Baseball Office, 8701 Loeds Road, Kansas City, MO 64129. **Telephone:** (816) 876-2285. **Fax:** 816-921-8755. **E-Mail Address:** jreed@fca.org. **Website:** www.fcabaseball.org. **General Manager/Head Coach:** Joe Reed.

JOPLIN OUTLAWS

Mailing Address: 5860 North Pearl, Joplin, MO 64801. **Telephone:** (417) 825-4218. **E-Mail address:** merains@mchsi.com. **Website:** www.joplinoutlaws.com. **General Manager:** Mark Rains. **Head Coach:** Chris Reddout.

NEVADA GRIFFONS

Mailing Address: PO Box 601. **Telephone:** (417) 667-6159. **E-Mail address:** jpost@morrisonpost.com. **Website:** www.nevadagriffons.org. **President:** Padrio Cladio. **General Manager:** Jeff Post. **Head Coach:** Ryan Mansfield.

OZARK GENERALS

Mailing Address: 1336 West Plainview, Springfield, MO 65810. **Telephone:** (417) 881-2920. **Fax:** (417) 881-2982. **E-Mail Address:** rda160@excite.com. **Website:** www.generalsbaseballclub.com. **General Manager/Head Coach:** Rusty Aton.

ST. JOSEPH MUSTANGS

Mailing Address: 2600 SW Parkway, St. Joseph, MO 64503. **Telephone:** (816) 279-7856. **E-Mail address:** Unavailable. **Website:** www.stjoemustangs.com. **President:** Dan Gerson. **General Manager:** Rick Muntean. **Head Coach:** Matt Johnson.

SEDALIA BOMBERS

Mailing Address: 2201 S. Grand, Sedalia, MO 65301. **Telephone:** (660) 287-4722. **E-Mail address:** jkindle@knobnoster.k12.mo.us. **Website:** www.sedaliabombers.com. **President/General Manager/Head Coach:** Jud Kindle. **Vice President:** Ross Dey. **Head Coach:** Jud Kendall.

TOPEKA GOLDEN GIANTS

Mailing Address: 3512 SE Colorado, Topeka, KS 66605. **Telephone:** (785) 266-7414. **E-Mail Address:** treb14@aol.com. **Website:** www.leaguelineup.com/goldengiants. **General Manager:** Brett Cowdin. **Head Coach:** Daniel Esposito.

MOUNTAIN COLLEGIATE LEAGUE

E-Mail Address: info@mcbl.net. **Website:** www.mcbl.net.

Year Founded: 2005.

Directors: Kurt Colicchio, Ron Kailey, Ray Klesh, Heidi Peterson.

Regular Season: 48 games. **2009 Opening Date:** May 30. **Closing Date:** Aug. 3.

Playoff Format: Second- and third-place teams meet in one-game playoff; winner advances to best-of-three championship series against first-place team.

Roster limit: 25 (college-eligible players only).

CHEYENNE GRIZZLIES

Telephone: (307) 631-7337. **E-Mail Address:** rkaide@aol.com. **Website:** www.cheyennegrizzlies.com. **Owner/General Manager:** Ron Kailey. **Head Coach:** Scott Laverty (Redlands, Calif.).

FORT COLLINS FOXES

Telephone: (970) 225-9564. **E-Mail Address:** info@fortcollinsfoxes.com. **Website:** www.fortcollinsfoxes.com. **Owner/General Manager:** Kurt Colicchio. **Head Coach:** Michael Bender (Montreat College, N.C.).

GREELEY GRAYS

Telephone: (303) 870-2523. **E-Mail Address:** rklesh@earthlink.net. **Website:** www.greeleygrays.com. **Owner/General Manager:** Ray Klesh. **Head Coach:** Dan Zuberbier.

LARAMIE COLTS

Telephone: (307) 742-2191. **E-Mail Address:** laramiecolts@msn.com. **Website:** www.laramiecolts.com. **General Manager:** Heidi Peterson. **Head Coach:** Ryan Goodwin (Northeastern, Colo., JC).

NEW ENGLAND COLLEGIATE LEAGUE

Mailing Address: 37 Grammar School Dr, Danbury, CT 06811. **Website:** www.necbl.com.

Year Founded: 1993.

Commissioner: Mario Tiani.

Division Structure: East—Lowell, Manchester, Newport, New Bedford, North Shore, Sanford. West—Danbury, Holyoke, Keene, North Adams, Pittsfield, Vermont.

Regular Season: 42 games. **2009 Opening Date:** June 4. **Closing Date:** July 31.

All-Star Game: July 18 at Holyoke.

Playoff Format: Top four teams in each division meet in best-of-three quarterfinals; winners meet in best-of-three divisional championship. Winners meet in best-of-three final for league championship.

Roster Limit: 25 (college-eligible players only).

DANBURY WESTERNERS

Mailing Address: 5 Old Hayrake Rd, Danbury, CT 06811. **Telephone:** (203) 797-0897. **Fax:** (203) 792-6177. **Website:** www.danburywesterners.com. **E-Mail Address:** westerners1@aol.com. **General Manager:** Terry Whalen. **Head Coach:** Jamie Shevchik.

HOLYOKE SOX

Mailing Address: 18 Cranberry Lane, Dedham, MA 02026. **Telephone:** (413) 652-9014. **Website:** www.holyokesox.com. **General Manager:** Barry Wadsworth. **Head Coach:** Darryl Morhardt.

KEENE SWAMP BATS

Mailing Address: 31 W. Surry Rd, Keene, NH 03431. **Telephone:** (603) 357-5464. **Fax:** (603) 357-5090. **Website:** www.swampbats.com. **General Manager:** Vicki Bacon. **Head Coach:** Marty Testo.

LOWELL ALL-AMERICANS

Mailing Address: PO Box 2228, Lowell, MA 01851. **Telephone:** (978) 454-5058. **Fax:** (978) 251-1211. **E-Mail Address:** info@lowellallamericans.com. **Website:** www.lowellallamericans.com. **General Manager:** Harry Ayotte. **Head Coach:** Jeff Kane.

MANCHESTER SILKWORMS

Mailing Address: 16 West St, Manchester, CT 06040. **Telephone:** (860) 559-3126. **Fax:** (860) 432-1665. **Website:** www.manchestersilkworms.org. **General Manager:** Ed Slegeski. **Head Coach:** Al Leyva.

NEW BEDFORD BAY SOX

Mailing Address: 4 Blinkoff Ct., Torrington, CT 06790. **Telephone/Fax:** (860) 482-0450. **Website:** www.nbbaysox.com. **General Manager:** Kirk Fredriksson. **Head Coach:** Unavailable.

NEWPORT GULLS

Mailing Address: PO Box 777, Newport, RI 02840. **Telephone:** (401) 845-6832. **Website:** www.newportgulls.com. **General Manager:** Chuck Paiva. **Head Coach:** Mike Coombs.

NORTH ADAMS STEEPLECATS

Mailing Address: PO Box 540, North Adams, MA 01247. **Telephone:** (413) 652-1031. **Website:** www.steeplecats.com. **General Manager:** Sean McGrath. **Head Coach:** Jeff Verplancke.

NORTH SHORE NAVIGATORS

Mailing Address: Frasier Field, Lynn, Mass. **Telephone:** Unavailable. **E-Mail Address:** philip@nsnavs.com. **Website:** www.nsnavs.com. **President:** Philip Rosenfield. **Head Coach:** Jason Falcon.

PITTSFIELD AMERICAN DEFENDERS

Mailing Address: 2 South St, Pittsfield, MA 01201. **Telephone:** (603) 883-2255. **Fax:** (603) 883-0880. **Website:** www.americandefenders.us. **General Manager:** Jon Tosches. **Head Coach:** Dr. Carroll Land.

SANFORD MAINERS

Mailing Address: PO Box 26, Sanford, ME 04073. **Telephone:** (207) 324-0010. **Fax:** (207) 324-2227. **Website:** www.sanfordmainers.com. **General Manager:** Neil Olson. **Head Coach:** Joe Brown.

VERMONT MOUNTAINEERS

Mailing Address: PO Box 586, Montpelier, VT 05602. **Telephone:** (802) 223-5224. **Website:** www.thevermontmountaineers.com. **General Manager:** Brian Gallagher. **Head Coach:** Moock Troy.

NEW YORK COLLEGIATE BASEBALL LEAGUE

Summer Address: 28 Dunbridge Heights, Fairport, NY 14450. **Winter Address:** PO Box 2516, Tarpon Springs, FL 34688. **Telephone:** (585) 455-3667. **Website:** www.nycbl.com.

Year Founded: 1978.

Commissioner: Dave Chamberlain. **President:** Stan Lehman. **Vice President:** Mark Perlo. **Treasurer:** Dan Russo. **Secretary:** Darin Williams.

Member Clubs: East—Amsterdam Mohawks, Bennington Bombers, Glens Falls Golden Eagles, Mohawk Valley Diamondawgs, Saratoga Phillies, Watertown Wizards. West—Alleghany County Nitros, Bolivar Oilers, Elmira Pioneers, Geneva Red Wings, Brockport Riverbats, Hornell Dodgers, Niagara Power, Webster Yankees.

Regular Season: 42 games. **2009 Opening Date:** June 4. **Closing Date:** August 9.

All-Star Game: July 14 at Shuttleworth Park; Amsterdam, NY.

Playoff Format: Eight teams, top four in each division. Best-of-three championship series format follows best of three divisional semifinals and finals.

Roster Limit: 25 (college-eligible players only).

NORTHWOODS LEAGUE

Office Address: 2900 4th St. SW, Rochester, MN 55902. **Telephone:** (507) 536-4579. **Fax:** (507) 536-4597. **Website:** www.northwoodsleague.com. **E-Mail Address:** curt@northwoodsleague.com

Year Founded: 1994.

President: Dick Radatz Jr.

Director of Operations: Curt Carstensen.

Division Structure: North—Alexandria, Brainerd, Duluth, Mankato, Rochester, St. Cloud, Thunder Bay. South—Battle Creek, Eau Claire, Green Bay, La Crosse, Madison, Rochester, Waterloo, Wisconsin.

Regular Season: 68 games (split schedule). **2009 Opening Date:** May 28. **Closing Date:** Aug. 16.

All-Star Game: July 21 at Thunder Bay.

Playoff Format: First-half and second-half division winners meet in best-of-three series. Winners meet in best-of-three series for league championship.

Roster Limit: 26 (college-eligible players only).

ALEXANDRIA BEETLES

Mailing Address: 1210 Broadway, Suite #100, Alexandria, MN 56308. **Telephone:** (320) 763-8151. **Fax:** (320) 763-8152. **E-Mail Address:** beetles@alexandriabeetles.com. **Website:** www.alexandriabeetles.com. **General Manager:** Shawn Reilly. **Head Coach:** Seth Maier (Wisconsin-Stout).

BATTLE CREEK BOMBERS

Mailing Address: 189 Bridge Street, Battle Creek, MI 49017. **Telephone:** (269) 962-0735. **Fax:** (269) 962-0741. **Email Address:** info@battlecreekbombers.com Website: www.battlecreekbombers.com. **General Manager:** Rick Lindau. **Head Coach:** Tom Fleenor (USC Sumter).

BRAINERD BLUE THUNDER

Mailing Address: PO Box 431, Brainerd, MN 56401. **Telephone:** (218) 824-3474. **Fax:** (320) 255-5228. **E-Mail Address:** info@lunkersbaseball.com. **Website:** www.brainerdbluethunder.com. **General Manager:** Joel Sutherland. **Head Coach:** Ryan Levendoski (Western Tech, Wis.).

DULUTH HUSKIES

Mailing Address: 207 W. Superior St, Suite 206, Holiday Center Mall, Duluth, MN 55802. **Telephone:** (218) 786-9909. **Fax:** (218) 786-9001. **E-Mail Address:** huskies@duluthhuskies.com. **Website:** www.duluthhuskies.com. **General Manager:** Craig Smith. **Head Coach:** Adam Stahl.

EAU CLAIRE EXPRESS

Mailing Address: 108 E. Grand Ave, Eau Claire, WI

54701. **Telephone:** (715) 839-7788. **Fax:** (715) 839-7676. **E-Mail Address:** info@eauclaireexpress.com. **Website:** www.eauclaireexpress.com. **General Manager:** Brett Schroedel. **Head Coach:** Dale Varsho.

GREEN BAY BULLFROGS

Mailing Address: 1306 Main Street, Green Bay, WI 54302. **Telephone:** (920) 497-7225. **Fax:** (920) 437-3551. **Email Address:** info@greenbaybullfrogs.com. **Website:** www.greenbaybullfrogs.com. **General Manager:** Dave Kost. **Head Coach:** Ronnie Nedset.

LA CROSSE LOGGERS

Mailing Address: 1223 Caledonia St, La Crosse, WI 54603. **Telephone:** (608) 796-9553. **Fax:** (608) 796-9032. **E-Mail Address:** info@lacrosseloggers.com. **Website:** www.lacrosseloggers.com. **General Manager:** Chris Goodell. **Assistant General Manager:** Ben Kapanke. **Head Coach:** Andy McKay.

MADISON MALLARDS

Mailing Address: 2920 N. Sherman Ave, Madison, WI 53704. **Telephone:** (608) 246-4277. **Fax:** (608) 246-4163. **E-Mail Address:** vern@mallardsbaseball.com. **Website:** www.mallardsbaseball.com. **General Manager:** Vern Stenman. **Head Coach:** C.J. Thieleke (Madison Area Tech).

MANKATO MOONDOGS

Mailing Address: 310 Belle Ave, Suite L-8, Mankato, MN 56001. **Telephone:** (507) 625-7047. **Fax:** (507) 625-7059. **E-Mail Address:** office@mankatomoondogs.com. **Website:** www.mankatomoondogs.com. **General Manager:** Kyle Mrozek. **Head Coach:** Mike Orchard (Central Arizona).

ROCHESTER HONKERS

Mailing Address: PO Box 482, Rochester, MN 55903. **Telephone:** (507) 289-1170. **Fax:** (507) 289-1866. **E-Mail Address:** honkers@rochesterhonkers.com. **Website:** www.rochesterhonkers.com. **General Manager:** Dan Litzinger. **Head Coach:** Rusty McNamara (UC Riverside).

ST. CLOUD RIVER BATS

Mailing Address: PO Box 5059, St. Cloud, MN 56302. **Telephone:** (320) 240-9798. **Fax:** (320) 255-5228. **E-Mail Address:** info@riverbats.com. **Website:** www.riverbats.com. **General Manager:** Marc Jerzak. **Head Coach:** Tony Arnerich (UC Berkeley).

THUNDER BAY BORDER CATS

Mailing Address: PO Box 29105, Thunder Bay, Ontario P7B 6P9. **Telephone:** (807) 766-2287. **Fax:** (807) 345-8299. **E-Mail Address:** baseball@tbaytel.net. **Website:** www.bordercatsbaseball.com. **General Manager:** Brad Jorgenson. **Head Coach:** Bobby Meier.

WATERLOO BUCKS

Mailing Address: PO Box 4124, Waterloo, IA 50704. **Telephone:** (319) 232-0500. **Fax:** (319) 232-0700. **E-Mail Address:** waterloobucks@waterloobucks.com. **Website:** www.waterloobucks.com. **General Manager:** Dan Corbin. **Head Coach:** Pete Lauritson (North Iowa Area CC).

WISCONSIN WOODCHUCKS

Mailing Address: PO Box 6157, Wausau, WI 54402. **Telephone:** (715) 845-5055. **Fax:** (715) 845-5015. **E-Mail Address:** info@woodchucks.com. **Website:** www.woodchucks.com. **General Manager:** Ryan Treu. **Head Coach:** Brandon Steele (Tusculum).

PACIFIC INTERNATIONAL LEAGUE

Mailing Address: 4400 26th Ave W, Seattle, WA 98199. **Telephone:** (206) 623-8844. **Fax:** (206) 623-8361. **E-Mail Address:** spotter@potterprinting.com. **Website:** www.pacificinternationalleague.com.

Year Founded: 1992

President: Steve Konek. **Commissioner:** Brian Gooch. **Secretary:** Steve Potter. **Treasurer:** Mark Dow.

Member Clubs: Everett Merchants, Seattle Studs.

Regular Season: 28 league games. **2009 Opening Date:** June 1.

Playoff Format: Top two teams playoff; winner goes to NBC World Series in Wichita, Kan.

Roster Limit: 30; 25 eligible for games (players must be at least 18 years old).

PROSPECT LEAGUE

Mailing Address: 5675 Feder Road, Columbus, OH 43228. **Telephone:** (614) 339-1164. **E-Mail Address:** commissioner@prospectleague.com. **Website:** www.prospectleague.com.

Year Founded: 1963 (as Central Illinois Collegiate League).

Acting Commissioner: Frank Pergolizzi.

Regular Season: 54 games. **2009 Opening Date:** June 4. **Closing Date:** Aug. 8.

All-Star Game: July 15 in Springfield, Illinois.

Playoff Format: Best-of-three; East division vs. West division champions.

Roster Limit: 26

BUTLER BLUESOX

Mailing Address: 1347 Gabby Avenue, Washington, PA 15301. **Telephone:** (724) 263-9874. **E-Mail Address:** butlerbluesox@ymail.com. **Website:** www.butlerbluesox.net. **General Manager:** Leo Trich. **Assistant GM:** Matthew Cunningham. **Head Coach:** Unavailable.

CHILLICOTHE PAINTS

Mailing Address: 59 N. Paint Street, Chillicothe, OH 45601. **Telephone:** (740) 773-8326. **Fax:** (740) 773-8338. **E-Mail Address:** bwickline@chillicothepaints.com. **Website:** www.chillicothepaints.com. **General Manager:** Chris Hanners. **President:** Shirley Bandy. **Vice President/General Manager:** Bryan Wickline. **Head Coach:** Unavailable.

DANVILLE DANS

Mailing Address: PO Box 1041 Danville, IL 62834. **Telephone:** (217) 446-5521. **Fax:** (217) 446-9995. **E-Mail Address:** jeaniecooke@danvilleareainfo.com. **Owners/General Managers:** Rick Kurth and Jeanie Cooke. **Head Coach:** Pete Paciorek (Principia, Calif., College).

DUBOIS COUNTY BOMBERS

Mailing Address: PO Box 332, Huntingburg, IN 47542. **Telephone:** (812) 683-3700. **E-Mail Address:** dcbombes@psci.net. **General Manager:** John Bigness. **Head Coach:** Brian Smiley.

DUPAGE DRAGONS

Mailing Address: PO Box 3076, Lisle, IL 60532. **Telephone:** (630) 241-2255. **Fax:** (708) 784-1468. **E-Mail Address:** mike@madisongroupltd.com. **Website:** www.dupagedragons.com. **General Manager:** Mike Thiessen. **Head Coach:** Mark Viramontes (San Diego).

HANNIBAL CAVEMEN

Mailing Address: 403 Warren Barrett Drive, Hannibal,

MO 63401. **Telephone:** (573) 211-1010. **Fax:** (573) 221-5296. **E-Mail Address:** hannibalbaseball@sbcglobal.com. **Website:** www.hannibalcavemen.com. **Owners:** Roland Hemond, Bob Hemond, Larry Owens and Dave Trogan. **Director of Baseball Operations:** Jay Hemond. **Head Coach:** Unavailable.

LORAIN NORTHCOAST KNIGHTS

Mailing Address: 578 East 30th Street, Willowick, OH 44095. **Telephone:** (440) 339-3291. **E-Mail Address:** jhayes2924@hotmail.com. **Website:** www.northcoastknights.com. **Owner:** Josh Hayes. **Director of Baseball Operations:** Mike Perry. **Head Coach:** Andy Jarvis.

QUINCY GEMS

Mailing Address: 300 Civic Center Plaza, Quincy, IL 62301. **Telephone:** (217) 223-1000. **Fax:** (217) 223-1330. **E-Mail Address:** rebbing@quincygems.com. **Website:** www.quincygems.com. **General Manager:** Rob Ebbing. **Head Coach:** Chris Martin.

RICHMOND

Mailing Address: 201 NW 13th Street, Richmond, IN 47374. **Telephone:** (765) 966-9999. **E-Mail Address:** duke@side1music.com. **Director of Business Operations:** Duke Ward. **Director of Baseball Operations:** John Cate. **Head Coach:** Unavailable.

SLIPPERY ROCK SLIDERS

Mailing Address: PO Box 496, Slippery Rock, PA 16057. **Telephone:** (724) 458-8831. **E-Mail Address:** mbencic@zoominternet.net. **Website:** www.theslipperyrocksliders.com. **Owner/General Manager:** Mike Bencic. **Head Coach:** Unavailable.

SPRINGFIELD SLIDERS

Mailing Address: 1415 North Grand Ave. E, Suite B, Springfield, IL 62702. **Telephone:** (217) 679-3511. **E-Mail Address:** info@springfieldsliders.com. **Website:** www.springfieldsliders.com. **General Manager:** Darren Feller. **Head Coach:** Jack Clark.

SOUTHERN COLLEGIATE BASEBALL LEAGUE

Mailing Address: 102 Pine Lake Drive, Indian Trail, NC 28110.

Telephone: (704) 635-7126. **Fax:** (704) 847-1455. **E-Mail Address:** SCBLCommissioner@aol.com. **Website:** www.scbl.org.

Year Founded: 1999.

Commissioner: Bill Capps. **President:** Jeff Carter. **Vice President:** Brian Swords. **Vice President of Marketing & Development:** Mark Dudley. **Secretary:** Larry Tremitiere. **Treasurer:** Brenda Templin.

Regular Season: 42 games. **2009 Opening Date:** June 1. **Closing Date:** July 23.

Playoff Format: No. 1 seed plays host to four-team, double-elimination tournament; begins July 23.

Roster Limit: 30 (College-eligible players only).

ASHEVILLE REDBIRDS

Mailing Address: PO Box 17637, Asheville, NC 28816. **Telephone:** (828) 691-3679. **General Manager:** Bill Stewart. **Head Coach:** Ken Bagwell.

CAROLINA CHAOS

Mailing Address: 142 Orchard Drive, Liberty, SC 29657. **Telephone:** (864) 843-3232, (864) 901-4331. **E-Mail Address:** brian_swords@carolinachaos.com. **Website:** www.carolinachaos.com. **General Manager/Coach:** Brian Swords (Southern Wesleyan, S.C.).

CAROLINA THUNDER

Mailing Address: 1443 Wedgefield Drive, Rock Hill, SC 29732. **Telephone:** (803) 366-2207, (803) 517-6626. **Fax:** (803) 980-7438. **E-Mail Address:** Ltrem@comporium.net. **General Manager:** Larry Tremitiere. **Head Coach:** Unavailable.

LAKE NORMAN COPPERHEADS

Mailing Address: PO Box 928, Cornelius, NC 28031. **Telephone:** (704) 892-1041, (704) 564-9211. **E-Mail Address:** jcarter@standpointtech.com. **Website:** www.copperheadsports.org. **General Manager:** Jeff Carter. **Head Coach:** Derek Shoe (Pfeiffer, N.C.).

MORGANTON AGGIES

Mailing Address: PO Box 3448, Morganton, NC 28680. **Telephone:** (828) 438-5351. **Fax:** (828) 438-5350. **E-Mail Address:** gwleonhardt@aol.com. **General Manager:** Gary Leonhardt. **Head Coach:** Anthony Dellinger (Wofford College).

SPARTANBURG BLUE EAGLES

Mailing Address: PO Box 4786, Cowpens, SC 29305. **Telephone:** (864) 444-4348. **E-Mail Address:** markdudley51@gmail.com. **General Manager:** Mark Dudley. **Head Coach:** Unavailable.

TENNESSEE TORNADO

Mailing Address: 1995 Roan Creek Road, Mountain City, TN 37683. **Telephone:** (423) 727-9111. **E-Mail Address:** tdr@maymead.com. **Owner:** Wiley Roark. **General Manager:** Tom Reese. **Head Coach:** Phillip Al-Mateen (East Tennessee State University).

TEXAS COLLEGIATE LEAGUE

Mailing Address: 735 Plaza Blvd, Suite 200, Coppell, TX 75019. **Telephone:** (817) 339-9367. **Fax:** (817) 339-9309. **E-Mail Address:** info@texascollegiateleague.com. **Website:** www.texascollegiateleague.com.

Year Founded: 2004.

Commissioner: Darren Hall. **Supervisor, Umpires:** John Ausmus.

Regular Season: 48 games. **2009 Opening Date:** Unavailable.

Playoff Format: Top two teams in each division meet in best-of-three division series. Winners meet in best-of-three series for league championship.

Roster Limit: 25 (College-eligible players only).

BRAZOS VALLEY BOMBERS

Mailing Address: 405 Mitchell St, Bryan, TX 77801. **Telephone:** (979) 799-PLAY. **Fax:** (979) 779-2398. **E-Mail Address:** info@bvbombers.com. **Website:** www.bvbombers.com. **Owners:** Uri Geva, Kfir Jackson. **General Manager:** Mike Lieberman. **Head Coach:** Brent Almbaugh.

COPPELL COPPERHEADS

Mailing Address: 509 W. Bethel Rd, Suite 100, Coppell, TX 75019. **Telephone:** (972) 745-2929. **E-Mail Address:** info@tclcopperheads.com. **Website:** www.tclcopperheads.com. **President:** Steve Pratt. **General Manager:** Jamie Murdock. **Head Coach:** J.T. Blair.

EAST TEXAS PUMP JACKS

Mailing Address: 1100 Stone Road, Suite 120, Kilgore, TX 75662. **Telephone:** (903) 218-GO ET. **Website:** www.pumpjacksbaseball.com. **General Manager:** Mike Lieberman. **Head Coach:** Stan Phelps.

MCKINNEY MARSHALS

Mailing Address: 6151 Alma Rd, McKinney, TX 75070. **Telephone:** (972) 747-8248. **Fax:** (972) 747-9231. **E-Mail Address:** info@tclmarshals.com. **Website:** www.tclmarshals.com. **Owner:** David Craig. **Owner/President:** Mike Henneman. **Executive Vice President/General Manager:** Ray Ricchi. **Director of Player Personnel:** Shayne Currin. **Head Coach:** Jim Gatewood.

VICTORIA GENERALS

Mailing Address: 3708 North Navarro, Suite B, Victoria, TX 77904. **Telephone:** (361) 485-9522. **FAX:** (361) 485-0936. **E-Mail Address:** info@baseballinvictoria.com. **Website:** www.victoriagenerals.com. **President:** Tracy Young. **Vice President of Baseball Operations:** Brad Haynes. **Head Coach:** Chris Clemons.

VALLEY LEAGUE

Mailing Address: 58 Bethel Green Rd, Staunton, VA 24401. **Telephone:** (540) 885-8901. **Fax:** (540) 885-2068. **E-Mail Addresses:** dbiery@valleybaseballleague.com, tthompson@valleybaseballleague.com. **Website:** www.valleyleaguebaseball.com.

Year Founded: 1961.

President: David Biery. **Executive Vice President:** Todd Thompson. **Media Relations Director:** Scott Musa.

Regular Season: 42 games. **2009 Opening Date:** May 31. **Closing Date:** July 27.

All-Star Game: July 6 at Covington.

Playoff Format: Eight teams; best-of-three quarterfinals and semifinals; best-of-five finals.

Roster Limit: 28 (college eligible players only).

COVINGTON LUMBERJACKS

Mailing Address: PO Box 171, Low Moor, VA 24457. **Telephone:** (540) 691-6351. **E-Mail Address:** covingtonlumberjacks@valleyleaguebaseball.com; jrh@alcovamortgage.com. **Website:** www.lumberjacksbaseball.com. **Owners:** Dizzy Garten, Jason Helmintoller. **Head Coach:** Andy Chalot.

FAQUIER GATORS

Mailing Address: PO Box 740 Warrenton, VA 20188. **Telephone:** (540) 341-3454. **Fax:** (540) 526-9444. **E-Mail Address:** gators@fauquiergators.org. **Website:** www.faquiergators.org. **Owners:** Alison Athey, Cecil Campbell. **Head Coach:** Paul Koch.

FRONT ROYAL CARDINALS

Mailing Address: 382 Morgans Ridge Road, Front Royal, VA 22630. **Telephone:** (540) 636-1882, (540) 671-9184. **Fax:** (540) 635-8746. **E-Mail Address:** frontroyalcardinals@valleyleaguebaseball.com. **Website:** www.frcardinalbaseball.com. **President:** Linda Keen. **Head Coach:** Bob Brotherton.

HARRISONBURG TURKS

Mailing Address: 1489 S. Main St, Harrisonburg, VA 22801. **Telephone:** (540) 434-5919. **E-Mail Address:** turksbaseball@hotmail.com. **Website:** www.harrisonburgturks.com. **Operations Manager:** Teresa Wease. **GM/Head Coach:** Bob Wease.

HAYMARKET SENATORS

Mailing Address: 42020 Village Center Plaza, Suite 120-50, Stoneridge, VA 20105. **Telephone:** (703) 989-5009. **E-Mail Address:** haymarketsenators@valleyleaguebaseball.com. **Website:** www.haymarketbaseball.com. **President/General Manager:** Pat Malone. **Head Coach:** Billy Shields.

LURAY WRANGLERS

Mailing Address: 1203 E. Main St, Luray, VA 22835. **Telephone:** (540) 743-3338. **E-Mail Addresses:** luraywranglers@valleyleaguebaseball.com. **Website:** www.luraywranglers.com. **President:** Bill Turner. **General Manager:** Greg Moyer. **Head Coach:** Mike Bocock.

NEW MARKET REBELS

Mailing Address: PO Box 1127, New Market, VA 22844. **Telephone:** (540) 740-4247, (540) 740-8569. **E-Mail Address:** nmrebels@shentel.net. **Website:** www.rebelsbaseball.biz. **President/General Manager:** Bruce Alger. **Executive Vice President:** Jim Weissenborn. **Head Coach:** Evan Brannon (Randolph Macon, Va.).

ROCKBRIDGE RAPIDS

Mailing Address: P.O Box 600, Lexington, VA 24450. **Telephone:** (540) 460-7502. **E-Mail Address:** rockbridgerapids@valleyleaguebaseball.com. **Website:** www.rebelsbaseball.biz. **General Manager:** Ken Newman. **Head Coach:** Mark Mace.

STAUNTON BRAVES

Mailing Address: 14 Shannon Place, Staunton, VA 24401. **Telephone:** (540) 886-0987. **Fax:** (540) 886-0905. **E-Mail Address:** stauntonbraves@valleyleaguebaseball.com. **Website:** www.stauntonbravesbaseball.com. **General Manager:** Steve Cox. **Head Coach:** Unavailable.

WAYNESBORO GENERALS

Mailing Address: 891 Shawnee Road, Waynesboro, VA 22980. **Telephone:** (540) 949-0370, (540) 942-2474. **Fax:** (540) 949-0653. **E-Mail Address:** waynesborogenerals@valleyleaguebaseball.com. **Website:** www.waynesborogenerals.com. **Owner:** Jim Critzer. **Head Coach:** Lawrence Nesselrodt.

WINCHESTER ROYALS

Mailing Address: PO Box 2485, Winchester, VA 22604. **Telephone:** (540) 667-7677. **Fax:** (540) 662-1434. **E-Mail Addresses:** winchesterroyals@valleyleaguebaseball.com, jimphill@shentel.net. **Website:** www.winchesterroyals.com. **President:** Jim Shipp. **Vice President/General Manager:** Jim Phillips. **Head Coach:** John Lowery, Jr.

WOODSTOCK RIVER BANDITS

Mailing Address: 2115 Battlefield Run Ct., Richmond, VA 23231. **Telephone:** (804) 795-5128. **Fax:** (804) 226-8706. **E-Mail Address:** woodstockriverbandits@yahoo.com. **Website:** www.woodstockriverbandits.org. **Owner/President:** Stu Richardson. **Vice President:** Glenn Berger. **General Manager:** Jerry Walters. **Head Coach:** Donn Foltz.

WEST COAST LEAGUE

Mailing Address: PO Box 8395, Portland, Oregon 97207. **Telephone:** (503) 764-9510. **E-Mail Address:** Wilson@westcoastleague.com. **Website:** www.westcoastleague.com.

Year Founded: 2005.

President: Ken Wilson. **Vice President:** Bobby Brett. **Secretary:** Dan Segel. **Treasurer:** Jim Corcoran.

Division Structure: East—Kelowna, Moses Lake, Spokane, Wenatchee. West—Bellingham, Bend, Corvallis, Kitsap.

Regular Season: 48 games. **2009 Opening Date:** June 5. **Closing Date:** Aug. 9.

All-Star Game: None.

Playoff Format: First- and second-place teams in each division meet in best-of-three semifinal series; winners advance to best-of-three championship series.

Roster Limit: 28 (college-eligible players only).

BELLINGHAM BELLS

Mailing Address: 1732 Iowa St, Bellingham, WA 98226. **Telephone:** (253) 606-3670. **E-Mail Address:** info@bellinghambells.com. **Website:** www.bellinghambells.com. **General Manager:** Derrel Ebert. **Head Coach:** Brandon Newell (Kansas).

BEND ELKS

Mailing Address: PO Box 9009, Bend, OR 97708. **Telephone:** (541) 312-9259. **E-Mail Address:** richardsj@bendcable.com. **Website:** www.bendelks.com. **Owner/General Manager:** Jim Richards. **Head Coach:** Scott Anderson.

CORVALLIS KNIGHTS

Mailing Address: PO Box 1356, Corvallis, OR 97339. **Telephone:** (541) 752-5656. **E-Mail Address:** dan.segel@corvallisknights.com. **Website:** www.corvallisknights.com. **President:** Dan Segel. **General Manager/Head Coach:** Brooke Knight.

KELOWNA FALCONS

Mailing Address: 201-1014 Glenmore Dr, Kelowna, B.C., V1Y 4P2. **Telephone:** (250) 763-4100. **E-Mail Address:** mark@kelownafalcons.com. **Website:** www.kelownafalcons.com. **General Manager:** Mark Nonis. **Head Coach:** Kevin Frady (Kansas).

KITSAP BLUEJACKETS

Mailing Address: PO Box 68, Silverdale, WA 98383. **Telephone:** (360) 692-5566. **E-Mail Address:** ricjansmith@comcast.net. **Website:** www.kitsapbluejackets.com. **Managing Partner/General Manager:** Rick Smith. **Head Coach:** Matt Acker (Green River, Wash., CC).

MOSES LAKE PIRATES

Mailing Address: 2165 Westshore Drive, Suite Arrr!, Moses Lake, WA 98837. **Telephone:** (509) 764-8200. **E-Mail Address:** bkirwan@mlpirates.com. **Website:** www.mlpirates.com. **General Manager:** Brent Kirwan. **Head Coach:** Steve Keller (Wenatchee Valley College).

SPOKANE RIVERHAWKS

Mailing Address: PO Box 19188, Spokane, WA 99219. **Telephone:** (509) 747-4991. **E-Mail Address:** zakheim@zak.com. **Website:** www.spokaneriverhawks.com. **General Manager:** Steve Hertz. **Head Coach:** Barry Matthews (CC of Spokane, Wash.).

WENATCHEE APPLESOX

Mailing Address: PO Box 5100, Wenatchee, WA 98807. **Telephone:** (509) 665-6900. **E-Mail Address:** sales@applesox.com. **Website:** www.applesox.com. **Owner/General Manager:** Jim Corcoran. **Head Coach:** Ed Knaggs.

WCL TRI-STATE

Mailing Address: PO Box 8395, Portland, Oregon 97207. **Telephone:** (503) 764-9510. **E-Mail Address:** Wilson@westcoastleague.com. **Website:** www.wccbl.com/tri-state.

WCL PORTLAND

Mailing Address: 21423 S.E. Salmon, Gresham, Oregon 97030. **Telephone:** (503) 665-2007. **E-Mail Address:** dalesteb@comcast.net. **Website:** www.wccbl.com/portland.

HIGH SCHOOL BASEBALL

NATIONAL FEDERATION OF STATE HIGH SCHOOL ASSOCIATIONS

Mailing Address: P.O. Box 690, Indianapolis, IN 46206. **Telephone:** (317) 972-6900. **Fax:** (317) 822-5700. **E-Mail Address:** baseball@nfhs.org. **Website:** www.nfhs.org.

Executive Director: Robert Kanaby. **Chief Operating Officer:** Bob Gardner. **Assistant Director/Baseball Rules Editor:** Elliot Hopkins. **Director, Publications/Communications:** Bruce Howard.

NATIONAL HIGH SCHOOL BASEBALL COACHES ASSOCIATION

Mailing Address: P.O. Box 12843, Tempe, AZ 85284. **Telephone:** (602) 615-0571. **Fax:** (480) 838-7133. **E-Mail Address:** rdavini@cox.net. **Website:** www.baseballcoaches.org. **Executive Director:** Ron Davini. **President:** Gary LaFevers (Buckeye Union HS, Buxkeye, Ariz.) **First Vice President:** Mark Gjormand (Madison HS, Herndon, Va.). **Second Vice President:** Steve Mandl (Washington HS, New York, N.Y.).

2009 National Convention: Dec. 3-6, 2009 at Tucson, Ariz.

NATIONAL TOURNAMENTS

IN-SEASON

AKADEMA PRO SPORTS BATTLE AT THE RIDGE

Mailing Address: Southridge HS, 19355 SW 1114th Ave., **Miami, FL 33157. Telephone:** (305) 322-2255. **Fax:** (305) 253-4456. **E-Mail Address:** edoskow@hotmail.com. **Website:** www.spartan-baseball.com

Tournament Director: Ed Doskow.

2009 Tournament: February 16-21 (three-game guarantee).

ANDERSON BAT NATIONAL CLASSIC

Mailing Address: P.O. Box 338, Placentia, CA 92870. **Telephone:** (714) 993-2838. **Fax:** (714) 993-5350. **E-Mail Address:** placentiamustang@aol.com. **Website:** nationalclassic.com

Tournament Director: Todd Rogers.

2009 Tournament: April 11-16 (16 teams).

BASEBALL AT THE BEACH

Mailing Address: P.O. **Box 1717, Georgetown, SC 29442. Telephone:** (843) 448-7149. **E-mail:** tchristy@horrycountyschools.net Website: www.baseballatthebeach.com.

Tournament Director: Tim Christy

2009 Tournament: Dates unavailable.

BLAZER SPORTCO SPRING BASH

Mailing Address: Durango HS, 7100 W. Dewey Dr., Las Vegas, NV 89113. **Telephone:** (702) 799-5850. **Fax:** (702) 799-1286. **E-Mail Address:** shknapp@interact.ccsd.net.

Tournament Director: Sam Knapp.

2009 Tournament: April 6-8 (39 teams).

FIRST BANK CLASSIC

Mailing Address: 10502 Utica Ave., Lubbock, TX 79424. **Telephone:** (806) 535-4505. **Fax:** (806) 791-4299. **E-Mail Address:** scottgwinn@suddenlink.net.

Tournament Director: Scott Gwinn.

2009 Tournament: March 12-14 (16 teams).

HORIZON CLEATS NATIONAL INVITATIONAL

Mailing Address: Horizon High School, 5653 Sandra Terrace, Scottsdale, AZ 85254. **Telephone:** (602) 867-9003. **E-mail:** huskycoach1@yahoo.com Website: www.horizonbaseball.com

Tournament Director: Eric Kibler.

2008 Tournament: March 16-19 (12 teams).

INTERNATIONAL PAPER CLASSIC

Mailing Address: 4775 Johnson Rd., Georgetown, SC 29440. **Telephone:** (843) 527-9606, (843) 546-3807. **Fax:** (843) 546-8521. **Website:** www.ipclassic.com.

Tournament Director: Alicia Johnson.

2009 Tournament: March 5-8 (eight teams).

LIONS INVITATIONAL

Mailing Address: 3502 Lark St., San Diego CA 92103. **Telephone:** (619) 602-8650. **Fax:** (619) 239-3539. **E-Mail Address:** peter.gallagher@sdcourt.ca.gov. **Website:** www.lionsbaseball.org

Tournament Director: Peter Gallagher.

2009 Tournament: April 6-9

MIDLAND TOURNAMENT OF CHAMPIONS

Mailing Address: Midland High School, 906 W. **Illinois Ave., Midland, TX 79701. Telephone:** (432) 689-1337. **Fax:** (432) 689-1335. **E-Mail Address:** barryrussell@esc18.net.

Tournament Director: Barry Russell.

2009 Tournament: March 5-7 (16 teams).

USA CLASSIC

Mailing Address: 5900 Walnut Grove Rd., Memphis, TN 38120. **Telephone:** (901) 872-8326. **Fax:** (901) 681-9443. **Email:** jdaigle@bigriver.net Website: www.usabaseballstadium.org.

Tournament Organizers: John Daigle, Buster Kelso.

2009 Tournament: April 1-4 at USA Baseball Stadium, Millington, TN (16 teams).

POSTSEASON

SUNBELT BASEBALL CLASSIC SERIES

Mailing Address: 505 North Blvd., Edmond, OK 73034. **Telephone:** (405) 348-3839. **Fax:** (405) 340-7538. **Website:** www.geocities.com/baja/ravine/1976

Chairman: John Schwartz.

2009 Oklahoma-Texas Series: Guthrie, OK, June 19-21

2009 Senior Series: Norman, OK, June 23-27

2009 Junior Series: McAlester and Wilburton, OK, June 12-17

2009 Sophomore Series: Edmond, OK, June 4-7

ALL-STAR GAMES/AWARDS

AFLAC HIGH SCHOOL ALL-AMERICA CLASSIC

Mailing Address: 10 S. Adams St., Rockville, MD 20850. **Telephone:** (301) 762-7188. **Fax:** (301) 762-1491. **Event Organizer:** Sports America, Inc. **President, Chief Executive Officer:** Robert Geoghan. **2009 Game:** Unavailable.

UNDER ARMOUR ALL-AMERICA GAME, POWERED BY BASEBALL FACTORY

Mailing Address: 9176 Red Branch Rd., Suite M, Columbia, MD 21045. **Telephone:** 410-715-5080. **E-Mail Address:** jason@baseballfactory.com. **Website:** baseballfactory.com/ Event Organizers: Baseball Factory, Team One Baseball. **2009 Game:** Unavailable.

GATORADE CIRCLE OF CHAMPIONS (National HS Player of the Year Award)

Mailing Address: The Gatorade Company, 321 N. Clark St., Suite 24-3, Chicago, IL, 60610. **Telephone:** 312-821-1000. **Website:** www.gatorade.com

SHOWCASE EVENTS

ALL-AMERICAN BASEBALL TALENT SHOWCASES

Mailing Address: 6 Bicentennial Ct., Erial, NJ 08081. **Telephone:** (856) 354-0201. **Fax:** (856) 354-0818. **E-Mail Address:** hitdoctor@thehitdoctor.com Website: thehitdoctor.com. **National Director:** Joe Barth.

AREA CODE GAMES

Mailing Address: 23954 Madison Street, Torrance, CA 90505. **Telephone:** (310) 791-1142 x 4424. **E-Mail Address:** andrew@studentsports.com. **Website:** www.studentsportsbaseball.com

Event Organizer: Andrew Drennen.

2009 Area Code Games: Aug. 5-10 at Long Beach, CA (Blair Field).

ARIZONA FALL CLASSIC

Mailing Address: 6102 W. Maui Lane, Glendale, AZ 85306 **Telephone:** (602) 978-2929. **Fax:** (602) 439-4494. **E-Mail Address:** azbaseballted@msn.com. **Website:** www.azfallclassic.com.

Directors: Ted Heid, Tracy Heid.

2009 Events

Four Corner Classic (Open HS, 16 & under)	Peoria, AZ, June 5-7
Peoria 4th of July All Star Game	Peoria, AZ, July 4th
Summer National Classic (2009 and Under)	Peoria, AZ, July 8-12
National 16U Summer Classic	Peoria, AZ, July 15-19
National 17U Summer Classic	Peoria, AZ, July 22-26
AZ Fall Invitational (2010 and Under)	Peoria, AZ, Oct. 9-11
AZ Senior Fall Classic (HS seniors)	Peoria, AZ, Oct. 15-18
AZ Junior Fall Classic (HS juniors)	Peoria, AZ, Oct. 23-25
AZ Sophomore Fall Classic (HS sophomore and Under)	Peoria, AZ, Oct. 30-Nov. 1
AZ NTIS Spring Training Camp	Peoria, AZ, Jan. 16-18, 2010

BASEBALL FACTORY

Office Address: 9176 Red Branch Rd., Suite M, Columbia, MD 21045. **Telephone:** (800) 641-4487, (410) 715-5080. **FAX:** (410) 715-1975. **E-Mail Address:** info@baseballfactory.com. **Website:** www.baseballfactory.com.

Chief Executive Officer: Steve Sclafani. **President:** Rob Naddelman. **Executive VP, Baseball Operations:** Steve Bernhardt. **Senior VP, College Recruiting:** Kelly Kulina. **VP, Finance:** Matt Frese. **VP, Operations and Marketing:** Jason Budden. **Sr. Director of Baseball Operations:** Andy Ferguson Sr. **Director of Instruction:** Matt Schilling. **Director of On-Field Sessions:** Jim Gemler. **Personal Recruiting Director:** Dan Mooney. **Creative Director:** Matt Kirby. **Player Development Coordinators:** Dan Forester, Steve Nagler, Dave Packer, John Perko, Patrick Wuebben, Ryan Koch, Chris Brown, Adam Darvick. **Director of SCR Program and UA National Tryouts:** Dave Wipkowski. **Director of Player Identification:** Josh Sunday.

Under Armour Pre-Season All-America Tournament: January 16-18 in Tucson, AZ (Kino Sports Complex)

Under Armour All-America Game: August 2009

2009 Under Armour National Tryouts & Signature College Recruiting Program Video Sessions: Various locations across the country. **Year round. Open to high school players age 13 – 18. Check www.baseballfactory.com for full schedule.**

BLUE-GREY CLASSIC

Mailing address: 68 Norfolk Road, Mills MA 02054. **Telephone:** (508) 376-1250. **Email address:** impactprospects@comcast.net. **Website:** www.impactprospects.com.

2009 events: Various dates, locations June-Dec. 2009.

COLLEGE SELECT BASEBALL

Mailing Address: P.O. Box 783, Manchester, CT 06040. **Telephone:** (800) 782-3672. **E-Mail Address:** TRhit@msn.com. **Website:** www.collegeselect.org.

Consulting Director: Tom Rizzi.

2008 Showcases: July 14-16, Norwich, CT; Aug. 4-6, Binghamton, NY.

IMPACT BASEBALL

Mailing Address: P.O. Box 47, Sedalia, NC 27342. **E-Mail Address:** andypartin@aol.com. **Website:** www.impactbaseball.com.

Operator: Andy Partin.

2008 Showcases: June 15, Pfeiffer University; June 16, Belmont-Abbey College; June 23, Lander University; June 30, Ferrum College; July 20-21, University of North Carolina.

EAST COAST PROFESSIONAL SHOWCASE

Mailing Address: 2125 North Lake Avenue, Lakeland, FL 33805. **Telephone:** (863) 686-8075.

Tournament Directors: John Castleberry. **Tournament Coordinator:** Shannon Follett.

2009 Showcase: Aug. 1-4, Lakeland, FL.

FIVE STAR BASEBALL SHOWCASE

Mailing Address: Champions Baseball Academy, 510 E. Business Way, Cincinnati, OH 45241. **Telephone:** (513) 247-9511. **Fax:** (513) 247-0040. **E-Mail Address:** toddmontgomery@championsbaseball.net. **Website:** www.championsbaseball.net.

Showcase contact: Mike Bricker

2009 Showcases: June 5-7 at Cincinnati, OH. July 9-12 at Cincinnati, OH.

PACIFIC NORTHWEST CHAMPIONSHIPS

Mailing Address: 42783 Deerhorn Road, Springfield, Or. **97478. Telephone:** (541) 896-0841. **Email Address:** mckay@baseballnorthwest.com. **Tournament Organizer:** Jeff McKay.

2009 Events: August 12-16 in Portland, Or. **State Prospect Games:** Southern Idaho, June 8-11 at Twin Falls H.S., Montana, June 8-11 in Three Forks, Washington Southwest, June 15-18 at Lower Columbia CC in Longview, Wa., Washington Metro, June 22-25 at Bellevue CC in Bellevue, Wa., Washington Northwest, June 29-July 2 at Glacier Peak H.S, Washington Metro South, July 6-9 at Tacoma CC, Washington East/Northern Idaho, July 20-23 at Columbia Basin CC, Oregon State, July 20-23 at Lane CC, Oregon Metro, July 27-30 at Wilsonville H.S.

PERFECT GAME USA

Mailing Address: 1203 Rockford Road SW, Cedar Rapids, IA 52404. **Telephone:** (319) 298-2923 Fax: (319) 298-2924. **E-Mail Address:** jerry@perfectgame.org. **Website:** www.perfectgameusa.com.

President, Director: Jerry Ford. **Vice Presidents:** Andy Ford, Jason Gerst, Tyson Kimm. **International Director:** Kentaro Yasutake. **National Showcase Director:** Jim Arp. **Scouting Directors:** Kirk Gardner, Kyle Noesen, David Rawnsley (WWBA), Greg Sabers. **Baseball Championship**

Director: Ben Ford. **WWBA Tournament Director:** Taylor McCollough. **League Director:** Steve James. **Director, Instruction:** Jim Van Scoyoc. **California Director:** Mike Spiers. **Mid-Atlantic Director:** Frank Fulton. **Northeast Director/State Showcase National Director:** Dan Kennedy. **Southeast Director:** Jeff Simpson. **Georgia Supervisor:** Billy Nicholson. **Director BaseballWebTV.com:** Tom Koerick Jr. **Supervisors BaseballWebTV.com:** Rick Stephenson, Matt Stephenson. **PGCrosschecker.com Director:** Allan Simpson. **PG National Academy Director:** Mike Chismar. **PerfectGameUSA.com writers:** Patrick Ebert, Jim McDonald, Jim Zellmann. **Vice President of Sales and Marketing:** Gary Keoppel. **Director of Sales and Marketing:** Austin Steines. **Merchandise Director:** Tom Jackson. **Merchandise Supervisor:** Dick Vaske. **Director of Information Technology:** David Mixon. **Building Manager:** Eric Oliver. **Business Manager:** Don Walser. **Office Managers:** Betty Ford, Nancy Lain.

2009 Showcase/Tournament Events: Sites across the United States, Jan. 5 – Dec. 30.

PROFESSIONAL BASEBALL INSTRUCTION—BATTERY INVITATIONAL

(for top HS pitchers and catchers)

Mailing Address: 107 Pleasant Avenue, Upper Saddle River NJ 07458. **Telephone:** (800) 282-4638. **Fax:** (201) 760-8720. **E-mail Address:** info@baseballclinics.com **Website:** www.baseballclinics.com/batteryinvitational.html

President: Doug Cinnella

Senior Staff Administrator: Greg Cinnella

General Manager/PR & Marketing: Jim Monaghan

2009 Showcase Events: November 5 & 6

SELECTFEST BASEBALL

Mailing Address: 60 Franklin Pl., Morris Plains, NJ 07950. **Telephone:** (862) 222-6404. **E-Mail Address:** selectfest@optonline.net. **Website:** www.selectfestbaseball.org Camp Directors: Bruce Shatel.

2009 Showcase: June 26-28.

TEAM ONE BASEBALL

(A division of Baseball Factory)

Office Address: 1000 Bristol Street North, Box 17285, Newport Beach, CA 92660. **Telephone:** (800) 621-5452, (805) 451-8203. **FAX:** (949) 209-1829. **E-Mail Address:** jroswell@teamonebaseball.com. **Website:** www.teamone-baseball.com.

Senior Director: Justin Roswell. **Executive VP, Baseball Operations:** Steve Bernhardt. **Director of On-Field Sessions:** Jim Gemler.

2009 Under Armour Showcases: Team One West: June 28 – June 30 in Costa Mesa, CA (Orange Coast College). **Team One South:** July 12 – 14 in Atlanta, GA (Emory University). **Team One North:** July 25 – 27 in Plymouth Meeting, PA (Plymouth Township Park). **Team One Futures Showcase:** October 23 in Peoria, AZ (Peoria Sports Complex)

2009 Under Armour Tournaments: Under Armour Southeast Tournament: June 5-9 in Jupiter, FL (Roger Dean Sports Complex). **Under Armour Southwest Tournament:** July 31 – August 4 in Peoria, AZ (Peoria Sports Complex). **Under Armour Fall Classic:** September 11-13 in Jupiter, FL (Roger Dean Sports Complex). **Under Armour Winter Classic:** December 27-30 in Tucson, AZ (Kino Sports Complex).

TOP GUNS PROSPECT DEVELOPMENT CAMPS

Mailing Address: 9323 N Government Way #307, Hayden, ID 83835. **Telephone/Fax:** (208) 762-1100. **E-Mail Address:** topgunsbss@hotmail.com. **Website:** www.top-gunsbaseball.com. **President:** Nick Rook.

2009 Camp: June 23-25, Las Vegas, NV

TPX TOP 96 COLLEGE COACHES CLINICS

Mailing Address: 6 Foley Dr. Southboro, MA 01772 **Telephone:** 508-481-5939

E-Mail Address: doug.henson@top96.com. **Website:** www.tpxtop96.com

Directors: Doug Henson, Dave Callum, Ken Hill

2008 Clinics: 44 clinics throughout the United States; see website for schedule.

YOUTH BASEBALL

ALL AMERICAN AMATEUR BASEBALL ASSOCIATION

Mailing Address: 331 Parkway Dr., **Zanesville, OH 43701. Telephone:** (740) 453-8531. **Fax:** (740) 453-8531. **E-Mail Address:** clw@aol.com. **Website:** www.aaaba.us.

Year Founded: 1944.

President: Doug Pollock. **Executive Director/Secretary:** Bob Wolfe.

2009 Events: Dates unavailable.

AMATEUR ATHLETIC UNION OF THE UNITED STATES, INC.

Mailing Address: P.O. **Box 22409, Lake Buena Vista, FL 32830. Telephone:** (407) 934-7200. **Fax:** (407) 934-7242. **E-Mail Address:** dan@aausports.org, kristy@aausports.org. **Website:** www.aaubaseball.org.

Year Founded: 1982. **Sports Manager, Baseball:** Dan Stanley

AMERICAN AMATEUR BASEBALL CONGRESS

National Headquarters: 100 West Broadway, Farmington, NM 87401. **Telephone:** (505) 327-3120. **Fax:** (505) 327-3132. **E-Mail Address:** aabc@aabc.us. **Website:** www.aabc.us.

Year Founded: 1935.

President: Richard Neely.

AMERICAN AMATEUR YOUTH BASEBALL ALLIANCE

Mailing Address: 1703 Koala Drive, Wentzville, MO 63385. **Telephone:** (636) 332-7799. **E-Mail Address:** clwjr28@aol.com. **Website:** www.aayba.com

President, Baseball Operations: Carroll Wood.

AMERICAN LEGION BASEBALL

National Headquarters: American Legion Baseball, 700 N. Pennsylvania St., Indianapolis, IN 46204. **Telephone:** (317) 630-1213. **Fax:** (317) 630-1369. **E-Mail Address:**

baseball@legion.org Website: www.baseball.legion.org.

Year Founded: 1925.

Program Coordinator: Jim Quinlan.

2009 World Series (19 and under): Aug. 14-18 at Newman Outdoor Field, Fargo, ND (8 teams).

2008 Regional Tournaments (Aug. 6-10, 8 teams): Northeast—Manchester, N.H.; Mid-Atlantic—Morgantown, W.V.; Southeast—Sumter, S.C.; Mid-South—Enid, OK; Great Lakes—Appleton, Wi; Central Plains—Excelsior, MN; Northwest—Medford, Or; Western—Fair Oaks, Ca.

BABE RUTH BASEBALL

International Headquarters: 1770 Brunswick Pike, P.O. **Box 5000, Trenton, NJ 08638. Telephone:** (609) 695-1434. **Fax:** (609) 695-2505. **E-Mail Address:** info@baberuthleague.org. **Website:** www.baberuthleague.org.

Year Founded: 1951.

President, Chief Executive Officer: Steven Tellefsen.

BASEBALL CHAMPIONSHIP SERIES

(A Division of Perfect Game USA)

Mailing Address: 1203 Rockford Road SW, Cedar Rapids, IA 52404 Telephone: (319) 298-2923 Fax: (319) 298-2924 E-Mail Address: taylor@perfectgame.org. **Website:** www.perfectgame.org/bcs/

Year Founded: 2005.

President: Andy Ford. **National Director:** Taylor McCollough

CONTINENTAL AMATEUR BASEBALL ASSOCIATION

Mailing Address: 1173 French Court, Maineville, Ohio 45039. **Telephone:** (513) 677-1580. **Fax:** 513-677-2586 E-Mail Address: lredwine@cababaseball.com. **Website:** www.cababaseball.com.

Year Founded: 1984.

Executive Director: Larry Redwine. **Commissioner:** John Mocny. **Executive Vice President:** Fran Pell.

DIXIE YOUTH BASEBALL

Mailing Address: P.O. Box 877, Marshall, TX 75671. **Telephone:** (903) 927-2255. **Fax:** (903) 927-1846. **E-Mail Address:** dyb@dixie.org. **Website:** www.dixie.org.

Year Founded: 1955.

Commissioner: Wes Skelton.

DIXIE BOYS BASEBALL

Commissioner/Chief Executive Officer: Sandy Jones, P.O. **Box 8263, Dothan, AL 36304. Telephone:** (334) 793-3331.

DIZZY DEAN BASEBALL

Mailing Address: P.O. Box 856, Hernando, MS 38632. **Telephone:** (662) 429-4365, (423) 596-1353 E-Mail Address: dizzydeanbaseball@yahoo.com. **Website:** www.dizzydeanbbinc.org.

Year Founded: 1962.

Commissioner: Danny Phillips. **Presdient:** Jimmy Wahl. **VP:** Bobby Dunn. **Secretary:** Billy Powell. **Treasurer:** D.B. **Stewart.**

HAP DUMONT YOUTH BASEBALL

(A Division of the National Baseball Congress)

Mailing Address: P.O. Box 83, Lexington, OK 73051. **Telephone:** (405) 899-7689. **E-Mail Address:** stevesmith@hapdumontbaseball.com. **Website:** www.hapdumontbaseball.com; www.oabf.net

Year Founded: 1974. **National Tournament Coordinator:** Steve Smith.

LITTLE LEAGUE BASEBALL

International Headquarters: P.O. **Box 3485, Williamsport, PA 17701. Telephone:** (570) 326-1921. **Fax:** (570) 326-1074. **E-Mail Address:** headquarters@LL.orgWebsite: www.littleleague.org.

Year Founded: 1939.

Chairman: Dennis Lewin.

President/Chief Executive Officer: Stephen D. **Keener. Chief Financial Officer:** David Houseknecht. **Vice President, Operations/Secretary:** Patrick Wilson. **Treasurer:** Melissa Singer. **Senior Communications Executive:** Lance Van Auken.

NATIONAL AMATEUR BASEBALL FEDERATION

Mailing Address: P.O. Box 705, Bowie, MD 20718. **Telephone:** (410) 721-4727. **Fax:** (410) 721-4940. **E-Mail Address:** nabf1914@aol.com. **Website:** www.nabf.com.

Year Founded: 1914.

Executive Director: Charles Blackburn.

NATIONAL ASSOCIATION OF POLICE ATHLETIC LEAGUES

Mailing Address: 658 W. Indiantown Road #201, Jupiter, FL 33458. **Telephone:** (561) 745-5535. **Fax:** (561) 745-3147. **E-Mail Address:** copnkid@nationalpal.org. **Website:** www.nationalpal.org.

Year Founded: 1914.

Executive Director: Mike Dillhyon. **National Program Manager:** Eric Widness.

PONY BASEBALL

International Headquarters: P.O. Box 225, Washington, PA 15301. **Telephone:** (724) 225-1060. **Fax:** (724) 225-9852. **E-Mail Address:** info@pony.org. **Website:** www.pony.org.

Year Founded: 1951.

President: Abraham Key.

REVIVING BASEBALL IN INNER CITIES

Mailing Address: 245 Park Ave., New York, NY 10167. **Telephone:** (212) 931-7800. **Fax:** (212) 949-5695.

Year Founded: 1989. **Founder:** John Young. **Vice President, Community Affairs:** Thomas C. **Brasuell.**

Email: rbi@mlb.com. **Website:** www.mlb.com/rbi

SUPER SERIES BASEBALL OF AMERICA

National Headquarters: 3449 East Kael Street., Mesa, AZ 85213-1773. **Telephone:** (480) 664-2998. **Fax:** (480) 664-2997. **E-Mail Address:** info@superseriesbaseball.com. **Website:** www.superseriesbaseball.com.

President: Mark Mathew

TRIPLE CROWN SPORTS

Mailing Address: 3930 Automation Way, Fort Collins, CO 80525. **Telephone:** (970) 223-6644. **Fax:** (970) 223-3636. **Websites:** www.triplecrownsports.com. **E-mail:** thad@triplecrownsports.com, sean@triplecrownsports.com **Director, Baseball Operations:** Thad Anderson, Sean Hardy.

U.S. AMATEUR BASEBALL ASSOCIATION

Mailing Address: 7101 Lake Ballinger Way, Edmonds, WA 98026. **Telephone/Fax:** (425) 776-7130. **E-Mail Address:** usaba@usaba.com. **Website:** www.usaba.com.

Year Founded: 1969.

Executive Director: Al Rutledge. **Secretary:** Roberta Engelhart.

U.S. AMATEUR BASEBALL FEDERATION

Mailing Address: 389 Bryan Point Dr. Chula Vista, CA 91914. **Telephone:** (619) 934-2551. **Fax:** (619) 271-6659. **E-Mail Address:** usabf@cox.net. **Website:** www.usabf.com.

Year Founded: 1997.

Senior Chief Executive Officer/President: Tim Halbig.

UNITED STATES SPECIALTY SPORTS ASSOCIATION

Executive Vice President, Baseball: Don DeDonatis III, 33600 Mound Rd., **Sterling Heights, MI 48310. Telephone:** (810) 397-6410. **E-Mail Address:** michusssa@aol.com.

Executive Vice President, Baseball Operations: Rick Fortuna, 6324 N. Chatham Ave., #136, Kansas City, MO 64151. **Telephone:** (816) 587-4545. **E-Mail Address:** rick@kcsports.org. **Website:** www.usssabaseball.org. **Year Founded:** 1965/Baseball 1996.

WORLD WOOD BAT ASSOCIATION

(A Division of Perfect Game USA)

Mailing Address: 1203 Rockford Road SW, Cedar Rapids, IA 52404. **Telephone:** (319) 298-2923 Fax: (319) 298-2924. **E-Mail Address:** taylor@perfectgame.org Website: www.worldwoodbat.com.

Year Founded: 1997.

President: Andy Ford. **National Director:** Taylor McCollough. **Scouting Director:** David Rawnsley.

YOUTH BASEBALL TOURNAMENT CENTERS

BASEBALL USA

Mailing Address: 2626 W. Sam Houston Pkwy. N., Houston, TX 77043. **Telephone:** (713) 690-5055. **Fax:** (713) 690-9448. **E-Mail Address:** info@baseballusa.com. **Website:** www.baseballusa.com.

President: Phil Cross. **Tournament Director:** Steve Olson. **Director, Marketing/Development:** Christina Yaya. **League Baseball:** Chip Nila. **Pro Shop Manager:** Don Lewis.

Activities: Camps, baseball/softball spring and fall leagues, instruction, indoor cage and field rentals, youth tournaments, World Series events, corporate days, summer college league, pro shop.

CALIFORNIA COMPETITIVE YOUTH BASEBALL

Mailing Address: P.O. Box 338, Placentia, CA 92870. **Telephone:** (714) 993-2838. **Fax:** (714) 961-6078. **E-Mail Address:** ccybnet@aol.com.

Tournament Director: Todd Rogers.

COCOA EXPO SPORTS CENTER

Mailing Address: 500 Friday Road, Cocoa, FL 32926. **Telephone:** (321) 639-3976. **Fax:** (321) 639-0598. **E-Mail Address:** athleticdirector@cocoaexpo.com. **Website:** www.cocoaexpo.com.

Athletic Director: Jeff Biddle.

Activities: Spring training program, instructional camps, team training camps, youth tournaments.

2009 Tournaments

President's Day Challenge, Feb. 13-16; Memorial Day Bash, May 23-25; Internationale, July 1-5; Cocoa Expo Summer Classic, Aug. 5-9; Labor Day Challenge, Sep. 4-7; Fall Challenge Oct. 17 -18.

COOPERSTOWN BASEBALL WORLD

Mailing Address: P.O. Box 530, Brick, NJ 08723. **Telephone:** (888) CBW-8750. **Fax:** (888) CBW-8720. **E-Mail:** cbw@cooperstownbaseballworld.com.

Complex Address: Cooperstown Baseball World, SUNY-Oneonta, Ravine Parkway, Oneonta, NY 13820.

President/Chairman: Eddie Einhorn. **Vice President:** Debra Sirianni.

2009 Tournaments (15 Teams Per Week): Open to 12U, 13U, 14U, 15U, 16U from July 4 through August 14.

COOPERSTOWN DREAMS PARK

Mailing Address: 330 S. Main St., Salisbury, NC 28144. **Telephone:** (704) 630-0050. **Fax:** (704) 630-0737. **E-Mail Address:** info@cooperstowndreamspark.com. **Website:** www.cooperstowndreamspark.com.

Complex Address: 4550 State Highway 28, Cooperstown, NY 13807.

Chief Executive Officer: Lou Presutti. **Program Director:** Geoff Davis.

2009 Tournaments: Weekly June 6–Aug. 29

DISNEY'S WIDE WORLD OF SPORTS

Mailing Address: P.O. BOX 470847, Celebration, Fl 34747. **Telephone:**: (407) 938-3802. **FAX:** (407) 938-3442. **E-mail address:** wdw.sports.baseball@disney.com. **Website:** www.disneybaseball.com.

Manager, Sports Events: Scott St George. **Sports Manager:** Emily Moak. **Tournament Directory:** Al Schlazer. **Sales Manager, Baseball:** Ryan Morris. **Sports Sales Coordinator, Baseball:** Kirk Stanley.

KC SPORTS TOURNAMENTS

Mailing Address: KC Sports, 6324 N. Chatham Ave., No. 136, Kansas City, MO 64151. **Telephone:** (816) 587-4545. **Fax:** (816) 587-4549. **E-Mail Addresses:** jay@kcsports.org, wally@kcsports.org Website: www.kcsports.org.

Activities: USSSA Youth tournaments (ages 6-18).

Tournament Organizers: Wally Fortuna, Jay Baxter.

U.S. AMATEUR BASEBALL FEDERATION

Mailing Address: 389 Bryan Point Dr. Chula Vista, CA 91914. **Telephone:** (619) 934-2551. **Fax:** (619) 271-6659. **E-Mail Address:** usabf@cox.net. **Website:** www.usabf.com.

Year Founded: 1997. **Senior Chief Executive Officer/President:** Tim Halbig.

INSTRUCTIONAL SCHOOLS/ PRIVATE CAMPS

ACADEMY OF PRO PLAYERS

Mailing Address: 140 5th Avenue, Hawthorne, NJ 07506. **Telephone:** (973) 772-3355. **Fax:** (973) 772-4839. **Website:** www.academypro.com. **Camp Director:** Dan Gilligan.

ALL-STAR BASEBALL ACADEMY

Mailing Addresses: 650 Parkway Blvd., Broomall, PA 19008; 52 Penn Oaks Dr., West Chester, PA 19382. **Telephone:** (610) 355-2411, (610) 399-8050. **Fax:** (610) 355-2414. **E-Mail Address:** basba@allstarbaseballacademy.com. **Website:** www.allstarbaseballacademy.com. **Directors:** Mike Manning, Jim Freeman.

AMERICAN BASEBALL FOUNDATION

Mailing Address: 2660 10th Ave. South, Suite 620, Birmingham, AL 35205. **Telephone:** (205) 558-4235. **Fax:** (205) 918-0800. **E-Mail Address:** abf@asmi.org. **Website:**

www.americanbaseball.org. **Executive Director:** David Osinski. **Chairman of the Board:** James R. **Andrews, M.D.**

THE BASEBALL ACADEMY

Mailing Address: IMG Academies, 5500 34th St. **W.**, Bradenton, FL 34210. **Telephone:** (941) 755-1000. **Fax:** (941) 739-7484. **Website:** www.imgworld.com.

BEN BOULWARE

Mailing Address: America's Baseball Camps, 3020 ISSQ. Pine Lake Road #12, Sammamish, WA 98075. **Telephone:** (800) 222-8152. **Fax:** (888)-751-8989. **E-Mail Address:** info@baseballcamps.com. **Website:** www.baseballcamps.com.

BUCKY DENT'S BASEBALL SCHOOL

Mailing Address: 490 Dotterel Road, Delray Beach, FL 33444. **Telephone:** (561) 265-0280. **Fax:** (561) 278-6679. **E-Mail Address:** staff@dentbaseball.com. **Website:** www.buckydentbaseballschool.com. **VP/GM:** Larry Hoskin.

DOYLE BASEBALL ACADEMY

Mailing Address: P.O. **Box 9156, Winter Haven, FL 33883. Telephone:** (863) 439-1000. **Fax:** (863) 294-8607. **E-Mail Address:** info@doylebaseball.com.

Website: www.doylebaseball.com. **President:** Denny Doyle. **Director:** Blake Doyle.

FROZEN ROPES TRAINING CENTERS

Mailing Address: 12 Elkay Dr., Chester, NY 10918. **Telephone:** (877) 846-5699. **Fax:** (845) 469-6742. **E-Mail Address:** info@frozenropes.com. **Website:** www.frozenropes.com. **Corporate Director:** Tony Abbatine. **Camp Director:** Dan Hummel.

MARK CRESSE BASEBALL SCHOOL

Mailing Address: 1188 N. Grove St., Suite C, Anaheim, CA 92806. **Telephone:** (714) 892-6145. **Fax:** (714) 892-1881. **E-Mail Address:** info@markcresse.com. **Website:** www.markcresse.com. **Owner/Founder:** Mark Cresse. **Executive Director:** Jeff Courvoisier.

MICKEY OWEN BASEBALL SCHOOL

Mailing Address: PO Box 4504, Springfield, MO 65808. **Telephone:** (417) 882-2799. **Fax:** (417) 889-6978. **E-Mail Address:** info@mickeyowen.com. **Website:** www.mickeyowen.com. **President:** Ken Rizzo. **Camp Director:** Tim Williams. **Clinician:** Tim Williams. **Advisor:** Howie Bedell.

MIKE DE SURVILLE

Mailing Address: US Sports Camps, 750 Lindaro Street, Suite 220, San Rafael, CA 94901. **Telephone:** (415) 479-6060. **Fax:** (415) 479-6061. **E-Mail Address:** baseball@ussportscamps.com. **Website:** www.ussportscamps.com.

NORTH CAROLINA BASEBALL ACADEMY

Mailing Address: 1137 Pleasant Ridge Road, Greensboro, NC 27409. **Telephone:** (336) 931-1118. **E-Mail Address:** info@ncbaseball.com. **Website:** www.ncbaseball.com.

Owner/Director: Scott Bankhead. **Assistant Director:** Chris Winterfeldt and Ben Barker. **Academy Director:** Ben Barker.

PENNSYLVANIA DIAMOND BUCKS

Mailing Address: 2320 Whitetail Court, Hellertown, PA 18055. **Telephone:** (610) 838-1219, (610) 442-6998. **E-Mail Address:** jciganick@moravian.edu. **Camp Director:** Jan Ciganick. **Head of Instruction:** Chuck Ciganick.

PROFESSIONAL BASEBALL INSTRUCTION

Mailing Address: 107 Pleasant Ave., Upper Saddle River, NJ 07458. **Telephone:** (800) 282-4638 (NY/NJ), (877) 448-2220 (rest of U.S.). **Fax:** (201) 760-8820. **E-Mail Address:** info@baseballclinics.com. **Website:** www.baseballclinics.com. **President:** Doug Cinnella.

RIPKEN BASEBALL CAMPS

Mailing Address: 1427 Clarkview Rd., Suite 100, Baltimore, MD 21209. **Telephone:** (800) 486-0850. **Fax:** (410) 823-0850. **E-Mail Address:** information@ripkenbaseball.com. **Website:** www.ripkenbaseball.com.

SHO-ME BASEBALL CAMP

Mailing Address: P.O. Box 2270, Branson West, MO 65737. **Telephone:** (800) 993-2267, (417) 338-5838. **Fax:** (417) 338-2610. **E-Mail Address:** info@shomebaseball.com. **Website:** www.shomebaseball.com. **Camp Director:** Christopher Schroeder. **Head of Instruction:** Dick Birmingham.

UTAH BASEBALL ACADEMY

Mailing Address: 389 West 10000 South, South Jordan, UT 84095. **Telephone:** (801) 561-1700. **Fax:** (801) 561-1762. **E-Mail Address:** kent@utahbaseballacademy.com. **Website:** www.utahbaseballacademy.com. **Director:** Bob Keyes

COLLEGE CAMPS

Almost all of the elite college baseball programs have summer/holiday instructional camps. Please consult the college section for listings.

SENIOR BASEBALL

MEN'S SENIOR BASEBALL LEAGUE

(25 and Over, 35 and Over, 45 and Over, 55 and Over)

Mailing Address: One Huntington Quadrangle, Suite 3NO7, Melville, NY 11747. **Telephone:** (631) 753-6725. **Fax:** (631) 753-4031.

President: Steve Sigler. **Vice President:** Gary D'Ambrisi.

E-Mail Address: info@msblnational.com. **Website:** www.msblnational.com.

2009 Events: World Series: Oct. 19-Nov. 7, Phoenix, AZ (25-plus, 35-plus, 45-plus, 50-plus 55-plus, 60-plus, 65-plus, 70-plus and Father/Son divisions). **Fall Classic:** Nov. 5-14, St. Petersburg, FL (25-plus, 35-plus, 45-plus, Father/Son Divisions).

MEN'S ADULT BASEBALL LEAGUE

(18 and Over)

Mailing Address: One Huntington Quadrangle, Suite 3NO7, Melville, NY 11747. **Telephone:** (631) 753-6725. **Fax:** (631) 753-4031.

E-Mail Address: info@msblnational.com. **Website:** www.msblnational.com.

President: Steve Sigler. **Vice President:** Gary D'Ambrisi.

2009 Events: World Series: Oct. 21-25, Phoenix, AZ (four divisions). **Fall Classic:** Nov. 5-9, Clearwater, FL (two divisions).

NATIONAL ADULT BASEBALL ASSOCIATION

Mailing Address: 3609 S. Wadsworth Blvd., Suite 135, Lakewood, CO 80235. **Telephone:** (800) 621-6479. **Fax:** (303) 639-6605. **E-Mail:** nabanational@aol.com. **Website:** www.dugout.org.

President: Shane Fugita.

2009 Events: Memorial Day Tournaments: 18 and over, 25 and over, 35 and over, 45 and over—May 23-25, Las Vegas, NV; 18 and over, 25 and over, 35 and over, 45 and over May 23-25, Atlantic City, NJ. Hall of Fame Tournament: 18 and over, 25 and over, July 2-5, Cooperstown, NY. Mile High Classic: 18 and over, 25 and over, 35 and over, 45 and over July 3-5, Denver, CO. NABA World Championship Series: 18 and over, 25 and over, 35 and over, 45 and over, 55 and over, Oct 1-Oct. 17, Phoenix, AZ. NABA World Championship Series Florida: 18 and over, 25 and over, 35 and over, 45 and over, 55 and over, Nov 5- Nov 8, Jupiter, FL. NABA Over 50 Baseball National Tournament: 48 and over, 58 and over, Oct. 26-31, Las Vegas, NV.

NATIONAL AMATEUR BASEBALL FEDERATION

Mailing Address: P.O. Box 705, Bowie, MD 20718. **Telephone:** (301) 464-5460. **Fax:** (301) 352-0214. **E-Mail Address:** nabf1914@aol.com. **Website:** www.nabf.com.

Year Founded: 1914.

Executive Director: Charles Blackburn.

2008 Events: College (22 and under), Toledo, OH, July 30-August 6; Major (unlimited), Louisville, KY, August 6-13.

ROY HOBBS BASEBALL

Open (28-over), Veterans (38-over), Masters (48-over), Legends (55-over); Family Affairs Division, Classics (60-over), Seniors (65-over), Women's open

Mailing Address: 2048 Akron Peninsula Rd., Akron, OH 44313. **Telephone:** (330) 923-3400. **Fax:** (330) 923-1967. **E-Mail Address:** rhbb@royhobbs.com. **Website:** www.royhobbs.com.

President: Tom Giffen. **Vice President:** Ellen Giffen.

2009 Events: World Series (all in Fort Myers, FL): Oct. 24-31—Open Division; Oct. 31-Nov. 7—Veterans Division; Nov. 7-14—Masters Division; Nov. 14-21—Legends Division, Classics Division, Seniors I & II Divisions (Seniors II tentative as of Feb. 1, call for update). Womens Open, TBA. Family Affairs (Father-Son) tournament in Tucson, AZ, tentative Sept. 30-Oct. 4.

DIRECTORIES
AGENT
SERVICE

AGENT DIRECTORY

ACES, INC.

Seth Levinson, Esq., Sam Levinson,
Keith Miller, Peter Pedalino, Esq.,
Mike Zimmerman
188 Montague Street 6th Floor
Brooklyn, NY 10312
718-237-2900
Fax 718-522-3906
aces@acesinc1.com

ALL STAR GROUP, INC.

Jaime Guillemard,
Francis A. Marquez, Esq.
Oscar Melendez
Hugo Catrain, Esq.
1302 Ponce de Leon Ave. Suite 302
San Juan, PR 00907
Fax 787-725-1339
www.asgbaseball.com
support@asgbaseball.com

DIAMOND STARS SPORTS MANAGEMENT

Lenard Sapp
5119 6th Avenue
Los Angeles, CA 90043
323-627-8882
Fax 323-294-4898
diamondstarsagent@sbcglobal.net

DOUBLE DIAMOND SPORTS MANAGEMENT

Howard A. Kusnick
Joshua A. Kusnick
401 East Las Olas Blvd Suite 1650
Fort Lauderdale, FL 33301
954-472-1047
Fax 954-527-8663
www.doublediamondsports
management.com
hkusnick@bellsouth.net

FRANK A. BLANDINO, LLC

Frank A. Blandino
204 Towne Centre Drive
Hillsborough, NJ 08844
908-217-3226
Fax 908-281-0596
Frank@blandinolaw.com

FULL CIRCLE SPORTS MANAGEMENT

Larry O'Brien, Barton Cerioni
23151 Moulton Parkway
Laguna Hills, CA 92653
949-206-0988
Fax 949-206-0963
www.fullcirclesm.com
info@fullcirclesm.com

IGLESIAS SPORTS MGMT

Ivan C. Iglesias,
Fernand Iglesias, General Counsel
2655 LeJeune Rd. #532
Coral Gables, FL 33134
305-446-9960
Fax 305-446-9980
Grndslm@aol.com

KDN SPORTS

Don Nomura
10801 National Blvd. Suite 525
Los Angeles, CA 90064
310-474-6700
Fax 310-474-6744

METIS SPORTS MANAGEMENT, LLC

Storm T. Kirschenbaum, Esq.
Two Towne Square Suite 800
Southfield, MI 48076
248-827-0510
Fax 248-281-5150
www.metissports.com
storm@metissports.com

MONACO LAW GROUP

Randell Monaco; Matthew R. Monaco
660 Newport Beach Center Dr. Suite 400
949-719-2669
Fax 714-374-9992
randell@monacolawoffice.com

PETER E. GREENBERG & ASSOCIATES, LTD

Peter E. Greenberg, Esq.,
Edward L. Greenberg, Chris Leible
200 Madison Ave., Suite 2225
New York, NY 10016
212-334-6680
Fax 212-334-6895

PLATINUM SPORTS & ENTERTAINMENT MANAGEMENT, LLC

Nick Brockmeyer – President,
Kenneth Powell, Chad McDermott,
Bert Fulk, Scott Casanover, Erik Johnson
123 N. 5th St.
St. Charles, MO 63301
636-946-0960
Fax 636-946-0283
www.psemagents.com
nbrockmeyer@psemagents.com

PRO AGENTS INC.

David P. Pepe, Bill Martin, Jr.
90 Woodbridge Center Drive
Woodbridge, NJ 07095
800-795-3454
Fax 732-726-6688
Pepeda@wilentz.com

PRO STAR MANAGEMENT, INC.

Joe Bick, Brett Bick
1600 Scripps Center
312 Walnut Street
Cincinnati, OH 45202
513-762-7576
Fax 513-721-4628
www.prostarmanagement.com
prostar@fuse.net; prostar2@fuse.net

REYNOLDS SPORTS MANAGEMENT

Larry Reynolds, Patrick Murphy,
Matthew Kinzer
2155 Chicago Avenue Suite 305
Riverside, CA 92507
951-784-6333
Fax 951-784-1451
www.reynoldssports.com

RMG SPORTS MANAGEMENT

Robert Garber, Esq., Brett Laurvick,
Robert Lisant, Matt Colleran
107 S. Vine St.
Hinsdale, IL 60521
630-986-2500; 630-986-0171
www.rmgsports.com

SOSNICK COBBE SPORTS

Matt Sosnick, Paul Cobbe, Matt Hofer,
Adam Karon, Jonathan Pridie
712 Bancroft Road #510
Walnut Creek, CA 94598
925-890-5283
Fax 925-476-0130
www.sosnickcobbesports.com
mattsoz@aol.com; paulcobbe@msn.com

STEVE MANDELL, ESQ.

Steve Mandell
220 W. Huron St. Suite 2001
Chicago, IL 60654
312-867-1900
Fax 312-867-1900

THE SPARTA GROUP

Michael Nicotera, Gene Casaleggio,
Sohail Shahpar, Esq.
140 Littleton Road Suite 100
Parsippany, NJ 07054
973-335-0550
Fax 973-335-2148
www.thespartagroup.com
frontdesk@thespartagroup.com

VERRILL DANA SPORTS LAW GROUP

David S. Abramson, Esq.
One Portland Square
Portland, ME 04101
207-774-4000
Fax 207-774-7499
www.verrilldana.com
dabramson@verrilldana.com

WEST COAST SPORTS MANAGEMENT

Dan Evans, Jim Lentine,
Bret Saberhagen, Scott Budner,
Felix Olivo, Donn Parris, Susan Evans
369 South Fair Oaks Ave.
Pasadena, CA 91105
626-844-1863; 626-844-1863
www.proballfirm.com
WCSMinfo@proballfirm.com

ZUCKER SPORTS MANAGEMENT

Herbie Zucker, Steve Zucker
333 W. Hubbard Suite 5B
Chicago, IL 60654
312-222-9999
Fax 312-494-1111
www.zuckersports.com
herbie@zuckersports.com

SERVICE DIRECTORY

ACCESSORIES

FOR BARE FEET

P.O. Box 159
Helmsburg, IN 47435
812-988-6674
Fax 812-988-1550
www.forbarefeet.com
kelly@forbarefeet.com

JUGS SPORTS

11885 S.W. Herman Rd.
Tualatin, OR 97062
800-547-6843
Fax 503-691-1100
www.jugssports.com
stevec@jugssports.com

ACCOUNTING

RESNICK AMSTERDAM LESHNER P.C.

633 Skippack Pike, Suite 300
Blue Bell, PA 19422
215-628-8080
Fax 215-643-2391
www.baseballaccountants.com
sxr@ral-cpa.com

APPAREL

CH SPORT

1400 Chamberlayne Ave.
Richmond, VA 23232
800-888-7606
Fax 804-643-4408
www.chsport.com
chouse601@aol.com

EBBETS FIELD FLANNELS, INC.

219 1st Ave. S. Suite 100
Seattle, WA 98104
206-382-7249
Fax 206-382-4411
www.ebbets.com
jcohen@ebbets.com

MINOR LEAGUES, MAJOR DREAMS

P.O. Box 6098
Anaheim, CA 92816
800-345-2421
Fax 714-939-0655
www.minorleagues.com
mlmd@minorleagues.com

MV SPORT INC.

88 Spence St.
Bay Shore, NY 11706
800-367-7900
Fax 631-435-8018
www.mvsport.com
baseball@wpmv.com

UNDER ARMOUR

1020 Hull St.
Baltimore, MD 21230
888-4-ARMOUR
www.underarmour.com

A/V CONTENT DELIVERY AND DISPLAY SYSTEMS

CLICK EFFECTS/SOUND & VIDEO CREATIONS, INC.

2820 Azalea Place
Nashville, TN 37204
615-460-7330
Fax 615-460-7331
www.clickeffects.com
fkowalski@clickeffects.com

BAGS

DIAMOND BASEBALL

11130 Warland Drive
Cypress, CA 90630
562-598-9717
Fax 562-598-0906
www.diamond-sports.com
info@diamond-sports.com

GERRY COSBY AND COMPANY

11 Pennsylvania Plaza
New York, NY 10001
877-563-6464
Fax 413-229-3492
www.cosbysports.com
gcmsg@cosbysports.com

BASEBALL CARDS

GRANDSTAND CARDS

22647 Ventura Blvd. #192
Woodland Hills, CA 91364
818-992-5642
Fax 818-348-9122
Gscards1@pacbell.net

BASEBALLS

DIAMOND BASEBALL

11130 Warland Drive
Cypress, CA 90630
562-598-9717
Fax 562-598-0906
www.diamond-sports.com
info@diamond-sports.com

JUGS SPORTS

11885 S.W. Herman Rd.
Tualatin, OR 97062
800-547-6843
Fax 503-691-1100
www.jugssports.com
stevec@jugssports.com

PICKLE-BALL, INC.

4700 9th Ave. NW
Seattle, WA 98107
206-632-0119
Fax 206-632-0126
www.pickleball.com
info@pickleball.com

SWINGBUSTER, LLC

P.O. Box 534
Selma, AL 36702-0534
877-4-BATAWAY
Fax 334-872-2990
www.swingbuster.com
cindyloumosley@hotmail.com

BATS

B45 BATS

825 Rue Raoul-Jobin
Quebec City, G1N 1S6
418-781-0194
Fax 418-877-6763
Pro Player Contact: Rick Kramer
301-346-1046
info@b45online.com
www.b45bats.com

BAMBOO BAT COMPANY

3555 Victory Blvd
Staten Island, NY 10314
718-698-0775
Fax 718-494-1583
www.bamboobat.com
info@bamboobat.com

BRETT BROS. SPORTS

East 9516 Montgomery St Bldg #14
Spokane, WA 99206
509-891-6435
Fax 509-891-4156
www.brettbros.com
brettbats@aol.com

BWP BATS

80 Womeldorf Lane
Brookville, PA 15825
814-849-0089
Fax 814-849-8584
www.bwpbats.com
sales@bwpbats.com

DINGER BATS

109 Kimbro St.
Ridgway, IL 62979
618-272-7250
Fax 618-272-5905
www.dingerbats.com
info@dingerbats.com

EASTON

7855 Haskell Ave. Suite 200
Van Nuys, CA 91406
800-632-7866
www.eastonsports.com

LOUISVILLE SLUGGER

800 W. Main St.
Louisville, KY 40202
800-282-2287
502-585-1179
www.slugger.com

MATTINGLY SPORTS

2 Enterprise Drive Suite 407
Shelton, CT 06484
866-627-2287
Fax 203-944-0284
www.mattinglysports.com
sales@mattinglysports.com

OLD HICKORY BAT COMPANY, INC.

P.O. Box 588
White House, TN 37188
866-PRO-BATS
Fax 615-285-0572
www.oldhickorybats.com
mail@oldhickorybats.com

RAWLINGS

510 Maryville University Drive Suite 110
St. Louis, MO 63141
866-678-GEAR
www.rawlingsgear.com

REEBOK

1895 JW Foster Blvd.
Canton, MA 02021
800-934-3566
www.reebok.com

SAM BAT (THE ORIGINAL MAPLE BAT)

54 Beech Street
Ottawa, ON K15 3J6
888-SAM BATS
613-725-3299
www.sambat.com
bats@sambat.com

SSK CORPORATION

514 Sebastopol Ave.
Santa Rosa, CA 95401
707-318-3610
Fax 707-566-6997
www.sskbaseball.com
robwilliams10@yahoo.com

BATTING CAGES

C&H BASEBALL, INC

2215 60th Drive East
Bradenton, FL 34203
941-727-1533
Fax 941-727-0588
www.chbaseball.com
danielle@chbaseball.com

JUGS SPORTS

11885 S.W. Herman Rd.
Tualatin, OR 97062
800-547-6843
Fax 503-691-1100
www.jugssports.com
stevec@jugssports.com

LOUISVILLE SLUGGER

800 W. Main St.
Louisville, KY 40202
800-282-2287
502-585-1179
www.slugger.com

MASTER PITCHING MACHINE, INC.

4200 NE Birmingham Rd.
Kansas City, MO 64117
800-878-8228
Fax 816-452-7581
www.masterpitch.com
info@masterpitch.com

MILLER NET COMPANY, INC.

P.O. Box 18787
Memphis, TN 38181
901-744-3804
Fax 901-743-6580

NATIONAL BATTING CAGES, INC.

P.O. Box 250
Forest Grove, OR 97116-0250
800-547-8800
Fax 503-357-3727
www.nationalbattingcages.com
sales@nationalbattingcages.com

NATIONAL SPORTS PRODUCTS

3441 S. 11th Ave.
Eldridge, IA 52748
800-478-6497
Fax 800-443-8907
www.nationalsportsproducts.com
sales@nationalsportsproducts.com

NETEX NETTING INC.

5128 Central Ave.
Delta, BC V4K 2H2
800-936-6388
Fax 604-946-8690
m.wilson@dccnet.com

SPORTS ATTACK

P.O. Box 1529
Verdi, NV 89439
800-717-4251
Fax 775-345-2883
www.sportsattack.com
info@sportsattack.com

WEST COAST NETTING

5075 Flightline Drive
Kingman, AZ 86401
928-692-1144/800-854-5741
Fax 928-692-1501
www.westcoastnetting.com
info@westcoastnetting.com

BLEACHERS/GRANDSTANDS

STURDISTEEL CO.

P.O. Box 2655
Waco, TX 76702
800-433-3116
Fax 254-666-4472
www.sturdisteel.com
rgroppe@sturdisteel.com

CAMPS/SCHOOLS

PROFESSIONAL BASEBALL INSTRUCTION

107 Pleasant Ave.
Upper Saddle River, NJ 07458
800-282-4638
Fax 201-760-8820
www.baseballclinics.com
info@baseballclinics.com

CAPS/HEADWEAR

EBBETS FIELD FLANNELS, INC.

219 1st Ave. S. Suite 100
Seattle, WA 98104
206-382-7249
Fax 206-382-4411
www.ebbets.com
jcohen@ebbets.com

MINOR LEAGUES, MAJOR DREAMS

P.O. Box 6098
Anaheim, CA 92816
800-345-2421
Fax 714-939-0655
www.minorleagues.com
mlmd@minorleagues.com

OUTDOOR CAP

1200 Melissa Lane
Bentonville, AR 72712
800-826-6047
Fax 479-464-5258
www.outdoorcap.com
sales@outdoorcap.com

TEAMHEADS

1331 NW Main St.
Lee's Summit, MO 64086
816-524-0316
Fax 816-554-3205
www.teamheads.com
sales@teamheads.com

CASH REGISTERS/ P.O.S. EQUIPMENT

CASIO AMERICA, INC

570 Mt. Pleasant Ave
Dover, NJ 07801
973-361-5400
Fax 973-537-8956
www.casio.com
lsampey@casio.com

CLEATS

NIKE

One Bowerman Drive
Beaverton, OR 97005
800-806-6453
www.nike.com

REEBOK

1895 JW Foster Blvd.
Canton, MA 02021
800-934-3566
www.reebok.com

CUP HOLDERS

CADDY PRODUCTS

73-850 Dinah Shore Drive Unit 115
Palm Desert, CA 92211
760-770-7299/800-845-0591
Fax 760-770-1799
www.caddyproducts.com
info@caddyproducts.com

EMBROIDERED EMBLEMS/ PATCHES

THE EMBLEM SOURCE

4575 West Grove Drive #500
Addison, TX 75001
972-248-1909
Fax 972-248-1615
www.theemblemsource.com
info@theemblemsource.com

ENTERTAINMENT

BIRDZERK!

P.O. Box 36061
Louisville, KY 40233
800-219-0899/502-458-4020
Fax 502-458-0867
www.birdzerk.com
dom@birdzerk.com

BREAKIN' BBOY MCCOY

P. O. Box 36061
Louisville, KY 40233
www.bboymccoy.com
dom@theskillvillegroup.com

MYRON NOODLEMAN

P. O. Box 36061
Louisville, KY 40233
www.myronnoodleman.com
dom@theskillvillegroup.com

TOTAL SPORTS ENTERTAINMENT + TSE GAMETIME

P.O. Box 2166
La Crosse, WI 54602
800-962-2471
Fax 608-782-4655
www.totalsportsentertainment.com
info@totalsportsentertainment.com

ZOOPERSTARS!

P.O. Box 36061
Louisville, KY 40233
800-219-0899/502-458-4020
Fax 502-458-0867
www.birdzerk.com
dom@zooperstars.com

FIELD EQUIPMENT

DIAMOND BASEBALL

11130 Warland Drive
Cypress, CA 90630
562-598-9717
Fax 562-598-0906
www.diamond-sports.com
info@diamond-sports.com

FIELD COVERS/TARPS

C&H BASEBALL, INC

2215 60th Drive East
Bradenton, FL 34203
941-727-1533
Fax 941-727-0588
www.chbaseball.com
danielle@chbaseball.com

COVERMASTER INC.

100 Westmore Dr 11-D
Rexdale, ON M9V5C3
800-387-5808
Fax 416-742-6837
www.covermaster.com
info@covermaster.com

NATIONAL SPORTS PRODUCTS

3441 S. 11th Ave.
Eldridge, IA 52748
800-478-6497
Fax 800-443-8907
www.nationalsportsproducts.com
sales@nationalsportsproducts.com

REEF INDUSTRIES, INC.

9209 Almeda Genoa
Houston, TX 77075
713-507-4251
Fax 713-507-4295
www.reefindustries.com
ri@reefindustries.com

FIELD WALL PADDING

ARTISTIC COVERINGS—SPORTS VENUE PRODUCTS

16444 Manning Way
Cerritos, CA 90703
877-599-9343
Fax 877-599-9335
michelle@accov.com
www.artisticcoverings.com

C&H BASEBALL, INC

2215 60th Drive East
Bradenton, FL 34203
941-727-1533
Fax 941-727-0588
www.chbaseball.com
danielle@chbaseball.com

COVERMASTER INC.

100 Westmore Dr 11-D
Rexdale, ON M9V5C3
800-387-5808
Fax 416-742-6837
www.covermaster.com
info@covermaster.com

NATIONAL SPORTS PRODUCTS

3441 S. 11th Ave.
Eldridge, IA 52748
800-478-6497
Fax 800-443-8907
www.nationalsportsproducts.com
sales@nationalsportsproducts.com

PROMATS ATHLETICS LLC

P.O. Box 2489
Salisbury, NC 28145
800-678-6287
Fax 704-603-4138
www.promatsathletics.com
pharvey@promatsathletics.com

WEST COAST NETTING

5075 Flightline Drive
Kingman, AZ 86401
928-692-1144/800-854-5741
Fax 928-692-1501
www.westcoastnetting.com
info@westcoastnetting.com

FIREWORKS

MELROSE PYROTECHNICS, INC.

4652 Catawba River Rd.
Catawba, SC 29740
800-771-7976
Fax 800-775-7976
www.melrosepyro.com
tom@melrosepyro.com

PYROTECNICO

P.O. Box 149
New Castle, PA 16103
800-854-4705
Fax 724-652-1288
www.pyrotecnico.com
info@pyrotecnico.com

ZAMBELLI FIREWORKS MANUFACTURING CO.

P.O. Box 1463
New Castle, PA 16103
724-658-6611
Fax 724-658-8318
www.zambellifireworks.com
sandy@zambellifireworks.com

FOOD SERVICE

CONCESSION SOLUTIONS INC

16022 26th Ave NE
Shoreline, WA 98155
206-440-9203
Fax 206-440-9213
www.concessionsolutions.com
theresa@concessionsolutions.com

GAME MANAGEMENT SOFTWARE/GAME OPS CONSULTING

TOTAL SPORTS ENTERTAINMENT + TSE GAMETIME

P.O. Box 2166
La Crosse, WI 54602
800-962-2471
Fax 608-782-4655
www.totalsportsentertainment.com
info@totalsportsentertainment.com

GAMES

APBA GAMES

P.O. Box 4547
Lancaster, PA 17604
800-334-2722
Fax 717-871-9959
www.apbagames.com
mrinaldi@apbagames.com

GIVEAWAY ITEMS

ALEXANDER GLOBAL PROMOTIONS

515 116th Avenue NE
Bellevue, WA 98004-5204
425-637-0610
Fax 425-637-0611
www.alexanderglobal.com
malcolm@alexanderglobal.com

RICO INDUSTRIES, INC./TAG EXPRESS

7000 N. Austin
Niles, IL 60714
800-423-5856
Fax 312-427-0190
www.ricoinc.com
jimz@ricoinc.com

SLINKY PRINT

800 Beaver Street
Hollidaysburg, PA 16648-1634
248-353-1693
Fax 248-353-1786
www.slinkyprint.com
bill@slinkyprint.com

GLOVES

BARRAZA PRO BASEBALL GLOVES

7060 Santa Anita Circle
Buena Park, CA 90620-3108
714-676-7846
www.barrazapro.com
cdayton@barrazapro.com

NIKE

One Bowerman Drive
Beaverton, OR 97005
800-806-6453
www.nike.com

OLD HICKORY BAT COMPANY, INC.

P.O. Box 588
White House, TN 37188
866-PRO-BATS
Fax 615-285-0572
www.oldhickorybats.com
mail@oldhickorybats.com

RAWLINGS

510 Maryville University Drive Suite 110
St. Louis, MO 63141
866-678-GEAR
www.rawlingsgear.com

REEBOK

1895 JW Foster Blvd.
Canton, MA 02021
800-934-3566
www.reebok.com

SSK CORPORATION

514 Sebastopol Ave.
Santa Rosa, CA 95401
707-318-3610
Fax 707-566-6997
www.sskbaseball.com
robwilliams10@yahoo.com

WILSON SPORTING GOODS

8750 W. Bryn Mawr Avenue
Chicago, IL 60631
800-333-8326
Fax 773-714-4595
www.wilson.com

H.S. SHOWCASE EVNTS/ SCOUTING SERVICES

SOCAL GOLD SCOUTING SERVICE

254 E. Grand Ave. Suite 201
Escondido, CA 92025
858-776-9361
Fax 760-738-8866
www.socalgoldscouting.com
rhabert@socalgoldscouting.com

ICE WRAPS

PRO ICE PRODUCTS

22612 Mojave Ln.
Mission Viejo, CA 92691
949-859-3795
Fax 949-859-4263
www.proice.net
proice@proice.net

INSURANCE

K&K INSURANCE

See our ad on the insde front cover!

1712 Magnavox Way
Fort Wayne, IN 46804
800-637-4757
Fax 260-459-5800
www.kandkinsurance.com
kk_general@kandkinsurance.com

LANYARDS AND ID ACCESSORIES

1888LANYARD.COM

P.O. Box 932
Nutting Lake, MA 01865
888-526-9273
Fax 781-229-5982
www.1888lanyard.com
1888_customerservice@1888lanyard.com

LIGHTING

MUSCO SPORTS LIGHTING, LLC

100 1st Ave. West
Oskaloosa, IA 52577
641-673-0411
Fax 641-673-4047
www.musco.com
rick.sneed@musco.com

MASCOTS

OLYMPUS FLAG & BANNER

9000 W. Heather Ave.
Milwaukee, WI 53224
414-355-2010
Fax 414-355-1931
www.olympus-flag.com
sales@olympus-flag.com

SCOLLON PRODUCTIONS, INC.

P.O. Box 486 1016 White Rock Rd.
White Rock, SC 29177
803-345-3922 x48
Fax 803-345-9313
www.scollon.com
rick@scollon.com

TEAMHEADS

1331 NW Main St.
Lee's Summit, MO 64086
816-524-0316
Fax 816-554-3205
www.teamheads.com
sales@teamheads.com

MUSIC/SOUND EFFECTS

CLICK EFFECTS/SOUND & VIDEO CREATIONS, INC.

2820 Azalea Place
Nashville, TN 37204
615-460-7330
Fax 615-460-7331
www.clickeffects.com
fkowalski@clickeffects.com

SOUND DIRECTOR

4380 SW Macadam Ave. Suite 540
Portland, OR 97239
503-963-3802/888-276-0078
Fax 503-963-3822
www.sounddirector.com
jj@sounddirector.com

NETTING/POSTS

C&H BASEBALL, INC

2215 60th Drive East
Bradenton, FL 34203
941-727-1533
Fax 941-727-0588
www.chbaseball.com
danielle@chbaseball.com

JUGS SPORTS

11885 S.W. Herman Rd.
Tualatin, OR 97062
800-547-6843
Fax 503-691-1100
www.jugssports.com
stevec@jugssports.com

L.A. STEELCRAFT PRODUCTS

P.O. Box 90365
Pasadena, CA 91109
626-798-7801/800-371-2438
Fax 626-798-1482
www.lasteelcraft.com
info@lasteelcraft.com

NATIONAL SPORTS PRODUCTS

3441 S. 11th Ave.
Eldridge, IA 52748
800-478-6497
Fax 800-443-8907
www.nationalsportsproducts.com
sales@nationalsportsproducts.com

NETEX NETTING INC.

5128 Central Ave.
Delta, BC V4K 2H2
800-936-6388
Fax 604-946-8690
m.wilson@dccnet.com

WEST COAST NETTING

5075 Flightline Drive
Kingman, AZ 86401
928-692-1144/800-854-5741
Fax 928-692-1501
www.westcoastnetting.com
info@westcoastnetting.com

NOVELTY ITEMS

BALLQUBE, LC

12146 CR 4233 W
Cushing, TX 75760
800-543-1470
Fax 903-863-5571
www.ballqube.com
sales@ballqube.com

RIXSTINE RECOGNITION

2350 "O" St.
Lincoln, NE 68510
800-347-3810
Fax 402-476-0968
www.homerunawards.com
tim@rixstine.com

TEAMHEADS

1331 NW Main St.
Lee's Summit, MO 64086
816-524-0316
Fax 816-554-3205
www.teamheads.com
sales@teamheads.com

PENNANTS, FOAM FINGERS & NOVELTY GIFTS

RICO INDUSTRIES, INC./TAG EXPRESS

7000 N. Austin
Niles, IL 60714
800-423-5856
Fax 312-427-0190
www.ricoinc.com
jimz@ricoinc.com

PITCHING AIDS

THROWTHECURVE.COM

107 Pleasant Ave.
Upper Saddle River, NJ 07458
800-282-4638
Fax 201-760-8820
www.throwthecurve.com

PITCHING CAGES

MOJO PITCHING CAGE

20609 Santa Lucia, Unit B
Tehachapi, CA 93561
661-822-5840
Fax 661-822-5837
www.mojosportsusa.com
jlewis@mojopitchingcage.com

PITCHING MACHINES

BETTER BASEBALL

1050 Mt. Paran Rd
Atlanta, GA 30327
404-467-4313
Fax 404-467-4573
www.betterbaseball.com
aga@betterbaseball.com

JUGS SPORTS

11885 S.W. Herman Rd.
Tualatin, OR 97062
800-547-6843
Fax 503-691-1100
www.jugssports.com
stevec@jugssports.com

MASTER PITCHING MACHINE, INC.

4200 NE Birmingham Rd.
Kansas City, MO 64117
800-878-8228
Fax 816-452-7581
www.masterpitch.com
info@masterpitch.com

PRO BATTER SPORTS

15 Old Gate Lane
Milford, CT 06460
800-513-1807/203-874-2500
Fax 203-878-9019
www.probatter.com
info@probatter.com

SPORTS ATTACK

P.O. Box 1529
Verdi, NV 89439
800-717-4251
Fax 775-345-2883
www.sportsattack.com
info@sportsattack.com

PLAYING FIELD PRODUCTS

BEAM CLAY

Kelsey Park
Great Meadows, NJ 07838
800-247-BEAM
Fax 908-637-8421
www.beamclay.com
sales@partac.com

See our ad on the insde back cover!

DIAMOND PRO (TXI)

1341 West Mockingbird Lane
Dallas, TX 75247
800-228-2987
Fax 800-640-6735
www.diamondpro.com
diamondpro@txi.com

L.A. STEELCRAFT PRODUCTS

P.O. Box 90365
Pasadena, CA 91109
626-798-7801/800-371-2438
Fax 626-798-1482
www.lasteelcraft.com
info@lasteelcraft.com

PRO'S CHOICE

410 N. Michigan Suite 400
Chicago, IL 60611
800-648-1166
312-331-9525
www.proschoice1.com
proschoice@oildri.com

POINT OF SALE ITEMS

BALLQUBE, LC

12146 CR 4233 W
Cushing, TX 75760
800-543-1470
Fax 903-863-5571
www.ballqube.com
sales@ballqube.com

NEW CONCEPTS SOFTWARE, INC.

P.O. Box 688
Roseville, MI 48066
586-776-2855
Fax 586-776-7433
www.ncsoftware.com
sales@ncsoftware.com

PRINTING

OLYMPUS FLAG & BANNER

9000 W. Heather Ave.
Milwaukee, WI 53224
414-355-2010
Fax 414-355-1931
www.olympus-flag.com
sales@olympus-flag.com

THEO DAVIS PRINTING (WES HARE)

1415 West Gannon Ave, Box 277
Zebulon, NC 27597
919-389-3459
Fax 919-269-5647
www.theodavis.com
wesh@theodavis.com

PROMOTIONS

SLINKY PRINT

800 Beaver Street
Hollidaysburg, PA 16648-1634
248-353-1693
Fax 248-353-1786
www.slinkyprint.com
bill@slinkyprint.com

THEO DAVIS PRINTING (WES HARE)

1415 West Gannon Ave, Box 277
Zebulon, NC 27597
919-389-3459
Fax 919-269-5647
www.theodavis.com
wesh@theodavis.com

TOTAL SPORTS ENTERTAINMENT + TSE GAMETIME

P.O. Box 2166
La Crosse, WI 54602
800-962-2471
Fax 608-782-4655
www.totalsportsentertainment.com
info@totalsportsentertainment.com

PROMOTIONAL ITEMS

B.I.G. BADGE USA

40 Citation Lane
Lititz, PA 17543
717-569-5797
Fax 717-569-2390
www.bigbadgeusa.com
tom.tulli@identicard.com

EVERYONE LOVES BUTTONS

20801 N. 19th Ave Suite 8
Phoenix, AZ 85027
623-445-9975
Fax 623-445-9979
www.elbusa.com
statman@elbusa.com

PROMOTIONAL ADVENTURES, INC.

16416 Labrador St.
North Hills, CA 91343
818-332-1381
Fax 818-332-1395
www.promotionaladventures.com
dustin@promotionaladventures.com

PHOENIX SPORTS, INC.

4226 6th Ave. South
Seattle, WA 98108
800-776-9229
800-776-4422
www.phoenixsportsinc.com
phoesports@aol.com

RICO INDUSTRIES, INC./TAG EXPRESS

7000 N. Austin
Niles, IL 60714
800-423-5856
Fax 312-427-0190
www.ricoinc.com
jimz@ricoinc.com

RIXSTINE RECOGNITION

2350 "O" St.
Lincoln, NE 68510
800-347-3810
Fax 402-476-0968
www.homerunawards.com
tim@rixstine.com

SLINKY PRINT

800 Beaver Street
Hollidaysburg, PA 16648-1634
248-353-1693
Fax 248-353-1786
www.slinkyprint.com
bill@slinkyprint.com

TCHOTCHKES

6440 Lusk Blvd.
Suite D110
San Diego, CA 92121
858-793-5322
Fax 858-793-5426

WIFFLE PROMOTIONAL PRODUCTS BY HOT TOPS

240 Long Hill Cross Road
Shelton, CT 06484
203-926-2067
Fax 203-944-6079
www.hottops.com
ppataky@hottops.com

RADAR EQUIPMENT

JUGS SPORTS

11885 S.W. Herman Rd.
Tualatin, OR 97062
800-547-6843
Fax 503-691-1100
www.jugssports.com
stevec@jugssports.com

SPORTS SENSORS, INC.

11351 Embassy Dr.
Cincinnati, OH 45240
888-542-9246
Fax 513-825-8532
www.sportssensors.com
adilz@cinci.rr.com

SEATING

STURDISTEEL CO.

P.O. Box 2655
Waco, TX 76702
800-433-3116
Fax 254-666-4472
www.sturdisteel.com
rgroppe@sturdisteel.com

SHOWCASES/PLAYER DEVELOPMENT

PROFESSIONAL BASEBALL INSTRUCTION - BATTERY INVITATIONAL

(pitchers/catchers - early November)
107 Pleasant Avenue
Upper Saddle River, NJ 07458
800-282-4638
Fax 201-760-8820
greg@baseballclinics.com

SPORTING GOODS

JUGHEAD SPORTS

107 Pleasant Avenue
Upper Saddle River, NJ 07458
800-282-4638
Fax 201-760-8820
www.jugheadsports.com

STADIUM ARCHITECTS

360 ARCHITECTURE

300 West 22nd St.
Kansas City, MO 64108
816-472-3360
www.360architecture.com
clamberth@360architecture.com

HOK SPORT

300 Wyandotte, Suite 300
Kansas City, MO 64105
816-221-1500
Fax 816-221-1578
www.hoksport.com
david.bower@hoksve.com

See our ad on page 6!

TICKETS

NEW CONCEPTS SOFTWARE, INC.

P.O. Box 688
Roseville, MI 48066
586-776-2855
Fax 586-776-7433
www.ncsoftware.com
sales@ncsoftware.com

NATIONAL TICKET CO.

P.O. Box 547
Shamokin, PA 17872
800-829-0829
Fax 800-829-0888
www.nationalticket.com
ticket@nationalticket.com

TRAINING EQUIPMENT

C&H BASEBALL, INC

2215 60th Drive East
Bradenton, FL 34203
941-727-1533
Fax 941-727-0588
www.chbaseball.com
danielle@chbaseball.com

JUGS SPORTS

11885 S.W. Herman Rd.
Tualatin, OR 97062
800-547-6843
Fax 503-691-1100
www.jugssports.com
stevec@jugssports.com

SPORTS SENSORS, INC.

11351 Embassy Dr.
Cincinnati, OH 45240
888-542-9246
Fax 513-825-8532
www.sportssensors.com
adilz@cinci.rr.com

SPORTS ATTACK

P.O. Box 1529
Verdi, NV 89439
800-717-4251
Fax 775-345-2883
www.sportsattack.com
info@sportsattack.com

SWINGBUSTER, LLC

P.O. Box 534
Selma, AL 36702-0534
877-4-BATAWAY
Fax 334-872-2990
www.swingbuster.com
cindyloumosley@hotmail.com

TRAVEL

BROACH BASEBALL TOURS

5821 Fairview Rd Suite 118
Charlotte, NC 28209
800-849-6345
Fax 704-365-3800
www.baseballtoursusa.com
info@broachsportstours.com

WORLD SPORT

P.O. Box 661624
Los Angeles, CA 90066
310-915-8007
Fax 310-915-7177
www.worldsport-tours.com
wrldsport@aol.com

TROPHIES/AWARDS

BALLQUBE, LC

12146 CR 4233 W
Cushing, TX 75760
800-543-1470
Fax 903-863-5571
www.ballqube.com
sales@ballqube.com

RIXSTINE RECOGNITION

2350 "O" St.
Lincoln, NE 68510
800-347-3810
Fax 402-476-0968
www.homerunawards.com
tim@rixstine.com

TURNSTILE ADVERTISING

ENTRY MEDIA INC

127 W. Fairbanks Ave #417
Winter Park, FL 32788
407-678-4446
Fax 407-678-1658
www.entrymedia.com
martin@entrymedia.com

UNIFORMS

EBBETS FIELD FLANNELS, INC.

219 1st Ave. S. Suite 100
Seattle, WA 98104
206-382-7249
Fax 206-382-4411
www.ebbets.com
jcohen@ebbets.com

WILSON SPORTING GOODS

8750 W. Bryn Mawr Avenue
Chicago, IL 60631
800-333-8326
Fax 773-714-4595
www.wilson.com

WINDSCREENS

C&H BASEBALL, INC

2215 60th Drive East
Bradenton, FL 34203
941-727-1533
Fax 941-727-0588
www.chbaseball.com
danielle@chbaseball.com

COVERMASTER INC.

100 Westmore Dr 11-D
Rexdale, ON M9V5C3
800-387-5808
Fax 416-742-6837
www.covermaster.com
info@covermaster.com

MILLER NET COMPANY, INC.

P.O. Box 18787
Memphis, TN 38181
901-744-3804
Fax 901-743-6580

NATIONAL SPORTS PRODUCTS

3441 S. 11th Ave.
Eldridge, IA 52748
800-478-6497
Fax 800-443-8907
www.nationalsportsproducts.com
sales@nationalsportsproducts.com

WEST COAST NETTING

5075 Flightline Drive
Kingman, AZ 86401
928-692-1144/800-854-5741
Fax 928-692-1501
www.westcoastnetting.com
info@westcoastnetting.com

INDEX

MAJOR LEAGUE TEAMS

MINOR LEAGUE TEAMS

INDEPENDENT TEAMS

OTHER ORGANIZATIONS